NAKED IN CYBERSPACE

NAKED IN CYBERSPACE

HOW TO FIND PERSONAL INFORMATION ONLINE

2nd Edition

Carole A. Lane

CyberAge Books

Information Today, Inc.
Medford, New Jersey

First printing 2002

Naked in Cyberspace
Second Edition

Copyright © 2002 by Carole A. Lane

Publisher's Note: The author and publisher have taken care in preparation of this book but make no expressed or implied warranty of any kind and assume no responsibility for errors or omissions. No liability is assumed for incidental or consequential damages in connection with or arising out of the use of the information or programs contained herein.

Many of the designations used by manufacturers and sellers to distinguish their products are claimed as trademarks. Where those designations appear in this book and Information Today, Inc. was aware of a trademark claim, the designations have been printed with initial capital letters.

Library of Congress Cataloging-in-Publication Data

Lane, Carole A.
  Naked in cyberspace / Carole A. Lane.--2nd ed.
    p. cm.
  Includes bibliographical references and index.
  ISBN 0-910965-50-1 (pbk.)
  1. Electronic public records--United States. 2. Records--United States--Computer network resources. 3. Biography--Research--United States--Computer network resources. 4. Investigations--Computer network resources. 5. Public records--United States--Electronic information resources. 6. Records--United States--Electronic information resources. 7. Biography--Research--United States--Electronic information resources. I. Title.

  JK2445.P82 L36 2002
  001.4'2'02854678--dc21

                                                                    2002004685

Printed and bound in the United States of America.

Publisher: Thomas H. Hogan, Sr.
Editor-in-Chief: John B. Bryans
Managing Editor: Deborah R. Poulson
Project Editor: Owen B. Davies
Production Manager: M. Heide Dengler
Copy Editor: Pat Hadley-Miller
Cover Design: Jaqueline Walter
Book Design: Kara Mia Jalkowski
Proofreader: Dorothy Pike
Indexer: Sharon Hughes

Dedication

This book is dedicated to the most important people I know:
Barry Wang, for his support and faith in me,
Skylar Wang, for regularly interrupting my work on the first edition for a cuddle,
for bragging about it ever since, and for being the son that I am so proud of,
and Alexandra Wang, for making all work on this edition nearly impossible,
but life so very wonderful.
I love you all infinity times infinity.

Table of Contents

Section III. Types of Personal Records

Section IV. Where Can I Find More Information?

Foreword

At the Privacy Rights Clearinghouse, we hear from people every day who are victims of identity theft, whose rights have been violated due to information illegally obtained about them, or who otherwise have had their privacy breached. A case in point ...

> Helen, fresh out of law school, walked into the district attorney's office on her first day on the job. She was eager to begin her new career. But instead of being greeted by the personnel officer, she was met by a police officer who arrested her and escorted her to the county jail. At first, Helen thought some of her friends, known for their pranks, were playing a practical joke. But when the officer began to book her, she realized this was no joke. She had been erroneously identified as an individual who had been arrested for marijuana possession. A bench warrant had been issued for "her" arrest when she did not show up for court.
>
> Then Helen put the pieces of the puzzle together. Her wallet had been stolen from her car several months ago. The thief must have used Helen's identity when arrested. Then, when the district attorney's office conducted a background check on Helen, they uncovered the arrest record on the data base that they accessed to determine whether their new employee had a criminal record. Helen was released on bail, and was soon able to convince the authorities that she was a victim of identity theft. She had learned an increasingly common lesson in this data-driven society: there is no such thing as a totally accurate data file; and erroneous information can have serious consequences for the individuals whose records are incorrect.

So why am I, a privacy advocate, writing the foreword for a book instructing you how to find personal information? It's simple, really. At the Privacy Rights Clearinghouse, we define privacy as the ability to control what is done with your personal information. We take a three-prong approach to taking control of your information:

- Be Aware

- Be Assertive

- Be an Advocate

This book, *Naked in Cyberspace*, provides a blueprint for the first prong: Be Aware. Be aware of how and when you give out personal information. Find out what information about you is stored in major industry and government data bases. *Naked in Cyberspace* not only explains where you can find your personal information in major industry and government databases, but also provides an education in locating your records in proprietary databases and on the Internet.

No central repository exists where you could review all of your personal information. If there were such a repository, we might face the bleak world portrayed by George Orwell in *1984*, where Big Brother was the all-seeing, all-knowing government entity who used that knowledge to control every aspect of life.

Your records are actually spread across the world in more places than you'd ever imagine. This book is a valuable resource in gaining an understanding of the myriad sources and uses for your personal information.

Even those of us in the privacy arena will acknowledge that there are valid reasons for maintaining personal records. For example, real property records are maintained by local government agencies so that the rights to the property can be verified and protected. They enable us to make sure that our property taxes are assessed fairly. Because credit payment histories are maintained in central clearinghouses, called credit reporting agencies, it is easier to obtain credit for auto purchases, home mortgages, and myriad other goods and services. Because we depend upon records such as these in order to do business and interact with government agencies, it is not likely that all of our personal information will become private at any time in the future.

However, while there are valid uses for personal information, there is also the potential for misuse of any of these records. It is vitally important that those using personal information comply with the laws that govern their use, and consider our need for privacy when developing plans and policies for collecting and handling personal records.

And where laws have not been proscribed to protect personal privacy, those who compile and use personal information should abide by a code of ethics called the Fair Information Principles. These include: consent, disclosure, access, correction, security, collection limitation, purpose specification, and accountability.

Here is where the second prong of the PRC's privacy motto becomes important: Be assertive! If you are aware of the major privacy laws that govern the use of personal information, and if you are cognizant of the Fair Information Principles, you are in a much better position to assert your rights. Do not be afraid to question uses of your personal information. You'd be surprised at how effectively you can assert yourself by calmly and firmly stating your position: "No, I don't provide my [you fill in the blank … Social Security number, date of birth, driver's license number …] for that use." Or, "If I give you that information, how can you assure me that you will keep it secure and it will not be used for any other purpose?"

It is also extremely helpful for those wanting to guard or reclaim their own privacy to understand which records they can control, and which are beyond their control, and why. *Naked in Cyberspace* addresses these important issues in a realistic, no-nonsense way, explaining the valid uses for your personal information while providing warnings about potential misuses to those who could be in danger (such as stalking victims). When you understand who can access your records, you can take steps to protect yourself further when necessary.

This leads to the third prong of our privacy protection motto: Be an advocate. An important aspect of *Naked in Cyberspace* is that it explains the legal environment surrounding those data sources that are protected by laws. Your arguments to lawmakers and industry representatives regarding the need for laws and business practices to protect personal data better carry more weight if they are backed up with solid facts.

Naked in Cyberspace is an invaluable resource, whether you want to learn to use personal information legitimately, or understand the extent to which your personal information is available to others. This book will greatly expand your knowledge of the "information marketplace." And it will help you to practice our privacy motto: Be aware, be assertive, be an advocate.

Beth Givens
Founder and Director, Privacy Rights Clearinghouse
www.privacyrights.org

Beth Givens is a recipient of the Brandeis Award from Privacy International and, in October 2001, received an award from the Foundation for Improvement of Justice for her work on behalf of victims of identity theft.

Acknowledgments

I would like to acknowledge all of the brilliant and supportive people in AIIP (the Association of Independent Information Professionals) who taught me well, encouraged me, and were never further away than my computer and modem. Special thanks to:

Marjorie Desgrosseilliers, for the brainstorming that started this book and for her ongoing support and her treasured friendship.

Helen Burwell, my wonderful technical editor on the first edition, for her endless patience and keen insight.

Mary Ellen Bates, who advised and encouraged me, and took me under her wing from my first dumb question on Section 0.

Colin McQuillan, a gifted writer who inspired the writer in me.

Reva Basch, for not laughing when I told her that I wanted to follow in her footsteps, and instead introduced me to her publisher.

Thanks to Owen Davies for his superb line editing and gentle prodding that kept me going through both editions, and to Deborah Poulson for her endless patience and support as my second edition manuscript evolved into a book under her direction.

Thanks to Jacqueline Walter for the wonderful original cover design, to Kara Jalkowski for her interior design, and to Production Manager Heide Dengler for putting it all together.

Thanks to Lisa Glandon and LexisNexis, and to the folks at Dialog Information, Inc., and DataStar, who all allowed me time and access to their databases so that I could find real examples to illustrate various types of records, and the power of their databases. Also, thanks to Gale Research Inc. and SilverPlatter Information, who provided the Gale Directory of Databases, a wonderful resource that was absolutely essential to my efforts to identify databases. Thanks also to Stuart Sandow, NIA Academy of Public Records Research, and Robert Heibel, Director, Research/Intelligence Analyst Program, Mercyhurst College, both of whom provided invaluable input on key chapters.

My sincere gratitude goes to my supporters and cheering squad, without whom this book would not be possible, and nothing else would be nearly as much fun: Melissa Sands, Tish and Dave Duesler, Hamideh Fatemi, Carlos Neucke and Liza Solis-Reyes, Bill Plachy, Doris Alvarez-Ramirez, Rachelle and Mike Garcia, Maggie Demirdjian, Mark and Gina Jennings, Michele and Steve Folan, Alan Schlein, Renee and Mike Andrade, Chuck and Debbie Mills, Ralph Burton, Chris Bernauer, Anne Peters, Elizabeth O'Hara, Jack Hurwitz, Holly Cartwright and Gene Krieser, Kent and Kande Thompson, Michelle Fort, Tom Garcia, David Agoff, Patricia Cordova, the wonderful women of the North County Association of Female Executives (NCAFE), and the rest of my family—the Santiagos, Lanes, Wangs, Goodwins, Zamichielis, Fromsons, Sands, Reyes, and Cannucciaris.

Finally, thanks to John Bryans, who made this book a reality.

Carole A. Lane
Vista, CA
2002

About the Web Site

www.technosearch.com/naked/directory.htm

The world of personal information online changes with each blink of the eye. While continuing improvements in the technologies that allow for the capture, storage, and sharing of data are tremendously important to online information searchers, perhaps no current trend promises a greater impact—at least in the near term—than the pace at which public records and proprietary databases are being made available on the Internet.

The limitations of any print volume covering Internet resources may be rather obvious: new sites appear every day, other sites are expanded to include new or enhanced databases, and still other sites disappear without a trace. In regard to the coverage of Internet resources in *Naked in Cyberspace*, the challenge for the author and publisher is to offer you the reader a way to keep abreast of new sites, databases, and developments.

Our approach is to offer you at our World Wide Web site a regularly updated directory of key Internet resources—including, wherever possible, active links to sites (you must have an Internet connection and WWW browser to utilize these links). This directory is designed to help you pinpoint sites offering specific types of information, and to keep you up-to-date on the trends and issues relevant to personal online research. It is being made available at no charge to you as a valued *Naked in Cyberspace* reader. Please be sure to read the important disclaimer that appears at the bottom of this page.

Disclaimer (please read carefully)

Neither publisher nor author make any claim as to the results that may be obtained through the use of the above mentioned links to Internet sites and resources, which are maintained by third parties. Neither publisher nor author will be held liable for any results, or lack thereof, obtained by the use of any links, for any third party charges, or for any hardware, software, or other problems that may occur as a result of using any links. This program of Internet resources and links is subject to change or discontinuation without notice at the discretion of the publisher.

Personal Records in Cyberspace

Chapter 1

Welcome to Cyberspace
(Check Your Clothes at the Door)

Oh sweet information superhighway,
what bring you me from the depths of cyberspace?

—Crow T. Robot, *Mystery Science Theater 3000*

Sitting here in my home office, what could I find out about you? What could you learn about me? How deeply could we probe into each other's private lives? And how many of our own closely held secrets are truly shielded from the prying keyboards of skilled researchers? Those questions are the seeds from which I have grown a busy research firm, tapping the wealth of online data to help my clients learn what they need to know about people, companies, and markets. They also are the seeds from which this book has grown. The answers will probably startle you.

In a few hours, sitting at my computer, beginning with no more than your name and address, I can find out what you do for a living, the names and ages of your spouse and children, what kind of car you drive, the value of your house, and how much you pay in taxes on it. From what I learn about your job, your house, and the demographics of your neighborhood, I can make a good guess at your income. I can uncover that forgotten drug bust in college. In fact, if you are well-known or your name is sufficiently unusual, I can do all this without even knowing your address. And, of course, if you become a skilled researcher, familiar with the online resources available to us all, you will be able to learn much the same things about me, or almost anyone else who piques your curiosity.

Whether you seek information about others or simply want to protect your own privacy, you need to know about finding personal information online, because there is not a lot of real privacy left and what little remains is disappearing fast. Very soon, we will all be "naked in cyberspace."

For most of us, that is a somewhat scary thought, and no one can be blamed for wishing to keep his or her private life private. Yet the growing availability of personal information has benefits that can be as important as the obvious potential dangers. There are many perfectly valid reasons to seek information about others.

If you have ever been curious about your ancestors or about lost relatives, you are a prime candidate for using some of the most common personal databases, the genealogical records compiled by churches, hobbyists, and historical societies around the world. Many of these archives are still available only as books and paper files. Yet a growing number of them can be obtained online and on CD-ROM. For many people, genealogy provides a fascinating and comparatively easy introduction to the vast universe of online information.

Most parents already know what it is like to help a child find information for a school report. These home information searches usually begin with a few minutes of thumbing through the nearest encyclopedia. This is a good way to start and one that cultivates research skills children will find useful throughout their lives. However, you may often find yourself making an unexpected trip to the library, where you, your child, and a helpful librarian sort laboriously through card files, reference works, and computerized indices to search out relevant books and magazine articles. These days, it can be faster, easier, and far more effective to tap into a few online databases, where the facts are readily available on almost any subject you can name. Professional writers and journalists use these resources daily as the most efficient means of gathering information for their books and articles.

In business, uses for online information abound. If you have applied for a job, sought credit or insurance, tried to rent an apartment or buy a house, or even made a substantial donation to charity, you almost surely have been the subject of many online information searches. Many employers routinely screen job applicants, and computerized databases now supply much of the information employers need. Financial institutions such as banks, credit card companies, and collection agencies use personal records to track assets, debts, and investments; identify potential clients; weigh credit risks; and locate "skips," debtors who move in the hope that creditors will be unable to find them. Insurance companies use personal records to screen out risky applicants, set rates, process claims, and investigate possible fraud. Landlords use computer and personal records to check out potential tenants. Attorneys use them to locate experts who can testify in civil and criminal trials and to find witnesses to crimes. Charitable organizations even use them to identify likely donors. And, of course, if you run a small business, own a house with a rental apartment, or contribute your free time to raise funds for a local charity, you will find the same personal records just as useful as these organizations did when they checked up on you.

Today most large institutions would be paralyzed without computerized personal records. The medical industry uses them to track and evaluate medical treatment, to match organ donors with patients who need a transplant, and to study illnesses and health risks. Government uses personal records in many thousands of computerized databases to assess taxes, dole out benefits, locate deadbeat parents, and carry out many of its other activities. Law enforcement uses personal records to identify and track criminals and witnesses to crimes. And while privacy laws justifiably restrict access to many of the records used by the medical community, government, and law enforcement, many institutional databases are available for at least limited private use.

It also is possible to make a business of research itself. I have done it. A few of the people who read this book may well join me. You could be one of them. Many information brokers (also known as information professionals or researchers) mine personal records to compile biographical information, gather competitive intelligence, or provide information in support of clients both in industry and in private life. List brokers use personal records to identify new markets, potential investors, or groups of people with common interests or characteristics that mark them as likely customers for specialty retailers. Private investigators use personal records to locate information about people, their assets, and their activities. Often, when someone vanishes "without a trace," she can be located without ever leaving the office, just by searching through the appropriate databases. By the time you finish this book, you should be able to master the basic skills needed to build a career finding information for clients in any of these fields—and gain the ability to provide for your own information needs.

Whatever your goal in searching for personal records, you will find it much easier to accomplish than it would have been twenty years ago, when most personal records existed only on paper. Your searches probably will be much more productive as well.

One reason is the sheer mass of information that is generated, and that others collect about us, as we pass through life. From the day we're born, our personal records begin to accumulate—in the hospital, perhaps at an obstetrician's office. Our birth certificate follows quickly and soon is filed down at City Hall. Then there are Social Security records, supplemented by school records, a driver's license, tenant records, voter registration, professional licenses, employment records, and tax records. Even the least active life today generates records at every turn.

When we actually *do* something, still more records appear. Most of us get married, rent a living space, establish some credit, buy a vehicle, subscribe to magazines. Many people get divorced, serve in the armed forces, commit crimes, write for publication, are interviewed, sue someone or are sued by them, join associations, answer ads for free goods or information, start businesses, make investments, or file for bankruptcy. Some, such as politicians and celebrities, spend nearly all of their time in the limelight and have every accomplishment, failure, or even rumor about them documented by the press. It all leaves a paper trail. Even if we remain in the shadows, comfortable within the illusion of our anonymity, almost everything we do can be tracked by almost anyone who chooses to go looking for it.

Today, paper trails have given way to "vapor trails"; far more of our records exist in the memories of computers than in paper files, much less the fallible memories of human beings. The availability of all those computerized databases is the second reason that personal research is so much easier and more productive today.

Before starting my research business, I worked as a systems analyst for many years. My job was to design computerized databases. It did not take me long to recognize that once information is entered into a database, it takes on a strange new life of its own, with benefits for searchers that go far beyond mere convenience. Computerized records are not just easy to call up and read; they can be manipulated, compared, and used to generate information that simply was not available before.

For example, consider a telephone book. When you use the printed version, you look up a person's name to find his address or phone number. That's about all there is to it. Put that same information into a computerized database, and suddenly it is transformed. You can still use a person's name to locate an address and phone number, but it does not end there. Now you can enter an address to find all the people or businesses with a telephone there, along with their phone numbers. If you have only a telephone number, you can enter it to find out whose it is and where they live.

But that is just the beginning. It takes 10,000 or so telephone books to store all the numbers for all the phones in the United States, far more than you would ever want cluttering your home or office. Yet a national telephone directory can be compressed into a few CD-ROMs that take up no more shelf space than a paperback book. If you do not want to buy all of that rapidly changing information, you can use the free national telephone directories available on the Internet without ever storing a single telephone book.

That convenience brings with it opportunities no printed directory can offer. If your search subject has an unusual name, you can search for the surname in a computerized directory and locate possible relatives across town or throughout the country. Much more sophisticated research is just as easy. Once you have found your subject's address, you can search for a range of addresses on either side and find the names and phone numbers of his or her neighbors. You can use a telephone database to learn how common a surname is within the United States or within a specific region. You can find out how many "Main Streets" there are in the U.S., how many cities are named "Lafayette," and exactly where to find "Success." (It's in Arkansas, of course.) All this from the stodgy old telephone book!

When information gets into a computer database, it can be indexed, searched, compared, summarized, shuffled, sliced, and diced almost any way you want, at lightning speeds and often from a terminal halfway around the world. It is this combination—thousands of vast, all-inclusive databases containing hundreds of millions of personal records, equipped with search facilities no mere book or filing cabinet can equal—that allows us to discover so much about each other without ever leaving our desks.

In the next several hundred pages, you will learn what these exciting, and occasionally troubling, new research tools can do for you. I will show you how to search online databases for the information you want, introduce you to the most important archives of personal records, and provide a reference guide to several thousand databases that can sometimes offer up exactly the information you need.

How This Book Is Organized

The five chapters of Section I are intended to give you a good general background on personal records—what is recorded in the world's databases and, in brief, how to go about finding it.

Database searching itself is introduced in Chapter 2. This is meant as a primer for those unfamiliar with the process of finding information in a database. In this chapter, you will discover some of the ways in which indices can help you to find the information you need.

Chapter 3 offers a look at the Internet and how it can be used to locate personal records, along with such consumer-oriented systems as CompuServe, America Online, and Prodigy. You will also find that many specific Internet sites are mentioned throughout this book; these references will point you to specific types of personal records that can be accessed on the Internet.

Three typical searches form the substance of Chapter 4. Here, the reader gets into the real-world practice of locating information. You will find that this is a kind of free-form exercise rather than a fixed procedure. At each step, the information found will guide the choice of the next database to try, the next question to ask. Experience also helps in making these choices, of course. As in computer programming, water skiing, or any other skill, you will get better with practice.

A discussion of privacy issues in Chapter 5 rounds out Section I. While not directly related to the "how-to" of searching, this is a subject that will influence many of the searches you perform. Much of the information that could theoretically be found online is off-limits to outside researchers, and there are tough laws to enforce these strictures. Whether they are tough enough, or restrictive enough, is still being debated. You may well see more limits in the future, enacted to control the kind of searching you are about to do.

Although *Naked in Cyberspace* can be read cover-to-cover, it is not necessary to do so. I recommend that you read Section I in its entirety. Even if you have had a little experience with online databases, these pages provide valuable information specific to searching for personal information. After that, Section II: How Personal Records Are Used supplies details of how to proceed with searches for certain kinds of personal information. The chapters in Section II will refer you to specific types of records to help with your search, which can be found in Section III: Types of Personal Records.

What Type of Research Interests You?

If you are looking for a lost love, a friend, or someone who owes you money, Chapter 6 will help you learn more about locating people.

Chapter 7 will provide the information you need for pre-employment screening, and if you manage a business Chapter 8 will tell you where to find potential employees online. Depending upon the types of positions you hire for, Chapter 12 may also be useful; it can guide you to experts in a wide variety of fields.

If you own or manage rental property, see Chapter 9 for tenant screening.

If you think you've already found your "one and only," but want to check him or her out before giving your heart, soul, and half your assets, see Chapter 10 for information on asset searching and Chapter 14 for private investigation. If you haven't found Mr. or Ms. Right, and money will influence your choice, Chapter 13: Prospect Research (Fundraising) can be used to figure out who has the money, and Chapter 14 can help you find out whether they are already married.

As a business person, you may need to size up the competition, as well as job applicants. Begin with Chapter 11, which describes how personal records can be used in competitive intelligence research. Chapter 7, on pre-employment screening, can help you to uncover valuable information about potential partners and others with whom you might be considering some type of financial arrangement. So can Chapter 10, on asset searching, and perhaps even Chapter 14, on private investigation, depending upon the situation.

If you are an attorney or involved in a lawsuit, an asset search can help you to decide whether your opponent has enough money to be worth suing or to finance a protracted court battle. See Chapter 10. And if you need an expert's testimony, Chapter 12 can be of help in finding the right expert witness.

Colleges and universities, nonprofit organizations, and volunteers hoping to raise funds for local charities should read Chapter 13 for information on the use of personal records in prospect research.

Anyone interested in private investigation will find that Chapter 14 provides a solid introduction to how personal records are used in this field. Professional investigators, however, will want to read all the chapters in Section II. Depending upon their clientele and specialties, private investigators may find themselves carrying out an asset search, trying to locate a missing person, seeking an expert, or looking for almost any other kind of personal information.

Each of these chapters will refer you to other parts of the book, where further explanation and assistance can be found.

Types of Personal Records

The third section of *Naked in Cyberspace,* Types of Personal Records, describes and illustrates the many types of personal records available in databases. Some of these records are open to everyone, and you may choose to gain access to them and use them in your research. Others are restricted by law or held in proprietary databases. You may qualify for access to them, or you may just want to know more about them in order to understand how much of your own life has been recorded in someone's computer files. In most cases, you have the right to obtain records about yourself, so many of these chapters also provide instructions for requesting your own records.

Adoptees seeking birthparents and birthparents seeking the children they once gave up for adoption should refer to Chapter 32.

Genealogists should jump directly to Chapter 34 for information on the types of genealogical records that can be found online. Chapter 6 provides information on locating people, which should be helpful to genealogists as well.

Where Can I Find More Information?

Section IV: Where Can I Find More Information? lists resources for the personal records researcher. Books addressing various types of research are listed first, followed by periodicals, and then organizations. Frankly, none of these chapters is exhaustive. Although you will find a great deal of information about personal records in *Naked in Cyberspace,* this book may not contain "all you ever wanted to know" about any particular subject, much less about all of the many kinds of records held in the world's computers or about every type of search that can now be carried out in cyberspace. I have tried to include all of the most important resources available, but filling the book with lesser materials would easily have doubled its size and price. And even then the book would have been incomplete, as new resources become available almost every day.

The appendices of this book list companies that produce databases containing information about people. Many are available online, while others can be purchased on CD-ROM. These lists are followed by listings of adoption registries, major bulletin-board vendors, public records producers and vendors, and other database vendors. Databases and vendors listed in these appendices are referred to throughout the book.

The appendices suffer from the same limitations as the reference material in Section IV. No list of databases or database vendors can ever be complete, since new resources appear almost daily. Nonetheless, this final section of the book will provide a great many resources with which to begin your search for personal information.

For updates to the Web sites listed in this book, turn to the *Naked in Cyberspace* Web site: www.technosearch.com/naked/directory.htm. This site provides a comprehensive listing of the personal records Web sites listed in *Naked in Cyberspace* and allows us to update the book as new resources become available.

Chapter 2

Database Searching

Database: Any collection of data, or information, that is
specially organized for rapid search and retrieval by a computer.
–Encyclopaedia Britannica

There is nothing terribly difficult about finding information in a database. Whether on a proprietary database, on the Internet, or on CD-ROM, electronic media invariably offer search facilities more sophisticated and convenient than anything a bound book or library could hope to provide. The real problems are knowing which databases to search and how to phrase your inquiry narrowly enough to avoid having all the useful information buried in mounds of dross. Those are the real subjects of this book. Before we get to them, however, there are some technical details to consider.

Equipment and Software

For some applications, like video editing, you really want the biggest, fastest, most expensive computer you can buy. Database searching is not like that. All that you really need is a computer capable of running software designed to work with the databases that interest you. For the Internet, however, a fast system with a fast modem can make the difference between your loving and hating the time you spend online.

For most online databases, any communications software will do. Since communications software is made for nearly any operating system, whatever computer you have almost surely can be used to access many online databases. There are exceptions, however. Some databases can be searched only through software that is custom-made for a particular vendor's products. In that case, access is limited to the types of computer for which the vendor provides software. Even databases that can be searched through generic communications software frequently offer custom programs that are more user-friendly or have features built in to save time and money or to track the cost of your searches. Database vendors such as LexisNexis and Factiva have made searching much easier by developing Windows software that even novices can use to access their systems efficiently. Today, more and more of these systems also are accessible through the Internet.

When building custom software, database vendors and third-party developers often create their products first for the Windows operating system, their largest market. Editions for the Apple Macintosh usually follow later, or may not be released at all. Of course, when software is improved or debugged, vendors follow the same priorities. Macintosh users can face long waits for Mac-compatible software, and they may be left out in the cold. This can be even more of a problem for those with machines still farther from the IBM-inspired mainstream.

If you plan to buy a computer for the sake of working with online databases, it makes sense to begin by learning whether the databases that interest you require any specific software. Then find out whether software upgrades for the different operating systems are released in any particular order. This may help you to choose your operating system and thereby narrow the list of computers suited to your task.

In the first edition of this book, I covered many of the CD-ROM databases then available. Although some are still included in this edition, many have been omitted to make room for additional coverage of Internet resources, which are far more accessible now.

A few databases are available on diskette, but since the space on a diskette is extremely limited, only the smallest are available in this format. (Since these databases usually are of interest only to specialists within very narrow fields and seldom are widely marketed, they are not covered in this book.)

Some databases also are available on magnetic tape, but modems and CD-ROM drives are far more common in both offices and homes today, and nearly all of the databases most of us will ever wish to use are available in at least one of these formats. If your interests are highly specialized and one of the products you need requires the use of magnetic tape, you should make sure that you can add a tape drive to your computer. This should not be a problem for most business systems.

Types of Online Database Vendors

In addition to the multitude of vendors now providing access to their databases through their own Web sites, there are many different types of online database vendors that offer access in a variety of ways.

Boutique Services

Some database vendors provide access only to their own databases. These stand-alone systems sometimes are referred to as "boutique" services. One example of a boutique service is Burrelle's Information Services (www.burrelles.com), which offers transcripts of television broadcasts such as *60 Minutes* and *The Oprah Winfrey Show*, and transcripts from Presidential press conferences, news documentaries, and radio broadcasts. Such a specialized service has much to offer, even though it does not include the databases of other companies.

Most public records vendors also qualify as boutique services. Boutique services can offer lower rates than might otherwise be the case, since they avoid an additional tier of resellers who make their profit by charging for access to the database. On the other hand, a boutique can also be a very expensive place to shop if its offerings are unique.

Multiproducer Database Vendors

Some of the larger database vendors, such as Dialog, offer not only their own databases, but also those of other companies. This strategy allows Dialog to provide more than 470 databases in its service, including news, business and industry information, book catalogs, patent and trademark filings, scientific literature, and so on. Most of the databases offered by Dialog are actually compiled by other companies.

A provider can make its databases available through multiple vendors, thereby broadening access to the database without having to provide the marketing or support that a large market otherwise would require. For example, Experian (formerly TRW) Business Profile Reports are available through several database vendors, including CompuServe (keyword: TRWREPORT) and Dialog, as well as directly through Experian Business Credit. If individuals have only occasional need for an Experian Business Profile, they are less likely to sign up for direct access through Experian, but they may find the reports through one of the other systems to which they subscribe.

Although you must pay the database vendor for access to the information, in addition to the database provider, signing up with a large database reseller can save you the time and expense of signing up with many different providers, not to mention the inconvenience of having to keep track of separate user IDs and passwords for every company that you deal with, as well as learning how to search each system efficiently.

Gateway Services

These database or consumer online service vendors provide access both to their own products and to the products of other database vendors. For example, CompuServe offers gateways to many other services available on the Internet.

CompuServe's IQuest provides access to some Dialog databases and to products from many other suppliers. IQuest offers everything from Dun and Bradstreet and Experian credit reports to company profiles, scientific and technical information, trademarks and patents, and newspapers. Although IQuest may be used commercially, searching IQuest is generally more expensive than direct access through the database vendors.

If a gateway service accesses a tape of the data, rather than the producer's actual database, the data available through the gateway may also be less current than what exists on the producer's or vendor's database. For only occasional use of a database, a gateway provides the convenience of ready access without having to sign up with another vendor. For regular use, it usually is more cost-effective to sign up directly with the database vendor, rather than with a gateway service.

Information professionals often use a combination of these resources, signing up with larger multiproducer vendors for a variety of databases, with some boutique services for specialized information, and gateway services for occasional use.

Types of Data

Although several vendors may offer a given database, this does not mean that they offer all of the same data. Sometimes a database is carried with full text, meaning that when you find the article or report you need, you will be able to read it all directly from the database on your computer screen, download it to your computer or hard drive, or print it out.

Bibliographic or indexing databases provide information about articles or reports available for your research topic and sometimes include abstracts or citations that give more details about the information from the text. However, they do not provide the full text itself. When a citation is found, it usually is necessary to order the text separately or to visit a library or courthouse to review the full record.

Some databases include a combination of bibliographic citations and full text.

Directory or dictionary databases provide specific, limited information about a well-defined subject. The telephone directory is the classic example, but many product listings and professional directories follow the same general format. This type of database may also include some text about the company or product.

Numeric databases consist of tables or statistics. Although numeric databases may also carry some text, their primary purpose is to provide statistical data.

Sometimes a database producer or vendor will add value to a product by offering information not originally provided on a database or by merging several databases together. Alternatively, they may choose to split the data from one database into several, offering information products tailored to more specific needs, sometimes at a lesser cost than for the full database.

The timeliness of data may vary from one vendor to another. Some databases are updated daily, others weekly, monthly, quarterly, or at longer intervals. Some databases are updated "periodically," which can mean anything.

At times, it is not how current the information is that matters, but how far back the records go. This varies from vendor to vendor and database to database.

For any of these reasons, you may find that you prefer accessing a particular database through one vendor rather than another, even if the contents are based on essentially the same information.

Search Languages and Methods

Online databases usually are organized to allow searching in certain fields that have been indexed. A given database may also be searchable by using terms found in the citations or abstracts of the articles. If the full text of an article is available, it sometimes may be searched as well, but you cannot assume that the text can be searched simply because it is available. Database producers and vendors may have their own unique indexing system, or they may use one that is shared by other information providers. All of this contributes to the complexity of searching a database.

Many databases allow searching based on Boolean logic. In its simplest form, Boolean logic allows the researcher to narrow a search by asking that the items retrieved have more than one thing in common (connecting search terms with the word AND), to broaden the search by asking that the items have at least one of the characteristics being requested (using OR), or to exclude undesired items from the set retrieved (using NOT). An example of a Boolean search would be:

(HUBCAP? AND ((RECREATIONAL(1w)VEHICLE?)
OR RV)) NOT IMPORT?

This search would retrieve articles in which both HUBCAPS and RECREATIONAL VEHICLES were mentioned, as well as those mentioning HUBCAPS and RVs, but it would exclude those in which the word IMPORT, IMPORTS, or IMPORTED were also found. It also would reject the word IMPORTANT and any others containing a word beginning with "IMPORT." The question mark is used in this example as a "wildcard," which takes the place of other characters. Any word that begins with IMPORT will be excluded from this particular search. Some databases use other symbols as wildcards, such as !, $, or *. Sometimes these symbols indicate that only one character may take the place of each wildcard, while in other cases, the wildcard substitutes for any number of letters. The term (1w), in this example, means that RECREATIONAL must appear within one word of VEHICLE, in the given order. This type of proximity operator also will vary from one database to the next. Proximity operators can be used to indicate that given words must be found near each other in any order, in a given order, or within the same paragraph, depending upon the search software.

On the Internet, some (but not all) search engines also use Boolean-type commands to search for matching Web sites. For example, AltaVista uses "+" before a search term to indicate that it *must* appear in pages matched. To exclude pages, AltaVista uses "-" before a search term. Rather than proximity operators, AltaVista uses quotation marks to indicate that a search term is actually a phrase, not individual words. This database also uses "*" as a wildcard at the end of a word to search for any words beginning with the given search term. These types of search operators are not always found on Internet search engines, so it is necessary to read a Help screen or view instructions for each search engine in order to learn how to find information with each most efficiently.

Each proprietary database provider and vendor has its own search language. The following are examples of some of the most common database search and retrieval functions and some of the commands used by database vendors.

Database Function	Dialog Command	LexisNexis Command
Select a database	**BEGIN** or **B**	**.cl** (change library) or **.cf** (change file)
Find	**SELECT** or **S**	(none)
Display	**TYPE** or **T**	**.fd** (first document)
Display one screen	**DISPLAY** or **D**	**.fp** (first page)
Save/Deliver later	**PRINT** or **PR**	**.pa** (print all)
Sign-Off	**LOGOFF** or **DISC** or **LOG** or **LOGOUT** or **OFF** or **BYE** or **QUIT** or **STOP**	**.so** (sign off)

Of course, these are simple examples. There are many more commands that accomplish variations of these and other search and retrieval tasks. There also are custom software packages built for searching these systems, each offering a different interface with its own menus and options. Many vendors have also developed more sophisticated software that can help you to locate hard-to-find items, sort sets of retrieved data, eliminate duplicate articles, rank them for relevance, and otherwise assist in your searches. The more sophisticated commands are rarely available through gateway systems, which is one more reason that information professionals often choose direct access.

Some databases also provide less sophisticated menus for searching. These commonly are menu-driven and are geared toward the novice or occasional user. Such menu systems are often found on the Internet. Gateway systems and public records vendors usually offer this type of search software. Public records vendors often provide menu-driven software, which makes it relatively simple to search for individual records, but may make it difficult or impossible to find groups of records with common characteristics or otherwise to construct a set of data in an automated way.

Before searching a database, especially through an expensive online service, it is important to obtain the manuals that document its use, to learn the procedures for searching out and retrieving data from it. If the database is not of the simplified, menu-driven variety, you also would do well to attend training classes offered by the producer or vendor. You will not only learn the basic search commands, but also may pick up some search tips that can save you a fortune in online costs.

When you are ready to begin your search, it pays to work out the most efficient search strategy, using the best commands available for that particular database, *before* logging on. When you are being charged by the minute, you have no time to waste looking up commands.

Make sure that you know the cost before ordering, displaying, or printing any of the documents you find online. Some vendors provide a command that allows you to check the cost before placing an order or issuing the print command. Sometimes this is found in a separate printed pricing guide. Also be aware of how long you are spending online, and of the cost-per-minute charges. Some systems offer a command to give you a minute-by-minute estimate. Others do not tell you until you log off, which is too late to avoid unpleasant billing surprises. More detailed information on costs associated with the use of online databases appears later in this chapter, under "Online Database Pricing and Fees."

Database searching, like most other skills, gets easier with practice. Some database vendors provide practice databases, practice user IDs, or free time on their systems so that you can get used to searching their databases. When these are provided for free, or at relatively low cost, they are great ways to get some inexpensive search practice. Some libraries offer access to databases, though these are often CD-ROM products rather than online databases. If a library near you offers a CD-ROM database for which the online search commands are the same (which is not always true), I recommend taking advantage of this, practicing and honing your search skills without the expense of an online database.

Some database vendors now are also offering a flat-fee option in which you can pay a single monthly fee for unlimited access to their databases. For inexperienced searchers or those who expect to make a great deal of use of those particular databases, this can be another cost-saving option.

In addition to practice databases and classes, several other resources can help you to become an efficient online searcher. There are books about searching, organizations for information professionals, information industry publications, and online and database conferences, all of which provide learning experiences and can assist you in keeping up-to-date with the latest search techniques and software.

If you do not have the expertise, time, or inclination to learn to search databases efficiently, you can also hire an information professional to perform the searching for you, so you do not have to do all this on your own. I will offer more thoughts about this option later in this chapter.

Delayed Retrieval

CD-ROM databases provide virtually instant access to the data included in them, slowed only by the speed of the computer used to search them. Online databases may also provide immediate access to even more vast amounts of data. On the other hand, they may serve only as an ordering mechanism by which to request a report. The actual data may not be delivered to you for a couple of hours, a day, a week, or even longer. This type of delayed retrieval is particularly common of public records systems. In fact, on some systems, you locate the report that you want through an online index, type in the command to retrieve the document, and then twiddle your thumbs while someone on the other end of the system either writes a letter to the agency (court, Department of Motor Vehicles, etc.) where the actual record is located or sends someone out to retrieve the document and eventually mails it back to you. But this beats the alternatives—doing without the information or hopping a plane to visit the agency in person.

Some bibliographic databases do not provide a way to order the full-text document you need. Where this is the case, you will have to track it down yourself or call a document delivery company to locate it and deliver it to you.

When comparing databases, it is important to distinguish whether the data is actually accessible online, whether there is any delay in retrieving it, and whether the vendor provides any way to order documents that are not available online.

Online Database Pricing and Fees

Have you ever tried to figure out which long-distance carrier really gives you the best telephone rates once you add in all the incentives and discount plans? Figuring out the cost of database research makes even that task look easy. The best adjective that I have heard used to describe database pricing is Byzantine. Database fees can be unreasonably complex, and many change in structure and form at random intervals. After the change, they may seem to cost less, while new hidden fees actually raise your bill. Database fees take you through a labyrinth where every turn hides a toll bridge. On the upside, if you do not like the way a database vendor prices its products, the fee structure probably will change and change again before you have had time to figure out the old one. Of course, you may not like the new pricing any better.

Each database vendor offers a pricing structure that combines its own unique selection of several basic patterns. Comparing them in order to decide which database will charge the least for a given article or report is more convoluted than comparing apples and oranges; it's more like comparing Irish setters, fire engines, and grapefruit.

Bear in mind that a database that seems to have lower prices can actually end up costing more if the vendor's search engine lacks the commands that let you extract your results in an efficient manner.

Some database vendors offer several pricing structures or options, so it may be necessary to compare pricing not only between vendors but also among the options offered by each vendor.

For a newcomer to online searching, flat-fee subscriptions can be an excellent choice, if only for their simplicity. Unfortunately, not all database vendors offer this option, and among those that do, many are priced too high for the occasional user.

Many, perhaps most, online database vendors charge a sign-up (or initiation, or membership) fee for access to their databases. These fees may be as little as $15 or $20, and may even be refunded in the form of usage credits. Some are more expensive. Sema Group InfoData AB - Rattsbanken, a vendor from Sweden, charges an initiation fee of $500. Many variables can change the initiation fee that some vendors charge.

After the sign-up fee come subscription fees, which may be charged monthly or at longer intervals. Again, these may be only a few dollars each month, or they may be quite expensive. Online Computer Library Center, Inc., (OCLC) charges $6,500 per year for some of its databases.

Instead of a subscription fee, or sometimes in addition to it, some vendors charge minimum usage fees. No matter how little you use the database during a given period, you will be charged at least that minimum fee. If you do use the database, the charges count against that minimum; when it is reached, additional charges begin to accrue. For low-volume users, a pay-as-you go plan can be a much better choice, even if the rates per hour and per report are higher. However, that option is not always available.

Most vendors charge an hourly fee for the use of their databases. A few services may be free, while many more are only a few dollars an hour. However, some are expensive. The highest charge I have encountered is $300 per hour. Additional fees usually are charged for the information you find, view, or print. Discounts are sometimes available for high-volume users or for those who pay in advance for a set number of hours. Vendors with multiple databases may charge a different rate for each one, or the databases may be grouped into several pricing levels. If several vendors carry the same database, each one will have its own pricing structure and hourly rate. Vendors may not all carry exactly the same data, and they may or may not provide an index that permits efficient searching for the type of data you need.

The list of possible charges goes on.

Many databases offer a choice of pre-formatted reports, each of which carries a different fee. You pay for exactly the information you want, and no more. The smallest unit of print may be the database record (or accession) number. Another common format is the KWIC (Keyword-In-Context) print, which provides a few lines of type surrounding the keywords that match your search request. Sometimes it is possible to select exactly the fields you wish to see displayed. There are further variations, depending on the vendor and database and on whether you view the record on the screen or have it e-mailed, faxed, or mailed to you. For Dun and Bradstreet Financial Records, fees can exceed $100 per report.

Add in copyright fees, which may be included in the cost of the database or billed separately, telephone and network charges, and a host of other charges, which mutate as vendors think up new ways to bill for their data.

All these variables make it even more important to compare prices among the various database vendors whose services you may wish to use. Unfortunately, vendors also make it nearly impossible to be sure which vendor's options will give you the most data for the most reasonable price. This is one area in which you must struggle along as best you can.

Copyright and Resale

Simply because information is available on a database does not mean that it can be used freely, without concern for copyright. If you buy or lease a CD-ROM database, copyright, use restrictions, and proprietary rights may all be defined on the packaging or within the database itself. For telephone directory databases, I have seen restrictions limiting use for commercial direct mail or telemarketing to no more than 250 listings per month. Alternatively, some telephone directory databases may be purchased with unlimited use, while others ban commercial use entirely.

Almost without exception, it is a severe violation of copyright for you to download records from one database to sell to another, or to resell any individual record to multiple users.

Online database vendors normally include copyright and use agreements in their contracts. Copyright statements are also found in the system documentation and on individual database records and reports.

If documents are ordered through a document delivery company, the firm usually charges a copyright fee, which is passed on to the publisher. If you go to a library and make copies of an article, you may already be in violation of a copyright. You may be able to pay the copyright directly to the publisher in order to remain in compliance. Rather than having to track down individual publishers yourself, it is also possible to set up an account with the Copyright Clearance Center to pay them the copyright fees for individual documents, which they will then distribute to the publishers for you.

Again, it is important that you become very familiar with copyright law if you plan to use databases or any other type of information for a commercial purpose.

Errors and Omissions

There is something uncommonly convincing about the information found in databases. Just as people once assumed that stories in the newspaper would not have been published if they were untrue, it is easy to believe that the information downloaded is valid. Yet you know that you cannot believe everything you see on TV or read in the paper. In the same way, you can't believe everything that you obtain from a database.

Some sources are more suspect than others. Information that is downloaded from a publicly accessible database, such as those created through voluntary contributions of their users, is particularly unreliable. However, even on proprietary databases errors may be found. Some errors are introduced at the time the data is created. For example, a news article can contain errors, which are not corrected or improved in any way by moving the article to a database. Some database records are based on information that individuals or companies contribute about themselves. These may be incorrect or incomplete, or at least present the information in an unrealistically flattering light. Some individuals will also go to great lengths to mask their identities, using pseudonyms, altering key identifying information, such as their birth dates, and otherwise making their records difficult to locate or to verify.

When moving the data from its original form to a database, additional errors may creep in. Typists can make mistakes while entering records. Records can be overlooked or indexed incorrectly, making them difficult to retrieve. This is extremely important to remember when searching for public records. One cannot guarantee that an individual has no criminal history simply because no criminal record was found. The record may not be available online, the vendor may not cover the geographic area or court where the record exists, or the record may be indexed incorrectly and impossible to retrieve. The vendor's software even may miss the record due to a program bug.

Many chapters in this book contain more specific warnings about certain kinds of information, but one rule applies to all database records: evaluate them as you would information obtained from any other source. Consider the source, the reputation of the vendor, and the possibility that the record may contain errors that must be reconciled through other sources or by ordering copies of original documents when conflicts are found or when validation of the information is extremely important.

Information Professionals or Brokers

You may have heard the term "information broker" (IB) or "information professional" (IP). Many other names also have been applied to this profession: freelance librarian, researcher or freelance researcher, cybrarian, finder, information consultant, information manager, information specialist, infopreneur, library consultant, and online researcher.

On occasion, much to the dismay of the profession, the press has written of "information brokers" when describing data thieves and others who break into computer systems or office file cabinets, pay off insiders, or otherwise obtain information illegally in order to sell it. As a result, some brokers who provide professional, legal, and ethical business or personal services avoid the title of "information broker" in order to avoid being tainted by the unsavory reputations of the dishonest and unethical, but newsworthy, minority. When I mention information brokers in this book, I will be referring to professionals and not to those who steal information or use it illegally.

Whatever the term, information brokers or professionals can be loosely defined as people who provide information for a fee and charge for their services. I will use IB and IP interchangeably throughout this section. Information broker is a bit of a misnomer, however, because it is not actually the information that an IB is normally selling. The information itself usually belongs to the database vendor. What the IB sells is expertise and the time it takes to locate whatever information the client requests.

Many IPs have a background in library science, but the advent of the "Information Age" has attracted people to the information field from nearly every profession and background. An information brokerage often operates as a sole proprietorship, but many are partnerships or corporations and some even serve as contracting agencies for many independent brokers.

An IP can provide the search expertise that a client needs but may not have the time, resources, or inclination to acquire. Database searching can be complex and expensive, and not everyone loves to do it. It sometimes makes more sense for researchers to contract with someone else for this service so that they can focus their attention and resources on other areas of their business.

If a company makes frequent use of databases or other types of research, it then may be more cost-effective to have researchers on staff and provide them with the ongoing training and resources to do their job efficiently. In-house researchers sometimes make use of IBs to handle business requests outside their field of expertise, or to locate information or search databases to which the company does not have access.

IBs do not offer exactly the same services. Some are subject specialists who offer a wide range of expertise and services from asset location to biomedical or engineering literature research. Others are generalists who will undertake many different forms of research. There are even IPs who do no online searching at all, whose expertise may be in telephone research, market analysis, teaching research, or some other specialty within the information arena. IPs such as these often contract with other IPs to obtain the information they need from online databases.

Information professionals charge according to their own pricing structures, at various rates. For small units of information, such as credit headers, it is common to see fees charged at a flat rate per report. Other types of information merit an hourly charge, which may range from $40 per hour to $250 per hour. Online and other expenses are often passed through to the client, with or without a mark-up. (Some database vendors prohibit information professionals from marking up their online fees, to avoid the perception of inflated online rates.) There are IBs who offer a not-to-exceed estimate, limiting their research efforts to your budget or to the charges they expect to incur. Other IBs will give a range within which the expenses will fall. Still others may quote a maximum number of hours and/or reports to be devoted to the project. IBs sometimes work on retainer, offering a certain amount of research or labor during a given period at a set rate.

If you are looking for an information professional to perform research on a contract basis, there are a couple of good resources for finding them. *The Burwell Directory of Information Brokers* (published by Burwell Enterprises, Inc.) is an international directory that lists IBs by specialty, geography, services offered, and other criteria.

Another resource is:

Association of Independent Information Professionals (AIIP)
7044 So. 13th Street
Oak Creek, WI 53154-1429
(414)766-0421
www.aiip.org

AIIP is a nonprofit organization whose "regular" members are all owners of information brokerages. AIIP also includes "associate" members, who either work for others or are interested in the profession.

Chapter 3

The Internet, Consumer Online Systems, and Personal Information

This just in: The Internet is not a fad.
　　　　　　　　　　　　–John Hoynes, *The West Wing* (1999)

By now, virtually everyone knows what the Internet is: a globe-spanning array of interlinked computer networks through which growing millions of people and companies exchange messages that range from product orders to scientific reports to singles ads. If you're already a devoted Web-head, netizen, or cybersurfer, you can skip this chapter. However, to those still unconverted, it may not be clear why the rest of us think the Net is so important. For anyone who needs personal information, it is a significant question.

The notion of a new communications medium, a new way to get information from one place to another, may not seem very profound. Neither the telephone nor the radio seemed all that important at one time either—Alexander Graham Bell imagined that his invention would be used primarily to carry music from the orchestra to distant listeners—yet each of these technologies changed the world. The Internet (along with the complementary consumer online systems—America Online, CompuServe, Prodigy, and their competitors) is the first truly new communications medium to appear since television.

It is a medium with advantages.

Like the telephone, the Net carries private messages from person to person and company to company. However, these "e-mail" messages are written, rather than spoken, and they can be sent and picked up from nearly anywhere at any time. For people who are on the move or who work unusual hours, this convenience can be important.

Also, Net messages are cheap, often far cheaper than the equivalent telephone call. For most people in many countries of the world today, Internet access is just a local phone call away. With the Net, that local call can carry your message to Singapore for the same price as a phone call to the house next door. One colleague who lives in a small New Hampshire town reports that a one-minute call to the next town, less than four miles away, costs $.75 during peak hours, while the call to send an e-mail message around the world is free!

In some ways, the Net is a lot like postal mail, known to Net citizens (or netizens), as "snail mail." The main difference is that messages flash around the world at the speed of light, rather than waiting to be carried by hand, truck, and air transport. This gives online messages a more conversational tone, with people often exchanging thoughts several times a day. ("Live" conferences also are possible on the Internet, but most Internet messages are posted and read at the participants' convenience.)

Like radio programs and newspaper articles, Internet messages also can be broadcast publicly to groups of people with common interests. Everyone who looks in on a Usenet newsgroup (an Internet bulletin board) can read everyone else's messages and reply to whichever message they wish. New newsgroups are created whenever enough people declare their interest. Unlike the radio or newspaper, however, virtually anyone can join in to reply, offer their own information and opinions, and share their ideas.

Larger works also are published on the Internet, including magazines, directories, and even complete books.

In a very real sense, everyone on the Internet is a potential advertiser or publisher. Thus, one can find home pages that promote nearly any type of business, topic, hobby, or interest. Companies all over the globe have set up home pages on the World Wide Web, which often include information about the company, its history, annual reports, press releases, and other items formerly available only in print or in proprietary research databases. Products and services are now bought and sold online, changing the business models of large and small companies all over the globe, and indeed the economy at large, as e-commerce restructures the ways in which the world conducts trade.

All these are examples of what the Internet has to offer, and to some extent what it all "means" will be inferred from these evolving resources. Yet it is still too early to predict confidently where the Net is ultimately headed. Although the first host was connected to ARPANET (the predecessor of the Internet) way back in 1969, it began only as a United States Defense Department network, used to support military research. Later it grew to include other government agencies, universities, and colleges, but it remained closed to the general public. Only in the last few years has the Internet opened to the general populace. Only since the World Wide Web was created (first proposed in 1989 by Tim Berners-Lee, but becoming gradually a reality between 1991 and 1994, when clients, browsers, and editors were created) did the Internet become easy enough to use and understand to attract businesses and consumers en masse.

While the Internet itself was still a government preserve, consumer online services began to appear. Over the years, they have grown into CompuServe (founded in 1969; offering online service in 1979), Prodigy (1988), America Online (1989), and other consumer-oriented bulletin board systems, each offering its own constellation of online databases and information services. In the 1990s, these online worlds merged, as the consumer systems provided gateways into the Internet and the online population exploded from a few hundred thousand to tens of millions. It is clear that some "critical mass" was reached long ago, that there now are enough people online to create viable new communities stretching across the entire planet.

The Internet is a global conference call, virtually free (depending on where you're calling from), and with just enough structure to keep it all from disintegrating into chaos. Online, people with any interest or expertise can find each other and exchange ideas all across the world as easily as they talk with their neighbors. They can discuss any topic, read and understand each others' views, and have their voices heard as well. Thus, they can build on each other's knowledge and reach new levels of understanding. One can only imagine where this will lead.

What the Internet Is Not

While the Internet is a fascinating and often useful means of communication, it is not the be-all, end-all panacea for all of a professional researcher's information needs. At least, not today.

Although billions of bytes of information flow across the Internet each day, the vast bulk of it is e-commerce, personal mail, discussion, or opinions shared by Internet users. Some of the information is valuable and may be found nowhere else, but much of it, from the researcher's point of view, is pure garbage. Putting information on the Internet does nothing to improve its quality, and it is often unclear whose opinions are being heard or who authored any particular Web page, article, or file that can be found and downloaded onto your computer. It is much like listening to the talk on the street, but the Internet neighborhood extends around the world. For some of us, the simple fact that information is found on a database or accessed via a computer gives it greater authority. Where the Internet is concerned, this is particularly unwise. For example, if you were attempting to obtain information about the reputation of an "expert" via the Internet, you might unknowingly find yourself talking with one of the so-called expert's close friends, or even with your candidate. For privacy, and sometimes for other reasons, many people use another name (or gender) while online, so you may not know who you're really talking to.

Another problem is that so much information is now accessible through the Internet that it can be virtually impossible to weed through it all to locate any specific fact. One needs a minimum of software to access the Internet, which is available free from many online vendors or Internet service providers; after that, dozens or hundreds of utilities and ancillary programs can be found online to help with navigating and searching the Net. However, the treasures that can be accessed through the Internet can be stored nearly anywhere, and many are not indexed. Despite the variety of search tools available, information can remain so well hidden that even the most experienced searchers cannot find it without knowing the address. The most useful sites for a given search may never be discovered without a great stroke of serendipity.

The Internet is only starting to be held to the same constraints that govern advertising on television or the radio, or in the newspaper. Nearly anyone can create a WWW home page, making it easy to invent a company on the Internet, add a directory naming oneself as a top executive, fabricate company history and press releases, and make any claim at all about that fictitious company, its products and services. Since no one owns the Internet, no one agency is responsible for policing it, and it is taking quite a while for the laws regulating truth in advertising to catch up with this new medium. The Federal Trade Commission (FTC) has prosecuted few cases of online fraud to date, even though existing laws can be applied to the online world, and many individuals have been defrauded by unscrupulous online vendors. Today, using Internet home pages, online zines, or other information published solely on the Internet to verify information about a person is risky, at best. Although information found on the Net may prove to be entirely correct, it should be verified through other sources whenever its accuracy is important to you.

One more thing: given all the free data that now is available over the Net, it is sometimes easy to forget that unique or otherwise valuable information is still worth paying for. The growing number of vendors that now allow access to their databases via the Internet have not suddenly decided to provide access for free. Some of the most useful databases that can be tapped through the Internet remain just as expensive as they were before they moved to the Net. Professional database vendors continue to require subscriptions and charge fees for access to their data. Using the Internet to access those databases has not changed that.

What Kinds of Personal Information Can You Find on the Internet and Consumer Online Systems?

Many types of personal records can be found on the Internet. For example, if you are interested in tracking down your ancestors, the Internet should be your first stop.

Through the Internet (as well as CompuServe's Roots forum and similar areas on other consumer online systems), genealogists are linking their lineages and contacting other researchers who will share their records around the globe. There are hundreds of genealogical sites on the Internet, with many simply dedicated to indexing the others. Along with a great deal of lineage information, one can find a searchable death index, rosters of Civil War combatants and a searchable database of Civil War soldiers and sailors, Medal of Honor citations, an index to British, German, and Loyalist officers of the American revolution, and a French and Indian War site that provides the names of French soldiers who went to Canada from 1755 to 1763. More recent collections include a Korean War KIA/MIA Database and the Vietnam Era Prisoner of War, Missing In Action Database. Further information about genealogical records can be found in Chapter 34.

Many consumer online systems offer online encyclopedias, which can be good sources for biographical information on historical as well as contemporary figures. More information about these databases can be found in Chapter 15.

Many recruiters and employers seeking potential new hires consider the Internet one of their most important resources. If you are looking for a job, putting your resume on the Net will make your availability known to recruiters and employers alike. Forums for certain interest groups, such as computer consultants and data processing professionals, already carry hundreds of resumes and job offers. Similar resources now appear for professions unrelated to computers. More information about recruitment and job searching can be found in Chapter 8.

Before looking for work at one of these sites, you should understand that anyone at all can read the information you include—not just those who might offer you a job. Your current employer might even see it. You should also be aware that anyone might be following the trail of your search, to find out what your interests are, and what you are posting. Services such as Google Groups (formerly Deja, now found on the Internet at http://groups.google.com) index Usenet newsgroups and even go so far as to provide an index of all of the messages that you post to any newsgroup. If you knew where someone spent his online time and had an index to all of the messages that were posted, you might learn more about that individual than anyone ever imagined possible—and all of this can be accessed on the Internet without the subject's knowledge. You would do well not to post more personal information online than you want the world to know; you never know who is listening.

If you were seeking information about someone who might reasonably use the Internet to search for a job, you might be able to locate a resume online as well. It could contain the person's home address and telephone number, educational background, family members, and personal interests, as well as employment history.

Many Internet accounts include a free or low-cost home page, so even netizens without a business to advertise are creating personal home pages, where they tell the world who they are and what interests them. These personal sites often include everything from their favorite recipes, hobbies, or music to pictures of their families and pets. Before spending time and money using expensive databases to find information about someone, it makes more and more sense to see whether the individual has a home page, either personally or professionally, where the very information needed may already be posted.

If you are trying to locate someone, the Internet and its commercial offshoots supply more than a dozen telephone directories. With these resources, the person you seek may be no more than a search or two away. Further information about telephone directories can be found in Chapter 17.

Other Internet search tools are designed specifically to help you find people who use the Internet. Finger and Whois are used to find out whether the person you are seeking has an Internet account, and the results of a search may even include a home address. Some of the consumer online services also make it possible to search member directories. For example, America Online allows you to search member "profiles," which include whatever information a member chooses to divulge. This may or may not include the subject's name. CompuServe allows searching by name, which may also be narrowed geographically. Further information about finding people who are online can be found in Chapter 6.

There are also dozens of general-purpose search engines and Internet indices, such as

- All4oneSearch Machine (http://leonardo.spidernet.net/Copernicus/831/search)
- AltaVista (www.altavista.com)
- CNET's Search.com (www.search.com)
- Dogpile (www.dogpile.com)
- Excite (www.excite.com)
- Galaxy (www.galaxy.com)
- Go.com (www.go.com)
- Google (www.google.com)
- HotBot (hotbot.lycos.com)
- Infospace (www.infospace.com)
- Lycos (www.lycos.com)
- Overture (www.overture.com)
- PeekABoo (www.peekaboo.net)
- WebCrawler (web.webcrawler.com)
- Webfilc (www.webfile.com)
- Yahoo! (www.yahoo.com)

These engines, along with their growing legion of competitors, can be used to search for the name of a person or company among the millions of World Wide Web pages, gopher sites, FTP files, and Usenet newsgroup postings. An index to search engines such as these can be found at Beaucoup! (www.beaucoup.com).

Unfortunately, names are often one of the least individual things about us. Searching for a particular "John Smith" among the millions of Internet users may turn up so many matches that it would take days to go through them all, with no guarantee that your subject was among them. If a person's name is uncommon, it is worth trying several of the search tools to see what they find, as each conducts the search in a different way. However, if you do not find the person you seek fairly quickly, do not waste too much time reading through all of the possibilities. Refer to Chapter 6 for further explanation of problems with names.

Even a company may share its name, but so many firms of every size are putting up their own home pages on the Internet that it is definitely worth a search or two if you are looking for someone who owns his own business. Employees are also sometimes listed on company home pages. Profiles of key executives can be found. So can annual reports, which usually list at least the members of the board and the top executives. On one of the corporate home pages I looked at, I even found profiles of the company's top scientists, along with lists of their inventions and contact information for each. I have found speeches by key executives that I would not have located on high-priced databases. It is not at all unusual to find a company's recent press releases included on its home page. Refer to Chapter 11 for information on gathering competitive intelligence on companies and individuals within companies.

Students may also be listed in an Internet student directory for their college or university, or perhaps in an Internet fraternity or sorority directory. Even some high school directories can be searched on the Net. People who have already graduated often can be found in an alumni directory. Associations often have their own Web sites, many of which include searchable member directories. There also are directories of experts, consultants, faculty, attorneys, and other professionals that can be searched on the Net. Further information about staff, professional, and other directories can be found in Chapter 18.

Adoptees and birthparents seeking one another can use the Internet to register their names with the Adoption Information Registry. If their names are matched, they will be put in contact with one another so that a reunion can be arranged. There are also Usenet newsgroups in which adoptees and birthparents provide assistance and advice to one another, including search assistance, and adoptee/birthparent classifieds are being compiled on the Internet as well. Similar help can be found through nearly all of the consumer online services. For additional information on adoption records, refer to Chapter 32.

For entertainers, sports heroes, and almost any type of celebrity, fans have compiled databases on the Internet. There are show business roundtables; soap opera, sports, and rock forums; photo libraries; and bulletin boards for fan clubs. These often include screen and television credits, upcoming concerts and appearances, fan reviews, photo libraries, and trivia. Fans also share stories of their personal encounters, opinions, and collective adoration with other fans through Usenet newsgroups and online mailing lists. Some television shows host their own forums in which they invite feedback on their episodes and take suggestions for future programs. It may even be possible to converse online with your favorite celebrities, as online vendors arrange "live chats" with rock stars, sports heroes, authors, stars of stage and screen, politicians, and other celebrities. If you need information about someone famous, the Internet can be a great resource. For further information on celebrity records, refer to Chapter 33.

Other databases being assembled by netizens deal in quotations (some you might recognize, some you might not) and obituaries (of the famous, as well as of the compilers' friends and family members). More about quotations can be found in Chapter 22, and information about obituaries and deaths can be found in Chapter 28.

Missing children also are listed on the Net, along with their photos, in the hope that someone will recognize them as a neighbor or schoolmate and contact the authorities. Registered sex offenders also are listed in order to notify communities of their presence. Information about these databases can be found in Chapter 21.

If you want information on a political figure, you can find Congressional directories, candidate profiles, political speeches, and many other valuable resources for political research on the Net. Information about political figures is common to many of the consumer online services. Further information about political records can be found in Chapter 35.

Public records are slowly coming to the Internet. For example, in some areas, court record indices may be found on the Net. Although most public records are still within the domain of commercial public records vendors, many of these vendors are now offering access to their systems through the Internet, or allowing people to order records through their Web sites. Further information about public records can be found in Chapter 31.

Some full-text books are accessible through the Internet, including some biographical works, and more are being uploaded each day. Refer to Chapter 15 for further information.

Original magazines, known as "zines" or "e-zines," are being published on the Net, and most print magazines and newsletters have Web sites that carry at least part of their contents or provide extra information about the articles that have appeared on paper. Many of these publications carry articles about individuals. For personal research, alumni magazines can be particularly helpful, as their news items usually list marriages, births, deaths, and accomplishments of the alumni.

Television, radio, and news programs also have Web sites, and some of these include recent stories about individuals. On more than one occasion, I have caught part of a news story on a television newscast and gone to the news program's Web site for additional details. Some of the newswire services also are providing their broadcasts through the Internet, sometimes linked to the home pages of companies that are mentioned in them. Additional information about news sources and transcripts can be found in Chapter 20.

If you know something about a person's interests, you may be able to find a Usenet newsgroup in which this person participates or where a colleague, friend, or family member can be found. Usenet newsgroups can be found through Google Groups (http://groups.google.com). The more you know about your subject, the easier it will be to gather additional information. If you believe in the theory that there are only six degrees of separation between all of us, it probably makes intuitive sense to you that one key to finding information about a person is to locate someone who knows someone, who knows someone, until you reach the circle of people who actually know the individual in question. With more people visiting the Internet every day, the chances get better all the time that people you are looking for, or at least someone who knows them, will be found online.

Finally, the Internet includes whatever information people care to share about themselves. This can be considerable. Companies wishing to market to people with particular interests gather names and Internet addresses of those participating in key newsgroups in order to target them for mailing lists and other marketing ventures. Although the online community generally frowns on this, it does illustrate that people are gathering information about us through our participation on the Net. Further information about mailing lists can be found in Chapter 19.

You will find Internet addresses for sites mentioned previously, as well as many others, listed throughout this book and at the *Naked in Cyberspace* Web site (www.technosearch.com/naked). This list can never be complete, and even if I had been able to include every site that a personal records researcher might find useful, the list still would have been inaccurate a week after it was finished. The Internet is evolving quickly. New sites appear daily, while old ones vanish or are transformed almost beyond recognition. No list of Net resources can ever be one-hundred percent accurate, but the sites in this book were updated continuously throughout the writing and production process, and the online version will be updated regularly. Please use the e-mail link to let me know of any promising resources you think I should include—as well as any obsolete listings that should be deleted.

Chapter 4

A Few Sample Searches

*I talk and talk and talk, and I haven't taught people in 50 years
what my father taught by example in one week.*

–Mario Cuomo

Any search for personal records begins with assessing the information at hand and determining the goals for the search. In this chapter, I will present three sample searches that illustrate how personal records are used with various pieces of starting information and different goals. More information on these and other types of search can be found in Section II: How Personal Records Are Used, but these examples will give you a good idea of how you can use personal records in your own life.

Locating a Person

The first sample represents the most universal type of search using personal records. Nearly everyone has someone that they would like to locate—an old friend, a first love, a lost family member, or someone who owes them money. I have performed searches such as this for creditors, attorneys trying to locate a witness, people looking for old friends and estranged family members, as well as locating many of my own old friends.

Each location search is somewhat unique, but they all start out with a list of the information at hand. (In Chapter 6, you will find the form I use to list all of the information known about the subject of a search.) In this case, it was an adoption search, and there were several good leads.

I had been contacted by a pre-adoptive mother (we'll call her Diane) who wanted to track down the birthparents of her infant to expedite the adoption. Diane's attorney had advised her that the adoption would go more smoothly if she obtained written consents from the birthparents directly. There was also a twist. The birthmother had been married to someone other than the birthfather at the times of the conception and birth, so Diane also wanted to locate the birthmother's husband to obtain his consent as well.

Diane had received the birth certificate for her infant. It contained the full name and birth date of the birthmother. The birthfather's first and last name were listed as well, but his birth date was unknown. (They had actually only met once, in a bar, so the spelling of his name was also in question.) Diane had received a copy of the marriage certificate for the birthmother and her husband, which contained their full names, dates of birth, names of their parents, and a 14-year-old address. With this much information, it was a relatively simple matter to track down the birthmother.

To make things even simpler, the birthmother and her husband had an unusual last name. I used an online phone directory (such as those listed in Chapter 17) and searched for anyone with that last name in California. Only eight listings were found. None of the listings matched their first names or first initials, but one gave a first initial that matched the husband's middle name. I ran an Address Update (which you can request through a public records vendor, if you do not have accounts with the credit agencies) and found that it was the husband's address; the record matched his full name and date of birth. I ran another Address Update for the birthmother, using that same address, and found that she had moved to a new address, which was provided. Both of their Address Update reports provided an additional piece of valuable information—their Social Security numbers. With that information, Diane would be almost guaranteed success in tracking them down again in the future, should she need to, such as in a medical crisis.

I searched the online telephone directory for the birthfather, but found no matches at all in California. This seemed odd because even if he was not listed, it seemed reasonable to assume that in a state as large as California there should be at least one person with the same surname. The failure made me question the spelling of his name all the more. Upon contacting the birthmother, I found that she had one more piece of information about the birthfather, which proved valuable. She had an old phone number for him. Using the telephone number, I went back to the online phone directory and searched for a match, through a reverse directory search. I found a listing for a woman whose last name sounded much like the one on the birth certificate, but was spelled differently. (It turned out to be the birthfather's mother, whom Diane did not wish to contact.) With the corrected spelling, I was able to run another Address Update report against the address found in the telephone directory and obtained the birthfather's current address.

Many other search procedures could have been used to obtain the same results, and this search could have taken other directions, depending on the information uncovered at each step. This was a best-case scenario; some searches are more difficult. However, this straightforward example demonstrates how easily personal records can resolve a problem that at first glance might seem all but impossible. It also illustrates how simple it can be to locate a person when you begin with good identifying information.

Searching for Assets

Our second example illustrates an asset search. You may wonder why you would ever need to conduct such a search. In fact, many people today use asset searches in different ways. Let us look at just a few.

People who are weighing a possible partnership or other financial arrangement sometimes worry about con men and women. Even if they do not doubt the basic honesty of their proposed partner, they feel better if they have first verified that the person they are dealing with has a realistic view of their assets. This can include anyone considering marriage!

Someone who is being sued may wish to size up the resources of the opposition. Similarly, people considering suing someone can perform an asset search to determine whether it is worth the expense of a lawsuit to go after what the other party owns. It does little good to win a costly suit if the other party has nothing to pay you.

Even charitable agencies have used asset searches to figure out where the big money is before targeting their fundraising efforts.

The asset searches that I typically perform are for financial businesses—companies that lend a great deal of money and want to know exactly what their debtors have to offer before going after them in court. In fact, many of their cases never make it to court because the information they bring with them to the deposition convinces the debtor that the company plans to go after *all* of their assets—and knows where to find them. A recent search went something like this:

First, as always, I started by looking over the information my client had provided. In this case, it amounted to credit reports from all three credit agencies (Equifax, Experian, and TransUnion). These reports provided a list of the debts owed by the subject, as well as his full name, date of birth, Social Security number, current and previous addresses, employer, and public records including a bankruptcy, a judgment, and two federal tax liens. Notable among the debts were real estate loans, which meant that there was most likely property to go after.

Having read and organized all of the data received on the credit reports, I ran my first search—an "Info:Probe," offered through one of the public records vendors (CDB Infotek, now ChoicePoint Online). When used to identify someone's assets, this service includes a search of this vendor's Bankruptcies, Liens and Judgments file, Civil Filings, Corporations and Limited Partnerships, FAA Aircraft Ownership, Fictitious Business Names, General Index, Judgment Docket and Lien Book, Real Property Ownership, Uniform Commercial Code Searches, and U.S. Coast Guard Watercraft File. An Info:Probe provides an inexpensive way to find out whether this public records vendor has any records on file for your subject before you spend the time and money to search individual files. In this case, a search of records for the Western states revealed the matches shown in Figure 4.1.

I then pulled each of the individual reports resulting from the Info:Probe search and read them over to determine which applied to my subject, and which were for someone with the same name. (ChoicePoint Online has placed a cap on the cost of the searches that result from an Info:Probe, so instead of costing several hundred dollars to pull all of these reports individually, the total was only $100.) Some of the records available online, such as those for real property, are fairly complete and require little further explanation (see Figure 4.2).

Other records, such as Uniform Commercial Code filings (UCCs), are merely indices, as shown in Figure 4.3.

The UCC record shown in Figure 4.3 does not provide the details of the debt or the collateral that was pledged, so I used the filing number to order copies of the records from a public records retriever. (If you need someone to retrieve records from a courthouse for you, many retrievers can be found through the National Public Records Research Association at www.nprra.org. You can also order records directly from courts in many cases.) The records arrived a day or two later, listing many additional assets that had been pledged against various debts.

I ran Info:Probe searches against each company name with which the subject was affiliated (which I found listed in various records, such as the Fictitious Business Name filings and Corporations and Limited Partnerships). This turned up additional UCC and Bankruptcy filings. I ordered copies of the files and found full financial statements including bank accounts, tax records, and many other undisclosed assets.

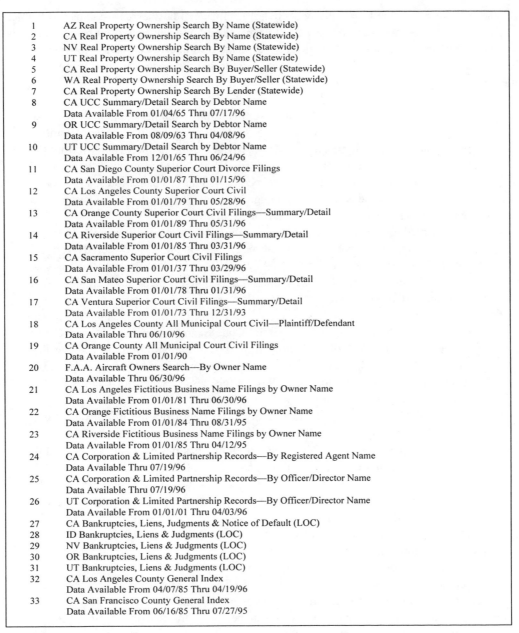

1	AZ Real Property Ownership Search By Name (Statewide)
2	CA Real Property Ownership Search By Name (Statewide)
3	NV Real Property Ownership Search By Name (Statewide)
4	UT Real Property Ownership Search By Name (Statewide)
5	CA Real Property Ownership Search By Buyer/Seller (Statewide)
6	WA Real Property Ownership Search By Buyer/Seller (Statewide)
7	CA Real Property Ownership Search By Lender (Statewide)
8	CA UCC Summary/Detail Search by Debtor Name Data Available From 01/04/65 Thru 07/17/96
9	OR UCC Summary/Detail Search by Debtor Name Data Available From 08/09/63 Thru 04/08/96
10	UT UCC Summary/Detail Search by Debtor Name Data Available From 12/01/65 Thru 06/24/96
11	CA San Diego County Superior Court Divorce Filings Data Available From 01/01/87 Thru 01/15/96
12	CA Los Angeles County Superior Court Civil Data Available From 01/01/79 Thru 05/28/96
13	CA Orange County Superior Court Civil—Summary/Detail Data Available From 01/01/89 Thru 05/31/96
14	CA Riverside Superior Court Civil Filings—Summary/Detail Data Available From 01/01/85 Thru 03/31/96
15	CA Sacramento Superior Court Civil Filings Data Available From 01/01/37 Thru 03/29/96
16	CA San Mateo Superior Court Civil Filings—Summary/Detail Data Available From 01/01/78 Thru 01/31/96
17	CA Ventura Superior Court Civil Filings—Summary/Detail Data Available From 01/01/73 Thru 12/31/93
18	CA Los Angeles County All Municipal Court Civil—Plaintiff/Defendant Data Available Thru 06/10/96
19	CA Orange County All Municipal Court Civil Filings Data Available From 01/01/90
20	F.A.A. Aircraft Owners Search—By Owner Name Data Available Thru 06/30/96
21	CA Los Angeles Fictitious Business Name Filings by Owner Name Data Available From 01/01/81 Thru 06/30/96
22	CA Orange Fictitious Business Name Filings by Owner Name Data Available From 01/01/84 Thru 08/31/95
23	CA Riverside Fictitious Business Name Filings by Owner Name Data Available From 01/01/85 Thru 04/12/95
24	CA Corporation & Limited Partnership Records—By Registered Agent Name Data Available Thru 07/19/96
25	CA Corporation & Limited Partnership Records—By Officer/Director Name Data Available Thru 07/19/96
26	UT Corporation & Limited Partnership Records—By Officer/Director Name Data Available From 01/01/01 Thru 04/03/96
27	CA Bankruptcies, Liens, Judgments & Notice of Default (LOC)
28	ID Bankruptcies, Liens & Judgments (LOC)
29	NV Bankruptcies, Liens & Judgments (LOC)
30	OR Bankruptcies, Liens & Judgments (LOC)
31	UT Bankruptcies, Liens & Judgments (LOC)
32	CA Los Angeles County General Index Data Available From 04/07/85 Thru 04/19/96
33	CA San Francisco County General Index Data Available From 06/16/85 Thru 07/27/95

Figure 4.1   Info:Probe

I repeated the whole process using the wife's name (which I found on their joint real property records) and found assets that were held under her name alone.

Then I went after vehicles registered under their names or their businesses. The necessary searches are offered by many public records vendors.

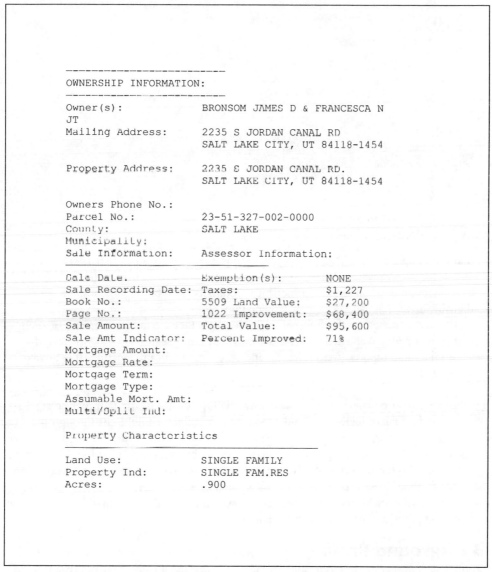

```
--------------------------------
OWNERSHIP INFORMATION:
--------------------------------
Owner(s):              BRONSOM JAMES D & FRANCESCA N
JT
Mailing Address:       2235 S JORDAN CANAL RD
                       SALT LAKE CITY, UT 84118-1454


Property Address:      2235 S JORDAN CANAL RD.
                       SALT LAKE CITY, UT 84118-1454


Owners Phone No.:
Parcel No.:            23-51-327-002-0000
County:                SALT LAKE
Municipality:
Sale Information:      Assessor Information:
                     _____
Sale Date.             Exemption(s):       NONE
Sale Recording Date:   Taxes:              $1,227
Book No.:              5509 Land Value:    $27,200
Page No.:              1022 Improvement:   $68,400
Sale Amount:           Total Value:        $95,600
Sale Amt Indicator:    Percent Improved:   71%
Mortgage Amount:
Mortgage Rate:
Mortgage Term:
Mortgage Type:
Assumable Mort. Amt:
Multi/Split Ind:


Property Characteristics
                     _____
Land Use:              SINGLE FAMILY
Property Ind:          SINGLE FAM.RES
Acres:                 .900
```

Figure 4.2   Real property record

Business credit profiles (offered through many professional research databases, but also available on Prodigy, CompuServe, and so on) were pulled for all of the businesses linked to the husband or the wife. This search provided several other public records for areas of the country not covered by the public records vendor. Copies of those documents were also ordered.

I searched news databases for further information about the husband, wife, and every business that they were affiliated with. Some newspapers publish a weekly column that lists properties sold in their area, and these uncovered still more properties

```
1 Filing Number:    91276700
Document Type:      UCC1—Financing Statement
File Date/Time:     02/20/1991 14:03
Debtor:             BRONSOM JAMES D
                    522 WEST 1500 SOUTH
                    SLC, UT 84115
Secured Party:      JOHNSTONE FINANCIAL SERVICES
                    P O BOX 3292
                    PORTLAND,OR 97208
Collateral:         A,A/R,EQ,FU,FX,INV,BILLS+
Microfilm:          822
Expire Date:        02/20/1996
```

Figure 4.3   Uniform Commercial Code (UCC) filing

that the couple owned. This search revealed no press releases or other news articles about their companies. When such records are found, they sometimes include announcements of important partnerships, contracts, or other significant changes in their business that can affect their financial position.

Finally, I looked on the Internet to find out whether the subjects or any of their companies had a Web site. In this case, they had not, but in other cases I have discovered annual reports, press releases, and other important information. It is always worth a check.

Since a great deal of money was at stake, my client probably would still plan to send someone out to conduct surveillance on the debtors. The investigator might sift through their trash, find out who they were meeting, and otherwise attempt to locate assets, such as off-shore accounts, that would not show up in the news or in the public records. What I provided from my computer would be the majority of what my client took to court, however, and would serve as the basis for further investigation. In many cases, such as when determining whether someone is worth suing or whether Prince Charming really owns a castle, the information you can gather using your computer will be more than sufficient.

A Background Profile

For the last sample search, I will show you how to construct a background profile from online sources. This particular case demonstrates the way a reporter might use personal records to learn about a public person. The template used in this example (see Figure 4.4) is important, and before you begin any background profiling of your own you may wish to create your own form, using the elements in my template which appears as Figure 6.1 on p. 50 under "Getting Started." The idea is to bring together as many relevant details as possible in order to create a comprehensive overview of the individual.

For this example, some simple Internet research was done on Microsoft Chairman Bill Gates. The actual work reported here is just a first step. An exhaustive search dealing with a subject as active and well-known as Gates could easily take months of work, but I will map out a reasonable path for continuing this effort. The same principles would guide any background research you might wish to undertake.

SUBJECT PROFILE

FULL NAME, ALIASES, NICKNAMES, MAIDEN NAME, MARRIED NAME: William (Bill) H. Gates

GENDER: M

BIRTHDATE AND/OR AGE: October 28, 1955

SOCIAL SECURITY NUMBER: No data provided at the Web site.

PHYSICAL DESCRIPTION: See photos at www.microsoft.com/billgates and www.microsoft.com/presspass/exec/billg/default.asp

DESCENT: No data provided at the Web site.

LAST ADDRESSES:
Grew up in Seattle.

EDUCATION:
In his junior year, Gates left Harvard University to devote his energies to Microsoft, a company he had begun in 1975 with his childhood friend Paul Allen.

In 1973, Gates entered Harvard University as a freshman.

Gates attended public elementary school and the private Lakeside School.

OCCUPATION/EMPLOYMENT: Chairman and Chief Software Architect for Microsoft; Founded Microsoft in 1975, along with Paul Allen.

Founded Corbis, which is developing one of the world's largest resources of visual information—a comprehensive digital archive of art and photography from public and private collections around the globe.

ORGANIZATIONS, AFFILIATIONS & AWARDS:

Sits on the board of ICOS, a company that specializes in protein-based and small-molecule therapeutics.

RELIGION: No data provided at the Web site.

MILITARY BACKGROUND: No data provided at the Web site.

LICENSES: No data provided at the Web site.

HOBBIES, INTERESTS:
In addition to his love of computers and software, Gates is interested in biotechnology.

Supports research into genetically modified food sources.

Gates is an avid reader, and enjoys playing golf and bridge.

RELATIONSHIPS (FAMILY MEMBERS, FRIENDS):
Gates was married on Jan. 1, 1994, to Melinda French Gates. The couple has two children: a daughter, Jennifer Katharine Gates, born in 1996; and a son, Rory John Gates, born in 1999.

2 sisters

Father, William H. Gates II, is a Seattle attorney.
Mother, deceased, Mary Gates, was a schoolteacher, University of Washington regent, and chairwoman of United Way International.

Steve Ballmer, Microsoft's president and chief executive officer (met at Harvard)

Paul Allen, childhood friend, founded Microsoft with Gates in 1975.

PUBLICATIONS:
Books:

In 1999, Gates wrote *Business @ the Speed of Thought*

The Road Ahead, published in 1995

Articles:

Bill Gates to Technology Professionals: Why We're Building .NET Technology, June 2001

Now for an Intelligent Internet, The World in 2001 (The Economist), Nov. 2000

Will Frankenfood Feed The World?, Time, Jun. 19, 2000

Yes, More Trade With China, Washington Post, May 23, 2000

The Case for Microsoft, Time, May 15, 2000

Enter "Generation i," Instructor, Mar. 2000

Product Distribution Goes Digital, IEEE Internet Computing, Jan. 2000

Beyond Gutenberg, The World in 2000 (The Economist), Nov. 1999

Everyone, Anytime, Anywhere, Forbes ASAP, Oct. 4, 1999

Microprocessors Upgraded the Way We Live, USA Today, Jun. 22, 1999

Why the PC Will Not Die, Newsweek, May 31, 1999

The Wright Brothers, Time, Mar. 29, 1999

Compete, Don't Delete, The Economist, Jun. 13, 1998

U.S. v. Microsoft: We're Defending Our Right to Innovate, Wall Street Journal, May 20, 1998

Who Decides What Innovations Go Into Your PC?, Wall Street Journal, Nov. 10, 1997

SUBSCRIPTIONS (MAGAZINES): No data provided at the Web site.

FINANCES (ASSETS):

Gates has donated the proceeds of both of his books to nonprofit organizations that support the use of technology in education and skills development.

An investor in a number of biotechnology companies
Has invested with cellular telephone pioneer Craig McCaw in Teledesic, which is working on an ambitious plan to employ hundreds of low-orbit satellites to provide a worldwide two-way broadband telecommunications service.

He and his wife have endowed a foundation with more than $21 billion to support philanthropic initiatives in the areas of global health and learning. To date, the Bill and Melinda Gates Foundation has committed more than $2 billion to organizations working in global health; more than $500 million to improve learning opportunities, including the Gates Library Initiative to bring computers, Internet Access and training to public libraries in low-income communities in the United States and Canada; more than $200 million to community projects in the Pacific Northwest; and more than $29 million to special projects and annual giving campaigns. More information on the Bill & Melinda Gates Foundation is available at www.gatesfoundation.org.

LAW HISTORY: No data provided at the Web site.

BANK ACCOUNTS: No data provided at the Web site.

POLITICS: Is in favor of permanent normal trade relations with China.

CREDIT CARDS: No data provided at the Web site.

Figure 4.4   Subject profile for Bill Gates

My first step in this search was to find out what information the Microsoft Corporation had published about him. I began with the official Bill Gates Web site on the Internet (www.microsoft.com/billgates/default.asp). There I found a detailed biography, which provided plenty of information from which to start an investigation. Speeches, articles, view papers relating to the

Internet and the future of technologies, and many other relevant topics were supplied for the consumption of both the press and anyone else interested in Gates or his views. With only the information published on Gates's own Web site, I was able to gather the data shown in Figure 4.4.

You will note that I was not able to fill in every element of the profile template from this one source, and you can easily understand why Gates's own Web site would not offer some of this information. Using any of the currently available Internet search engines and simply entering "Bill Gates," you can begin to fill in some of the blanks. There are hundreds of thousands of sites and documents on the Net that mention, discuss, or quote Gates. For instance:

- Barnes & Noble lists 57 books with the words "Bill Gates" in the title www.barnesandnoble.com

- Biography.com's Biography of Bill Gates search.biography.com/print_record.pl?id=15061

- *Forbes* World's Richest People www.forbes.com/worldsrichest

- Bill Gates: *The Road Ahead* Web site www.roadahead.com

- *Business @ the Speed of Thought* Web site www.speed of thought.com/index_home.html

- AskMen.com's Biography of Bill Gates www.askmen.com/men/business_politics/33_bill_gates.html

- The Microsoft Boycott Campaign (including many links to Bill Gates information) http://msbc.simplenet.com

- Bill Gates Speaks (quotations attributed to Bill Gates) http://people.blinx.de/wahn/GatesTalk.htm

- Bill Gates Personal Wealth Clock www.webho.com/WealthClock

- The Bill Gates Net Worth Page http://web.quuxuum.org/~evan/bgnw.html

- Bill Gates Collectibles at eBay (including the coin and the paper doll book!) http://search.ebay.com (after searching for Bill Gates)

Searching the Web for clues about Mr. Gates's religious convictions, I found assertions that he is the Anti-Christ, but I decided to look further anyway. I found an article "In Search of the Real Bill Gates" in *Time* magazine, in which he discusses plans for the religious education of his daughter at www.time.com/time/magazine/archives.

In case you haven't realized it already, the biggest problem you will encounter in searching the Internet for information about a public figure like Gates is an overabundance of data. To wade through everything posted online about Gates, and then tackle the all-important task of verifying what is fact and what is fiction, is simply not practical. Therefore, if I were an investigative reporter writing a piece on Mr. Gates, I would search Internet sites and documents only to the point where I felt all the elements listed in my template were addressed in reasonable detail. I would then take this data and draw up a timeline, attempting to cover every period of his life. Friends, family, and associates would be placed in the appropriate time slots. So would employers, significant events in Gates's life, and so on.

To verify the data, and continue to round out the profile, I'd gather up all biographies on Gates available, including the books. I would search online biographical book directories, biographical index directories, and biographical directories (such as *Who's Who in American Politics*, which is available online). Given Gates's renown, additional biographical information might also be found in encyclopedias (searchable online, as well as on CD-ROM and in print).

I would also want to know which political campaigns or Political Action Committees Mr. Gates had contributed to. This information could be found in several databases and publications that are searchable online.

My next search would include news databases, where I would flush out further biographies and details to place into my subject profile and timeline. One of the things an investigative reporter would look for in the timeline are gaps. If there is a gap in the subject's employment, or a period when the subject's whereabouts are not accounted for, that interval would be targeted for further investigation. Conflicts in the information could also signal a potentially important area for investigation.

News articles about people who have gathered a great deal of press usually save me quite a bit of time in my own research, since I can quickly gather information that others may have taken weeks or months to uncover.

I would also want to start following Gates's paper trail, both manually and online, hoping to verify or disprove all of the information found. I would send public record retrievers out to gather records that are not yet available online, starting with his birth certificate, while I ran online searches of public records systems and retrieved any record for William H. Gates III, his wife, his family members, any other alias found, starting in the Seattle area and then branching out nationally and even internationally. These searches would include driving records, criminal records, civil records, real property records, and so on. Similar searches could be conducted for all known family members and could even extend to friends and business associates.

An asset search, such as the one in the previous example, would seek out personal and business assets, which, in this case, amount to billions of dollars. I would also expect to find some of this reported in the news, since there has been considerable interest in Gates's wealth.

I might even search for the Gates family tree to find out about skeletons in the family closet. The Internet could be very helpful in locating others who had information on his family and who might be willing to share whatever records they had gathered.

An investigative reporter would likely want to contact many of the people whom this process identified as friends, family members, and associates, in order to gather first-hand information and uncover new facts as well. All of this background work done on the computer could be used to lay the groundwork for interviews, uncover discrepancies or gaps in a person's history, and help to target certain areas for more intense investigation.

Similar background profiles can be created for those who are not well-known, starting with the information at hand, rather than published biographies—an employment application in the case of a job applicant; a residential history in the case of a potential tenant. Although little or no information about your subject may have appeared in the news, and while you might find nothing at all on the Internet, use every tool at your disposal in searching for additional information. You may be surprised how much you can find out online about "ordinary people" through a concerted effort and by your willingness to use multiple sources of public records.

The key to research is in understanding the types of records that are available, and then conducting a methodical search, carefully documenting the information found, along with its source, questioning discrepancies, verifying all data before accepting it as fact, and looking for loose ends. You will find this true of genealogical research, locating people, biographical research, or any other type of research, including all of the many types of research that are based on personal records.

If you find any of these searches alarming or upsetting in their intimacy, please go on to the next chapter, where privacy is discussed.

Chapter 5

A Word About Privacy

A secret is not something unrevealed,
but something told privately, in a whisper.

Marcel Pagnol, French playwright

Before moving on to the core of this book to discuss where personal records may be found and how they can be used, one more subject must be considered. This is the matter of privacy. It is a concern, not only when learning to search through personal records, but every time personal research is undertaken. It probably has occurred to you already. I have given talks on the subject of "Personal Records Online" from one end of the country to the other, and on each occasion someone in the audience has raised questions of privacy.

This is a subject that invites an emotional response. Few of us relish the fact that others have access to a great deal of personal information about us, or could have with surprisingly little effort. However, most of us would claim the right to investigate the background of others, at least under certain circumstances—for example, if we were hiring a nanny to care for our children, an advisor to handle our investments, or a live-in companion to watch over an elderly parent. As much as we all wish to protect our own right to privacy, we all accept that this right is not absolute. Whether it is appropriate for us to invade someone's privacy, or for them to invade ours, sometimes calls for delicate judgment. In some cases, the question has been answered for us.

Privacy Laws

Legislation offers our privacy some protection. There are laws restricting access to personal information, such as the Privacy Act of 1974 (Public Law 93-579, 5 U.S. Code 552a), which sets limits on the collection and transfer of personal data by government agencies and lets citizens sue agencies that violate the act. Other laws guarantee access to personal information. For example, the Information Practices Act (California Civil Code 1798-1798.76), a California law, gives the right to see otherwise confidential personal information in records concerning oneself. Federal law restricts access to credit information to those with a legitimate need for it, such as banks to which we have applied for a loan. State laws restrict access to many different kinds of personal information, while some records are protected in one state, but not in another. Our medical records are somewhat protected from use without our permission. However, much of our personal information is simply unregulated.

Even where laws do protect our privacy, they are a fragile barrier. Science has long sought to define the natural laws that govern the world around us and sometimes help us to predict the future. I have proposed a similar hypothesis that may someday prove to be a law of information; in fact, I refer to it as "Lane's First Law of Information":

If information exists in one place, it exists in more than one place.

Credit information provides a good example. Access to personal credit information is regulated by the Fair Credit Reporting Act (Public Law 91-508) and is generally considered to be one of the more private areas of our personal records. Yet it is not as difficult to obtain credit information as many people probably believe. Assuming that

- the credit agencies do their part in protecting credit information and allow access to it only to those with a legally "permissible purpose"

- a computer hacker does not illegally break into the credit agency's computer system

- an employee of the credit agency does not illegally obtain or sell the information

where else might someone also find the information held by credit agencies?

Credit card companies have records that include your credit card numbers, anything that you voluntarily filled in on the credit application, your credit limit and balance, and the details of each credit transaction and payment. Only part of their information is sent to the credit agencies, where it can be used by stores and others in deciding whether to extend credit or make a loan. Before issuing a credit card, a credit grantor undoubtedly will have pulled a copy of your full credit report, which will later be stored in the company's files. An employee probably will have reviewed your credit application and credit report in order to decide whether or not to extend credit to you; in that case, the information may also exist in the memory of at least one employee at every business from which you have requested credit. Another credit report may be pulled later in order to assist the company in deciding whether to raise your credit limit or cancel your card. Again, some of the individuals involved in this process become familiar with your credit history. All this information may be placed on file by each company or agency that pulls your credit report.

Others may become aware of your spending by observing whom you pay for what. If you are famous, such observations may be more memorable; they may even be profitable for the observer. Even for those of us who are not celebrities, our family members, friends, and anyone who happens to be nearby may watch when we sign our credit card receipts. A stranger may not care how much you spend, but if your face later appears on the front page of their newspaper, it may take on greater significance. You need not have become implicated in a major scandal or crime to trigger this sort of recollection. All it would take is the local newspaper's photograph of you singing with the church choir or setting out on a camping trip with the local Cub Scouts. Although this will not provide a complete picture of your credit history, it could supply a valuable clue.

Store clerks, waiters, mail-order business staffers, and many others put through your credit transactions, keeping copies for their establishments. Not only does the employee have information about your purchase, but others in the company have access as well. Duplicate copies of credit slips may also be found in their trash.

Speaking of trash, what would yours tell us? Many people, if not most, drop credit card receipts, bills, bank statements, and other revealing information into their own trash without shredding them. Others gain legal access to all that information the moment you place it on the curb. These scraps of paper all can reveal small pieces of your credit history.

Another source of information may be current, previous, or even prospective employers. Employment applications often include a clause requesting your permission to obtain your credit history. Once received from the credit agency, this information may be attached to your employment application or kept in your employee file.

Whether you rent or own your home, you probably have given your permission to obtain your credit history before moving in. It probably is still on file for your current home, and perhaps even for previous dwellings.

Law enforcement agencies may also have reason to track your purchases or to obtain copies of your credit report. Your records may even be subpoenaed to court as part of a case that involves you, your family, or your associates, and if you have ever been divorced, goodness knows what type of financial information will make its way into the proceedings. All of it may become part of the public record, available to anyone who takes the trouble to find it.

So you see, information about you that may be protected by the credit agencies also exists in many other places, all of which are generally unregulated. This is true not only for credit records, but for most types of personal information.

For that reason, I am amazed when I read articles in the newspaper stating that someone has been found to be paying an informant off for "inside" information. I am almost amused to find that some of these cases involve ridiculously high payments for information that can be legally obtained elsewhere for much less money, and often even free, by simply looking through sources such as public records. Is it laziness, ignorance, or both? A little imagination would go a lot further in finding legal avenues to nearly any type of information.

I do not advocate obtaining any type of information illegally. In this book, you will not find instructions on how to hack into systems or gain illegal access to protected information. *Naked in Cyberspace* serves as an inventory of the computer databases that store information about us and a textbook for how to use them. Reading it should help you to understand the many sources of personal information, whether public or private. After that, it is up to your own imagination to find legal sources, rather than seeking out illegal ones, or to go through the proper legal channels to request copies of records that are privately held—or to protect your own records to the limited extent that still is possible.

Technology and Personal Information

As computers have made it easier to search for personal records, they have eroded our privacy. This process can only accelerate in the years to come.

Most of the personal records available today have been available for many years. However, they have been relatively inaccessible. This includes public records, which theoretically have always been open to inspection, but for many purposes were too inconvenient to obtain. Just a few years ago, acquiring public records meant going to the effort and expense of traveling to the courts, records halls, and other buildings where the originals are stored, only to spend further hours sifting through archives or waiting in long lines for copies. This was enough to discourage most people from undertaking any but the most critical investigation.

Even in the early days of the computer age, information searching remained inconvenient. Records existed only on large, expensive mainframe computers, and they could be accessed only from a terminal in the same building. It still was necessary to visit the repository or to order records and wait for them to arrive by mail. The long, broad trail of records that we all leave behind remained difficult and tedious to follow.

Today, computers are networked, and information that exists in a database in Maryland or California is no farther away than your desktop PC in Texas or Illinois. With a handheld Internet device, it is right there in your palm. Hardware and software costs have fallen so dramatically that an estimated 50 percent of American households now own at least one computer; in business, personal computers are all but universal. So is access to information. Today, simple curiosity is motive enough for some people to investigate their neighbors, friends, and associates. Our beloved privacy is largely an illusion.

Other technologies are further eroding the walls around our lives. Powerful databases now can be developed on a PC, and massive amounts of data can be stored there on a CD-ROM or hard disk. As a result, sensitive information now is stored routinely in small computers distributed throughout a business, in what is known as client-server architecture. Putting the information at the client's site—in the end-user's small computer rather than the corporate mainframe—can reduce the security of the data. Rather than being locked inside one system whose access was closely controlled and monitored, information often exists at many sites, where it may be relatively unprotected.

High-speed networks now allow computers to send and receive information from town to town or halfway across the world within seconds. Systems like America Online, CompuServe, and Prodigy are bringing these networks into the home, and the Internet is linking them all into a single, globe-spanning super-network. Growing millions of individuals throughout the world are gaining access to vast quantities of information stored at universities, government sites, and many other institutions.

As these networks have grown, "hackers," or "crackers," have made a sport of breaking into distant computers electronically and exploring their contents at will. We often think of hackers as electronic muggers or terrorists who may secretly alter the records on computer systems, erase data or programs, or even bring whole networks to a halt. Frightening as this image can be—can you imagine the chaos a hacker could cause by attacking an air-traffic control system?—hackers who destroy records or make it impossible to access them do little to harm our privacy.

Not all hackers are destructive, however. Many "sport hackers" pit their wits against computer security systems for the pure intellectual thrill of defeating the security measures that defend computers and networks. Ironically, the hackers' intent only on amusement pose a greater threat to our privacy than their destructive colleagues. In addition to peeking into the records they find on the databases they "crack," hackers have been known to share their victories, posting telephone numbers, passwords, and break-in strategies on electronic bulletin boards so that others can admire their expertise. In this way, even beginning hackers have picked up the information necessary to invade our private information.

Somewhere between the sport hacker and the destructive hacker lies the data thief. These specialists break into computer systems for the specific purpose of obtaining the information stored inside. They may not harm the data or the computer systems that they invade; it usually is in their interests to leave no trace of their activities. However, they do invade our privacy and steal information to which they have no right.

There is no way to quantify exactly how seriously the various forms of hackers threaten our privacy. No one really knows how many hackers there are, nor how capable they may be, and new security measures are making it more difficult to gain unauthorized access to computers. However, it is clear that technology is also putting our records at greater risk.

Databases now can store information in one format and almost instantly translate it to another. Thus, it is becoming easier to combine or compare data from different sources. Information collected, and perhaps even volunteered, at different times and for different purposes can now be bought, sold, traded, and manipulated to offer new information products, identify new markets, and otherwise expand its use. Privacy no longer means quite so much when someone can manipulate information freely, pass it to others, and use it for purposes we never approved.

Not all databases are easy to use. Even some that are publicly accessible or are available by subscription can be terribly complex and difficult to navigate. Today, it still may prove impossible to find a certain piece of information in an efficient or cost effective manner. This has stopped some people from acquiring data that they otherwise would seek. But this obstacle is shrinking all the time. To make their products easier for unskilled researchers to use, database vendors are developing sophisticated new "front ends" for their systems. Some vendors allow clients to phrase their inquiries in "natural languages" that approach everyday English. Others use the point-and-click menus familiar to almost anyone with a personal computer. The need to learn Boolean logic and sophisticated search commands is passing quickly. One more defense around our personal information is being stripped away.

Artificial intelligence (AI) software allows computers to mimic some of the decisions by which human experts do their jobs. In the near future, it may enable any novice researcher to ferret out information as efficiently as the most skilled professional can today. AI also is being used to develop "intelligent agents," software that someday may help us all to navigate the vast array of computers and databases linked to the world's networks.

As all this is taking place, multimedia accessories and software are making computers easier and more exciting to use, and network theoreticians have long promised that computers would merge with television. The result will be interactive TV, which promises to open vast new quantities of information to fast, easy access. The first stage of this development can be seen as Web TV.

In years to come, it may be possible to request information from anywhere in the world and have it delivered to our televisions. It will not be mere data anymore, but graphs, charts, timelines, images, and video with all the simplicity and impact of TV. This remarkable new access to knowledge will revolutionize our educational systems, communication, and the way we view information in general.

A *Last* Word About Privacy

By now, it should be clear that Lane's First Law of Information has a corollary:

> If information exists anywhere, no matter how carefully guarded,
> it exists somewhere else, where virtually anyone can gain access to it.

If privacy is important to you today, you must understand what personal records are being stored, how they are used, and who has access to them. You will find that information in the pages to come. Where possible, I have also included instructions for obtaining copies of your own records from the agencies that store them and for removing your records from their files. You can find a list of books about privacy in "Books," the first part of Section IV: Where Can I Find More Information?. You may also wish to subscribe to periodicals that specialize in issues of privacy or even to join organizations involved in defining or protecting privacy. Lists of these resources too are available in Section IV. Many online resources also can help you learn more about your privacy rights. Indices to these resources are available on at least three Internet sites:

1. http://dir.yahoo.com/government/Law/Privacy

2. the Privacy Rights Clearinghouse home page at www.privacyrights.org

3. the Electronic Privacy Information Center at www.epic.org

The old brand of privacy, the kind we enjoyed because people simply could not find our records, is almost history. In just a few years, we will no longer be able to control our information, nor even to restrict access to it effectively; neither will anyone else be able to control theirs. As a result, we will be forced to develop new standards, new laws, and a whole new way of viewing privacy and access to information.

In practical terms, all that really is left for us is to learn to use this new, almost universal access to its best advantage, and perhaps to play a rear-guard defensive action on behalf of our own records. By the time you finish reading *Naked in Cyberspace*, you should be more prepared to do both.

How Personal Records Are Used

Chapter 6

Locating People

All that is gold does not glitter;
not all those that wander are lost.

–J. R. R. Tolkien, *The Fellowship of the Ring*

Many of us have wished at one time or another that we could locate someone. Almost every-one has lost track of an old friend, a relative, or an old flame, and who would not wish to locate someone who owed them money? This personal need to find people is one shared with many pro-fessions, all of which are growing to depend more and more on the use of personal records now available online.

> **Law Enforcement**—Members of the law enforcement community routinely need to locate people who are witnesses to crimes, previous victims, crimi-nals, and so on.

> **Attorneys**—With the criminal justice system chronically overburdened, underfunded, and short of manpower, a criminal case can take months or more before it gets to court; a civil suit, even longer. By that time, key wit-nesses may have moved away or been lost, and must be located prior to the court date.

Probate attorneys must also sometimes locate heirs before a will can be executed. If you wish to obtain rights to something (a patent, trademark, mineral rights, and so on), an attorney can assist you by tracking down the owner and obtaining the necessary signatures.

In the most dramatic example, a capital murder case, an attorney may need to locate people from a person's past, perhaps all the way back to that person's childhood. Attorneys may want to provide character witnesses or "re-construct" a person's life, in order to convince a judge and jury that their client should not receive the death sentence. Under these most dire of circumstances, locating a person could actually mean the difference between life and death.

Attorneys routinely use private investigators, process servers, information brokers, and even paralegals to locate people.

> **Process Servers**—Process servers are hired by attorneys or the court to locate persons who are ordered to appear in court.

Skip Locators—When someone moves without notifying their creditors, a skip locator may be called to track down the person. Skip locators (or bounty hunters) can also be hired to locate people who have jumped bail. This is probably the most dangerous type of work in locating people. It can also be the most difficult. Unlike most of the people you might need to find, a bounty hunter's quarry deliberately leaves as few clues to his whereabouts as possible.

Private Investigators—Private investigators are hired not only by attorneys, but also by businesses and individuals to locate people for many reasons.

Creditors—Creditors and collection agencies often need to locate people who owe money and move unexpectedly. This includes people who must track down a former spouse or lover in order to collect on child support payments.

Information Brokers/Researchers—During the course of research, an information broker sometimes needs to locate an expert in order to gain information about subjects being researched; or to update previously published findings.

Employers and headhunters (employment agencies) sometimes hire an information broker to locate someone in order to make a job offer. Even when the current employer is known, it is sometimes desirable to locate the person's home address and approach them there rather than at the job in order to make a competitive offer.

Holders of patents, trademarks, and copyrights must also be found and contacted in order to purchase the property or to negotiate the rights to use it.

Although many other types of professionals need to locate people, they do not all have the expertise or experience to perform database research efficiently. In that instance, an information broker can be a valuable ally. Information brokers are often hired by attorneys, process servers, skip locators, private investigators, and others to locate people or to provide the part of the picture that can be found on databases or through other types of research.

Adoptees and Birthparents—Birthparents sometimes wish to locate an adoptee in order to assure themselves that the adoptee is well or to reunite with their offspring. Adoptees also often wish to locate their birthparents in order to obtain information such as family medical history or in hopes of a reunion. Natural siblings and other relatives also initiate such searches at times.

Alumni Associations—Alumni associations often attempt to locate former students in order to plan high school and college reunions. Schools also search for members in order to solicit funds from them.

Family Members—It is not unusual today for people to marry more than once, to have children with more than one partner, or to blend their families through remarriage, forming stepfamilies and all of the resulting relationships. When families break apart, for whatever reason, people can lose touch with natural and stepfamily members, and later they may wish to locate them in order to re-establish those relationships.

Friends and Other Loved Ones—Nearly everyone has lost track of a friend or former loved one at some point in their lives. For those who wish to find someone, many will hire a private investigator or information broker to find the individual. Others can do so on their own. This is becoming easier for those who know how to make use of computer databases, consumer online systems, and the Internet.

Getting Started

The first and most important task in locating a person is to document all of the information you have, and all that you gain on each step of your search. I use a specific form (see Figure 6.1) to assist me with this task. Some of the questions on this form may not seem relevant, but they can all provide leads to additional resources that might be used to locate the subject. All documents and notes from each contact or search are attached to the profile, which is updated as new information is received until all avenues have been fully explored, the budget has been exhausted, or the subject has been found.

From this point forward, each search is unique. There is no exact formula for which databases are searched first, or how many are examined. I wish that I could lay out some methodical search procedure so that you would always succeed, or at least be certain that any possible clues have been unearthed, but in fact there is some luck involved in locating people, in addition to your analytical and search skills.

I had, for example, occasion to search for a niece of a client, who had not been seen by her father's side of the family since she was two years old. At the time of the search, the subject was approaching the age of 30. Prepared for a long and arduous search, I started with one of the earliest pieces of information that I received. I contacted the medical records department at the hospital in which the subject was born. A kindly clerk let it slip that the subject had been a patient of the hospital until she was in her teens, which was a leap forward by many years. This alone was a stroke of luck because the family believed that she had moved to another state at the age of two.

Pleased with that information, I went out to dinner. By the time I returned, the subject of the search had called and left a number where she could be reached. Upon contacting her, I found out that the medical records clerk had, of her own volition (and against hospital policy), called the emergency contact on the subject's admission records. The contact turned out to be an aunt on the mother's side of the family, who called her niece, and passed on my number. The niece was thrilled to be put in contact with her two aunts and grandmother, whom she had always wanted to find, but whom she had not known how to locate.

The only database search that was performed for that project was to check a telephone directory to locate the hospital. I hope that this illustrates the following points. First of all, don't overlook any detail that you have in front of you; any lead may prove to be important when it is explored. Second, don't expect all of the answers to be found on a database. Although computers and databases are wonderful resources, they are still just tools, and a telephone is every bit as important a research tool. Third, enlist allies whenever possible. If you are courteous when requesting information on the telephone, you will be more likely to receive assistance and even advice, which may be just the tidbit you need to track the person down.

TechnoSearch, Inc.
SUBJECT PROFILE

FULL NAME, ALIASES, NICKNAMES, MAIDEN NAME, MARRIED NAME:

GENDER:

BIRTHDATE AND/OR AGE:

SOCIAL SECURITY NUMBER:

PHYSICAL DESCRIPTION:

DESCENT:

LAST ADDRESSES:

EDUCATION:

OCCUPATION:

ORGANIZATIONS:

RELIGION:

MILITARY BACKGROUND:

LICENSES:

HOBBIES:

SEARCH REASONS:

RELATIONSHIPS (FAMILY MEMBERS, FRIENDS):

SUBSCRIPTIONS (MAGAZINES):

POSSIBLE LOCATION (ANY IDEAS YOU MAY HAVE):

FINANCES (ASSETS):

LAW HISTORY:

BANK ACCOUNTS:

POLITICS:

CREDIT CARDS:

Figure 6.1   Subject profile form

The Problems with Names

Before spending money for an online search, there are a few potential problems that you should be aware of. Finding people by scanning through personal records often requires more background information than simply knowing their names.

    1. Names are not unique. A name by itself will rarely provide a positive identification. In the telephone book for a community of only 50,000 people, I

recently counted no fewer than 11 men named David Smith and 12 named Robert Johnson. Literally dozens of names were shared by two or three men or women, many with the same middle initial. Where the subject's location is unknown, the problem of duplicate names is far worse.

2. Nicknames may be used. When searching for a person in a database, you should be aware that your subject may be listed under a nickname. You probably would automatically search for Robert under Bob, Bobby, Rob, and Robbie, and even his initials, but you may have no way of knowing that a particular Robert is known as Moose or ChooChoo, so a database search may miss their records entirely. Likewise, a person known as Al at work may actually sign his proper name, Elvyn, on legal documents, while the newspaper article written about his softball team may list him as Doc, as he's known to his teammates. You might not find him at all without this knowledge.

3. Aliases. People sometimes also use more than one name. While most often thought of in connection with criminals seeking to evade the law, there also are many legitimate reasons for individuals to adopt other names. For example, women (and very rarely men) often take on their spouse's names after marriage. Some women continue to use their maiden names. Some women continue to use their maiden names professionally, but socially use their spouse's surname.

   Adoptees usually take on the adoptive parent's last name. Often the first name is changed as well, if the adoption occurs early in the child's life. Adult adoptees are frequently given the option of choosing which name they would like to use, and can select an entirely new name if they wish.

   People sometimes change their names simply because they don't like the ones they were given, or because they wish to avoid the notoriety that their names carry. For example, you may recall that Jeff Gillooly, Olympic skater Tonya Harding's ex-husband, went to court to change his name to something less notable after his release from prison.

   A writer may also use an entirely different pen name. For instance, Stephen King has written several books under the name Richard Bachman.

   An actor may take on a screen name. Some actors will go to court to have their names changed legally, while others will continue to use their given names everywhere except on the screen, in order to maintain whatever privacy is available to them offscreen.

4. Middle names. Some people use their middle names, but still sign legal documents with their proper names. A database may list either or both.

5. People, particularly women, compound their own last names at times, using both their maiden and married names. On some databases, the first last name is entered as a middle name. On others the two last names are

run together. On still others, a hyphen may appear between the names. Sometimes one of the last names is simply dropped.

6. First names are also sometimes abbreviated, as in F. Scott Fitzgerald. If a database lists F as the first name, a search for the full first name (i.e., Francis) may not turn up a single match, even though there are many records dealing with your subject. Some database software is sophisticated enough to cope with these situations. Most software is not.

7. Misspellings and typographical errors are not as uncommon as you would hope. People entering names or other information into a database sometimes make mistakes, which makes it difficult, if not impossible, to locate the record. When a database is indexed, the indexer can also make mistakes, confusing a last name with a middle name, and so on. You've probably heard the expression "Garbage in, garbage out" (or GIGO). That pretty much says it all.

8. Common names are sometimes handled differently than uncommon names by the application software. When a common name is entered, the application software may require that other identifiers match as well before returning the record in question, especially if the software was designed with privacy in mind. Without additional information, it sometimes is not possible to reach the threshold of certainty at which the system will return the matching record. For example, a match to a person's name alone is not sufficient for locating a credit record. Other matches to home address, Social Security number, birthdate, spouse's first name or initial, and so on are all considered in determining whether the person in the database does in fact match the inquiry that was entered.

9. Ethnic variations sometimes can make it challenging to locate a record. For example, there are countries in which a woman commonly uses her mother's maiden name, rather than her father's surname. This can lead to some confusion when the woman enters the United States. You may find some records under one surname, while others are listed under the other. Vietnamese, Chinese, and other names with sounds that are unfamiliar to some Americans often confuse people entering the information into the database, as well as those searching for it. It is not unusual to find first and last names transposed in such cases, or to find variant spellings. For example, former Chinese Premier Zhou Enlai might be found under the more common spellings Chou En Lai or Chou En-Lai, in which case the last name might be indexed as Chou, Lai, or En-Lai.

10. Indexing variations. Some databases lack a standard convention for indexing names. In those cases, it may be necessary to search for the name in several ways. Variations that I've found include:

Surname, First Name
Surname, First Name, Middle Initial
Surname, First Name, Middle Name

Surname, First Initial
Surname, First Initial, Middle Initial
Surname, First Initial, Middle Name
First Name, Surname
First Name, Middle Initial, Surname
First Name, Middle Name, Surname
First Initial, Surname
First Initial, Middle Initial, Surname
First Initial, Middle Name, Surname

On databases that charge per search, trying all of these variations could be expensive. If a combined search is possible, that would certainly be preferable in this case, but not all databases will allow a combined search. Some databases do not index the names at all, making it necessary to search the text of the article, rather than a defined field.

11. Few databases can recognize the difference between Doe (as in John Doe) and DOE (the acronym for the Department of Energy). When news databases are searched for names such as these, a good many erroneous matches may be found before a real hit is identified.

Excluding articles in which the term "energy" is used may inadvertently drop some of the hits that you wanted. Even excluding articles with exact matches on "Department of Energy" may drop an article that names John Doe from Albuquerque in the same article that happens to mention someone from the DOE. LexisNexis does have a command for searching for words in capitals (i.e., ALLCAPS(DOE)), so that these can be excluded, and another command to identify words with only one capital (i.e., CAPS(DOE), which will identify instances of Doe), but this system is an exception. These problems with names usually can be overcome, but you should be aware of them before conducting a database search.

Databases Used

Many factors influence the choice of databases that you use to locate a person. Nearly any type of personal record can be useful under the right circumstances. Section III of this book, "Types of Personal Records," describes the types of database records used in personal research.

The following questions and explanations will illustrate how databases often are chosen. When reading them, try to imagine that you are looking for someone, and that these questions are being asked by someone who will help you to select the databases to be searched.

What Do You Know About the Person?

I am always surprised when a former spouse or lover does not even have the Social Security number of someone he or she was married to or had a child with. Good identifying information is the key to locating a person. When unique or complete identifying information is available, it may take only a single search to locate the person. When it is not, many searches may be necessary in order to fill in these gaps before the final search is possible. Some of the best identifiers are Social Security number and date of birth. Although it is possible to find a person without this information, having it can shorten a search considerably. Knowledge of these identifiers also makes it possible to verify whether any of the records found actually belong to the person that you are looking for.

Armed with a Social Security number, the first thing that I would do would be to run a search for it through the credit agency databases. In many cases, this is all that is needed to locate a person who is not hiding, and uses a credit card, holds a mortgage, or uses some other form of credit.

Is the Name Unique?

If I were looking for a person with a name as uncommon as Engelbert Humperdink, I would begin by simply searching a telephone directory. The odds would be pretty good that any Engelbert Humperdinks found would either be the person I was searching for, or at least a close relative of his, who might know his whereabouts.

For unique surnames, it may be worthwhile to use a telephone directory database to locate all of the people in the country who share that surname in order to locate family members of the person being sought. Early in the Clinton years, several newspapers ran human-interest stories pointing out that there are extremely few people with the surname Rodham in the United States, and all of them are related to Hillary Clinton.

How Long Has It Been Since You Knew Where This Person Was?

When looking for someone who has recently moved, several databases might provide an address update. The Postal Change of Address or Publisher's Change of Address searches offered by some of the public records vendors would be excellent choices.

An online telephone directory might have the updated record before it could be found elsewhere. A telephone directory that allows for address searches could also be used to identify former neighbors who might know where the person had moved.

The consumer credit databases might have been updated by a creditor that was notified of the change of address. In that case, an Address Update (or Finders) search could provide the new address and possibly the telephone number. Even if creditors have not been given a new address, if the subject is shopping for a new car or applying for more credit, recent inquiries on the subject's credit profile might lead you to their approximate whereabouts.

When many years have passed since the person's location was known, I am more likely to try one of the "wild card" searches offered by a public records vendor, such as the People Locator: Info Probe, offered by ChoicePoint Online. A search such as this can save much time and money by combining several searches into one, and with luck turning up at least a lead or two.

Is the Person Hiding?

The problem often becomes more difficult when someone is known to be hiding, perhaps from creditors. In this case, I might not search records that the individual would be likely to know about, such as telephone directory listings and real property records, or I might search these sources using the names of children, spouse, or associates. I would also look for voter registration records, not only in the subject's name, but the names of the spouse and any adult children who might either live at home or use their home address for voting registration while away at school.

I might also try more obscure public records, such as Fish and Game licenses. People who are keeping a low profile may not be so careful about these records, as they might not understand that these can now be searched online.

Is the Person Famous? An Expert?

If a person were famous, I would be more likely to check news databases for information about the individual's whereabouts. I would also check professional directory databases such as BASE-LINE - Celebrity Contacts, for information on how to contact the celebrity, or other professional directories to find out where this person worked.

For an expert, I might look for anything that this person had written or anything that had been written about this person in order to find his or her affiliations. A database such as the LC MARC: Name Authorities database (available from the U.S. Library of Congress Information System) could be useful in this respect, as it identifies names listed by the Library of Congress.

For people who are well-known in their field, I might also put a message on an online newsgroup or forum in an area visited by their fans or colleagues, if the search were not confidential.

Are There Friends or Relatives Who Might Be Located as an Alternative?

When a person is hard to locate, it is often worthwhile locating his or her parents, children, or other close relatives, who may tell you where the person is. Even former spouses can be helpful, especially if they have children in common.

Once I was trying to locate a client's lost uncle, who had not been seen in more than 20 years. Although elderly, he was not listed on any of the death indices that I checked, and I had no reason to believe that he was dead, other than that he had not reconciled with his family for so many years. I knew that he was divorced, and that he and his former spouse had adopted a child. It was believed that he and his ex-wife might have reconciled later. Unable to find the uncle, I looked for his ex-wife and found that she was listed on the death index. This led me to send for her death certificate. It did not list the uncle (her husband), but their son was listed as next of kin, along with his address. Upon contacting him, I learned that his father had died many years before in a traffic accident. I could have been looking for the subject for a very long time if I had not branched out to look for family members instead.

How Old Is the Person?

If the person you're seeking is elderly, it is important to rule out death before proceeding to other searches. Refer to Chapter 28: Death Records for databases that can be used to assist you in this task. Even a young person may have died, so this possibility can never be completely overlooked.

A person's age might also be considered in determining the likelihood that he or she would be credit-active. A person who is young or aged would be less likely to have active credit than people in their twenties through sixties, so a search of the credit records could be more productive for that age group. When a person in his or her thirties or forties does not turn up on the credit files, I begin to wonder whether there is some problem with the information I've been given, or whether there is some likelihood that the person is living on the streets.

If the subject is of driving age, I would want to check for a driving record. Even though the DMV will no longer release a driver's home address, it would help to narrow my search by determining that the subject is licensed within a given state.

For someone old enough to pursue a profession, professional licenses might also be worth checking. People in their mid-years might also show up in marriage and divorce records, or other civil suits, or even have a criminal record, all of which might be found online. Real property records should also be explored for people in their thirties (and younger) through their sixties (and older), and since these are available statewide for many states (rather than at only the county level, as many other public records are), it is possible to cover a broad area fairly quickly. There are many additional public record indices available online, any of which may contain information about the individual that you're seeking. These are important resources for people who need to locate others.

If the person you're seeking is of college age, he or she may belong to a fraternity, sorority, or co-educational organization. Some fraternities, sororities, and co-eds are maintaining online sites, especially on the Internet. Some of the Internet sites that are attempting to link all of the fraternities, sororities, and co-eds online can be found at

> GreekPages.com
> www.greekpages.com/index2.cfm
>
> greekspot.com
> www.greekspot.com

The home pages that are linked to these addresses normally include the location of the sorority, fraternity, or co-ed (which can be used to contact the organization and inquire whether the student you're seeking is a member), along with a brief list of officers and advisors. Some of these sites also include a list of their full roster, which may be all that you need to track down the student you are looking for.

University students who are not members of a fraternity or sorority can also sometimes be found online, because student directories are springing up online at many colleges and universities, both in the United States and abroad. Lists of college and university home pages can be found at the following sites:

> www.mit.edu:8001/people/cdemello/univ.html
>
> www.indiana.edu/~librcsd/internet/Colleges_and_Universities
>
> http://geowww.uibk.ac.at/univ

A searchable list of American Universities can also be found at www.clas.ufl.edu/CLAS/american-universities.html.

For a person who has already graduated from a college or university, many additional Internet sites might be worth reviewing. There is no shortage of alumni associations that now have home pages on the Internet. Many of them list brief biographies and contact information for individual alumni. Some of these sites also carry alumni publications that list marriages, babies, promotions, and other types of alumni news.

High school alumni associations are also creating home pages on the Internet, so people of any age beyond high school might be found at such a site. Since more people do graduate from high school than college, such sites may grow into an even more valuable resource in the future.

Yahoo! is indexing college and high school alumni associations at http://d1.dir.snv.yahoo.com/education/organizations/alumnae_i_associations. A fee-based site that is linking individuals from high schools all over the U.S. and Canada is ClassMates.com, located at www.classmates. com. Another site, gradFinder, is also indexing students from high schools and elementary schools throughout the world. Their address is www.gradfinder.com.

Age can also help you to decide whether the subject may have served or be serving in the military. Military City offers searches of its database of active military, reserve/guard, and veterans at www.militarycity.com/newsroom/locator.html. A registry for military personnel, veterans, and their families is found in the American War Library at http://members.aol.com/veterans. Military Network also has many links to military locator sites on the Internet and is located at www. military-network.com.

What Is Your Relationship to the Person?
Why Are You Looking for Him or Her?

Access to certain databases will depend upon your purpose for the search. For example, if you are a creditor, you probably have a signed authorization allowing you to retrieve the full credit profile of the subject, and you have permissible purpose according to the Fair Credit Reporting Act. If you have neither permission nor permissible purpose, you may not have access to all of the details provided on the credit report, but you can use the credit headers to provide location information.

The Department of Motor Vehicles, in most cases, will no longer provide home addresses of individuals; however, if you are a process server and are pursuing a subject for a legal case, you may be able to gain access to this information directly from the DMV, online or in person.

If you are a friend or relative, you can expect more cooperation from your subject's other friends and relatives than a creditor would receive. On the other hand, if you are a creditor, you can expect more cooperation from ex-spouses (who might be located online), other creditors (found on the credit report), and other people who have sued the subject (whom you can find on the civil records).

If you are looking for long-lost relatives for genealogical purposes, the less expensive resources should probably be utilized, as there is generally no rush for the information. If there is a life-or-death purpose for the search, no expense can be spared, so the choice of databases will be wide open.

If you are an adoptee searching for a birthparent, adoption registries may already have record of a parent who is looking for you; likewise, these registries can aid birthparents searching for the offspring that they gave up for adoption. These registries should certainly be considered first.

If you are looking for someone whom you plan to sue, or who might run away if this person knew you were looking for him or her, more discretion would be called for. Posting online messages asking for anyone with information to contact you, or otherwise enlisting help from others, may not be an option. It is possible that the person that you're looking for may also use the system where your message is posted, or a friend or relative may tip the person off.

If you'd like to find out whether someone is a member of one of the online systems, it is possible to search the membership directory on some of the consumer online services. For example, CompuServe allows members to search the membership directory by name, and will return the city, state, and e-mail address of those persons found whose names match. On the Internet there are also tools for searching for a person, including the "WHOIS" server, which can lead you to the system that they are accessing the Internet from. Network Solutions' WHOIS server can be found at www.netsol.com/cgi-bin/whois/whois. Other WHOIS servers can be found at http://dir.yahoo.com/Computers_and_Internet/Internet/Directory.Services/Whois. There is also a "finger" server, which searches for matches on e-mail addresses and returns real names. Brett's Web to Finger Gateway can be found at www.rickman.com/finger.html.

There are also missing persons sites on the Internet, at which anyone can enter the information that they know about someone they're seeking, in hopes that someone will see it and offer information. Some of the people listed are old friends, some are parents, and so on. Sites such as these can be found at:

Missing Persons Bulletin Boards & Registries/Reunion.com/
highschoolalumni.com
www.highschoolalumni.com

PeopleSite
www.peoplesite.com

Summary

Although I cannot cover every possible way in which a person might be located, I hope that you have begun to understand how the many types of records available online can make the task easier, and that these examples have sparked your imagination. Each situation is unique, and a great deal of your success will depend not only on your knowledge of the resources available, but on your analytical and research skills. As I have said, there is also some luck involved, and it certainly helps to have good instincts and intuition.

You should also know that not everyone can be located. (For example, labor leader Jimmy Hoffa has been missing since the late 1970s.) For those who can be located, the time and budget available for the search are not always sufficient to complete the task. Although an impressive list of database resources is available, sometimes surveillance or legwork can prove more productive; in that case, you may want to hire a private investigator rather than taking on such a task by yourself.

On the other hand, many people can be located with no more in hand than a national telephone directory database, which can sometimes be found at your local public library, and on the Internet. If you decide to pursue a search on your own, there are organizations that can provide assistance and advice, and which may also share database resources among their members. Organizations focused on adoptee/birthparent searches, genealogical research, private investigation, process serving, public records research, and skip tracing all participate in locating people from their own perspectives. You can find listings of all of these types of organization in Section IV: Where Can I Find More Information—Organizations.

There are search guides for adoptees, birthparents, and genealogists as well as books about public records research, some specifically written about locating people. Listings of all of these can also be found in Section IV: Where Can I Find More Information—Books.

Last of all, many periodicals can help you to keep up with changes in the technology, new databases being introduced, advice, and techniques for locating people. Such publications may focus on adoptee/birthparent searches, genealogical research, investigative journalism, or private investigation. Listings of many of these periodicals are also included later in Section IV: Where Can I Find More Information—Periodicals.

Good luck and happy hunting!

Chapter 7

Pre-Employment Screening

Integrity without knowledge is weak and useless,
and knowledge without integrity is dangerous and dreadful.

–Samuel Johnson

If you are not screening job applicants, you probably have been screened as one. If you are in a responsible position and likely to attract the attention of corporate headhunters, you may go through some level of pre-employment screening even if you have not applied for a job, most likely without ever becoming aware of it. Not so many years ago, someone could make almost any claim on a job application, secure in the near-certain knowledge that the lie would never be found out. It was simply too much trouble to check most claims, so relatively few employers did more than a cursory follow-up; many did not even bother to call former employers to confirm the applicant's job history. In the last decade, this situation has changed dramatically. We live in a less trusting and more litigious society today, and thanks to computers, information is much easier to come by. At most major companies and many smaller ones, pre-employment screening is now routine, and it is likely to be increasingly comprehensive.

Prospective employees are screened in order to protect a company. At a basic level, no employer wants to get stuck with an employee who has lied about his (or her) work history or capabilities, and cannot do the job. It is much easier and less expensive to screen out such people as applicants than to fire them later.

Company assets also can be put at risk when someone is hired under a false identity, or when the person has ulterior motives for seeking employment. Employers risk embezzlement and fraud by employees who have access to company funds. Customer funds may similarly be put at risk by a thieving or inept investment counselor, banker, accountant, or anyone else given the responsibility for or access to their money.

Trade secrets can be just as vulnerable when an unscrupulous employee is hired. A company's reputation can suffer at the hands of an employee who does not deal well with customers or is out to sabotage the company. An unskilled programmer can bring a company's information systems to a halt if her code fails to operate or degrades the system's performance, and it might even damage the existing systems. A company that cannot access its own information could be shut down in a matter of days.

These risk factors may seem to be limited to those involving key executives, but even a maintenance person or janitor often receives a master key to an apartment building or office complex in order to clean up or make necessary repairs. They then could steal tenants' belongings or gain access to untold amounts of proprietary information.

Moving up to the top of the risk hierarchy, lives can be put in danger by a poor hiring choice. A pilot or bus driver need only suffer a momentary lapse in order to cause massive destruction and loss of life. Someone with drug or alcohol problems or a medical condition that might cause a blackout would be a poor choice for such a position, and I would not want to see them in the operating room, or entrusted with the care of a child or otherwise helpless person. A building contractor who uses poor quality materials or cuts corners, an elevator repair person who does not properly inspect and maintain all of the elevators, a security guard who falls asleep on the job— there are any number of cases in which a single unqualified person could endanger the lives of employees, customers, and the public at large.

Violence in the workplace also is a very real danger today, and one for which employers must assume some responsibility. When a new hire covers up a history of mental instability or violence, fellow employees, customers, employers, and the public could be put at risk. If a violent incident does occur, the employer will have to answer for it, and not only to the employees, customers, and families who have suffered. Employers may also find themselves in a court of law, accused of criminal negligence in hiring such an individual.

Although an employer may not wish to be suspicious of job applicants, or to intrude upon their privacy, the safety and well-being of other employees and customers, as well as the good of the company, must all be weighed in deciding how much pre-employment screening to perform. This is balanced against the amount of risk the company is comfortable in shouldering.

What Is Pre-Employment Screening?

Pre-employment screening can take many forms. The employment application is normally the starting place. At a bare minimum of screening, employers usually call to verify information provided on a job application. Even if all of that information checks out, this is far from a thorough employment screening, as only the information volunteered by the applicant will then have been confirmed.

Merely calling telephone numbers supplied on a job application can make it exceedingly simple for someone to fake a work history. After all, the employer may not really know who they are calling. There are companies that, for a fee, will verify whatever a customer asks them to, pretending to be the previous employer and providing a glowing review of their work history. An applicant's friends may be willing to do the same.

Even legitimate employers often are far from candid when they receive a call to verify the person's work experience. Most will verify the dates of employment, salary, and job title. Fewer will provide an evaluation of work performance, job responsibilities, whether the employee left on good terms, and whether he or she is eligible for re-hire, and this information is becoming more difficult to obtain. Many employers now fear being sued by former employees who are refused a job because of negative information provided for a pre-employment screening. Such suits are surprisingly common and occasionally are successful.

At least one online vendor/public records search service advertises that it can shield employers from such suits if they provide negative information on a former employee. This is because the vendor has credit bureau status, which allows it to ask such questions without fear of a lawsuit.

This is not to say that references should not be called. In fact, not calling to verify the references given could be considered negligent. However, when these calls are made, the telephone numbers should be looked up or obtained from Directory Assistance (or an online telephone directory), and the personnel or human resources office should be requested, rather than the name of the person that the applicant has provided. This probably will not uncover a company that has been set up as a phony reference shop, but one might be able to catch someone who has named a best friend as a former employer, or someone waiting at home for your call to XYZ Corporation. However, even when the proper connections are made to a real former employer, you should not expect too much from the calls, and most employers should not stop there.

A number of databases can assist in pre-employment screening, and some of them can reveal important information that the job applicant failed to divulge.

Professional Licenses, Certifications, and Registrations

For fields in which a person must maintain a professional license, certification, or registration, the applicant may be asked to supply a copy of the license. For some employers, this may be sufficient verification of licensing; however, a real con artist may go so far as to forge a license. Without obtaining verification from the licensing authority (the Department of Consumer Affairs, Department of Health Services, Department of Professional Regulation, Division of Consumer Affairs, Bureau of Professional and Occupational Affairs, or other licensing bureau, which varies from state to state), an employer may not be able to detect a forgery.

Licensing authorities can often be contacted directly to verify a license. Some public records vendors also provide access to databases of professional license holders, which can be used to verify the status of a license. For example, KnowX offers a search that can verify licenses held by an individual in various fields, which can include the fields in the states noted in Figure 7.1.

Other vendors offer their own combinations of licenses for a variety of states, so many employers may find that they can perform all license verification for applicants in their field conveniently from their own computers.

Licenses also appear in biographical databases and professional directories, but I would not recommend these as a means of pre-employment verification, as this information may have been supplied by the job applicant, and it seems unlikely that anyone would update it when a person's license has lapsed.

Professional license searches are also now appearing on the Internet, through state, county, or city Web sites, or on the Web sites of the licensing agencies. These can be useful in tracking down a person in a given field, as they often contain the licensee's address. Some sources of licenses, certifications, and registrations are listed at the *Naked in Cyberspace* Web site.

Motor Vehicle Records

A company may also use motor vehicle records for employee screening, and these records may be obtained online as well. Certainly a clean driving record and a valid driver's license would be desirable for anyone who will be driving as part of their work responsibilities. Employers should know of any limitations on the applicant's ability to drive (such as restrictions on night driving or the types of vehicles that they may operate) in order to make sure that the appropriate accommodations can be made, if necessary.

If the employee will be supplied with a company vehicle, the employer may feel that it's important to know if there are accidents on her or his record, and if so, who was at fault.

STATE	SOURCE
AK	Alaska Occupational (Professional licenses)
AL	Alabama Licensed Physician File
	Alabama Licensed Social Workers
AR	Arkansas Licensed Dentists/Hygienists/Assistants
	Arkansas Licensed Nurse File (All nurses)
	Arkansas Licensed Optometrists
	Arkansas Licensed Pharmacists
AZ	Arizona Licensed Dentists and Hygienists
	Arizona Licensed RNs LPNs and CNAs & APRNs
	Arizona Licensed Physician Data
	Arizona Licensed Physician's Assistant
	Arizona Licensed Psychologists
	Arizona Licensed Respiratory Care Practitioners
	Arizona Licensed Veterinarians
CA	State of California Licensed Professionals
	State of California Real Estate Licenses
CO	Colorado Professional Licenses
CT	Connecticut Health Professions Licenses
	Connecticut Licensed Pharmacists
DC	D.C. Licensees in Medicine and Osteopathy
	District of Columbia Licensed Professionals
DE	Delaware Certified Nurses Aides
	Delaware Licensed Dentists
	Delaware Licensed Nurses (RN/LPN)
	Delaware Licensed Optometrists
	Delaware Licensed Pharmacists
	Delaware Licensed Physicians (MD, DO, PA)
	Delaware Licensed Psychologists and Social Workers
	Delaware Respiratory Therapists
	Delaware Licensed Physical Therapists & Veterinarians
FL	Insurance Agents Licensed in State of Florida
	Members of the Florida Bar (Attorneys)
	Florida Board Licenses including Tobacco and Alcohol
	Florida Health Professions License

	Florida Notaries
	Florida Nursing Licenses
	Florida Realtors and Brokers Licenses
GA	Georgia Professional Licenses
IA	Iowa Licensed Health Professionals
	Iowa Licensed Nurses
	Iowa Licensed Veterinarians
ID	Idaho Licensed Dentists
	Idaho Licensed Professionals 2
	Idaho Board of Medicine, Health Professions
	Idaho Licensed Nurses (RN & LPN)
	Idaho Licensed Veterinarians
IL	Illinois Licensed Professionals & Temp Professionals
KS	Kansas Licensed Health Examiners
	Kansas Licensed Nurses (RNs)
	Kansas Licensed Optometrists
KY	Kentucky Licensed Chiropractors
	Kentucky Licensed Dentists
	Kentucky Licensed Nurses (RN & LPN)
	Kentucky Licensed Pharmacists
LA	Louisiana Licensed Dentists
	Louisiana Practical Nurse Examiners
	Louisiana Licensed Optometrists
	Louisiana Licensed Physicians
MA	Massachusetts Board of Licensed Physicians
	Massachusetts Professional Licenses (incl. Health)
MD	Licensed Maryland Dentists
	Maryland Licensed Dietitians
	Maryland Board of Nursing
	Maryland Licensed Nurse (LPN/RN)
	Maryland Licensed Optometrists
	Maryland Licensed Pharmacists
	State of Maryland, Licensed Physicians
	Maryland Licensed Podiatrists
	Maryland Licensed Social Workers
	Maryland Licensed Speech & Language Therapists

	MD Licensed Therapists (PA/Radiologist/Respiratory
	Maryland Licensed Occupational Therapists & Assts.
ME	Maine Licensed Dentist
	Maine Licensed Nurses (RN/LPN)
	Maine Licensed Physicians
	Maine Licensed Professionals
MI	Michigan Notaries Public
	Michigan Professional Licenses
MN	Minnesota Licensed Dietitians and Nutritionists
	Minnesota Licensed Health Professionals
	Minnesota Licensed Nurses (RNs, LPNs,)
	Minnesota Licensed Optometrists
	Minnesota Licensed Physicians
	Minnesota Licensed Speech & Language Pathologists
	Minnesota Licensed Veterinarians
MO	Missouri Licensed Health Professions
	Missouri Licensed Nurses (RNs & LPNs)
MS	Mississippi Licensed Dentists
	Mississippi State Department of Health
	Mississippi Board of Nursing
	Mississippi Licensed Pharmacists
	Mississippi Licensed Psychologists
	Mississippi Licensed Social Workers
MT	Montana Licensed Physicians
NC	North Carolina Licensed Chiropractors
	North Carolina State Board of Dental Examiners
	North Carolina Board of Nursing—RNs & LPNs
	North Carolina Licensed Optometrists
	North Carolina Licensed Pharmacists
	North Carolina Medical Board—Physicians
	NC Physical Therapists & PT Assistants
	North Carolina Licensed Veterinarians
ND	North Dakota Certified Nurses Aides
	North Dakota State of Board of Dental Examiners
	North Dakota Licensed Nurses (RN/LPN)
	North Dakota Board of Pharmacy
	North Dakota Licensed Physical Therapists

	North Dakota Board of Veterinary Medical Examiners
NE	Nebraska Health Professional Licenses
NH	New Hampshire Licensed Midwives
	New Hampshire Licensed Nurses (RN/LPN/CNA)
	New Hampshire Licensed Optometrists
	New Hampshire Licensed Pharmacists
	New Hampshire Licensed Physicians & Assistants
	New Hampshire Licensed Physician Assistants
	New Hampshire Licensed Podiatrists
	NH Speech Language Pathologists & Respiratory Care
	New Hampshire Licensed Physical Therapist
	New Hampshire Licensed Occupational Therapists
	New Hampshire Licensed Veterinarians
NJ	New Jersey Licensed Professionals
NM	New Mexico Licensed Midwives
	New Mexico Licensed Nurses—RN/LPN
	New Mexico Licensed Psychologists
NV	Nevada Licensed Osteopaths
	Nevada State Board of Pharmacy
	Nevada Licensed Medical Doctors
OH	Ohio Professional Licenses
	Ohio State Board of Psychologists Examiners
	Ohio Licensed Respiratory Therapists
OK	Oklahoma Licensed Chiropractors
	Oklahoma Licensed Dentists
	Oklahoma Licensed Osteopathics
	Oklahoma Board of Nursing—Licensed Midwives
	OK Licensed Physicians Ass't, Podiatrists, Physicians
	Oklahoma Licensed Optometrists
	Oklahoma Board of Pharmacy
	Oklahoma Licensed Physicians & Disciplinary Action
	Oklahoma Licensed Respiratory Therapists
	Oklahoma State Veterinary Board
OR	Oregon Lawyers
	State of Oregon, Licensed Contractors & Landscapers
	Oregon Dentist
	Oregon Nurses (RN, LPN, CNA, NP)

	Oregon Board of Pharmacy
	Oregon Licensed Physicians
	Oregon Licensed Psychologists
	Oregon Licensed Real Estate Professionals
	Oregon Board of Clinical Social Workers
	Oregon Licensed Radiographic Technologists
PA	Pennsylvania Professional Licenses
RI	Rhode Island Licensed Health Professionals
	Rhode Island Medical Licensure & Discipline
SC	South Carolina Licensed Health Professionals/Physicians
	SC Ambulance Services, Paramedics, and EMTs
	South Carolina Licensed Podiatrists
	SC Licensed Speech Pathologists & Audiologists
SD	S. Dakota Licensed Health Professionals & Physicians
	South Dakota Licensed Nurses (LPN/RN)
	South Dakota Licensed Veterinarians
TN	Tennessee Licensed Health Professionals
TX	TX Registered Architect, Interior Design & Landscape
	State Bar of Texas (Lawyers)
	Texas Board of Barber Examiners
	Texas Professional Counselors
	Texas State Board of Public Accountancy
	Texas Board of Nurse Examiners
	Texas Licensed Optometrists
	Texas Licensed Pharmacists and Pharmacies
	TX Medical Examiners
	Texas Licensed Podiatrists
	Texas Licensed Professionals
	Texas Licensed Real Estate Agents
	Texas Licensed Land Surveyors
	TX Physical & Occupational Therapist & Assts.
	Texas Licensed Veterinarians
UT	Utah Professional Licenses
VA	Virginia Licensed Health Professionals
VT	Vermont Licensed Medical Physicians
	Vermont Licensed Professions

WI	Wisconsin Professional Licensees/Credential Holders
WV	West Virginia Doctors of Osteopathy
	West Virginia Licensed Nurses (RNs) & (LPNs)
	West Virginia Medical Doctors, Physicians' Asst., & DOs
WY	Wyoming Licensed Chiropractors
	Wyoming Licensed Nurses (LPN/RN/CNA)
	Wyoming Licensed Optometrists
	Wyoming Licensed Podiatrists
	Wyoming Licensed Physical Therapists

Figure 7.1 KnowX Professional License Search

If a company's group insurance policy excludes pre-existing conditions, a company may also choose to check motor vehicle records for evidence of personal injury accidents, which may be excluded from their coverage for a period after employment.

For further information about driving records, please refer to Chapter 27.

FAA Airmen

If an applicant is being hired as a pilot, a search of the FAA Airmen Directory can be executed online through many public records vendors, in order to verify a pilot's license.

Some of these vendors are accessible on the Internet as well, including KnowX, which offers this search at www.knowx.com.

Consumer Credit Records

The credit agencies offer a variation on their normal credit report for use specifically in pre-employment screening (usually dropping the birth date, and containing other slight variations in content and format), but employers may also pull the regular credit report. Both reports require the permission of the job applicant. The credit and employment reports are used by many employers to determine whether a prospective employee has been responsible about his own finances. For employees being hired in the financial arena, this may take on greater importance. After all, would you want to hire a financial advisor who had a history of bad debts?

A person who will be given access to and authority over company funds or customer accounts may be required to have a squeaky clean credit record and low debt ratios in order to be entrusted with that type of responsibility.

The credit record can also be used to verify some of the information given by the job applicant. For example, the Social Security number often appears on the credit report header. The number is not normally verified with the Social Security Administration when a person is obtaining credit, so verifying the number on the job application against that on the credit report will only show whether the applicant is consistent with the number given to others, and not that it is correct. If several Social Security numbers are found on the credit report, and they do not appear to be a result of a creditor's transposition or typing errors, one may wonder why the applicant is using various numbers, and may suspect some type of fraud. If the Social Security number is completely invalid, meaning that it falls within a range not yet issued by the Social Security Administration, the credit record may also contain a warning to that effect.

Previous employers' names and addresses also sometimes appear on a credit or employment report. If the information displayed does not correspond to that on the job application, the discrepancy should be resolved with the job applicant. If the applicant's reported employment history implies that he lived in one part of the country at a given time, but the credit record shows addresses in other areas, this again should be resolved.

A company may also perform a Social Security number search against the credit files in order to identify any other names used by the individual, as well as anyone else who may be using the same Social Security number to obtain credit. When several individuals are using the same Social Security number and appear to be living at the same address, one possibility is that the Social Security number may be shared by a group of individuals who are in the country illegally. If only one other, apparently unrelated, person is using the same Social Security number, either that individual or the applicant may be doing so in error. This is not uncommon, but it should be cleared up. A Social Security number may also display as invalid or belonging to a deceased person on the credit file. Calling this to the applicant's attention may prompt him to re-check the number and correct it, as the person may simply have forgotten the number, rather than be attempting to perpetrate any kind of fraud.

It's important that employers who use credit records to pre-screen employees remember that what appears on the credit report is not necessarily correct. As explained in Chapter 25: Consumer Credit Records, mistakes can be made, and records from more than one individual can be erroneously combined. With this in mind, one should not assume that an applicant is lying when a discrepancy is found, but discrepancies should be followed up on and resolved to the employer's satisfaction.

Consumer Credit Records may be obtained online from the three national credit agencies, or through any of the hundreds of credit bureaus, or public records vendors, some of which may be found on the Internet.

An Alternative Social Security Number Screening Device

Even without access to consumer credit records, anyone can perform a crude type of Social Security number screening, using a software tool found on the Internet or other consumer online systems. From time to time, I have run across Internet sites that, when given a Social Security number, will return the state and approximate year of issuance, and validate that the number is within the range of those issued by the Social Security Administration. One such site is offered by Informus Corporation at www.informus.com/hdocs/intrpt.html.

I have seen similar software available for downloading from online forums on CompuServe and other consumer online systems. With a little searching (in forums for genealogy, private investigation, and locating people) you can often obtain a copy of this type of software online.

Although this type of search does not verify that the Social Security number belongs to any given person, it can raise questions if a person's Social Security number was issued before that individual was born or in a state in which that person has never lived.

Earnings History

A company may also choose to verify an applicant's earnings history from the Social Security Administration (SSA). This can be particularly useful when the information cannot be confirmed by an employer, such as when they have gone out of business or their records have been destroyed in a fire or other accident. Although a company cannot directly access the SSA database to screen their applicants, earnings information from the SSA is made available, with the applicant's consent, by at least one employment screening company:

Edge Information Management Inc.
One Harbor Place
1901 South Harbor City Boulevard
Suite 401
Melbourne, FL 32901
(800)725-3343
www.edgeinformation.com

Not all earnings are reported to the SSA. There is a maximum amount that an employer must report for an employee, and the maximum has increased from year to year. When the Social Security Administration opened for business in 1937, the maximum was only $3,000. By 1966, this figure had more than doubled to $6,600. A decade later (1976), the maximum was $15,300, and by 2000, the maximum had increased to $76,200. Although these maximums may cover a majority of Americans, the earnings records will not encompass many CEOs, top entertainers, or others at the high end of the earnings spectrum.

The earnings history from Edge Information Management Inc. can be ordered online, but the records are not immediately accessible. The information obtained by Edge is uploaded to their system at a later date, and may then be accessed by the employer.

Education Verification

An employer may want to verify the applicant's educational background. The first check should be to verify that the school is a legitimate college or university. A search of Peterson's College Database (available online through CompuServe Information Services, Inc., Dialog and Factiva) can be performed to locate the school if it is a legitimate one. For a graduate school, a search of Peterson's GradLine (available online through CompuServe Knowledge Index and Dialog) can also be used to verify its legitimacy. If the school is not found on one of these databases, it may be necessary to contact the accrediting association to make sure that the degree claimed is not from a diploma mill. For information about accrediting agencies, contact the Council for Higher Education Accreditation (www.chea.org).

If the school is legitimate, the employer would then want to verify the years of attendance and degrees attained by the applicant. I have not yet seen a system that makes it possible to access school records databases directly; however, some companies offer online systems through which an educational verification can be ordered. After the information is obtained from the school, it is uploaded to their system and accessed by the client. Some schools require the consent of the applicant; others do not.

Employment History

Employment verification usually is performed on the telephone, but may also be ordered online through some of the employment screening companies. After the information is obtained from the former employer, it is uploaded to the employment verification system and can then be accessed by the prospective employer.

Worker's Compensation History

An employer may wish to obtain details of any previous worker's compensation claims filed by prospective employees before hiring them. They may wish to spot an applicant who has filed frequent claims or who seems to be particularly accident prone, as well as to identify pre-existing injuries that their group insurance company may wish to know about.

Many states will release information about previous worker's compensation claims. Some states require the applicant's authorization, while others do not. A few will not release the information even with authorization.

For many states, a worker's compensation claims history may be ordered online through some employment screening companies. After the information is obtained from the state or district office, it is uploaded to the employment verification system and can then be accessed by the employer.

For further information about worker's compensation records, please refer to Chapter 30: Medical and Insurance Records.

Occupational Safety and Health Administration Records

Records on industrial inspections and accidents are obtained from the U.S. Department of Labor, Occupational Safety, and Health Administration (OSHA) and are sold by many public records vendors (such as ChoicePoint Online). Employers may wish to obtain information on accidents involving an applicant, just as they would worker's compensation records.

For further information about OSHA records, please refer to Chapter 30.

Medical Records

Medical records are usually confidential; however, insurance companies are routinely given access to medical histories of millions of Americans. Employers who self-insure their employees may also have access to the complete medical records of their employees through firms such as the Medical Information Bureau (MIB). For further information about this company, please refer to the Medical Insurance Databases section of Chapter 30.

Public Records

Public records can also be used in pre-employment screening. A criminal records check in each county where an applicant has lived, going back several years, might reveal a history of violence, embezzlement, or other crimes that could have a direct bearing on an applicant's employment.

Some employers will wish to check the credit headers to determine whether the applicant has lived in other states or counties where a previous criminal record might be located.

For employment in criminal justice, federally chartered or insured banking institutions or securities firms, or state or local government, the National Crime Information Center (NCIC) database may also be used to check for criminal records nationally. Please refer to Chapter 26: Criminal Justice Records for more information about this database.

Civil records could also reveal a suit involving a previous employer or fellow employee, which could be of interest no matter which side was suing. If a prospective employee has been sued for fraud, this would be a definite red flag for most employers. Before hiring the applicant, the employer would need to be completely satisfied with the explanation for such a suit.

Personal injury lawsuits might also be found in the civil records, which might be used to identify pre-existing injuries, which the employer's group insurance company may wish to know about.

A great deal of additional information might be gleaned from public records. For further information, please refer to Chapter 31: Public Records.

Combined Pre-Employment Searches

Public records vendors and pre-employment screening companies often offer combined pre-employment screening packages. These may include any combination of the reports listed earlier, conveniently packaged into a single request.

Other Pre-Employment Databases

Employers also sometimes use proprietary databases to screen their employees. For example, Employers Mutual Association United/Stores Protective Association (EMA-SPA), in Simi Valley, California, is a not-for-profit company that keeps private files on previous employees of their member companies (which include Circuit City, Reno Air, department stores, and other companies, for a total of approximately 150 firms). These "incident files" catalog people who were fired because their bosses concluded that they were stealing, using drugs, or harassing co-workers while on the job, among other things. Shoplifters caught by department stores are also named.

Most of the estimated 200,000 people on file with EMA-SPA do not know that their names are on file, and many (if not most) have never been arrested for their purported wrongdoings. This means that they may have had no opportunity to defend themselves, and yet, their future employment opportunities at any of the member firms may be limited by their presence on this database. I would not be surprised to see the demise of this and similarly "private" databases as their existence becomes more widely known.

Summary

An employer has a variety of means for prescreening potential employees, and many databases can help with the process. Not all prescreening work can be accomplished on a computer, however. No database can entirely remove the need for an interview with the applicant, and not all types of records are available online. Military records, for example, cannot be obtained online, but may be obtained for use in the prescreening process by submitting the appropriate request form to the service in question. There also are aptitude tests and technical interviews specific to many occupations.

A thorough screening depends in large part on the information supplied by the applicant, and on the employer's ability to verify each pertinent fact and find any holes in the information supplied. The application should account for all periods since the applicant began working (or at least several years), including where they were living and working at all times. Gaps in their residential or employment history could indicate a problem period and should be discussed with the applicant.

Employers may also use other screening devices, such as integrity and honesty tests, drug tests, handwriting analysis, psychological assessment, and physical exams, in hopes of further reducing their risk of hiring a problem employee. Although there has been some controversy over the effectiveness of these methods, some employers do feel that administering these tests does at the very least discourage potential employees from applying for a job if they know that they have something to hide.

There are legal limitations on the types of records that can be used in pre-employment screening, and, in some cases, the age of the records that can be considered is regulated. The Fair Credit Reporting Act, for example, limits the employer to considering only the last seven years for most types of credit records used in pre-employment screening. It also requires that an applicant be told when rejected for a job because of information on a credit report or investigative consumer report. A patchwork of other state and federal laws (including civil rights acts and laws barring discrimination against the disabled) govern prescreening in various areas of the country. It is incumbent on the employer to be aware of these laws and to adhere to them in all prescreening of prospective employee. The Legal Information Institute at Cornell Law School provides a couple of Internet Web sites that might be worth examining for this type of legal information:

> U.S. Employment Law
> www.law.cornell.edu/topics/employment.html
>
> U.S. Employment Discrimination Law
> www.law.cornell.edu/topics/employment_discrimination.html

These sites may also lead you to other legal or employment sites where further information can be found.

Of course, one should always consult an attorney for interpretation of the laws and how they apply to one's own situation.

Again, please remember that databases do contain errors, so no prescreening process should rely solely on the computer. Employers should obtain authorization from applicants before delving into their backgrounds and should discuss any findings with them. Only in this way can an employer avoid unfairly denying employment to a qualified individual.

For more information on pre-employment screening, see Section IV: Where Can I Find More Information?. Listed here are books that include additional sources and methods among the Background Research/Investigative Reporting Books and Public Records Research Guides. Organizations of employers sometimes also provide information on screening potential employees. You might additionally consider subscribing to periodicals such as those listed under Pre-Employment Screening and Recruitment Publications, also found in Section IV.

On the Internet, you can also locate many companies that perform pre-employment screening or sell reports that can be used for this purpose, as well as Usenet newsgroups and mailing lists on which such issues are discussed.

Chapter 8

Recruitment and Job Searching

*The crowning fortune of a man is to be born to some pursuit
which finds him employment and happiness, whether it be to
make baskets, or broadswords, or canals, or statues, or songs.*

–Ralph Waldo Emerson

A few years ago the only reason to use a computer when searching for a job was in writing up a resume. Recruiters hardly needed a computer at all. That is no longer true. In fact, so many recruiters now operate online that a sizeable directory is published just to keep track of them all, *The Best Directory of Recruiters On-Line* (www.recruitersinteractive.com or www. bestrecruiters.com/6.html).

Online job postings are now routine, and job-seekers upload their resumes to online bulletin boards, employment services, and directly to companies at an ever-increasing rate. In fact, it is difficult to imagine finding a job in some industries (such as in data processing/computers) or at professional or executive level positions without the use of online resources or databases.

Applicants once sent resumes containing detailed work histories and personal information directly to companies that advertised their job openings in the newspapers. Now a resume may travel far beyond those bounds, being downloaded from online services by executive search firms, company recruiters, and others who can use the information to size up their competition.

Job applicants, company recruiters, executive search firms, and businesses are all continuing to adjust to this new employment arena. Let us look at some descriptions and examples of the employment information now available and how it is being used.

Job Seekers

People seeking employment have always had to reveal personal information such as home address and telephone number. Their resumes have often included information such as employment history, responsibilities, professional accomplishments, salary history, educational background, professional association memberships, awards received, and references.

Today, resumes are being uploaded to online bulletin boards and databases, where they can be accessed not only by a particular company that interests the applicant, but in some cases by nearly anyone with a computer. Job seekers should keep this in mind when deciding what to include in their online resumes.

General Resume Databases

Many of the online systems offer resume databases. Following are a few examples of general resume databases (or databanks) that can be used to seek out prospective employees. They can also be used by employers intent on finding out whether their own employees are looking elsewhere, so job searchers beware:

- CSI National Career Network (available online through Star Temporaries, Inc.) contains resumes of job-seekers and lists of employment opportunities from potential employers.

- E-Span Job Search (available online through CompuServe Information Service) contains descriptions of job openings and a second database of resumes posted by job candidates.

- The National Resume Bank (available online through Callassure) contains qualifications summaries submitted by those seeking work in many employment sectors.

Since it seems that nearly everyone in the world has their own Internet home page (okay, I am exaggerating—slightly), resumes can also be found at individual Internet sites as well as in collections of resumes found all over the Internet, such as:

America's Job Bank
www.ajb.dni.us

Jobs.net
www.jobs.net

JobsOnline.com
www.JobsOnline.com

Recruiters Online Network
www.recruitersonline.com

While some sites allow virtually anyone to view your resume, others allow you to be more selective. For example, HotJobs.com (www.HotJobs.com) provides the ability to block companies from viewing your resume if you have not applied to them for a job. Monster.com (www.monster.com) allows you to activate your resume so employers can view it, or to store it privately for your own use. Careerbuilder (www.careerbuilder.com/index.html) allows you to block certain companies (such as your employer) from viewing your resume. Headhunter.net (www.headhunter.net) allows you to conceal your identity while you look for a job on their site, and to hide your resume from employers if you wish, allowing you to send it to individual companies yourself. BestJobsUSA (www.bestjobsusa.com) offers a "Resume Masking" option, which hides the identifying information on your resume. JobOptions (http://ww1.joboptions. com/jo_main) allows you to post your resume publicly, or to post it privately but allow others to search for any of the information on it, or to post it privately and to make all identifying information (including your name) nonsearchable.

Military Personnel

For resumes of enlisted personnel, warrant officers, commissioned officers, and persons separated from the National Guard and Reserve forces, who will soon be leaving the military and seeking employment as civilians, you can look to the Military in Transition Database (available online through MILITRAN, Inc.).

College Students Seeking Employment

For resumes of college students or recent graduates, you can look to MonsterTrak.com (www.jobtrak.com).

Hot Prospects

Recruiters can use resumes posted online to locate hot prospects for job openings. They may also use professional and staff directory databases, such as those listed in Appendix D and described in Chapter 18: Staff, Professional, and Other Directories, in order to identify individuals in key positions who may have the required experience and expertise for a position they are trying to fill.

News databases can be used to identify the movers and shakers in an industry. Mergers and acquisitions, executive changes, and other events taking place within companies are often detailed in the news. Recruiters and competitors can use this information to determine when the time is ripe for spiriting away key employees with a better offer.

Additional information and resources for identifying hot prospects for recruitment can be found in Chapter 12: Identifying an Expert, as much of that information can also be applied to recruitment.

Job Openings

All of the Web sites mentioned to this point also contain job openings. There are others that list job openings without listing resumes, such as E Span Job Search (available online through CompuServe Information Service).

Job seekers who are not anxious to upload their resumes to a database or Web site where their current employer might see it can use these same sites and services to search for current job openings and apply to the companies, either directly or through the service.

Some of these services also allow job seekers to set up a profile or an "agent" to search for the ideal job. The service will e-mail matching listings to them periodically.

Classified Ads

Although there are many news databases available online, most news databases omit the classified ads. This is also true on the Internet; although most newspapers can now be found on the Internet, most do not include their classified section.

There are classified employment ads that can be found on the Internet, however. These include sites specifically designed to publish classified ads collected from various newspapers, such as

AdQuest3D
www.adquest3d.com

Job Search Bookmarks-Search Newspaper Classifieds
www.cashvalley.net/newspapers.html

Other sites provide Internet ad space for anyone wanting to publish a classified ad (for a fee), such as

>AdMamma.com
>www.admamma.com

>Classified Internet Inc.
>www.classifiedinet.com/NetAdvertise.htm

>ClassifiedToday
>www.classifiedtoday.com

Openings Within a Geographic Area

People seeking a position within a specific geographic area may find that there is an online service specifically designed to suit their needs. For example, workers who have been "downsized" in the San Francisco Bay Area might start their job search at BayArea.com: (http://careers.bayarea.com) or at Jobs & Careers (http://jobscareers.com). People seeking summer jobs in Alaska should consider Alaska Wildland Adventures (www.awasummerjobs.com).

Openings Within an Industry

Some databases are focused on jobs in a particular industry. Examples of these include IBIS-CUS (available online through Association IBISCUS), which contains, among other things, a list of employment opportunities for development specialists. (Refer to Appendix N for this database vendor.) Similar information can be found on the Internet.

Jobs in radio and television can be found at the Corporation for Public Broadcasting Employment Outreach Project, at www.cpb.org/jobline. The Navy Jobs Home Page is located at www.navyjobs.com. People seeking jobs in the academic arena can also visit the Academic Position Network, which is searchable by state, and located at www.apnjobs.com.

High tech jobs are the focus of BrassRing.com (www.brassring.com), dice.com (www.dice.com), and techies.com (www.techies.com).

People seeking seasonal work in a ski resort should go to Natives (www.natives.co.uk/index.htm).

Thrill seekers may find their ideal job at ActionJobs (www.actionjobs.com), a site dedicated to jobs in Adventure Travel, Alaska, Cruise Ships, Entertainment, Forestry and Firefighting, Resorts, Ski and Snowboarding, Professional, and other action jobs.

Online mailing lists can also be used to notify people of openings in their field. For instance, mailing lists for those seeking computer jobs can be found at A1A Computer Jobs Mailing Lists (www.home.earthlink.net/~rko153/a1a/).

Some of the general resume databases mentioned earlier also maintain sections for specific industries, or allow searches by industry as well.

Openings Within Specific Companies or Agencies

Many companies and various branches of government now maintain their own online job bulletin boards on their Web sites, which applicants can use to find openings for which they are qualified.

Magazines and Newsletters

Some online newsletters and magazines include not only articles, but job openings as well. An example is Career Magazine located at www.careermag.com.

Summary

The ways in which jobs are advertised and applicants are recruited have been transformed in recent years. The economy, technology, and the availability of online (and particularly Internet) access have all played a large part in the changing employment scene.

Job hunters in many fields will operate at a growing disadvantage if they lack access to the online resources used by companies and recruiters who are looking for them. Recruiters who cannot take advantage of the online systems, databases, and the Internet will similarly be operating at a disadvantage.

This chapter has provided only an introduction to the many online resources available to job seekers and their would-be employers. Additional online sites can be found on America Online and various other consumer online systems. Many publications, such as those listed under Pre-Employment Screening and Recruitment Publications (see Section IV: Where Can I Find More Information?—Periodicals), may contain useful information for navigating some of the online resources available for recruitment, and may also explain the legal issues involved in recruitment and hiring. Still more resources are listed in the comprehensive database of personal information resources available at the *Naked in Cyberspace* Web site (www.technosearch.com/naked/directory.htm).

For many workers seeking jobs, employers offering jobs, and recruiters trying to pair the two, online systems have already become essential. This will ultimately affect the nature and volume of personal information floating around cyberspace.

Chapter 9

Tenant Screening

Quite frankly, that's why I was so glad to find this great
apartment. You'd be surprised how hard it is to get a place
in the city. Never mind that most folks are hesitant to rent to
a slime-based organism, much less one with intentions of
taking over the world ...

–Thrakkorzog, *The Tick*

If you have ever rented a house, condominium, apartment, or any other type of property, you are probably already aware that landlords and property management companies typically screen prospective tenants in some way before allowing them to take possession of a property. Some of this screening may take place on the telephone, calling references such as an employer and previous landlords and verifying whatever information the prospective tenant supplied on the rental application. Many online databases also can alert property owners and managers to additional information that a would-be renter may not have volunteered.

Credit Records

Probably the most common type of database used for tenant screening is a credit database. A credit profile can be used to show a person's history of good credit, which will reveal whether they are responsible about their debts and will be likely to pay their rent. It can also uncover a history of late payments and bad debts, which might make the person a less desirable tenant.

Use of a credit profile will not allow a landlord to foresee all possible problems that might arise with a tenant, nor provide information on all past rental problems. Most of the information on the credit files relates to credit cards and loans, so things like late rental payments are not normally reflected.

You should also know that there are variations in the records carried by the three national credit agencies, as described in Chapter 25: Consumer Credit Records. Landlords who routinely pull a credit report from only one credit agency should be aware that one of the other credit agency databases may offer additional information on the prospective tenant.

A landlord may choose to deal only with the credit agency that is the most well established (has the most reporting companies on file, better coverage of public records, etc.) in their area of the country; however, when screening tenants from other regions, another credit agency's report may be more complete. It can be expensive to pull credit records for each prospective tenant from all three agencies, yet failing to do so can increase the risk of renting to a bad debtor.

Public Records

Public records can also provide information on a person's rental history. For example, civil records can include suits by previous landlords to recover payment for property damage inflicted by the prospective tenant. Real property records can include foreclosures under the applicant's name. Criminal records may show a history of violence, possibly even involving previous neighbors or landlords, or current members of their household. These are all problems that any landlord might want to know when deciding between several prospective tenants.

Many public records vendors are now offering packages of searches to be used specifically for tenant screening.

Tenant Databases

Many databases have been built specifically for tenant screening. In fact, approximately one hundred companies maintain proprietary tenant screening databases across the country. First American Registry is an automated computer service that links some of these databases, allowing property managers access to landlord-tenant court records from more than 1,000 courthouses in 25 states. This service also allows access to credit reports, landlord-reported tenant histories, wanted fugitive searches, skip tracing, risk scores, and many other services designed for the property management industry. For additional information about this database, contact:

First American Registry, Inc.
11140 Rockville Pike #1200
Rockville, MD 20852
(800) 999-0350
(301) 881-3400
(301) 984-7312 FAX
www.firstamregistry.com or www.residentscreening.com

Similar services are offered by American Tenant Screen, Inc. (www.atshome.com).

Summary

Tenant screening involves legal issues, which can vary from one state to another. For example, a landlord may not have the right to consider certain records as part of the tenant screening process, or there may be limitations on how many years of history may be considered for particular types of records such as bankruptcies. Landlords who screen prospective tenants should become thoroughly knowledgeable about the laws governing tenant screening in their area.

For legal information on landlord-tenant laws, you might also visit the Legal Information Institute (of Cornell Law School) on the Internet. Among their sites, U.S. Landlord-Tenant Law can be found at www.law.cornell.edu/topics/landlord_tenant.html, and the Plain-Person's Guide to Minnesota Landlord-Tenant Laws is available at http://tenant.net/Other_Areas/Minnesota.

For further information about tenant screening, many publications regularly carry articles that discuss resources for tenant screening, along with legal issues for landlords and property management companies. Some of these are included later in this book under Property Management

Publications in Section IV: Where Can I Find More Information?—Periodicals. On the Internet, you can also peruse TenantNet, the Online Resource for Residential Tenants' Rights at www.tenant.net. *The Rental Property Reporter* is a newsletter for landlords, which can be found on the Internet at www.rentalprop.com. Real estate-oriented resources can also be found at RealtyGuide International at http://www.xmission.com/~realtor1.

There are also usenet newsgroups such as alt.invest.real-estate, realtynet.invest, alt.real-estate-agents, and alt.business.property on the Internet, where discussions of property rights and rental practices regularly take place.

In addition, property management organizations such as those listed under that heading in Section IV: Where Can I Find More Information?—Organizations can provide more information and publications in this field.

On the Internet, you can also find many sites for companies that specialize in tenant screening services, such as Metropolitan Tenant Information Services, Inc. (www.tenant-screening.com), Tenant Check (www.infotel.net/tenantcheck), Tenant Screening Credit (www.tsci.com), and Tenant Screening Services Inc. (www.onlinescreening.net).

You'll also find Web pages for attorneys specializing in landlord rights and commercial property information.

Landlords should also be aware that any type of database can carry errors, and denying housing to someone should not be taken lightly, nor based solely on a problem surreptitiously discovered on a database. This can be especially true on the Internet. I strongly advise obtaining written permission from prospective tenants before performing any type of tenant screening and, if a problem is discovered, discussing the results with the applicant before ruling them out as a tenant. It is possible that there is a bad debt that can be explained or that a record found belongs to another individual entirely. (This is not an uncommon occurrence.) Unless a landlord discusses possible problems with rental applicants, the applicants may have no way to explain or correct the problem and may be unfairly denied housing.

Chapter 10

Asset Searches

I'm tired of Love: I'm still more tired of Rhyme.
But Money gives me pleasure all the time.

–Hilaire Belloc

Who Needs an Asset Search?

Performing an asset search may be the furthest thing from your mind today, but there are a few instances in which almost anyone may find themselves needing to do just that. So, who does need an asset search?

Anyone Who Is About to Sue Someone

At some point in your life, you may have occasion to sue someone. You may have an ironclad case, miles of proof, and all of the reasons in the world for wanting to sue someone. You may even be 100 percent sure that you will win the case—hands down.

Before spending big bucks on legal fees, it might be wiser to spend a few dollars finding out whether the person that you are thinking of suing has anything worth suing for. If you're suing because someone owes you money, it is entirely possible that they don't have it to pay you. In that case, your sense of satisfaction upon winning your case may vanish when you realize that there is no way for you to satisfy the judgment and that you now have legal fees to pay as well.

If it turns out that the person you're suing is wealthy, that information could also be valuable if a settlement is offered.

If you decide to go ahead with the suit, and you win, knowledge of your opponent's assets might also make it easier to satisfy the judgment and recoup your expenses.

Anyone Being Sued

If you are being sued by someone, it might also pay to know your opponent's financial position. This might help you to gauge their seriousness at pursuing the suit or the likelihood of their accepting an out-of-court settlement. If, as part of the suit, they claim that you have damaged their financial position, you may also want to gather evidence to the contrary.

Anyone Going into Business with Someone

If you are about to go into business with someone, especially someone whose financial backing you'll be relying on, you would do well to obtain as full a picture of their financial position as possible. If they are committing to sharing the business's ongoing expenses in exchange for partial ownership, investigating whether they are in a position to fulfill their end of the agreement may save you from hardship later.

Anyone Extending a Substantial Amount of Credit to Someone

If someone asks you for a loan, or asks you to perform any type of service now in exchange for payment to be made at a later date (i.e., after they liquidate some funds, after they get paid for the project that they're working on, after the cow jumps over the moon), they may not be telling you that several other people are already waiting in line for the money, or that the IRS has already filed a tax lien on their future assets. An asset search can help you to weigh the situation before putting your own assets at risk.

What Types of Records Are Available?

Real Property

A home represents the largest asset many Americans will ever own. Real property records will identify homes owned by an individual as well as land and business properties. These can be found online for many areas of the country.

You should also be aware that people who are trying to hide their income sometimes pour money into an existing asset such as their home equity, thereby paying down the mortgage while protecting the funds (if their property is protected by homestead law).

Bank Accounts

Banks do not give individuals or private investigators access to lists of their account holders or to their account information online. Public records can, however, sometimes lead you to identify bank accounts. Some of the company databases also sometimes list the name of the bank or banker, which can help you to locate their bank accounts, as explained in Chapter 23: Bank Records. Examples of databases that include this banking information for at least some of their company records follow:

- ABC Europe Production Europex (available online through FIZ Technik and STN International)

- Business Who's Who of Australia (available online through Dun and Bradstreet and on the Internet at http://bww.dnb.com.au)

- COMLINE Japanese Corporate Directory (available online through DataStar)

- Company Intelligence (available online through DataStar, Dialog, and Nexis)

- Dun's Market Identifiers (available online through Dun and Bradstreet)

- Hoppenstedt Germany (available online at www.companydatabase.de)

- KOMPASS Israel (available online through Dialog)

- Standard and Poor's Register—Corporate (available online through CompuServe's Knowledge Index, Dialog, Lexis, and Nexis)

Refer to Appendix N for the addresses of the vendors above, except for CompuServe, which can be found in Appendix L, and Dun and Bradstreet, which is listed in Appendix M.

Bank loans may also be found on credit records. Since people often obtain loans from banks where their accounts are held, any loan from a bank found on a credit report may warrant further investigation.

Motor Vehicles

Department of Motor Vehicle records can be used to locate motor vehicles, including automobiles, trucks, trailers, commercial vehicles, motor homes, buses, motorcycles, off-road vehicles, and snowmobiles. Many public records vendors, as well as some of the DMVs, offer online searching of these files.

Boats

The DMV also registers motorized boats in their vessel registration files, and many of these can be searched online. Watercraft of 27 feet or more, or 5 net tons or more, can also be found on the U.S. Coast Guard Watercraft file offered by some of the public records vendors, including Lexis.

Aircraft

The Federal Aviation Administration registers all individuals and businesses that own aircraft throughout the United States. These records vendors also offer these records.

Business Assets

Along with such personal assets as a home and car, people may own very significant business assets. Corporate and Limited Partnership records, Fictitious Business Name Statements (or DBAs—Doing Business As), and Uniform Commercial Code filings (in which they may promise business assets as collateral for a loan) can all point you to businesses in which a person has a financial interest. This information is offered by public records vendors.

Many company databases and company Web sites list principals and key executives of businesses. The persons named may have financial interest in the companies that they operate as well.

Stock Ownership

Many databases identify owners of companies that are more than 5 percent public, information that must be declared on Form 13D to the Securities and Exchange Commission. Some of these databases also identify the holdings of company officers, directors, and principals owning 10 percent of a company's equity.

Company databases also sometimes list shareholders. Examples of databases that include names of shareholders are:

- Analysis (available online through ARK Information Services)

- CIFARBASE (available online through Center for International Financial Analysis and Research, Inc. and GENIOS Wirtschaftsdatenbanken)

- COMLINE Japanese Corporate Directory (available online through DataStar)

- Company Credit Reports (available online through COSMOSNET)

- Company Intelligence (available online through DataStar, Dialog, and Nexis)

- Datastream Company Accounts (available online through Primark Corporation)

- Dunsmarketing (available online through Questel Orbit)

- FP Corporate Survey (available online through Infomart Dialog and Infomart Online)

- INFOCHECK (available online through DataStar and The Infocheck Group, Ltd.)

- Insider Trading Monitor (available online through CDA/Investnet, Dialog, and Factiva)

- Jordans Shareholder Service (available online through Jordans Ltd.)

Refer to Appendix N for the addresses of the vendors above.

Some public records vendors, such as Information America, also offer a stock ownership search among their asset searching services. Information America's stock search details stock transaction and holding information for directors, executive officers, and shareholders who control at least 10 percent of stock in a public company. Proposed sales notices of restricted securities are also included.

For more information on this subject, see Chapter 11: Competitive Intelligence.

Charitable and Political Contributions

Large contributors to political candidates can be found in the news, as well as on many databases (as explained in greater detail in Chapter 35: Political Records).

Philanthropists can also be found in the news, and on the fundraising databases described in Chapter 13: Prospect Research (Fundraising).

People who make large contributions to charitable or political causes usually have substantial assets behind those contributions, so this type of information can help you to gauge the size of the assets that you are going after.

Civil Records

During civil suits, business holdings and personal assets often become part of the public record. Detailed information that would not otherwise be public may be subpoenaed by the courts or found in the discovery process by the attorneys involved in the case.

During a divorce, assets of both parties are normally presented to the court, and agreement is reached as to how they can be split most equitably. A spouse may be aware of hidden assets that they wish to share in, so they may present this evidence in court, where it again becomes public record. They may have even hired a private investigator to locate offshore accounts, penthouses purchased for mistresses, or money earned through illicit activities. In the worst divorce cases, scandalous amounts of information can be uncovered.

The civil record indices offered by public records vendors can point you to the location of civil suits, which may then be obtained from the court or records building in order to find out what has already been uncovered in previous cases.

Criminal Records

If a person has been tried for fraud, grand theft, embezzling, or other financial crimes, it is possible that a good deal of the financial dealings and assets may be documented in the criminal records. Although this level of detail won't be found online, the criminal record indices offered by many public records vendors can point you to the existence and location of this information.

Probate Records

If a person has inherited money, jewelry, art, real property, or other valuable items, this may be found in probate records, which sometimes can be searched online through public records vendors. Again, the online records are only an index to the actual records, which exist at the county court or records building.

Tax Liens, Bankruptcies, and Judgments

Detailed financial records are normally introduced during bankruptcy proceedings. Tax liens and judgments can also provide records of assets and debts. All of these records can be found online in many areas of the country through public records vendors.

Some databases offered by more mainstream business, financial, or news database vendors focus on business litigation or personal and corporate bankruptcies. Suits, judgments, satisfactions, bankruptcies, and foreclosures all can be found on databases such as these:

- Bankruptcies and Defaults (available online through Thomson Financial Securities Data) provides information on companies that have filed for bankruptcy.

- The Bankruptcy Datasource: Data Pages (available online through Nexis) provides information on companies with assets greater than $50 million that have gone into bankruptcy since 1984.

- Bankruptcy Records (available online through Information America) contains bankruptcy records for individuals and businesses in the U.S.

- Duns Legal Search (available online through Dun and Bradstreet Business Credit Services) contains public record information for businesses in all U.S. states.

- SANP, also known as Italian National Archive of Protests or Italian National Defaulters File (available online through CERVED International, S.A.) contains default information on individuals and corporations, from the official default bulletin of local Chambers of Commerce.

- SCRL Defaillances (available online through DataStar and Questel Orbit) contains announcements of current liquidation and bankruptcy judgments by French commercial courts prior to their publication in the Bulletin Officiel des Annonces Civiles et Commerciales (BODACC).

Refer to Appendix M for Information America and Nexis (listed under LexisNexis), and to Appendix N for the addresses of the remaining vendors.

Company databases also frequently carry legal information about firms, including bankruptcies, civil suits, and judgments. Refer to Appendix C for examples of company databases.

News articles and newswires also describe financial difficulties encountered by some businesses, including bankruptcy judgments. They also record profits, business mergers, and other such information. Federal Filings Business Newswire (available online through Factiva) is one newswire that often contains financial information. This database provides proprietary news, financial data, and investment research from the U.S. Securities and Exchange Commission (SEC), other U.S. federal government agencies, Capitol Hill, and bankruptcy courts.

Some of the news database producers have separated bankruptcy and other financial notices into their own searchable databases. For example:

- CAPA (available online through BELINDIS) contains more than 134,000 citations to public notices appearing in the Moniteur Belge, the Official Journal of Belgium. It covers persons and companies that declared bankruptcy or who have applied for a deed of arrangement with creditors, as well as persons deprived of certain rights (i.e., legally disabled) or placed under guardianship.

- The Daily Reporter (available online through Bell & Howell Information and Learning and as part of Business Dateline, which is available online through CompuServe, Dialog, Factiva, OCLC EPIC, and Nexis) contains bankruptcies, liens, notices (e.g., bidding, circuit court, city), and permits (building, burial, and so on) listed in the *Daily Reporter* (Milwaukee, Wisconsin) newspaper.

Refer to Appendix N for the addresses of these vendors.

Credit records also list such public records as bankruptcies, liens, and judgments on personal and business credit profiles. The credit agencies also sometimes offer additional databases for searching business litigation as well. One such database is the Business Litigation Database, offered by Trans Union LLC (www.transunion.com). This database contains court records on companies from New York and New Jersey, including information on suits, judgments, satisfactions, bankruptcies, foreclosures (for New Jersey only), and federal, state, and city tax liens.

Credit Information

Debts are not the only thing that you can find on credit records. A loan from a mortgage company may indicate that your subject is paying for property, which may be listed under another name. Vehicle loans or inquiries from car dealers may lead you to other vehicles owned by an individual, even though they may not be registered in your subject's name.

When someone has a great deal of credit card debt but indicates that they have no assets, you can't help but wonder where the money was spent. This may cause you to do more digging into their assets or lead an attorney to request additional documentation to corroborate their story of where the money went.

As noted earlier, public records also are sometimes included on credit records.

Although all three national credit agencies offer credit records online, along with numerous credit bureaus throughout the country, anyone wishing to access personal credit information must have permissible purpose, as defined by the Fair Credit Reporting Act (FCRA). For more information, please refer to Chapter 25: Consumer Credit Records. However, the FCRA does not restrict access to business credit records.

Universal Commercial Code Indices

Universal Commercial Code (UCC) filings can be very helpful in documenting assets that have been used as collateral for loans. The online indices do not contain detailed asset information, but they do allow you to locate the records so that the full detail can be obtained from the courts. Please refer to Chapter 31: Public Records for additional information about these records.

Assets in the News

Additional personal and business assets are sometimes discovered in the news. A magazine or newspaper article may cover a fundraiser being held on someone's yacht, or their purchase of fine art at a Sotheby's auction. At times, even detailed financial information is revealed in the news.

For example, Bill Gates's wealth has been well-documented. *Forbes* magazine lists him among the world's richest people, and in a January 2000 article *Forbes* listed his personal wealth at about $85 billion, with nearly all of it in Microsoft stock. Of course, it's hard to keep up with his billions, so there are several other unofficial Web sites dedicated to just that (including the Bill Gates Net Worth Page at www.quuxuum.org/~evan/bgnw.html and the Bill Gates Personal Wealth Clock at www.webho.com/WealthClock). *US News Online* contains diagrams of his $97 million home overlooking Lake Washington, including detailed descriptions of room dimensions, decorating motifs, and special features (www.usnews.com/usnews/nycu/tech/billgate/gates.htm). Many of his charitable contributions have also made the news, including when he and his wife, Melinda, donated $1 billion over the next 20 years to finance college scholarships for minority students (*Los Angeles Times*). Some of their other charitable efforts are documented on the Bill and Melinda Gates Foundation page (www.gatesfoundations.org/default.asp).

What's Missing?

Bank Accounts

A person may have funds in banks from one end of the country to the other. Although some public records can point to bank accounts, there may still be funds held in many bank accounts that you will not discover online.

Insurance Policies

Unless an insurance policy is discovered as an asset in a public record (such as a divorce settlement), you may not be aware that the subject is insured. One reason that these can be important is that a person might prepay a policy (especially one that gathers interest) in order to hide assets there.

Assets in Areas that Are Not Online

Many counties, courts, and other agencies have not yet made their records accessible online. Even when a public records vendor offers a statewide search, the fine print often notes that the search accesses all available counties. This can leave broad gaps in what is actually searched.

If records are gathered in a haphazard manner, the vendor may well miss some records when they are entered into the online system. For example, a public records vendor may actually go to the county court and pick up and scan a stack of new files every Friday. This procedure can miss a file that is being used in court on that day or sitting on someone's desk.

When records are scanned or manually entered into a system, some of the writing on the records may not be legible or can be misread. In that case, the record may be indexed in such a way that it will never be found online.

Assets Held Under Aliases or Unknown Associates

Although you may be able to anticipate some of the names under which assets are hidden (i.e., names of relatives, close friends, business associates, and businesses) and perform searches under them, assets may still elude you if they are listed under aliases or have been transferred to associates of whom you're unaware.

One way to uncover some of these assets is to perform an online search for real estate taxes that are billed to a person's mailing address. But even this precaution will overlook real estate that is not linked to an individual through any known address or name, just as it will miss other assets that remain hidden.

Money

If a person is trying to hide assets, he may purchase savings bonds, cashier's checks, or just keep cash in a home safe or hiding place. Database searching alone will seldom help much in discovering this.

Offshore Holdings

If a person is sending money to offshore accounts, you may have no way of discovering this online. For this reason, attorneys will sometimes subpoena telephone and fax records, overnight delivery receipts, passports, travel agency records, and hotel receipts (which often note telephone calls made). This sometimes can reveal suspicious activities, such as calls to Switzerland or trips to the Cayman Islands.

Summary

Although many assets can be discovered online, it may still be necessary to hire a private investigator specializing in asset investigation, and/or to subpoena additional records from the individual, in order to gain a full assessment of their financial status. Database searching skills are becoming increasingly important and can make an asset search more efficient and thorough, but investigative skills, analytical skills, and experience continue to be of greatest importance.

For additional information on performing asset searches, consider reading books on background research and investigative reporting, such as those listed in this book in Section IV: Where Can I Find More Information?—Books. You may also find books specifically on asset searching or private investigation, which should also be included on your reading list.

Organizations that you can learn from include those focused on asset searching, debt collection, fundraising/prospect research, legal research, private investigation, and public records research. Lists of these types of organizations are also included in Section IV under "Organizations."

Publications focused on competitive/business intelligence, fundraising/prospect research, investigative journalism, and private investigation can also provide information on different perspectives on asset searching. See "Periodicals" in Section IV.

Chapter 11

Competitive Intelligence

Knowledge itself is power.

–Francis Bacon

Competitive intelligence is loosely defined as gathering information about your business competitors. It includes collecting knowledge of your industry and anything that can affect the industry or the business. This knowledge can encompass factors such as technological developments, shifts in the economy, changes in legislation and regulations, and mergers and acquisitions. Databases, on the Internet and on proprietary systems, can make the task of tracking all of these areas much more manageable.

On the personal side, competitive intelligence includes knowledge of the people involved in the industry. Businesses are made up of people, and changes in that composition can have dramatic effects on businesses and industries.

Who's Who?

In order to track personnel, you must first identify them. You can find the names of some key players in any industry mentioned in the news whenever articles are written about their companies.

There also are dozens of company/business databases that include the names and positions of key personnel and company contacts. A list of business credit and financial databases that include personal information can be found in Appendix C.

One more way to identify key personnel is to search business and professional directory databases online. (Refer to Appendices D and E for these listings.)

The Internet is extremely useful as a source for this type of information. Companies, both large and small, now maintain their own World Wide Web home pages on the Internet. Many of these sites include press releases and the names of key individuals within a company. At the least, these listings include the names of the CEO, president, or other spokesperson. Sometimes the names of scientists or those responsible for important developments within the company are also listed. A few Web sites give access to the entire corporate directory. These listings are not standard, or necessarily searchable as a database would be, but they can add details that would not easily be found otherwise.

Corporate Musical Chairs

The departure of a company president or chief executive officer is quite newsworthy and will often coincide with some type of shake-up in the company, frequently taking the form of a reorganization. The classic move for new management is to streamline the operation, cutting costs, eliminating functional redundancies, and sometimes replacing the old guard with their own trusted people.

Companies looking for a clear opportunity to get a jump on their competition can take advantage of times like these, hoping that the upheaval taking place inside their competitor's company will delay the introduction of new products and services into the market. Continually scanning the newspapers and newswires for announcements of the departure of key executives and appointments of new executives is vital to companies whose market position is dictated by their ability to get a product to market first. For public (as well as some private) companies, a change of key executives may also cause the generation of an SEC filing, which can also be searched online at www.sec.gov.

Current Awareness

Current Awareness, Alert Service, Selective Dissemination of Information, and SDI are all names for the continuous monitoring of a particular subject or set of subjects. This is a common practice in competitive intelligence research, where the need for information never ends and seldom is limited to any single topic. Some of the database vendors offer automated current awareness searches. Vendors make it possible to enter search terms along with a search interval—daily, weekly, biweekly, monthly, and so on. The system then repeats the search automatically at the stated interval and sends the results into the researcher's online mailbox. This saves the time required to perform the same search repeatedly, and it often costs less. Not all systems can automate Current Awareness searches yet. To use the rest, the searcher must rerun the query by hand as often as necessary.

For competitive intelligence, it is important to set up the Current Awareness parameters to search not only for company and personnel names, but for appointments, promotions, resignations, retirement, and other significant changes in personnel that can affect competitors. When the target company is a subsidiary of a larger corporation, the important changes may be made at another, higher level of the organization, so you must be sure to also include the parent company and other affiliated companies in the search.

Companies themselves must also continually search for Web sites and Usenet newsgroup messages on the Internet for rumors about their products and services, in order to respond to concerns by customers and dispute any untrue claims made by competitors or detractors. Internet rumors, whether founded or not, have been responsible for damaging the reputations of companies such as Neiman Marcus, Tommy Hilfiger, Intel, McDonalds, and Nike. There are Web clipping services such as CyberAlert (www.cyberalert.com) and Northern Light's Alert Service (www. northernlight.com/docs/alerts_help_about.html) that continually scour the Internet and provide articles that match your search criteria. Some of these services are free, while others are sold on a subscription basis (some monthly; some annually). Companies can make use of these services to find out what's being said about them, or about their competitors. Refer to Chapter 20: News for further information about Web clipping services.

Where Have They Been? What Have They Done?

Once you have identified the key players in an industry, you will want to know more about them in order to try to predict what they might do next. Online databases can assist you in locating or developing your own biographical dossier on each person. Some of the best predictors of future actions can be found in their past, so you will want to know where they have worked and what they have accomplished before. Executives with a history of turning companies around and making them profitable can be considered important adversaries; they should be watched closely.

You may also be able to identify their previous business associates, who might be able to provide insight into their character and work style. In a close-knit industry, it is sometimes possible to find a friend of a friend who knows the former business associate and can set up an interview. It is also possible that some former associates are already on your own staff.

There are executives who, although extremely successful, are difficult to work with. News articles have been known to go on at length about a successful, albeit demanding, explosive, or domineering personality. Executives with a history of sexual harassment, drunk driving, or other problems that can affect the workplace are also sometimes exposed in the news. All of this information may be found through a database search reaching back several years. Former associates can also provide this type of information.

A problem personality can create hard feelings among colleagues and subordinates. When a problem is identified at another company, it may be possible to take advantage of that information by courting and then pirating away some of the competition's best people. This can have the dual effect of improving one's own business and crippling the opposition.

What Are They Thinking?

Listening closely to the competition is important, as they will sometimes explain their plans for their company in great detail. Their predictions for the future of the industry often reveal the direction in which their company is moving. Interviews with key executives, or articles or books by them, should always be read with this in mind.

CEOs and high-level executives are frequently called upon to give speeches, which reveal their assessment of the industry, along with their predictions for the future. Speeches such as these can sometimes be found on a company's Web page. Executives may even have occasion to testify before Congress; if so, their names will appear in such sources as *Congressional News*, which is searchable online. (Refer to Chapter 35 for information about political records.)

Impressions and summaries of speeches often make their way into the news, but the most important competitive details, and the context of any statements made, can sometimes be lost in these synopses. In fact, the article may offer little more than the speaker's name, the topic, and where the speech took place. When this is the case, it may still be possible to contact the organization that sponsored the speech and order a copy of the conference or meeting materials handed out to the attendees. The organization may also post the text or slides from a presentation on its own Web site.

On the other hand, when a speech is attended by a knowledgeable business analyst, the ensuing article can include not only key points made in the speech, but further analysis and insights into the speaker's impact on the industry.

Excerpts of notable speeches by prominent businesspeople can sometimes be found online in the newsletter *The Executive Speaker* (available through Nexis and on the Internet at www.executive-speaker.com).

The complete text of speeches can also be found in a few of the databases. Riksdagstrycket, ANF (available online through Rixlex) covers speeches by members of the Swedish Parliament. Dansk Nationallitteraert Ariv (available on the Internet through Det Kongelige Bibliotek at www.kb.dk) provides the full text of Danish literary works within fiction, fairy tales, lyrics, drama, letters, speeches, historical sources, and other literature.

Predictions also are sometimes found on a company's home page on the Internet. The full text of speeches are sometimes included, and annual and interim reports also sometimes contain this kind of information.

There is nothing like seeing your competition in action. If you would like to attend a meeting that an important executive will be attending, or where she will be speaking, in order to draw your own conclusions, and possibly even have the opportunity to question him or her directly, you can find scheduled conferences, events, trade fairs, and meetings listed on many databases. Three of the most prominent are FAIRBASE (available online through DataStar, FIZ Technik, and Gesellschaft fur Betriebswirtschaftliche Information mbH (GBI)), the Washington Daybook (available online through Factiva and on the Internet at web.fnsg.com), and Global Meeting Line (available online through Global Meeting Line, Inc.).

A call to the conference registrar can often confirm whether any of the executives that you are tracking will speak or attend. If you cannot attend an upcoming conference or meeting, tapes, transcripts, or other handouts can frequently still be obtained, sometimes even before the event.

Transcripts from radio and television broadcasts, many of which can be found in online databases, also can offer an excellent chance to find out what an executive is thinking.

Stock Ownership

As part of their compensation package, many executives receive stock in their company. They may also purchase shares on their own. There is nothing unusual or particularly revealing about that. What can be telling is a change in the ownership patterns. For example, if several members of a company's board were to dump all of their stocks suddenly, you could bet that something was brewing. If a company executive regularly accrued a given number of stocks each year and then uncharacteristically sold them all at once, that might be a step toward leaving the company. If a company president immediately sold off all the company stocks received each year as part of his or her compensation package, one might also question their emotional investment or faith in the company.

Several databases can be used to monitor the purchase and sale of company stocks by key executives and major shareholders. Please refer to Chapter 10: Asset Searches for examples.

Business Predictions Hidden in Public Records

Sometimes public records can reveal a company's plans. For example, when a company buys real estate, it may plan to expand or relocate. If a company wants to keep that information confidential, it may purchase the property under the name of an executive or the corporate attorney.

A company may also hide public transactions under a separate name that has been set up for this purpose. Searching for fictitious business name statements (or DBAs—Doing Business As) under the names of key executives can sometimes reveal the existence of another business being operated under an executive's name. Corporation and Limited Partnership records can also expose this.

When a company is having financial or legal difficulties, the principals also will sometimes start a new corporation before declaring bankruptcy and/or closing the old business. For competitive intelligence research, the formation of a new corporation under the names of a competitor's key executives should at least cause you to investigate further.

Inventions and new products developed by scientists or others within a company may be patented in the name of the inventor or employee rather than in the company's name. Searching the patent databases under the names of key personnel as well as companies can alert you to an impending change in products or reveal new products that they may plan to introduce to the market. Likewise, they may trademark the names of new products before introducing them to the marketplace, and a search of the trademark databases can be helpful in discovering them.

If executives purchase property a fair distance from their employers, one might also suspect that they are planning to move on. Of course, there are other possibilities, such as a vacation home or an investment; you should not jump to conclusions based on this type of information alone.

As a last example of the usefulness of public records, when an executive is in trouble due to drunk driving, assault, or other criminal convictions, it does not take too much of a leap to conclude that changes in the company will result from a conviction.

Summary

Companies that regularly study competitors have found online research to be of tremendous assistance in this task. This is not only because of the depth and breadth of the information available, or the convenience of accessing it from the office, but also because database vendors and information providers will keep the company's interest confidential.

Competitive intelligence, however, does not normally stop at database research. Primary research, such as talking with people in the industry and with their competitors, suppliers, and customers, is another important part of developing a complete picture of an industry.

Companies that want information about their competitors can discreetly search the databases in order to track both developments in the industry and the activities of their competition; however, calling the competitors and finding someone willing to talk, send information, or provide their insights into the business and the industry are tasks usually best handled by a third party, such as a market research firm or information brokerage. After all, how much time would you be willing to spend educating your competitors?

For further information on competitive intelligence, you can learn from professional research organizations such as the Society of Competitive Intelligence Professionals (SCIP at www.scip.org), which is listed in Section IV: Where Can I Find More Information?—Organizations.

Books on competitive intelligence, background research, and investigative reporting such as *Millennium Intelligence: Understanding and Conducting Competitive Intelligence in the Digital Age* by Jerry P. Miller and *Internet Business Intelligence: How to Build a Big Company System on a Small Company Budget* by David Vine can also shed some light on the subject. Periodicals focused on competitive and business intelligence, investigative journalism, and private investigation may give you additional insight into this type of research. These periodicals are all listed in Section IV.

There are excellent competitive intelligence sites available on the Internet. One of them, offered by Fuld and Company, contains an Internet Intelligence Index, which includes links to more than 600 intelligence-related Internet sites at www.fuld.com/i3/index.html.

Another site, CorporateInformation (www.corporateinformation.com), offers thousands of research reports on public companies, industry research and analysis reports, and links to company profiles at other sites.

Hoovers Online (www.hoovers.com) provides a mix of free and fee-based information on companies, along with a Business Directory, providing links to industry news, directories, statistics, conferences, trade shows, and events, and so on.

Each of these sites provides an excellent starting place for competitive intelligence, and each will lead you to a multitude of other resources available for your research.

Chapter 12

Identifying an Expert

An expert is one who knows more and more about less and less.
—Nicholas Murray Butler

There are many definitions of an expert. Webster defines an expert as "having, involving, or displaying special skill or knowledge derived from training or experience." Oscar Wilde had another definition: "An ordinary man away from home giving advice." The first time I was paid to travel 3,000 miles to give a speech, I knew that I officially qualified as an expert, by Oscar Wilde's definition if not by Webster's.

There are many reasons to need an expert and just as many definitions under which one might qualify. In order to find the right expert, you need to know how the experts' special knowledge will be used.

How Are Experts Used?

Preparing a Legal Case

Attorneys frequently rely on experts to testify in court. Forensic experts may be needed to explain a type of testing or to validate or dispute a test result being used as evidence. A medical expert may testify to the likelihood of a person coming out of a coma intact, when the family is petitioning to turn off life support.

Not all experts are from scientific fields. An expert from law enforcement may be called upon to explain the proper administration of a chokehold or how to subdue a person under the influence of PCP. Pyrotechnic experts may testify to the inherent dangers of using fireworks and the proper procedures for avoiding accidents. A financial expert may be asked to explain what a junk bond is and how risky this type of investment is in financial terms.

Experts such as these often are called into court to testify in hopes of lending further credence to the attorney's argument before the judge or jury. In these cases, the expert's credentials (degrees, positions held, years of experience, membership in professional associations, and awards won), previously published opinions, experience testifying in court, agreement with the attorney's position, ability to express ideas clearly and succinctly, ability to stand up to cross-examination, willingness and availability to testify in court, personal warmth before a jury, and many other factors may be weighed in seeking the ideal expert witness.

Planning a Meeting

A conference planner may need to identify many experts for any given meeting. An expert may be needed to give the keynote speech, to serve on panels, or to lecture on a variety of topics. In order to attract greater attendance, more renowned experts will often be preferred, especially as the keynote speaker.

When a panel of experts is to appear at a conference, it usually is best that they hold a variety of opinions or can speak from various perspectives or experience in order to ensure a lively discussion. A debate may also be planned, in which one expert is needed to present the pro argument, while the other presents the con. In other conference sessions, a speaker may be sought to teach a basic or advanced class on a topic requested by the previous year's attendees.

Conference planners must often balance the need for big names with the desire to present certain topics that are of most interest to the attendees.

Recruiting New Employees

Recruiters, or "headhunters," as they often are called, are frequently asked to find prospective employees with a given level of expertise in a specified field. In some cases, the best candidates hold similar positions in competing organizations and must be identified. In other cases, a company may wish to pursue a new venture and needs someone who can advise them, possibly on a contract basis. The recruiter must normally rely on the employer to define criteria that the candidate must meet and then find prospects who fit the profile.

Pursuing the Unknown

Nearly all researchers must at some time locate an expert to help with their research. Information brokers or researchers, such as myself, often find that an expert can cut through a great deal of information quickly, explaining the most significant points and providing insight and direction that can cut a research project's life cycle in half. The expert may be a scientist or technician who can put complex ideas into simpler language, or it may be an industry insider who can bring a historical perspective to current events in the business or help to read current signals for indications of what might happen next.

Scientific researchers also need to locate experts in order to discuss previous research findings, determine whether additional research is underway, but not yet published, or even to bring these experts in to collaborate on a project with other experts.

The expert's experience and accomplishments may be irreplaceable. In choosing an authority to consult, these may be given more weight than other credentials, such as degrees and current professional associations.

Producing a Talk Show

The explosion of talk shows appearing nearly every hour on several competing television stations, not to mention radio, brings up an obvious question: How in the world do the producers find enough guests who are worth watching? For some programs, it is not terribly difficult. There seems to be no shortage of people eager to talk about how they cheated on their spouse with another family member, got more than one woman pregnant at a time, or hate their twin. Other talk shows focus on celebrities, so their need for outside experts may also be small. However, some talk shows invite experts on to educate and enlighten us, to debate political issues, or at least to provide perspective or glib repartee on sensational topics.

Each talk show has its own criteria for what makes both an expert and a good talk show guest. It may not be enough to be the author of a new book, president of a university, the victorious attorney from a famous legal case, the head of a nonprofit organization, or even a Nobel prize winner.

Guests must also be able to speak up, keep pace with the show, and perhaps mix in just the right amount of humor and entertainment value.

Writing an Article, Book, Play, or TV Show

Journalists often seek out experts for interviews or quotes. They sometimes also need to find experts on each side of an argument, in order to present both sides fairly, so the experts' published opinions can help narrow the field.

Authors of books and screen plays also consult with experts in order to obtain facts and anecdotes that can add texture to a story, opinions on whether something reads realistically, or sometimes just to learn the language that a character might use.

Television writers on shows like *ER* have experts on the set who teach the actors how to do everything from taking a temperature to performing open heart surgery, or at least how to appear as if they can. Cop shows often use consultants from law enforcement as well. Even soap opera writers call in experts to advise them about a story line from time to time, such as when a character will be struggling with drug dependence or AIDS.

In these cases, the expert's ability to tell a story, or relate to the story being told, adding anecdotes and nuances that make the tale ring true, may be his or her most valuable assets. Experience and knowledge are essential, but their title or credentials will be more important to a journalist than to a screen or soap opera writer who is gathering information, rather than quoting the source. Experience as a consultant on a television or movie set (especially on a successful film or series) may also weigh heavily in establishing someone as an expert. The entertainment industry does, after all, understand film credits.

How Can You Identify an Expert?

Expert Witness Directories

Attorneys have the advantage of being able to turn to directories of experts when they need an expert witness. The individuals listed in these directories have normally established themselves as experts within their fields, as well as having indicated their willingness to appear in court to testify. Any of the following directories, all available online, might be used in order to locate expert witnesses:

- ExpertNet (available online through West Group—Westlaw) contains information on physicians available to serve as expert trial witnesses or consultants to attorneys in medical malpractice and personal injury cases.

- Forensic Services Directory (available online through West Group— Westlaw) contains the names of scientific, medical, and technical experts available to serve as expert trial witnesses or consultants to attorneys, corporations, and the government.

- Technical Advisory Service for Attorneys (available online through West Group—Westlaw) contains information on individuals in a variety of occupations available to serve as expert witnesses or as consultants to attorneys.

Refer to Appendix M for the address of this vendor.

Many other expert witness directories can be found on the Internet. For example, ExpertPages.com, is offered by Advice Company at http://expertpages.com. ExpertLaw.com is available at www.expertlaw.com/experts. An Expert Witness & Consultant Directory, offered by Rominger Legal, is located at www.romingerlegal.com/expert. The Expert Witness Network can be searched at www.witness.net.

The American Society for Testing and Materials offers the ASTM Directory of Scientific and Technical Consultants and Expert Witnesses at www.astm.org/consultants. The National Directory of Expert Witnesses from the Claims Providers of America is available for purchase or searchable online at www.claims.com. The Los Angeles County Bar Association sponsors the site expert4law.org, which includes a searchable directory of experts and consultants at www. expert4law.org/ewc. The Internet Directory of Expert Witnesses is available at www. expertwitness.com. ExpertWitnesses Online includes directories for the U.S. and U.K. at www.onlineexperts.net. The U.K. Register of Expert Witnesses can be found at www.jspubs.com. Expert witnesses can be found at law.com Texas at http://www5.law.com/tx.

Links to other expert witness directories available on the Internet can be found on the Americans for Effective Law Enforcement, Inc. (AELE) Law Enforcement Legal Center Web site at www.aele.org/Exlinks.html.

Professional directories are another source of experts. Directories for many professions are available online; many are listed in Appendix D. The advantage a database directory offers over the same information in book form is that it usually can be searched by not only a person's name, but by his field of expertise, geographic location, degrees, and many other useful criteria. This makes it possible to review the credentials of a known expert as well as to discover other potential experts based on your own criteria. Some of the professional directory databases that are most useful in identifying an expert include:

- BEST Great Britain (available online through Cartermill Ltd.), which contains qualifications for scientists and researchers in U.K. public sector institutions.

- Information USA (available online through CompuServe; refer to Appendix L for the address), which contains information on free or low-cost information, grants, or other resources available from U.S. state and federal government agencies. Among other things, this database includes names and telephone numbers of some 9,000 experts in various fields.

- Texas Faculty Profiles (available online through Texas Innovation Network System [TINS]) contains profiles of experts at some 50 public and private Texas universities in all science and engineering disciplines, as well as medicine, agriculture, arts and humanities, and business.

Refer to Appendix N for the addresses of these vendors, except where otherwise noted.

Association Directories

Associations are an important resource for any researcher. Associations often maintain libraries of information that might otherwise be impossible to tap into. There is an association for virtually any trade, hobby, or interest in the world. If you doubt it, stop by a library and peruse a print copy of the Encyclopedia of Associations.

Associations also are a valuable resource for locating experts who know everything you ever wanted to know about ferrets, yo-yos, aircraft commutators, natural childbirth, or almost any other subject. Databases of associations that are available include:

- Associations Canada: Directory of Associations in Canada (available on the Internet by subscription through Micromedia Limited, Voyageur at www.mmltd.com/voyageur/voyageur.htm), which contains information on active international, foreign, national, interprovincial, and provincial associations in Canada.

- Associations Unlimited (available on the Internet by subscription through GaleNet at www.galenet.com/servlet/ProdList), which contains detailed descriptions of international and U.S. national, regional, state, and local membership organizations in all fields.

- Deutsche Unternehmensberater (available online through GENIOS Wirtschaftsdatenbanken), which contains biographical profiles of 300 members of the German Association of Consultants.

- Directory of Associations in Israel (available online through Israel National Center of Scientific and Technological Information [COSTI]), which contains information on scientific organizations, technical associations, industrial laboratories, and research institutes in Israel.

- DIRLINE, the Directory of Health Organizations (available on the Internet at http://dirline.nlm.nih.gov), which contains information on organizations that provide information in their areas of specialization.

- Encyclopedia of Associations (available online through Dialog and Nexis), which provides detailed descriptions of international and U.S. national, regional, state, and local membership organizations in all fields.

- Encyclopedia of Associations: National Organizations of the United States (available on the Internet by subscription through GaleNet at www.galenet.com/servlet/ProdList), which contains detailed descriptions of national organizations.

- Human Rights Internet, Organizational Database (HRIO) (available on the Internet by subscription through Human Rights Internet at www.hri.ca/welcome.cfm), which contains information on organizations concerned with human rights and social justice.

- National Trade and Professional Associations of the United States (available on the Internet by subscription through INFOTRAC at http://infotrac.galenet.com), which contains directory listings for national trade associations, professional societies, technical organizations, and labor unions in the United States.

- Soviet Public Associations Directory (available online through MagnaTex International., COMMUNICATE!, and SovInfoLink), which contains information on associations, institutions, and organizations in the Commonwealth of Independent States (C.I.S.).

- Verbande, Behorden, Organisationen der Wirtschaft (available online through Gesellschaft fur Betriebswirtschaftliche Information mbH (GBI) (VBO)), which contains profiles of German and international institutions and associations.

Refer to Appendix N for the addresses of these vendors, except where available on the Internet as noted.

Company Directories

Company directories can be another good source of experts. Almost anyone in a key position of an important company could be assumed to have some expertise and insight into the industry. In a smaller or close-knit industry, it is not too unusual to find a company insider who has also worked for the competition and has something to say about them as well.

Business credit and company financial databases, such as those found in Appendix C, often are indexed by position, making it easy to identify company presidents, some senior executives, corporate attorneys, and a variety of other positions, which vary from one database to the next.

Staff directories of politicians and those in the political arena can also be found online. Refer to Political Directories in Chapter 35 for further information.

Some companies have also set up their own online directories or databases. More and more of these resources are now found on the Internet, however, and can be located through any of the standard Net search tools. Any company site may contain a company directory.

Biographical Databases

Biographical directories in print are seldom very useful in identifying experts because the entries are usually listed in name order and may not be indexed by specialty, experience, or other useful criteria. Once converted to computer media, however, biographical databases take on whole new dimensions. Suddenly it becomes possible to find experts by a combination of indexed fields and free-text searching, which can help to pinpoint the people with the attributes you need. Examples of biographical databases can be found in Appendix A.

Articles That Cite an Expert

Another way to identify an expert is to take another expert's word for it. If writers of articles in respected trade journals often cite someone as an expert, that person may at least be worth consideration and further research.

Some databases, such as SciSearch on Dialog, have defined fields for cited authors, cited inventors, and cited references. This makes it much easier to determine how important a cited work is, or how often an expert is cited, without confusing the author of a given article with writers who are cited within the piece.

Dialog's search software offers a command that allows one to "RANK" the results of a field. RANK cited authors, and it provides a list of authors according to the number of times other writers have cited their publications, providing the number of citations for up to 50 authors. If you need the most-cited authors in articles over the last two years, you can first narrow your set by date before RANKing the results. When looking for experts, the RANK command can be very useful.

Articles Written by an Expert

Expertise in a field can also be assessed by their published works. When a potential expert is identified, you can look at what they have written in order to find out whether their publications touch on subjects of interest and to gain some understanding of their work and opinions.

Authors who have written a great deal about a subject can also be identified through use of the RANK command (on Dialog), by RANKing the author field. For example, using the PsycINFO database on Dialog, I searched for dissociative personality disorder (also known as multiple personality). Many other search terms could be used, but for the sake of the example, only this one was chosen. This search resulted in 1,245 matching articles. I narrowed the sample by selecting only those articles published between 1997 and 2001; this left 261 hits. RANKing that set by author resulted in a listing of the top 50 authors, ten of whom are included here:

Dialog RANK Results

```
--------------------
RANK: S5/1-261   Field: AU−  File(s): 11
(Rank fields found in 261 records—413 unique terms) Page 1 of 52

RANK No. Items  Term
-------- -----  ----
    1     10  ROSS, COLIN A.
    2      9  KLUFT, RICHARD P.
    3      9  VAN DER HART, ONNO
    4      7  ET AL
    5      7  PUTNAM, FRANK W.
    6      5  BOON, SUZETTE
    7      5  BREMNER, J. DOUGLAS
    8      5  FRASER, GEORGE A.
    9      5  LYNN, STEVEN JAY
   10      5  NIJENHUIS, ELLERT R. S.
```

Be aware that even writers who have published a great deal on a given subject may turn out to be journalists, rather than practitioners. If you are looking for expert practitioners rather than expert journalists, some of the entries found may need to be discarded.

Of course, not all publications are available online, so an expert who writes for airline magazines and other publications found only in print may not be located through an author search.

Encyclopedias can also be useful for identifying experts: Simply find out who wrote the section that pertains to your field of interest. The author will be an expert, almost by definition. Refer to Appendix F for a list of encyclopedia databases available online or on CD-ROM.

Award Winners

People who win awards may also be considered experts in their fields. Announcements of awards can often be found in trade journals, newsletters, and even newspapers and newswires. Many of these news publications can be found online. You might pay particular attention to newspapers in the geographic area of the organization that is bestowing the awards, in order to find an announcement or list of the winners.

If you anticipate an upcoming competition or annual awards ceremony, you might also ask the organization that will be giving the awards to send you the announcement of the winners as soon as possible, or find out from them where the announcement will be released. Checking their Web site may also provide this information. The awarding organization should also be able to provide contact information on all winners and contestants.

Transcripts from Other Legal Cases

When looking for expert witnesses (or experts to be interviewed), one useful technique is to look at similar legal cases and find out who testified in them. Legal databases such as Lexis and Westlaw can provide this type of information. For example, Jury Verdict and Settlement Summaries (available online through Lexis and Westlaw) contain summaries of personal injury jury verdicts and settlements. For each case, this database provides verdict or settlement amounts, case type, state and county where the case was tried or settled, party names, attorney names, expert witness names, and other factual information. Refer to Appendix M for the addresses of these vendors.

When you know that your opposition's attorneys plan to call an expert witness, check legal databases for previous cases in which their expert has testified to find out how well the expert has done, whether he or she is likely to stand up under cross-examination, and whether the statements made in court are consistent with the information likely to be presented in your case.

Other background information, such as professional history and published works, can be important. In some cases, a complete background check may be warranted in order to avoid unpleasant surprises that could discredit your expert witness in court.

Experts Who Have Testified Before Congress

You will find more than politicians in Congress. Depending upon the issue being debated, you might find witnesses from nearly any industry or background. For example, you might be surprised to learn that the late musician Frank Zappa once testified before Congress rather eloquently on the subject of censorship.

If you agree that a person who has testified before Congress should be considered an expert, several databases may be helpful. The following databases include the names of witnesses who have testified before Congressional committees:

- Congressional Information Service, Inc. (CIS) (available on the Internet by subscription through LexisNexis at www.lexisnexis.com/academic/3cis/cisMnu.htm, which among other things contains abstracts of testimony given by individual witnesses or groups of witnesses.

- CQ Committee Action Votes and Rosters—Committees Database (available online through Congressional Quarterly Inc. [CQ] [COMMITTEES]), which provides comprehensive analysis of all committee and subcommittee action and votes, and includes, among other things, a witness list for each action.

- CQ Committee and Floor Schedules (available online through Congressional Quarterly Inc. [CQ] [SCHEDULE]), which provides schedules for the U.S. House of Representatives, Senate, joint committees, conference committees, and floor votes for the next day up to three months ahead, and includes names and affiliations of witnesses for each meeting or hearing.

- FactSearch (available on the Internet by subscription through OCLC FirstSearch Electronic Collections Online at www.ref.oclc.org/html/ eco_frames.html), which among other things contains materials, with accompanying comparative statistical content, extracted from testimony presented at Congressional hearings by witnesses considered to be experts in their field.

Refer to Appendix N for the addresses of these vendors, except where available on the Internet as noted.

Transcripts from Talk Shows

If you are looking for an expert with experience on talk shows, you should be aware that transcripts from many television shows and radio broadcasts can also be found online. Several are described in Chapter 20: News.

You can also search book directory databases (such as those listed in Appendix B) in order to locate additional sources for talk show hosts. One of the best, the Yearbook of Experts, Authorities & Spokespersons (also known as the Talk Show Guest Directory), published by Broadcast Interview Sources, is available on the Internet at www.yearbook.com.

The Internet and Consumer Online Systems

There is no shortage of expertise represented on the Internet. Using AltaVista (one of the many Internet search engines), I searched for EXPERTS and found 2,143,385 Web sites (as of July 2000). I found another 2,861,025 sites for CONSULTANTS. I selected sites at random and found a mix of commercial services, companies involved in expert systems, lists of experts in particular fields, and searchable databases, among other things. Usenet newsgroups, Internet mailing lists, and World Wide Web pages all could help to identify and locate an expert in a particular field.

Lists of Usenet newsgroups for almost every conceivable topic can be found through the indices at http://dir.yahoo.com/Computers_and_Internet/Internet/Chats_and_Forums/Usenet/By_ Subject or through Google Groups (formerly Deja) at http://groups.google.com.

Forums offered by other vendors (such as America Online, CompuServe, and Prodigy) can also contain a wealth of information, along with the advice of experts or contact with the experts themselves.

Appendix L contains a list of the main bulletin board vendors. Each of these services has an online directory, which is updated frequently as new forums and services are added. The best way to keep up with the ever-changing canvas of the Internet is to become familiar with the various search tools and indices that can be used to navigate the Internet and discover current sites. The next best method is to rely on Internet books and directories such as the many varieties of Internet "Yellow Pages" and the various magazines that provide information about the Internet, lists of sites, and ways of using the Internet for research. Some of these can be found in Section IV: Where Can I Find More Information?—Periodicals.

There are many Internet sites and databases that I have found interesting for locating experts. One such database, Speakers Online, contains biographical information on many authors, celebrities, and other speakers who can be hired as speakers. Examples of the speakers found on this site

Gloria Allred	David Horowitz
Peter Arnett	Dr. Henry Kissinger
Dave Barry	John McLaughlin
Jim Bouton	Deborah Norville
Stephen Covey	Jennifer O'Neill
Governor Mario Cuomo	Prime Minister Shimon Peres
Alfonse D'Amato	Pat Riley
Mike Ditka	Cokie Roberts
Linda Ellerbee	Al Roker
Vince Ferragamo	Patricia Schroeder
Roy Firestone	Beverly Sills
Steve Forbes	Kathy Smith
President Gerald Ford	Gloria Steinem
Al Franken	Bob Woodward
Mitzi Gaynor	Zig Ziglar
John Gray	

Figure 12.1   Speakers online

are listed in Figure 12.1. Additional speaker bios from this database can be found at http://speakers.com/website/speakersonline.asp.

Faculty experts can be found from the following Web sites:

Brandeis
www.brandeis.edu/news/experts.html

DePaul University
http://penguin.depaul.edu/newsbureau/mrfind.html

Georgetown University
http://experts.georgetown.edu

Lehigh University
http://www2.lehigh.edu/page.asp?page=expertstopics

Marymount University
www.marymount.edu/news/experts/index.html

Notre Dame University
www.nd.edu/~prinfo/faculty/index.html

Purdue University
http://news.uns.purdue.edu/UNS/newsweb.experts.html

Queen's University
www.notes.queensu.ca/Find/Expert.nsf

San Jose State University
www.sjsu.edu/news_and_info/experts/lastnameN.html

University of Michigan
www.umich.edu/~newsinfo/exphompg.html

University of Mississippi
www.olemiss.edu/experts

University of Oregon
http://comm.uoregon.edu/experts

USC
http://uscnews3.usc.edu/experts/index.html

Washington State University
http://experts.wsu.edu

Wayne State University
http://141.217.20.182/experts.html

University of Wisconsin-Madison
http://experts.news.wisc.edu

Expert faculty sites such as these can be found for many other universities as well. These sites often are set up by the university public affairs office to assist the press in locating faculty experts. A list of college and university home pages can be found at www.mit.edu:8001/people/cdemello/univ.html.

Summary

After reading this chapter, it should be clear that there are many definitions for an expert, and nearly limitless ways to identify them.

After identifying experts, one normally must still locate them and speak with them in order to determine whether they are really suited to your purpose, whether they are willing to assist you, and whether they are available at the time needed. You can refer to Chapter 6: Locating People for further information about how to find them.

Once all this is done, the final decision of who is the best suited for the job often is a subjective one. The database resources available should help to identify prospective experts in nearly any area, but the ultimate choice should not be left to a database.

For further information on identifying experts, there are publications such as the newsletter, *The Expert and the Law* (available online through Nexis), which covers the application of scientific, medical, and technical knowledge to litigation, along with the Online Research and Database publications listed in Section IV: Where Can I Find More Information?—Periodicals. The magazine *ONLINE* also has carried excellent articles on the use of databases in order to locate experts. Organizations such as the professional research organizations and the legal research organizations listed in Section IV: Where Can I Find More Information?—Organizations can also be good sources of additional information.

Chapter 13

Prospect Research (Fundraising)

Philanthropy is almost the only virtue which is sufficiently appreciated by mankind.

–Henry David Thoreau

Another use of personal records is for prospect research, which is one piece of the fundraising effort. When an organization is looking for donations, it seldom makes sense to spend limited resources sending mailings or contacting people who do not have much money. Rather than going after a few dollars from many people, organizations may find it more productive to go after larger sums from fewer donors. Prospect research seeks to identify those people who are most likely to donate funds.

Prospect research typically involves more than personal records. Businesses, foundations, and even the government can also be good prospects for donations or grants.

Prospect researchers also normally use more than database resources. Print directories, newspapers, and magazines that are not yet online can be just as useful. Personal knowledge of the social elite or the aid of someone who travels in wealthy social circles may be the most valuable resource that an organization can have in obtaining funds.

Nonetheless, online databases and Web research can help to identify many people who have the resources and possibly the willingness to donate large sums to a good cause.

News

Online news databases and news Web sites can be of great assistance to a prospect researcher. Articles talk of people's assets and personal wealth every day. News articles even rank the wealthiest people in America, or the wealthiest people in computers or other industries.

When a celebrity speaks out for a cause, it can bring them to the attention of organizations supporting it. For example, after actress Susan Sarandon was arrested at a protest of the police shooting of West-African immigrant Amadou Diallo, smart human rights organizations surely added her to their lists of prime candidates for donations. Likewise, since Martin Sheen was arrested at a nuclear weapons protest, anti-nuke organizations would consider him an excellent prospect.

Large donations can also be found in the news, such as when someone pays to add a new wing to a hospital. Even organizations with unrelated causes may add these donors to their lists simply because of their wealth and their demonstrated willingness to give to a good cause.

Campaign Contributions

Information about campaign contributions can also identify individuals who have money and may be willing to donate it. For further information about campaign contributions, please refer to Chapter 35: Political Records.

Public Records

Public records can sometimes aid in assessing wealth. Real property records, for example, can reveal whether someone is a renter or owns a particular home, and whether the home is an expensive one. Performing a search using a person's name, it also is possible to locate all of the homes and real property that he or she owns in a state. The geographic coverage for this type of searching varies from vendor to vendor, but some statewide searches are available.

Most public records systems require a name or an address in order to perform a real property search, so searching by the value of the home in order to locate all of the expensive homes within an area is seldom possible. There are a couple of exceptions to this rule though. DataQuick Information Systems (www.dataquick.com) and Experian (www.experian.com) can both provide this type of information. Refer to Appendix M for their addresses.

Telephone Directory Databases

Even telephone directories can be used to locate wealthy prospects. When one wealthy person is identified, a telephone directory database able to search by address can reveal any neighbors who have listed telephone numbers. Public records vendors sometimes offer "neighbor" searches that provide similar data. It is possible that a wealthy person's neighbors may include renters and others who may not be wealthy. After all, not every rich person lives among the rich. However, there are neighborhoods in which wealth is the rule, rather than the exception, and telephone directory databases can be used to scour these neighborhoods, street by street, in order to locate candidates who are at least suspected of having wealth. Refer to Chapter 17: Telephone Directories for further information.

Mailing Lists

Mailing lists of wealthy individuals and philanthropists can be purchased on diskette, or even downloaded online. Though sometimes costly, this is probably the quickest, easiest way for an organization to acquire a database of hundreds or thousands of wealthy prospects. Some lists target individuals who have donated large amounts in the past. Others target those who have donated to a particular type of cause or who have made multiple donations. Other lists consist of people who own expensive cars, or have almost any type of interest, hobby, or profession. People with an expensive hobby or a well-paid profession might be wealthy or at least have sufficient income to be considered as prospects.

For further information on mailing lists, please refer to Chapter 19: Mailing Lists.

Foundations and Grants Databases

There are foundations and grants databases such as the Foundation Directory (www.fcon line.fdncenter.org), Foundation Grants Index, and GRANTS (www.oryxpress.com/grants.htm), all available online through Dialog. Rather than identifying individual philanthropists, these databases list organizations that provide money to worthwhile causes. For additional information about foundations and grants, some home pages on the Internet index many other sites. These include the Foundation Center's Home Page at www.fdncenter.org and Information about the Grants Database located at www.oryxpress.com/grntdb.htm.

Summary

Although many databases assist in seeking funds, most prospect researchers supplement them with other information sources. When prospective contributors are identified, some must still be located. Contact must then be made with them. This can take many forms, and if that step is not accomplished tastefully, eliciting sympathy and conveying the necessary information inoffensively, even the best prospect list may produce few contributions.

Fundraising must include not only research skills and experience, but marketing savvy, public relations, and great people skills, in order to obtain the best results.

For further information on prospect research and fundraising, please refer to Section IV: Where Can I Find More Information? for listings of periodicals and organizations. Information about additional publications can be found at the following Web sites:

Philanthropy News Digest (on the Foundation Center's
Web site)
www.fdncenter.org

Philanthropy Journal (the journal of Philanthropy Australia)
www.philanthropy.org.au/research/7-02-journal.htm

Foundation News and Commentary (on the Council on Foundations'
Web site)
www.foundationnews.org

Council on Foundations Publications Catalogue
www.cof.org/applications/publications

A few more Internet sites that may be of interest to prospect researchers follow:

The Philanthropy News Network Online
www.pnnonline.org

The Office of Development Research at Northwestern University—
Philanthropy/Non-Profit Bookmarks
http://pubweb.nwu.edu/~cap440/bookmark.html

The Grantsmanship Center
www.tgci.com

Society of Research Administrators' GrantsWeb
www.srainternational.org/newweb/grantsweb/index.cfm

Chapter 14

Private Investigation

Investigation may be likened to the long months of pregnancy,
and solving a problem to the day of birth. To investigate a
problem is, indeed, to solve it.

–Mao Tse-Tung

Private investigation involves more than database searching. Investigators are also called upon to provide protection and security, surveillance, and other "hands-on" services that cannot be performed from behind a desk. Insurance companies and attorneys both commonly rely on private investigators (PIs). Businesses and individuals turn to private investigators as well.

Many private investigators use subterfuge (or pretense), disguises, inside contacts (in the police department, telephone company, or banks, for example), and electronic devices in their assignments. These all are far beyond the scope of online research and will not be covered here. However, many private investigators are coming to rely on the use of online databases, the Internet, and CD-ROM databases as important components of their investigative toolbox. These are the subject of this chapter.

Public Records

Private investigators have always relied on various types of public records. This used to involve spending hours or days digging through physical records at county court houses and records buildings. This is still necessary in some cases, but online indices to public records are now available for many areas of the country, mostly via fee-based online services. Online investigation allows an investigator to do a more thorough job of locating public records, while reducing the need to travel from one courthouse to another or to hire investigators in other areas to search for records that may not even exist. When a record appears in an online index, the investigator can then visit the courthouse or send someone to pick up a copy of the full record. Sometimes it even is possible to order a physical copy through the online system.

The ability to search for records across an entire state, or even nationwide, and to search through civil, criminal, probate, and other records at one time has made online databases much more cost effective than old-fashioned "legwork." The bottom line is that a private investigator can do a more thorough job in less time, for less money, and dedicate more of the budget to other types of investigative work. Refer to Chapter 31 for further information about public records.

Motor Vehicle Records

Many private investigators also rely heavily on motor vehicle records. Private investigators who provide surveillance need to be able to identify people who come and go from a watched location, as well as who is seen with their target. The ability to run a quick database search to learn who owns a vehicle makes it possible to perform this task much more efficiently. Refer to Chapter 27 for further information about motor vehicle records.

Telephone Directories

Telephone directories also are extremely useful in investigative work, but PIs often require information that standard phone books cannot supply. Often, the investigator must perform a reverse directory search; instead of simply looking up someone's telephone number, it is necessary to begin with a number or an address and find a name. This is possible through some of the online telephone directories, including some of those found on the Web.

Sometimes old telephone directories are more helpful than the current version. Until recently, this forced investigators to store old phone books from across the country. Even then, searching through dozens of bound directories was never easy.

CD-ROM telephone directories make it possible to store phone directories from the entire country in an inch of shelf space, or less. They also make it far more convenient to search for someone across a wide geographic area, to locate everyone with a given surname in order to track down relatives, to search by address in order to find out who lives at a given location, and to search by address range in order to locate a person's current or former neighbors.

Some CD-ROM telephone directories are available exclusively by lease, with upgrades provided only after the previous discs are traded in. These may be an attractive choice for other professions, but they are not generally as useful to investigators who are not disposed to giving up old phone directories, whatever their form. Not all CD-ROM databases allow different types of reverse directory searches. Some vendors charge a premium for their databases with all of these capabilities, and a lesser price for their databases that provide only a name search. These factors often influence an investigator's choice of telephone directory databases. Refer to Chapter 17 for further information on telephone directories.

Not All Private Investigators Use Databases

Not all private investigators use online services or the Internet. This depends in part on the PI's specialty. Although I can't think of a single area of investigation that would not benefit from the availability of additional information, some private investigators do not feel that they need online research. Some PIs simply are not inclined to spend the time or expense in developing online research skills. For these PIs, information brokers/researchers can provide this service, thereby freeing them to pursue other areas of investigation.

Researchers can search not only public records, but business, news, and legal databases, filling in company and industry financial information, news, product announcements, names of key executives, information on expert witnesses, and other pieces of the investigative puzzle. Even investigators who are loathe to touch a computer can benefit from the databases now available through an intermediary. Information brokers offer a valuable resource to many private investigators, while other PIs are honing these skills themselves in order to expand their investigative capabilities.

The Internet

The advent of the Internet is also changing the investigator's trade in some ways. Private investigators who had previously worked alone now may find a wide range of colleagues available to help them in all areas, at any time of the day or night. Investigative techniques and resources can be shared, friendships forged, referrals made, and partnerships formed, all through the use of the Internet. When investigators need help in a distant city, or even another country, or need someone with special expertise, or access to resources that they lack, one of their online colleagues often can supply just what they need.

The Internet carries Usenet newsgroups, such as alt.private.investigator, where investigators converse, offer advice, and share their opinions and techniques.

The PI Mall is described by its sponsor, the National Association of Investigative Specialists (one of the largest national PI associations and also publisher of *PI Magazine*), as "a one-stop shop for finding a Private Investigator on the World Wide Web." At the PI Mall, you can view different Private Investigator Web sites, search for a PI in your state, and shop for PI shirts and books. If you are interested in becoming a PI, the PI Mall offers encouragement and resources. You can find the PI Mall at www.pimall.com.

A list of Investigative Associations on the Internet can be found at www.pimall.com/nais/links.c.html. Bombet, Cashio, and Associates has also compiled an impressive list of state, regional, national, and international investigative associations, as well as other investigative links at www.intersurf.com/~lizcabom/links2.html.

There is also no shortage of private investigators who have put up their own home pages on the Internet. Visiting these, or the sites noted above, will lead you to an almost unending chain of additional sites of interest to private investigators.

Further Information

Many books address particular aspects of investigation, such as surveillance, fraud investigation, background investigation, and public records research. A list of books on public records research and another list on background research and investigative reporting are both included in Section IV: Where Can I Find More Information?—Books.

If you are serious about investigation, you might also consider joining one of the organizations for private investigators. A list of some of these organizations also appears in Section IV: Where Can I Find More Information?—Organizations: Investigative Journalism and Private Investigative Organizations.

Finally, many publications can teach you more about the field of private investigation. These include not only magazines about private investigation, such as *The Legal Investigator* (www.nali.online.org/nalipublications.html) and *PI Magazine* (www.pimag.com), but also publications dealing with competitive/business intelligence, investigative journalism, online research, and databases. Lists of these types of publications are also provided in Section IV: Where Can I Find More Information?—Periodicals.

Types of Personal Records

Chapter 15

Biographies

There is properly no history; only biography.
—Ralph Waldo Emerson

For "one-stop shopping" on the personal information superhighway (to borrow a much over-used phrase), biographies are a great place to start. There are many from which to choose.

Biographical Book Directories

Biographical books often contain information that it has taken someone else years to dig out. Autobiographical books may include personal revelations and a perspective that could be found nowhere else.

Although many directories can be used to search for books about a person, a single database search can scan through many of these directories at once, providing a list of the books in print, as well as those out of print.

For example, the Books In Print database (available online through Dialog, EBSCO Publishing, K.G. Saur Verlag GmbH & Co., OCLC EPIC, OCLC FirstSearch Catalog, Nexis, Ovid Technologies, Inc., SilverPlatter Information, Inc., and on the Internet at www.booksinprint. com/bip) includes all of the information in the most current printed editions of all of the following publications:

- *Books In Print*
- *Subject Guide to Books In Print*
- *Books In Print Supplement*
- *Forthcoming Books*
- *Children's Books In Print*
- *Subject Guide to Children's Books In Print*
- *Complete Directory of Large Print Books and Serials*
- *Paperbound Books In Print*
- *Books Out-of-Print* (last ten years)

- *Publishers, Distributors and Wholesalers of the United States (Bowker's Publisher Authority Database)*

- *Words On Cassette*

A search of this database for the subject "Diana, Princess of Wales" yields 210 listings, one of which is shown in Figure 15.1.

```
Title:                      Princess Diana
Author:                     Walter G Oleksy
Publication Date:           2000
Publisher:                  Lucent Books
ISBN:                       1-56006-579-6
Item Status:                Active Record
Binding Format:             Trade Cloth
Edition:                    illustrated
Pages:                      112
Price:                      $18.96 Retail (Publisher)
                            $19.96 Retail (Ingram)
Available Through:          Baker & Taylor Books
Series Title:               People in the News Ser.
Age Range:                  9 to
Grade Range:                4 to 12
Audience:                   Juvenile Audience
Bowker Subjects:            DIANA, PRINCESS OF WALES, 1961-1997
General Subjects (BISAC):   BIOGRAPHY & AUTOBIOGRAPHY / Royalty
Children's Subjects:        DIANA, PRINCESS OF WALES, 1961-1997
LCCN:                       99-053455
LC Call#:                   DA591.A45D53535 2000
Dewey #:                    941.085/092 B
Physical Dimensions:        6 x 9 x .53 in.
                            .7 lbs.
Synopsis/Annotation:        The life of the Princess of Wales including her
                            childhood, royal courtship and marriage, public and
                            private life, divorce, humanitarian efforts, and
                            untimely death.
```

Figure 15.1 Sample *Books in Print* listing

If I were interested only in books that are still in print or are forthcoming, and that are available in bound form (excluding audio and video formats), another search could narrow the list to 121 books, including such listings as:

- *Diana: Her True Story in Her Own Words*

- *Diana: A Princess and Her Troubled Marriage*

- *Princess*

- *Princess Diana: Glitter, Glamour, and a Lot of Hard Work*

- *Little Girl Lost: The Troubled Childhood of Princess Diana by the Woman Who Raised Her*

- *Diana in Private: The Princess Nobody Knows*

- *Princess Diana: The Palace Years*

- *The Diana I Knew: The Story of My Son's Nanny Who Became the Princess of Wales*

- *Diana: Queen of Hearts*

- *Diana, Princess of Wales: A Tribute in Photographs*

- *How God Sees Princess Diana*

- *Mensajes de la Princesa Diana Desde la Cuarta Dimension*

- *Princess Diana: A Celebration in Her Memory, Althorp, 1998*

- *Princess Diana, the House of Windsor and Palm Beach: America's Fascination with "The Touch of Royalty"*

- *The Prince and Princess of Wales: A Royal Colouring Album*

- *Diana and Prince Charles Fashion Paper Dolls in Full Color*

- *Debrett's Illustrated Fashion Guide—The Princess of Wales*

- *Two Royal Women: The Public and Private Lives of Fergie and Di*

Reviews of the books can also be extracted from this database, making it possible to evaluate them before deciding which to order or to track down. This type of database can be of great assistance when researching what has been written by or about someone.

On the Internet, bookstores such as Amazon.com (www.amazon.com) and Barnes and Noble (www.barnesandnoble.com) allow shoppers to search for books, including biographies. At Amazon.com, you can search for books by title, author, or subject or browse by subject, such as Biographies and Memoirs. Barnes and Noble also has a Biographies section. Refer to Appendix B for a listing of additional book directory databases.

Biographical Books

Actual books are now being made available online, and many are biographical works. For example, if you consider the Bible, the Book of Mormon, and the Koran to be biographical works, versions of each can be found in full text on the Internet.

Other biographies available on the Internet include:

- *The Autobiography of Benjamin Franklin*

- *My Bondage and My Freedom and Narrative of the Life of Frederick Douglass (American writer, orator, abolitionist and former slave)* by Frederick Douglass

- *Letters of a Woman Homesteader* by Elinore Pruitt Stewart

- *Personal Memoirs of U.S. Grant* by Ulysses S. Grant

- *The Rough Riders* by Theodore Roosevelt

- *Up from Slavery: An Autobiography* by Booker T. Washington

For listings and locations of other online books, sometimes referred to as e-books, you can visit the following sites:

Antique Books
www.antiquebooks.net

Bartleby.com
www.bartleby.com

netLibrary
www.netLibrary.com

Gemstar eBook!
www.gemstar-ebook.com

Philologos Religious Online Books
www.philologos.org

TeleRead
www.teleread.org

UT Books on the Internet
www.lib.utexas.edu/books/etext.html

Alex Catalog of Electronic Texts
www.infomotions.com/alex

Encyclopedias

Encyclopedias have probably been used to study historical figures since the first was invented in the year 961. (I got that date from an encyclopedia!) Putting today's encyclopedias into electronic databases has had a number of benefits, aside from the added excitement of sound bytes and video action.

First, an electronic encyclopedia is likely to have much better search capabilities than any printed volume can. Searching for a name can point out all of the places where it occurs in the encyclopedia, so you are less likely to miss a citation.

Second, electronic encyclopedias may be updated more frequently than the print version, and may contain relatively current information about people and events. For this reason, electronic encyclopedias should rightfully be considered even when researching contemporary persons and events.

Third, electronic encyclopedias are often relatively inexpensive compared to the print version, and access to the online version often is included with subscriptions to services such as America Online or Prodigy, or offered free on the Internet. A CD-ROM encyclopedia is sometimes thrown in for free when purchasing a CD-ROM drive or a computer.

A last benefit is that a whole set of encyclopedias with rich multimedia features can fit onto a single CD-ROM or DVD disk, or can be accessed through online services. For people with space problems, this represents a change for the better.

Encyclopedias can be found at the following Web sites:

Columbia Encyclopedia
www.bartleby.com/65

Encyclopedia Americana Online
http://ea.grolier.com

The Knowledge Adventure (Kids) Encyclopedia
http://www.knowledgeadventure.com/features/kids

Refer to Appendix F for a listing of other general encyclopedia databases.

Biographical Index Directories

Many companies produce biographical directories. These directories may be general, containing information about notable people from virtually any walk of life, or they may target specific groups, such as attorneys, women in science, or Asian Americans. So many biographical works are now available in electronic form that there are databases that index the directories themselves.

Biography Master Index (BMI), produced by Gale Group (and available online through Dialog), contains more than 12.7 million citations to biographical information appearing in more than 3,400 editions and volumes of more than 1,250 source publications, covering more than 4.4 million persons who have distinguished themselves in hundreds of fields.

A search of BMI for actor Jack Nicholson renders three extensive listings comprising a total of 129 citations. See Figure 15.2 for excerpts from these listings.

Please note that these are only excerpts; many additional citations for Jack Nicholson are available on BMI. As this example demonstrates, this type of search can guide you to many of the biographical directories and dictionaries that contain information about a person.

Other databases used to index biographical works include:

- American Genealogical Biographical Index (available on the Internet at www.ancestry.com/search/rectype/biohist/agbi/main.htm)

- Wilson Biography Index (available online through H.W. Wilson Company, OCLC EPIC, OCLC FirstSearch Catalog, Ovid Technologies, Inc., and SilverPlatter Information, Inc.)

- World Biographical Index (available online through K.G. Saur Verlag GmbH and Co. and on the Internet at www.saur-wbi.de)

These databases contain references to information in biographies, autobiographies, memoirs, journals, diaries, biographical fiction, critical studies, juvenile literature, and periodicals, publications like *Who's Who,* major biographical dictionaries, handbooks, and directories.

Biographical Directories

After searching the biographical index directories, the next step is to search the indexed directories. Unfortunately, not all biographical directories are available online yet, so you may have to track down some of the sources manually.

Nicholson , Jack
1937-
Number of Citations: 98

A Biographical Dictionary of Film. By David Thomson. New York: Alfred A. Knopf, 1994. (BiDFilm 94)
Biography Index. A cumulative index to biographical material in books and magazines. Volume 25: September, 1999-August, 2000. (BioIn 25)
Biography News. A compilation of news stories and feature articles from American news media covering personalities of national interest in all fields. Volume 1, Numbers 1-12. Edited by Frank E. Bair. Detroit: Gale Research, 1974. (BioNews 74)
The Cambridge Biographical Encyclopedia. Second edition. Edited by David Crystal. Cambridge: Cambridge University Press, 1998. (CamBiEn)
The Cambridge Dictionary of American Biography. Edited by John S. Bowman. Cambridge: Cambridge University Press, 1995. (CamDcAB)
Celebrity Register. Third edition. Edited by Earl Blackwell. New York: Simon & Schuster, 1973. (CelR)
Celebrity Register, 1990. Detroit: Gale Research, 1990. (CelR 90) Biography contains portrait.
Chambers Biographical Dictionary. Sixth edition. Edited by Melanie Parry. New York: Larousse Kingfisher Chambers, 1997. (ChamBiD)
Contemporary Authors. A bio-bibliographical guide to current writers in fiction, general nonfiction, poetry, journalism, drama, motion pictures, television, and other fields. Volume 143. Detroit: Gale Research, 1994. (ConAu 143)
Contemporary Theatre, Film, and Television. A biographical guide featuring performers, directors, writers, producers, designers, managers, choreographers, technicians, composers, executives, dancers, and critics in the United States, Canada, Great Britain and the world. Volume 32. Earlier editions published as @it1Who's Who in the Theatre.@it2 (ConTFT 32)
Current Biography Yearbook. "1995." New York: H.W. Wilson Co., 1995. (CurBio 95) Biography contains portrait.
Dictionary of the Arts. New York: Facts on File, 1994. (DcArts)
Dictionary of Twentieth Century Culture. Volume 1: "American Culture After World War II." Edited by Karen L. Rood. Detroit: Gale Research, 1994. (DcTwCCu 1)
The Facts on File Encyclopedia of the Twentieth Century. Edited by John Drexel. New York: Facts on File, 1991. (FacFETw)
The Film Encyclopedia. By Ephraim Katz. New York: Thomas Y. Crowell, 1979. (FilmEn)
The Filmgoer's Companion. Fourth edition. By Leslie Halliwell. New York: Hill & Wang, 1974. Later editions published as "Halliwell's Filmgoer's Companion." (FilmgC)
Gangster Films. A comprehensive, illustrated reference to people, films, and terms. By Michael L. Stephens. Jefferson, NC: McFarland & Co., 1996. (GangFlm)
Halliwell's Filmgoer's Companion. Ninth edition. By Leslie Halliwell. New York: Charles Scribner's Sons, 1988. Earlier editions published as "The Filmgoer's Companion." (HalFC 88)
The International Dictionary of Films and Filmmakers. Fourth edition. Volume 3: @it1Actors and Actresses.@it2 Edited by Tom Pendergast and Sara Pendergast. (IntDcF 4-3) Biography contains portrait.
International Motion Picture Almanac. 1996 edition. New York: Quigley Publishing Co., 1996. (IntMPA 96)
The International Who's Who. 63rd edition, 2000. (IntWW 00)
Italian Film. A who's who. By John Stewart. Jefferson, NC: McFarland & Co., 1994. (ItaFilm)
Legends in Their Own Time. New York: Prentice Hall General Reference, 1994. (LegTOT)
Michael Singer's Film Directors. A complete guide. Ninth international edition. Edited by Michael Singer. Los Angeles, CA: Lone Eagle Publishing Co., 1992. (MiSFD 9)
Motion Picture Performers. A bibliography of magazine and periodical articles, 1900-1969. Compiled by Mel Schuster. Metuchen, NJ: Scarecrow Press, 1971. (MotPP)
The Movie Makers. By Sol Chaneles and Albert Wolsky. Secaucus, NJ: Derbibooks, 1974. The "Directors" section begins on page 506. (MovMk)
The New York Times Biographical Service. A compilation of current biographical information of general interest. Volume 17, Numbers 1-12. Use the annual Index to locate biographies. (NewYTBS 1986) Biography contains portrait.
Newsmakers. The People behind Today's Headlines. 1989, Issue 2. Detroit: Gale Research, 1989. Issues prior to 1988, Issue 2, were published as "Contemporary Newsmakers." Use the "Cumulative Newsmaker

Index" to locate entries. Biographies in each quarterly issue can also be located in the annual cumulation. (News 89-2) Biography contains portrait.

One Hundred Years of American Film. Edited by Frank Beaver. (OnHuYAF) Biography contains portrait.

The Oscar Stars from A-Z. By Roy Pickard. London: Headline Book Publishing, 1996. (OsStAZ)

The Oxford Companion to Film. Edited by Liz-Anne Bawden. New York: Oxford University Press, 1976. (OxCFilm)

Who's Who. An annual biographical dictionary. 153rd Year of Issue, 2001 New York Palgrave 2001 (Who 2001)

Who's Who in America(reg;) [Marquis(TM)]. 55th edition, 2001. (WhoAm 2001)

Who's Who in Entertainment(reg,) [Marquis(TM)]. Third edition, 1998-1999. New Providence, NJ: Marquis Who's Who, 1997. (WhoEnt 98)

Who's Who in Hollywood. The largest cast of international film personalities ever assembled. Two volumes. By David Ragan. New York: Facts on File, 1992. (WhoHol 92)

Who's Who of the Horrors and Other Fantasy Films. The international personality encyclopedia of the fantastic film. First edition. By David J. Hogan San Diego: A.S. Barnes & Co.; London: Tantivy Press, 1980. (WhoHrs 80)

Who's Who in the World(reg;) [Marquis(TM)]. 18th edition, 2001. New Providence Marquis Who's Who 2000 (WhoWor 2001)

The World Almanac Biographical Dictionary. By the editors of "The World Almanac." New York: World Almanac, 1990. (WorAlBi)

The World Almanac Book of Who. Edited by Hana Umlauf Lane. New York: World Almanac Publications, 1980. Use the "Name Index," which begins on page 326, to locate biographies. (WorAl)

Figure 15.2 Biography Master File excerpts

One of the biographical databases now available online is Marquis *Who's Who* (available through Dialog and CompuServe's Knowledge Index). It contains more than 790,000 profiles drawn from:

- *Who's Who in America*
- *Who Was Who in America*
- *Who's Who in the East*
- *Who's Who in the Midwest*
- *Who's Who in the South and Southeast*
- *Who's Who in the West*
- *Who's Who in the World*
- *Who's Who of American Women*
- *Who's Who in Finance and Industry*
- *Who's Who in American Law*
- *Who's Who in Entertainment*
- *Who's Who in Advertising*

The individual biographies in this directory range from a few lines to a few pages and may list not only a person's professional accomplishments, but personal information about the subject's family, home address, and more. Since the subjects themselves provide the information collected in many of these directories, they may volunteer facts that would not otherwise be found or be public knowledge. However, information may also have been concealed or presented in an unrealistically favorable light.

A search of the Marquis *Who's Who* database (via DIALOG) for actor Sir Anthony Hopkins renders the listing found in Figure 15.3.

Using a biographical directory such as this, you may find details that would be difficult and time-consuming to dig out elsewhere. These listings can also sometimes note political and religious affiliations, avocations, and even home addresses.

The information can be very detailed and extremely helpful when researching a famous person, but you will also find many lesser known and unknown people in these directories. Although Carole A. Lane is far from a household name, I received applications from several of the biographical directories shortly after starting my research business, so you never know who will turn up in one of these, or what they will divulge.

There are also many, many biographical databases available on the Internet. A few examples of these follow:

Biographical and Pictorial Archive of the Russian Nobility
www.geocities.com/~tfboettger/gallery

Biographical Dictionary
http://www.s9.com/biography

Biographical Directory of the United States Congress
http://bioguide.congress.gov/biosearch/biosearch.asp

Biography.com
www.Biography.com

The Blue Flame Café (a biographical dictionary of the great blues singers)
www.blueflamecafe.com

Chinese Biographical Database
www.lcsc.edu/cbiouser

Distinguished Women of Past and Present
www.DistinguishedWomen.com

Mexico/Arizona Biographical Survey
www.mexicoarizona.com

Additional links to biographical information on the Internet can be found at www.bemorecreative. com/links-bioinfo.htm. Refer to Appendix A for a listing of additional databases that contain biographies.

Biographical News

Hundreds, if not thousands, of newspapers are now available online. These range from national papers such as the *New York Times* to local papers such as *Grants Pass Daily Courier*. Some of

```
00157183
Hopkins, Anthony (Philip), Sir

Record Status: ACTIVE
Marquis Volume:
Who's Who in the World 18
Who's Who in the World 17
Who's Who in the World 16
Who's Who in America 55
Who's Who in America 54
Who's Who in America 53
Who's Who in Entertainment 4
Who's Who in Entertainment 3
Who's Who in Entertainment 2
Who's Who in America 51
Who's Who in America 52
Who's Who in the World 14
Who's Who in the World 15
Who's Who in Entertainment 1
Who's Who in America 48
Who's Who in America 49
Who's Who in America 50
Who's Who in the World 11
Who's Who in the World 12
Who's Who in the World 13
Who's Who in America 47
Who's Who in the World 10
Who's Who in America 44
Who's Who in America 45
Who's Who in America 46
Who's Who in the World 9
Occupation: actor
Born: Dec. 31, 1937  Port Talbot South U.K.
Parents: Richard Arthur and Muriel Annie (Yeates) H.
Family: married Petronella Barker, 1967 (div. 1972); 1 child,
Abigail; married Jennifer Ann Lynton, Jan. 13, 1973.
Sex: Male
Education:
student Welsh Coll. Music and Drama Cardiff, 1954-56
student Royal Acad. Dramatic Art London 1961-63
DLitt (hon.) Wales 1988
Fellow (hon.) St. David's Coll. Lampeter, 1992
Career:
ind. stage, screen, TV actor 1963-
Civic/Military Information:
Made London stage debut in Julius Caesar, 1964; mem. Nat. Theatre Co.,
1966-73; appeared in Juno and the Paycock, 1966, A Flea in Her Ear, 1966,
Three Sisters, 1967, The Dance of Death, 1967, As You Like It, 1967, The
Architect and the Emperor of Assyria, 1971, A Woman Killed with Kindness,
1971, Coriolanus, 1971, The Taming of the Shrew, 1972, Macbeth, 1972,
Equus (Best Actor award N.Y. Drama Desk, Best Actor award Outer Critics
Circle, Best Actor award Am. Authors Celebrities Forum), N.Y.C., 1974-75,
(L.A. Drama Critics award), L.A., 1977, The Tempest, L.A., 1979, Old
Times, N.Y.C., 1983, The Lonely Road, London, 1985, Pravda, Nat. Theatre,
London, 1985-86 (Olivier award 1985, Stage Actor award Variety Club),
King Lear, Nat. Theatre, London, 1986-87, Anthony & Cleopatra, Nat.
Theatre, London, 1987, M Butterfly, Shaftesbury Theatre, London, 1989,
```

(also dir.) August, 1994; films include (debut) The Lion in Winter, 1968, Hamlet, 1969, The Looking Glass War, 1970, When Eight Bells Toll, 1971, Young Winston, 1972, A Doll's House, 1973, The Girl from Petrovka, 1974, Juggernaut, 1974, A Bridge Too Far, 1977, Audrey Rose, 1977, International Velvet, 1977, Magic, 1978, The Elephant Man, 1979, A Change of Seasons, 1980, The Bounty, 1984 (Film Actor award Variety Club), The Good Father, 1985, 84 Charing Cross Road, 1986 (Best Actor award Moscow Film Festival 1987), The Dawning, 1988, Silence of the Lambs, 1991 (Acad. award for Best Actor 1992, Best Actor award Chgo. Film Critics 1992, Best Actor award Boston Film Critics 1992, Best Actor award N.Y. Film Critics 1992, Film Actor award Variety Club 1992, Best Film Actor award BAFTA 1992), Freejack, One Man's War, 1990, Spotswood/The Efficiency Expert, 1990, Howard's End, 1991, Bram Stoker's Dracula, 1992, Chaplin, 1992, Remains of the Day, 1993 (Acad. award nominee for Best Actor 1994, Best Actor award L.A. Film Critics Assn. 1993, Best Actor award Nat. Soc. film Critics (U.S.A.) 1993, BAFTA UK best film actor award, Guild of Regional Film Writers UK Best Actor award, Variety Club UK Film Actor award 1993, Japan Critics Best Actor in a Fgn. Film award), Shadowlands, 1993 (Best Actor award Nat. Bd. Rev. 1993, Best Actor award L.A. Film Critics Assn. 1993, Best Actor award Nat. Soc. Film Critics (U.S.A.) 1993), the Trial, 1993, The Road to Welville, 1993, Legends of the Fall, 1994, The Innocent, 1995, Nixon, 1995 (Acad. award nominee for Best Actor 1996), August, 1996, Surviving Picasso, 1996, The Edge, 1997, Amistad, 1997, The Mask of Zorro, 1998, Meet Joe Black, 1998, Instinct, 1999, Titus, 1999, Mission Impossible II, 2000; BBC-TV series War and Peace (Best TV Actor award Soc. Film and TV Arts), 1972; TV shows include A Heritage and Its History, 1968, Vanya, Hearts and Flowers, Three Sisters, The Peasant's Revolt, Dickens, Danton, The Poet Game, Decision to Burn, War and Peace, Cuculus Canorus, Lloyd George, Q.B. VII, 1971, Find Me, A Childhood Friend, Possessions, All Creatures Great and Small, 1975, The Lindbergh Kidnapping Case, 1976 (Emmy award), Victory at Entebbe, 1976, Dark Victory, Mayflower: The Pilgrim's Adventure, 1979, The Bunker, 1980 (Emmy award), Peter and Paul, 1980, Othello, BBC, 1981, Little Eyolf, BBC, 1981, The Hunchback of Notre Dame, 1982, A Married Man, 1984, The Arch of Triumph, CBS, 1984, Hollywood Wives, ABC, 1984, Guilty Conscience, CBS, 1984, Blunt, BBC, 1985, the Tenth Man, CBS, 1988, Across the Lake, BBC, Heartland, BBC, Great Expectations, 1989, Disney Primetime, To Be The Best, 1990, others.
Memberships:
Decorated Comdr. of Order of Brit. Empire, 1987, Knights Bachelor, 1993, Comdr. of Order of Arts & Letters, France, 1996.

MAILING ADDRESS:
Office
 CAA
 9830 Wilshire Blvd
 Beverly Hills
 CA
 90212-1804
 Marquis Who`s Who(r) (Dialog® File 234): (c) 2001 Reed Elsevier Inc. All
              Rts Res. All rights reserved.

© 2001 The Dialog Corporation

Figure 15.3   Marquis Who's Who record

these papers are carried with the full text of the articles, while others are only indexed or carry abstracts of the articles, which can be ordered separately.

Magazines, journals, and newsletters also are available online, providing coverage of nearly every interest under the sun, including many biographical articles.

You can usually find at least partial coverage of the current issue of a newspaper or magazine, journal or newsletter at the publication's own Web site. Many of these sites also provide searchable online archives of previous issues. Any of these news sources may contain biographical articles. Some of the database vendors segment biographical articles into separate databases or database sections in order to simplify search and retrieval. Others provide search indices on persons named in the articles, while still others must be searched in their entirety in order to locate information about a person.

A few examples of biographical databases taken from news sources (and all available online through Nexis) are:

- *The Associated Press* Candidate Biographies

- *New York Times* Biographical File

- *Washington Post* Biographical Stories

Television programs also feature biographical pieces on personalities from all fields, and transcripts from some of them are now available online. The television show *Biography* provides a great deal of biographical information, including a database of biographies and information on upcoming programs at www.biography.com.

Biography has inspired several other biographical programs, including:

Bravo Profiles
www.bravotv.com/sections/shows.php

Lifetime's Intimate Portrait
www.lifetimetv.com/shows/intimate/index.html

VH1's Behind the Music
www.vh1.com/insidevh1/shows/btm

Some programs, although not solely dedicated to biographies, have also done an excellent job of presenting biographical shows on a regular basis, normally involving crimes, including:

A&E's City Confidential
www.aande.com/tv/shows/cityconfidential.html

A&E's Investigative Reports
www.aande.com/tv/shows/ir

Crime Stories (on CourtTV)
www.courttv.com/onair/shows/crimestories

Mugshots (on CourtTV)
www.courttv.com/onair/shows/mugshots

Refer to Chapter 20 for further information about news sources.

The Internet

Anyone newsworthy can generate enough interest for a group of netizens to create another Usenet newsgroup or Web page. If your subjects are appearing in the news, you can use one of the Internet search engines to find out whether newsgroups or Web pages are discussing them.

One caveat: The information found on the Internet may be best characterized as opinion. There are experts on the forums to whose opinions you might not otherwise have access, and a great many learned people do participate. You may even find the neighbor or childhood friend of the person you're interested in. That said, much misinformation is also shared online, and you should consider the information at best as hearsay, to be verified elsewhere if it is important to you.

Chapter 16

General Indices

*Knowledge is of two kinds. We know a subject ourselves,
or we know where we can find information upon it.*

–Samuel Johnson

Whenever you look for information, a general index search on a professional online service can provide an excellent starting place. An index can guide you to other files or databases (usually offered by the same vendor) containing information about your subject. One example of a general index is Dialog's DIALINDEX.

DIALINDEX

A search of DIALINDEX (available online directly through Dialog, as well as on the Internet through DialogWeb at http://products.dialog.com/products/dialogweb) points you to other databases on Dialog's system in which your search terms were found. In the following example, I searched all of Dialog's files (using SET FILES ALL) to locate databases that contain information about Oscar-winning actress Marisa Tomei (searching for MARISA within two words of TOMEI). No fewer than 93 different databases on this system contained one or more matching records. I have listed some of the resulting records here:

Processing your request …
DIALINDEX®
[Rule]

Your select statement is 'S MARISA (2N) TOMEI'.

[Select All]
[Clear Selections]   [Begin Database]

File	Database Name	Hits
9:	Business & Industry (TM)	22
15:	ABI/INFORM®	11
16:	Gale Group PROMT® (1990–present)	222
18:	Gale Group F&S Index (TM)	2
20:	Dialog Global Reporter	356
47:	Gale Group Magazine Database	262

88:	Gale Group Business A.R.T.S. (SM)	103
111:	Gale Group National Newspaper Index (TM)	47
141:	Readers' Guide Abstracts Full Text	128
147:	The Kansas City Star	36
148:	Gale Group Trade & Industry Database (TM)	188
149:	Gale Group Health & Wellness Database (SM)	4
211:	Gale Group Newsearch (TM)	16
258:	AP News (January 2000 to present)	85
261:	UPI News (June 1999–present)	35
262:	Canadian Business and Current Affairs Fulltext	33
275:	Gale Group Computer Database (TM)	2
281:	ONTAP® Gale Group Marketing & Advertising Reference Service®	1
287:	Biography Master Index	2
299:	Magill's Survey Cinema	10
382:	Baton Rouge Advocate	5
387:	Denver Post	33
392:	Boston Herald	88
397:	Las Vegas Review-Journal	12
420:	UnCover®	24
426:	LC MARC - Books	1
427:	Fort Worth Star-Telegram	64
433:	Charleston Newspapers	35
435:	Art Abstracts	5
436:	Wilson Humanities Abstracts Full Text	8
471:	New York Times® - Fulltext (90 Days)	9
474:	New York Times Abstracts	23
476:	Financial Times Fulltext	17
477:	The Irish Times	7
482:	Newsweek (TM)	7
483:	Newspaper Abstracts Daily	211
484:	Periodical Abstracts PlusText (TM)	278
486:	(Long Beach) Press-Telegram	89
487:	Columbus (Georgia) Ledger-Enquirer	11
489:	(Fort Wayne) The News-Sentinel	3
490:	Tallahassee Democrat	8
492:	(Phoenix) The Arizona Republic/The Phoenix Gazette	143
494:	St. Louis Post-Dispatch	167
497:	(Fort Lauderdale) Sun-Sentinel	132
498:	Detroit Free Press	51
532:	Bangor Daily News	1
536:	(Gary) Post-Tribune	11
538:	(Boca Raton) The News	1
539:	Macon Telegraph	2
541:	SEC Online (TM) - Annual Reports	1
542:	SEC Online (TM) - 10-K and 20-F Reports	2
545:	Investext®	23
553:	Wilson Business Abstracts Full Text	19

716:	(Los Angeles) Daily News	154
717:	The Washington Times	144
718:	Pittsburgh Post-Gazette	139
719:	(Albany) The Times Union	107
720:	(Columbia) The State	36
721:	Lexington Herald-Leader	39
722:	The Cincinnati Post/The Kentucky Post	81
723:	The Wichita Eagle	68
724:	(Minneapolis) Star Tribune	48
726:	South China Morning Post	4
727:	Canadian Newspapers	989
728:	Asia-Pacific News	37
731:	The Philadelphia Daily News	47
732:	San Francisco Examiner	57
733:	The Buffalo News	89
734:	Dayton Daily News	91
735:	St. Petersburg Times	53
736:	Seattle Post-Intelligencer	57
738:	(Allentown) The Morning Call	118
739:		115
740:	(Memphis) The Commercial Appeal	35
741:	(Norfolk) The Ledger-Star/The Virginian Pilot	45
742:	(Madison) The Capital Times/Wisconsin State Journal	27
743:	(New Jersey) The Record	150
744:	(Biloxi) Sun Herald	8
747:	(Newport News) Daily Press	3
748:	Asia-Pacific Business Journals	1
749:	Latin American News	74
750:	Emerging Markets and Middle East News	11
755:	New Zealand Papers	26
756:	Daily and Sunday Telegraph	7
757:	Mirror Group Publications	62
766:	Kalorama Information Market Research	2
781:	ProQuest Newsstand (TM)	617
788:	(Myrtle Beach) The Sun News	1
810:	Business Wire (1986–Feb 1999)	31
813:	PR Newswire (1987–Apr 1999)	54
861:	UPI News (1996–May 1999)	44
929:	Alburquerque Newspapers	10
979:	Milwaukee Journal Sentinel	33
980:	Sarasota Herald-Tribune	19
990:	Dialog NewsRoom - Current	831

There are 141 databases matching your statement 'S MARISA (2N) TOMEI'.

As you might expect, many of the files that contain mentions of this actress are news files. You might be surprised to see that many cross into the financial arena, as the names of the actors and actresses in a film will often be mentioned when box office numbers and profits are tallied. Some biographical databases also contain information about Ms. Tomei.

When you are looking for a person of less renown, a DIALINDEX search sometimes can also point you to an article in a local newspaper where a person may be mentioned for participation in a group such as the Chamber of Commerce or the PTA, or where his or her promotion or wedding has been announced. One should not assume that indices such as these are useful only for researching the famous.

The previous example also turned up a few articles in the financial files, including File 542: SEC Online 10-K Reports and File 545: Investext. One might have overlooked these files when searching for information about Ms. Tomei, and this illustrates one of the ways in which a general index search can be particularly useful. General indices can point you to information whose existence you would not have suspected otherwise, or take you in new directions after you have exhausted other possibilities.

Since the search criterion in this case was imprecise (searching for the word MARISA within two words of TOMEI), you also should be aware that the articles found may have nothing to do with the actress. References to JAMES TOMEI AND MARISA SMITH or JOHN MARISA OF TOMEI INTERNATIONAL would also meet this search criterion. When searching for someone whose name is as unusual as Marisa or Tomei, I would use this imprecise kind of search and take the chance of a few poor matches.

When many references are found or when a subject's name is common, I would suggest adding other terms to your search criteria to screen out poor matches. The danger is that you may miss valuable information if your search criteria are too stringent or exclusive. You must balance these two factors in your search strategy. A search for Bob Dole, for example, would identify a great many pointers to other databases (and even more if one included references to Robert Dole), but some references would be for persons other than the former Republican Senator. Because his name is so common, one must either use more specific search criteria or retrieve and sift through a great many poor matches in order to uncover the occasional gem.

For information about using Dialog on the Internet, you can select the DialogWeb product at the main site (www.dialog.com) or go directly to DialogWeb at http://products.dialog.com/products/dialogweb.

FamilyFinder Index

There are many CD-ROM databases produced for genealogical research. You can find quite a few (if not the majority) of them at the Family Tree Maker Online home page (www.familytreemaker.genealogy.com).

If you are interested in researching a person's lineage, a search of the FamilyFinder Index at the Family Tree Maker Online site will reveal whether the name appears in any of the following sources:

- Family Archives—Now 254 in the Collection!

- The Internet

- GenealogyLibrary.com

- Message Boards

- Family Home Pages, Civil War Databases on FamilyTreeMaker.com

- Virtual Cemetery

- The World Family Tree Collection

- World Family Tree Online Subscriptions (Volumes 1–50)

- Super Bundle 7 (World Family Tree Volumes 33–37)

- Super Bundle 8 (World Family Tree Volumes 38–42).

Refer to Chapter 34 for further information on genealogical records.

Public Records Indices

Public records vendors sometimes offer general indices that can point you to their other databases of public records. These databases are extremely useful in locating people or information when you have only a name and no obvious starting place for your search. Examples of public records general indices are ChoicePoint Online's Info:PROBE and KnowX's Quick and Easy Searches.

ChoicePoint Online's Info:PROBE Searches

ChoicePoint Online offers several general index searches, called Info:PROBE searches, for use in locating information on individuals or businesses. These probes do not provide the actual records. Instead, when you search for a name, the probes provide a list of databases that contain information that matches it.

For individuals, the Info:PROBE will search such databases as:

- Bankruptcies, Liens, and Judgments

- Bureau of Consumer Affairs

- Chiropractic Index and Disciplinary Action

- Civil Filings

- Contractor Licensing

- Corporate and Limited Partnerships

- Criminal Filings

- FAA Aircraft Ownership

- FAA Airmen Directory

- Fictitious Business Names

- General Index

- IRS Enrolled Agent

- IRS Tax Practitioners/Preparers

- Medical Board

- National Death Locator

- OSHA

- People Tracker

- Professional Licensing Indexes

- Real Estate Licensing

- Real Property Ownership

- Secretary of State/Department of State Indexes

- State Board of Equalization

- Uniform Commercial Code Filings

- Watercraft

For businesses, the Info:PROBE will search such databases as:

- Bankruptcies, Liens, and Judgments

- Business Directory

- Chiropractic Index and Disciplinary Actions

- Civil Filings

- Corporate and Limited Partnerships

- FAA Aircraft Ownership

- Fictitious Business Names

- General Index

- IRS Enrolled Agent

- IRS Tax Practitioners/Preparers

- Medical Board

- OSHA

- Professional Licensing Indexes

- Real Property Ownership

- Secretary of State/Department of State Indexes

- State Board of Equalization

- Uniform Commercial Code Filings

- Watercraft

Either type of Info:PROBE will select databases based on which are available in the state or geographic region selected. For further information about ChoicePoint Online's databases, refer to their Web site at www.choicepointonline.com.

KnowX

KnowX, a product of Information America, is available on the Internet on a pay-as-you-go basis at www.knowx.com. KnowX offers several general or "Quick and Easy" searches that will point you to their databases that match your search criterion. In other words, you can enter a name, and they will point you to any of their databases that have information on that person. These are grouped in the following ways:

- Assets
- Background Check
- Name Availability
- Owners and Officers
- Professional Licenses
- Reverse Address Lookup
- Reverse Phone Number Lookup
- The Ultimate Business Finder
- The Ultimate People Finder

Quick and Easy (general index) searches make it easy, even for the novice, to figure out which databases to search when looking for a particular type of information on an individual. Refer to the KnowX Web site for further information.

Chapter 17

Telephone Directories

The telephone book is full of facts,
but it doesn't contain a single idea.

–Mortimer Adler

Telephone directory databases would seem to be pretty self-explanatory. They contain names, addresses, and telephone numbers. So why are there so many telephone directory databases available online?

Geographic Differences

As might be expected, one factor that differentiates the various telephone directory databases is geography. For example, the Base de Dados Mope database (available online through Lda Mope) includes listings for Portugal, the Azores and Madeira Islands, and Cape Verde.

Online telephone directory databases typically cover a wider area than the print editions. Many American directories include all of the United States, for example. Some of the directories combine several countries; the EuroPages (www.europages.com) includes more than thirty.

Residential vs. Business

Another difference between telephone directory databases is that, like print telephone directories, some carry residential listings while others list businesses. Some directories include both.

Subject Area

Telephone directory databases, especially those for businesses, may also concentrate on specific industries.

Currentness

When selecting an online telephone directory database, the contents must be up-to-date. The directory data may be updated semi-annually, quarterly, monthly, or on an ongoing basis. This could mean as often as hourly for an online database.

This does not mean that someone dealing with personal records would necessarily want the most current database. Private investigators have been known to hang onto old telephone books in order to locate where people "used" to be, as well as for use in verifying names or places, and CD-ROM products present an excellent alternative to print or online versions for this reason. They also save quite a bit of space over print editions.

A few producers of CD-ROM telephone directories lease their products, but do not sell them. These companies require customers to return previous versions of their discs in order to receive more current editions. This requirement makes their products somewhat less attractive for investigative work.

One should not assume that an online system is more current solely because it theoretically could be updated dynamically. Although online databases may be updated from one minute to the next, some are actually revised less often than the CD-ROM versions. If records are updated only once every quarter, or even less frequently, some records will be out-of-date, and newer records will be missing.

Accuracy

One telephone directory may claim to list 11 million businesses, while another claims 10 million, and another 9.2 million. The numbers alone do not tell the complete story. The accuracy of the data may also vary.

Because some directories are created directly from tapes from the telephone companies, the data in them may be cleaner. Other directories may be created from multiple sources, making them more complete, but some of their sources could also be less accurate.

If directory producers wish to add numbers, they may not remove old listings. Instead, they may replace an old listing only when a new record is received, thus leaving the database littered with out-of-date entries.

At the other end of the spectrum, some database producers contact each business at least once each year to verify their listings. You can expect to pay a premium price for this level of accuracy.

Added Content

Business telephone directories may contain a great variety of added content in order to make them more usable and valuable. One of the most frequent additions is the Standard Industrial Classification (SIC), which identifies the primary industry, and sometimes secondary or additional industries, in which each business operates. For some businesses, the SIC code can be very clear. For others, especially those that manufacture a variety of products or whose services are not clearly identified by a single SIC code, the code may be less valuable, or even confusing. The SIC code may be supplied by the business itself or assigned by the telephone directory producer, so the same business may be coded differently in various databases.

Added content may also include the number of employees, names of owners, directors, executives, staff, or key personnel, yellow page category, size of yellow page advertisement, and year in which the business was first listed in the directory.

Contents may vary even among residential telephone directories. People Finder, for example, lists not only the names, addresses, and telephone numbers for individuals, but includes dates of birth, residence type, length of residence, and family members and their dates of birth.

Older versions of the CD-ROM telephone directories sometimes included unlisted telephone numbers, which have been acquired from public records and sources outside of the telephone companies. In later versions, most producers have omitted unlisted numbers from their telephone directories.

Search Capabilities

Among the most important features of any database are its search capabilities. Telephone directories are no exception. For residential listings, some of the options available include searches by name, address, a range of addresses, telephone number, Soundex code, and partial names and indices. Alternative search capabilities can dramatically increase the value (and often the price) of telephone directory databases.

For example, assume that you have checked a printed telephone directory for someone, but your subject has since moved away and you cannot locate a new listing. If you can extract names and addresses of people living nearby (through a range of address searches), a former neighbor may help you to locate your subject. With a partial name search or index, you can locate others with the same surname, and thereby find relatives in other areas of the country or even beyond.

Consider how a telephone number search can be used in concert with Caller-ID. When someone calls, Caller-ID displays the telephone number on a small screen. When you call an 800 or 900 number for information (or any number, for that matter), you may think that you are doing so anonymously. In fact, the vendor on the other end of the line may be using Caller-ID to log your telephone number; this is a common practice, and growing more so each day. The number can then be used to search a telephone directory database in order to find your name, address, and possibly additional information. You may never even know that this is happening. If you begin to receive mail offers or telephone solicitations after calling a company from your home or business, this is one way that you may have ended up in their database.

If you wish to reclaim your telephone anonymity, you can buy another device that blocks your telephone number from being sent to Caller-ID, or your telephone company may block Caller-ID for you, or you can use a pay phone for more anonymity.

Use Restrictions

Most telephone directory databases restrict the use of their data in one way or another. One of the most basic restrictions is that you cannot download all of their data and sell it as your own product. (This is true of almost any database on the market.) A product may also carry the restriction that it may be used only by the purchasing end-user, and may not be loaned, rented, put on a network, or otherwise made available to or shared with others.

A telephone directory database compiler may restrict its product from use in generating commercial mailing lists or telemarketing. One of the ways that it enforces this restriction is to pepper the databases with a false listing here and there. When a solicitation is received under the false listing, the producer discovers which company is making the offer. Violators are easily caught.

Further restrictions may include the number of records that you can download in any given period. Some telephone directory databases carry no such restrictions and allow unlimited downloads and use. If you intend to create mailing lists, be sure to verify that there are no use restrictions before purchasing a CD-ROM product or signing up with an online carrier.

Price

One last factor that differentiates the various telephone directory databases is price. Like other databases, telephone directories carry many different pricing structures. Some online databases require hourly and/or per search charges, while CD-ROM products entail the cost of purchase or lease. One unusual aspect of telephone directory prices is that the same data can be charged at dramatically different rates, depending upon how you access it.

Using telephone directory databases for personal research often requires more than one product, so some comparison shopping can be important. It may be useful to own a CD-ROM database (many of which are currently priced in the $100 range, or less) and dial into an online database as a secondary source. If you have an ongoing need for this type of information, you may also find that alternating your CD-ROM purchases and updates between two or more vendors provides greater coverage.

Telephone Directories on the Internet

Telephone directories can also be found on the Internet. For example, you can search Switchboard for business and residential listings at www.switchboard.com.

Yahoo! People Search, which includes a search for e-mail addresses, can be found at http://people.yahoo.com.

The Bigfoot Directory can be found at www.bigfoot.com.

InfoSpace offers several white and yellow page directories, as well as a celebrity search, reverse searches (allowing you to search by e-mail, address, or phone number), and a set of world directories, at www.infospace.com.

AT&T AnyWho Info allows you to search for a person or business at www.anywho.com.

Lycos offers WhoWhere?, which includes several types of People Searches, including searches for Home Pages, Celebrities, People in the News, and Government Officials at www.whowhere. lycos.com.

InfoUSA.com includes Directory Assistance, which can be searched by business name, person name, yellow page category, as well as a reverse search by phone number at www.abii.com/homesite/da.html.

The Ultimate White Pages, containing several telephone directory searches, can be found at: www.theultimates.com/white.

Another site, PeopleSearch.net, searches many telephone directories simultaneously at www.peoplesearch.net.

infobel.com also contains several international directories at www.infobel.com/World.

411 Locate includes several directories, including a reverse telephone directory (searchable by phone number rather than name), and is available at www.411locate.com.

An electronic yellow pages called AllBusiness can be found at www.allbusiness.com/directory/index.jsp.

The Federal White Pages enables you to locate Federal employees at http://directory.gov.

Other telephone directories lie hidden within additional Internet sites. Many such directories list university faculty and/or students. For example, the Campus Directory for Murdoch University in Perth, Western Australia, can be found at http://quokka.murdoch.edu.au/directory.

Other telephone directories can be found at Internet sites all over the world. One site that can help you to identify many of them can be found at Telephone Directories at www.teldir.com/eng.

Another index to telephone directories is offered by Yahoo! at http://dir.yahoo.com/Reference/Phone_Numbers_and_Addresses.

For Further Information

This book offers several additional sources of information about specialized telephone directories. Refer to Appendix J for a listing of telephone directory databases. Refer to Appendix C for business credit and company financial databases that include personal information. Refer also to the Appendix D listing professional and staff directory databases and Appendix E for other directory databases containing employee information. The databases listed in each of these sections may also be used as telephone directories.

Chapter 18

Staff, Professional, and Other Directories

Professional: (n) A person with a high degree of knowledge or skill in a particular field: ace, adept, authority, dab hand, expert, master, past master, proficient, wizard.

—Roget's II: The New Thesaurus,
Third Edition

When you need information about people, professional and organizational directories have much to offer.

Staff Directories

Staff directories list personnel who belong to a single organization. These directories may serve as telephone books for the organizations, or may actually contain detailed information about the personnel on staff. An example of a staff directory is the California State Government Directory, available online from Information for Public Affairs, Inc. (IPA)—StateNet.

Many staff directories for government offices and educational institutions are available on the Internet. Examples of these include:

> Arkansas State Directory (state agencies)
> www.state.ar.us/government.html

> North Star Minnesota Government Information and Services
> www.state.mn.us/dir/index.html

> Washington State Department On-Line Government Telephone Directory
> (includes state agencies, educational institutions, and many local
> government organizations)
> http://dial.wa.gov:80/EmployeeDirectory/LocalFrames.asp

> CSU (Connecticut State University) Telephone Directory
> www.ctstateu.edu/cgi-bin/tel.cgi

> University of Sussex (UK) Staff Directory
> www.sussex.ac.uk/USIS/phone/index.shtml

Refer to Appendix D for additional examples of staff directories.

Professional Directories

Professional directories may concentrate on a specific occupation or a range of occupations. One example is Artists in Canada (available online through Canadian Heritage Information Network), a database containing biographical information on visual artists along with artisans, architects, designers, and others who have lived and worked in Canada.

Some online professional directories target executives, physicians, physicists, astronomers, and attorneys, as well as members of many other professions.

The Martindale-Hubbell Law Directory is one of the best-known professional directories. Martindale-Hubbell contains information about lawyers and legal services. Listings for attorneys include the attorney's name, firm name, address, telephone number, date of birth, college of first and additional degrees, law school, fields of law, court admissions (e.g., local, state, federal), scholastic and legal honors, Martindale-Hubbell rating (when available), membership(s) in bar associations, clients, languages, biography, firm size, and legal services. The Martindale-Hubbell Law Directory is available online through Lexis as well as on the Internet as the Martindale-Hubbell Lawyer Locator at www.martindale.com/xp/Martindale/home.xml.

If I were a prosecuting attorney about to face famed lawyer Johnnie Cochran in court, a quick search of the Martindale-Hubbell would certainly help me to size up the competition. You can hardly imagine an attorney who has received more awards than Mr. Cochran, as you can see in Figure 18.1, taken from the Martindale-Hubbell site on the Internet.

West's Legal Directory is available on the Internet at web2.westlaw.com. Simons European Law Directory is located at www.simons-law.com.

Another example of a professional directory is the Complete Directory of Law Officer's Personal Home Pages (http://search.officer.com/officersearch).

Healthlinks.net provides directories of healthcare professionals, associations, and businesses at www.healthlinks.net. The National Capital Area Chapter of the American Translators Association provides a Directory of Translators and Interpreters at www.ncata.org/main.html-ssi. There's even an international directory of professional dog waste removal services at www.pooper-scooper.com.

Refer to Appendix D for additional examples of professional directories.

Ancillary Directories

Other online directories also sometimes include employee information. Examples of these can be found among company and business directories. Many contain listings of key personnel, management, executives, contacts, and sometimes even shareholders.

Refer to Appendix C for business credit and company financial databases, many of which contain personal information. Refer to Appendix E for additional examples of other directory databases containing employee information.

MARTINDALE-HUBBELL ® LAW DIRECTORY

Practice Profiles Section

JOHNNIE L. COCHRAN JR.
Law Offices of Johnnie L. Cochran, Jr. A Professional Corporation
4929 Wilshire Boulevard, Suite 1010
Los Angeles, California 90010
(Los Angeles County)
Telephone: 323-931-6200
Fax: 323-931-9521

POSITION: Member

PRACTICE-AREAS: Personal Injury; Entertainment; Sports Law; Professional Liability; Business Litigation; Mass Tort Litigation; Criminal Law; Civil Rights Law.

ADMITTED: 1963, California; 1966, U.S. District Court, Western District of Texas; 1968, U.S. Supreme Court

LAW-SCHOOL: Loyola University (J.D., 1962); University of Southern California

COLLEGE: University of California at Los Angeles (B.S., 1959)

TEXT: Recipient: Criminal Trial Lawyer of the Year, Los Angeles Criminal Courts Bar Association, 1977; Pioneer of Black Legal Leadership Award, Los Angeles Brotherhood Crusade, August 1979; Outstanding Law Enforcement Office of 1979, California Trial Lawyers Association; Trial Lawyer of the Year, Hon. Loren Miller Award, John M Langston Bar Association, 1982-1983; Equal Justice in Law Award, Legal Defense Fund, National Association for the Advancement of Colored People; Distinguished Alumni Award, UCLA Black Alumni Association, March 1988; Alumni Award of Excellence in Professional Achievement, UCLA, June 1988; Outstanding Criminal Defense Attorneys, Southern California, July 1989; Trial Lawyer of the Year, The Los Angeles Trial Lawyers Association, January 1991; Trial Lawyer of the Year Award, Criminal Courts Bar Association, 1977; 1990 Trial Lawyer of the Year; Kappa Alpha Psi, 1991; Civil Rights Lawyer of the Year Award, L.A. Chapter of the NAACP Legal Defense Fund; Presidential Award, L.A. Chapter of the NAACP; Lifetime Achievement Award, Pasadena Branch, NAACP, 1991; Man of the Year, Los Angeles International Airport Kiwanis Club, 1991. Deputy City Attorney, Criminal Division, City of Los Angeles, 1963-1965. Assistant District Attorney of Los Angeles County, 1978-1982. Former Adjunct Professor of Law: Trial Tactics and Techniques, UCLA School of Law and Loyola University, School of Law. Member, Board of Directors: Los Angeles Urban League; Oscar Joel Bryant Foundation; 28th Street Y.M.C.A., L.A. Family Housing Corp., Los Angeles African American Chamber of Commerce, Airport Commissioners City of Los Angeles; American Civil Liberties Union Foundation of Southern California; Lawyers Mutual Insurance Company. Special Counsel, Chairman of the Rules Committee, Democratic National Convention, June 1984. Special Counsel, Committee on Standard of Official Conduct (Ethics Committee) House of Representatives, 99th Congress. Lawyer Representative, Central District of California, Ninth Circuit Judicial Conference, August 1990. President, Black Business Association of Los Angeles, California, 1989. Fellow, American Bar Foundation.

MEMBER: State Bar of California (Co-Chair, Board of Legal Service Corps., 1993); American College of Trial Lawyers.

BORN: October 2, 1937, Shreveport, Louisiana

ISLN: 908322976

Maintains law offices at more than one place

Figure 18.1   Martindale-Hubbell record

Chapter 19

Mailing Lists

*Let advertisers spend the same amount of money improving
their product that they do on advertising and they wouldn't
have to advertise it.*

—Will Rogers

Do you receive catalogs, telemarketing calls, junk mail? If so, your name is on a mailing list database, and probably more than one. Direct marketing companies buy, sell, and trade your name and "profile" to companies that hope you may be interested in their products or services. More than 10,000 lists of data about individuals are now available for rent. This is a multibillion dollar industry.

If you are interested in mailing to a particular segment of society, be it people of a certain religion or financial status, people suffering from any illness or ailment you can name, those who enjoy cross-stitch or hockey, those who buy into "get rich quick" schemes, or those who hold certain political beliefs, mailing list brokers can provide mailing lists of these individuals from their databases. Some brokers will even supply the list on diskette so that you can form your own database or easily load it into your contact management software or spreadsheet.

Along with mailing lists available for rent, there are databases (some online, but more on CD-ROM) from which you can extract your own mailing list data.

You may wonder how mailing list companies know so much about you, your beliefs, and your spending habits. There are more sources of mailing list information than you probably have ever imagined, and those sources range from the innocent to some that might be thought of as either inventive or invasive, depending upon your perspective.

Telephone Directories

Telephone directories represent one of the most innocuous sources for mailing lists. The only personal information that you might guess when compiling a mailing list from a telephone directory is a person's sex, and not even that is certain any more.

If you have read Chapter 17, you know that some telephone directory databases now include date of birth, residence type, length of residence, and other family members and their birth dates. This makes it possible, using this single source, to develop a mailing list targeting a much more specific marketing group.

If you plan to develop your own mailing list from a telephone directory database, be sure to check it over thoroughly before buying. Many of the telephone directories that include residential listings strictly prohibit their use in mailing lists. (If, on the other hand, you wish to develop a mailing list of companies, you should have little difficulty finding a telephone directory database to accommodate you, either online or on CD-ROM.)

One CD-ROM residential telephone directory database, Address Maker, lists residents of Japan and allows you to print mailing labels for the Japanese market. Another database, OzOnDisc, lists residences and businesses in Australia; it also enables the creation of mailing lists and labels. Phonedisc New York and New England includes businesses, residences, and government offices served by the New England Telephone and New York telephone companies in Connecticut, Maine, Massachusetts, New Hampshire, New York, Rhode Island, and Vermont; it is also a mailing list tool. Other examples can be found, but limitations vary from vendor to vendor and version to version; you will need to evaluate them before buying.

One step away from extracting your own data is Donnelley's master file, an online database that contains data on 84 million households. It can be accessed remotely from another computer, allowing you to obtain list counts based on your own parameters. You can then order mailing labels for a geographic or custom-defined market area, rather than extracting the data yourself.

Refer to Appendix J for other examples of Telephone Directory databases, many of which are used to produce mailing lists.

Other Directories

With a little help from professional or trade directories, it is easy to compile mailing lists based on occupation. American Book Trade Directory, which lists bookstore owners and managers, is used for this purpose. The Martindale-Hubbell Law Directory is used to produce mailing lists of attorneys (selectable by legal specialty, gender, age, geographic area, or school of graduation), as is the Directory of Intellectual Property Attorneys. The Directory of Engineering and Engineering Technology Undergraduate Programs contains information about undergraduate engineering and engineering technology deans and is sold as a mailing list. Various hospital directories are used to compile databases of specialists in many medical fields. The Rocky Mountain Petroleum Directory and similar ones from the Mid-continent, Northeast, and Gulf states provide information for mailing lists of professionals in the petroleum field. Many additional examples can be found for other professions and industries.

School directories are used to compile mailing lists of high school and college students, who make up additional marketing groups.

If you want a mailing list from any of these sources, a mailing list broker should be able to help in locating the one you want. Do ask about any licensing restrictions before buying or renting any lists. Some lists allow unlimited use, but most do not. If the list you want is available on diskette (some are not), its use may be limited to one year after the purchase date. Some lists allow only one-time use, and you must pay for each subsequent mailing. In order to discourage multiple uses, many companies will not even provide the data on diskette. A list with one-time use may be prohibitively expensive if you plan to send several mailings to the same people over the coming year. I have been told that it takes four exposures before prospective clients recognize a company's name. If that is true of your industry, I suggest you either buy a list that allows unlimited use for a period long enough to allow at least four mailings, or budget to repurchase the list four times. If you can send only a single mailing, you may be wasting your money.

Some directory databases can be accessed directly to compile your own mailing lists. The Capital Source, available online and on diskette, is one. It lists persons and organizations in the United States government, corporations, media, and professional organizations located within the metropolitan Washington, DC, area. For each person or organization, this database provides name, department or organization name, contact name and title, office or business address, political party, street address, city and state, ZIP Code, and telephone number. The software makes it possible to generate mailing labels. Another database, Aviation Compendium (available on CD-ROM), contains names and addresses of Canadian and United States aircraft registrants, airmen, pilots, air traffic controllers, airport facility owners, facility managers, mechanics, inspectors, medical examiners, and air taxi operators. This database can also be used in developing mailing lists.

Appendix C contains business credit and company financial databases that also identify individuals within the companies, and many of these databases can also be used to create mailing lists. Appendices D and E contain other examples of directory databases, many of which can be used in developing your own mailing lists.

Although many organizations include membership directories on their Web sites, using this information to create a mailing list is often discouraged, or even prohibited. It is best to check with the organization before pirating their mailing list, or their members may object or even "blackball" you as an undesirable vendor in the future.

Magazine Subscriptions

If you subscribe to almost any magazine today, you can bet that your name is being sold on its mailing list. What you read can be very telling, as so many magazines are tailored to very specific audiences and tastes.

Artists; antique collectors; auto mechanics; auto racing enthusiasts; business owners; children; classic car collectors; aviation enthusiasts; brides-to-be; Corvette owners; the elderly; entrepreneurs; expectant and new mothers; the gay and lesbian community; off-road vehicle owners; parents; people of any race, religion, and ethnicity; sailing enthusiasts; step-parents; and women all are targeted for mailing lists, based on the magazines they receive.

Magazine publishers each have a composite image of their target readers. They may sell their lists of subscribers based on those composites, which will typically include the percentage of women vs. men, average income, median age, and many additional details. For example, you could undoubtedly guess that nearly all of *Latina Magazine*'s subscribers are Hispanic, but the publishers also know that 75 percent of its subscribers are women, and their median age is 29, making those subscribers a target audience for particular types of goods and services.

Another type of mailing list that can be created from magazine subscriptions is a "new mover" list. When you or a third party, such as the post office, notifies a magazine that you subscribe to of your new address, that type of information can be used to create such a mailing list. New movers could be good targets for grocery and video stores, insurance companies (for either renters' or homeowners' policies), restaurants, gardeners, and a variety of other consumer-oriented retail businesses.

Associations and Membership Groups

Ramada business card members earn points for each stay in a Ramada Inn or Hotel. They also earn their place on another mailing list. Likewise, restaurants sometimes sell lists of children's names and birthdays when they are signed up for birthday clubs or kids clubs, and they may do the same for adult membership groups. Frequent Flyer programs can be great sources for locating people who may be interested in hotel discounts, new luggage, or other travel bargains.

Many trade associations also sell their membership lists. The American Dental Association and the American Pharmaceutical Association sell mailing lists of their members. So do the American Vocational Association (for vocational educators) and the Special Libraries Association (for corporate librarians). If you want to market to attorneys, the American Bar Association and the Los Angeles County Bar Association both sell their membership lists. The American Academy of Family Physicians, the Institute of Packaging Professionals (IOPP), and the Society of Decorative Painters all sell their membership lists for use in mailing lists.

Even B'nai Brith, a cultural and fraternal Jewish organization, sells its membership file. So do many fan clubs.

In theory, you can ask the organizations you join not to sell your name as part of a mailing list. However, one member of a national dating service opted out of having her personal information and single status sold to the masses, and was later distressed to receive a flurry of offers for singles. The dating service explained that an ex-employee had stolen a copy of its membership database and sold it to a mailing list firm. This type of theft is always possible when there is a profit to be made. Even the most private membership information can turn up in a mailing list at some point.

Call-Ins/Write-Ins/Buyers

Have you ever written or called to buy something that was offered on the television or radio or in a mailing? Have you ever entered a contest or purchased anything at all through the mail? Of course you have, and these are other sources of mailing lists.

One mailing list of this type includes individuals who watch live opera from the Met on public TV. Another lists those who watch E! Entertainment Television. Do you wonder how anyone knows what you are watching? They are not monitoring your television signal, although cable companies could probably do that. The people on the Met's list responded to an offer for a sample of the Met's Teleguide, which had been advertised during the broadcast. E! Entertainment Television ran a sweepstakes on their cable station and then sold a mailing list of the contestants. These are just two of many ways in which TV stations can gather information about who is watching. People who send videos into "America's Funniest Home Videos" also are placed on a mailing list, whether or not they actually are accepted as contestants on the show.

Radio Shack asks for name, address, and telephone number at the time of each purchase, even when you pay cash, and then uses this information to build its own mailing list.

If you have ever bought advertising space of any kind, there is a better than even chance that you have been added to at least one advertiser's list by now.

Buyers are sometimes asked to complete questionnaires about their interests and will provide information about their "lifestyle characteristics" and demographics, such as sex, age, occupation, marital status, home ownership, credit card usage, ages of children at home, geography, income, and political party. Unlisted telephone numbers are routinely volunteered. Questionnaires may even collect information such as the type of breakfast cereal that customers eat, their make of car, the brand of diapers their baby wears, and more. Quaker Oats once offered buyers of its Cap'n Crunch cereal "high value" coupons and a wristwatch for filling out this type of questionnaire. Among other things, Quaker Oats wanted to know consumers' opinions on firearm ownership, school prayer, and mandatory drug testing. If not for use on mailing lists, what in the world would a cereal manufacturer want with that kind of information? I can't imagine how it might have helped in any of their advertising campaigns, but that is the only other possibility that I have come up with.

Asking people to fill out questionnaires in order to receive "free" information can also provide facts that would be hard to compile otherwise. These questionnaires sometimes become mailing lists for single mothers, heads of households, divorcees, widows, and other consumer groups.

Did you know that mailing lists even single out people with particular ailments? These are sometimes compiled when you request treatment information, fill a prescription, or fill out a survey or questionnaire. The following list contains selections available from the "ailments" database of only one company, along with their record counts.

QUANTITY

6,086,205	Allergies/Hay Fever
107,097	Alzheimer's Disease
493,746	Angina
4,465,401	Arthritis/Rheumatism
2,081,264	Asthma
2,867,553	Back Pain
101,413	Birth Defects
1,082,284	Bladder Control and Incontinence
495,134	Bleeding Gums/Gingivitis
325,275	Bronchitis
381,749	Clinical Depression
7,407	Congestive Heart Disease
1,296,317	Diabetes
13,071	Eczema
87,969	Emphysema
176,951	Epilepsy
191,470	Estrogen Deficient
18,882	Excessive Perspiration
817,129	Frequent Headaches
1,700,531	Frequent Heartburn
320,463	Gastritis
107,685	Glaucoma
415,992	Gum Problems
837,249	Hearing Difficulty
476,131	Heart Disease
3,283,446	High Blood Pressure
2,681,986	High Cholesterol
13,145	Hyperthyroidism
211,727	Insomnia
23,000	Irritable Bowel Syndrome
9,652	Kidney Disease
122,850	Lactose Intolerant
1,980,173	Migraines
385,239	Motion Sickness
129	Multiple Sclerosis

1,037,323	Nasal Allergies
365,295	Osteoporosis
706,294	Other Allergies
109,248	Parkinson's Disease
299,421	Physical Handicap
246,679	Prostate Problems
320,034	Psoriasis
213,813	Sensitive Skin
730,911	Sinuses/Sinusitis
1,107,966	Thinning Hair and Baldness
1,283,573	Ulcer
277,615	Visual Impairment/Blindness
196,677	Warts

Could you ever have imagined that excessive perspiration or gingivitis could make your name valuable to a direct marketing firm?

Book clubs typically sell lists of their customers, sometimes creating separate lists such as "coffee table book purchasers." Other catalog companies do likewise, separating their customers into groups such as those who purchase children's goods. Some credit card companies also segment their customers into broad tiers such as "Rodeo Drive Chic," "Fifth Avenue Sophisticated," "Fashion Conscious," and "Value Seeker," based on spending habits. This segmentation makes their mailing lists more marketable, as they target more and more specific spending groups.

If you participate in online discussions on the Internet or other bulletin board systems, you should be aware that posting your address or telephone number can also make that information available to mailing list vendors and others. There are companies that regularly troll the online bulletin boards, hoping to pick up this type of information in order to compile their lists. (You never know who is listening when you're talking online.)

Other information can be *inferred* from your purchasing habits. For example, a purchaser of a ship-to-shore radio probably also owns a boat or a yacht, so buying one may place you on a list of boat owners, whether you actually own a boat or not. Other things can also be gleaned from sales data, and not just by the marketing firms. One car rental company that sold its list later received many complaints from customers whose spouses drew an entirely different inference when they received a mail order offer declaring that their recent rental of a car entitled them to a discount from another company. If you rent a car in hopes of sneaking around on your spouse, you might want to reconsider that plan.

Some companies place newspaper or magazine ads offering free goods or information, or "too good to be true" products or ideas. Some of these companies simply want to get your name and address in order to sell it on their mailing lists. "Opportunity Seeker" lists can be compiled this way. For instance, a company can place an ad offering a way to make millions for a mere $20 investment. If you send in your check, you may not only have bought their "get rich quick" scheme (which may not be worth the price of the stamp), but also paid to have your name added to an "Opportunity Seeker's" list. If you continue to answer similar ads, marketers may elevate your status from "Opportunity Seeker" to "Sucker," and the offers will *really* start to pour in!

If you want to find out how long it takes your name to circulate from one contact to the world, try this little experiment. When filling out personal information, alter the way your name is listed by adding or deleting a middle name, changing a middle initial, or making some other slight variation that you can recognize, yet that will not make it impossible to deliver your mail. You can then track the time that it takes this new identity to spread from one company to another.

Warranty Registration Cards

Another source for mailing lists is the warranty registration cards that we all fill out after making a purchase or receiving a gift. For example, if you have ever bought a Black & Decker appliance and sent in the warranty card, you may have been placed on one of several mailing lists, depending upon the product you registered. Minolta, the maker of photographic equipment, sells the information from its warranty cards as well.

The facts requested on warranty registrations can be quite detailed, including information about other products that you own and sometimes even a whole questionnaire of personal data. One type of question that makes your name and profile very saleable involves what you *plan* to purchase in the future. If you were selling microwave ovens, wouldn't you like to have a list of people who plan to buy one in the next few months? If you fill out a warranty card checking off the box that states that you plan to buy a new VCR, computer, washing machine, or anything else in the next six months, and you are suddenly deluged with offers for them, you can bet that it is no coincidence.

As I understand it, you do not actually even need to send in warranty cards in order for your purchases to be covered under warranty. However, I have not yet been able to bring myself to believe this, so I still fill them out and send them in. I fill them out *imaginatively*, however, picking and choosing the interests for which I would like to receive catalogs in the future.

If you have relatives or clients who play golf and you do not, you might consider checking off golf as one of your interests anyway, in order to receive free golfing catalogs and other offers that you can pass on to them, or to use the catalogs to buy gifts for them. If the warranty card asks whether you play occasionally or frequently, you can bet that marketers are interested in each group. Perhaps a golf shop has found that people who play occasionally seldom have their own clubs, shoes, or various golf goodies, so they may send their catalogs to the "occasional" group. Maybe a golf resort has found that their target group is only those who play frequently, so they will send their discount coupons and brochures to the "frequent" group.

If you can imagine how the information that you give out might be used, you stand a better chance of receiving the types of offers that you will actually enjoy.

Friends and Family

You may not be the only one volunteering information that places you on a mailing list. Mailing lists are also created from information volunteered by your associates. When MCI Communications Corp. started the Friends and Family discount calling plan, it was not the first company to ask for referrals to other prospective customers. For years, mail order companies have been asking their customers to provide names and addresses of others who might enjoy their catalogs. The record, CD, and book clubs even offer free merchandise if you can convince your friends to sign up for a membership.

Telephone Inquiries

As noted in Chapter 17, merely placing a phone call may land you on a mailing list, even when you do not give out your name or address. This can happen while you listen to a recorded message, without speaking to a soul. With Caller-ID, the company at the other end of the phone may be able to capture your telephone number and then use a reverse telephone directory (indexed by telephone number rather than name) to add your name and address to its database. When you dial an 800 number, you have saved them some of the trouble, as the telephone company reports their callers on their bill.

Companies may also call and request your participation in a survey, and then use the information gathered in creating mailing lists.

Attendees

If you attend a gallery opening or special exhibition, a class or workshop, a beauty show, computer show, or other trade show, you've guessed it by now: These are also sources of mailing lists.

Donors

If you have contributed to any type of cause—to back a political candidate, support an environmental protest, or to help cure a disease, for instance—you probably have noticed a significant increase in the number of requests you receive. A donation can be "the gift that keeps on giving." Beyond your donation, the recipient may continue to make money by selling your name and profile to others who also would like a bit of your cash.

Politically based donor lists include the Beer-Bellied Reactionary Republicans list (contributors said to be dedicated to preserving "American ideas and traditions"), and the Blue and White Jewish Donors list (donors to pro-Israel candidates). Others include Taxpayers for Government Reform (donors to the balanced budget amendment, line item veto, tax reduction, and other Congressional reform issues), and the Fund for the Feminist Majority Donors (donors to an organization founded to promote feminist issues and leadership for women in government, business, education, law, media, and medicine).

There are many, many lists of donors who contribute to animal protection causes: Animal Activist Donors, Anti-Cruelty Donors, Animal Legal Defense Fund donors list, In Defense of Animals Donors, International Wildlife Coalition Donors, People for the Ethical Treatment of Animals Donors, Save the Whales Donors, Super Ocean Activists donors list, World Wildlife Fund Donors, and the ASPCA donors list are among them.

Lists of donors to health causes also are plentiful. Among the causes whose donors can be found on mailing lists are the Arthritis Foundation, cerebral palsy, heart research, Alzheimer's research, the International Eye Foundation, the March of Dimes, Paralyzed Veterans of America, and the SIDS (Sudden Infant Death Syndrome) Alliance. There are many others. One list includes people who have formerly donated to the Epilepsy Foundation of America. The Muscular Dystrophy Association markets several specialized lists of its contributors, including Catholic, Hispanic, and Jewish donors, "mail responsive donors," donors who have contributed more than once, and those who have responded to the organization's annual telethon. Additional lists include donors to any one health cause, and those who have contributed to more than one, or who have contributed more than once to any similar cause. These sometimes are called "sympathetic donor lists," or something of the sort.

Government Agencies

Government agencies also provide information for mailing lists. If you own any type of aircraft, the Federal Aviation Administration (FAA) may have sold your name and profile. The Coast Guard may have sold your information when you registered a boat with them, and the Federal

Communications Commission (FCC) may have done the same when you registered your ship-to-shore radio.

Technically these organizations may not have "sold" your information. When "selling" is prohibited, they might instead charge for the effort that it takes to compile the information and then give the data away free. What it nevertheless comes down to is that the year, make, and model of your aircraft, boat, or yacht may be listed in a database, along with the information it will take to contact you.

Most of us give the Post Office change-of-address forms when we move. They then contract with several companies to process changes of address so that our mail will continue to get to us after we've moved. This is another source for "new movers" lists.

State licensing boards for pharmacists, surveyors, marriage and family therapists, and other professions are yet another source. State insurance departments license agents and agencies to sell property, casualty, life, and disability insurance, and can be a source for mailing lists specifying agents licensed to sell any of these.

Public Records

Although it is possible to compile mailing lists from public records, this process can be extremely labor-intensive to do on your own using court documents. For most types of records, you would have to collect the records one at a time, read through them, locate the names and addresses, and scan or input them into a computer or type them onto mailing labels.

Some of the public records databases available online could be useful in compiling specialized lists, but most public records vendors allow searching only record by record, using personal names rather than parameters such as "all divorcees in Cleveland during 1995," which would be more useful for compiling mailing lists. This may be good news for those of you who were hoping that such intimate details as your divorce would remain somewhat private, but it probably is only a matter of time before these are all automated and the search capabilities are improved.

This is not to say that there are no public records databases suitable for use in building mailing lists. One database convenient for this purpose is Real Estate on CD-ROM. This database includes four sets of tax assessor data and map information on real estate in various United States county and city jurisdictions. Users can search by address, map/parcel number, sales price, date of title transfer, year built, tax amount, properties owned by lender, and absentee owner, and can print mailing labels for selected groups of owners. A similar database, the Massachusetts and Connecticut Real Estate Transfer Database, and another, RealScan Systems (containing data on commercial, industrial, and residential property for three counties in Florida), can also be used for generating mailing lists. Refer to Appendix M for information on public records producers and vendors.

If you are hoping to build a mailing list based on a type of public record that cannot yet be searched easily online or on CD-ROM, you may have better luck renting an existing list rather than starting from scratch. One such mailing list is the New Bankruptcies/Judgments/Tax Liens list (available from New Residata Marketing Services, Inc.). This list includes people who are suffering from difficult economic times. It is compiled from many public records sources across the country and includes individuals who have filed for bankruptcy, incurred federal and/or state tax liens, or who had legal judgments levied against them. Refer to Section IV: Where Can I Find More Information?—Books for additional sources of mailing list directories.

Online Mailing Lists and Spam

Internet mailing lists used to represent one of the few areas in which people had some control over whether their name remained on it. Members who did not wish to remain on an online list could usually have their names removed before they were passed on or sold for the creation of other lists. Many Internet service providers (ISPs) prohibit the sending of unsolicited junk mail online (referred to as "spamming"). Even where this practice is not prohibited, it can result in loss of online privileges if the ISP receives many complaints against a particular person or company.

Nonetheless, the spamming rate continues to increase. Mailing list vendors are using software to capture data about individuals and their interests as they travel through cyberspace. E-mail address lists are being compiled, sold, and resold daily. Software such as DynamicMailer claims to send more than 20,000 e-mails per hour, and Prospect Mailer 2000 reports to make it possible to send over 50,000 e-mailings in about an hour, both costing less in time and expenses than a fraction of what similar postal mail would cost. Given these factors, I would not predict much slowing of this type of advertising.

Internet service providers are attempting various methods of controlling the spam, blocking e-mail being received from certain parties, requesting that members return any message that they find offensive to the sending party, or sending copies of solicitations to their ISP for follow-up.

Although the Internet is not regulated by any one ISP, Internet users have developed their own ways of controlling the Net's use as an advertising medium. When advertisers post messages on Usenet newsgroups, members can make their irritation abundantly clear. One or more members may "flame" (publicly denounce) the offending company or person, letting everyone who reads their messages know what they think of the solicitations. If the advertising messages continue, extremely irate members may set up their computers to send repeated messages to the offending company or person; these messages may number in the thousands each day, filling the online advertiser's mailbox and making it difficult if not impossible for the advertiser to receive any orders or inquiries. If recipients of spam also send complaints to the advertiser's Internet service provider, many ISPs will drop repeat offenders from their services. The advertiser can go to another provider to set up a new account, but probably will have lost orders in the meantime, incurred charges for obtaining the new account, and suffered other inconveniences. This has not been successful in stopping most advertisers and marketers from spamming individuals on the Net, but it does deter them from advertising online in Usenet newsgroups.

Now that e-mail can be transferred from one online service to another, advertisers are finding ways to circumvent the prohibitions of the Internet service providers. Efforts continue to be made on behalf of the members to slow or stop advertisers from deluging members with unwanted solicitations.

Mailing List Swapping

Companies who own their own mailing lists sometimes trade them with other firms, in order to expand their marketing reach. If a company says that it does not sell its mailing list, this does not always mean that it does not trade it or give it away, either free or for the price of processing the data.

Finding an Existing Mailing List

If you are interested in renting an existing mailing list, rather than compiling one of your own, you might want to use a directory to search through the tens of thousands of lists now available. One of the most comprehensive mailing list directories in print is SRDS Direct Marketing List Sources, from Standard Rate and Data. Oxbridge Communications, Inc., has its own database, called the National Directory of Mailing Lists; it is reported to contain information on some 20,000 mailing lists. The company also produces a print directory of the same name. Refer to Section IV: Where Can I Find More Information?—Books for additional sources of Mailing List Directories.

You can even locate information on some mailing lists through an Internet search. One site, Liszt, the Mailing List Directory, claims to have subscription details for more than 90,000 online mailing lists. It can be found at www.liszt.com. Liszt's mailing list categories include:

Arts (206 lists)
Crafts, Television, Movies ...

Books (102 lists)
Writing, Science_Fiction,
Life_and_Works_of ...

Business (178 lists)
Finance, Jobs, Marketing ...

Computers (250 lists)
Hardware, Database, Programming ...

Culture (298 lists)
Gay, Jewish, Parenting ...

Education (112 lists)
Distance_Education, Academia, Internet ...

Health (271 lists)
Medicine, Allergy, Support ...

Humanities (254 lists)
Philosophy, History, Psychology ...

Internet (78 lists)
WWW, Business, Marketing ...

Music (216 lists)
Bands, Singer-Songwriters, Genres ...

Nature (123 lists)
Animals, Environment, Plants ...

News (50 lists)
International, Regional, Politics ...

Politics (96 lists)
Environment, Activism, Human_Rights ...

Recreation (366 lists)
Games, Autos, Sports ...

Religion (111 lists)
Christian, Jewish, Women ...

Science (97 lists)
Biology, Astronomy, Chemistry ...

Social (100 lists)
Regional, Religion, Kids ...

Remember that these lists are not commercial mailing lists of people to be spammed, but voluntary special-interest communities whose members use e-mail to exchange information and opinions about their subject, and often the kind of off-topic gossip found in any other small town. To contact them, you will have to join the list, sometimes after a screening process. List members often are at least as irritated by unexpected commercial messages as participants in newsgroups. Many lists have specific rules against commercial messages and moderators or list owners to enforce them. A single courteous product announcement on a mailing list will seldom evoke more than a few minor protests, particularly if it comes from someone who has already established himself as a valued member of the group. Repeated infractions will get you bounced from the list and earn the kind of reputation that discourages business from intolerant Net users.

For commercial lists, a mailing list broker should be able to help you locate or sort through the mailing lists available to find one that will fit your needs. You can find mailing list brokers listed in the telephone book yellow pages of any large city. One print directory that includes mailing list brokers, along with their specialties, is *Direct Marketing Market Place: The Networking Source of the Direct Marketing Industry*, published by National Register Publishing.

Mailing List Expenses

Vendors usually charge a base price (a price per thousand records) for their lists, with further charges that depend upon the type of output requested (cheshire labels, pressure-sensitive labels, magnetic tape, diskette, or 3x5 cards), shipping costs, and additional selection criteria (such as telephone numbers, age, gender, geography, and income level). If the list is unique, the charges will be higher, and marketers usually charge a premium for re-use of the list, if multiple uses are allowed at all.

Each vendor sets its own minimum number of records (often 5,000) that may be rented or a minimum charge for use of its lists. Many vendors also place restrictions on how their lists can be used, often requiring the right to approve any piece before it is mailed.

Stopping the Junk Mail and Telemarketing Calls

If junk mail and telephone solicitors are driving you crazy, you may want to have your name removed from their lists. The only way to get rid of all junk mail and telephone solicitations is to pay off all of your bills, close out all of your accounts, cancel all of your credit cards, and move without having any of your mail forwarded. You might also need to change your name in order to keep them from tracking you down. From that point on, ride only public transportation to keep your name out of the DMV, and do not buy any other type of transportation that requires a license or registration (such as a motorcycle, boat, or aircraft). Do not maintain any type of professional license, or take part in a profession where you might be listed in a directory. Make all purchases in cash, do not request anything through the mail or respond to any type of solicitation, and just to be on the safe side, don't get a telephone. You probably will have to give up your friends and family as well.

Short of this, you can take somewhat more reasonable steps that at least should significantly cut down on your junk mail and telephone solicitations.

Don't:

- Send a change-of-address form to the Post Office, as that probably will add your name and address to a "new movers" list, as well as provide a mechanism for all of the companies currently sending you junk mail to receive updates. Notify friends, family members, creditors and business contacts directly instead.

- Give out personal information to everyone and anyone who asks.

- Print your telephone number on your checks or give it out any more than necessary.

- Fill out warranty registration cards. If you must send them in, do not provide any more than the minimum required information identifying the product purchased, its serial number, and your name and address. (Be especially sure not to include your unlisted telephone number.)

- Participate in birthday clubs, buyers' clubs, or membership organizations.

Do:

- Get a new unlisted telephone number to cut down on telemarketing calls, or at least omit your address to cut down on new mail solicitations.

  According to the Federal Telephone Consumer Protection Act, all telemarketers in the United States (except for nonprofit, tax-exempt organizations and charities) must maintain a "do not call" list of those who do not wish to be contacted. This still allows them to call you once each year before you can take legal action against them, but it may help.

- Tell telephone solicitors that you want to be put on their "do not call" list.

- Call to place telephone orders for products or goods from a pay phone or from your office, rather than from home.

- Tell mail order companies, 800 and 900 number operators, and other companies that you call, in answer to television, radio, magazine and newspaper advertisements, that you do not wish to be put on any mailing lists, to have your telephone number or name sold, or to receive calls from them.

- Write to each company that sends you an offer, and ask to be taken off its mailing lists.

- Let charities that you contribute to know that you do not want your name or information sold or released, or make all donations anonymously.

- Contact each of the major companies that compile street-address directories and ask to be removed from their present and future listings:

  - R.L. Polk & Company

  - Haines and Company Inc.

  - Donnelley Marketing, Inc.

Refer to Appendix O for these companies.

In New Zealand, Parliament passed legislation mandating that direct marketers may not buy, sell, rent, or exchange personal information without permission from the individual. Violators are subject to a fine of up to $30,000 per violation. In Canada, consumers are given the opportunity to have their names removed from lists at least once every three years. In the United States, there is little to stop anyone from buying, selling, or trading consumer names, addresses, and profiles for use in mailing lists, but you are not completely on your own.

You can sign up with the Direct Marketing Association's (DMA) Telephone Preference Service to have your name and phone number added to their "do not call" list. This will only get your message to members of the Direct Marketing Association, but it will cut down on what you receive. (Refer to Appendix O for the address.)

You may also consider joining one of several privacy groups that will list your name in their directories and send it to hundreds of companies, threatening legal action if they solicit you. This will not eliminate all junk mail, but it will reduce the burden. One such group is Private Citizen, Inc. (PCI) (www.private-citizen.com). Junkbusters (www.junkbusters.com) provides form letters and advice for ridding yourself of junk mail. Refer to Appendix O for the addresses of these associations. The Federal Trade Commission (www.ftc.gov/privacy/protect.htm) provides instructions for "opting out" from mailing lists from credit bureaus, DMV's, and direct marketers on their site.

Opting out of mailing lists will take some time, effort, and continued diligence on your part, and it is doubtful that you will ever stop receiving junk mail entirely or permanently. As long as junk mail remains an effective advertising medium, companies will continue to fill your mail boxes, both in the real world and online, with offers and advertisements.

Chapter 20

News

Spies are of no use nowadays. Their profession is over.
The newspapers do their work instead.

–Oscar Wilde

Most of us probably would select the news as one of our first resources when looking for information about a prominent person. However, the news can provide information about virtually anyone. With the various news media churning out story after story, day in and day out, even the most obscure topics and least famous people can find their way onto a talk show or into a magazine or newspaper story.

News Directories

Online databases are rich with information culled from newspapers, newswires, magazines (and their online equivalent, "zines"), journals, and even television and radio broadcasts. So many sources for news are available online that entire directories are dedicated to tracking and cataloging them. *Fulltext Sources Online* (available in print and online through Information Today, Inc.) tracks publications that are carried in full text, and their listings number in the thousands. (Additional news databases can be found in such publications and databases as *Gale Directory of Online, Portable, and Internet Databases*, available in print from Gale Group and online through Dialog.)

Many additional news directories are available. Some are dedicated to tracking newsletters or periodicals only, while others contain a combination of news sources, many of which are not yet online in any form. Although news directories will not guide you to individual articles in which a given person is mentioned, they can be very useful in pointing you in the right direction.

Other directories can be similarly used to locate industry publications or local newspapers, and to find out which of them can be searched online. Newspaperlinks.com is an online directory of newspapers, which can be found at www.newspaperlinks.com/home.cfm.

Another directory, Newspapers.com (www.newspapers.com), provides links to newspapers by name, city, or category.

Yahoo! also provides a directory of newspapers at http://dir.yahoo.com/news_and_media/newspapers/index.html.

For European publications, if you do not know the publisher or you don't know which publications to contact, you might try the European School Culham (click on Secondary, and then Links to European Newspapers), located at www.esculham.fsnet.co.uk.

CollegeNews.com provides a directory of Campus Newspapers at www.collegenews.com/campusnews.htm.

For publications that cannot be searched online, you might then call the publisher, which often can be found by a search of online publications directories. Many keep an in-house index or database that could reveal whether that publisher has written about your subject. Alternatively, you might visit a university library that carries back issues of the magazine or journal or microfiche of the newspaper.

Another good source for the text of newspapers or local business journals not available online is the library in the publication's home town, which you can find using a telephone directory database. The reference librarian may be able to help in searching back issues for you or may arrange to lend microfiche of their back issues to a library near you, so that you can search through them yourself.

Newspapers

Newspapers can supply information about almost anyone. Most carry the "big stories," as you would expect, but smaller newspapers also routinely mention people who are involved in local groups, such as the PTA or the Girl Scouts. Anyone who gets married, is promoted, or dies may be listed among their announcements. Local businesspeople are mentioned for their involvement in the Chamber of Commerce, the Rotary Club, and similar groups, and are sought for quotations when events could affect their businesses or the local economy. Traffic accidents, county fairs, and dozens of everyday events can make their way into newsprint. Even children may be mentioned or featured for winning at spelling bees or science fairs or for bringing in a prize lamb at the 4-H Club.

Something else one can find in smaller newspapers is information about arrests. Although not generally newsworthy by big-city standards, the arrest of a local citizen for solicitation or drunk driving can be big news in a small town. In fact, some communities have taken to publishing the names of all "johns" caught for solicitation of prostitutes in the local papers, in order to shame their citizens into better behavior.

If you wish to search through newspapers for articles about someone, there are a few variables to consider. First, not all newspapers are yet available online, so you may need to use a news directory (online or in print) to locate the papers in the subject's region and learn how you can best access them.

Some newspapers are found online only as citations and abstracts. This is useful for locating the articles that interest you, but you may then need to contact the newspaper, a local library, or a document delivery company to obtain a copy of the full article. Some database vendors also allow for online ordering of the articles.

Databases have been compiled from selected biographical articles appearing in the *New York Times* and *Washington Post*. Segregating this information into its own database (as Nexis has done for each of these papers) makes searching it much more convenient.

Bell & Howell Information and Learning (formerly UMI/DataTimes), Factiva, Dialog, and LexisNexis all offer large numbers of newspapers online. When you do not know where the information might be found, online systems such as these allow you to search across dozens of newspapers at once, which can save a great deal of time and expense.

Some databases also combine news sources, drawing from newspapers, newswires, magazines, journals, and television and radio transcripts. Examples of these can be found later in this
chapter under "Combined News Databases."

Newswires

Newswires are a good place to look for business information such as press releases, product
announcements, legal actions, company acquisitions, announced earnings and dividends, and
expansion plans; civic, cultural, and scientific events; and developments in politics and government. Source organizations include public and private companies, associations, political parties,
unions, sports and entertainment organizations, educational and scientific institutions, and government agencies.

Personal data that can be gathered on the wires typically includes announcements of promotions and changes in management, especially in the upper ranks of large corporations. News
about celebrities, politicians, sports stars, and others in the news are also found there. One
newswire database, Associated Press—Candidate Biographies (available on Nexis), contains the
text of biographical newswires about political candidates.

Nearly anything that anyone cares to put in a press release and pay a newswire company to
broadcast may be found in a newswire database. Newswires can even include photographs.

The information on the newswires tends to be brief, but full feature articles sometimes follow,
if the story is picked up by other news media. That is often the hope of those issuing press
releases on the wires.

Some newswires carry only a certain type of news. For example, E-Wire (available at
http://ens.lycos.com/e-wire) contains news releases covering environmental topics. There are
many financial and economic newswires, such as Federal Filings Business Newswire (available
through Factiva and as part of several other databases) and Japan Economic Newswire Plus
(JEN) (available through Dialog, Factiva, Nexis, and as part of Lexis Country Information
Service).

Several newswires carry a broader spectrum of subjects. One of the best known is UPI News,
from United Press International. UPI News (available through AT&T EasyLink Services, Dialog,
and through CompuServe's Knowledge Index) includes national and international news; current
events; the political scene at the federal and state government levels; business, financial and
sports news, columns and commentaries; and standing features. Gannett News Service (available
online through Bell & Howell Information and Learning and Nexis) is another example, carrying national and international news, features, finance, and sports stories, with an emphasis on
state and regional stories. Kyodo News Wire (available online through NIFTY-SERVE) covers
Japan's current events, internal politics, governmental news, economics, and business; it also
includes coverage of American and European dealings with Japan, and news from the Pacific
Rim.

Current newswires can also be found now on the Internet, and it is not unusual for companies
to republish their press releases on their own Web pages. Thus, the Net is becoming a great place
to start your search for news on top executives of a company.

Some of the many newswires that you will find on the Internet include the following:

@Brint.com (Business and Technology) News Wire
www.brint.com

Business Wire
www.businesswire.com

Canada NewsWire
www.newswire.ca

Cole's Newswire and News Inc.
www.colegroup.com/nw

Lebanon.com News Wire
www.lebanon.com/news/newswire/index.htm

PR Newswire
www.prnewswire.com

US Newswire
www.usnewswire.com

Video News Wire (from PR Newswire)
www.videonewswire.com

Using any search engine, you can find many additional newswires on other topics and geographic regions.

Magazines

Hundreds, if not thousands, of magazines can be found online. Like the newswire databases, some magazine databases are dedicated to a single publication. For example, there are databases such as *AutoWeek, BYTE, Canadian Mining Journal, Fortune, LIFE, Public Utilities Reports* (containing the full text of Public Utilities Fortnightly), and *The Washington Quarterly*, to name but a few.

If you know or suspect that one of these publications contains an article about someone you are researching, you should be able to locate and extract the story within a few minutes if it exists on one of these databases.

Other databases include many magazines among their sources. For example, Magazine Index (available online through DataStar, Dialog, and CARL Corporation, and on the Internet through CompuServe's Knowledge Index, and on the Internet: DataStarWeb at www.dialog.com/info/products/datastar-index.shtml, DialogWeb at www.dialogweb.com, and InfoTrac (Gale Group) at http://infotrac.galenet.com) contains articles from more than 400 general-interest and consumer magazines.

Additional databases include articles from magazines and from other news media, such as newspapers and newswires. Examples of these can be found later in this chapter.

Most magazines also now maintain a Web site or other presence on the Internet. Such a site may include past or present issues, or portions of either.

One of the sites indexing magazines available on the Net is provided by Yahoo! at http://dir.yahoo.com/news_and_media/magazines. Another can be found at Lycos at http://dir.lycos.com/News/Magazines. Another index, focusing on Information Technology magazines and e-zines can be found on the compinfo.ws site at www.compinfo-center.com/itmags.htm.

Journals

Do you remember the commercial in which a group of women in an office building breathlessly ogle a shirtless hunk of a construction worker while he drinks a can of Diet Coke? This ad raised a bit of a furor in advertising circles and caused some controversy between people who found the ad to be sexist and those who were amused to see men treated as sex objects.

If you were starting an advertising agency and decided to find and recruit the genius who created this ad, you would not have to look far. Hundreds of trade journals are available online, and several among them address the advertising industry. *Adweek,* for example, is available on Nexis. A quick search of *Adweek* reveals far more than the name of the person who created the Diet Coke ad. Writer Ann Cooper turned out an entire article about him for the April 11, 1994, Eastern Edition. Within the article, you could obtain the following information to aid in your recruiting efforts:

Name: Lee Garfinkel
Age: 39 (at the time the article was written)
Marital Status: Married
Father's Background: Shoe Salesman from 175th Street in the Bronx
Current employer:
> Lowe & Partners/SMS (a $500 million agency), since November 1992
> Located in the Grace Building, Sixth Avenue, New York (corner office)

Current position: Chief Creative Officer and Vice President
Salary: In the high six figures
Previous Employment: (in reverse chronological order)
> Star Copywriter at BBDO (for 3 years)
> Starting as Junior Copywriter, ending as Creative Director at Levine,
> Huntley, Schmidt & Beaver
> Stand-Up Comic

Business Associates:
> Andy Langer, CEO at Lowe & Partners/SMS
> Frank Lowe, Chairman at Lowe & Partners/SMS
> Martyn Straw, Head of Planning at Lowe & Partners/SMS
> John Hayes, President at Lowe & Partners/SMS
> Barbara Siegel, Copywriter at Lowe & Partners/SMS
> Peter Cohen, at Lowe & Partners/SMS and previously at Levine, Huntley,
> > Schmidt & Beaver
> Todd Godwin, at Lowe & Partners/SMS and previously at Levine, Huntley,
> > Schmidt & Beaver
> C.J. Waldman, at Lowe & Partners/SMS and previously at Levine, Huntley,
> > Schmidt & Beaver
> Leslie Stern, at Lowe & Partners/SMS and previously at Levine, Huntley,
> > Schmidt & Beaver
> Richard Ostroff, at Lowe & Partners/SMS and previously at Levine, Huntley,
> > Schmidt & Beaver
> Bob Nelson, at Lowe & Partners/SMS and previously at Levine, Huntley,
> > Schmidt & Beaver

Amy Borkowsky, at Lowe & Partners/SMS and previously at Levine, Huntley,
  Schmidt & Beaver

Tony DeGregorio, creative partner at Levine, Huntley, Schmidt & Beaver

Current Agency Accounts:

Diet Coke (a $70 million account)

Hanson, a bricks-and-chemical conglomerate

Grey Poupon

Fresca

Sprite

Smirnoff (handled out of the London office)

Cinzano

Accounts That Got Away:

Thom McAn shoes

Comedy Central

Burger King

Previous Agency Accounts:

Pepsi, for which Mr. Garfinkel won awards (at BBDO); worked on M.C. Hammer's
  "Feelings" commercial; "Logo" (the ad with Cindy Crawford); and "Shady Acres"
  Matchbox Toys at Levine, Huntley, Schmidt & Beaver

Reading this article, you could also find out a great deal about Garfinkel's personal management style and reputation, his manner of dress, and even details of his office decor, which
includes a rubber donkey's head! Subsequent articles in 2001 and 2002 mention his heavy mus-
tache, additional accounts, commercials, associates, his home recording studio and songwriting
talent, his exit from Lowe Lintas, and subsequent career moves.

If you were planning to recruit him, these articles would provide a wonderful starting place for
your background research. You might find that you have business associates in common, who
might provide an introduction or additional background information. You could identify
Garfinkel's current and previous ads to get a better understanding of his creative capabilities. If
you knew anyone who worked for any of the accounts that got away, you might find out why they
did. All of this information could give you an advantage in recruiting or negotiating.

These types of articles could also be extremely useful for companies providing competitive
intelligence to other advertising agencies. One may think of trade journals as being rather dry and
lifeless reading, but from the perspective of a researcher, I consider these types of articles quite
full of juicy details.

Many journals can also be found on the Internet. Please refer to the "Zines" section of this
chapter, as well as the "Combined News Databases" section for examples of sites indexing journals found on the Net.

Zines

Zines, sometimes called e-zines or e-journals, are online publications. They may be published
as online editions of familiar magazines, or they may be entirely new publications that exist only
online.

Because anyone can publish a zine and add it to the Internet, zines can have a considerably different look and feel than the print publications you are used to. You may find information in them
that you would not find elsewhere. You may also find strong language and even stronger opinions.

Be aware that many zines lack the credibility of print publications, and the writers and publishers could even take pains to maintain their anonymity while publishing pure lies. If you read something about someone in a zine, always consider the source.

The online medium also lends itself to the exchange of views between readers about the publications, sometimes including online discussion with the authors or the publisher. This type of interchange is much more immediate and interactive than the "letters to the editor" section of print publications, and it adds another dimension to the zines.

Many zines are free to the reader, but some are e-mailed only to paying subscribers. Unlike print publications, it would be possible for a zine publisher to offer partial purchase so that a subscriber could pay for only the parts of the zine of interest.

So many zines are being published that several Internet Web sites are dedicated to keeping track of them and/or reviewing their work, along with other online news sources. Please refer to "Combined News Databases" later in this chapter for examples of those sites. One site that is dedicated to indexing only zines is EZine-Universe.com at http://ezine-universe.com.

Searching zines for articles about a particular individual can be an arduous task, especially if the publisher has not indexed the publication with the searcher in mind. Thus, the researcher can easily miss these sources.

Another site, Scholarly Journals Distributed via the World Wide Web (from the University of Houston Libraries), is available at http://info.lib.uh.edu/wj/webjour.html.

Newsletters

These days, it seems like almost every organization is publishing a newsletter. These newsletters can provide valuable information on current topics in any field of research. They can be filled with recaps of meetings, elections, and events, including the names of many of their members. People who do not otherwise write professionally can sometimes have their arms twisted to contribute an occasional article to a newsletter.

Some newsletter databases combine more than one newsletter. One of the largest, combining more than 500, is Newsletter Database, from Gale Group (available online through Bell & Howell Information and Learning, DataStar, Dialog, European Information Network Services, Factiva, FT PROFILE, I/PLUS Direct, and STN International, and on the Internet through DataStarWeb at www.dialog.com/info/products/datastar-index.shtml, DialogWeb at www.dialogweb.com, and InfoTrac (Gale Group) at http://infotrac.galenet.com). Dozens of others cover one or more newsletters. Newsletters provide more avenues for finding information about individuals participating in organizations, associations, or professions.

Many additional newsletters can be found on the Internet. Some of the best sites indexing these can be found within Yahoo!, such as:

Business Newsletters
http://dir.yahoo.com/news_and_media/business/newsletters

Computer Newsletters
http://dir.yahoo.com/business_and_economy/business_to_business/
computers/industry_information/newsletters

Electronic Commerce Newsletters
http://dir.yahoo.com/business_and_economy/business_to_business/
electronic_commerce/news_and_media/newsletters

Health Newsletters
http://dz.dir.snv.yahoo.com/health/news_and_media/newsletters

Law Newsletters
http://dz.dir.snv.yahoo.com/government/law/news_and_media/
newsletters

Market Information and Research Newsletters
http://dz.dir.snv.yahoo.com/business_and_economy/shopping_and_
services/financial_services/investment_services/market_
information_and_research/newsletters

Travel and Transportation Newsletters
http://dl.snv.yahoo.com/business_and_economy/shopping_and_
services/travel_and_transportation/newsletters

A search of Yahoo! for "Newsletters" will provide indices to a great many more newsletters, categorized by subject.

Television and Radio Transcripts

If you have watched any news or talk shows lately, you've probably heard the announcement at the end of the program telling where to call or write for transcripts of the show. The same companies often make those transcripts available online as well. Transcript databases are useful in locating people who have appeared on talk shows or on the radio. They also can help you to find out what has been said about someone. If it is your job to book talk show guests, transcript databases can tell where else someone has appeared and what he or she has talked about. You can also use these databases to find out whether other shows have recently covered the topic that you are planning. If you know or even suspect that the person you are researching has written a book or been involved in anything controversial, there is a good chance that a transcript database will help you to identify any live interviews on television or radio. Talk show transcripts often appear in Burrelle's Broadcast Database (available online through Bell & Howell Information and Learning and Burrelle's Information Services) and Burrelle's TV Transcripts (available online through Bell & Howell Information and Learning).

LexisNexis also carries several transcripts databases within its news library. It includes not only news transcripts, but same-day transcripts for newsworthy trials.

For international news, you might also consider CNN News Transcripts (available online through Bell & Howell Information and Learning and LexisNexis). Refer to Appendix N for addresses of these vendors except where otherwise noted.

A few additional online databases are somewhat more limited or subject specific in the transcripts that they offer. For example, Reuters Transcript Report (available online through Congressional Quarterly Inc., Nexis, and Reuters, Ltd.) provides word-for-word record transcripts of Washington, DC, political news and events. Transcripts: News Events and Congressional Hearings (available online through Congressional Quarterly, Inc.) contains verbatum transcripts of newsworthy congressional committee hearings and executive branch press briefings.

Television and radio transcripts can also be found on the Internet, although these are often limited to the most current news. Some television stations are indexed at: http://dir.yahoo.com/news_and_media/television/stations.

Many television and radio programs also maintain their own presence on the Internet, America Online, CompuServe, or Prodigy. This presence often is announced during or after their broadcast. These sites sometimes include transcripts or information about recent broadcasts and usually include an e-mail address where further information can be requested. Examples of these sites include:

Good Morning America
http://abcnews.go.com/sections/GMA/index.html

The Rosie O'Donnell Show
http://rosieo.warnerbros.com/pages/rosieo/home.jsp

Martha Stewart Living
www.marthastewart.com

Politically Incorrect with Bill Maher
http://abcnews.go.com/primetime/politicallyincorrect/index.html

The View
http://abc.go.com/theview/main.html

Today
www.msnbc.com/news/TODAY_Front.asp

Combined News Databases

Many news databases combine a number of news sources, including newspapers, newsletters, newswires, magazines, journals, and television and radio transcripts. These databases may contain full text or only citations and abstracts of the articles or transcripts. Databases that cross many news media are an excellent choice for a fishing expedition when you do not know whether any information is available about a person.

Combined news databases can be subject-specific, such as:

- Computer ASAP, which concentrates on the computer industry.

- Ethnic NewsWatch, which focuses on ethnic and minority newspapers, magazines, and journals.

- PROMT (Predicasts Overview of Markets and Technology), concentrating on companies, markets, products, and technologies for major international, national, and regional manufacturing and service industries.

Some databases combine just a couple of types of these news sources. Examples of these include:

- The Business Library, which includes business, trade, and industry publications.

- McGraw Hill Companies Publications Online, which includes a large selection of magazines and newsletters.

- Reuters TEXTLINE, including major daily and financial and business newspapers and journals.

- Trade & Industry Database, taken from business, trade, and industry journals.

Some Internet sites also index multiple news sources. An example of such a site is NewsDirectory.com, which provides links to both newspapers and magazines at http://newsdirectory. com.

News Clipping Services, Current Awareness, and Selective Dissemination of Information

If you are not able to keep up with all of the news but need to keep track of a competitor, a celebrity, or any other topic, news clipping services can provide a solution.

A news clipping service can scan a set of publications or databases at regular intervals—daily, weekly, monthly, quarterly, or on any schedule you like. Search parameters are selected ahead of time, and the results may be delivered online, via fax, by overnight delivery, or via "snail mail" (the U.S. Postal Service).

Many online vendors offer the ability to set up your own automated clipping or current awareness service. You can enter the search statements ahead of time, identify databases to be searched, set the interval at which you'd like to repeat the search, and specify your preferred delivery method. For complex searches or databases that you do not have access to, you might also consider using an information professional who can provide this service for you. For those publications that are not available online, it may be necessary for you to find a newsclipping service that specializes in the clipping of print publications.

A dozen or more vendors now offer free clipping services on the Internet. In some cases, headlines and "basic" articles are free, while the full text of some articles may be obtained only by subscribers who pay a monthly fee for access to "premium" publications or wire services.

Online Newsgroups

Online newsgroups (sometimes referred to as online bulletin boards, forums, roundtables, or Usenet newsgroups) are far more than the equivalent of their predecessors, the thumbtack bulletin boards of the past. Online newsgroups now provide an international public forum for posting questions, opinions, and information and for holding discussions and debates between people around the globe.

Whatever the subject, there is probably a newsgroup where you can meet others with a similar interest and discuss issues near and dear to you.

When traveling among these newsgroups, you will soon notice that there are different rules for different boards. The number one rule on most newsgroups states whether or not advertising is allowed on the board. Another rule often states that republishing anything that appears on the newsgroup is prohibited; this can actually be a matter of copyright infringement. Other rules have to do with proper etiquette (or "netiquette") for any bulletin board. Typical netiquette rules may prohibit the use of offensive language or discourage personal attacks.

Large providers of newsgroups, such as America Online, CompuServe, and Prodigy, usually appoint or hire a system operator (Sysop), or host, for each forum, to ensure that the rules are obeyed, to bar access for those who refuse to obey the rules, and to try to keep participation active on the board. (For systems that accept paid advertisements, the time you spend online can translate to advertising dollars for them.) The largest newsgroup system of all, the Internet, is more of a free-for-all, where individual members take it upon themselves to police the boards in which they participate.

A little time spent reading the participants' messages will quickly reveal the unique personality of each forum or newsgroup. Since each forum serves as a microcosm of diverse people with one or more similar interests that brought them to the board, one forum can have a very different feel or personality from another. On one, you may find a virtual community where members support one another, offering advice and assistance, forming friendships, doing business together, and otherwise becoming a somewhat cohesive group. Participants in these groups often remain with them for years. On another forum, members curse, debate, and harangue one another; pontificating on any given point or issue; and YELL AT EACH OTHER AT THE TOP OF THEIR LUNGS (by using uppercase characters) whenever they see a message they disagree with. Visitors to these groups often move on fairly quickly to less contentious neighborhoods.

Some boards serve as a meeting or messaging place for people who at other times meet face-to-face. On others, the members use aliases, maintain relative anonymity, and never meet or correspond in any other way.

Before becoming too involved in a newsgroup, it is best to spend a little time visiting to find out not only what the rules are, but whether the board offers a community or group of people with whom you want to converse.

Appendix L contains a list of some of the major consumer online service vendors, which include online forums, bulletin boards, or newsgroups. On the Internet, there are tens of thousands of Usenet newsgroups. Newsgroups come and go, often dying for lack of participation, so expect the list of available boards on any of these systems (and most especially on the Internet) to change continuously.

When you are looking for information about people, newsgroups can help in a number of ways. First, there is the chance that the person you are looking for may also participate in a newsgroup, so you may be able to make direct contact. Some newsgroup vendors (such as CompuServe) allow online searching of their membership directories, providing at least an e-mail address, and sometimes more. Although no single membership directory exists for the Internet, there are mechanisms for finding people using their names or e-mail addresses. For those who value their privacy, there also are businesses and a few free services, such as Anonymizer.com (www.anonymizer.com) that will relay any messages through its own e-mail address in order to mask the original sender's identity.

If you know someone's interests, you might ask around in the newsgroups that you think he or she would be most likely to join. Even if the person does not participate in the forum, his or her associates may, and they may be willing to put you in contact.

If you are looking for information about a celebrity, there may be a fan club forum that can fill you in on every film, commercial, or television show that the celebrity has appeared in; the names of family members and friends; the next scheduled appearance; and even what he or she eats for breakfast. The celebrity may even participate in the forum from time to time.

If you want information about respected authorities in any field—engineering, nuclear science, law, cardiology, astrology, or astronomy—a forum can often provide access to others who are very familiar with their work and who can point you to a wealth of information. It is possible to gather a great deal of information about an expert's professional reputation by posting your questions in a forum devoted to his or her field of expertise.

You may even find that you are talking to current or former neighbors or co-workers of your subject. Keep in mind that most forums are public vehicles, so this is not the place for gathering sensitive information about subjects without their knowledge.

You should also be aware that the messages that you post on a newsgroup may have a longer life than you intended. There are Internet search engines designed to search the archives of current and past messages, so anyone now or in the future may look up all of the messages that you've ever posted. Keep that in mind before writing anything private or inflammatory.

Information found on a newsgroup should also be taken with a grain of salt. After all, you probably do not even know for sure who you are talking to. It is best to use the forum to gather leads to more hard-core facts, rather than accepting what you hear as factual.

Chapter 21

Photographic Images

"Whoever controls the media—the images—controls the culture."
 –Allen Ginsberg

Any large newspaper receives hundreds of photographs each day. Among those photos are pictures of celebrities, politicians, and people from every walk of life. Over the last decade or two, but especially during the last few years, digital imaging has begun to replace old-fashioned chemical film. This has enhanced our ability to capture, store, index, and manipulate photographs and to transmit them around the world. Digital cameras have become the tools of photojournalists and newspapers, advertising agencies, and even artists. Sophisticated equipment can already scan and store up to 100 images at one time. There are Web sites that are loaded with JPEG images that can be captured by virtually anyone and transmitted over the Internet to others. A single CD can store 3,000 to 8,000 thumbnail images (small low-resolution "condensations" of the digitized photographs) or approximately 75 to 100 low compression, high-resolution images, and DVDs have even greater capacity.

At the same time, computer programmers have developed software to capture photos from the wire services, along with their header and keyword information, and pull them into databases. Such a system can capture and file thousands of photographs each day.

Once pictures have entered these databases, photo editors can locate and retrieve their choice of images on nearly any subject. What used to take hours of paging through photographs can now be accomplished in minutes if the database is well indexed and the search software is well designed. The pictures can then be cropped, sharpened, colorized, manipulated in dozens of ways, and scaled to fit the space available for them.

Photo Stock Agencies

Newspapers are not the only industry to take advantage of these developments. Many photo stock agencies have also gone digital, and some of them can be found on the Internet. A directory of stock photo sources is included in the Creative Directory Catalog at www.creativedir.com.

If you are on a limited budget, you will be pleased to know that some stock photos have become available as shareware or are available for free if credited properly to the photographer. The Internet has enabled even amateur photographers to share their work with the worldwide online community. If you are looking for a photograph of anyone famous, or a picture of an anonymous person participating in just about any type of activity, there is a good chance that you can find unpublished shots from amateurs and professionals alike. Online photographic forums, fan sites, and photographers' Web pages all can lead you to photographers who have pictures to share.

News Services

Although many database vendors still offer news only in text form, services such as NewsCom (www.newscom.com) are now offering text, photos, and graphics. Some of the sources included in NewsCom's service are the *New York Times News Service, Reuters, Washington Post News Service*, and *Los Angeles Times Syndicate*. Newspapers offered on the Internet generally carry the full graphics of the print version.

Business Periodicals and Magazines

Many business periodical and magazine Web sites incorporate text and photos, just as they appeared in the original publications. These databases can be useful if you want to find out what someone in a magazine or periodical looks like, but re-use of the photographs may be prohibited except by prior arrangement with the publisher.

Missing Children and Loved Ones

Photographic image databases now are being used to aid in locating missing children and other loved ones. The Internet carries many databases that provide descriptions and images of criminally abducted children and their suspected kidnappers. Information supplied by law enforcement agencies worldwide includes physical description, date of disappearance, and investigation information, including agency name, address, telephone number, investigating officer, agency case number, and the FBI's NCIC number. Photos in these databases sometimes include simulated age progression photos that show how the child might look now.

Some of the missing children's sites on the Internet are:

> The Missing Children Database, from the National Center for Missing and Exploited Children
> www.missingkids.org

> Child Search National Missing Children Center
> www.childsearch.org

> Gallery of Missing People
> www.lionshouse.org/dorian/index.htm

> Garden of Missing Children Society
> www.gomcs.org

> Missing Youth Foundation
> www.discoveromaha.com/community/groups/missingyouth/index.html

> National Missing Children's Locate Center USA
> www.cnnw.net/~nmclc

> Child CyberSEARCH Canada
> www.childcybersearch.org

Criminals

Alleged Abductors

Missing children databases may also carry photos of the child's alleged abductor, when known. One such site, the Parental Abductors' section of the Fugitive Hunter's Top 100 Fugitives Web site, can be accessed through www.fugitivehunter.org.

Registered Sex Offenders

There has been a great deal of controversy over whether and how communities are to be notified when registered sex offenders move into their neighborhoods. With the passing of the federal statute known as Megan's Law, after the New Jersey girl whose death inspired it, states are required to find a way to notify communities of registered sex offenders living in their areas. This notification can take many forms: alerting school administrators and neighborhood watch groups, issuing press releases, setting up 900-numbers, which the public can call to find out if someone they suspect is registered, or even holding town hall meetings. Additional methods include the creation of CD-ROM databases containing information and photographs of registered sex offenders, which are now being made available upon request by some police and sheriff stations. In some cases the Internet is also being used to identify registered sex offenders. Examples of Sex Offender sites include:

> The Sex Offender site
> www.sexoffender.com

> The Sex Offender's Who's Who (provided by the Virginia
> State Police)
> www.realtycom.net/megans-law.htm

The FBI's Ten Most Wanted Fugitives

If you want to know who the FBI's Ten Most Wanted Fugitives are, you don't need to travel to FBI headquarters in Washington, DC, or even to your local post office. Pictures and background on the FBI's Ten Most Wanted Fugitives can now be viewed on the Internet at www.fbi.gov/mostwant/topten/fugitives/fugitives.htm.

Photos Included in Other Databases

Photos are included in many other types of database, both online and on CD-ROM. Multimedia encyclopedias are filled with photographs of scientists, inventors, and important figures in history. Additional databases that can help in tracking down a needed photograph include the following:

- AccuNet/AP Photo Archive (available online through AccuWeather, Inc.) enables users to view and print out AP photographs of historical and current news stories, from 1844 to the present.

- CP Pictures Archive (available online through The Canadian Press) contains an archive of famous Canadian photos such as sports figures, government officials, and others.

- The Internet Movie Database—Photo Galleries (available on the Internet at http://us.imdb.com/Sections/Gallery).

- Palmer's Full Image Online (available online through Bell & Howell Information and Learning), which contains 100 years of images from the Times of London.

Other databases can be found that target many other areas of interest. Any of them may contain photographs as well, especially on the Internet or on CD-ROM. Refer to Appendix H for further examples of databases containing photographic images.

Video

Thousands of places are being videoed every day and shown on the Internet. The locations can range from an office showing people at work, to a castle across the globe, or a taxi cab. Even day-care centers are starting to broadcast video from their classrooms so that parents can check in on their children while at work. If you know someone who works in a building with a Webcam, it may be possible to sit at your computer and watch them all day long. One site that is attempting to index Webcam sites is WebCam Central at www.camcentral.com.

If this trend continues, there will be fewer and fewer places left on the planet where people can be sure that they are not under surveillance by the masses.

Chapter 22

Quotations

A book that furnishes no quotations is, me judice,
no book it is a plaything.

–Thomas Love Peacock

As you know, public statements can be more telling than anything a biography or resume reveals. Consider the comments former House Speaker Newt Gingrich made in a lecture as part of the televised history course "Renewing American Civilization," which he taught for Mind Extension University. If you were wondering where Speaker Gingrich stands on issues concerning gender differences, he shared his views that women "have biological problems being in a ditch for 30 days because they get infections," while "a male gets very, very frustrated sitting in a chair all the time because males are biologically driven to go out and hunt giraffes."

These curious revelations were quoted in many newspapers that can be searched online and were rebroadcast on television news programs. Anyone writing a biography or an investigative profile may find news sources well worth searching for quotes that reveal the subject's thoughts and motivations.

If you are looking at a historical or famous person, there is a good chance that a search through news files will unearth a quotation from an interview or a reference to something the subject is reported to have said. In addition to newspaper databases, there are news databases focusing on newswires and television and radio transcripts. Refer to Chapter 20 for additional information about searching the news.

Speech Databases

If you wonder about an executive's statements or views, you might consider also searching sources such as *The Executive Speaker*, which is published by a company of the same name. In this newsletter, available online through LexisNexis, you can find a bibliography of speeches made by executives since 1980, and the organizations that heard them. Part of each speech is also available, but the full text of the speech must be ordered off-line. "Executive Speeches," a full-text database of speeches offered by the same company, is included in the ABI-INFORM database carried by many database vendors including BRS, DataStar, Dialog, FT Profile, Info Globe, STN, and Westlaw.

Quotations Databases

Many databases specialize in quotations. These quotations are generally brief, but they can provide a glimpse of the speaker's views. Consider persons as ultimately quotable as Albert Einstein or Oscar Wilde. During their lifetimes, many quotations were attributed to them on topics ranging from God to mathematics, art to women.

Bartleby.com Quotations combines several reference works including *Columbia World of Quotations*. A search for Albert Einstein provides 41 quotations, most of which reveal sober reflections, including one of my personal favorites:

> "My religion consists of a humble admiration of the illimitable superior spirit who reveals himself in the slight details we are able to perceive with our frail and feeble minds."

There are 399 quotations attributed to Oscar Wilde in this database. Although most are colored by his rapier wit, others reveal a more serious side of his views. A recurring theme involves his image of women, such as in "Women love us for our defects. If we have enough of them, they will forgive us everything, even our gigantic intellects" and "The strength of women comes from the fact that psychology cannot explain us. Men can be analysed, women ... merely adored." Such quotations could cause a biographer to speculate on misogynist tendencies that may have biased his relationships, and following that theory, to concentrate much of a biography on exploring those relationships.

Additional quotation databases can be found as follows:

Bartlett's Familiar Quotations
www.bartleby.com/100

Simpson's Contemporary Quotations
www.bartleby.com/63

Quoteland.com (a quote reference source that takes suggestions
for additional quotes)
www.quoteland.com

Additional Internet sources for quotations are indexed by Yahoo! at http://d5.dir.dcx.yahoo.com/reference/quotations. Additional quotation links may be found in the Love Quotes Encyclopedia at http://lovequote.com. There's even a site for David Letterman's Top 10 List at www.cbs.com/latenight/lateshow/topten.

Some of these collections contain disclaimers stating that quotations have not been verified, so be sure to confirm them elsewhere if they are important to you. Refer to Appendix I for additional quotations databases.

Professional and Technical Papers Presented

If a presentation is given at a conference, a professional or technical paper may well provide essentially the same information. From it, you might find material worthy of quotation. One database that carries such papers is Ei Compendex, provided by Engineering Information, Inc. This database includes summaries of journal articles, technical reports, and conference proceedings, referencing more than 5,000 sources. Database vendors now carrying this database include DataStar and Dialog.

Published Articles

People's written words can also provide wonderful insight into their character and views. If someone has written articles for newspapers, magazines, journals, or newsletters, it is often possible to locate these works through a database search. Many databases provide bibliographic information, abstracts, or even the full text of articles.

An example is Academic Index, provided by the Gale Group. This database (carried by DataStar, Dialog, and CARL Corporation) indexes more than three million records from more than 1,550 scholarly, technical, and business journals.

Many similar databases focus on scientific journals, popular magazines, newspapers, and newsletters. Most well-known publications are also available on the Internet today, but they do not always carry the full text of the print editions, and many are limited in how far they go back into the previous issues. Searching across many publications at once is also much, much faster on the fee-based systems such as Dialog and LexisNexis. Refer to Appendix G for directories of other news databases.

Published Books

To locate books written by a particular author, check with databases such as Books In Print, produced by R.R. Bowker, which provides information about them. Booksellers like Amazon.com (www.amazon.com) and Barnes and Noble (www.barnesandnoble.com) are also very useful in searching for books. Refer to Appendix B for a list of databases that index books.

You may also find relevant quotations in biographies written by others about the person. Refer to Chapter 15 for additional information about searching for biographical books.

As entire books are slowly being placed on the Internet and on CD-ROM, it is possible, in some cases, to search complete texts for the best or most telling quotations.

When searching the Internet for additional quotation sites, I ran into The Commonplace Book at www.internetbookinfo.com/ibic/Commonplace-Book.html. The Commonplace Book is described as "an edited collection of striking passages noted in a single place for future reference." Anyone with Internet access can submit favorite passages with proper attribution, and once verified, the proposed entry may become part of this virtual book of quotations.

Political Speeches

Many historic U.S. speeches and addresses are now available on the Internet. Chapter 35 provides further information about these documents.

College Dissertations

If you need quotations from someone's doctoral thesis, you may be in luck. One bibliographic database indexes virtually every American dissertation granted at accredited North American universities since 1861. Dissertation Abstracts Online is produced by Dissertation Publishing, UMI, and is carried by Dialog. Selected masters theses have also been included since 1962. Abstracts of the doctoral records have been included since July 1980, and those for masters theses have been included since the spring of 1988. Since 1988, the database also has included citations for dissertations from 50 British universities. Although the full dissertation is not available in the database, a copy can be ordered online.

Canadian masters and doctoral theses are microfilmed, published, and cataloged by the National Library of Canada. A bibliography of Canadian theses is available through the National Library of Canada. Refer to Appendix N for the address.

Chapter 23

Bank Records

*A bank is a place where they lend you an umbrella in fair
weather and ask for it back when it begins to rain.*

−Robert Frost

For someone about to file a lawsuit, or to file for divorce, or in any other situation where he
or she might wish to measure someone's financial standing, bank records can be a very telling
information source. Because of this, bank records also are among the most closely guarded. Yet
if bank records themselves are not readily accessible, other personal records, both online and off,
can still reveal a lot about the funds these institutions hold.

Personal Bank Accounts

When speaking about personal records, I am often asked, "Can you find out about someone's
personal bank accounts?" Of course you can, but not through a database search.

Well, that is not entirely true. A database search might help in a few roundabout ways.
Although public records will not provide direct access to bank accounts, they can put you on the
trail of them, as well as other financial records.

For example, you can use a database search to locate divorces in the civil indices. You still
must obtain a copy of the actual divorce documents, as the details of the divorce are not yet
online. Somewhere within the paperwork of the divorce you often will find financial records of
either or both parties. Other civil records include tax liens and civil suits, and the papers filed in
these cases can also contain records of bank accounts. Bankruptcies and Uniform Commercial
Code (UCC) filings found online can likewise lead you to legal documents containing bank
account information. Even criminal records can contain banking information if a person's crime
was embezzlement or some other type of theft. Of course, the funds may have been seized or
spent before the information does you any good. Refer to Chapter 31 for further information
about searching for these public records.

Other database searches may lead you to a person's business banking accounts, and there is
the possibility that personal accounts are with the same bank. Refer to Chapter 24 for information about searching for business bank accounts.

If you have a legally permissible purpose for obtaining a credit report, such as when you are
a creditor, you may find records of bank loans, bank credit cards, or credit inquiries from various banks listed on the credit profile. Any of these may point you to the bank where the subject's

personal or business funds are maintained. Refer to Chapter 25 for information about searching consumer credit records.

One database available online and on CD-ROM does contain personal banking information, but it is limited to listings of approximately 3,100 executives. It is Simmons Top Management Insights from Simmons Market Research Bureau, Inc. (Please refer to Appendix N for the address.) The information for the Simmons Top Management Insights database is collected through interviews and questionnaires, so bank account information is only there if the executive agrees to supply it. Many do not.

None of these methods or sources is guaranteed to turn up bank accounts, and even when they do, you still may need a subpoena to obtain the bank balances, or a court order to get at the funds. If you are looking for bank accounts in connection with a legal case, your attorney may be able to acquire the information through the legal discovery process or obtain proper legal authorization to gain the information from other sources, such as the person's accountant.

Several companies and individuals now offer to sell bank account information over the Internet. If someone promises to find personal bank accounts for you, he or she may be using methods that have nothing to do with databases. He or she may be paying off insiders in the banks for information, something I strongly recommend against trying or allowing anyone else to do on your behalf. He or she may be sifting through the person's trash, which can provide bank statements and receipts revealing not only account numbers, but the balances as well. Telephone records could reveal overseas calls to banks, which may be where the funds are hiding. "Garbology," the study of garbage, is legal in most places once the trash hits the curb, so if you value your privacy be aware of what you throw away.

Many other techniques have been used to locate bank accounts. One could follow people around waiting for them to go to the bank, stand behind them in the supermarket, or even tail them through the shopping mall, hoping to watch over their shoulder as they write a check. Alternatively, send them a check for a few dollars, calling it a refund or prize of some type, and hope that they will deposit it into their personal bank account. Once it has been deposited, the bank information can be obtained from the back of the returned check. Some people have been known to engage in deception in order to elicit banking information. If someone calls you, claiming to be from your bank and asking to confirm information on your accounts, call them back at the bank before volunteering anything. Better yet, go to the bank to clear up any problems. It would be rare for a bank to call and ask for the very keys that would open your accounts to thieves and con artists.

These all are common means of finding information about a person's bank accounts, some legal, some not. What no individual can do is dial directly into a database and access another's personal banking information without the person's permission. While banks must have this capability in order to transfer funds and cash checks, they do not produce such databases for individuals, nor do they produce mailing lists of their banking customers. Even check verification systems usually rely on a combination of records of past bad checks and telephone calls to banks in order to verify that the checks that you write will be good.

If someone "guarantees" that he or she can provide personal banking information, this is a red flag. If this person cannot tell you what his sources are, there is the good chance that the methods are illegal, and I recommend steering clear of this individual. I would not even consider putting my business or myself at risk by unknowingly being involved with anyone else's illegal activities, or purchasing stolen data. There are legal means of obtaining banking information, as we have seen, but none of them brings "guaranteed" results.

Unclaimed Funds

There is a site on the Internet where you can identify bank accounts, and that is at the National Association of Unclaimed Property Administrators' Web site. If you or someone you know is suspected of having a bank account that has been forgotten, you can search this site by state to find links to state search sites, or to obtain the forms needed to send in a search request, depending upon the state. You can find the NAUPA site at www.unclaimed.org.

Business Bank Accounts

If you are looking for a business's banking information, rather than an individual's, a quick database search may provide a pointer to their accounts.

There are business databases that list bank references or affiliations. Examples of such databases follow:

- ABC Belge pour le Commerce et l'Industrie (available on CD ROM and on the Internet at www.abc-d.be)

- ABC der Deutschen Wirtschaft (available on CD-ROM from ABC pour le Commerce et l'Industrie C.V.)

- ABC Europe Production Europex (available online through FIZ Technik and STN International)

- ABCDienstverleners (available online through ADC voor Handel en Industrie C.V., DataStar, Gessellschaft fur Betriebswirtschaftliche Information mbH, and LexisNexis)

- ABC Germany (available online through DataStar and FIZ Technik)

- ABC voor Handel en Industrie (available online through ABC voor Handel en Industrie C.V., DataStar, Gessellschaft fur Betriebswirtschaftliche Information mbH, and LexisNexis)

- Base de Dados Mope (available online through Lda Mope)

- BISNES Plus (available online through DataStar and INFOTRADE N.V.)

- BizEkon News—Soviet Business Directory (available online through Gessellschaft fur Betriebswirtschaftliche Information mbH, Lexis, and SovInfoLink)

- Business Who's Who of Australia (available online through Dun and Bradstreet)

- COMLINE Japanese Corporate Directory (available online through DataStar)

- Company Intelligence (available online through DataStar, Dialog, and Nexis)

- COMPUSTAT (available online through ADP Network Services, Inc., CompuServe, Interactive Data Corporation, FactSet Data Systems, Inc., Standard and Poor's Compustat, Vestek Systems, Inc.)

- DBRISK (available online through Dun and Bradstreet France S.A.)

- Dun's Market Identifiers Australia (available online through Dun and Bradstreet Australia)

- Dun's Middle Market Disc (available on CD-ROM through Dun and Bradstreet)

- Dun's Million Dollar Disc (available on CD-ROM through Dun and Bradstreet)

- DunsPrint Canada (available online through Dun and Bradstreet Canada)

- DunsPrint Worldwide (available online through Dun and Bradstreet Ltd.)

- Experian Business Credit Profiles (available online through CompuServe, Dialog, and on the Internet at www.experian.com/cgi-bin/bcredit.cgi)

- Hoppenstedt Germany (available on the Internet at www. companydatabase.de)

- ICC Full Text Accounts (available online through DataStar, Dialog, and FT PROFILE)

- INFOCHECK (available online through DataStar and The InfoCheck Group, Ltd.)

- KOMPASS-FRANCE (available online through Kompass France S.A.)

- KOMPASS Israel (available online through Dialog)

- Luxemburgs ABC voor Handel en Industrie (available online through ABC voor Handel en Industrie C.V., DataStar, and LexisNexis)

- SDOE (available online through CERVED International S.A. and DataStar)

- SICE: Foreign Trade Information System (available online through Organization of American States, General Secretariat)

- Teikoku Japanese Companies (available online through Dialog)

Although all of these databases have fields for bank references, this information is not always provided. You may find it in one database, but not another, and the bank listed in one database may disagree with that provided in another. Annual reports or financial statements, available either online or directly from the company, may supply further banking information; bank balances may even be included.

Uniform Commercial Code (UCC) filings found on public records databases can also point to records that contain business bank accounts, as can bankruptcies, tax liens, and judgments. Again, the actual case documents must be acquired from the courts in order to obtain this level of detail. Refer to Chapter 31 for further information on UCC filings.

Business banking information is easier to acquire through legal means than personal banking information; yet if someone offers to provide it for you, it would still be wise to ask about his or her sources. Along with database searches, both legal and illegal means can be used to obtain banking information, and you should be aware of which you are paying for along with any inherent risks.

For further information about business financial records, please go on to Chapter 24.

Business Credit and Company Financial Records

Have more than thou showest,
Speak less than thou knowest,
Lend less than thou owest.

—William Shakespeare, *King Lear*

Many business financial records are widely available through online databases on professional systems, on CD-ROM, and on the Internet. Some databases contain only information on publicly traded companies, while others list both public and private firms. Certain databases address particular industries exclusively, such as banks or manufacturers. Others cross industry boundaries. Sources, details, and currentness also vary. Some contain hidden treasures for anyone seeking personal information.

Appendix C lists business credit and company financial databases. This list has been limited to databases that also contain information about individuals. Others, such as Experian's Business Credit database, are also useful when assessing a business owner's assets. When a company is a sole proprietorship, its assets and debts may represent a large portion of the individual's finances as well.

Business credit and company financial databases can help to identify business relationships, as they often list key personnel including executives and officers, auditors, attorneys, bankers, and others.

Along with business associates within a company, these databases can at times help to identify principal suppliers and customers of a business. People at each of these companies could be interviewed for further information if one were attempting to compile a complete dossier on an executive, business owner, or company.

Salary information occasionally is found in company financial databases, such as INFOCHECK. A few of the company databases also list the main shareholders, along with their holdings.

Biographical information may also be stored on company financial databases. Biographies such as these are normally limited to the principals of the companies.

Public Records

Databases such as Dun's Legal Search (available online through Dun and Bradstreet Business Credit Services) contain public record information, including parties to lawsuits. Parties to a suit are not necessarily limited to the principals of the company, so almost any employee could conceivably turn up in such a database.

Other business databases limit their public records to a single type of record, such as the Bankruptcy DataSource: Data Pages (available online through Nexis and Thomson Financial Securities Data and on the Internet at www.bankruptcydata.com/datasource_index.htm).

Business credit databases often list Uniform Commercial Code (UCC) filings, which can include property owned by the company that has been used to secure a loan. Alternatively, a UCC could also be filed when the company lends money or extends credit to one of its own customers or associates.

Sources of Business Financial Information

Annual and quarterly reports, and other business financial data may be filed with the U.S. Securities and Exchange Commission (SEC). This information is accessible on various databases, as well as on the Internet at www.sec.gov.

Additional financial reports can often be found on company Web pages.

When assessing a person's wealth based on a company's value, you should be aware that the company itself may have provided the information. It may give an overly optimistic view of the firm's position, or a strongly negative picture if that serves the company's purposes. Without independent verification or some insight into the company and the industry, one could easily be misled.

For some of these databases, company financials have been audited by independent accounting firms. This lends more credibility to their figures.

Financial information can also be independently gathered, using combinations of sources such as the company's creditors, stock value, news, public records, and independent analysis. This provides a composite of the company's financial position, reputation, and expectations for future growth or decline.

When a person's finances are primarily tied up in their business, researching the business's finances takes on much greater importance.

Chapter 25

Consumer Credit Records

The rich are different from you and me
because they have more credit.

–John Leonard

Before discussing consumer credit records, there are some important restrictions to be aware of. Because people are so protective of their financial information, consumer credit databases are among the most heavily regulated in existence. There are stiff penalties for their misuse.

The Fair Credit Reporting Act (FCRA)

The Fair Credit Reporting Act (Public Law 91-508) ensures that consumers are treated fairly and that information disseminated about their credit standing is accurate. If you use the credit files, it is imperative that you become familiar with its content and abide by it.

Copies of the FCRA can be found at any law library or on the Internet. For example, I obtained a copy from the Federal Trade Commission site at www.ftc.gov/os/statutes/fcra.htm.

Section 604 of the FCRA, as shown in Figure 25.1, details "permissible purpose" for obtaining consumer credit reports.

Credit Databases

Most larger creditors, such as credit card companies, department stores, and banks, report their information to all three agencies (Equifax, TransUnion, and Experian). Smaller creditors, such as jewelry stores, smaller lending institutions, and public records providers may not. Each of the national credit agencies has distinct strengths within certain regions of the country, due largely to reports from thousands of smaller creditors and reporting agencies.

Another issue is "depth of file," technical jargon that indicates how long creditors have reported to an agency. One credit agency may have more depth of file than another within a certain part of the country.

Each agency has developed its own unique, proprietary algorithm or matching system for determining which records (among billions) belong to each consumer. This secret formula is held almost as tightly as the recipe for Coca Cola. As a result of their matching system, credit reports from one agency will include more records—some of which may

§ 604. Permissible purposes of consumer reports [15 U.S.C. § 1681b]

(a) In general. Subject to subsection (c), any consumer reporting agency may furnish a consumer report under the following circumstances and no other:

(1) In response to the order of a court having jurisdiction to issue such an order, or a subpoena issued in connection with proceedings before a Federal grand jury.

(2) In accordance with the written instructions of the consumer to whom it relates.

(3) To a person which it has reason to believe

(A) intends to use the information in connection with a credit transaction involving the consumer on whom the information is to be furnished and involving the extension of credit to, or review or collection of an account of, the consumer; or

(B) intends to use the information for employment purposes; or

(C) intends to use the information in connection with the underwriting of insurance involving the consumer; or

(D) intends to use the information in connection with a determination of the consumer's eligibility for a license or other benefit granted by a governmental instrumentality required by law to consider an applicant's financial responsibility or status; or

(E) intends to use the information, as a potential investor or servicer, or current insurer, in connection with a valuation of, or an assessment of the credit or prepayment risks associated with, an existing credit obligation; or

(F) otherwise has a legitimate business need for the information

(i) in connection with a business transaction that is initiated by the consumer; or

(ii) to review an account to determine whether the consumer continues to meet the terms of the account.

(4) In response to a request by the head of a State or local child support enforcement agency (or a State or local government official authorized by the head of such an agency), if the person making the request certifies to the consumer reporting agency that

(A) the consumer report is needed for the purpose of establishing an individual's capacity to make child support payments or determining the appropriate level of such payments;

(B) the paternity of the consumer for the child to which the obligation relates has been established or acknowledged by the consumer in accordance with State laws under which the obligation arises (if required by those laws);

(C) the person has provided at least 10 days' prior notice to the consumer whose report is requested, by certified or registered mail to the last known address of the consumer, that the report will be requested; and

(D) the consumer report will be kept confidential, will be used solely for a purpose described in subparagraph (A), and will not be used in connection with any other civil, administrative, or criminal proceeding, or for any other purpose.

(5) To an agency administering a State plan under Section 454 of the Social Security Act (42 U.S.C. § 654) for use to set an initial or modified child support award.

(b) Conditions for furnishing and using consumer reports for employment purposes.

(1) Certification from user. A consumer reporting agency may furnish a consumer report for employment purposes only if

(A) the person who obtains such report from the agency certifies to the agency that

(i) the person has complied with paragraph (2) with respect to the consumer report, and the person will comply with paragraph (3) with respect to the consumer report if paragraph (3) becomes applicable; and

(ii) information from the consumer report will not be used in violation of any applicable Federal or State equal employment opportunity law or regulation; and

(B) the consumer reporting agency provides with the report, or has previously provided, a summary of the consumer's rights under this title, as prescribed by the Federal Trade Commission under section 609(c)(3) [§ 1681g].

(2) Disclosure to consumer.

(A) In general. Except as provided in subparagraph (B), a person may not procure a consumer report, or cause a consumer report to be procured, for employment purposes with respect to any consumer, unless--

(i) a clear and conspicuous disclosure has been made in writing to the consumer at any time before the report is procured or caused to be procured, in a document that consists solely of the disclosure, that a consumer report may be obtained for employment purposes; and

(ii) the consumer has authorized in writing (which authorization may be made on the document referred to in clause (i)) the procurement of the report by that person.

(B) Application by mail, telephone, computer, or other similar means. If a consumer described in subparagraph (C) applies for employment by mail, telephone, computer, or other similar means, at any time before a consumer report is procured or caused to be procured in connection with that application--

(i) the person who procures the consumer report on the consumer for employment purposes shall provide to the consumer, by oral, written, or electronic means, notice that a consumer report may be obtained for employment purposes, and a summary of the consumer's rights under section 615(a)(3); and

(ii) the consumer shall have consented, orally, in writing, or electronically to the procurement of the report by that person.

(C) Scope. Subparagraph (B) shall apply to a person procuring a consumer report on a consumer in connection with the consumer's application for employment only if--

(i) the consumer is applying for a position over which the Secretary of

Transportation has the power to establish qualifications and maximum hours of service pursuant to the provisions of section 31502 of title 49, or a position subject to safety regulation by a State transportation agency; and

(ii) as of the time at which the person procures the report or causes the report to be procured the only interaction between the consumer and the person in connection with that employment application has been by mail, telephone, computer, or other similar means.

(3) Conditions on use for adverse actions.

(A) In general. Except as provided in subparagraph (B), in using a consumer report for employment purposes, before taking any adverse action based in whole or in part on the report, the person intending to take such adverse action shall provide to the consumer to whom the report relates--

(i) a copy of the report; and

(ii) a description in writing of the rights of the consumer under this title, as prescribed by the Federal Trade Commission under section 609(c)(3).

(B) Application by mail, telephone, computer, or other similar means.

(i) If a consumer described in subparagraph (C) applies for employment by mail, telephone, computer, or other similar means, and if a person who has procured a consumer report on the consumer for employment purposes takes adverse action on the employment application based in whole or in part on the report, then the person must provide to the consumer to whom the report relates, in lieu of the notices required under subparagraph (A) of this section and under section 615(a), within 3 business days of taking such action, an oral, written or electronic notification--

(I) that adverse action has been taken based in whole or in part on a consumer report received from a consumer reporting agency;

(II) of the name, address and telephone number of the consumer reporting agency that furnished the consumer report (including a toll-free telephone number established by the agency if the agency compiles and maintains files on consumers on a nationwide basis);

(III) that the consumer reporting agency did not make the decision to take the adverse action and is unable to provide to the consumer the specific reasons why the adverse action was taken; and

(IV) that the consumer may, upon providing proper identification, request a free copy of a report and may dispute with the consumer reporting agency the accuracy or completeness of any information in a report.

(ii) If, under clause (B)(i)(IV), the consumer requests a copy of a consumer report from the person who procured the report, then, within 3 business days of receiving the consumer's request, together with proper identification, the person must send or provide to the consumer a copy of a report and a copy of the consumer's rights as prescribed by the Federal Trade Commission under section 609(c)(3).

(C) Scope. Subparagraph (B) shall apply to a person procuring a consumer report on a consumer in connection with the consumer's application for employment only if--

(i) the consumer is applying for a position over which the Secretary of Transportation has the power to establish qualifications and maximum hours of service pursuant to the provisions of section 31502 of title 49, or a position subject to safety regulation by a State transportation agency; and

(ii) as of the time at which the person procures the report or causes the report to be procured the only interaction between the consumer and the person in connection with that employment application has been by mail, telephone, computer, or other similar means.

(4) Exception for national security investigations.

(A) In general. In the case of an agency or department of the United States Government which seeks to obtain and use a consumer report for employment purposes, paragraph (3) shall not apply to any adverse action by such agency or department which is based in part on such consumer report, if the head of such agency or department makes a written finding that--

(i) the consumer report is relevant to a national security investigation of such agency or department;

(ii) the investigation is within the jurisdiction of such agency or department;

(iii) there is reason to believe that compliance with paragraph (3) will--

(I) endanger the life or physical safety of any person;

(II) result in flight from prosecution;

(III) result in the destruction of, or tampering with, evidence relevant to the investigation;

(IV) result in the intimidation of a potential witness relevant to the investigation;

(V) result in the compromise of classified information; or

(VI) otherwise seriously jeopardize or unduly delay the investigation or another official proceeding.

(B) Notification of consumer upon conclusion of investigation. Upon the conclusion of a national security investigation described in subparagraph (A), or upon the determination that the exception under subparagraph (A) is no longer required for the reasons set forth in such subparagraph, the official exercising the authority in such subparagraph shall provide to the consumer who is the subject of the consumer report with regard to which such finding was made--

(i) a copy of such consumer report with any classified information redacted as necessary;

(ii) notice of any adverse action which is based, in part, on the consumer report; and

(iii) the identification with reasonable specificity of the nature of the investigation for which the consumer report was sought.

(C) Delegation by head of agency or department. For purposes of subparagraphs (A) and (B), the head of any agency or department of the United States Government may delegate his or her authorities under this paragraph to an official of such agency or department who has personnel security responsibilities and is a member of the Senior Executive Service or equivalent civilian or military rank.

(D) Report to the congress. Not later than January 31 of each year, the head of each agency and department of the United States Government that exercised authority under this paragraph during the preceding year shall submit a report to the Congress on the number of times the department or agency exercised such authority during the year.

(E) Definitions. For purposes of this paragraph, the following definitions shall apply:

(i) Classified information. The term 'classified information' means information that is protected from unauthorized disclosure under Executive Order No. 12958 or successor orders.

(ii) National security investigation. The term 'national security investigation' means any official inquiry by an agency or department of the United States Government to determine the eligibility of a consumer to receive access or continued access to classified information or to determine whether classified information has been lost or compromised.

(c) Furnishing reports in connection with credit or insurance transactions that are not initiated by the consumer.

(1) In general. A consumer reporting agency may furnish a consumer report relating to any consumer pursuant to subparagraph (A) or (C) of subsection (a)(3) in connection with any credit or insurance transaction that is not initiated by the consumer only if

(A) the consumer authorizes the agency to provide such report to such person; or

(B) (i) the transaction consists of a firm offer of credit or insurance;

(ii) the consumer reporting agency has complied with subsection (e); and

(iii) there is not in effect an election by the consumer, made in accordance with subsection (e), to have the consumer's name and address excluded from lists of names provided by the agency pursuant to this paragraph.

(2) Limits on information received under paragraph (1)(B). A person may receive pursuant to paragraph (1)(B) only

(A) the name and address of a consumer;

(B) an identifier that is not unique to the consumer and that is used by the person solely for the purpose of verifying the identity of the consumer; and

(C) other information pertaining to a consumer that does not identify the relationship or experience of the consumer with respect to a particular creditor or other entity.

(3) Information regarding inquiries. Except as provided in section 609(a)(5) [§ 1681g], a consumer reporting agency shall not furnish to any person a record of inquiries in connection with a credit or insurance transaction that is not initiated by a consumer.

(d) Reserved.

(e) Election of consumer to be excluded from lists.

(1) In general. A consumer may elect to have the consumer's name and address excluded from any list provided by a consumer reporting agency under subsection (c)(1)(B) in connection with a credit or insurance transaction that is not initiated by the consumer, by notifying the agency in accordance with paragraph (2) that the consumer does not consent to any use of a consumer report relating to the consumer in connection with any credit or insurance transaction that is not initiated by the consumer.

(2) Manner of notification. A consumer shall notify a consumer reporting agency under paragraph (1)

(A) through the notification system maintained by the agency under paragraph (5); or

(B) by submitting to the agency a signed notice of election form issued by the agency for purposes of this subparagraph.

(3) Response of agency after notification through the system. Upon receipt of notification of the election of a consumer under paragraph (1) through the notification system maintained by the agency under paragraph (5), a consumer reporting agency shall

(A) inform the consumer that the election is effective only for the 2-year period following the election if the consumer does not submit to the agency a signed notice of election form issued by the agency for purposes of paragraph (2)(B); and

(B) provide to the consumer a notice of election form, if requested by the consumer, not later than 5 business days after receipt of the notification of the election through the system established under paragraph (5), in the case of a request made at the time the consumer provides notification through the system.

(4) Effectiveness of election. An election of a consumer under paragraph (1)

(A) shall be effective with respect to a consumer reporting agency beginning 5 business days after the date on which the consumer notifies the agency in accordance with paragraph (2);

(B) shall be effective with respect to a consumer reporting agency

(i) subject to subparagraph (C), during the 2-year period beginning 5 business days after the date on which the consumer notifies the agency of the election, in the case of an election for which a consumer notifies the agency only in accordance with paragraph (2)(A); or

(ii) until the consumer notifies the agency under subparagraph (C), in the case of an election for which a consumer notifies the agency in accordance with paragraph (2)(B);

(C) shall not be effective after the date on which the consumer notifies the agency, through the notification system established by the agency under paragraph (5), that the election is no longer effective; and

(D) shall be effective with respect to each affiliate of the agency.

(5) Notification system.

(A) In general. Each consumer reporting agency that, under subsection (c)(1)(B), furnishes a consumer report in connection with a credit or insurance transaction that is not initiated by a consumer, shall

(i) establish and maintain a notification system, including a toll-free telephone number, which permits any consumer whose consumer report is maintained by the agency to notify the agency, with appropriate identification, of the consumer's election to have the consumer's name and address excluded from any such list of names and addresses provided by the agency for such a transaction; and

(ii) publish by not later than 365 days after the date of enactment of the Consumer Credit Reporting Reform Act of 1996, and not less than annually thereafter, in a publication of general circulation in the area served by the agency

(I) a notification that information in consumer files maintained by the agency may be used in connection with such transactions; and

(II) the address and toll-free telephone number for consumers to use to notify the agency of the consumer's election under clause (I).

(B) Establishment and maintenance as compliance. Establishment and maintenance of a notification system (including a toll-free telephone number) and publication by a consumer reporting agency on the agency's own behalf and on behalf of any of its affiliates in accordance with this paragraph is deemed to be compliance with this paragraph by each of those affiliates.

(6) Notification system by agencies that operate nationwide. Each consumer reporting agency that compiles and maintains files on consumers on a nationwide basis shall establish and maintain a notification system for purposes of paragraph (5) jointly with other such consumer reporting agencies.

(f) Certain use or obtaining of information prohibited. A person shall not use or obtain a consumer report for any purpose unless

(1) the consumer report is obtained for a purpose for which the consumer report is authorized to be furnished under this section; and

(2) the purpose is certified in accordance with section 607 [§ 1681e] by a prospective user of the report through a general or specific certification.

(g) Furnishing reports containing medical information. A consumer reporting agency shall not furnish for employment purposes, or in connection with a credit or insurance transaction, a consumer report that contains medical information about a consumer, unless the consumer consents to the furnishing of the report.

Figure 25.1 Permissable Purpose according to the Fair Credit Reporting Act

not belong to the subject. Another agency will err on the side of caution, showing only records that meet more stringent matching criteria.

The last factor differentiating credit agencies is price. Each charges a stiff fee for becoming a subscriber, monthly minimum fees regardless of use, and record fees that vary with volume. If you pull only an occasional report or a few each month, you will be charged top dollar for them. Those prices could drop to pennies if you regularly pull large volumes of reports. If you only have occasional need for credit reports, it would probably be to your benefit to go through a third party in order to retrieve credit records. There are credit bureaus all over the country, many of which access all three credit agencies. Some will pull records without charging sign-up fees or minimum monthly quotas of reports, and for the occasional user this could represent significant savings.

Searching the Credit Files

Due to the need to protect credit history information about individuals, access to the credit databases is restricted to certain "inquiry types" or standard types of searches. An individual may not search across the records in order to identify groups of individuals with similar characteristics. This process is meant to provide access to singular records, on a one-by-one basis only.

This is not to say that records for multiple individuals will never appear as the result of a single inquiry. At times, more than one person's records match the inquiry criteria. For example, if a father and son had the same name and lived at the same address, it is likely that one inquiry would call up records for both individuals, especially if the date of birth were not included on the inquiry. With some credit agencies and bureaus, it is also possible to enter a dual or joint inquiry in order to access the combined records of a husband and wife. However, credit agencies generally intend to restrict searches so that only one individual's records are accessed and displayed for each inquiry processed.

For this reason, you will not find the "wild card" search capabilities that are available with other databases. In other words, one cannot enter SMITH, J to retrieve credit records for all of the Jane, John, and Joe Smiths in the database. Neither can one enter a name without an address. If the minimum necessary information for the inquiry type is not complete, the system will return an error message, rather than a credit report.

Even if the minimum information is entered, the system may require further data. This can occur if the name is as common as Smith or Jones, or Rodriguez or Sanchez, or the address is as common as Main Street or a post office box. A search may also fail if the matching system weighs any part of the data less heavily, for whatever reason, and the remaining details do not meet the credit agency's matching threshold. In these cases, the system may not be able to determine whether the record is for the same person, and it may not display the information.

Unfortunately, entering too much information can also bring negative results. For example, if you enter a date of birth, middle initial, or Social Security number that conflicts with information reported by the lender, the credit agency's matching system may determine that it probably is not for the same person.

As you can see, the way the inquiry is entered can affect the results of the search, and there may be additional factors about a single inquiry that can make the process more complex, depending upon each credit agency's matching system.

As noted earlier, the matching system or algorithm for each of the credit agencies is unique, and one of their most carefully held secrets. Thus, it is not always apparent why the same inquiry can yield different results from one credit agency reporting system to another, or why entering slightly different inquiries into the same system bring more or less complete results. This can occur not only because of differences in the data held within their files, but due to differences in how the inquiry is processed and the data is matched. For these reasons, one credit agency's system is sometimes preferable to another, given a specific inquiry. It may also be necessary to enter more than one inquiry for a single individual in order to gain the most complete information possible.

Credit Agency Reports

Several types of reports are generated from the credit databases. Some contain credit information and are thereby regulated by the Fair Credit Reporting Act. Others contain what is considered "identifying" information only, without credit information, and are, therefore, unregulated; however, the threat of regulating this type of data is always present and under debate.

The information contained in credit agency reports can be considered unverified. In other words, the credit agency stores the information on its files, but does not generally confirm it unless the consumer disputes the facts of the credit history.

If the consumer fills out a credit application and notes an employer on the form, that information may be entered into the system as part of an inquiry by a lender who is considering extending credit to the individual. The employer's name may then appear in the consumer's file and will be displayed on subsequent reports, although no one has verified that the consumer is actually employed.

There also are occasions when one person's identifying information is similar to another's and their credit histories become mixed.

For these reasons, if a credit report is being used as part of a credit granting or employment decision, it is best to verify all information with the subject, or with independent sources such as creditors and employers.

Consumer Credit History Reports

The consumer credit report contains credit information for an individual. It may also contain certain public records such as bankruptcies, liens, and judgments against a consumer. In addition, some identifying information appears about the consumer. Certain identifiers can always be expected:

- Inquiry information (the information that you entered in order to request the credit report)
- Consumer name
- Consumer address

Several other pieces of identifying information also may be displayed. It should be noted that not one of the three credit agencies stores or displays all of the following information:

- Age
- Year of birth
- Date of birth
- Home telephone number
- Previous addresses
- Employer's name

- Employer's address

- Position

- Salary

- Date on which the employment was first reported

- Date employed

- Date on which the employment was verified

- Previous employer's name

- Previous employer's address

- Marital status

- Number of dependents

- Spouse's first initial or name

- Spouse's Social Security number

- Spouse's employment information

Warning messages may appear for a number of reasons, including suspicion of fraud. They may be displayed if the person has been reported deceased, if the Social Security number lies outside the valid range, or if the address is known to be nonresidential, such as a hospital or jail. Refer to "Fraud/Alert/Prevention/Detection" later in this chapter for further explanation.

If there is credit information on file for the consumer, the credit information displayed may include:

- Reporting credit grantor's name

- Credit grantor's identifier

- Consumer's account number

- Type of account

- Terms of account

- A code to identify the consumer's relationship or association with the account (sometimes referred to as the Equal Credit Opportunity Act code, or ECOA code)

- Date the account was opened

- Balance date

- Date of the consumer's last payment

- Original amount of the loan

- Credit limit

- High balance amount

- Charge-off amount

- Current balance

- Monthly payment amount or estimated monthly payment amount

- Account status

- Status date

- Amount past due

- Payment history

- Collateral

- Original creditor

- Oldest opening date of an account

- Newest reporting date of an account

- Names of those who have inquired about the consumer, their identifiers, their account numbers, dates of the inquiries, and the types, terms, and amounts of their credit lines to the consumer

- Name, address, and telephone number of the credit agency office or credit bureau nearest the consumer's home address (so that the consumer can be referred there to clear up any errors appearing on the report)

- Report messages: these may warn of a variation in the identifying information (such as a transposition in the Social Security number), warn of an invalid ZIP Code, or contain a statement from the consumer (such as when an account is in dispute)

- Summary counts, which may include the number of trade lines displayed, number of public records, total balance of installment loan accounts, total balance of real estate loans, total balance of revolving charge accounts, recent inquiries for the given Social Security number, recent inquiries for the given address, number of times the accounts have been delinquent, total dollars past due for each loan type, and total percentage of revolving credit available to the consumer

- Risk scores (used for evaluating the risk of extending credit to the consumer)

- Names of lenders who appear on the report, their identifiers, their addresses, and telephone numbers

If there is public record information on file for the consumer, the report displayed may include:

- Court name

- Case number

- Filing date

- Plaintiff
- Court code
- Amount
- Type of public record

Employment Reports

The employment report may be essentially the same thing as a credit report. It may appear in a different format, depending upon the credit agency.

A few of the items on the normal credit report are suppressed from the display when the report is pulled for employment purposes:

- Age
- Year of birth
- Date of birth
- Marital status
- Number of dependents
- Account numbers

The credit agency may offer additional pre-employment screening, such as drug testing or employment verification, in addition to this report. This varies by agency.

Collection Reports

The collection report is essentially the same thing as a credit report. It contains the same information as the credit report, in addition to a code indicating that the consumer is repaying bills through debt counseling.

Consumer Reports

Consumer reports are essentially credit reports that are issued to consumers about their own credit history. Refer to the end of this chapter for instructions on requesting a copy of your own credit report.

Address Update Reports

When Address Update reports do not contain credit information, they normally can be purchased without meeting FCRA criteria for permissible purpose. I say "normally" because this seems to lie in a gray area and may be interpreted differently by each of the credit agencies, depending upon what they display on their report. In fact, FCRA standards have at times been applied when Address Update reports have been requested for famous persons, such as highly placed elected officials.

The Address Update report is used to locate people who have moved. It is used by creditors, alumni and charitable associations, along with other organizations. To order this report, you must enter a consumer's name and last known address in order to determine whether there is a more current address on the credit agency's file. The consumer's full identifying information will appear, if found.

This report may also include the addresses and phone numbers of people living near the consumer's current residence. It may include a list of creditors (without the details of the tradelines), an indicator noting that there are public records on file, and an indicator that a bankruptcy is on file.

Figure 25.2 shows an example of an Address Update report. I have taken the liberty of condensing and changing many of the details.

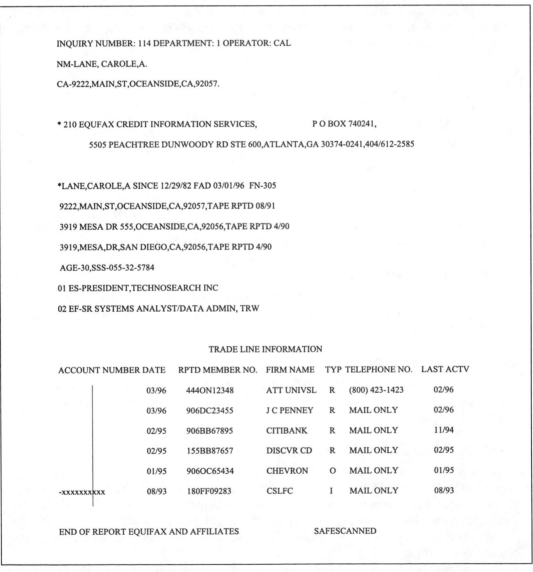

INQUIRY NUMBER: 114 DEPARTMENT: 1 OPERATOR: CAL

NM-LANE, CAROLE,A.

CA-9222,MAIN,ST,OCEANSIDE,CA,92057.

* 210 EQUFAX CREDIT INFORMATION SERVICES,   P O BOX 740241,
        5505 PEACHTREE DUNWOODY RD STE 600,ATLANTA,GA 30374-0241,404/612-2585

*LANE,CAROLE,A SINCE 12/29/82 FAD 03/01/96 FN-305

9222,MAIN,ST,OCEANSIDE,CA,92057,TAPE RPTD 08/91

3919 MESA DR 555,OCEANSIDE,CA,92056,TAPE RPTD 4/90

3919,MESA,DR,SAN DIEGO,CA,92056,TAPE RPTD 4/90

AGE-30,SSS-055-32-5784

01 ES-PRESIDENT,TECHNOSEARCH INC

02 EF-SR SYSTEMS ANALYST/DATA ADMIN, TRW

TRADE LINE INFORMATION

ACCOUNT NUMBER	DATE RPTD	MEMBER NO.	FIRM NAME	TYP	TELEPHONE NO.	LAST ACTV
	03/96	444ON12348	ATT UNIVSL	R	(800) 423-1423	02/96
	03/96	906DC23455	J C PENNEY	R	MAIL ONLY	02/96
	02/95	906BB67895	CITIBANK	R	MAIL ONLY	11/94
	02/95	155BB87657	DISCVR CD	R	MAIL ONLY	02/95
	01/95	906OC65434	CHEVRON	O	MAIL ONLY	01/95
-xxxxxxxxxx	08/93	180FF09283	CSLFC	I	MAIL ONLY	08/93

END OF REPORT EQUIFAX AND AFFILIATES   SAFESCANNED

Figure 25.2   Address update report

Address Verification Reports

Address Verification reports do not contain credit information and are therefore unregulated.

This report often is used by mail order and catalog companies that ship goods to people who place orders using credit cards. The consumer's name, address, and credit card number are entered on the inquiry. A verification message is returned indicating whether the address and credit card number match those on the credit agency's file, and the consumer's full name and address appear, if found.

If the consumer has recently moved, the addresses may not match, so this form of conflict does not necessarily indicate that any type of fraud is being perpetrated. If a match is not found, the shipper is advised to contact the consumer and verify the information prior to shipment.

Social Security Number Search Reports

Social Security Number Search reports do not contain credit information and are therefore unregulated. This report is used in locating people, especially those who have changed their names, due to marriage or other circumstances. Upon entering a Social Security number, the credit agency returns a report listing names and addresses of consumers that it links to that number, along with the rest of their identifying information.

An example of a Social Security Number Search report is shown in Figure 25.3. I have again condensed and changed many of the details.

Fraud Alert/Prevention/Detection Reports

The fraud detection report may be combined with the credit report, or it may be ordered separately. If ordered separately, it does not contain credit information, and is therefore unregulated.

INQUIRY NUMBER: 115 DEPARTMENT: 1 OPERATOR: CAL

DTEC-055-32-5784

SSN ISSUED -72 STATE ISSUED-CA

M1 OF 1 NM-LANE,CAROLE.A CA-9222,MAIN,ST,OCEANSIDE,CA,92057,01/95

FA-3919 MESA DR 555,OCEANSIDE,CA,92056,08/91 ES-PRESIDENT,TECHNOSEARCH INC

SS-055-32-5784

END OF REPORT EQUIFAX AND AFFILIATES

Figure 25.3   Social Security Number Search report

When requesting the fraud detection report, the consumer's name and address is entered, along with the Social Security number, if available. The credit agency checks the address against its files of addresses belonging to hospitals, jails, mail drops, and businesses. It also checks the address against residential addresses that have been used for fraudulent purposes in the past.

If received on the inquiry, the Social Security number is checked to verify that it is within the range issued by the Social Security Administration, that it is a valid number (one that does not contain invalid combinations of digits, such as -00- in the fourth and fifth positions), and that the Social Security Administration does not show the holder as deceased.

Employment information may also be checked against that on file. The telephone number may be checked against a file of invalid or fraudulent numbers.

Counts are also displayed for the number of recent inquiries against the Social Security number and against the address.

Figure 25.4 shows an example of a Fraud Detection summary on an individual who is not committing fraud; it was excerpted from a consumer credit report.

FACS+ SUMMARY:

INPUT SSN ISSUED 1972-1974

FROM 06-01-02 # OF INQS WITH THIS SSN=0

FROM 06-01-02 # OF INQS WITH THIS ADDR=4

Figure 25.4   Fraud Detection summary

Examples of Additional Credit Services

Credit agencies offer additional services for the financial industry. These vary from agency to agency, and the following list is not exhaustive. The agencies often add new services to match or improve on those of the competition.

- A Skip Locator service can be activated to notify a creditor if one of its accounts applies for credit elsewhere or if a new address is placed on the file.

- A Bankruptcy service can be activated to notify a creditor if one of its accounts declares bankruptcy.

- A Signal service continuously monitors accounts according to the creditor's own criteria in order to notify creditors when a consumer's account requires action, such as raising or lowering the credit limit.

Similarly, the credit agency may scan its entire credit files according to the lender's criteria and identify consumers who will then be offered credit. (That is why you may receive offers for pre-approved lines of credit from time to time.) These lists may be further screened by matching against other lists, and psychographic characteristics, in order to identify a targeted market for a company's services or goods.

- Collection letters may be sent to delinquent consumers on the creditor's behalf.

- A Credit Watch service regularly provides consumers with a copy of their own credit reports and/or notifies them if someone inquires about their credit or reports a derogatory line of credit for them.

- An instant update service allows a creditor to flag an account immediately when a problem arises.

- A Positive ID service is offered (to public utility companies) to verify the identity of a consumer. If the Social Security number is not found or matched, the Department of Motor Vehicles records may be accessed for verification. A G.A.D. (Government Agency Disclosure)/Motor Vehicle Report may also be offered (to investigative companies) to verify identity.

- Tenant screening services are offered to landlords and property management companies.

- Insurance personal property claim records are used to assist insurance underwriters in processing claims and detecting fraud.

- One service, Verifind, helps to locate owners of unclaimed assets— lost depositors, shareholders, and policyholders.

Credit Bureaus

As mentioned earlier, hundreds of credit bureaus offer information from the three national credit agencies. Many have access to reports from all three agencies. In order to make these reports easier for their clients to read, some bureaus edit the credit information into a standard format, so that their clients do not have to learn to read the differing reports from Equifax, TransUnion, and Experian.

Another option that credit bureaus sometimes offer is to pull credit reports from one, two, or all three credit agencies and combine them into a single report, in order to furnish a more complete credit profile.

Credit bureaus may also collect credit or public record information, provide independent verification services such as employment or education verification, or in other ways add value to the information provided by the credit agencies.

Consumer Rights

If you are concerned about your credit records, you can request a copy of your credit reports by contacting each of the credit agencies and following their procedures. If you have recently been denied credit, employment, or insurance due to the information provided on your credit report, each agency will furnish a copy of its report for free.

If you see an error on your credit record, you may contact the credit agency, which will then verify the information by checking with the source. If whoever reported the information agrees that there has been an error, the record will be deleted from your credit report. If they insist that the information is correct, you may either take your dispute to the creditor for resolution or write a short statement explaining the dispute to the credit agency and ask that it be placed on your credit record.

Requesting a Copy of Your Credit Report

Equifax

If you have been denied credit, employment, or insurance within the last 60 days due to the information provided by Equifax, you may request a free copy of your Equifax credit report by calling (800)997-2493, and following their instructions for automated or mail-in requests. You may also order through their Internet site at www.equifax.com. Mail-in requests should be sent to:

Equifax Inc.
P.O. Box 105496
Atlanta, Georgia 30348-5496

For mail-in requests, you will need to furnish:

- Full name (including Jr., Sr., II)

- Social Security number

- Current and previous addresses within the last five years

- Date of birth

- Signature

- Telephone number (home)

I still suggest calling first, as the company's voice system provides specific instructions, and the mailing address does change periodically. This information should be verified before sending your request.

If you have not been denied credit recently, you may request a copy of your Equifax credit report by writing to the preceding address, furnishing the same information, and including the required fee of $8, or ordering via the Internet. If your spouse would also like a copy of the report, this must be requested separately.

TransUnion

You may request a free copy of your credit report through TransUnion's interactive voice response system or via mail, if you meet either of these criteria:

1. You have been denied credit, employment, or insurance in the last 60 days, and the company used a TransUnion credit report.

2. You are a resident of Colorado, Georgia, Massachusetts, Maryland, New Jersey, or Vermont.

If you meet one of these criteria, you may order your credit report by calling (800)888-4213 or via mail to the address below.

Whether or not you qualify for a free report, you may request a copy of your TransUnion credit report by writing to:

TransUnion LLC
Consumer Disclosure Center
P.O. Box 1000
Chester, PA 19022

For mail-in requests, you will need to furnish the following:

- First, middle and last name (including Jr., Sr., III)

- Current address

- Previous addresses in the past two years, if any

- Social Security number

- Date of birth

- Current employer

- Phone number

- Signature

- Applicable fee

The fee varies by location of residence:

- California $8.00

- Connecticut $5.00

- Maine $2.00

- Minnesota $3.00

- Virgin Islands $1.00

- Other states $8.50

If you are a resident of a state other than Colorado, Georgia, Maryland, Massachusetts, New Jersey, or Vermont, you may also order your credit report via the Internet at www.transunion.com.

Experian (Formerly TRW)

If you have been denied credit, employment, or insurance within the last 60 days, based on your Experian credit report, you may request a free copy of your credit report. You also are entitled to one free report every 12 months upon request if you can certify one of the following:

1. You are unemployed and plan to seek employment within 60 days.

2. You are on welfare.

3. Your report is inaccurate due to fraud.

You may order your report by calling (888)EXPERIAN (888-397-3742), or by writing to:

Experian National Consumer Assistance Center
P.O. Box 2104
Allen, TX 75013-2104

For a mail-in request, you must furnish:

- Your full name (including generation, such as Jr., Sr., III)

- Current address

- City, state, zip

- Social Security number

- Date of birth

- If you've lived at your current address less than five years, you will also need to list your previous addresses for a five-year period

- Spouse's first name (if married)

- Your signature

- The appropriate fee

The fee for your credit report varies by state:

- California $8

- Connecticut $5 for your first copy each year (plus $.30 tax); $7.50 for additional copies (plus $.45 tax)

- Colorado $8 (plus $.28 tax for Denver residents); you also are entitled to a free report each calendar year

- Georgia $8; you also are entitled to two free reports each calendar year

- Hawaii $8 (plus $.32 tax)

- Illinois $8 (plus $.48 tax for Chicago residents)

- Maine $2

- Massachusetts $8; you also are entitled to a free report each calendar year

- Maryland $5 (plus $.25 tax); you also are entitled to a free report each calendar year

- Minnesota $3

- New Jersey $8; you also are entitled to a free report each 12-month period

- New Mexico $8 (plus $.40 tax)

- New York $8 (plus $.66 tax)

- South Carolina $8 (plus $.40 tax)

- South Dakota $8 (plus $.48 tax)

- Texas $8 (plus $.66 tax)

- Vermont $7.50; you also are entitled to a free report each calendar year

- Washington DC $8 (plus $.46 tax)

- West Virginia $8 (plus $.48 tax)

You may also order your credit report through Experian's Web site at www.experian.com.

Foreign Consumer Credit Records

Many credit agencies operate outside of the United States. In order to obtain foreign credit records, you can call or write to the foreign credit agency, or to the credit agency in your own country, in order to have them obtain and send the records. Gaining online access to foreign credit systems is seldom possible from within the United States. Neither do the United States credit agencies allow direct access to their systems from outside of the United States. However, they will send credit records upon request, so long as the inquiry meets the permissible-purpose requirements of the FCRA. Figure 25.5 shows examples of foreign credit agencies.

Limitations on the Records Displayed on Credit Reports

There are legal limitations on what can be included on a credit report, and the length of time that it can appear. These limitations are defined in the Fair Credit Reporting Act and include the following:

- Bankruptcies (under Title 11) must not remain on the report for more than ten years after the date of adjudication or order for relief.

- Lawsuits and judgments must not remain on the report for more than seven years after the date of entry or until the governing statute of limitation expires, whichever is longer.

- Paid tax liens must not remain on the report for more than seven years after payment.

Argentina
Experian
Reconquista 672
Piso 8
(C1003ABN) Buenos Aires
Argentina
Tel: (54) 11 4311 1267
Fax: (54) 11 4312 2721

Experian Argentina (formerly Fidelitas SA)
Reconquista 661
Piso 4
1003 Buenos Aires
Argentina
Tel: (54) 11 4315 6700
Fax: (54) 11 4315 6690

Organizacion Veraz S.A. (in partnership with
Equifax)
Tacuarí 202, 1º Piso
(C1071AAF) Buenos Aires, Argentina
Telefax 4348-4300
www.veraz.com.ar

Australia
Experian
Level 5
553 St. Kilda Road
Melbourne 3004
Australia
(61) 3 9249 9888
Fax (61) 3 9521 3645

Experian
Suite A
6th Floor
100 Arthur Street
North Sydney
NSW 2060
Australia
Tel: (61) 2 9409 9888
Fax: (61) 2 9954 5708

Austria
Experian Deutschland GmbH
Kaiserstrasse 84
Stiege 1
Tür 4
1070 Wien
Austria
Tel: (43) 1 524 91 981
Fax: (43) 1 524 91 989

Belgium
Experian

Kotrijksesteenweg 400 d
B-9000 Gent
Belgium
(32) 9 244 6340
Fax (32) 9 244 6341

Brazil
SCI Equifax
R Sertório,Maj, 332, VL Buarque,
São Paulo, SP, 01222000
Telephone: (0XX11)-2369000
Telephone: 0800 118854
Fax: (0XX11)-2590631
www.sci.com.br/indexb3.htm

Experian Brasil Ltda
Av. Roque Petroni Jr. 999
13 andar
Sao Paulo - SP
04707-910
Brasil
Tel: (55) 11 5185 2806
Fax: (55) 11 5185 2899

Canada
Equifax/Creditel Inc.
Box 190 Jean Talon Station
Montreal, Quebec H1S 2Z2
(800) 465-7166
(514) 493-2314
Fax (514) 355-8502
www.equifax.ca

Experian
170 University Ave
Suite 502
Toronto, Ontario M5H 3B3
Tel: (1) 416 593 7906
Fax: (1) 416 593 7909

TransUnion Canada, Inc.
170 Jackson ST East
Hamilton, Ontario Canada
L8N3K8
(905) 525-0262

Chile
DICOM (Equifax)
Miraflores
353 Pisos 6, 7 y 8
Santiago, Chile
638-1573
Fax 633-1573
https://www.dicom.cl/

El Salvador

DICOM CENTROAMERICA S.A. (partially
owned by Equifax)
San Salvador
El Salvador
(503) 278-5000

France

Experian
85 Avenue Piere Grenier
92517 Boulogne-Billancourt Cedex
France
(33) 1 46 10 53 00
Fax (33) 1 46 10 53 49
www.experian.fr

Germany

Experian Deutschland
Airport Center - Haus D
Flughafenstr. 52b
22335 Hamburg
(49) 40 53 28 99 0
Fax (49) 40 53 28 99 33 (March 1998)
www.experian.de

Hong Kong

Experian
Suite 806, 8th Floor,
AXA Centre,
151 Gloucester Road,
Wanchai,
Hong Kong
Tel: (852) 2722 5037
Fax: (852) 2877 7803

India

Equifax Venture Infotek Limited (EVI)
3, A to Z Industrial Estate,
Lower Parel,
Mumbai - 400 013,
Maharashtra State,
India.
91 22 498 3257 (Dir.)
91 22 496 8983/84 (EPABX)
Fax 91 22 497 4941
www.evi-india.com

Italy

Experian
Galleria Passarella, 1
Scala ovest, 6 piano
20122 Milan
Italy

Tel: (39) 02 777 113 1
Fax: (39) 02 777 113 208

Experian
Cinecitta 2
Palazzo Experian
Via U Quintavalle 68
00173 Rome
Italy
Tel: (39) 06 724 221
Fax: (39) 06 7242 2480

Japan

Central Communications Bureau Inc. (CCB)
Chiyoda-ku, Tokyo
Japan

Mexico

Datacredit (a joint venture of Experian)
Mexico

Equifax de Mexico, S.A.
Monterrey, Mexico

Monaco

Experian Scorex SAM
Athos Palace
2 Rue de la Lujernetta
MC98000
Monaco
(377) 97 98 54 54
Fax (377) 97 98 54 55 (March 1998)
www.experian-scorex.com

Netherlands

Experian Nederland
Savannah Tower
Savannahweg No. 17
3542 AW Utrecht
(31) 30 2 41 71 11
Fax (31) 30 2 41 71 00
www.experian.nl

New Zealand

Equifax New Zealand
P.O. Box 5446
Wellesley Street
Wellington
New Zealand
www.equifax.co.nz
0800 730 740

Peru

Infocorp Equifax
www.infocorp.com.pe

Philippines
Experian
11/F PSE Bldg.
East Tower, Suite 1109
Ortigas Centre
Pasig City
Philippines
(632) 635 42 53
(632) 635 42 57
Fax (632) 635 42 98

Portugal
Credinformações-Informações de Crédito
Lda
Av Praia Vit² 71,4°-A - Lisboa
1050-183 LISBOA
Portugal
213 112 600
213 112 666

Experian
Centro Empresarial Sintra Nascentre Ed 14
Av Almirange Gago Coutinho 132/134
2710 Sintra
Portugal
Tel: (351) 21 910 5590
Fax: (351) 21 910 5595

South Africa
Experian
Experian House
The Ambridge
Vrede Avenue
Douglasdale
Sandton 2021
Johannesburg
South Africa
(courier address)
or
PO Box 98183
Sloane Park 2152
South Africa
(postal address)
Tel: (27) 11 799 3400
Fax: (27) 11 463 3985

Spain
ASNEF/Equifax
www.asnefequifax.es

Experian Bureau de Crédito
Orense, 58
28020 Madrid
Spain

Tel: (34) 91 417 9350
Fax: (34) 91 555 6929

Turkey
Kredi Kayit Burosü (a partner of Experian)
Istanbul
Turkey

United Kingdom
Experian
39 Houndsditch
London EC3A 7DB
(44) 171 623 5551
Fax (44) 171 621 9596

Experian
Talbot House
Talbot Street
Nottingham
NG1 5HF
United Kingdom

Infocheck-Equifax UK
Capital House
25 Chapel Street
London, NW1 5DS
0171 298 3000
Fax 0171 723 1999
www.infocheck.co.uk
or
708 20th Floor, 3rd Avenue
New York, NY 10017
(800) 729-9054
Fax (212) 867-3212 (March 1998)
www.equifax.co.uk

Figure 25.5   Foreign credit agencies

- Collection or charged-off accounts must not remain on the report for more than seven years.

- Records of arrest, indictment, or conviction of a crime must not remain on the report for more than seven years after the date of disposition, release, or parole.

- Any other adverse item must not remain on the report for more than seven years.

However, the FCRA does make some exceptions to these rules.

Other factors may also limit the information displayed on a credit report. For example, smaller creditors may not report to any of the credit agencies, or may report to only one or two rather than all three. Some do not report all of their accounts on a monthly basis, instead reporting only those accounts that are late or unpaid. If a credit agency believes that a creditor's records contain too many errors, it may choose not to accept records from that source. In an effort to assure that the date limitations of the FCRA are adhered to, a credit agency may choose to purge records at some time before the required date.

Public records may not be collected from certain courts or jurisdictions and, therefore, are not represented on the credit report. Errors can occur when these records are collected, and some may be missed as a result. There also may be a delay in the collection of these records or in placing them on the credit files.

Summary

Although credit reports provide a great deal of valuable information, they do not represent a complete picture of a person's worthiness for credit, employment, or insurance. Studies have shown that 50 percent or more of the credit reports pulled contain errors. For these reasons, any information shown on a credit report should be verified before a decision is based upon it.

Chapter 26

Criminal Justice Records

Facts, Hercule, facts! Nothing matters but the facts.
Without them the science of criminal investigation is
nothing more than a guessing game.

–Inspector Jacques Clouseau, *A Shot in the Dark*

According to the FBI's Uniform Crime Reports, approximately 11.6 million crime index offenses were committed in 2000: 15,517 people were murdered; 90,186 forcible rapes occurred; there were 407,842 robberies and approximately 2 million burglaries; and 910,744 aggravated assaults took place. An estimated 14 million arrests (excluding traffic violations) were made during this period.

Every one of these crimes triggered a long and complex series of procedures designed first to catch and then to convict the criminal, documenting the process at every step of the way. At the crime scene and in the following hours and days, investigators gather evidence, take statements from witnesses, weigh the results of forensic tests, and search through criminal histories contained in computerized databases to find possible suspects. Physical evidence such as fingerprints, hair, body fluids, and fibers may be gathered, and can even be computer matched against other samples already in databases from prior arrests. From the arrest, through pretrial hearings, perhaps a grand jury hearing, the trial itself, and sentencing, each agency involved in the case may start its own file, search databases for records at the local level as well as in the state repository and perhaps even the FBI's Interstate Identification Index, and draw its own conclusion. When the convict is committed to prison, and when he or she is eventually released, still more records are created.

Although some of these databases are accessible only to law enforcement personnel, your knowledge of them will give you a better idea of the types and amount of personal information that are being gathered in computerized form. In addition, many of the records created throughout the criminal justice processes are matters of public record and can be accessed by anyone for any reason. For example, court documents are, for the most part, public records. When looking for criminal records, you will find Court Dockets and Criminal Record Indices are available online for many areas of the country. Case Transcripts and Case Summaries may also include details of criminal cases. Please refer to Chapter 31: Public Records for further information about these records and databases. Additional information on criminal cases may be found in the news. Please refer to Chapter 20 for information on news databases. Although criminal court records are not typically made available online in full text, computer indices to these records are very useful when searching for records of past crimes and seeking the location of the physical files.

A new development in criminal justice is the introduction of the Webcam, allowing Internet surfers to come inside jails via camera, viewing prisoners, guards, and visitors live. Crime.com (www.crime.com) provides "jail cams," featuring various views inside Maricopa County jail in Phoenix, Arizona. Crime.com also provides the latest crime news, Sex Offender databases, Most Wanted photos, and data for various cities across the country, crime statistics and demographics, information on all of the prisons in the U.S., and a variety of other crime information.

Criminal Justice Databases

The Department of Justice is a huge organization, made up of over 38 separate component departments, and describing the databases used within its framework is no small task. In fact, the department spends $1.5 billion on information technology each year. This tremendous expenditure pays for administrative functions, but most of it is spent on information systems and databases that are primarily used to gather information about people.

During the course of our lifetimes, there is a fairly good chance that at least one of these systems will contain some information about almost all of us. Even the most law-abiding citizens can experience the theft of a vehicle or a home break-in, or witness other crimes. We are all candidates for inclusion in a criminal justice database. This does not mean that any single database holds information about all of us, however. Thus far, each law enforcement agency maintains its own systems, and information passes between them only under narrowly controlled conditions.

Many criminal justice systems use proprietary technology that makes it difficult to exchange information. Much information is exchanged manually by copying and sending documents, making telephone calls, or meeting with other law enforcement personnel. In order to streamline operations, and provide greater efficiency and effectiveness, information systems are now being developed with interoperability in mind.

What follows is a partial list of databases used in law enforcement that contain personal records, emphasizing those in general use, those with far-reaching impact on criminal justice, and those I found to be the most interesting in my search for personal data.

Advance Passenger Information System

The Advance Passenger Information System (APIS) allows inspectors to conduct computer queries on U.S.-bound passengers while their flights are still en route. This system is supported by the Interagency Border Inspection System (IBIS), which links databases of several inspection agencies. Further information about this system can be found on the U.S. Customs Service Web sites at www.customs.gov/impoexpo/tools/archives/vol2n02/apismgr.htm and www.customs.gov/impoexpo/tools/archives/vol2n01/moujul.htm.

Automated Fingerprint Identification System

Fingerprints are scanned into the Automated Fingerprint Identification System (AFIS), where ridge details and other identifying characteristics are digitized in such detail that the system can find a match among the millions of fingerprints previously scanned. Card-scan devices can be used to enter standard inked fingerprint cards into the system. Live-scan devices can capture fingerprint images directly from subjects' fingers, which are rolled onto scanning pads. The AFIS equipment can also lift a latent fingerprint at a crime scene. These advances make it possible to capture, scan, and transmit fingerprints from a squad car or crime scene to the AFIS, match the prints against those in the database, and transmit the results back to the officer in the field.

The AFIS is due to be incorporated into the FBI's Integrated Automated Fingerprint Identification System, which will be made up of the three segments: the Automated Fingerprint Identification System (AFIS) segment, the Interstate Identification Index (III) segment, and the Identification, Tasking, and Networking (ITN) segment.

Booking Logs

Law enforcement agencies normally create daily written records of suspects who are booked. These records may show up in the local newspaper, in a police database, or even on the Internet. For example, the Booking Log for San Diego County, providing name, sex, race, and date of birth of all suspects who are booked, can be found at www.co.san-diego.ca.us/cnty/cntydepts/safety/sheriff/bookings.html. The booking log for Gwinnett County, Georgia can be found at www.gwinnettcountysheriff.com/Docket%20Book.htm.

Carnivore System

Carnivore is the FBI's Internet wiretap system. Carnivore is attached either when law enforcement has a court order under the Electronic Communications Privacy Act (ECPA) permitting it to intercept in real time the contents of the electronic communications of a specific individual, or allowing it to obtain the "numbers" related to communications from or to a specified target.

Unlike a traditional wiretap of a conventional phone line, Carnivore gives the FBI access to all traffic over the ISP's network, not just the communications to or from a particular target. Carnivore, which is capable of analyzing millions of messages per second, purportedly retains only the messages of the specified target. Further information about Carnivore can be found at the FBI's Web site at www.fbi.gov/hq/lab/carnivore/carnivore.htm.

Central Repository

All 50 states, Puerto Rico, and the District of Columbia have established central repositories for their criminal history records. These repositories are state databases used to maintain criminal history records of those arrested for felonies or serious misdemeanors. (The definition of a felony and a serious misdemeanor can vary from state to state, so reporting is not always consistent.) According to a survey conducted by SEARCH for the Bureau of Justice Statistics, more than 59 million individual offenders were included in state central repositories by the end of 1999. Records of reportable arrests and their eventual disposition are maintained within the central repositories. Disposition data can include decisions by the police to drop all charges, the prosecutor's decision not to prosecute, court decisions such as convictions and sentences, confinement in a correctional facility, or release from incarceration.

Each central repository includes a Master Name Index (MNI), which has been automated in most states. The MNI identifies each individual whose criminal records appear in the repository. Some contain a felony flag, which indicates whether the individual has arrests or convictions for felony offenses. When the MNI contains a felony flag, it can be especially useful for such purposes as presale firearm checks, criminal investigations, or setting bail.

Federal regulations exclude traffic violations and certain other petty offenses from these "criminal history records" in systems built or operated with Federal funds, so few state repositories maintain them. Juvenile offenses were omitted until 1992 (except where the juvenile was tried as an adult), but they are now included in some of the state repositories. Neither records of

Federal offenses nor records from other states are included. When a local agency requests a national record check, the request is routed from the central repository to the FBI.

Consolidated Asset Tracking System (CATS)

CATS is a multiagency computer system managed by the Asset Forfeiture Management Staff, JMD. CATS provides a consolidated asset forfeiture database for both administrative and judicial cases. This is used to track information and support operations in all of the asset forfeiture program's business functions, including seizure, custody, notification, forfeiture, claims, petitions, equitable sharing, official use, and disposal.

Further information about CATS can be found at the U.S. Department of Justice site at www.usdoj.gov:80/oig/i9702/i9702p1.htm.

Combined DNA Index System (CODIS)

CODIS consists of national and regional DNA databases that assist in investigating sex offenses and violent crime. It is accessible through the NDIS, the National DNA Index System. This is a combined effort of the FBI and state DNA laboratories, and has been installed in over 100 laboratories in 47 states, as of 2001.

DNA can be obtained from a wide range of body fluids and other materials, including blood, semen, mouth swabs, body hair, and many other materials. DNA extracted from one of these samples is unique to an individual, with the exception of identical twins; unlike fingerprints and other identifying characteristics, it remains unchanged throughout a person's lifetime. The CODIS databases consist of data representations of DNA profiles; no medical samples are stored.

CODIS uses two indices to generate investigative leads where biological evidence is recovered. The Convicted Offender Index contains DNA profiles of those convicted of felony sex crimes and other violent crimes. The Forensic Index contains DNA profiles from crime scene evidence such as samples of hair, semen, or blood where victims or suspects have not yet been identified. There is also a Population File, which contains DNA types and allele frequency data from anonymous persons intended to represent major population groups found in the United States. This database is used to estimate statistical frequencies of DNA profiles.

In the future, additional indices will be added to CODIS: The Victims Index will contain DNA records from victims, living or dead, from whom DNA may have been carried away by perpetrators. The Unidentified Persons Index will contain DNA from body parts, human remains, and individuals who do not disclose their identities to police. The Unidentified Persons Reference Index will contain DNA records from missing persons and their close biological relatives.

Further information about CODIS can be found on the FBI's Web site at www.fbi.gov/congress/congress00/dadams.htm or at www.fbi.gov/hq/lab/codis/indexl.htm.

A similar database, the National DNA Database (NDNAD), has been developed in Britain. The Criminal Justice and Public Order Act 1994 empowered British police to take biological samples from people charged with, or reported for, recordable offenses including murder, attempted murder, manslaughter, sexual offenses, and other crimes. Since that time, DNA databases have been developed, or are under development in other countries throughout the world, including China, Austria, Canada, Scotland, and Australia.

Counterdrug Information Indices System (DRUGX)

This joint FBI-Drug Enforcement Administration (DEA) drug index database serves as a pointer to enable investigators in Federal agencies to obtain and share information on drug-related cases. Additional information about this, and many other FBI databases and programs, can be found on their Web site at www.usdoj.gov/jmd/orginfo/irm/irm_majend.html.

Criminal Records

Court records of criminal cases are stored throughout the courts and record halls of America. A growing number of these records are now indexed on databases, making it possible for anyone to locate them using the databases of a public records or legal database vendor. Background checks and employment screening typically include searches of criminal records for each county in which a subject is known to have lived. As not all of these records are yet automated, it may still be necessary to conduct manual records searches and to order copies of the original case documents in order to gain a full understanding of the details of a case. Please refer to Chapter 31: Public Records for further explanation of criminal records that are accessible to the public.

Many courts have created Internet sites at which you can find instructions for obtaining records. Record indices may also be searched through these sites in the future. There is an index to court-related Web sites, which can be found at the National Criminal Justice Reference Service at www.ncjrs.org/courwww.html.

Another index, including state, Federal, and even international court sites, can be found at the National Center for State Courts Web site, located at www.ncsconline.org/Information/info_court_web_sites.html.

El Paso Intelligence Center Database (EPIC)

For more than 20 years, the El Paso Intelligence Center (EPIC) has maintained the Drug Enforcement Agency's database of drug dealers and traffickers, used by Federal, state, and local law enforcement agencies. EPIC has agreements for data exchange and analysis of information with other Federal agencies involved in reducing the flow of drugs, supporting law enforcement in all 50 States, the District of Columbia, Guam, Puerto Rico, the U.S. Virgin Islands, American Samoa, the U.S. Forest Service, National Marine Fisheries, Bureau of Prisons, Amtrak, and the Department of Defense, as well as 20 foreign countries.

Additional information about EPIC can be found on the U.S. Department of Justice site at www.usdoj.gov/dea/programs/epic.htm.

Escapees

There are now escapee databases and Web sites accessible through the Internet. For example, the Colorado Department of Corrections (www.doc.state.co.us) provides an Escapee database on its site. So do the Departments of Correction for the following states:

North Carolina
www.doc.state.nc.us

Oregon
www.doc.state.or.us (in their Absconds and Escapees site)

South Carolina
www.state.sc.us/scdc (in their Fugitives database)

South Dakota
www.state.sd.us/corrections/corrections.html

Tennessee
www.state.tn.us/correction

The Automated Biometric Identification System (IDENT)

IDENT is an electronic system that stores fingerprints and photos of people caught trying to enter the country illegally. It is designed primarily to flag criminals and people who repeatedly try to cross the border illegally, and to share the Immigration and Naturalization Service's information with other law enforcement agencies.

Information about IDENT can be found on the U.S. Immigration and Naturalization Service Web site at www.ins.usdoj.gov/graphics/aboutins/foia/ereadrm/reference/majorinfosys/ident_9.htm.

The Inappropriate Communications/Threat Information System (IC/TIS)

The IC/TIS system contains identifying information and background data on persons who have directly threatened or pose a violent threat to people protected by the U.S. Marshall Service, information concerning the threat, and threat-related investigative information. This system is used to plan and carry out security operations for the protection of Federal judges, court officials, witnesses, and jurors.

Further information about IC/TIS can be found at the U.S. Marshall Service's Web site at www.usdoj.gov:80/marshals/readingroom/ic-tis.html.

Inmate Databases

Of course, police and corrections agencies maintain records of who they have incarcerated, but you may not have realized that some of these agencies have posted them on the Internet as well. One such site, Who's In Jail—Sheriff's Inmate Log for San Diego, California, allows searching by inmate name or inmate number, and provides name, sex, race, and date of birth of the inmate. You can find this site at www.co.san-diego.ca.us/cnty/cntydepts/safety/sheriff/whosin.html.

The Georgia Department of Corrections also provides an Offender Query, allowing you to search for prison inmates and view photos, physical descriptions, lists of offenses, and incarceration history at http://fugitives.dcor.state.ga.us/default.html.

The Illinois Department of Corrections provides an Inmate Search on its site at www.idoc. state.il.us/inmates/search.htm.

The Michigan Department of Corrections offers access to its Offender Tracking Information System on its site, located at www.state.mi.us/mdoc/asp/otis1.html, while the Indiana Department of Corrections provides an Offender Search at www.IN.gov/indcorrection.

The Minnesota and Pennsylvania Departments of Corrections offer Offender Locators on sites at http://info.doc.state.mn.us/publicviewer/main.asp and www.cor.state.pa.us/locator.html, respectively.

North Carolina provides a Search for offenders at www.doc.state.nc.us/offenders.

The Ohio Department of Rehabilitation and Correction provides a list of Inmates on Death Row at its site at www.drc.state.oh.us/public/deathrow.htm.

For Federal inmates, the Federal Bureau of Prisons provides a searchable inmate database at its Web site www.bop.gov.

INS Passenger Accelerated Service System (INSPASS)

The INS Passenger Accelerated Service System (INSPASS) was first introduced in 1993. The INSPASS kiosk, which is similar to an automated bank teller machine, uses a hand geometry biometric image to validate the identity of travelers, query requisite databases, and record the results of the inspection. This is meant to speed the inspection of frequent travelers who enroll in the system and receive a special card, and to speed the flow of legal traffic through U.S ports-of-entry.

Further information about INSPASS can be found on the U.S. Immigration and Naturalization Service Web site at www.ins.usdoj.gov/graphics/publicaffairs/factsheets/passfs.htm.

Integrated Automated Fingerprint Identification System (IAFIS)

The Integrated Automated Fingerprint Identification System (IAFIS) is being developed by the FBI for state-of-the-art fingerprint identification and criminal history data services. It is expected to improve dramatically the fingerprint processing services that the FBI provides to 72,000 Federal, state, and local law enforcement and criminal justice agencies. The IAFIS project is divided into three major segments: the Identification Tasking and Networking (ITN) system, the Interstate Identification Index (III), and the Automated Fingerprint Identification System (AFIS). Additional information about IAFIS can be found on the FBI Web site at www.fbi.gov/pressrel/pressrel99/iafis.htm.

Interagency Border Inspection System (IBIS)

The Interagency Border Inspection System (IBIS) is an automated lookout system that links the databases of several inspection agencies, including airports, land border ports, and seaports. This is aimed at strengthening the country's security against terrorists, drug traffickers, and criminals. IBIS also supports the Advance Passenger Information System. Further information about IBIS can be found by searching for IBIS on the U.S. Customs Service site at www.customs. gov/travel/ travel.htm.

The Interpol-U.S. National Central Bureau System

Interpol maintains an interrelated electronic and computerized communications system, which is spread across the United States and around the world. Interpol's U.S. National Central Bureau has developed a system in which known felons who have been indicted in U.S. District Courts for distribution of narcotics or money laundering, but who have evaded prosecution by fleeing the country, can be entered into the Interpol network in order to assist in locating them and returning them to the United States.

Additional information about Interpol and its 178 NCBs around the world can be found on the Interpol Web site at www.interpol.int.

Interstate Identification Index (III)

The FBI's Interstate Identification Index (III) holds information about persons arrested for felonies or serious misdemeanors under state or Federal law. The index includes identifying information, FBI numbers, and State Identification numbers (SIDs) from each state or Federal file holding information about an individual. According to the Bureau of Justice Statistics, 41 states were members of the Interstate Identification Index by April 2000. States that do not participate in the

III may still voluntarily submit records to be stored in the FBI files, which may then be searched as part of the III process.

When an III inquiry is received and a matching record is found, the III automatically sends a record request to the state repository holding the information about the person.

The III is one of the three databases utilized by the National Instant Criminal Background Check System (NICS), which is the system that provides information to gun dealers prior to allowing a potential customer to purchase a firearm. Additional information about NICS can be found by searching the FBI Web site at www.fbi.gov/search.

The Jewelry and Gem Database

The Major Theft/Transportation Crimes Unit at FBI Headquarters maintains a computerized database of jewelry thefts and robberies as reported by law enforcement agencies and the jewelry industry. Suspect descriptions and images, modus operandi, and stolen jewelry descriptions and images all are analyzed in an effort to link isolated and seemingly disparate crimes. Additional information about this database can be found on the FBI Web site at www.fbi.gov/hq/cid/jag/database.htm.

Joint Automated Booking System (JABS)

The Joint Automated Booking System (JABS) is a Department of Justice initiative to develop a nationwide automated booking system. Its primary goal is to streamline the identification and processing of Federal offenders throughout the criminal justice system. The idea is to minimize the processing time for booking an offender, eliminate redundant data collection, provide accurate information in a timely manner, and facilitate information sharing among Federal law enforcement entities. JABS provides an electronic means to collect, store, and transmit photographic, fingerprint, and biographical data on offenders when they are booked.

To check the progress of the Joint Automated Booking System, search for announcements on the U.S. Department of Justice Web site at http://search.usdoj.gov/compass or at the U.S. Marshall Service Web site at www.usdoj.gov:80/marshals/readingroom/jointa.html.

Judicial Protection Information System (JPIS)

The Judicial Protection Information System (JPIS) contains records on U.S. Marshall Service protectees who have been directly threatened or are subject to violent threat and consists of identifying data and other personal information, district, information on the type and source of threat, how the threat was made, and the expenditure of funds and allocation of resources related to the threat.

Additional information about JPIS can be found on the U.S. Marshall Service Web site at www.usdoj.gov:80/marshals/readingroom/judpro.html.

Justice Detainee Information System (JDIS)

The Justice Detainee Information System (JDIS) consolidates four USMS applications: Warrant Information Network (WIN), Prisoner Tracking System (PTS), Automated Prisoner Scheduling System (APSS), and Automated Booking System (ABS) to produce a centralized database containing the majority of prisoner data records collected by the U.S. Marshall Service. JDIS is currently in development mode.

For further information, check the U.S. Marshall Service Web site at www.usdoj.gov:80/marshals/readingroom/jusdet.html.

Motor Vehicle Records

Law enforcement officers regularly use driver's license data, driving histories, motor vehicle registrations, and other Motor Vehicle Records (MVR) data. For further information on this data, please refer to Chapter 27: Department of Motor Vehicles.

National Crime Information Center (NCIC)

First established by the FBI in 1967, the National Crime Information Center (NCIC) is a system used by all branches of law enforcement, as well as criminal justice agencies. The NCIC system contains information about wanted, missing, and unidentified persons (such as children, amnesia victims, and unidentified dead bodies). These records are used for criminal history searches, which may be included in the pre-employment screening process for criminal justice employment, employment by a federally chartered or insured banking institution or securities firm, or by state or local governments. NCIC is also used as part of the background screening process for licensing pursuant to a state statute approved by the U.S. Attorney General.

The National Child Search Act of 1990 requires that law enforcement agencies immediately accept all reports concerning a missing child and enter a record with the child's description into NCIC. That information then becomes available to all of law enforcement throughout the United States, Puerto Rico, the U.S. Virgin Islands, and Canada.

NCIC also includes several other types of records. It catalogs burned, decomposed, and skeletonized remains in order to provide a central clearinghouse for unidentified remains found by different agencies, and to aid in the identification of victims in the event of a catastrophe. It records stolen items, including vehicles, license plates, boats, guns, articles of personal property, and securities. It contains a file of Canadian warrants, as well as warrants of deportation for wanted criminal aliens. The Secret Service protective file (also part of NCIC) provides information on individuals who may pose a threat to the President or other authorized protectees.

More recent enhancements (NCIC 2000, which went live in July of 1999), added images to NCIC, including mugshots of suspects, tattoos, crime scenes, evidence, and fingerprints. These changes improved law enforcement's ability to convey and access these types of information whenever and wherever needed. Also added were enhanced name searching capabilities, a search of right index-finger prints, sexual offenders, persons on probation or parole, persons incarcerated in Federal prisons, and various other improvements to the previous system. Since the introduction of NCIC 2000, this system encompasses 17 databases. Further information about NCIC2000 can be found at www.fbi.gov/pressrel/pressrel99/ncic2000.htm.

National Drug Pointer Index System (NDPIX)

The National Drug Pointer Index System (NDPIX) is a pointer system developed by the Drug Enforcement Administration (DEA) to allow participating Federal, state, and local agencies to determine whether a current drug investigative suspect is under active investigation by other participating agencies. Additional information about the NDPIX can be found on the DEA Web site at www.dea.gov/programs/ndpix.htm.

National Fingerprint File (NFF)

The National Fingerprint File (NFF) contains fingerprints of all the individuals in the Interstate Identification Index (III), described earlier in this chapter. The NFF can be searched to identify individuals who give false names to police or employers in an attempt to hide their criminal pasts.

National Incident-Based Reporting System (NIBRS)

The National Indicent-Based Reporting System (NIBRS) is a long-range effort to modernize law enforcement data collection in order to provide a truer, more complete picture of crime. It is currently being used in several states and tested in others, but it is not expected to be completely online until 2010.

The 52 distinct data elements to be collected under NIBRS will include much more detailed information about the criminal offense, the victim, the offender, and any property involved. These records are expected to give law enforcement a broader view of criminal activity in the United States, because NIBRS will also collect data on 22 Group A crime categories made up of 46 offenses, instead of the eight serious offenses that now make up the FBI's Crime Index. It will also collect data on 11 Group B crime categories.

The FBI will use this data to analyze certain types of offenders and crimes, such as drug-related robberies, hate crimes, domestic violence, and crimes in which alcohol was a factor.

Additional information about NIBRS can be found on the FBI Web site at www.fbi.gov/publish/nibrs/nibrs.htm or at Search—The National Consortium for Justice Information and Statistics site at www.search.org/nibrs/default.asp.

National Instant Criminal Background Check System (NICS)

In accordance with the Brady Act, NICS was established in November of 1998 as a national system that checks available records on persons who are disqualified from receiving firearms. It allows Federal Firearms Licensees (FFLs) to find out immediately whether receipt of a firearm by a prospective transferee would violate United States Code or state law. NICS checks criminal records, protective/restraining orders, records on wanted persons, individuals involuntarily committed to mental institutions as well as those declared incompetent, records of unlawful drug users, illegal aliens, individuals dishonorably discharged from the military, and persons who have renounced their U.S. citizenship.

Further information about NICS can be found on the FBI Web site at www.fbi.gov/hq/cjisd/nics/index.htm.

Prisoner Tracking System (PTS)

The Prisoner Tracking System (PTS) is an enhanced automated system in support of the handling of Federal prisoners in U.S. Marshall Service district offices and suboffices. All prisoner data that is necessary to track prisoners under the purview of the U.S. Marshalls is entered into the PTS/Prisoner Population Management System. Further information about the PTS can be found on the U.S. Marshall Web site at www.usdoj.gov:80/marshals/readingroom/pripro.html.

Regional Information Sharing Systems (RISS)

The Regional Information Sharing Systems (RISS) program is an innovative, federally funded program to support law enforcement efforts to combat organized crime activity, drug trafficking, criminal gangs, and violent crime. The six regional projects of RISS—MAGLOCLEN, MOCIC,

NESPIN, RMIN, ROCIC, and WSIN—provide member law enforcement agencies in all 50 states with a broad range of intelligence and investigative support services.

For more information, you can visit the RISS Web site at www.iir.com/riss.

Registered Sex and/or Violent Offenders

Citizens have the right to notification if they have registered sex or violent offenders in their neighborhoods. This is something that parents in particular want to know. More and more communities, law enforcement, and government agencies are making this information available on the Internet at sites such as www.sexoffender.com. For additional sites, see the *Naked in Cyberspace* Web site.

SENTRY

The SENTRY network provides for the processing of inmates at all phases of incarceration including admission, release, transfer, and furlough. For further information about SENTRY, refer to the Federal Bureau of Prisons' Web site at www.bop.gov:80.

Threat Analysis Information System (TAIS)

The Threat Analysis Information System (TAIS) contains identifying information and background data on persons who have directly threatened or pose a violent threat to USMS protectees, information concerning the threat, and threat-related investigative information.

For further information about TAIS, refer to the U.S. Marshall Service's Web site at www. usdoj.gov:80/marshals/readingroom/threat.html.

Victim Notification System (VNS)

The Justice Department has unveiled plans for a computer system that will enable victims of violent Federal crimes and their families to track the whereabouts of their attackers and the status of their cases in the justice system. The Victim Notification System (VNS) is intended to head off the potentially traumatic situation in which a victim of rape, assault, or another violent crime crosses paths with the convicted attacker, not even having known that the assailant was out of prison.

Similar systems in New York, Texas, Arkansas, Nebraska, North Carolina, Ohio, Alabama, California, and New Jersey utilize the VINE (Victim Information and Notification Everyday) system, developed by Appriss, Inc. Appriss also will provide the technology for the national Victim Notification System. For additional information about VINE, or VNS, refer to the Appriss, Inc., Web site at www.appriss.com.

Violent Gang and Terrorist Organizations File (VGTOF)

The Violent Gang and Terrorist Organizations File (operational since 1995 as a component of NCIC) contains information on members of violent gangs and terrorist organizations and pointers to other contacts within law enforcement who can share further information. In the past, it has been especially useful in identifying gang members by their monikers, or nicknames.

Since the terrorist attacks of September 11, 2001, this file has taken on greater importance, being utilized as an important tool for information sharing about the subjects of counterterrorism investigations, by federal, state, and local law enforcement agencies. The sharing of VGTOF data is just one of the measures taken to support and respond to the mission of the newly formed Office of Homeland Security, created for the prevention of future terrorist attacks.

Other Uses for Criminal Records

Criminal history records can be extremely important in many aspects of police work. For example, when police officers stop someone for a traffic violation or loitering, they need to know whether the person is wanted for a crime, has a history of violence, is a prison escapee, or has failed to comply with the terms of parole, probation, or bail. Having this information will better prepare the officers before approaching the person, and can even save their lives. When a firearm or other dangerous weapon is found in the possession of a felon, that represents another felony, for which the police can arrest the person. The availability of complete, updated criminal history records to officers in the field is vital to police work. Criminal records are also used to perform pre-employment background checks.

International Criminal Justice Organizations

In addition to the databases used within the United States criminal justice system, some international databases are shared by multiple countries, in order to coordinate their criminal justice efforts. Other databases developed for use within one country may be accessed by international criminal justice organizations in order to share the information with other countries, and cooperate in apprehending criminals across borders.

Information about some of these cooperative organizations follows.

Europol

Europol is the European Law Enforcement Organization. The current mandate of Europol includes the prevention and combat of criminal activities where there is reason to believe that an organized criminal structure is involved and two or more of the organization's member states are affected. These activities include:

- illicit drug trafficking

- crimes involving clandestine immigration networks

- illicit vehicle trafficking

- trafficking in human beings including child pornography

- forgery of money and means of payment

- illicit trafficking in radioactive and nuclear substances

- terrorism

- illegal money-laundering activities in connection with these forms of crime

For further information about Europol and their computer systems, refer to the Web site at www.europol.eu.int.

Interpol

The International Criminal Police Organization, known as Interpol, was formed in 1923. It currently includes 178 member countries around the world. A list of the member countries can be found on the Web site at www.interpol.int/Public/Icpo/Members/default.asp.

In 1985, Interpol embarked upon an extensive program of modernization, which created two databases of interest here. These are the computerized criminal information records stored at the General Secretariat and the Message Response Branch, which speeds responses to inquiries for information received by member countries. Prior to this, Interpol's criminal records consisted of more than four million cards, all which had been accessed manually.

A worldwide telecommunications network now links each member country's National Central Bureau (NCB) to all other NCBs and the General Secretariat in Lyons, France. The NCBs serve as links between the law enforcement agencies of member countries.

Further information about Interpol can be found on the organization's Web site at www.interpol.int.

The World Customs Organization (WCO)

Established in 1952 as the Customs Co-operation Council, the World Customs Organization (WCO) is an independent intergovernmental body consisting of 151 member governments. Its mission is to enhance the effectiveness and efficiency of Customs administrations. For further information, refer to the WCO Web site at www.wcoomd.org.

The World Customs Organization, the United Nations International Drugs Control Programme (UNDCP) and Interpol, have joined forces in a drug data sharing project. Each organization has contributed the details of more than 10,000 worldwide seizures of drugs made by Customs administrations, police authorities, and other law enforcement agencies since 1998. The initiative will involve regular coordinated data sharing to maintain and improve awareness of international drugs trafficking activity and trends.

Criminal Justice Bulletin Boards and Web Sites

There are many bulletin boards and Web sites on which criminal justice information, techniques, and experience are shared. For example, the National Criminal Justice Reference Service (NCJRS) is a federally sponsored information clearinghouse for people around the world involved with research, policy, and practice related to criminal and juvenile justice and drug control. Their Web site provides information about Office of Justice programs, project funding opportunities, national and international criminal justice news, legislation, criminal justice conferences, and other criminal justice services and organizations. The site also offers access to hundreds of criminal justice publications, including the group's own newsletters, *JUSTINFO* and *JUVJUST*. For further information about NCJRS, refer to the Web site at www.ncjrs.org.

Through the Justice Technology Information Network (JUSTNET), users have access to interactive bulletin boards on a variety of topics, a comprehensive database of law enforcement products and technologies, and National Law Enforcement Technology Center (NLECTC) publications. Their Web site is located at www.nlectc.org.

The JUSTNET Web site also provides links to hundreds of other criminal justice resources available on the Internet.

Many courts have their own independent bulletin boards. The National Center for State Courts (www.ncsconline.org/Information/info_court_web_sites/html) maintains a directory of court-related Web sites at their site.

Police and sheriff's departments maintain Web sites as well. Web sites such as CopSeek.com provide directories of thousands of other law enforcement sites on the Internet. CopSeek.com can be found at www.copseek.com.

Law schools also sometimes operate independent bulletin boards, and usually are represented on the Internet with their own Web sites.

The databases listed in this chapter do not represent all of the criminal justice databases used to store or track information about people. Neither do they come close to representing all of the databases used within the criminal justice system, as many additional databases are used that do not contain information about individuals at all, or contain such information only incidentally. For example, litigating organizations within the criminal justice system also use legal research databases, such as those offered by JURIS (www.juris.com/public/default.asp), Lexis (www.lexis.com), and Westlaw (www.westlaw.com). Other databases are used to catalog stolen art or spent ammunition. There also continue to be technological developments that can be combined with the criminal justice databases and systems, in order to provide more efficient access to criminal justice records or simplify the booking process. All these applications are beyond the scope of this book.

For Further Information

For further information about databases used within the criminal justice system, many additional resources are available.

Publications

Many databases provide indices to criminal justice publications. For example, the National Criminal Justice Reference Service (NCJRS) maintains a database of abstracts for more than 160,000 criminal justice books, documents, and reports published by the U.S. Department of Justice, other local, state, and Federal government agencies, international organizations, and the private sector.

Individual criminal justice publications from all over the world can be found on the Internet at their own sites:

> Justice Action Australia
> www.justiceaction.org.au
>
> The Australian and New Zealand Journal of Criminology
> www.australianacademicpress.com.au/Publications/anzjc/crim1.html
>
> The British Journal of Criminology
> http://www3.oup.co.uk/crimin
>
> The Canadian Journal of Criminology
> www.wimsey.com/~ccja/angl/cjc.html
>
> Journal of Scandinavian Studies in Criminology and Crime Prevention
> www.tandf.co.uk/journals/tfs/14043858.html

Additional databases that index criminal justice publications include the following:

- CINCH: The Australian Criminology Database (available on the Internet at www.informit.com.au/show.asp?id=CINCH), which contains citations, with some abstracts, to over 300 journals on corporate crime, corrections, court procedures, criminals, criminal law, deaths in custody, drug offenders, and related subjects

- Criminal Justice Abstracts (available online through Westlaw), which contains citations, with abstracts, to journals, reports, books, dissertations, magazines, and newspapers covering criminal justice topics

- Criminal Justice Periodical Index (CJPI) (available online through Dialog), which contains citations to articles in magazines, journals, newsletters, and law reporting publications on administration of justice and law enforcement

- Criminology and Criminal Justice (available on the Internet at www.izum.si/cobiss_eng.html), which contains bibliographic information on articles, books, Congress, and other materials from the field of criminology

- Law Enforcement and Criminal Justice Information Database (available online through International Research and Evaluation [IRE]), which contains citations, with some abstracts, to the literature on law enforcement and criminal justice

- Legal Resource Index (available online through CARL Corporation, DataStar, Dialog, Lexis, and Westlaw), which contains citations, with selected abstracts, to articles published in key law journals, bar association publications, and legal newspapers

Other collections of criminal justice journals are available in full-text online. These include:

- ABA Standards for Criminal Justice (available online through Westlaw), which contains the complete text of guidelines and standards relating to the administration and development of the criminal justice system

- APB Online (available on the Internet at www.apbnews.com), which contains extensive and up-to-date news, information, background, and other material on police and criminal justice issues

The University of Nebraska–Lincoln's Department of Criminal Justice has provided a partial list of Criminology/Criminal Justice Related Journals at www.unl.edu/crimjust/JOURNALS.html.

There are magazines and newsletters that you can subscribe to, such as the *Law Enforcement Bulletin*. Recent issues of this publication can be found on the Internet at www.fbi.gov/publications/leb/leb.htm.

Criminal justice newsletters can also be subscribed to, or accessed online:

- Computer Fraud and Security Bulletin (available online as part of the Newsletter Database on Bell and Howell Information and Learning, DataStar, Dialog, European Information Network Services, Factiva, FT Profile, I/PLUS Direct, and STN International), which contains the complete text of this newsletter on computer crime and on prevention methods and related commercial products

- Money Laundering Alert (available online through Lexis), which contains the complete text of this newsletter covering legislative, regulatory, enforcement, and international developments in the area of money laundering controls and asset forfeiture

CIA publications can be found at www.odci.gov/cia/publications/pubs.html.

Many additional publications track specific types of laws, cases filed, and their progress. Examples include:

- BNA Antitrust and Trade Regulation Daily (available online through Lexis and Westlaw), which provides comprehensive reports on legislative, regulatory, and judicial developments affecting restrictive trade practice law

- BNA California Environment Daily (available online as part of BNA Daily News from Washington through Dialog, Nexis, and Westlaw) contains information on legislative activities, regulations, and standards affecting California environmental law

- Business Law Brief (available online through FT Profile and Nexis), which contains the complete text of Business Law Brief, a monthly newsletter on significant developments in international business law

- Weekly Criminal Bulletin (available online through Lexis, Nexis, and QL Systems Limited), which contains more than 32,000 summaries of judgments in criminal cases tried in the Federal and provincial courts in Canada

Other Criminal Justice Resources

Many other Internet sites are dedicated to criminal justice:

The United Nations Crime and Justice Information Network (UNCJIN)
www.uncjin.org

The Central Intelligence Agency
www.cia.gov

The Department of Justice
www.usdoj.gov:80

The FBI Home Page
www.fbi.gov

The FBI Home Page contains information about the mission of the FBI, along with information about the top crimes that the FBI is currently investigating. You can also find information about the FBI's Ten Most Wanted Criminals at www.fbi.gov/mostwant/topten/tenlist.htm.

Dozens of additional sites for individual police departments can be found on the Internet, and they are rapidly multiplying in number. The Police Officer's Internet Directory can also provide links to many other Internet sites of interest to police officers. This site can be found at www. officer.com.

Whether you are a layperson, a police officer, an attorney, or anyone else involved in the criminal justice system, nearly unlimited resources are now available online to help you in understanding more about criminal justice, or in actually doing your job. In fact, it is hard to imagine those in the criminal justice system doing their jobs today without extensive use of the online systems now available.

Chapter 27

Department of Motor Vehicles

Just think about it. Our whole world is sitting there on a com-
puter. It's in the computer, everything: your DMV records, your
social security, your credit cards, your medical records. It's all
right there. Everyone is stored in there. It's like this little elec-
tronic shadow on each and everyone of us, just, just begging for
someone to screw with, and you know what? They've done it to
me, and you know what? They're gonna do it to you.

—Angela, *The Net*

The Department of Motor Vehicles (DMV) in each state maintains several types of records on individuals. These include identifying information, the status of driver's licenses, records of violations, license suspensions, and accident records. The DMV also maintains vehicle and vessel registrations and histories.

Identifying Information on Individuals

The DMV maintains identifying information on individuals, for use on driver's licenses and identification cards. This information typically includes:

- Driver's license or identification card number (in some states, the Social Security number is used)

- Driver's full name

- Aliases (aka's, maiden names)

- Residential address

- Mailing address

- Birth date

- Sex

- Height

- Weight

- Color of eyes
- Color of hair
- Photo

All of this information, except for the photo, is available online for nearly all states. However, the law restricts who has access to the residential addresses on these records. This is explained in greater detail at the end of this chapter.

Driver's License Data

In addition to the identifying information, driver's license data also includes:

- Status (valid, expired, suspended, revoked)
- Class of license (single vehicle, 3-axle house car, motorcycle, etc.)
- Date issued
- Expiration date
- Extension code (out-of-state, renewal by mail, military, etc.)
- Restriction code (corrective lenses required, may not drive on weekends or holidays, court restrictions, artificial limb required, under seat cushion required, must be accompanied by licensed adult, etc.)
- Duplicate issuance date
- License held code (surrendered by the court, withheld by DMV, etc.)

Driving Records

Accident and violation information is not only used in hiring a chauffeur or delivery person. It has also been used to locate individuals and track their whereabouts on a given date. If you were being sued for damage to another's vehicle or for personal injury resulting from a fender bender and the claim appears suspicious, it could be worth obtaining a copy of the plaintiff's driving record in order to find out whether damage to the vehicle has been reported before or the person appears to be particularly "accident prone." For the full details of an accident, you would still want to request the full accident report from the jurisdiction noted on the record, as the online information is brief, and valuable details may be hidden in the paper documentation.

A driving record may also include any of the following data:

- Violation or accident date (up to seven years for major violations; up to three years for minor violations)
- Abstract of the court's record indicating a conviction
- Court case disposition code
- Court docket or citation number

- Assigned code number

- Location of court

- Accident involvement

- Financial responsibility file number

- Coded report numbers

- License plate number

- Notice of failure to appear in court (FTA)

- Notice of failure to pay a court-imposed fine (FTP)

- Conviction date

- Statute(s) violated (number)

- Statute abbreviation

- Departmental action

- Date departmental action order was mailed

- Effective date of departmental action

- Vehicle code number authorizing departmental action

- Ending date of departmental action

- Reason for departmental action

- Date of service of departmental action

- Code for service of departmental action

- Financial responsibility file number

Vehicle Registrations

The DMV registers vehicles, including automobiles, trucks and commercial vehicles, trailers, motor homes, buses, motorcycles, off-road vehicles, and snowmobiles. Registration records make it possible to identify vehicles owned by an individual or company. This is useful for asset searches, especially where expensive vehicles are involved. Spouses and other relationships also sometimes appear on vehicle registration records as co-owners.

Vehicle registration records are not only useful for law enforcement, but are particularly helpful for surveillance work. Vehicle license plate numbers can be taken down at a surveillance site and later used to identify whose vehicles were coming and going from the location. Of course, the driver may be someone else altogether, and some of the vehicles may turn out to be rental vehicles, but these records often do provide invaluable leads.

Vehicle registrations include a Vehicle Identification Number (VIN). For vehicles manufactured since 1981, the VIN has been standardized into the following format:

- Digit 1—Nation of Origin (1=USA, 2=Canada, 3=Mexico, 4=Joint venture, in USA, 6=Australia, 9=Brazil, J=Japan, K=Korea, L=Taiwan, S=England, V=France, W=Germany, Y=Sweden, Z=Italy)

- Digit 2—Make (A=Imperial or Chrysler, B=Dodge, C=Chrysler, F=Ford, G=General Motors, J=Jeep, M=Mercury, P=Plymouth)

- Digit 3—Type of Vehicle (3=Passenger car, 4=Minivan/Multipurpose Vehicle, 7=Pickup)

- Digit 4—Passenger Safety (B=Manual Seat Belts, G=Dual Air Bag System) or GVWR and Hydraulic Brakes (E= 3,001–4,000 lb, F= 4,001–5000 lb, G= 5,001–6,000 lb, H= 6,001–7,000 lb)

- Digit 5—Car Line (usually the body series; for example, B=Cherokee - 2WD (RHD), J=Cherokee–4WD (LHD), N=Cherokee–4WD (RHD), T=Cherokee–2WD (LHD), X=Grand Cherokee–2WD (LHD), Y=Wrangler–4WD (LHD), Z=Grand Cherokee–4WD (LHD))

- Digit 6—Series (among Jeeps, 1=Sport (Wrangler), 2=SE, 4=Sahara, 5=Laredo, 6=Sport (Cherokee), 7=Limited/Country) or Quality Level (1=Economy, 2=Low, 4=High, 5=Premium, 6=Special)

- Digit 7—Body Style (2=2-Door Hardtop, 4=LWB Van, 5=SWB Van, 6=4-Door Sedan, 7=2-Door Wagon, 8=4-Door Wagon, 9=2-Door Open Body (w/Soft or Hard Top))

- Digit-8—Engine Size (P=2.5 Liter, I-4, MPI, S=4.0 Liter, I-6, MPI, Y=5.2 Liter, V8, MPI)

- Digit 9—Check Digit (used to validate the VIN)

- Digit 10—Year of Manufacture (A=1980, B=1981, C=1982, D=1983, E=1984, F=1985, G=1986, H=1987, J=1988, K=1989, L=1990, M=1991, N=1992, P=1993, R=1994, S=1995, T=1996, V=1997, W=1998, X=1999, Y=2000)

- Digit 11—Assembly Plant (A=Auburn Hills, C=Detroit (Jefferson North), L=Toledo #1, P=Toledo #2)

- Digits 12-17—Production/Sequence Number

Vessel Registrations

The DMV also registers motorized boats and vessels. Vessel registration records are used for asset searches when it is suspected that the subject may own a boat. Vessel registrations include:

- Vessel identification number

- Manufacturer

- Hull number

- Year of manufacture

- Length measurement of vessel

- Hull material code

- Vessel hull type code

- Body type model abbreviation

- Type of propulsion

- Legal owner

- Residential address

- Mailing address

Vehicle/Vessel Histories

In addition to current registration information, vehicle and vessel histories reveal where a vehicle or vessel came from. Vendors of this information sometimes offer different pricing, depending upon how many years you want to go back when checking a vehicle/vessel history.

Vehicle histories can be used to show a relationship, such as when one party purchases a vehicle or vessel from another. They can also be used to show how someone has hidden assets, as when they transfer vehicles and vessels to other family members and friends.

Problem Driver Pointer System

The Problem Driver Pointer System (PDPS) is an electronic database allowing users to identify drivers who have DUI (driving under the influence) and other major traffic convictions, or who have suspended or revoked licenses due to serious violations in any state. The PDPS is managed by the National Driver Register, which maintains an index of the records and pointers to the corresponding state records. It is not managed by the state DMV.

The PDPS is used by government and employers to screen prospective employees. It is not open to investigators. Individuals may submit requests for information about themselves directly to the National Driver Register.

National Driver Register
NHTSA, NTS-24
400 7th Street, SW, Room 6124
Washington, DC 20590

How to Access DMV Records Online

Some vehicle records that are available online must be acquired in two steps. First they are ordered online; they cannot actually be retrieved until a day or two later, after DMV employees have had time to search them out manually and the vendor has time to type them into its own system. Other vendors purchase tapes from the DMV and allow access to their systems or sell CD-ROMs of the data, which quickly become obsolete unless they are updated regularly. In some states, it is also possible to retrieve online data directly from the DMV.

Many public records vendors offer DMV records as well. For example, ChoicePoint Online offers driving records for 47 states, searches of vehicles by owner name in 37 states, and searches by license plate or VIN number in 47 states. New York records are returned immediately, but in most other states, records are returned in one or two business days.

Many additional online vendors offer DMV data, not just those that trade in public records. Some, like CARFAX in Virginia, Trans-Union DATEQ Network Inc. in Georgia, Explore Information Services in Minnesota, Pollock & Co. in Connecticut, and Experian Target Marketing Services in Texas, specialize in DMV data and offer records for several states. Some companies, such as Database Technologies, Inc., in Florida, provide complete records for law enforcement and offer private citizens access to only a portion of the records. Some companies, such as Intelligence Network, Inc., in Florida, offer records for a single state. Refer to Appendix M for these vendors.

Regulations on Accessing DMV Records

Regulations for accessing DMV records vary from state to state. When you purchase records online, it is the vendor's responsibility to explain the regulations and verify that you meet the requirements necessary to access the records for a given state.

California's restrictions originated in 1990, when state legislators adopted a law barring release of home addresses except under special circumstances. This law was passed after the murder of actress Rebecca Schaeffer, who was shot by an obsessed fan who had obtained her home address from the DMV with the assistance of a private investigator. DMV address information from vehicle registrations has also been used to track down doctors who perform abortions, as well as women who visit their clinics, to harass them, threaten them, or incite violence against them.

These facts spurred Senator Barbara Boxer from California to introduce an amendment entitled the "Protection of Information in State Motor Vehicle Records," which she attached to the Crime Bill (Omnibus Crime Control Act). The amendment would extend restrictions on DMV information to all states. At the same time, Representative Jim Moran from Virginia introduced a similar bill in the House of Representatives. In September of 1994, Congress passed the Omnibus Crime Control Act with the amendment. This law restricts access to name, address, telephone number, and other personal information held by each state DMV.

Several exceptions are contained in the law, now known as the Driver's Privacy Protection Act of 1994, allowing access for government use, insurance industry claims and underwriting purposes, driver safety disclosures, employment verification, and even for surveys, marketing, or solicitations. People are allowed to request that their information not be made available to firms collecting data for mailing lists or for building their own databases. Full compliance with this law was not required by the states until September of 1997. A copy of the full act may be found at www.nydmv.state.ny.us/dppact.htm or www4.law.cornell.edu/uscode/18/2721.html.

Since the passing of the Driver's Privacy Protection Act (DPPA), most vendors on the Internet no longer allow access to home address information from DMVs, but they do still sell driving histories and vehicle ownership information. As you probably realize by now, there are still many other sources for home address information, so the passing of the DPPA did very little to protect those who are in serious danger from those who would harm them.

Chapter 28

Death Records

We owe respect to the living; to the dead we owe only truth.

−Voltaire

Death records today are widely available in several computerized forms. This has made it efficient and relatively inexpensive to locate information on the computer about someone who has died.

Although examples supplied in this chapter deal with people whose names you may recognize, the death records databases contain records for millions of people, relatively few of whom are famous. Anyone who has died may be included.

Social Security Death Index

The primary source of automated death information is the Social Security Administration (SSA). The SSA has kept records of deaths in the United States since the late 1930s. The SSA usually learns that a person has died when someone claims a death benefit or when the agency is notified to stop Social Security payments to a person. Although the SSA does not have records of all deaths, its records do cover 64 million names. Thus, this agency is a rich resource for genealogists and others.

The Social Security Death Index records consist of:

- The individual's name and Soundex code (Refer to Chapter 34 for explanation of Soundex codes.)

- Dates of birth and death

- Social Security number and state where it was issued

- State of residence at death

- ZIP Code of last known residence and the primary location it is associated with (for approximately 77 percent of the records)

- ZIP Code of the address where the death benefit payment was sent and the primary location it is associated with (for 15 percent of the records)

The Social Security Administration licenses its records to several vendors. Each of these vendors sets its own price for access to the records, and the prices vary widely. For example, a "nationwide death search" can cost $75 for a single online search, $15/hour for as many searches as you like, $40 for a CD-ROM database containing all of the records from 1937 to the present, or it can be free on the Internet. There are many other prices for this same data, depending upon the vendor.

The Social Security Death index is available on the Internet as a free service from Ancestry Search at www.ancestry.com/search/rectype/vital/ssdi/main.htm. A search of this database for the late actress and *The Sopranos* star, Nancy Marchand, produced the results shown in Figure 28.1.

Figure 28.1   Social Security Death Index

Knowing Ms. Marchand's date of birth, I am able to identify the second record as the correct match. So you see, having some good identifying information can help at every stage of researching a person.

Public Records Vendors

Many additional public records vendors offer searches of Social Security Death Records, often under trade names such as "Decedent Trace" and "National Death Search." The date ranges, update schedules, and prices for these searches can vary significantly. In most cases, the vendors allow a search on only one name at a time, using predefined fields, and charging a fee for each search attempt.

A notable exception is the Social Security Number Death Master File search on Lexis. This search includes only the records from 1962 to the most recent quarter, but Lexis allows the same search capabilities as on the firm's other databases. It is possible to search for a range of names, or even a combination of names (such as Robert or Bob) in the same search. The content of Lexis's Social Security number Death Master File is listed as:

- Name of deceased individual
- Social Security number
- Date of death
- Date of birth
- State/country of residence
- ZIP Code of last residence
- ZIP Code of recipient of death benefits

Not all of the information is necessarily present for each record.

Public records vendors may also offer death records indices from other sources, as well. ChoicePoint Online, for one, offers death records indices from the California and Texas Departments of Health.

Probate records include wills, financial and property information, lists of next of kin, lists of claims against the estate, personal information about the deceased, and details of how the decedent's property was distributed. ChoicePoint Online also offers an online Superior Court Probate index for California, which provides a file date, file number, and case title. Although not particularly telling in itself, you may use this information to order the full probate record from the court.

The Occupational Safety and Health Administration (OSHA) maintains records of workplace accidents and fatalities, which are indexed and searchable online through several public records vendors including Westlaw, Information Resource Services Company (IRSC), and ChoicePoint Online. ChoicePoint allows searching of these records nationally by accident victim name. Basic information is available online, but for an additional fee, ChoicePoint will supply further details, including the victim's age, injury information, part of the body affected, events and factors causing and contributing to the accident, and so on.

Wrongful deaths (motor vehicle and other types) may also be found online in the civil records, and this information is offered by many public records vendors. Criminal records may also contain murder, manslaughter, self-defense, and accidental deaths as well.

Genealogical databases may also carry deaths among their vital records. For further information about these databases, please refer to Chapter 34: Genealogical Records.

Cemetery Records

Cemetery caretakers normally keep records of the names and death dates of those buried, as well as maps of the grave sites. They may also keep more detailed records, including the names of the deceased's relatives. In addition to these paper records, there are tombstones, which can provide information such as birth and death dates and the names of other family members. The best place to find cemetery records are in the cemeteries, of course. Often, when there is no longer a caretaker of the cemetery, records can be found in the holdings of local libraries, archives, or historical societies. Some of this information can also now be found online. Two Web sites have been designed to access cemetery records all over the world (although only a few countries are currently listed).

>   Cemetery Records Online (Interment.net)
>   www.interment.net

>   Cemetery Junction Directory
>   www.daddezio.com/cemetery

Using these sites, you can locate the grave site of individuals, as well as vital statistics such as dates of birth and death.

War Records

If you believe that someone you are looking for may have died or been declared missing in action in the Vietnam War, the Wall on the Web site (http://grunt.space.swri.edu/thewall/thewallm.html) contains the names of the people who are memorialized on the Vietnam War Memorial Wall in Washington, DC.

A second source is the Virtual Wall Vietnam Veterans Memorial, located at www.VirtualWall.org. Korean War veterans can be found on the Korean War Databases site at www.koreanwar.org/html/korean_war_databases.html. Civil War Soldiers and Sailors can be found on the Civil War Soldiers & Sailors System at http://www.itd.nps.gov/cwss.

For living military, VetFriends.com offers searches of veterans and active duty military personnel at its site www.vetfriends.com. Military Locators can also be found at Military.com (www.military.com) and at Military Connections (www.militaryconnections.com).

Deaths in the News

When the famous die, you can expect to find information about them and their deaths in newspapers, magazines, and often even television or radio transcripts. News of a celebrity's death is often accompanied by information summarizing the subject's accomplishments and events in their lives. Refer to Chapter 33 for further information about celebrity deaths.

The news also contains articles about the deaths of less-celebrated individuals. People who die in accidents or who suffer violent deaths are often featured in news stories. Even those who die under normal circumstances may be mentioned within other articles or may be featured in an obituary, particularly in local newspapers, many of which are now available online. Obituaries usually also list surviving family members, which can provide a lead to further information about the subject.

News database vendors sometimes make it simpler to search for the deceased by coding obituaries in such a way that they are easy to locate. For example, Factiva uses the code N/OBT to identify obituaries in its Press Release Wires.

Genealogists are also interested in obituaries, so there have been some efforts made at compiling obituary databases from newspapers. For example, Legacy.com offers an obituary finder searching more than 1,000 newspapers, searchable by name, keyword, or newspaper at its site (www.legacy.com/legacyhome.asp).

FREE Obituaries On-Line can be searched at www.king.igs.net/~bdmlhm/obit_links.html. Obituary Daily Times is a compilation of daily obituaries by volunteers at www.rootsweb.com/~obituary. D'Addezio.com provides obituaries at www.daddezio.com/catalog/cemndx03.

html. Obituary Central offers several searchable databases, including Canadian obituary links, a Ship Search of early passenger lists, special obituary collections, and so on at www.obitcentral. com/obitsearch.

There also are sites for people to register obituaries for their own loved ones on the Internet, including The Virtual Memorial Garden (www.monument.to/vmg) and The WorldWide Cemetery (www.cemetery.org).

Deaths in Other Databases

Many other databases offer death records online. Some are covered in other chapters of this book. For example, biographical databases (discussed in Chapter 15) contain the date or at least the year of death for thousands of persons, few of whom are famous. Some of the quotations databases (discussed in Chapter 22) also contain the year of death for persons who are quoted. Encyclopedias normally carry this information as well, when referring to someone now deceased.

The Demographic Data Base (in English and Swedish) contains historical demographic and social data on 365,000 individuals listed in 19th-century Swedish church records and other historical sources. Records date from 1800 to 1895, with some coverage extending back to 1700. Typical data items include parish catechetical examination register, register of births, register of deaths, register of marriages, register of migration, date of birth, place of birth, name(s), legitimate or illegitimate birth, and twinship. Also included are demographic events data such as date of death, date of marriage ceremony, change of residence within parish or across border, previous and later domicile, trade (profession), social status, civil status, and position in family household. Kinship relations data including parents, spouses, children, and source of information is also included. Demographic Data Base is available online from Umea Universitet.

There also are Web sites dedicated to dead musicians, dead porn stars, and other deceased celebrities. These can be found in Chapter 33.

Chapter 29

Tax Records

*Well, fancy giving money to the Government! Might
as well have put it down the drain. Fancy giving money
to the Government! Nobody will see the stuff again.
Well, they've no idea what money's for—Ten to one they'll
start another war. I've heard a lot of silly things, but,
Lor'! Fancy giving money to the Government!*

–A. P. Herbert

It will either disappoint or relieve you to know that the Internal Revenue Service does not release federal income tax records to online searchers simply for the asking. Nor do they post them on the Internet. However, this does not mean that income tax information can never be found through the use of online systems.

Franchise Tax Records

Franchise tax records include both personal and business tax returns. Although most of the information on these returns is considered confidential, some states do make at least part of it available online. This can help in determining the standing of a domestic or foreign corporation.

This nonconfidential information can include the name of the corporation, address, phone number, date opened for business within the state, officers and directors, corporation number, tax year, filing date of return, name and title of person signing the return, tax due date, and amount of delinquent taxes.

Board of Equalization Records (or State Sales Tax Board)

State sales tax records may be found online for some states. In California, for example, the state Board of Equalization values state assessed property, oversees local property tax assessment, hears appeals from the Franchise Tax Board, and collects a wide variety of business taxes. These taxes include the Alcoholic Beverage Tax, Cigarette Tax, Emergency (911) Telephone Users Surcharge, Energy Resources Surcharge, Hazardous Waste and Substance Taxes, Insurers Registration Tax, Motor Vehicle Fuel Tax, Private Railroad Car Tax, Sales and Use Tax, Solid Waste Disposal Fee, Timber Yield Tax, and Use Fuel Tax.

If someone wishes to avoid paying sales tax on goods bought for resale (paying tax on their sales instead), they must apply for a Sales and Use Tax permit. Records such as these are kept by the State Sales Tax Board or a similar agency. For some states, these permits can be found through an online search of the state Board of Equalization records, which are provided by some of the public records vendors.

Property Tax Records

Real property records contain property tax information and, for many counties, can be found online through public records vendors. This information normally is collected from the county assessor's office.

The county assessor's office also collects taxes on unsecured property such as aircraft and boats, but that information is not generally available online. Real property tax records from County Assessors in selected states are now available on Westlaw from Experian REDI Property, with more states to be added as they become available.

Although not available online as real property records, you may search Federal Aviation Administration (FAA) records for aircraft registrations through public records vendors, or the U.S. Coast Guard Watercraft database for merchant and recreational vessels weighing five net tons or more (approximately 27 feet or more). In some states, the Department of Motor Vehicle records include information about smaller boats. However, none of these records indicate the value of the craft or the amount of taxes paid. That information must still be obtained from the county assessor's offices, which have not yet made this information available online.

Income Tax Records Within Public Records

If you fail to pay taxes, a federal, state, or county tax lien may be filed. Public records vendors routinely offer online tax lien indices, sometimes grouped with bankruptcies and judgments into a single search. When a matching record is found, only the basic information will be listed online, but you can then request a copy of the actual records from the court. These may provide more detailed tax records for an individual or a business.

Bankruptcies can also be expected to include detailed financial records, including tax returns, which can be requested from the court or records center once you have located the case online.

Another great place to find income tax records is in the records of a civil suit, particularly for tax-related cases. If a person has a dispute with the IRS settled in court, details of the person's financial affairs may all be found in the court documents.

Divorce cases, child custody, and support actions all are found to be good sources for tax returns and other financial information. Online civil records indices are available from many public records vendors, and again, the full record can then be requested in order to obtain details of a person's financial position, frequently including income tax records.

Uniform Commercial Code (UCC) indices also are available online. Their presence indicates that a financial statement is on file with the Secretary of State, which may be available at the county level as well. Income tax records are sometimes included in the financial statements. For more information on UCC filings, please refer to Chapter 31: Public Records.

Chapter 30

Medical and Insurance Records

Whatsoever things I see or hear concerning the life of men, in my attendance on the sick or even apart therefrom, which ought not to be noised abroad, I will keep silence thereon, counting such things to be as sacred secrets.

–An excerpt from the Hippocratic Oath

Are medical records private? People probably would like to think so. Of all the matters you may consider to be "sensitive information," your health is among the most personal. Have you had a facelift? Lost a breast to cancer? Had a venereal disease? For most people, information about these and many, many other types of personal health matters are expected to remain private.

The truth is that despite their sensitivity, medical records are not as discreetly held as individuals would hope. Let's take a few minutes to consider how medical information is processed today.

Databases of medical records exist in doctors' offices, hospitals, pharmacies, and medical facilities of all types. Some of these databases are standalone systems. Many others are part of integrated systems that link the records of one department or medical facility to those of another. In Wisconsin, this concept has grown into the Wisconsin Healthcare Information Network, or WHIN, which transmits laboratory results, transcribed medical reports, patient demographics, and insurance claims between doctors' offices, hospitals, and insurance companies throughout the state.

Linking medical databases lets patients' medical records follow them throughout a hospital stay, and potentially throughout their lives. This is more efficient than maintaining independent records, and by giving doctors and nurses more information about the patient's medical history and condition, it can improve medical care itself. This added knowledge can eliminate redundant tests and treatments, and it can be especially important in an emergency. Information about past treatments, medical conditions, current prescriptions, and allergies can save a patient's life.

Take the simple case of a physician administering a new medication. If the patient is not questioned, is unconscious or disoriented and unable to answer, or for whatever reason does not report taking a medication, the doctor could unknowingly administer conflicting medications or treatment. This could further endanger the patient's health. Unreported allergies to drugs are an even greater danger; patients die each day because of them. Better access to the patient's medical history can prevent such mishaps.

Healthcare information is being automated in large and small ways today. Even companies outside of the healthcare field are involved. Medical Manager Corporation (formerly Physician Computer Network, Inc.) provides practice management systems to more than 185,000 physicians throughout the U.S., offering doctors computerized billing and electronic links to hospitals, labs, and insurance companies.

McKesson HBOC, Inc., Shared Medical Systems Corp., Health Systems Design Corporation, Sunquest Information Systems, Inc., Health Management Systems, Inc., and IDX Systems Corp. are additional examples of companies linking doctors, hospitals, clinics, pharmacies, and other medical facilities to patient medical records.

Medical Registries

On an even larger scale, there are databases that track the incidence and results of particular types of injury, disease, or treatment. These medical registries also identify patients to be contacted for research into their illnesses.

Cancer registries were among the earliest types of medical database developed, and they remain the most numerous and highly detailed registries in operation today. In the United States, local hospital databases were consolidated during the 1950s and '60s into several regional and state cancer registries. The National Cancer Act of 1971 marked the beginning of the "war on cancer." Among many other provisions, it instructed the United States National Cancer Institute (NCI) to create a continuous system of national cancer surveillance. Two years later, the NCI established the Surveillance, Epidemiology, and End Results (SEER) program, which operates as a network of cancer registries for state and regional populations. The SEER program does not attempt to monitor all types of cancer, nor does it cover all populations. SEER data is accumulated from selected areas of the nation, currently 11 population-based cancer registries and three supplemental registries, accounting for approximately 14 percent of the United States population. The supplemental or "expansion" registries increase the coverage to approximately 26 percent. Information on more than 3 million in situ and invasive cancer cases is included in the SEER database, and approximately 170,000 new cases are accessioned each year within the SEER catchment areas. The SEER registries routinely collect data on patient demographics, primary tumor site, morphology, stage at diagnosis, first course of treatment, and follow-up for vital status. The SEER Program is the only comprehensive source of population-based information in the United States that includes stage of cancer at the time of diagnosis and survival rates within each stage.

Many other medical registries in the U.S. track such disorders and conditions as:

- AIDS

- Alzheimer's Disease and Dementia

- Angiofollicular Lymph Node Hyperplasia (AFH)

- Congenital Malformations

- Coronary Artery Surgery

- Endocarditis Prophylaxis Failure

- Epidermolysis Bullosa (EB)

- Eye Trauma

- Football Head and Neck Injury

- IDDM (Insulin-Dependent Diabetes Mellitus)

- In Vitro Fertilizations

- Mushroom Poisoning

- Percutaneous Transluminal Coronary Angioplasty (PTCA)

- Tuberculosis

- Trauma

There are international registries for a variety of medical data. The Caitlin Raymond International Registry of Bone Marrow Donor Banks (www.crir.org) combines the resources of independent regional bone marrow registries in the United States with those of other registries. As an international registry, it has access to the names of more than 2.7 million donors internationally. Similarly, the International Fetal Surgery Registry is accumulating data that may determine the efficacy and safety of the various surgical procedures performed on fetuses.

Medical registries have proved to be remarkably valuable in this kind of research. Since the first computerized trauma registry opened at Cook County Hospital in Chicago in 1969, hospital trauma registries have been used primarily to assess the quality of medical care and to pinpoint necessary changes in treatment. Data from the National Eye Trauma System Registry has also helped to identify ways to prevent occupational eye injuries, such as wider use of safety glasses and improvement of engineering controls. In Virginia, a legislative subcommittee used data from the Virginia Statewide Trauma Registry to support a bill to regulate the use of all-terrain vehicles.

Organ, bone, and tissue donor registries operate as waiting lists for those needing a transplant, as well as tracking patients who have received them. For example, the Scientific Registry of the United Network for Organ Sharing, established in late 1987, has tracked thousands of cardiac transplant procedures since its inception. Its data revealed that patients face greater risk of death in heart centers that seldom perform a transplant than they do in centers where doctors get more practice in the procedure. These statistics could be used to justify closing some cardiac treatment centers in order to keep the remaining centers busy or, alternatively, to justify changes in training or procedures at the less active centers. Though intuitively unsurprising in this case, such information often makes the difference between true medical knowledge and informed guesswork.

One of the best known successes of registry-based medical research came from the National Football Head and Neck Injury Registry. Established in 1975, this database tracks serious injuries of the cervical spine caused by participation in football. Analysis of registry data revealed that so-called "freak accidents," in which football players were paralyzed by neck fractures were primarily caused by the use of a tackle in which the player strikes his opponent with the top of his helmet, much like a battering ram. As a result of this work, game rules and coaching techniques were changed to eliminate the use of this tackle. This has dramatically reduced the incidence of quadriplegia since 1976.

Despite these and many other successes, American medical registries are still in the embryonic stage. One reason for this is the lack of unique medical identifiers for each U.S. citizen. For many reasons, registry operators would like to key each person's medical records to an individual code that would follow people throughout life, much like the Social Security number. However, this raises privacy concerns, as well as the fear that identifiers will in some way make medical care more impersonal. Part of the controversy over the United States National Healthcare Reform Initiative in 1994 centered on this issue.

Norway and Sweden have used this kind of identifier for decades now. In Norway, each citizen is assigned a national identification number shortly after birth. The number is structured so as to link the baby's records to the mother's records and, in most cases, to the father's. This becomes part of the Medical Birth Registry, which records all live births and stillbirths with a gestational age of at least 16 weeks. Registration is compulsory and is performed by midwives. As of 1994, about 1.5 million births had been registered. Future medical treatments are tracked by the birth registry number. This code is also recorded on death certificates, making computer linkage of birth and death certificates simple and direct.

Sweden has a Medical Birth Registry similar to Norway's. More than 99 percent of births in Swedish hospitals have been recorded since this registry was established in 1973.

Privacy issues aside, the assignment of unique identifiers makes it possible to track people's health throughout their lives. Research that would be difficult, costly or even impossible using American medical registries is little more than a database search in Sweden and Norway. For example, in Sweden and Norway physicians can perform a search to find out what percentage of AIDS patients also have cancer. The link between birth and death records makes it easy to extract longevity figures for patients who received fetal surgery. Even more fundamentally, doctors can determine how many people in the general populace suffer from any given malady. Because medical registries in the United States are generally limited to patients who have experienced one specific illness or treatment, it is nearly impossible to correlate their data. Such comparisons can sometimes identify factors common to several disorders or prove that a factor often seen in one disease also occurs among patients not afflicted by the illness. This can provide clues that could lead to the development of a vaccine or even a cure. Because American medicine does not use personal identifiers, you may well be overlooked for life-saving new medical treatments.

Of course, we must weigh these benefits against the need for privacy. No one is likely to suggest that you be given unrestricted access to another's medical histories. What the medical profession struggles to achieve is a balance that respects privacy, yet makes it possible to use individual medical data to find cures for disease, prevent injuries, and improve medical care. I hope that in the near future that balance will be found.

Access to Medical Records

Physicians, nurses, and other medical professionals are trained to treat patient records with the utmost confidentiality. Although they sometimes must discuss a patient's condition or share a patient's records, those circumstances are supposed to be limited to professional medical consultation or discussions with insurance carriers.

However, many others also have access to a patient's medical information: admissions staff, laboratory personnel, X-ray technicians, pharmacists, insurance billing personnel, medical records transcriptionists and filers, and personnel from virtually every other department or office in a hospital or physician's office. Private and public review organizations and auditors may look at medical records in order to assess the level of care offered by a hospital or a physician, to investigate possible healthcare fraud, or to improve the efficiency or reduce the cost of healthcare.

Still more people routinely handle sensitive medical records. Insurance companies receive copies in order to process payment claims. Government agencies receive the records in order to process claims on their services. Some of these agencies contract with third parties, companies like Computer Sciences Corporation, in order to process the claims. In this case, a third party receives the medical records as well. The Health Care Financing Administration in Washington manages Medicare and Medicaid claims, with computer databases now processing more than half of its claims electronically. Private insurance companies also are automating their claims processing. In 1997, nine regional electronic data interchange (EDI) network providers collaborated to form ShareNET, promoting the creation of a virtual private network for healthcare electronic data interchange administrative transactions, linking payors and providers in several states. Today, ShareNET is the nation's leading healthcare electronic data interchange (EDI) consortium. Such electronic systems may reduce the chance for claims processors to look through patient records, but they may provide greater opportunity to break into the records electronically.

Employers may also receive full access to the medical records of their employees. When a company insures its own employees rather than paying for outside coverage, each medical treatment is reported to the employer in order to process the insurance claims. Rather than the relative anonymity of an insurance company, the treatment records and medical information may be processed by a co-worker. This could lower "office gossip" to a whole new level.

Medical Insurance Databases

In an effort to stop fraudulent insurance claims, some insurance companies have even created their own databases of medical records. Perhaps the largest of these databases is that of the Medical Information Bureau (MIB), a nonprofit company founded in 1902 by the medical directors of fifteen insurance companies. Today, MIB maintains up to seven years of medical records on millions of people in the United States and Canada. Not everyone who applies for a life, health, or disability insurance policy is recorded in MIB's database. Insurance companies decide whether or not to file a report with MIB and, if so, what should be in it. Serious medical conditions generally are reported, along with other factors that might affect someone's life expectancy, such as a poor driving record or a taste for dangerous sports. This information may come from the individual's insurance application, a physical examination, a physician, or the insurer's own investigation, which may include a search of public records.

If you have been rejected for insurance, or charged a higher premium, you might do well to request a copy of your MIB report:

> Medical Information Bureau (MIB)
> P.O. Box 105
> Essex Station
> Boston, MA 02112
> (617)426-3660
> (781)461-2453 Fax
> www.mib.com/html/home.html

You can download a copy of the "Request for Disclosure" form from the Web site. If there is a report on you, it will usually arrive about a month after you send in MIB's request form. If the report contains errors, notify the bureau so that it can tell you how to make a correction.

Public Records

Any system so complex as the ones that now distribute medical records far and wide allows the possibility of abuse. Most physicians today are extremely sensitive to the ethical issues that surround patient confidentiality. On rare occasions, a doctor might slip and discuss a patient's medical condition inappropriately, but such transgressions probably are more rare in medicine than in most other professions, with the possible exception of the clergy. However, the farther medical records circulate, the greater the risk that they will be released improperly. To prevent this, individuals depend both on handling procedures and on the ethical sense of the people who handle them. This system works surprisingly well.

Nonetheless, private investigators sometimes can uncover surprising amounts of medical information about you. Does this mean that they have broken into medical facilities, computer systems, or insurance companies, or paid informants to breach confidentiality? Not necessarily. While they may have followed their subject in and out of the doctor's office or found medical receipts in their garbage, there often are ways to learn medical secrets that are both legal and easier than "dumpster diving." Medical information can also overflow into public records.

Civil Records

Lawsuits can uncover a great deal of information about specific incidents in a person's medical history. Personal injury suits often describe a particular accident in great detail, and many discuss other facts relating to a person's health. Product liability suits may describe injuries that the plaintiff believes were caused by a poorly designed or defective product. Suits against a health insurance company may provide itemized lists of treatments, along with details of a patient's medical condition. Malpractice suits certainly would describe a patient's condition and treatment. Even judgments granted to a physician or hospital for nonpayment of medical bills can provide details of a patient's care.

A physician's notes may be subpoenaed to court as part of a case, and these notes sometimes extend beyond description of the incident in question, such as a traffic accident. They may describe mental health, the health of other family members, and provide a transcript of everything else that the patient and physician have ever discussed.

When income tax returns make their way into the public record—which can happen in any lawsuit, including divorce—large deductions for medical expenses can reveal the existence of a possibly serious medical condition.

Public records vendors provide some online indices to lawsuits, but it is necessary to request a copy of the case file itself in order to review the details.

A company in Chicago found a niche in the public records arena by offering a database to physicians, which allowed them to search for malpractice suits filed by any given patient. It is unclear how this information was used: whether physicians discussed their findings with the patient or in some way took precautions against future malpractice suits. If they used information about prior suits to deny patients treatment, this in itself might lead to future litigation. Perhaps that is why I can no longer verify the existence of this company.

Motor Vehicle Records

Some additional information can also be gleaned from the state DMV. A driver's license may note driving restrictions, such as the need for glasses. A driving history including drunk driving incidents may suggest a problem with alcoholism. If accidents are noted, description of a serious injury may also be included.

Worker's Compensation Records

Companies such as Avert and Informus Corp. provide databases of Worker's Compensation filings. These filings include information such as:

- Name of employee
- Employee's Social Security number
- Type of injury
- Nature of injury
- Extent of injury
- Part of body affected
- Accident type
- Relevant dates
- Name of employer
- Insurance carrier

Refer to Appendix M for listings of these companies.

News

Searching the news databases may uncover stories about traffic or industrial accidents, assaults, and other incidents that involve injuries. When a patient is famous or a ground-breaking medical procedure is performed, intimate details of the person's health may be reported as well.

Although this is not a primary source of medical information, anything can turn up in the news. Before the advent of news databases, searching each individual newspaper for the unlikely event that such an incident might be mentioned was not efficient. The news databases now make it quick and easy to search broad spans of newspapers, newswires, and television and radio transcripts.

For further information about news databases, please refer to Chapter 20.

Mailing Lists

Some mailing list companies now compile lists of people with ailments ranging from arthritis to Parkinson's disease, broken down by age, sex, income, marital status, and as many other factors as one could name.

These mailing lists may be compiled from information obtained directly from the patients, such as the Hillsdale-High Blood Pressure Sufferers list, which is compiled from direct mail questionnaires. People who subscribe to specialty publications, such as *Diabetes Self-Management* magazine, will find themselves on a specialty mailing list, where it is assumed that they are diabetic. Anyone who purchases a diet or exercise product by telephone or mail may end up on one of the many diet and fitness lists. Some lists are even more specific, such as the Jewish Vegetarians list offered by R.C. Direct, Inc., which includes "buyers of books, as well as inquirers about Jewish Vegetarianism and the humane treatment of animals and the Jewish approach to diet and health." Experian Target Marketing Services even offers a list providing height and weight of individuals.

Huge mailing lists are compiled through responses from questionnaires inserted in packages, as well as mailings and magazine and television ads that offer information about medications to people who call or write. A few years ago, half a million viewers in sixteen states called a toll-free number given on a television commercial to find out the pollen count in their ZIP Code area. As a result, many of the callers received sales pitches for allergy medication from Warner Lambert, the ad's sponsor.

Even some pharmacies and physicians now sell information from their databases to drug-makers or mailing list companies.

Major drug companies such as Merck, SmithKline Beecham, and Eli Lilly, have engineered corporate takeovers of companies that distribute drugs to consumers. The hottest targets are companies that administer corporate prescription benefit plans and those that sell prescription drugs by mail. Eli Lilly's acquisition of PCS Health Systems, for example, gave the pharmaceutical company direct access to 50 million patients.

For further information about mailing lists, please refer to Chapter 19.

OSHA Records

Reports from the Occupational Safety and Health Administration (OSHA) are available online through ChoicePoint Online and some of the other public records vendors. These reports detail information such as:

- Accident descriptions
- Address
- Business or establishment name
- Federal region
- Inspection type and scope
- Number and type of violations
- Number of employees
- OSHA area office
- Penalties
- Standard Industrial Classification (SIC) Code
- Union status

Some of these reports include the details of accidents, including the names of people involved in them. However, vendors may index them by business name, making it more difficult to search for information about an individual. It may be necessary to search for each business that the person has worked for in order to find out whether he or she has ever been involved in an accident that was reported to OSHA.

These records are also carried by legal database vendors, such as Westlaw. In this case, searching for individuals may be simpler.

Although OSHA records are not a primary source for medical information, they do remain another possible location for details of a person's medical condition.

Medical Details Viewed by the World

There now are Web sites that broadcast surgeries and medical procedures live over the Internet. In June of 1998, the first Internet broadcast of a woman giving birth was watched by millions. America's Health Network broadcast this event, and many surgeries such as balloon angioplasty, laparoscopic hysterectomy, and even surgery inside a woman's womb. The site has since disppeared.

Another site, Lifespan (www.lifespan.org/staywell/videosurgery.html), has been broadcasting surgery videos, including such procedures as ACL knee repair, cataract surgery, and "keyhole" heart surgery.

Even some stars share their medical information online. Singer Carnie Wilson had her gastric bypass surgery broadcast over the Internet. On sites like A Doctor in Your House.com (www.adoctorinyourhouse.com), celebrities discuss their medical conditions and treatments, including Jill Eikenberry's breast cancer, Larry King's coronary artery disease, and Roger Moore's skin cancer.

Every day, the nonfamous share intimate details of their medical conditions on the Internet, at support sites, on newsgroups, and in chat rooms. Although rarely signing their names, their messages are identified by their e-mail addresses, which can often be traced back to them, especially if they print it on their business cards and give it to friends and associates.

Concern for the Future

The technology is already in place for tracking your purchases at the supermarket. After your groceries are scanned at the checkout counter, you may have scanned in your own debit or check-cashing card, thereby linking those purchases to your identity. The supermarket may scan your check into their system, thereby identifying you, clearing your check, and linking you to your purchases. Today, this may do no more than make you the happy recipient of a tailor-made set of store coupons, and few would argue against that innocuous use. However, it soon will be possible to extract more intimate information from such data. Suppose insurance companies paid supermarkets a premium for access to that information. (This could be quite a profit center for the supermarkets.) Insurance companies could then determine who smoked too much, who ate too much junk or fatty foods, who might have a problem with alcohol, whose diet relied too heavily on beef or dairy products, and so on. This type of information could be used to define high-risk groups, assessing premiums, or even denying insurance coverage.

If you knew that your next purchase of a pint of Ben & Jerry's Bovinity Divinity ice cream would send up a red flag at your insurance carrier, would that change your buying decision or would you merely start paying cash?

Just a little food for thought.

Chapter 31

Public Records

The noblest motive is the public good.

–Sir Richard Steele

Public records include hundreds of types of records that are kept in order to protect the public's interests. For example, real property records are stored in order to establish the legal owner of a property. This is important not only to the person claiming the property, but to potential buyers. If legal title could not be established in this way, none of us would have protection from con artists who sell a property they do not own, or sell a property to more than one buyer.

Corporate and limited partnership records exist so that the owner(s) of a business can be identified and legal liability can be established. This is meant to assist in pursuing legal satisfaction when a company is involved in fraudulent activities or other wrongdoing, or if its products are found to do harm.

You not only have a right to public records, but you actually already own them. Americans have established laws determining which types of records must be kept; who must create, store, and maintain them; and under what circumstances, if any, the government may deny access to those records. In most cases, you do not need a reason for wanting the records. It is none of the government's business why you want to know who owns a home or a business, what it is worth, or any other matters of public record. As taxpayers, you pay for the storage and retrieval of public records, and you pay the salaries of the public employees who assist in this process. In most instances, the government must provide free access to the records to anyone who asks; it may only charge a fee if someone wishes to obtain copies.

Today, many types of public records are available online through public records vendors and court records systems, and even through the Internet. In fact, the availability of public records through the Internet is the single largest boon to personal research in years. These records can be extremely useful to those in various areas of personal research.

Limitations of Online Public Records

As convenient and useful as it is to be able to reach out from your computer to obtain public records existing in courts and record halls throughout the land, there are several limitations to the public records now available online. First of all, only a small portion of all public records information can yet be found online. This situation is improving, but it will be some time before you are able to use a personal computer to tap into all the public records that you might wish to use in personal research.

Most online files of public records today consist of indices, rather than detailed records. It often is necessary to locate the records through the indices and then order copies of the physical documents to learn what you need to know. This is changing very slowly—some records have been scanned and made available online, but this is not yet the norm.

Some jurisdictions and courts still have not automated their records or even their indices, so you will not find those online. Others may index only particular types of record. Even when public records vendors offer a "statewide" or "nationwide" search, they may mean that it includes all counties or courts that provide online access to that type of record, rather than all courts. This is not always clear in vendor advertising or documentation, or on the Web sites where public records are found.

As with any other type of database, errors can occur when the public records indices are built. Many of these difficulties are discussed in Chapter 6: Locating People.

Records can also be missed when the indexing takes place. If physical records are scanned in order to make them available online, a file may be out of place when its turn arrives and miss the indexing process altogether.

Public records vendors normally sell more current records than older ones, and some older records may not legally be used in pre-employment or credit screening. Some public records vendors begin collecting their records at a given date and never fill in the earlier data. For these reasons, it is often difficult to locate older public records online.

In addition, collection methods can delay the availability of some recent records. If the online vendor or court records system offers direct access to the database at the city, county, state, or Federal agency where the records are actually stored, the records that one accesses will be as up-to-date as possible. Anything less than that will introduce lag-time between the agency's records (which may already be backlogged) and the vendor's database. This delay may vary from one jurisdiction to another; access to some records may be delayed for three months or more.

Records filed in a municipality may not appear in the county records until much later. Cities may report to counties monthly, or only semi-annually, and the counties may not report to the states until much later. Information may even be held at the local level because the people involved are the record-keeper's friends or relatives.

Many public records vendors offer limited search capabilities. The sophisticated search engines found on some of today's online services are rarely encountered in the public records arena. In fact, many vendors allow only the most elementary menu-driven searches, with nothing even close to Boolean logic (AND, OR, and NOT) capabilities. One seldom finds a public records database that can be searched for groups of individuals with similar characteristics. An exception to this is Lexis, which provides the same search capabilities for public records as for its news and legal databases.

This is not to say that a single inquiry will never result in the display of records for more than one individual. At times, several records match the inquiry criteria and are displayed. Some vendors will display a warning message when this occurs, or a summary of the possible record matches so that you can select the ones you wish to see in detail, rather than pay for all of them.

As for court record systems, in most states, PACER provides access to civil and criminal records from United States District Courts, as well as bankruptcy records. The actual case record content varies and is determined by each local district. Some districts keep all open and closed cases on their databases, whereas others maintain only open cases and purge records after cases are closed. Similar court records systems include NIBS-BRASS, CHIP, and ACES (Appellate Court Electronic Services), also known as EDOS (Electronic Dissemination of Opinions System). Others are emerging in courts throughout the country, each with its own content and search capabilities.

All of these circumstances can omit public records from online systems and make useful information more difficult to obtain. These are imperfect processes, so the current online public records systems should still be viewed as evolving tools, rather than final solutions.

Types of Public Records Available Online
Arrests

Although records of arrests may be viewed on the blotters sitting in police stations across the land, arrest records are not generally available through online public records systems. This is probably for the best, as arrests are not convictions and under the criminal justice system should not be held against the accused. Furthermore, certain minorities clearly have been subject to arrest in certain areas due only to their ethnicity, and not their activities, so consideration of arrests could bear unfairly on those groups. With these factors in mind, one should be very cautious about the use of arrest records.

This does not mean that arrests never show up online. Many newspapers routinely carry stories about people who have been arrested for local crimes, and most of these can be found online.

You can also find a few police blotters (also known as booking logs or arrest logs) listed in newspapers that are accessible through the Internet, such as those listed by the following:

> The News-Times (Danbury, Connecticut), Police Reports
> www.newstimes.com/news/today/police.htm
>
> The Journal Tribune (York County, Maine)
> www.journaltribune.com/pswkd.html
>
> The Lincoln Journal Star (Nebraska)
> www.journalstar.com/police_blotter
>
> The Concord Monitor (New Hampshire)
> www.cmonitor.com/index/policelogs.shtml
>
> The Portsmouth Herald (New Hampshire), Police Logs
> www.portsmouthherald.com/news/index.htm
>
> The Daily Egyptian (the paper of Southern Illinois University
> at Carbondale), News
> www.dailyegyptian.com

The St. Paul, Minnesota, Police Department has created a Web site to display those arrested for prostitution or for hiring prostitutes in its fair city, in order to combat this vice at www.stpaul.gov/ depts/police/prostitution.html. Toronto In FOCUS (www.torontoinfocus.com/police.shtml) includes the police blotter for Toronto, Ohio. The Police Log for East Haven, Connecticut, is at http://nearhome.com/ct/easthaven/police/blotter/list.html. The Hillsborough County, Florida,

Sheriff's Office publishes arrests on its Web site (www.hcso.tampa.fl.us/pub/default.asp?/Online/sname01); the Greensboro, North Carolina, Police Department lists its arrest log at www.ci.greensboro.nc.us/police.

Celebrity arrests may be featured in all news media as well. In fact, there is even a Web site called Famous Mugshots that publishes arrest photos of celebrities at www.mugshots.org. Unfortunately, a subsequent release, dismissal, or acquittal may go unreported in the same news databases that are filled with stories of the arrest.

Please refer to Chapter 20 for further information about coverage of arrests in the news.

Bankruptcy Records

Bankruptcy is a legal process under Federal law intended not only to ensure fairness and equality among creditors, but also to help debtors by enabling them to start anew with property exempted from their liabilities, unhampered by the pressure and discouragement of previous debts. A person is not bankrupt until adjudicated bankrupt under Federal law. A corporation is not bankrupt until it performs an "act of bankruptcy" or proceedings in bankruptcy have been instituted by or against it.

Bankruptcy information can be found on many public records systems and court records systems, as well as on consumer credit reports, business credit reports, and company financial databases. Bankruptcies can include voluntary and involuntary adjudication of a debtor under Chapter 7, Chapter 11, or Chapter 13, as well as relief of the debtor by reorganization and readjustment, which is under Chapter 11. Chapter 12 bankruptcies, which apply to family farmers, can also be found online.

On the Internet, it is possible to search for bankruptcies. Publications sites such as *BayouBusiness NewsWire* (www.bayoubusiness.com/legal) provide public notices of bankruptcies within their region. The American Bankruptcy Institute posts headlines about bankruptcies on its site at www.abiworld.org/headlines/todayshead.html. Idaho bankruptcies can be found at www.id.uscourts.gov/doc.htm.

Bankruptcies are sometimes listed within Grantor/Grantee Indices. Refer to that section of this chapter for examples of these indices that can be searched online.

There are also many fee-based services offering bankruptcy records. Some of these offer free searches, but charge for detailed records. An example is BankruptcyData.Com (www.bankruptcydata.com/findabrtop.asp).

When a bankruptcy record is located through any online system, many more details usually are available on file at the court. It is still necessary to obtain copies of those records in order to gain a complete picture of the bankruptcy, or a person's finances.

Birth Records

Many birth records can now be found on the Internet. Some of these are stored at genealogical sites, which may include older as well as current records (as noted by date ranges). Others are made available through government agencies, and are usually fairly current. Numerous Web-based sources of birth records are available through the *Naked in Cyberspace* Web site.

If you are looking for someone's birthday, you can also try to find her at Anybirthday.com (anybirthday.com/search.htm); however, if the name is not unique, it will be difficult to determine whether you've found the correct person's birthday.

Please refer to Chapter 34: Genealogical Records for further information about birth records found online, such as those found in cemetery records, church records, birth notices, and family histories.

Business Licenses

Business licenses are necessary in order to do business in many areas of the country. These are sometimes administered by a city, a state, or a licensing agency. Business licenses can be useful in locating a person or the subject's business assets. See the *Naked in Cyberspace* Web site for examples of business licenses that can be found on the Internet.

Business Public Filings

Although sometimes grouped as Business Public Filings, these include bankruptcies, tax liens, and judgments on businesses. Please refer to those reports individually in this chapter.

Campaign Contributions

Please refer to Chapter 35: Political Records for information about tracking campaign contributions.

Certificates of Listings or Secretary of State Filings

A certificate of listing, from the Secretary of State, lists the types of records that are on file for a specific corporation. Typical records would include:

- Corporate identification number
- Corporation name
- Type(s) of document(s) on file

Certificates of Merger

A certificate of merger, from the Secretary of State, indicates that two or more corporations have merged. Typical records include the following:

- Corporate identification numbers
- Corporation names

Certificates of Name Reservation

A company may reserve a business name with the Secretary of State for a short period (typically 10 to 60 days), during which time the company is incorporating under that name or changing the previous corporate name. These records can provide clues as to what a competitor is planning. Typical certificates of name reservations include:

- Business name to be reserved
- Name of party reserving business name
- Address of party reserving business name

Certificates of Nonfiling

A certificate of nonfiling indicates that there are no records on file with the Secretary of State for a given corporation, either active or inactive. This is useful in fraud investigations, as well as for those companies wishing to find out whether a corporation name has been used within a state. (Note that an unincorporated company may still be using the name.) A typical certificate of nonfiling record will list only the corporation name.

Certificates of Status

A certificate of status from the Secretary of State indicates the existence and current standing of a corporation doing business within a state. Typical records include:

- Corporate identification number

- Corporation name

- Corporate status

Civil Court Records

Civil court records can be obtained from the superior, supreme, district, justice, municipal, small claims, city, or circuit courts, as well as courts of common pleas. Online civil records may include civil, probate, and family law (such as dissolution of marriage—divorce, legal separation, nullity, dissolution with Uniform Child Custody Act, and summary dissolution) cases. Civil court records can be used to locate court minutes, court dockets, and civil case files. They are available from public records vendors as well as court records systems and sometimes on the Internet.

Refer to Court Case Summaries later in this chapter for examples of sites containing civil court records.

Construction and Water Resource Permits

Although not usually available online, construction and water resource permits for North Dakota can be found at the following Web sites:

Construction Permits
www.swc.state.nd.us/4DLink/4dcgi/DamSearchForm

Drainage Permits
www.swc.state.nd.us/4DLink/4dcgi/DrainSearchForm

Water Permits
www.swc.state.nd.us/4DLink/4dcgi/PermitForm

Consumer Public Filings

Although sometimes grouped as consumer public filings, such filings often include bankruptcies, tax liens, and judgments for individuals. Please refer to those reports individually elsewhere in this chapter.

Corporate Records or Corporate Document Listings

Sometimes grouped as corporate document listings or corporate records, these searches can include articles of incorporation, certificates of acquisition, mergers, and name changes.

The Articles of Incorporation is the legal instrument that creates a corporation, pursuant to the general corporation laws of the state. Public records vendors typically obtain articles of incorporation and limited partnership records from the Secretary of State. These records aid in locating the name of the registered agent in order to serve process on a company and make it possible to obtain the legal name of a business when conducting a fraud investigation.

All of the corporate records can also be very useful in locating assets or backgrounding an individual. They conceivably could even help someone in searching for a job. For example, if my dream were to work for Steven Spielberg, a quick online search could point me to several companies in which Spielberg has a financial interest where I could begin my job search.

The online treasure trove of corporate filings can be found on the Securities and Exchange Commission site (www.sec.gov) in its Edgar Archives.

Many of the corporations databases are now available and searchable via the Internet through the Secretaries of State, Departments of Commerce, or sometimes other organizations within a state. The *Naked in Cyberspace* Web site includes numerous relevant links.

Corporate Tax Records

Corporate tax records typically include:

- Corporate filename
- Current year's tax assessments
- Current year's payments
- Previous year's tax assessments
- Previous year's payments

Court Case Transcripts

Copies of actual court transcripts can be ordered online through services such as Westlaw and LEXSEE, on the Lexis service. These services typically require a case citation in order to retrieve a document. Thus, it is sometimes necessary to search the court indices for this information before retrieving copies of the actual case transcripts.

Court Case Summaries

Summaries of cases, court dockets, details of verdicts, and settlements can be found in the legal journals, such as those in the Lexis Verdicts Library. Records such as these can be very helpful in obtaining a quick synopsis of a case, as well as in locating and checking the credentials of expert witnesses and attorneys. Attorneys use such information to size up the competition and to gather fodder for the impeachment of witnesses.

Case summaries can also sometimes be found on the Internet through county or court sites. These sometimes include only civil records, only criminal records, or various types of records. Case summaries can also sometimes be included in the Grantor/Grantee Indices, as noted later in this chapter. See the *Naked in Cyberspace* Web site for a list of case summary sources.

Court Dockets

A court docket lists the cases on a court's calendar. Court docket information is now available online through several court records systems, such as the PACER (Public Access to Court Electronic Records) system, NIBS-BRASS, CHIP, and ACES (Appellate Court Electronic Services), also known as EDOS (Electronic Dissemination of Opinions System). It is also often available within the case summaries found on the Internet. Refer to Court Case Summaries earlier in this chapter for further information.

Criminal Records

Criminal records are created, stored, updated, and tracked throughout the criminal justice system. When criminal cases reach the courts, they normally become a matter of public record. (An exception to this is for juvenile cases, which usually are sealed from public view.) Criminal court records can be filed at the municipal, superior, or federal courts. Typical criminal records found on public records systems include:

- Court
- Case or file number
- Case title
- Date filed
- Close date
- Defendant name
- Defendant date of birth
- Additional or cross-defendant name or plaintiff name
- List of charges
- Violations

These records can be found on public records systems, and sometimes on the Internet. Refer to Court Case Summaries, earlier in this chapter, for examples of sites containing Criminal Court Records.

Death Records

Death records can sometimes be found through public records vendors, as well as on the Internet in some cases. Those found on the Internet may include fairly current records, but may also be limited to older records collected by genealogists. Links to death records sources are available on the *Naked in Cyberspace* Web site.

Please refer to Chapter 28 for further information about death records and to Chapter 33 for celebrity deaths. Also refer to Chapter 34 for genealogical records of death, including those taken from cemetery records and family histories. Obituaries and death notices can also be found in the news, so refer to Chapter 20 for news.

Divorce Records

Divorce records can be found in the Civil Court Indices, or sometimes separated into their own databases. ChoicePoint Online, for example, offers a divorce index for Nevada, and another for Texas. The *Naked in Cyberspace* Web site includes numerous links to divorce records sources on the Internet.

Please refer to the discussion of civil court indices mentioned earlier in this chapter for further information about divorce records. Note that Grantor/Grantee Indices also sometimes contain divorce filings.

Federal Tax Liens

A federal tax lien is a lien of the United States on "all property and rights to property" of a taxpayer who fails to pay a tax for which that person is liable to the Federal government. It reaches not only all property owned by the taxpayer when the lien arises, but also property that otherwise would be exempt by state law from the reach of creditors.

Please refer to the discussion of tax liens later in this chapter, which also deals with state and county tax liens.

Fictitious Name Statements

Fictitious Name Statements (aka Doing Business As, DBAs, Fictitious Business Names, or assumed names) provide information on filings that reflect the intent of an individual or company to conduct business under a fictitious name. These can be very useful in competitive intelligence research, and are also used to locate people and to determine an individual's business affiliations. The information provided typically includes:

- File number
- File date
- Business name
- Business address
- Owner name

Sources of Fictitious Name Statements available on the Internet can be found at the *Naked in Cyberspace* Web site.

Please note that Fictitious Name Statements can also sometimes be found within Grantor/Grantee Indices, so please check that section of this chapter for further information.

Franchise Tax Board Status Letters

The Franchise Tax Board Status Letter is the official certificate from the State Franchise Tax Board, which reveals a corporation's ability or inability to transact business within the state. Typical online indices to these records include:

- Corporate identification number
- Corporation name
- Status

- Actions taken by the Franchise Tax Board (as a result of unpaid tax liability)

These records can typically be found through a search of corporate and limited partnership records.

For Texas, the Franchise Tax Board Status Letter, along with listings of officers and directors, can be found at http://ecpa.cpa.state.tx.us/coa/coaStart.html.

Grantor/Grantee Indices

Grantor/grantee records, maintained by some counties, can be a catch-all place for various types of record. They may include abstracts of judgment, death distribution decrees, deeds, property transfers, fictitious name filings, financing statements, homesteads, liens, notices of default, powers of attorney, reconveyances, satisfactions of judgment, UCC financing statements, case summaries, and up to 400 document types. Some public records vendors carry an index to grantor/grantee records, although they may contain only a selection of these records, such as property transfers. Some counties have made these records available on the Internet, grouped as public records, official records, or county recorder records. The *Naked in Cyberspace* Web site features a number of useful links.

Hospital Liens

Hospital liens may appear as part of a Judgment Docket and Lien Book search, grouped with bankruptcies, liens, and judgments, or otherwise appear in some type of online lien index. They can also be found within Grantor/Grantee Indices in some cases.

For Benton County, Arkansas, hospital liens can be searched on the Internet, listed under Other Public Records, Medical Liens at www.co.benton.ar.us.

Please refer to the discussion of liens later in this chapter for further information.

Judgments

A personal judgment, usually referred to simply as a judgment, is rendered against an individual or an entity such as a corporation for the payment of money damages. Typical judgment indices include:

- Case or lien number

- Creditor name

- Debtor name

- Filing and release dates

- Liability amount

Judgments can sometimes be found within Court Case Summaries or Grantor/Grantee Indices. Please refer to those sections of this chapter for further information.

Lawsuits

Please refer to the discussion of court dockets, civil court indices, case transcripts, court case summaries, and judgments earlier in this chapter.

Liens

Liens may include hospital liens, mechanic's liens, and sidewalk liens. A public records vendor may offer each of these as separate searches, or liens may be grouped together into one search. Online vendors sometimes group liens into a "Liens and Judgments" search, or Judgment Docket and Lien Book search. For example, ChoicePoint Online offers the New York State Supreme Court Judgment Docket and Lien Book, which includes civil judgments, hospital liens, mechanic's liens, building loans, lis pendens, sidewalk liens, and Federal tax liens. Typical records include the following information:

- Attorney name

- Creditor name

- Debtor address

- Debtor name

- Effective date

- Expiration date

- Filing type

- Judgment or lien amount

- Satisfaction date

- Third party

Records such as these are used in fraud investigation, background searches, skip tracing, asset searching, and so on

Please refer also to the discussion of tax liens later in this chapter for additional information.

Limited Partnership Records

Please refer to corporate and limited partnership records discussed earlier in this chapter.

Lis Pendens

Lis pendens are pending lawsuits. Notices of lis pendens are required in some jurisdictions to warn others (such as prospective purchasers) that the title to a property is in litigation, and that they will be bound by any judgment. Lis pendens may also appear in the Judgment Docket and Lien Book. Please refer to the discussion of liens earlier in this chapter for further information.

Marriage License Indices

Marriage license information is very useful for locating people. Women may not appear on other records, because their names have changed with marriage. Marriage license indices can be used to identify the new surname.

Marriage license information found online is often limited to older records collected by genealogists. Where current records are found, a copy of the marriage license can also be ordered, which may provide the actual address at the time of the marriage.

Examples of marriage licenses that can be found on the Internet include American Marriages before 1699, located at www.ancestry.com/search/rectype/inddbs/2081.htm. Additional sites can be found at the *Naked in Cyberspace* Web site.

It is sometimes possible for a couple to obtain a "confidential" marriage license. These marriage licenses do not require a blood test, as they are offered only to couples who are already cohabiting. These licenses may be missing from the marriage indices, as it is assumed that the couple would want to protect the fact that they cohabited prior to marriage. Thus, the fact that no marriage license is found does not prove that none exists. Please refer to Chapter 34: Genealogical Records for additional marriage record information found in church records and family histories and marriage notices found in the news.

Mechanic's Liens

A mechanic's lien is "one created for the purpose of securing priority of payment of the price or value of work performed and materials furnished in erecting or repairing a building or other structure, and as such attaches to the land as well as buildings and improvements erected thereon." Please refer to the discussion of Liens and to Grantor/Grantee Indices earlier in this chapter for further information.

Name Changes

Although these records are not usually found online, you can search for name changes for Massachusetts (1780–1892) at www.ancestry.com/search/rectype/inddbs/3280.htm.

Notice of Default/Notice of Sale

A Notice of Default (sometimes referred to as a Notice of Sale) identifies a failure to discharge a duty or make payments on a loan. This most often refers to a failure to make payments on a mortgage loan. These records are filed at the county recorder's office, but some of the public records vendors offer them online. These records typically include:

- Filing date

- Filing number

- Debtor name(s)

- Debtor address

- Court location

- Document information

- Tax assessor's parcel number

- Tax assessor's lot number

- Tax assessor's map number

- Actual street address of property

Occupational Safety and Health Act Records

In 1970, Congress passed the Occupational Safety and Health Act in an attempt to protect employees against being injured or contracting illnesses in the course of their employment. This empowered the Occupational Safety and Health Administration (OSHA) to inspect business premises and to impose civil and criminal injunctions and penalties where safety violations are found. Some public records vendors have obtained OSHA records from the United States Department of Labor, Occupational Safety and Health Administration, and make them available online. These records can help in competitive intelligence research, background investigations, and sometimes in locating people. Typical records include:

- Accident information

- Accident victim name

- Administrative payment information

- Business address

- Business name

- Company debt on file with OSHA

- Failure to abate history

- Hazardous substances found during inspection

- Hours spent in inspection

- Inspection office

- Inspection officer

- Number of employees

- OSHA file entry date

- Penalties assessed

- Reason for inspection

- Scope of inspection

- SIC Code

- Total number of violations cited

OSHA records can now also be searched on the Internet at www.osha.gov/oshstats; however, it is not possible to search by injured party through this site.

Patents

A patent for an invention is the grant of a property right to the inventor, issued by the Patent and Trademark Office (PTO). The term of a new patent is 20 years from the date on which the application for the patent was filed in the United States or, in special cases, from the date an earlier related application was filed, subject to the payment of maintenance fees.

U.S. patents can now be searched online at www.uspto.gov/web/menu/pats.html, http://patents.uspto.gov/patft/index.html, or www.delphion.com/simple. International patent applications can be searched on the PCT Database at http://ipdl.wipo.int.

Links to these and additional online patent databases can be found at the *Naked in Cyberspace* Web site.

Personal Property Filings

Refer to Real Property Ownership.

Probate Records

Probate records (wills and the documents proving their legality and validity) are indexed online in some jurisdictions. Typical records include:

- Case title

- File date

- File number

- Name of decedent

Probate records are sometimes found on the Internet (see the *Naked in Cyberspace* Web site for examples). Probate records also can sometimes be found within Court Case Summaries or Grantor/Grantee Indices. Please refer to those sections of this chapter for further information.

Real Property Ownership

Real property records, usually obtained from county recorder and tax assessor records, are available on many public records systems. In fact, several systems (like Damar and DataQuick) have been designed specifically for real property records and are used extensively by real estate and title agents. These records are also very useful for asset investigation, as a home represents the largest asset for many people.

Real property ownership records may include not only ownership information and property transfers, but refinances, construction loans, and seller carry-backs (in which the seller of the property is also the lender). Searches by owner name, property address, and mailing address are all available through public records systems, some at the county level, and others combining several counties or "statewide" (with the limitations explained earlier). These searches are performed in order to locate all of the properties owned by a person or business, as well as the history of ownership and current title of a property.

Real estate systems can also offer searches using the other property characteristics, such as the number of bedrooms and bathrooms, price, and area.

Real property records for many areas of the country can now be searched on the Internet; see the *Naked in Cyberspace* Web site for a listing.

Please refer to Chapter 34: Genealogical Records for additional land records. Refer to Grantor/Grantee Indices earlier in this chapter, as real property records often are contained in those records. Note that personal property records may also be found at the same Web sites as real property records.

Registered Sex Offenders

Please refer to Chapter 26: Criminal Justice Records for further information about these records.

Sales and Use Tax Permits

Sales and Use Tax Permits, from the State Board of Equalization or Comptroller's Office, represent information about individuals and companies that pay sales tax and have either an active or inactive taxpayer ID assigned. Files include corporations, limited and general partnerships, and sole proprietors. Information listed from these permits includes:

- Taxpayer name
- Taxpayer address
- Type of business
- Outlet information

SEC Reports

Securities and Exchange Commission (SEC) Reports are available through many online systems, such as the Disclosure database on Lexis. SEC filings are not found on as many public records systems as on other, more mainstream, systems, but they may be found on either. SEC reports include various SEC filings, company profiles, quarterly financials, and annual financials. These reports are useful in asset investigation, competitive intelligence research, and can even be used in locating people. Records can include any of the following information, derived from annual reports, 10-K forms, 20-F forms, 10-Q forms, and proxy statements, or any other SEC filing:

- Annual assets and liabilities
- Auditor company name
- Balance sheet
- Company address
- Company telephone number
- Current dividends
- CUSIP number
- Dun's number
- Earnings per share
- Exchange symbol
- Fiscal year and date
- Five year summary of sales

- Forbes number

- Forms filed with the SEC (with dates)

- Fortune number

- Latest annual data date

- Latest quarterly data date

- Latest weekly data about prices

- Legal counsel

- Market value

- Names of 5 percent owners

- Names of insiders

- Names of officers, directors, nominees

- Net income

- Number of employees

- Number of shareholders

- Outstanding shares of stock

- Previous dividends

- Shares held by officers and directors

- SIC Code

- Stock transfer agent

- Subsidiaries

- Ticker symbol

- Trade dates

- Trade highs/lows/closing prices

- Trade volume

Many SEC reports can also be found on EDGAR, the Electronic Data Gathering, Analysis, and Retrieval system, at the SEC Web site (www.sec.gov).

EDGAR performs automated collection, validation, indexing, acceptance, and forwarding of submissions by companies and others that are required by law to file forms with the U.S. Securities and Exchange Commission.

Not all documents filed with the Commission by public companies are available on EDGAR. Companies were phased into the system over a three-year period that ended on May 6, 1996. As of that date, all public domestic companies were required to make their filings on EDGAR, except for filings made to the Commission's regional offices and filings made on paper because of a hardship exemption. Third-party filings with respect to these companies, such as tender offers and Schedules 13D, are also filed on EDGAR.

Electronic filing is banned for some documents, and consequently those records will not be available on EDGAR. Other documents may be filed on EDGAR voluntarily, but are not mandatory, and consequently may or may not be available on EDGAR. For example, Forms 3, 4, and 5 (security ownership and transaction reports filed by corporate insiders), Form 144 (notice of proposed sale of securities) and Form 13F (reports filed by institutional investment managers showing equity holdings by accounts under their management) may be filed on EDGAR at the option of the filer. Similarly, filings by foreign companies are not required to be filed on EDGAR, but some of these companies do so voluntarily.

Servitude and Emancipation Records

Although these records are not routinely available online, there is a database including more than 2,000 transactions found in Illinois governmental records involving servitude and emancipation of Africans and, occasionally, Indians in the French and English eras of colonial Illinois (1722–1790) and African-Americans in the American period of Illinois (1790–1863). The Archives (www.sos.state.il.us/departments/archives/servant.html) extracted the names of servants, slaves, or free persons and masters, witnesses, or related parties from selected governmental records to produce this database.

Sidewalk Liens

Please refer to the discussion of liens earlier in this chapter for more information.

Statements and Designations by Foreign Corporations and Amendments

Corporations doing business in one state while incorporated in another may be found in the Statements and Designations by Foreign Corporations and Amendments. Typical records include:

- Corporate identification number

- Corporation name

As you can see, very little information is provided in this type of index; however, it is sufficient to obtain copies of the actual records, where details may be found.

Statements of Domestic Stock Corporations

Please refer to corporate and limited partnership records discussed earlier in this chapter.

Tax Liens

Tax liens can include federal, state, and county tax liens. Typical tax liens found online include:

- Court

- Lien number

- Tax board certificate number

- Date of lien

- Debtor name

- Doing Business As (DBA)

- Cross-debtor name

- Secured party/plaintiff name

- Amount of lien

On many public records systems, tax liens are also included in a grouped search of bankruptcies, liens, and judgments. Tax liens can also be found on consumer credit and business credit reports.

Please refer to the section on liens that appears earlier in this chapter for further information.

Trademarks

A trademark is a word, name, symbol, or device that is used in trade with goods to indicate the source of the goods and to distinguish them from the goods of others. A servicemark is the same as a trademark except that it identifies and distinguishes the source of a service rather than a product.

Trademark rights may be used to prevent others from using a confusingly similar mark, but not to prevent others from making the same goods or from selling the same goods or services under a clearly different mark. Trademarks used in interstate or foreign commerce may be registered with the Patent and Trademark Office.

Federally registered (or pending) trademarks can be searched through the Trademark Electronic Search System at http://tess.uspto.gov/web/menu.tm.html or through Trademark Applications and Registration Retrieval at http://tarr.uspto.gov.

International Trademark Applications are searchable through Madrid Express at http://ipdl.wipo.int.

Additional searchable trademark databases are listed on the *Naked in Cyberspace* Web site.

Uniform Commercial Code Indices (UCC)

The Uniform Commercial Code (UCC) was adopted to assure national uniformity when describing goods, timber, or crops that are pledged as security for a loan. These filings offer protection against debtor bankruptcy, insolvency, or default.

If household goods or furnishings are pledged, these records are filed in the county where the debtor lives or where the goods are located. If timber or crops are pledged, these records are filed in the county where the timber or crops are grown. If business or farm equipment, accounts payable, inventory, or trust receipts are pledged, these records are filed with the Secretary of State or Department of Commerce. UCC filings are now available online (see the *Naked in Cyberspace* Web site for useful links).

UCC filings are also sometimes found within the Grantor/Grantee Indices, as noted earlier in this chapter.

Voter Registration Records

Voter registration records are available online through some of the public records vendors. These records are particularly useful for locating people, as they provide a name and address, as well as a birth date, which often is absent from public records and can help to identify individuals with common names.

Voter registration records typically include:

- Name of voter

- Address of voter

- Date of birth

- Party identification

- Registration date

- Voter identification number

- Voting district number

See the *Naked in Cyberspace* Web site for links to voter registration records sources.

Court Records Systems

In addition to the various public records vendors who are making public records accessible online, the federal courts have introduced services that permit online public access to court information. These services include ACES (EDOS), PACER, and similar systems developed separately by various districts, operating under names such as NIBS-BRASS and CHIP.

Electronic Dissemination of Opinions System (EDOS)

First introduced in 1989, the Electronic Dissemination of Opinions System (EDOS) (or Appellate Court Electronic Services, aka ACES) is an electronic system of appellate court information and decisions. Records include slip opinions, court oral arguments, calendars, court rules, notices, press releases, and reports. This service includes Federal Circuit Courts, as well as some District and Bankruptcy courts.

Public Access to Court Electronic Records (PACER)

Also introduced in 1989, PACER (Public Access to Court Electronic Records) is an electronic public access service that provides online access to court case information and court dockets from Federal Appellate, District and Bankruptcy courts, and from the U.S. Party/Case Index.

RACER (Remote Access to Court Electronic Records) is software (developed by Wade Systems, LLC; www.wadesystems.com) that provides access to PACER, using the Internet, rather than dial-up networks. You will sometimes find PACER services listed under PACER, and others listed under RACER. For further information about PACER, you can visit the PACER Service Center at http://pacer.psc.uscourts.gov.

For a directory of PACER and other similar services, refer to the Directory of Electronic Public Access Services to Automated Information in the United States Federal Courts, at http://pacer.psc.uscourts.gov/pubaccess.html.

Circuit court cases can also be searched through the sites listed at www.courses.unt.edu/chandler/SLIS5647/WorkBook/Week1/FCCCLaw.html.

Other Types of Records Available from Public Records Vendors and County Sites

Business Credit Records

Dun and Bradstreet, Experian, and other vendors offer business credit records. These records are provided directly by these vendors but are also available on some of the mainstream systems, such as Dialog, and from public records vendors as well. Please refer to Appendix C for examples of business credit and company financial databases, and the systems that offer these databases. Additional information can be found in Chapter 10: Asset Searches.

Consumer Credit Records

Many public records vendors offer consumer credit records, address updates, Social Security number searches, and other credit-based records. Please refer to Chapter 25: Consumer Credit Records for further information.

Death Records (from Social Security Benefits Records)

The Social Security Administration (SSA) is usually notified of a person's death when a beneficiary dies or the death benefit is claimed. These records are not public, but the Social Security Administration does make them available through many public records vendors, and they can now also be found on the Internet. Please refer to Chapter 28: Death Records for additional information about SSA records, as well as many other types of death records.

Dog Tag Registrations/Licenses

Dog tag licenses are not usually a matter of public record, yet some are found online at city or county Web sites (see the *Naked in Cyberspace* Web site for examples).

Federal Aviation Administration Records

The Federal Aviation Administration (FAA) maintains records on all currently registered individuals or businesses that own aircraft throughout the United States, as well as an FAA Airmen Directory. Federal Aviation Administration ownership information includes:

- Description of the aircraft
- Owner address
- Owner name
- Registration information

FAA Airmen Directory records include:

- Name of airman
- Mailing address of airman

- Certificate class

- Date of last medical exam

Aircraft owners and pilots, aviation medical examiners, and A & P (Airframe & Powerplant) mechanics can now be found on the Internet as well, at www.landings.com.

Fish and Game Licenses

Fish and Game Licenses may seem relatively trivial as public records go, but they actually can be very useful. For example, someone who is hiding from creditors may not realize that a fishing trip can leave an automated paper trail that others can follow from across the country, leading them directly to his or her location.

Although many jurisdictions don't make it possible to search these records online, the North Dakota Game and Fish Inquiry System (www.state.nd.us/gnf/inquiry/pubsysinq.html) allows you to search for those licensed to hunt in North Dakota.

General Indices

Public records vendors sometimes offer a general index search, which allows you to search all, or a portion, of the vendors' databases at once. These indices identify which databases contain records matching the individual's name or other search criteria. Although vendors may levy an additional charge for this index search, the fee is sometimes credited against subsequent fees on searches that result from the general search. Please refer to Chapter 16 for further information about General Indices.

Military Locators

Public records vendors also sometimes offer a service whereby they provide the location of active military personnel and military retirees who are receiving benefits. Please refer to Chapter 6 for further information about military locators.

Missing Persons

Although missing persons are usually handled by police agencies, missing persons reports are not criminal records. Nor are they public records. For want of a better place to put them, they are included here, because missing persons information now appears online at many county Web sites, as well as the sites of private agencies, police, and sheriff departments. A list of Missing Persons URLs can be found at the *Naked in Cyberspace* Web site.

A great many missing-person Web sites are dedicated to people who want to post messages to a lost love, an old friend, a birthparent, or a child who has been adopted.

Motor Vehicle Records

Motor vehicle registrations, driving records, and driver's license information are offered by many public records vendors. Please refer to Chapter 27: Department of Motor Vehicles for more information about these records.

National Address Search

National address searches can be as simple as a national telephone directory search (as described in Chapter 17), or they may include several other searches, such as postal change of address, publisher's change of address, and even real estate. Please refer to these specific types of record elsewhere in this chapter for more information.

National (Postal) Change of Address

The U.S. Postal Service provides national change of address (NCOA) records through many vendors in order to expedite address updates. Some of the vendors that receive these records are public records vendors, who then sell the individual records upon request.

Professional/Occupational Licenses

Professional license indices are available online through many public records vendors, as well as through Web sites of the agencies that issue licenses and government sites. The records are normally obtained from various individual licensing agencies, and are sometimes combined into a multilicense search.

Please refer to Chapter 7: Pre-Employment Screening for additional information about professional licensing databases. Refer also to Federal Aviation Administration (FAA) Records, earlier in this chapter, for aviation-related licenses.

Publishers' Change of Address

Magazine publishers receive notifications of changes of address from their subscribers. Even those hiding from a creditor sometimes update the publishers of magazines in order to take their subscriptions with them to their new addresses. Some publishers sell these records to public records vendors, who then sell individual records upon request.

Telephone Directory Searches

Many public records vendors offer location or surname searches based on telephone directories. They sometimes also offer reverse directory searches, allowing you to look up a telephone number or address and find the person who owns it, and neighborhood searches, which provide a range of names and telephone numbers for the homes surrounding a targeted home. Some vendors also use warranty card data, census information, and mailing lists to add length of residence and approximate income levels of occupants; one such service is Infoscan, offered by ChoicePoint Online. Please refer to Chapter 17: Telephone Directories for more information on searching telephone directories.

Utility Company Records

You can occasionally find an individual's water, electric, sewer, cable, or gas company records available on a public record vendor's system. These records are seldom available to the public directly through the utility company, so their presence online represents an even more valuable resource for investigators.

Vendor Registrations and Licenses

Although not necessarily a matter of public record, vendor registrations and licenses can be found on some public records systems, as well as on the Internet (see the *Naked in Cyberspace* Web site for a list of URLs).

Watercraft Ownership Records

Watercraft ownership records from the U.S. Coast Guard can be found online through some of the public records vendors. These records contain information on merchant and recreational vessels weighing no less than five net tons (approximately 27 feet or more) that are owned by U.S. citizens or corporations. These records can be useful in locating assets of an individual or corporation. The data included in these records follows:

- Certificate status
- Home port
- Official ID number
- Owner name
- Owner address
- Service type
- Trade indicator
- Vessel description
- Vessel name
- Vessel size
- Vessel weight

The Port State Information Exchange Vessel Search is now available on the Internet at http://psix.uscg.mil/Default.asp.

Worker's Compensation Records

Worker's Compensation statutes establish the liability of employers for injuries or sicknesses that arise out of and in the course of employment. Worker's compensation records typically include:

- Date of birth
- Date of injury
- Filing date
- Injury duration
- Injury type
- Name of injured party
- Social Security number

Records such as these are offered by some public records vendors.

Grouped Searches

Public records vendors sometimes group their searches in various ways in order to make them more attractive or to provide a better value to the buyer. For example, a real property search might include several counties or states. Another vendor might group bankruptcies, tax liens, and judgments into a single search. A civil records search can include records from both municipal and superior courts. Several searches can also be packaged into a more general Asset Search or People Finder grouping. Some group searches may even include all public records that the vendor has on file. Many other varieties of grouped search can be found on public records systems. Although grouped searches are sometimes offered at a discount from the individual search prices, other vendors may charge a premium price for grouped search packages. As with most types of public records found online, wide price variations are common.

Other Services Available from Public Records Vendors

Document Retrieval

Although many databases found online supply only indices to the actual records, public records vendors sometimes allow customers to order an actual document to be retrieved from the court or records facility. The records may be available in a few hours, days, weeks, or even months, and they may be delivered in a variety of ways, including online (on the public records system or through e-mail), fax, overnight delivery, or the U.S. Postal Service.

On-Site Court Searches

Not all public records are even indexed online at this time. For those records that are not, some public records vendors let customers order a search and then perform the actual search at the court or records building. At that point, the records may be delivered by any of the methods listed previously.

Screening and Verification Services

Public records vendors sometimes offer value-added services based in part on public records or database records. These may include pre-employment screening, tenant screening, or similar services, which may also involve database searches, as well as calling previous employers, landlords, schools, or other agencies that have records that are not available online.

Services could even include administration of honesty test instruments, drug testing, or other pre-employment screening having little or nothing to do with database records.

Summary

Public records contain a wealth of information about individuals and their business dealings. Many types of personal research, such as asset searching, pre-employment screening, and locating people, are extremely dependent upon these records. As public records continue to be made more accessible, such research is becoming easier to do well.

What exists online today is a small portion of the public records that are actually stored. I do not expect all public records to become available online within my lifetime, but many more types will become available as the marketplace demands and is willing to pay for them. How quickly a given record arrives online will also depend upon how it is collected and stored. In other words, some records will reach the online market because of demand, while others will become available simply because they are already automated and easy to load into a public records system. Online vendors are also beginning to offer foreign public records, both domestically and abroad.

Eventually, this may make it possible to perform global asset searches and to locate people who have left the country, using online resources.

In selecting a public records vendor, it is important to consider the geographic area that you anticipate needing records from, the types of records that you anticipate using, the searches and services available from the vendor (including online ease-of-use, document retrieval, and other factors influencing whether the records are accessible, and readable), and price (which may include online time, report fees, fees per printed line of information, fax fees, and on-site document retrieval charges).

In addition to the various public records vendors available by direct dial, growing numbers of fee-based public records databases are accessible through the Internet. Many are listed in Appendix M and are linked to from the *Naked in Cyberspace* Web site.

Many state public records and other government databases are also available through government office sites on the Internet.

Additional Internet sites link you to fee-based public records retrievers and services that can perform online searches for you and services that offer online access directly to their systems (rather than going through the Internet).

To learn more about searching public records, several public records research guides are listed later in Section IV: Where Can I Find More Information?—Books, and public records research organizations appear in Section IV: Where Can I Find More Information?—Organizations.

Chapter 32

Adoption Records

*The test of the morality of a society is
what it does for its children.*

–Dietrich Bonhoeffer

Adoption records are open and available in many countries, including Australia, Colombia, England, Finland, France, Holland, Israel, New Zealand, Scotland, and Sweden. In most of the United States, however, adoption records remain relatively confidential. The exact rules governing them vary from one state to another.

Adoptees, birthparents, siblings, and other relatives who wish to locate each other can and do use many databases to aid in their search. Public records, telephone directories, and other databases can provide valuable clues, and sometimes will lead to the hoped-for reunion. Other databases have been built specifically for adoptees, birthparents, and others seeking reunions with lost relatives. How useful these resources are depends in part upon how much they know about one another,

Adoption/Reunion Registries

Adoption or reunion registries are databases in which a person registers (sometimes free, but often for a small fee) in order to help those who may be trying to find them. This type of database is normally passive; registry owners make no effort to locate a person. You must search the registry for known identifying characteristics such as the name, date of birth, and place of birth. If you find a match, or someone finds your information, the registry provides the information needed to make contact.

Some adoption and reunion registries are active registries, in which the agency actively searches for people on behalf of their registrants. This is normally a fee-based service, charged at a premium above the registry fee.

The grandmother of all reunion registries is the International Soundex Reunion Registry (ISRR). (Refer to Appendix K for the address and telephone number.) The ISRR registers adoptees, siblings, and birthparents, and also many others seeking reunions; runaways, kidnap victims, missing relatives, MIAs, POWs, and abandoned children are all candidates for inclusion in the system. The ISRR can also be contacted on the Internet at www.isrr.net.

Many other adoption and reunion registries are operated by private organizations, and some of these feed into the ISRR or other registries. Some states also operate adoption registries, as do some adoption agencies. For example, the New York State Department of Health has placed information and an application for joining the Adoption Information Registry on the Internet at www.health.state.ny.us/nysdoh/consumer/vr.htm. Figure 32.1 describes how the New York Adoption Information Registry works, in the agency's own words.

What Is the Adoption and Medical Information Registry?

The Adoption and Medical Information Registry in the New York State Department of Health provides three services.

- First, it helps adult adoptees to obtain general nonidentifying information about their adoptions and birthparents.
- Second, it facilitates the exchange of identifying information among adult adoptees and their birthparents.
- Third, it enables adoptees to obtain medical information provided by birthparents after the adoption is finalized.

What Information Is Available?

The registry has three kinds of information: nonidentifying, identifying, and medical.

Nonidentifying Information

Nonidentifying information can be given to an adopted person who is at least 18 years of age without the registration or consent of the birthparents. It may include the following details about the birthparents:

- ages at the time of the adopted person's birth
- heritage, including their nationalities, ethnic backgrounds, and race
- education (number of school years completed)
- general appearance—height, weight, color of eyes, skin, hair
- religion
- talents, hobbies, special interests
- occupations
- health histories at the time of the adopted person's birth
- facts and circumstances related to the adoption
- name of the agency that arranged the adoption, if any

However, all of this information may not have been recorded. Nonidentifying information can be given only to the adopted person. It cannot be released to the adoptive parents, birthparents, sisters or brothers, or anyone else.

Information about the birthparents will be obtained from the records that may be on file with the New York State Department of Health, the New York City Department of Health, the court that finalized the adoption, and the agency (if any) that arranged the adoption.

Identifying Information

Identifying information includes the names and addresses of the adopted person and his or her birthparents. Identifying information cannot be released unless the adoptee is at least 18 years of age and the adopted person and the birth mother and father all register with the Adoption and Medical Information Registry.

If only one birthparent was required to sign the surrender agreement or consent to the adoption, then the registration of the other parent is not needed.

The New York State Department of Health is not allowed to ask adopted persons or their birthparents to join the Adoption and Medical Information Registry or to contact them in any way to obtain a registration.

Before identifying information is released, the New York State Department of Health will check to make sure that the adopted person and all required birthparents are registered. If so, each person will be contacted to make sure that he or she still consents to the exchange of names and addresses. If even one of the necessary parties has not registered or does not give final consent, no identifying information will be released.

Medical Information

Only medical information voluntarily submitted by a birthparent and certified by a licensed healthcare provider may be accepted by the Adoption Medical Information Registry. The information must be on the healthcare provider's letterhead, including the healthcare provider's name, address, telephone number, and signature. Medical information is medical or psychological information, which was learned after the adoption was finalized and which would be of significance to the adoptee when providing his or her healthcare provider with a family medical history. Medical risk factors, hereditary diseases, or other conditions should be reported if the information will promote the adoptee's health or cause the adoptee to seek medical advice or treatment.

When an adoptee registers, any nonidentifying medical information already provided by a birthparent is shared immediately with the adoptee. Thereafter, any medical updates submitted by the birthparent will be forwarded to the adoptee. If the birthparent has not submitted any nonidentifying medical information, the adoptee is notified that no medical information is currently available.

When a birthparent registers, a search of the adoptee file is made to determine if the adoptee is registered. If the adoptee is registered, the medical information is shared with the adoptee. If the adoptee is not registered, the information is kept until the adoptee registers.

Who Can Register?

Adoptees and their birthparents may register. However, there are restrictions based on where the adoptee was born and adopted as well as the adoptee's age.

In all cases, the adoptee must have been both born and adopted in New York State. If it is found that the adoptee was not both born and adopted in New York State, the adoptee or birthparent applicant will be notified that the registration cannot be accepted.

To register for identifying information and general nonidentifying information, the adoptee must be at least 18 years of age.

To register for medical information, there is no age restriction. However, if the adoptee is under 18 years of age, an adoptive parent must sign the application.

Siblings, spouses, grandchildren, aunts, uncles, or any other relatives or friends of the adoptee or birthparent may not register.

How Do You Register?

Adoptees who want to join the Adoption and Medical Information Registry must complete and submit an application. If the adoptee is under 18 years old, an adoptive parent must sign the application. In this case, only post-adoption medical information made available by a birthparent may be released. Identifying information and general nonidentifying information about the birthparents cannot be released unless the adoptee is at least 18 years old. An adoptee may register for one or all of the services available.

Birthparents who wish to make postadoption medical information available to adoptees or to register for identifying information must complete and submit an application. Medical information must be submitted on the medical care provider's letterhead. The medical care provider's name, address, telephone number, license number, and signature must be included. Identifying information cannot be released unless the adoptee is at least 18 years old.

How Long Will It Take?

The time needed to process each application varies according to what has happened since the adoption. Several sources, including the Vital Records Sections of the New York State and New York City Departments of Health, the court of adoption, and the adoption agency, must search their records. It will take at least six months to obtain nonidentifying information. Identifying information cannot be released until all necessary parties to the adoption have registered and consented to the release of the information. This can take years or may never take place at all. Medical information already submitted by birthparents will be shared with the adoptee or adoptive parents when they register. A registered adoptee cannot receive medical information until a birth parent has submitted it.

Figure 32.1   New York Adoption Information Registry

Registries such as these sometimes require the birthparents' consent for their natural children to gain access to their records. When the adoptee contacts the agency, if the birthparent's consent is not on file, the request may be denied unless a court order requires the information in a medical emergency. Adoption registries may also require that adult adoptees give consent before releasing their location to their birthparents. A few state registries record confidentiality requests, rather than release consents.

Each registry sets its own requirements and regulations for matching persons. For example, there often is a minimum age requirement, which varies from state to state. Minors usually are not given access to their birth records until they have reached the age of 18, 19, 21, or 25, depending upon the state. In some cases, the adoptive parent must give consent before the records are released, or the records can be released to a younger adoptee with parental consent. Some agencies require that both birthparents consent before the records are released, if both appear on the original surrender. In yet other cases, the agency must verify the consent with the person before the records are released. Laws surrounding adoptees' rights to their records are changing, so a person born on one date may be denied access to records, while someone born in the same state a year later may be granted access, or vice versa.

Many additional reunion registries can be located and contacted on the Internet:

AdoptionRegistry.Net
www.adoptionregistry.net

BirthQuest Online International Searchable Database
www.birthquest.org

Black Market Adoptee's Registry (U.S. and Canada)
www.geocities.com/Heartland/Garden/2313/index.htm

British Columbia's Adoption Reunion Registry
www.adoptionreunion.net

Central Adoption Registry for the Texas Department of Health
www.tdh.state.tx.us/bvs/car/car.htm

Free International Adoption Registry (at Adoption Triad Outreach)
www.atonetwork.org/Registry.htm

Illinois Adoption Registry
www.idph.state.il.us/vital/iladoptreg.htm

Maternity Home Registry
www.crashers.com/search/1form.html

Searching for Siblings Registry
http://sibsearch.8m.com

The Seekers of the Lost International Free Adoption and Missing Persons
Registry
www.seeklost.com

Twins & Triplets Search Registry
http://hometown.aol.com/CEEART/index10.html

Vermont Adoption Registry
www.state.vt.us/srs/adoption/registry.html

So many adoption/reunion registries are now available on the Internet that a search engine has been developed to search several of them at once:

AdoptionRetriever.com
www.adoptionretriever.com

News Groups

Many online news groups and forums focus on adoption. Participants in these news groups frequently offer information about state regulations, new legislation, search advice, and personal experiences. Participants often send out pleas for assistance to "anyone who knows who my parents are" and similar requests.

On the Internet, some of the Usenet Newsgroups dedicated to adoption issues include:

- alt.adoption

- alt.adoption.agency

- alt.adoption.issues

- alt.adoption.searching

- soc.adoption.adoptees

- soc.adoption.parenting

Similar forums are available through the consumer online systems.

Adoption Information

Adoption information can be found on the Internet, at the following sites:

Adoptees Resources Home Page
http://psy.ucsd.edu/~jhartung/adoptees.html

Adopting.com
www.adopting.com

Adoption.com
www.adoption.com

AdoptioNetwork
www.adoption.org

Jewish Adoption Resources
www.starsofdavid.org/adopt_resources.htm

These sites will point you to many others, where further adoption information is shared.

Adoption/Reunion Publications

The fast-growing list of publications on the Internet now includes adoption/reunion publications, such as Reunions Magazine (www.reunionsmag.com) and Seeker Magazine (www.the-seeker.com). Refer to Section IV of this book for additional Adoptee/Birthparent Search Publications.

Adoption Legislation

If you are about to embark on a search for your birthparent or a natural child who was given up for adoption, you might want to know about adoption laws in the state in which you or your child were born, adopted, or both. Westlaw Family Law Library contains the complete text of United States Federal court decisions, statutes, and regulations, state court decisions, specialized files, and texts and periodicals dealing with family law. These resources include such topics as abortion, adoption, custody, divorce, juvenile delinquency, marriage, and minors' rights. A similar family law library can be found on Lexis.

Search Master California Practice Library (available on CD-ROM from Matthew Bender & Company, Inc.) and California Family Law: Practice and Procedure, 2nd Edition cover all contemporary family law areas and offer guidance through all of the procedural and substantive laws arising in cases of dissolution, adoption, and other areas.

Listings and discussions of state laws can also be found on many of the news groups noted earlier.

Children Available for Adoption

For people seeking children to adopt, databases can definitely help. For example, Parents.com provides a registry of women, men, and couples who are facing an unplanned pregnancy and are looking for the right parents to adopt their child at www.parentprofiles.com.

Parents seeking a child to adopt can also contribute detailed letters and photos to Adoption Online.com (www.adoption-registry.com).

The National Adoption Exchange (available online through National Adoption Center [NAC]) contains information on thousands of children with special needs available for adoption. For further information, contact the National Adoption Center at http://nac. adopt.org.

The Jewish Children's Adoption Network maintains a similar registry of adoptable children needing Jewish homes, and a registry of Jewish families who are interested in considering children for adoption. Further information can be obtained from the Jewish Children's Adoption Network at www.starsofdavid.org/jcan.htm.

Chapter 33

Celebrity Records

*A celebrity is a person who works hard all his life to become
well known, then wears dark glasses to avoid being recognized.*

–Fred Allen

Any type of record can include information about celebrities. The famous buy and sell property, go into business, use credit cards, and obtain medical care, much like anyone else. Of course, even routine events such as a day of work or a date can become a news event when a celebrity is involved, so news sources take on a higher priority when the people being researched are famous.

This chapter identifies some additional databases useful in researching celebrities. When seeking information on someone who is famous, these databases represent supplemental sources, which often are used in combination with conventional sources such as public records.

Biographies and Credits

As noted earlier in Chapter 15: Biographies, much information about celebrities is contained in biographical and autobiographical form. Databases such as Marquis Who's Who (www.marquiswhoswho.com) abound with facts on celebrities, as well as other people who are notable in their fields.

The contents of a record vary, depending upon whether the information was provided by the subject or somebody else. A record sometimes contains a more complete list of honors and accomplishments if it was contributed by the biographee. For example, the record for composer Quincy Jones, reportedly contributed by Jones himself, includes an extensive list of honorary degrees and an extremely impressive catalogue of creative works. Figure 33.1 lists his awards.

AWARDS:

AWARDS Recipient 76 Grammy nominations, 26 Grammy awards, numerous
Readers Poll awards Downbeat Mag., Trendsetters awards Billboard Mag.,
GoldenNote award ASCAP, 1982, Image award NAACP, 1974, 80, 81, 83, 90,
91,Hollywood Walk of Fame, 1980, Man of the Yr. award City of Hope,
1982, Whitney Young Jr. award Urban League, 1986, Humanitarian of Yr.
award T.J. Martell Found., 1986, Lifetime Achievement award Nat. Acad.
Songwriters, 1989, Grammy Living Legend award, 1990, Grammy award
for Best Jazz instrumental, individual or group 1994 for "Miles and
Quincy Live at Montreux", Scopus award Hebrew U., 1991, Spirit of
Liberty award People for the Am. Way, 1992; named Entrepreneur of the
Yr. USA Today/Fin. News Network, 1991; film biography: Listen Up: The
Lives of Quincy Jones, 1990.

(extracted from LexisNexis)

Figure 33.1   Marquis Who's Who Record for Quincy Jones

Frank Sinatra's record is equally impressive, but it was compiled by Marquis. Perhaps as a result, it also includes a list of ex-wives (see Figure 33.2).

FAMILY: married Nancy Barbato, Feb. 4, 1939 (div.); children: Nancy, Frank Wayne, Christine; married

Ava Gardner (div.); married Mia Farrow, 1966 (div.); married Barbara Marx, 1976

Figure 33.2   Marquis Who's Who Record for Frank Sinatra

This information might not have been provided if Mr. Sinatra had contributed the record. Although children from previous marriages often are found on these records, many biographees omit information about their former spouses.

When a record has been contributed by the biographee, Marquis can be a good source for information about one's interests that you may not see elsewhere. Examples of celebrity interests include that for David Letterman, as shown in Figure 33.3.

Avocations: baseball, basketball, auto racing, running

Figure 33.3   Partial Marquis Who's Who Record for David Letterman

For Jerry Seinfeld:

Political/Religious Affiliation: Jewish

Avocations: Zen, yoga

Figure 33.4   Partial Marquis Who's Who Record for Jerry Seinfeld

This does not imply that Marquis does not compile personal information on its own. For example, did you know that Jay Leno used to work as a Rolls-Royce auto mechanic and delivery man? His record, compiled by Marquis, also includes his interest in antique motorcycles and automobiles. Of course, if you watched *The Tonight Show* for about a week, you would probably pick up this information there.

Another set of databases, these specifically used to track the entertainment industry, are BASELINE (available online through Nexis or directly through BASELINE, INC., and on the Internet as Baseline.Hollywood.com, at www.pkbaseline.com). On Nexis, the BASELINE databases include:

- Box office grosses
- Celebrity bios
- Celebrity contacts
- Company profiles
- Film/TV credits

- In production credits

- Industry personnel credits

- Latest grosses

The biography for the late director, screenwriter, and producer, Stanley Kubrick, shown in Figure 33.5 is a good example of what you can expect from the Celebrity Bios database.

If you were about to interview a celebrity, it would also be very useful to have a list of their professional credits handy in advance. BASELINE's Film/TV Credits and Industry Personnel Credits files offer that information.

The Biography Resource Center, from Gale Group, (available online through Gale Group) includes data from more than fifty Gale databases, including Contemporary Authors, Encyclopedia of World Biography, and Almanac of Famous People, as well as full text content from 270 periodicals. Information about this source can be found on the company's Web site at www.galegroup.com.

Many other entertainment databases also provide film credits. They include:

- Cinematografia (CINE) (available online through Ministerio de Educacion y Cultura (ESPANA))

- Hollywood Hotline (available online through America Online, AT&T Easylink Services, CompuServe, Delphi Internet Services Corp., and Youvelle Renaissance Group GEnie; refer to Appendix L for these addresses)

- Mini Reviews (available on the Internet at www.minireviews.com)

Refer to Appendix N for addresses of these vendors, except where available on the Internet as noted.

The Internet Movie Database is another collection of information, this one compiled with the help of many participants and submissions. It has become a commercial site, supported by advertisers, but searching the database remains free. The Internet Movie Database is available at http://us.imdb.com, www.moviedatabase.com, and http://uk.imdb.com.

Star biographies can also be found on the Internet Stars Site (www.internet-stars.com) and at Chinastar.com (dedicated to Chinese stars) (http://1chinastar.com/index1.shtml).

Although these can be wonderful resources, whenever a database is assembled from voluntary submissions, you must always take extra care to verify the information found there.

Of course, many fans have compiled biographies of their favorite stars on their own Internet sites, or on fan club sites to which they contribute. One site that attempts to track these sites, along with the celebrity "official sites" is the Celebrity Showcase, located at http://up4u.net/links.

There are also many database and Internet sources for music celebrity information, such as the following:

- All Music Guide (available on the Internet at www.allmusic.com), which provides a biographical database of artists, including lists of their music, influences, people who they've worked with (a good source for interviews about a musician), books written about them, and so on.

```
Stanley Kubrick

    OCCUPATION: director; also screenwriter and producer

    BORN: in Bronx, New York, July 26, 1928 (male).

    DIED: March 6, 1999 in Hertfordshire, England at the age of 70. Cause of
        death: heart attack.

    NATIONALITY: American

    EDUCATION: Attended William H Taft High School in Bronx, New York (1946).
        Classmates included singer Eydie Gorme.
        Attended City College in New York, New York. School now known
        as City University of New York.
        Attended Columbia University in New York, New York. Enrolled as
        a non-matriculating student while working at Look magazine.

    OTHER OCCUPATIONS: photographer

    MILESTONES:
        1945: Photograph taken by Kubrick of a newsdealer on the day of
            President Franklin Roosevelt's death bought by Look
            magazine; Kubrick subsequently hired as a photographer for the
            magazine and worked there from 1946-1950
        1951: First short film as director (also screenwriter, director of
            photography and producer), the 16-minute documentary "Day of
            the Fight", about boxer Walter Cartier whom Kubrick had
            photographed for Look magazine
        1953: First medium-length film as director (also director of
            photography), the documentary "The Seafarers"
        1953: First feature film as director (also director of photography,
            editor and producer), "Fear and Desire"
        1955: Founded (with James B Harris) Harris-Kubrick Productions;
            partnership lasted through "Lolita" (1962)
        1956: Scripted first Harris-Kubrick production "The Killing" from
            Lionel White's thriller "Clean Break"
        1957: Adapted (along with Calder Willingham and Jim Thompson)
            Humphrey Cobb's World War I novel "Paths of Glory", starring
            Kirk Douglas; as an indictment of war, compared to Lewis
            Milestone's "All Quiet on the Western Front" and Jean Renoir's
            "La Grande Illusion"
        1957: Signed contract with MGM but released after making no films
        1960: Hired by Marlon Brando to direct the Western "One-Eyed Jacks";
            left the project after six months; Brando went on to direct
            (date approximate)
        1960: Replaced Anthony Mann as the director of "Spartacus", at the
            time the most expensive movie ever made in America
        1961: Moved to Great Britain, which stood in for America in "Lolita";
            based in London ever since
        1963: Scripted along with Terry Southern and Peter George from
            George's novel "Red Alert" the apocalyptic black comedy "Dr
            Strangelove, or How I Learned to Stop Worrying and Love the
            Bomb"; also directed, produced and served as special
            photographic effects designer; Kubrick garnered Academy Award
            nominations for Best Picture, Best Director and Best
            Screenplay
        1968: Wrote, produced, directed and designed the effects for "2001: A
            Space Odyssey"; received Oscar for Best Special Effects and
            nominations as Best Director and for Best Screenplay
        1971: Produced, directed and adapted "A Clockwork Orange" from the
            Anthony Burgess novel; received Academy Award nominations for
            Best Screenplay and Best Picture and as Best Director
        1975: Last feature for five years, "Barry Lyndon"; wrote, produced
            and directed; again personally nominated for Best Picture,
            Best Director and Best Screenplay
        1980: Returned to features with screen adaptation of Stephen King's
            "The Shining"
        1987: First feature in seven years, "Full Metal Jacket", based on
            Gustav Hasford's novel "The Short Timers"; shared an Academy
            Award nomination for Best Screenplay
```

1996: Announced casting of Tom Cruise and Nicole Kidman in feature
"Eyes Wide Shut" and began lensing in November; completed
shooting in 1998; film released posthumously in the summer of
1999

BIOGRAPHY:
One of the most consistently fascinating filmmakers of the last four
decades, Stanley Kubrick saw his work praised and damned with equal
vigor. Just as his singularly brilliant visual style won him great
acclaim, his unconventional sense of narrative often elicited critical
scorn. Above all, he remained a unique artist in a medium dominated
by repetition and imitation. If his ambitious vision had at times
exceeded his capacity to satisfy the demands of mainstream filmmaking,
this chink in his armor was perhaps a strength in disguise, and only
served to highlight the distinctiveness of Kubrick's cinema.
     After some success as a photographer for Look magazine in
the late 1940s, the young Kubrick produced and sold several
documentaries before attempting a pair of self-financed low-budget
features--"Fear and Desire" (1953) and "Killer's Kiss" (1955), which,
in scenes like the warehouse finale of the latter, already gave hints
of the disturbing images to come. Working with producer James B
Harris, Kubrick was able to graduate to professional cast and crew
with his next effort, "The Killing" (1956), a well-paced, assured,
cynical drama about a race track heist. At a time when independent
filmmakers were still relatively rare, critics justly began to take
notice.
     "Paths of Glory" (1957) marked Kubrick's emergence as a major
director. This WWI saga is a sharp, intelligent, superbly acted
indictment of military practice and psychology as well as a powerful
piece of filmmaking that synthesized the lessons the director had
learned about composition and camera movement. Although his next
effort plays today as a more personal effort on producer-star Kirk
Douglas's part than it does on Kubrick's, the director showed that he
could function within mainstream Hollywood with "Spartacus" (1960),
his first--and only--work-for-hire. Critics praised the visual aspects
of this widescreen, Technicolor epic a notch above the standard
super-spectacle of the 1950s. As he had in "Paths of Glory", Kubrick
depicted the "weird disparity" between the aesthetics of warfare and
its human consequences.
     Kubrick left for England in 1961, searching for greater
independence and greater control of his films. He has worked there
ever since, developing and producing meticulously crafted yet markedly
different films. "Lolita" (1962) was an adaptation of Vladimir
Nabokov's controversial novel about a middle-aged man's infatuation
with a 12-year-old girl. Though Kubrick has since complained that
over-zealous censors kept him from exploring the story in
appropriately lubricious detail (two years were even added to Lolita's
age), the film stands today as a superb example of understated, double
entendre comedy.
     The ironic touch displayed in "Lolita" exploded to cosmic
proportions with "Dr Strangelove or: How I Learned to Stop Worrying
and Love the Bomb" (1964), perhaps the most deliciously satirical
comedy of the last three decades. (Ironically, the project began as a
serious thriller about the possibility of nuclear Armageddon.)
Kubrick's dark laughter at man's penchant for destroying himself
reinforced what some reviewers had noted at the time of his overly
analytical "The Killing", that he was a "cold" director, and the
reputation has followed him to this day.
     Despite some moral backlash, the successes of "Lolita" and
"Strangelove" earned Kubrick the freedom to choose his own subjects
and, more importantly, to exert total control over the filmmaking
process, a rare freedom for any director. The first product of this
license was the science-fiction classic (and quintessential late 60s
"head" movie), "2001: A Space Odyssey" (1968). Five years in the
making, this film redefined the boundaries of the genre and
established visual conventions, filmic metaphors and special effects
technology that have remained standards for the industry well into the
90s. As visually hypnotic as it was daring in narrative (little
dialogue, no final explanations, a time span of eons), "2001" made
Kubrick a cultural hero. Despite initial mixed reviews, it has proven
to be as stylistically influential as any film released in the last 30

years.

Further cementing his anti-establishment reputation, Kubrick
followed "2001" with another futuristic work, "A Clockwork Orange"
(1971), adapted from the novel by Anthony Burgess. No critic could
take an uncommitted stance toward this film about a violent and amoral
punk (played by Malcolm McDowell), whose ruthless behavior is
reconditioned by the--equally diabolical--state. Kubrick's camera
moved with an audacity unrivaled in contemporary cinema, causing fans
to gush unequivocally and detractors to decry what David Thomson
called "his reluctance to let a plain or simple shot pass under his
name." Anyway you sliced it, there was no denying who was in charge of
a Kubrick film.

"Barry Lyndon" (1975) was a bold attempt to bring modern
techniques to bear upon a narrative set in the 18th century. Kubrick
spent as much technical effort and expertise recreating the lighting
and imagery of Thackeray's novel as he had done inventing a future in
his two previous films. Although a commercial failure, "Barry Lyndon"
fits logically into the Kubrick oeuvre, a dour fable of humanity
trapped in the same determinism that had colored his previous work. In
that respect he is a latter-day Sophocles, whose characters can never
escape their inexorable fate.

Kubrick's adaptation of Stephen King's horror novel "The Shining"
(1980), is perhaps his most autobiographical work. He had long ago
retreated to his Overlook Hotel (Chilwickbury Manor in
Buckinghamshire) just as the writer and his family do in the film.
Jack Torrance's isolation is Kubrick's, and by choosing a blocked
artist as his main character, he shows his fear at the specter of
being unable to create. His typically "cold" analysis may have robbed
the film of the trademark terror horror fans expect, but "The Shining"
is funny, endlessly interesting and pure Kubrick, with Jack the linear
descendant of that ape in "2001", brandishing his bone as weapon.

Kubrick's Vietnam movie, his adaptation of Gustav Hasford's "Full
Metal Jacket" (1987), is essentially two movies in one. The first
section, Marine basic training on Parris Island that culminates in the
suicide of Private Gomer Pyle (Vincent D'Onofrio), is so powerful that
it simply overwhelms the second half, where Kubrick's sets and East
London locale make a poor substitute for Southeast Asia. Though
compelling, well-acted and certainly in keeping with his recurring
theme of dehumanization, "Full Metal Jacket" paled in comparison to
the tropical splendor of Francis Ford Coppola's "Apocalypse Now"
(1979), proving that sometimes, in the interest of verisimilitude, a
director needs to go farther than a two-hour drive from home.

The time needed for Kubrick to recharge his creative batteries
became increasingly long. Five years passed between "Barry Lyndon" and
"The Shining", then seven before "Full Metal Jacket", and more than
ten years would pass until Kubrick allowed his next film "Eyes Wide
Shut" (1999), starring Tom Cruise and Nicole Kidman, to meet the gaze
of the public. True to form, the pedantic filmmaker labored
excessively, assigning great importance to each and every image the
camera would record, and endlessly reshooting scenes until achieving
the exact look he desired. His control over every aspect of his films
assured his legacy as a great craftsman, but his isolation and
monomaniacal intensity may have obscured his genius. Kubrick once
said, "I think that one of the problems with 20th-century art is its
preoccupation with subjectivity and originality at the expense of
everything else." If he had chosen not to reveal much of himself in
his films in order to give us the "everything else", we must accept
his enormous gifts while lamenting the high price of obsession.

AWARDS:
Received Locarno Film Festival Golden Sail Award for "Killer's Kiss"
(1959).
Received New York Film Critics Circle Award for Best Director for "Dr.
Strangelove or: How I Learned to Stop Worrying and Love the Bomb"
(1964).
Received Writers Guild of America Award for Best-Written American
Comedy for "Dr. Strangelove or: How I Learned to Stop Worrying and
Love the Bomb" (1964). Shared award.
Received British Film Academy Award for Best Film for "Dr. Strangelove
or: How I Learned to Stop Worrying and Love the Bomb" (1964).
Received British Film Academy Award for Best British Film for "Dr.

Strangelove or: How I Learned to Stop Worrying and Love the Bomb"
(1964).
Received British Film Academy United Nations Award for "Dr.
Strangelove or: How I Learned to Stop Worrying and Love the Bomb"
(1964).
Received Oscar for Best Special Effects for "2001: A Space Odyssey"
(1968).
Received New York Film Critics Circle Award for Best Motion Picture
for "A Clockwork Orange" (1971).
Received New York Film Critics Circle Award for Best Director for "A
Clockwork Orange" (1971).
Received National Board of Review Award for Best Director for "Barry
Lyndon" (1975). Tied with Robert Altman ("Nashville").
Received BAFTA Award for Best Director for "Barry Lyndon" (1975).
Received Directors Guild of America D W Griffith Award (1997). 26th
recipient of the award established in 1953.
Received Venice Film Festival Golden Lion for Career Achievement
(1997).
Received BAFTA Britannia Award (1999). Presented posthumously; BAFTA
announced that the award would be renamed in Kubrick's honor.
Received BAFTA Academy Fellowship (2000). Presented posthumously;
Michael Caine was also cited.

FAMILY MEMBERS:
        Father: Jacques Leon Kubrick. aka Jacob Leonard Kubrick. Doctor. The
                son of Polish and Romanian Jews; married Kubrick's mother on
                October 30, 1927.
        Mother: Gertrude Kubrick (nee Perveler).
        Sister: Barbara Mary Kubrick. Born on May 21, 1934.
        Daughter: Katherine Kubrick. aka Katherine Bruhns. Natural daughter of
                Werner Bruhns and Christiane Kubrick; looked upon Kubrick as
                her father and adopted his surname.
        Daughter: Anya Renata Kubrick. Born on April 6, 1959; mother, Susanne
                Christiane Harlan; survived him.
        Daughter: Vivian Kubrick. aka Abigail Mead. Screenwriter. Born on
                August 5, 1960; mother, Susanne Christiane Harlan; shot
                documentary film of Kubrick making "The Shining" (for which
                she worked in the art department), screened on the BBC arts
                program "Arena" in 1980, parts of which made it into another
                documentary "The Invisible Man", shown on England's Channel
                4 in 1996; had a bit part in "2001" (1968); composed the
                original music for "Full Metal Jacket" (1987) under the
                pseudonym Abigail Mead; survived him.

COMPANIONS:
        wife: Toba Etta Metz. Born on January 24, 1930; highschool
                sweethearts; married in 1947; divorced in 1952; worked as
                dialogue director on "Fear and Desire" (1953).
        wife: Ruth Sobotka. Dancer. Married in January 1955; divorced c. 1957;
                was art director in "The Killing" (1956); also acted in
                "Killer's Kiss" (1955) as the heroine's sister in the
                flashback sequences.
        wife: Susanne Christiane Harlan. aka Susanne Christian; Christiane
                Kubrick. Painter, former actor. Married in April 1958;
                appeared in "Paths of Glory" (1957) as the young woman
                singing the German song at end; had been previously married
                to Werner Bruhns with whom she had a daughter Katherine;
                mother of Kubrick's two daughters; survived him.

AFFILIATIONS:
        Jewish.

BIBLIOGRAPHY:
        "The Making of Kubrick's 2001" by Jerome Agel (ed.) (1970).
        "Kubrick" by Michel Cimet (1980).
        "Stanley Kubrick: A Guide to References and Resources" by Wallace
        Coylee (1980).
        "The Films of Stanley Kubrick" by Daniel De Vries (1973).
        "A Cinema of Loneliness" by Robert Philip Kolker (1980). Kubrick
        discussed along with other American filmmakers of the 1970s.
        "Stanley Kubrick: Inside a Film Artist's Maze" by Thomas Allen Nelson

(1982).
"Stanley Kubrick: A Film Odyssey" by Gene D Philips (1975).
"Stanley Kubrick: A Biography" by Vincent LoBrutto (1996). Publisher:
Donald I Fine.
"Perspectives on Stanley Kubrick" by Mario Falsetto, editor (1997).
Publisher: G K Hall & Co.
"Stanley Kubrick Directs" by Alexander Walker (1999). Publisher: W W
Norton & Co.
"Eyes Wide Open: A Memoir of Stanley Kubrick" by Frederic Raphael
(1999). Publisher: Ballantine Books.
"Kubrick" by Michael Herr (2000). Publisher: Grove Press.
"Kubrick: Inside a Film Artist's Maze" by Thomas Allen Nelson (2000).
Publisher: Indiana University Press.

NOTES & QUOTES:
"I'm distrustful in delegating authority, and my distrust is usually
well founded." --Stanley Kubrick.

"I tried with only limited success to make the film as real as
possible but I was up against a pretty dumb script which was rarely
faithful to what is known about Spartacus. If I ever needed convincing
of the limits of persuasion a director can have on a film where
someone else is the producer and he is merely the highest paid member
of the crew, 'Spartacus' provided proof to last a lifetime." --Stanley
Kubrick quoted in "World Film Directors" Volume II 1945-1985, edited
by John Wakeman (New York: H W Wilson Company.)

"There is no doubt that there's a deep emotional relationship between
man and his machines, which are his children. The machine is beginning
to assert itself in a very profound way, even attracting affection and
obsession.
    "There is a sexiness to beautiful machines. The smell of a Nikon
camera. The feel of an Italian sports car, or a beautiful tape
recorder. . . . Man has always worshipped beauty, and I think there's
a new kind of beauty afoot in the world." --Stanley Kubrick to The
New York Times in 1968, at the time of the release of "2001."

"He does not believe in biting the hand that might strangle him."
--critic Hollis Alpert.

"He is a brilliant filmmaker, but he does not do well in the final
test--as a man." --"A Clockwork Orange" star Malcolm McDowell on
Kubrick.

" . . . I think the enemy of the filmmaker is not the intellectual or
the member of the mass public, but the kind of middlebrow who has
neither the intellectual apparatus to analyze and clearly define what
is meant nor the honest emotional reaction of the mass film audience
member. And unfortunately, I think that a great many of these people
in the middle are occupied in writing about films. I think that it is
a monumental presumption on the part of film reviewers to summarize in
one terse, witty, clever Time Magazine-style paragraph what the
intention of the film is. That kind of review is usually very
superficial, unless it is a truly bad film, and extremely unfair."
--Stanley Kubrick to Robert Emmett Ginna from an unpublished 1960
interview (From Entertainment Weekly, April 9, 1999.)

"He didn't like stupidity, razzmatazz, celebrity. Stanley refused to
accept that drainage of his spirit." --novelist and friend David
Cornwall (aka John Le Carre), quoted in Newsweek, March 22,
1999.

"He not only understood humanity, he understood it too well. He had no
love of humanity. He was a misanthrope." --Alexander Walker, author of
"Stanley Kubrick Directs."

LAST UPDATE DATE: July 21, 2000

Figure 33.5   BASELINE.Hollywood.com record

- BN-OPALINE (available on Biblioheque Nationale de France; information about this database can be found on the Internet at www.bnf.fr), which contains full bibliographic descriptions of records, tape recordings, compact discs, multimedia products, and videotapes that are produced or distributed in France; details available here include the composer, performer, producer, brand name, and distributor.

- Dansk Musikfortegnelse (available online through Det Kongelige Bibliotek), which covers all music published in Denmark and foreign music that has a connection with Denmark.

- FONO (available online through Sveriges Kungl), which contains references to music CDs, cassettes, and records in Sweden.

- MAPOP (available online through GENIOS Wirtschaftsdatenbanken and on the Internet at www.munzinger.com), which contains biographies of people involved in the music industry (in German).

- Nordisko (Norsk musikkfortegnelse:lydfestinger) (available online through University of Oslo Library), which contains full bibliographic descriptions of cassettes and compact discs of recorded music and catalogs in Norway.

- RockNet (available online through CompuServe, and NIFTY-Serve; refer to Appendix L for CompuServe, which contains news of the rock music industry, including announcements and reviews of albums, concerts, and Music Television (MTV) events, as well as interviews with rock stars and radio and record industry personnel.

Refer to Appendix N for these vendors, except where available on the Internet as noted.

The WWW Music Database covers the music scene much as the Internet Movie Database covers the movie industry. It resides at www.roadkill.com/MDB. Another music database, Gracenote, can be found at www.cddb.com.

Similar databases can be found for foreign music, such as the French music database, netmusik.com (www.netmusik.com), and the Swiss Music Guide, music.ch (http://guide.music.ch).

Sports celebrities can be found on many sports databases. Two examples follow:

- Computer Sports World (available online through DBC Sports—Computer Sports World and on the Internet at www.cswstats.com), which contains information on professional and collegiate sports.

- Primeros Puestos del Deporte Espanol (available online through Ministerio de Educacion y Cultura (ESPANA)), which contains information on approximately 1,000 medals and other honors won by Spanish athletes in international sports competitions.

Upcoming Projects

If you are wondering what your favorite stars are up to, you can search for upcoming projects, using BASELINE's In Production (Inpro) database, available online through Nexis and through

Baseline.Hollywood.com at www.pkbaseline.com. This database is very useful for identifying projects in production, upcoming projects and appearances, and even rumors of future projects. Records from this database typically include such information as:

- Film title
- Status
- Genre
- Location
- Production company
- Phone number
- Date when shooting began
- Date when shooting finished
- Distributor
- Producer(s)
- Director(s)
- Credits
- Cast
- Casting
- Publicity
- Synopsis
- Notes
- Language

Another source for information on upcoming projects of your favorite celebrities is to check with their fan clubs, or their "official" Web sites. A search of the Internet can provide contact information for hundreds of fan clubs and official and unofficial Web sites, as well as information about their past, present, and future projects.

Contact Information and Business Relationships

If you want to get in touch with your favorite celebrity, BASELINE's celebrity contacts database is a good choice. You will not find the star's home address here; the contact provided is usually the celebrity's agency or management company. These contacts can put you in touch with the celebrity if they feel that you have a valid reason to contact their client, such as an interview or a role to cast, and they can tell you where to send your fan mail. An example of the contact information that you will find for Laura Dern is shown in Figure 33.6.

There also are Internet sites that provide contact information for fans. One such site is Celebrity Addresses Online at http://celebrity-addresses.com. The Celebrity Address Emporium

```
    Laura Dern

              OCCUPATION: actor / producer / director

                 AGENCY: International Creative Management
                  PHONE: (310)550-4000
                         (212)556-5600

            MGR. OFFICE: Hofflund/Polone Management
                  PHONE: (310)859-1971

             PR OFFICE: Wolf-Kasteler
                  PHONE: (310)205-0618


              Copyright 1997 by Hollywood.com, Inc. All rights reserved.
```

Figure 33.6   BASELINE Celebrity Contacts record

attempts to catalog actual celebrity addresses and/or contact information (www.springrose.com/celebrity). Fanzine magazine provides celebrity contacts at www.fanzine.co.uk.

The Star Archive (www.stararchive.com) catalogs physical, contact, and e-mail addresses submitted by fans and collects comments from people who test the addresses, noting whether their requests for autographed photos are answered.

BASELINE Company Profiles can also serve to provide additional background information about individuals in the entertainment industry. For example, if I wanted to know what a producer was involved in, I could search Company Profiles to find his production company. The company record could be used to identify business associates, any of whom might provide valuable insights for a profile of the producer.

News

Although any news database may provide information on celebrities, you might want to focus on entertainment-related or sports publications first. Some of the entertainment and news databases available online include:

- AGORA-SPORTS (available online through DataStar and Europeenne de Donnees [ASPO]), which contains news items on sports and sporting events

- *Billboard* (available online through Bell and Howell Information and Learning and Nexis, as well as part of the PROMT database, which is carried by Bell and Howell Information and Learning, DataStar, Dialog, FT Profile, Genios, Wirtschaftsdatenbanken, I/PLUS Direct, Questel-Orbit, STN International, and on the Internet at www.billboard.com/billboard/index.jsp).

- *Box Office* (available on the Internet at www.boxoff.com)

- *Entertainment Weekly* (available online through Nexis and on the Internet at www.ew.com/ew)

- *The Hollywood Hotline* (available online through AT&T EasyLink Services, CompuServe Information Services, Delphi Internet Services Corp., and Youvelle Renaissance Group—Genie and on the Internet at www.hollywoodhotline.com)

- *The Hollywood Reporter* (available online through Bell and Howell Information and Learning and Nexis, as well as part of the PROMT database, carried by the systems noted earlier, and on the Internet at www.hollywoodreporter.com/hollywoodreporter/ index.jsp)

- *People Magazine* (available online through CompuServe Information Services and on the Internet at http://people.aol.com/people/index.html)

- *Rolling Stone Online* (available on the Internet at www. rollingstone.com)

- *Screen Digest* (available online as part of the Newsletter database, which is carried by Bell and Howell Information and Learning, DataStar, Dialog, European Information Network Services, Factiva, FT Profile, I/PLUS Direct, and STN International, and on the Internet at www.screendigest.com)

- The Sports Network (available online through The Sports Network and Nexis and on the Internet at www.sportsnetwork.com/ home.asp), which contains news on professional and collegiate sports

- *TV Guide* (available on the Internet at www.tvguide.com)

Refer to Appendix M for Nexis, listed under LexisNexis, and to Appendix N for the addresses of the remaining vendors, except where available on the Internet as noted.

Of course, since celebrities are involved, one might take a bit more skeptical look at what appears in the news. Mistakes, rumors that later prove false, and even outright lies are printed about celebrities every day.

Locating information on sports stars can also be assisted by searches of sport publications such as:

- *The Olympics Factbook* (available online through Nexis)

- *The Sporting News* (available on the Internet at www.sportingnews.com)

- *Sports Illustrated* (available online through CompuServe and Nexis and as part of the Magazine ASAP and Time Publications databases as listed in Appendix G, and on the Internet at http://sportsillustrated.cnn.com)

Refer to Appendix N for the vendors above, except where available on the Internet as noted.

Many other excellent sports news Web sites are found on the Internet, where you can locate information on anyone in sports. Some of the most important include:

- CBS SportsLine.com (available on the Internet at www. sportsline.com)

- ESPN.com (available on the Internet at http://espn.go.com/main.html)

- FoxSports.com (available on the Internet at http://foxsports.lycos.com)

- MSNBC Sports (available on the Internet at www.msnbc.com/ news/SPT_Front.asp?ta=y)

- USA Today Sports (available on the Internet at www.usatoday.com/sports/sfront.htm)

To locate other sports sites, you can use the sports directory created by Yahoo! at http://d2.dir. snv.yahoo.com/recreation/sports.

Refer to Appendix N for these vendors, except where available on the Internet as noted.

Online News Groups

It sometimes is possible to converse directly with celebrities online. The consumer online systems (America Online, CompuServe, Prodigy, and others) often arrange for online conferences with actors, writers, or musicians, where individuals who participate are able to "talk" online with them. For news of upcoming online conferences, refer to the consumer online systems directly (listed in Appendix L).

Certain celebrities have found the online world to be a convenient medium for communication with friends and fans alike. Stars can use screen names or aliases to talk with people on a level that they may not be able to achieve any longer in the "real" world, because they can meet and make friends without being recognized by fans. In fact, many celebrities have gone online under other names in order to listen in on what their fans were saying about them, or even to participate in critiquing their competition. Chat rooms dedicated to particular celebrities can be found on the consumer online systems, as well as on the Internet. There are also news groups on the Internet dedicated to particular celebrities, such as those beginning with alt.fan., as well as those used to share information on all celebrities, such as alt.gossip.celebrities and alt.showbiz.gossip. You can locate news groups such as these, and search through several years' worth of past messages for material of interest, with the help of sites such as Google Groups (formerly Deja, now at http://groups.google.com).

From time to time, someone intent on "outing" the celebrities publishes a list of e-mail addresses and pseudonyms of the famous and circulates it online. Many of the addresses and pseudonyms are then changed. This cat-and-mouse game continues.

Internet Sites

Nearly all television shows have Web sites today. Many of these sites include chat rooms or news groups so that fans can discuss their views, under the watchful eye of the show's producers or the television network.

Since the entertainment industry is of such interest to so many people, new Internet sites that contain information on actors, actresses, movies, television shows, and nearly anything else about the industry spring up almost daily. Some of these sites are being indexed on the Internet at sites such as:

Celebrity Link
www.celebrity-link.com

HollywoodNetwork.com
http://hollywoodnetwork.com/indexmain.html

The Special TV Resources
www.specialweb.com/tv

Yahoo! Entertainment
http://d2.dir.snv.yahoo.com/entertainment

Zap2it.com
www.zap2it.com/index

Music resources are also being indexed at sites such as:

About's Music/Arts and Entertainment Index
http://home.about.com/arts

Lycos' Music Directory
http://music.lycos.com

Yahoo!'s Music Directory
http://d2.dir.dcx.yahoo.com/entertainment/music

Sports sites can be found on the Internet, indexed through sites such as:

About's Sports Index
http://home.about.com/sports

Yahoo!'s Recreation: Sports Resources
http://d1.dir.dcx.yahoo.com/recreation/sports

Celebrity Deaths

On the Internet, there are many sites that list celebrity deaths, including Dead People Server, which not only lists those celebrities who have died, but also tells you which are alive whom you probably thought were dead (http://dpsinfo.com/dps.html). The Bone Orchard (www.brians driveintheater.com/dead.html) lists deceased B-movie stars. Dead Porn Stars (http://customersare funny.com/pornlist/deadpornstars/deadpornstars.htm) lists dates and causes of death for stars of the blue screen.

There are several sites dedicated to dead musicians, such as:

The Dead Musician's Page
www.songsearch.net/dead.htm

Fuller Up: The Dead Musician Directory
www.elvispelvis.com/fullerup.htm

We'll Always Remember, the Rock Obituary Site
www.hotshotdigital.com/tribute.html

There is even a Web site where you can bet on which celebrity will die next, and win cash and prizes. The Lee Atwater Dead Pool can be found at www.stiffs.com. Another site, DEADquiz (www.deadquiz.com), allows you to take an interactive quiz to identify who's alive and who's dead. SearchBug.com allows you to search for the graves of famous people at www.searchbug.com/peoplefinder/graves2.asp. You can view photos of their headstones, as well as gather additional facts, at the Funeral Guy's site, located at www.funeralguy.com/celebs.html. I even came across a Web site displaying photos of dead celebrities at their funerals, autopsies, and death scenes, but it is really just too gruesome for me to list it.

Please refer to Chapter 28 for additional sources for death records, which would also apply to celebrity records.

Summary

Although it is not possible to offer a comprehensive list of information sources for celebrity research within a single chapter (in fact, it could fill an entire book at this point), the information presented here should give you some starting places for your research and illustrate the ways in which fans and vendors alike are compiling personal data about the famous. Many of the other databases presented throughout this book are at least as useful for researching the famous as they are for learning about the average citizen. With this many information resources available (in addition to "sources close to ...," garbacologists, and the paparazzi), it is no wonder the tabloids are never at a loss for stories!

Chapter 34

Genealogical Records

There are secrets in all families.

–George Farquhar

Genealogical research has come a long way. Although information about one's lineage is still frequently gathered from notes made in family Bibles and stories passed down from generation to generation, it is now just as likely to be collected online.

Genealogists often become masters of public records research and are some of the heaviest users of census, church, military, and burial records. Genealogists may also use most of the various other types of personal records described in this book. Libraries of genealogical information are available in print, on microfiche, and on CD-ROM across the country and in many other parts of the world. Genealogists can utilize all of these in the quest for their roots.

Along with these resources, databases are produced specifically for genealogical research, and home-grown databases filled with family records, personal recollections, and research are copied and transmitted from one person to the next around the world every day. A plethora of genealogical resources now appear on the Internet as well, including the catalog of the Church of the Latter-Day Saints, the largest collection of genealogical information in the world. In fact, it is estimated that there are now more than one million Web pages dedicated to genealogy!

Software

Genealogists can choose from many computer programs with which to store their findings. Their choice of software is important, because the use of standardized record formats read and written by the software can automate the process of sharing genealogical findings. This automation can make it possible to locate quickly whole branches of one's family, sometimes adding hundreds of relatives to a family tree within minutes. It can also link living relatives all around the world who are researching their shared heritage.

Before adding your lineage to a database, you must put records into the format required by that particular site. Although it may be possible to download lineage information from a database without any particular genealogical software program, having software that can accept and utilize the records in an automated fashion can assist a researcher considerably, especially when hundreds or thousands of records are downloaded at once.

Other factors influencing the genealogist's choice of software may include hardware requirements, maximum records allowed, types of relationships allowed (i.e., multiple marriages, stepfamilies, adoptions, etc.), the software's ease of use, graphical capabilities, and price.

The list of software available for genealogical research is enormous. Some programs are commercial products, while others are available as shareware; copies can be downloaded on a trial basis, and if you like them, you can send the fee for a registered copy and receive technical support from the company.

For additional information on genealogical software, you can refer to the list of Genealogical Research Publications in Section IV: Where Can I Find More Information?—Periodicals, many of which carry reviews, announcements, comparisons, and articles about various genealogical software. *Computers in Genealogy* and *Genealogical Computing* provide this focus and might be good choices to start with.

You may also look to genealogical news groups for discussions, reviews, and working copies of genealogical software. For example, soc.genealogy.computing is focused on discussions of genealogical software, fr.comp.applications.genealogie deals with French genealogical software, and no.fritid.slektsforsking.it specializes in Norwegian genealogical computing. You can search news groups through sites such as http://groups.google.com or through the newsgroup reader on your Internet browser.

A list of Commercial Genealogical Sites, many of which are genealogical software companies, can also be found on the Internet at www.genhomepage.com/commercial.html. Additional information about the use of computers in genealogy can also be found at www.genealogytoolbox.com/computers.html.

Standard Genealogical Record Formats

Before viewing genealogical records, you will need to know something about the format in which they appear. There are several formats for genealogical records that can make them more readable and useful to genealogists. Some of them have been standardized in order to automate sharing lineage data. A few of the most common standardized formats for genealogical research follow.

GEDCOM

The GEDCOM (GEnealogical Data COMmunications) format, introduced by the Church of Jesus Christ of the Latter-Day Saints in 1984, has evolved over the last couple of decades, and several versions have been developed during that time. Today, GEDCOM is the format most commonly used by genealogical software. However, this elongated format requires so much disk space and processing capacity that some genealogical databases and Web sites prohibit its use. The GEDCOM format nonetheless has become the standard for genealogical databases and is now the form most often used for exchanging lineage data.

PAF

PAF (Personal Ancestral File) is the traditional format of the Church of Jesus Christ of the Latter-Day Saints.

Ahnentafel

An Ahnentafel is an ancestor table in which each position in a pedigree is given a unique number. This format is rarely used in online systems, and since it is not as easily read as an ancestor or pedigree chart, it is less frequently used by those placing their lineage on their own Web pages. It is, however, over a century old and is still found in genealogical research.

Tiny-Tafel

The Tiny-Tafel format, first introduced in 1986 in *Genealogical Computing Magazine*, presents an abbreviated snapshot of a genealogical database. It is machine readable and used to match lineage information among databases and people that can utilize it.

The Tiny-Tafel contains one line of text for each family line, giving the surname, locations, and the time period represented by that line, along with codes that signify the researcher's degree of interest in receiving information concerning the ancestors or descendants of that line. Not all genealogical information fits into this abbreviated format, which is used for matching, rather than for storing or sharing full records. When Tiny-Tafel is used to query other databases and a match is found, a copy of the full records from the matching database can be requested and sent in a more complete format, such as GEDCOM.

In addition to these common formats, various genealogical software programs store data in their own proprietary formats, which are not generally transferable between programs. For example, Family Tree Maker for Windows stores data in files with an FTW extension, signifying the program's own format. This software does allow you to alternatively export data in a GEDCOM format, however, for sharing with users of other programs.

You can now find genealogical records posted on the Internet in nearly any format imaginable.

Soundex Codes

Genealogical records are frequently indexed using Soundex Codes, which are helpful in locating records containing variant spellings. (Although particularly common in genealogy, Soundex Codes are used for many other types of databases as well.)

Assigning a Soundex Code is fairly simple. The first letter of the name is maintained, so, for example, with Eichenlaub (one of my family names), the first code is E. After the first letter, vowels are dropped, as are the letters h, w, and y, and any second consecutive occurrence of a letter. For Eichenlaub, this leaves CNLB. The remaining letters are coded according to the following assigned numbers:

1 = B, F, P, V

2 = C, G, J, K, Q, S, X, Z

3 = D, T

4 = L

5 = M, N

6 = R

For Eichenlaub, coding CNLB (the remaining consonants) would translate to 2541, so the total Soundex Code for that name would be E2541.

NAME	E	I	C	H	E	N	L	A	U	B
SOUNDEX	E		2			5	4			1

Although a Soundex Code could have any number of characters, the codes are usually limited to 4, so E2541 would be shortened to E254. This could result in all of the matches for Eichenlaub shown in Figure 34.1.

Some of these (noted in boldface) are close to Eichenlaub, and might be attributed to misspellings, transpositions, typing errors, or variations or evolution of the same name, while others seem to have little relation to Eichenlaub at all. This demonstrates how Soundex can assist you in finding variant spellings, as well as a wide variety of mismatches.

Further information about Soundex and an automated Surname to Soundex Converter can be found on the Internet at www.geocities.com/Heartland/Hills/3916/soundex.html. Rootsweb's Soundex Converter can be found at http://resources.rootsweb.com/cgi-bin/soundexconverter.

Using Soundex Codes (rather than names) to search for records can save a genealogist countless hours reading name by name to find variations, especially when using a microfilm or microfiche reader, or printed records. Having a database with the ability to search both by name and Soundex Code can not only save time, but catch records with misspellings that might have been missed.

Where to Get Started

Genealogical Networks and Consumer Online Systems

At about the same time the Tiny-Tafel format was being developed, around 1986, the idea of connecting the various online genealogical bulletin boards around the country started to take shape. These connections would enable genealogists to exchange queries and genealogical data through an online network that would eventually reach around the world. (Although the Internet did exist at that time, it was not yet generally available to individuals outside of government or academia.) When the first two genealogical bulletin boards were connected later that year (using a program named Fido; hence, referred to as FidoNet), that was the beginning of the National Genealogical Conference. Although FidoNet still unites around 30,000 systems today, the Internet has now eclipsed FidoNet for sharing genealogical information. Further information about FidoNet can be found at http://fidonet.fidonet.org.

Internet genealogical newsgroups can be found by searching "genealogy" through services such as Liszt's Usenet Newsgroups Directory at www.liszt.com.

Further information about genealogy and genealogical bulletin boards (or newsgroups) can be found through GenForum (http://genforum.genealogy.com), Irene's Genealogy Post Forum (www.thecore.com/~hand/genealogy/post), Yourfamily.com—The Genealogy Bulletin Board (www.yourfamily.com/bulletin.cgi), or Rootsweb Message Boards (http://boards.ancestry.com/mbexec?htx=main&r=rw).

Genealogy-related mailing lists can also be found at Genealogy Resources on the Internet—Mailing Lists, at www.rootsweb.com/~jfuller/gen_mail.html or by searching "genealogy" at Liszt's mailing list directory, at www.liszt.com.

Although genealogical bulletin boards continue to exist on CompuServe, America Online, and other popular consumer online systems, the Internet is now carrying the majority of the world's online genealogical research traffic. I recommend spending some time on a genealogical bulletin board, news group, or forum for anyone getting started with online genealogical research. The

EAKENWALDER, EASHNAULT, EASNLAUFF, ECENHOWLER, ECHMALIAN, ECHONALS, **ECKENLAUB**, ECKENLE, ECKENLEVY, ECKENLEY, ECKENWALDER, ECKENWEILER, ECKENWELLER, ECKENWILDER, ECKENWILER, ECKMUELLER, ECKMUL, ECKMULLER, ECNELL, ECNOLS, EGENLAAD, EGENLAUF, EGENLER, EGENLRET, EGENOLF, EGGENWEILER, EGGENWELER, EGGENWILER, EGMALIN, EGNAEL, EGNAL, EGNALL, EGNEL, EGNELL, EGNYALOVICII, **EICHANLAUB**, EICHANLMOYER, EICHENHOLTZ, EICHENHOLZ, **EICHENLABU**, EICHENLAMB, EICHANLANB, EICHENLANG, **EICHENLAUB**, **EICHENLAUBX**, EICHENLAUF, EICHENLAUL, EICHENLAULE, EICHENLAUT, EICHENLIEB, **EICHENLOB**, **EICHENLOUB**, EICHENLOUF, EICHENMILL R, EICHENMILLER, EICHENMILLER, EICHENMUELLER, EICHENMILLER, EICHNALD, EICHNOLZER, EICHUNLAND, EICKENLAMB, EICKENLAND, **EICKENLAUB**, EICHENLOFF, EISENLOH, **EIGANLAUB**, **EIGANLUB**, **EIGENLAUB**, **EIKENLAUB**, EISENHELD, EISENHOLT, EISENLA, EISENLAHR, EISENLANE, EISENLARD, EISENLATH, EISENLAU, EISENLAUER, EISENLEFFEL, EISENLEIMOR, EISENLERGER, EISENLISE, EISENLOAD, EISENLOEFFEL, EISENLOFFEL, EISENLOH, EISENLOHR, EISENLONE, EISENLOR, EISENLORD, EISENLOT, EISENLOW, EISENLREY, EISENMULLER, **EISHENLAUB**, EISMILD, EISMUELLER, EKHAML, EKMALIAN, EKNOWLES, ESCAMELLA, ESCAMILLA, ESCAMILLA II, ESCAMILLA MA, ESCAMILLA-CO, ESCAMILLAS, ESCAMILLIA, ESCAMILLO, ESCANELLA, ESCANELLAS, ESCANELLE, ESCANILLA, ESCANILLAS, ESCANUELA, ESCANUELAS, ESCHEMULLER, **ESCHENLAUB**, ESCHENLAUER, ESCHENLOHR, ESCHENWALD, ESCOMILLA, ESCONUELAS, ESENLY, ESHENWALD, ESHMAEL, ESHMALYAN, ESHMILLER, ESHMLE, ESKAMALEN, ESKENLOPH, ESKMULLER, ESMAEL, ESMAIELOF, ESMAIL, ESMAILKA, ESMAILZADEH, ESMAL, ESMEAL, ESMEL, ESMELE, ESMIEL, ESMIOL, ESMMEL, ESMOIL, ESMOLD, ESMUELT, ESMULLER, ESNAL, ESNAOLA, ESNAULT, ESNEALT, ESNEAULT, ESNELL, ESNEWALL, ESNLER, ESQUEMAULT, ESQUINALDO, ESQUINLIN, ESSANLOW, ESSENHOLM, ESSENLOHR, ESSIN/ELSIN, ESSMILLER, ESSMUELLER, ESSMULLER, ESWINNEL, EUKENLHARGER, EUSMULER, EXAMILIOTIX, EYSAMLIN

Figure 34.1   Soundex search results for Eichenlaub

information and advice shared in these forums can save you a great deal of time in your research and point you to many valuable resources, as well as establish friendships and support for people interested in genealogy.

Genealogical Search Engines (Name Indices)

When starting out your genealogical research, a genealogical search engine can be a valuable resource. When you don't know where records for your family exist, a genealogical search engine can point you to databases or Web sites where these records may be found.

Before searching online, you should keep in mind that genealogical records do contain errors. After all, reading and writing have not been common skills in all cultures at all times, so names on records may have been recorded as approximations of their phonetic sound. As noted earlier, Soundex Codes can be very helpful in identifying various forms of the same name.

Genealogical search engines tend to take one of two forms. The first type searches across the Internet for Web pages and databases that have been indexed by surname, place, date, or any other criteria useful in matching pedigrees to the information that you enter. Examples of this type of genealogical search engine include the following:

> FamilyTreeMaker.com's Find Family
> http://familytreemaker.genealogy.com/all-search.html

> GENDEX—WWW Genealogical Index
> www.gendex.com/gendex

> GenealogyPortal.com
> www.genealogyportal.com

> RootsWeb.com (aka WorldConnect Project)
> www.rootsweb.com

> Surname Springboard
> www.allenlacy.com/spring.htm

The second type of genealogical search engine searches a list or database for names, places, and/or dates to find other genealogists (rather than actual data) who have information on that lineage. It can point you to people who have already researched your family and are willing to share their discoveries. It also can contain queries by others who are looking for information about your family. This type of search engine can save a great deal of time and trouble when starting out your research, as you may find genealogists who have done most of the work on your lineage already, or who have unique family collections that would not otherwise be found. Examples of this type of genealogical search engine include:

> The RootsWeb Surname List
> http://rsl.rootsweb.com

> GeneaNet
> www.geneanet.org

One of the nicest things about doing genealogical research is that other researchers are usually happy to share their findings, advice, and sometimes their own research resources, even with strangers. It is not unusual for one researcher to look up information for another, send copies of his or her own records, or even to visit a church or cemetery to obtain information that a far-off correspondent otherwise would find difficult to acquire. Linking researchers through online networks such as FidoNet and the Internet has extended the reach of genealogists around the world.

General Genealogical Collections and Web Sites

There are many genealogists who have spent countless hours indexing all of the genealogical sources that they can lay their hands on. These indexed sources now include Web sites. It is not unusual to find a collection of genealogical links displayed on any genealogist's Web site. Some have taken this task to an extreme, attempting to index all of the genealogical sites that can now be found on the Internet. Since the number of sites has ballooned to upwards of a million, this is no small task, nor one that has been accomplished by anyone entirely.

Rather than try to list all genealogical sites, I will refer you to those who have already taken on this challenge. Some of the best efforts at indexing the Internet's genealogical sites include:

Cyndi's List (which is also now available in book form, and currently boasts more than 90,000 links!)
www.cyndislist.com

Helm's Genealogical Toolbox
www.genealogy.tbox.com

The Genealogy Home Page
www.genhomepage.com/full.html

About's Genealogy Guide
http://genealogy.about.com

Refer to Chapter 15: Biographies for Biographical Index Directories, and Chapter 16: General Indices for other databases that can be used as starting points for your research.

Genealogical Registries (Pedigrees)

Genealogical registries are used to collect family pedigrees, often contributed by researchers and covering many families. Pedigrees can help a genealogist to identify relatives, locate existing records, and supplement what is already known about families, adding names, dates of important events, and links to other family members—even entire branches at once. When a residence or date of a family event is found on a pedigree, these can provide starting places to search for other records such as church records, vital records, or census records. You can contact local churches, archives, libraries, and county recorders to locate these original records, which may provide additional information about the individual. In addition, when the submitter's name is included in the registry or collection of pedigrees, a genealogist may be able to contact the individual who submitted the pedigree to obtain or share additional information, obtain copies of original documents, or even photographs.

Collections of pedigrees may take the form of private registries, maintained by genealogical associations. An example of this is the genealogical collection of the Church of Jesus Christ of

Latter-Day Saints. The catalog of their collection can be searched at www.familysearch.org/Eng/Search/frameset_search.asp.

The LDS catalog contains a great deal of genealogical data such as names, dates, places, and so on. However, its greatest value is that it makes it possible to view copies of the original documents at family history centers (genealogical libraries), after using the catalog to obtain the identifying data (Batch Numbers, Dates, Source Call Numbers, Printout Call Numbers) for the records that you are seeking.

The Library of Congress, America's national library, has one of the world's premiere collections of U.S. and foreign genealogical and local historical publications. The Library's genealogy collection began as early as 1815, when the government purchased Thomas Jefferson's library. Through generations of international giving, these family history collections today contain more than 40,000 compiled family histories and more than 100,000 U.S. local histories. The Library also collects local histories from around the world. Researchers seeking information from other countries will find strong collections for western Europe, especially the British Isles and Germany. For further information, you can visit the library's Internet site at www.loc.gov/rr/genealogy.

Another collection of pedigrees that is well worth searching on the Internet is Ancestry World Tree www.ancestry.com/search/rectype/usersub/worldtree/main.htm.

You can use the General Genealogical Collections and Web sites mentioned earlier to identify many others.

Census Records

The first United States census was taken in 1790. It has been updated every ten years since, as required by the Constitution, in order to count America's citizens and apportion taxes among the states. A few limited censuses were also taken during colonial times, and interim head-counts have been taken in several states in between the national censuses.

Census records are the backbone of American genealogy. In fact, since data for individual households or persons is not published for 72 years (and is only available prior to that time to the government, the parties named, and, under certain circumstances, their descendants), individual census records remain almost the exclusive domain of genealogists.

The information gathered for the census has changed over the years. Between 1790 and 1840, the census included various statistics, but only the names of the heads of households were collected. That, along with the number of children, other adults, total persons in the household, and other counts, have been used by genealogists to validate other data, and provide leads to identifying additional offspring.

Since 1850, the names of all persons living in a household have been collected, along with their ages, sex, and race. The place of birth of each person in the household and his or her relationship to the head of the household have been collected since 1880. In 1890, the length of each person's present marriage was added to the census, along with the number of children born and the number still living. For the genealogist, all of these details are golden, and since many people in past generations could not read or write, written records may not have existed before the census provided them.

Only eleven states participated in the first census. Additional territories and states were added over time. The following chart lists the first year that each of the states began participating in the census:

Year	State
1790	Connecticut, Maine, Maryland, Massachusetts, New Hampshire, New York, North Carolina, Pennsylvania, Rhode Island, South Carolina, Vermont
1800	Delaware, District of Columbia
1810	Kentucky, Louisiana, Virginia, West Virginia, Georgia, Illinois, Indiana, Michigan, Mississippi, Ohio, Tennessee, Wisconsin
1830	Alabama, Arkansas, Florida, Missouri, New Jersey
1840	Iowa
1850	California, Minnesota, New Mexico, Oregon, Texas, Utah, Kansas, Montana, Nebraska, Nevada, North Dakota, South Dakota, Washington, Wyoming
1870	Arizona, Colorado, Idaho
1890	Oklahoma, Alaska, Hawaii

In some cases, counties within a reporting state have been omitted, and complete states sometimes have been missed in a subsequent census, even after the state began participating. Tax lists have been substituted in some cases where states were not yet reporting or records were missing. During some years, certain counties from one state were included in the census for an adjacent state. Some pages of the early census schedules have been damaged or lost over time. As a result of all this, some knowledge of the history of the census, along with the history of the territories and states, can be helpful in locating information about prior generations that has been obtained through the census records.

Most of the 1890 census records were destroyed in a fire at the Commerce Department. The remaining records are now maintained at the National Archives in Washington, DC, and are no longer directly accessible by the public. They are being preserved in order to avoid further wear on the original records. Copies and microfiche of the census data are now made available at the LDS Church, Family History Centers, some libraries, at genealogical organizations in various parts of the country, and may even be purchased by individual genealogists on CD-ROM.

Family History Centers (listed on the Internet at www.genhomepage.com/FHC/fhc.html) and public libraries that maintain genealogical collections may also make these databases available to the public.

Since the census schedules are normally listed in household order on the microfiche, rather than by name, locating a family's information can be an extremely laborious task. The ability to search a census database instead of using a name, or occupation and city, or other combinations of identifying information, in order to pinpoint the exact address or other identifying information before accessing the microfilmed census records is a great advance for genealogical research. Knowing where a family lived also provides a starting place for genealogists to search for other types of records, such as church records of marriages, baptisms, and deaths and county records of births, marriages, and deaths.

You can also find census indices posted online from time to time. For example, I have found the 1890 U.S. Census Index posted in CompuServe's Roots Forum library. The 1871 Ontario Census Heads of Households can be found (in several compressed files all beginning with 1871) on the Internet at ftp://FTP.CAC.PSU.EDU/pub/genealogy/text/data.

The Census of Norway for 1801, 1865, and 1900 are searchable through the National Archives of Norway at http://digitalarkivet.uib.no/index-eng.htm. The 1850 Census for Wyoming County, Virginia, can be found at ftp://FTP.CAC.PSU.EDU/pub/genealogy/text/data/WyoCoWV1.850.

Church Records

Church records contain evidence of births, baptisms, marriages, and deaths and are an excellent source for genealogists, or anyone doing personal research. Unfortunately, these records were not accessible for many years. Many church records have now been collected and placed on CD-ROM or online for genealogical use. Examples can be found at the following Web sites:

Dauphin County (PA) Church Records (1744–1844)
www.ancestry.com/search/rectype/inddbs/4934.htm

Charles, York County (VA) Parish Records (1648–1789)
www.ancestry.com/search/rectype/inddbs/3479.htm

Mexican Parish Records (1751–1880)
www.ancestry.com/search/rectype/inddbs/3947.htm

Announcements (Newspaper, Meeting, Etc.)

Births, marriages, and deaths are often announced in the newspapers. These are sometimes collected by genealogists or genealogical vendors and made available on CD-ROM or online. Examples of this type of record can be found at the following sites:

Colusa Newspaper Records in California (1876–1884)
www.ancestry.com/search/rectype/inddbs/3956.htm

Clay County (MO) Marriage Notices from the Liberty Chronicle and the
Liberty Advance (1852–1900)
www.ancestry.com/search/rectype/inddbs/5430.htm

Columbia, South Carolina, Newspaper Marriage and Death Notices
(1792–1839)
www.ancestry.com/search/rectype/inddbs/3399.htm

Additional information about searching the news for personal information can be found in Chapter 20.

Announcements can also take the form of meeting minutes, such as when the Quakers held their Monthly Meetings and announced births, marriages, and deaths. These announcements have also been collected:

Chappaqua, Westchester County (PA), Quaker Records (19th Century)
www.ancestry.com/search/rectype/inddbs/4968.htm

Duchess County (NY) Quaker Records
www.ancestry.com/search/rectype/inddbs/4702.htm

Family Bible Records

For generations, records of births, baptisms, marriages, and deaths were written in family Bibles, and passed down from generation to generation. There are efforts to transcribe and collect these listings from families and make them available to others via the Internet. These efforts include:

The Bible Archives (TBA)
www.geocities.com/Heartland/Fields/2403

Bible and Family Records Index at Connecticut State Library
www.cslib.org/bible.htm

Family Bible Records (held by the Argyle Township Court House Archives in Nova Scotia)
http://ycn.library.ns.ca/~ipatcha/archives/vitals/fambbl.htm

Birth Records

Of course, what genealogist would not want copies of all of their relatives' birth records? A birth record contains information such as the mother's full maiden name, the father's full name, the name of the baby, the date of the birth, and the name of the county where the birth took place. Many birth records also include other information, such as the birthplaces of the baby's parents, the addresses of the parents, the number of children that the parents have, the race of the parents, and the parents' occupations.

A birth record index can reveal that a particular birth record containing an ancestor's name exists, and provide the location. Looking at the information in the birth index, which contains much of the information available on the original birth record, can help you to determine whether the information is for a specific ancestor or just someone with the same name. It can also supplement what is already known about a family, allowing the genealogist to fill in missing information. Each birth record index usually provides the child's name, birth date, and birth location. With this information, you can contact the county and get a copy of the original birth record or search for other evidence such as a newspaper announcement, which may provide more details about the family.

Examples of some of the birth records found online include:

Birth Records (contributed by individual genealogists)
www.carolyar.com/BirthRecordsmain.htm

Saskatchewan (Canada) Birth Records (from the Alberta Family History Society)
www.afhs.ab.ca/registry/regsk_birth.html

Genealogists collect birth information from a variety of sources in addition to the official records (those filed with government offices such as county recorders). Newspaper announcements, family Bibles, census records, church records, and baptismal certificates are also excellent sources of birth information. Many of these records can now be found online. More information about these types of record can be found later in this chapter.

Marriage Records

A marriage record can provide the bride's and groom's full names, the date of the marriage, and the name of the county where the marriage took place. Many marriage records also include other information, such as the names and birthplaces of the bride's and groom's parents, the addresses of the bride and groom, information about previous marriages, and the names of the witnesses to the marriage.

A marriage record index can reveal the existence of a particular marriage record with an ancestor's name, thereby saving a genealogist much time and effort. The information in the marriage index can be reviewed to decide whether the information is for a specific ancestor or just someone with the same name. It can also be used to add to what is already known about a family. Each marriage index usually gives the county of marriage, marriage date, and the spouses' names. With this information, you can contact the county and get a copy of the original marriage record or find a newspaper announcement, which may offer more facts about the bride, groom, and their families.

Examples of online marriage records include:

> Autauga County (AL) Marriage Index for 1829–1898
> http://searches.rootsweb.com/cgi-bin/autauga/auta-mar.pl
>
> Baker County (FL) Marriages for 1877–1930
> www.rootsweb.com/~flbaker/mgs.html

Records of marriage can be found at county court houses, in church records, and in newspaper announcements. Collections of each of these types of records can now be found online. Refer to those sections of this chapter for further information.

Death Records

Genealogists can gain a great deal of information from death records. A death certificate not only details information about the death, but also provides dates of birth and next of kin. Of course, genealogists recognize that the information is only as good as the knowledge of the person providing it, and since the decedent cannot be consulted, errors are not uncommon. These mistakes can also be compounded by the same types of error found on other public records, such as those introduced when the records are transcribed from handwritten form to databases. It is the genealogist's challenge not only to locate valuable death records, but to identify errors in them and determine the truth.

Death records can take so many forms that an entire chapter of this book has been dedicated to them (Chapter 28). Those sources used most by genealogists include public records (Chapter 31), church records, and newspaper announcements (Chapter 20). Death records have been collected by many genealogists and are also available as genealogical collections on CD-ROM and online. Examples of these include:

> Death Records (contributed by individual genealogists
> and others)
> www.carolyar.com/Deathrecords.htm

Quebec (Canada) Death Records (from the Alberta Family Histories Society)
www.afhs.ab.ca/registry/regqc_death.html

California Death Records
http://userdb.rootsweb.com/ca/death/search.cgi

Cemetery Records

Even cemetery inscriptions can sometimes be found on the Internet now. Examples of these include:

Cross Creek (PA) Cemetery History
www.ancestry.com/search/rectype/inddbs/4616.htm

Aiken County (SC) Cemetery Inscriptions
(St. Thaddeus Church Cemetery, Bethany Cemetery, Milbrook Baptist Church Cemetery, First Baptist Church Yard Cemetery, St. John Methodist Church Cemetery)
www.ancestry.com/search/rectype/inddbs/4437.htm

Bennington (VT) Cemetery Inscriptions
www.ancestry.com/search/rectype/inddbs/3990.htm

Refer to Chapter 28: Death Records, Cemetery Records for further information.

Obituaries

Any news database may include obituaries, but genealogists have also developed several obituary databases. These include:

The Boston Jewish Advocate Obituary Database
www.jewishgen.org/databases/advocate.htm

Deaths Extracted from the New Zealand Herald, 1993
www.geocities.com/Heartland/6123/dth_names.html

Canadian Obituary Links
www.geocities.com/cribbswh/obit/canada.htm

The Social Security Death Index

The Social Security Death Index (SSDI) has been obtained from the Social Security Administration and made available on the Internet. This database is one of the largest and easiest to access databases used for genealogical research. It contains records of death where the Social Security Administration was notified. The SSDI can be found at http://ssdi.genealogy.rootsweb.com.

Immigration Records

When family members emigrated from one country to another, it was not always possible to stay in touch, especially in times of war or strife when families were scattered. Immigration records are now becoming accessible on the Internet, making it possible to track lost branches of your family and to identify additional family members and travel companions. Examples of online immigration records include:

> American Family Immigration History Center—Ellis Island
> www.ellisislandrecords.org
>
> inGeneas—Canadian passenger and immigration records
> www.ingeneas.com
>
> Emigration List for Bergen Harbour (Norway) 1874–1924 (in the National
> Archives of Norway)
> http://digitalarkivet.uib.no/index-eng.htm

Land (Real Property or Deed) Records

Where vital (birth, marriage, and death) records were not always kept in the past, land records normally were. They can serve as valuable links to your ancestors, as well as to living relatives. Deed records can show not only land that was transferred (and along with it, names, dates, and locations), but ownership of other types of property (such as cattle), and the transfer of ownership of slaves.

Examples of land records available online include the following:

> Federal Land Records for Arkansas
> www.rootsweb.com/~usgenweb/ar/fedland.htm
>
> Dominion Land Grants (Manitoba, Saskatchewan, Alberta, and the railway
> belt of British Columbia, c. 1870–1930) Canada
> www.archives.ca/02/020111_e.html
>
> Wisconsin Land Records
> http://searches.rootsweb.com/cgi-bin/wisconsin/wisconsin.pl

Refer to Chapter 31: Public Records for additional real property records available online.

Military Records

Family folklore is filled with stories about relatives who were war heroes or who fought in famous battles. Records of those who have served can now often be found online. Examples of these include the Civil War Soldiers and Sailors System (CWSS), which is a searchable database that contains names of Union and Confederate soldiers and sailors, plus the regiments that they served in. This database can be found at www.itd.nps.gov/cwss.

The French and Indian War site (http://web.syr.edu/~laroux) is dedicated to the French soldiers who went to Canada from 1755 to 1763 to fight in the French and Indian War. The Korean War KIA/MIA Database can be found at www.koreanwar.org/html/korean_war_databases.html, while the Vietnam Veterans Memorial Wall Page can be found at http://thewall-usa.com. The Commonwealth (UK) War Graves Commission, Debt of Honour Register is located at www.cwgc.org.

There is a full-text listing of Medal of Honor Citations now available on the Internet at www.army.mil/cmh-pg/moh1.htm. This includes the following sections:

Full-Text Citations

- Civil War (A–L)

- Civil War (M–Z)

- Indian War Campaigns

- Interim 1866–1870

- 1871 Korean Campaign

- Interim 1871–1898

- War with Spain

- Philippine Insurrection

- China Relief Expedition (Boxer Rebellion)

- Interim 1901–1911

- Action Against Outlaws—Philippines 1911

- Mexican Campaign (Vera Cruz)

- Haiti 1915

- Interim 1915–16

- Dominican Campaign

- World War I

- Haiti Campaign 1919–1920

- Second Nicaraguan Campaign

- Interim 1920–1940

- World War II Black Medal of Honor Recipients

- World War II (A–F)

- World War II (G–L)

- World War II (M–S)

- World War II (T–Z)

- Korean War

- Vietnam (A–L)

- Vietnam (M–Z)

- Somalia

- Special Legislation

Combined Records

Genealogical collections sometimes include combinations of records for a geographic area, an ethnic (racial, national, religious, or cultural) group, or some other subject area. Some collections are commercial databases, while others are compilations by groups of genealogists or individuals who have placed their data online for use by others.

Refer to General Genealogical Collections and Web sites earlier in this chapter for links to all types of genealogical Web sites grouped by religion, race, nationality, and so on.

Summary

Not all information found on genealogical databases is necessarily accurate, so genealogists must do more than access these records. They must also research the information that they find, locate corroborative documentation to prove or disprove relationships and histories, weigh that evidence against their other data, and resolve any discrepancies and conflicts they find. As new technology eases the process of gathering information, genealogists are able to dedicate more time to evaluating and verifying the information they have amassed.

It should be noted that genealogical research is not limited to family ties from many generations past. Since most genealogists are acutely interested in tracing and documenting their own family histories, the contemporary records of family members are often quite complete. As this data is being shared at increasing velocity, it may even be useful in locating people or providing fodder for investigative journalists. Individuals trying to hide from creditors or guarding their privacy may not realize that their aunt, grandfather, or another relative is broadcasting information about them across genealogical networks around the world. The battle between the thirst for information and the right to privacy may take some interesting turns in the genealogical arena.

For additional information about genealogical records and research, many genealogical research guides are available. Some of them are listed in Section IV: Where Can I Find More Information?—Books. Other types of research guides, such as those for public records research can assist genealogists as well. Chapter 15: Biographies offers additional avenues of genealogical research.

A partial list of genealogical periodicals also appears in Section IV: Where Can I Find More Information?—Periodicals.

There are hundreds of genealogical research organizations all over the world, and they are filled with people who are glad to help others with their research, as well as to share their own research resources and findings. A list of genealogical research associations also can be found in Section IV: Where Can I Find More Information?—Organizations. Many of these fellow genealogists can also be found online on any of dozens of genealogical newsgroups now available.

Although no one could hope to provide everything you ever wanted to know about genealogical research in one chapter, or even one book, the resources listed in this chapter can take you well on your way to finding your own roots, or give you the tools that can lead you to them.

For additional information on genealogical research, you can't do better than to spend some time in the Family History Library of the Church of Jesus Christ of Latter-Day Saints, 35 North West Temple Street, Salt Lake City, UT 84150, (801) 240-2331.

In addition to genealogical resources that are highlighted in this chapter, some very helpful microfilm collections are available for genealogists. They can be located through the National Archives and Records Administration (NARA), which can be found on the Internet at www.nara.gov/genealogy.

   NARA's collections include census records, military records, and immigration records. As microfilm has limited search capabilities, and requires hardware that is not common to most PC users, some companies (such as ArchivalCD, at www.archivalcd.com) can convert microfilm or personal record collections into searchable CD databases for commercial or personal use. With these advancements, as well as the movement of genealogy onto the Internet, genealogy has become a very exciting, high-tech hobby, and a great training ground for personal records researchers.

Chapter 35

Political Records

*Politics is perhaps the only profession for
which no preparation is thought necessary.*

–Robert Louis Stevenson

If you need to locate or research a political figure, there are dozens of databases to help you. Book directories, including those offered by online bookstores such as Amazon.com (www.amazon.com) and Barnes and Noble (www.barnesandnoble.com), can identify books written about politicians, past and present. Public records databases can supply information on their backgrounds, and genealogical records can provide details of their lineage and relations. Online political news groups can also turn up valuable insights and leads to information about politicians, candidates, and events.

Political News

Since politicians live much of their lives in the public view, news databases can be rich resources for political research. Transcripts of the *MacNeil/Lehrer News Hour* (available on the Internet at www.pbs.org/newshour), *CNN News* transcripts (available online through Bell and Howell Information and Learning and LexisNexis and at www.cnn.com/TRANSCRIPTS), and other political radio and television programs may include discussions in which a politician who interests you has taken part or has been a topic of debate.

Political publications can also provide valuable insight. The online selections include such publications as:

- *The American Spectator* (available online through Nexis)

- *BNA Washington Insider* (available online through Lexis, Nexis, and Westlaw)

- *California Journal* (available online through Information for Public Affairs—StateNet and Nexis)

- *CQ Governing magazine* (available online through Congressional Quarterly)

- *CQ Weekly Report* (available online through Bell and Howell Information and Learning and Congressional Quarterly)

- *Department of State Dispatch* (available online through Lexis)

- *National Journal* (available online through Bell and Howell Information and Learning, Factiva, Legi-Slate, Lexis, and Nexis)

- *Roll Call* (available online through Bell and Howell Information and Learning, Infonautics Corporation, and Nexis)

- *Washington Post* (available online through Bell and Howell Information and Learning, Dialog, European Information Network Services, Factiva, FT Profile, Legi-Slate, NewsBank, Nexis, and Westlaw and on the Internet at www.washingtonpost.com)

- *Washingtonian* (available online through Nexis)

- *Washington Times* (available online through Bell and Howell Information and Learning and Dialog)

A search of regional and local publications can also be helpful. For example, if you were researching the Kennedys, you should search the *Boston Globe* in particular. It is available online through Bell and Howell Information and Learning, CompuServe's Knowledge Index, Dialog, and Nexis.

Several newswire services have a political focus and can be searched online. They include:

- The Associated Press-Campaign News (available online through Nexis and on the Internet at http://wire.ap.org)

- Federal News Service (available online through Federal News Service directly and on the Internet at web.fnsg.com)

- Reuters Transcript Report (available online through Congressional Quarterly, Nexis, and Reuters Ltd.)

- US Newswire (available online through Bell and Howell Information and Learning, Dialog, Factiva, NewsBank, Inc., NewsEdge Corporation, and Nexis, Reuters Information Services)

Political Directories

A number of directories can be used to locate politicians and political staff members. Directories, such as *The Capitol Source* (available on Nexis) and *The Congressional Staff* (available on Congressional Quarterly), provide a "Who's Who" of Washington.

Another government directory can be found on the Internet at www.fedworld.gov. Congressional Directories can also be found at http://clerkweb.house.gov/mbrcmtee/mbrcmtee.htm; senate directories can be found at www.senate.gov.

Links to Embassy staff directories and Congressional Foreign Affairs personnel can be found at www.embassy.org.

There also are directories for lobbyists, such as the *California Lobbyists/PACs Directory* (available online through Information for Public Affairs—StateNet), which provides information on lobbyists, lobbyist employers, and political action committees (PACs) registered in the state of California.

Many state directories also are available through the Internet, such as those for Minnesota (www.state.mn.us/dir) and Pennsylvania (www.pennsylvania.com/government.html).

On the Internet, you can find government directories for other countries as well. For example, several government directories for Canada can be found at http://canada.gc.ca/directories/direct_c.html, and Australian government directories can be found at www.directory.gov.au.

The Internet provides other government directories for countries throughout the world through such sites as http://dir.yahoo.com/government/countries.

Biographies

Who's Who in American Politics is included in the Bowker Biographical Directory database, which is available online through Dialog and Nexis.

The Congressional Member Profile Report database (on Lexis and Nexis) supplies biographical information on members of the U.S. Congress. Each record includes name, party, elected office, terms served, birth date, gender, religion, race, former occupation, education, and military service. CQ Member Profiles (available online through Congressional Quarterly, Inc.) offers analytical biographies of all voting members of U.S. Congress. It provides personal data (birth date, occupation, family, political career, military experience, and religious affiliation); descriptions of members' style at home and in Washington, with insight on their personality, influence, and priorities; state or district description and demographics, election and campaign finance history; party and Presidential support ratings; committee assignments; key vote studies; and interest group ratings. Committee Membership Profile Report (available online through Lexis and Nexis) contains information on all U.S. Congressional committees and subcommittees.

Congressional biographies can be found on the Internet at www.house.gov/MemberWWW.html. Staff members of the committees and subcommittees of the U.S. Congress are also found through the index (www.house.gov/CommitteeWWW.html). Biographies of Presidents, Congressional members, and state politicians can also be found on the Internet at www.vote-smart.org.

CQ INFO (available online through Congressional Quarterly) provides profiles of candidates running for federal office, lists of state governors, and the complete text of special reports and reference files on topics addressed by the U.S. Congress since the beginning of the 100th Congress. AP Alert/Political (available online through Bell and Howell Information and Learning) covers local, state, and national politics. One of the files included in this service contains biographies, including a biographical sketch, political history, and vital statistics. The Almanac of American Politics (available online through Nexis and Legi-Slate) also provides descriptions and analyses of persons and events in American politics. This almanac can also be found on the Internet at http://nationaljournal.com.

Voting Records/Politics

CQ Committee Action Votes & Rosters—Committees Database (available online through Congressional Quarterly) provides comprehensive reporting and analysis of all committee and subcommittee actions and votes, including markups and all amendments, and covers all U.S.

House of Representatives, Senate, joint and conference committee and subcommittee hearings, markups, and executive sessions.

CQ Weekly Report (available online through Bell and Howell Information and Learning and Congressional Quarterly) includes summaries of subcommittee work, investigations, hearings, and debates; reports of votes; and floor actions.

The Legi-Tech database (available online through Legi-Tech) covers voting records for members of the U.S. Congress and of the California, New York, and Washington state legislatures.

StateNet 50-State Legislative Reporting (available online as part of Westlaw Federal Case Law Library) contains status information and summaries of bills currently before state legislatures and the U.S. Congress, along with name, address, telephone number, district, party affiliation, and committee memberships for all state legislators.

StateNet: California (available online through Information for Public Affairs, Inc.—StateNet) is a legislative tracking service specializing in California politics. It includes state legislators' voting records. Other versions of this database for Illinois, Michigan, Ohio, and Pennsylvania also are available.

There is also a national nonpartisan, nonprofit organization called Project Vote Smart, which offers a database containing the voting records of Presidents, members of Congress, and state politicians. This database is accessible on the Internet at www.vote-smart.org.

Money

If you would like to know who has contributed to a candidate's campaign, how much money a politician has made for speaking engagements, or the financial history of a member of Congress, you can find this information from several online sources.

The Political Action Committee Report (available online through Lexis and Nexis) contains information on donations from political action committees to U.S. Congressional members. FEC Campaign Finance Information (available online through Nexis) and Federal Election Commission Direct Access Program (available online through the U.S. Federal Election Commission) both contain information on persons participating in Presidential, Senatorial, and Congressional races, as well as contributions to candidates for Federal offices by supporters, including political action committees (PACs), and individual contributors of $250 or more.

The Federal Election Commission also provides a nonpartisan Federal candidate campaign money page on the Internet at www.tray.com.

On this site, you can search by candidate name, by contributor name, or even by occupation, among other searches. Just for fun, I used the occupation search to look for contributions by actors, and the result read like a Hollywood Who's Who. I might also have searched for Entertainer, Director, Producer, or other entertainment industry occupations to find out where the Hollywood elite are sending their contributions.

Seeing who a person contributes funds to can provide insight into political views and priorities. Viewing frequent contributions to certain types of candidates or political action committees, you might also infer that the contributor has a great deal of conviction and commitment toward certain causes. For example, what might you infer from the contributions made by actor Warren Beatty as shown in Figure 35.1?

The Legi-Tech database (available online through Legi-Tech) lists political contributions and lobbyist activities for members of the U.S. Congress and the state legislatures of California, New York, and Washington. StateNet: California (available at www.statenet.com/about/products) includes campaign contributions to state legislators.

BEATTY, WARREN
6/30/98 $293.00
LOS ANGELES, CA
ACTOR -[Contribution]
CAROL MOSELEY-BRAUN FOR US
SENATE 1998 INC
Senate Image Not Available from FEC

BEATTY, WARREN
3/4/98 $1,000.00
BEVERLY HILLS, CA 90210
ACTOR -[Contribution]
A LOT OF PEOPLE SUPPORTING TOM
DASCHLE
Senate Image Not Available from FEC

BEATTY, WARREN
4/28/99 $1,000.00
LOS ANGELES, CA 90017
ACTOR -[Contribution]
RE-ELECT CONGRESSMAN KUCINICH
COMMITTEE
[View Image]

Beatty, Warren Mr.
4/12/00 $1,000.00
Beverly Hills, CA 90210
Actor -[Contribution]
NADER 2000 PRIMARY COMMITTEE INC
[View Image]

Beatty, Warren Mr.
4/12/00 $1,000.00
Beverly Hills, CA 90210
Actor -[Contribution]
NADER 2000 GENERAL COMMITTEE INC
[View Image]

Beatty, Warren Mr.
5/31/00 $1,000.00
New York, NY 10022
Self employed -[Contribution]
GORE/LIEBERMAN GENERAL ELECTION
LEGAL AND ACCOUNTING COMPLIANCE
FUND
[View Image]

Beatty, Warren Mr.
4/14/00 $2,000.00
New York, NY 10022
Self employed/Actor -[Contribution]
GORE 2000 INC
[View Image]

Beatty, Warren Mr.
5/31/00 -$1,000.00

New York, NY 10022
-[Contribution]
GORE 2000 INC
[View Image]

BEATTY, WARREN
12/31/93 $5,000.00
LOS ANGELES, CA 90000
ACTOR -[Contribution]
DNC SERVICES
CORPORATION/DEMOCRATIC NATIONAL
COMMITTEE
[View Image]

BEATTY, WARREN
5/23/90 $1,000.00
BEVERLY HILLS, CA 90210
DIRECTOR/ACTOR/PRODUCER -
[Contribution]
PEOPLE FOR MRAZEK

BEATTY, WARREN
5/23/90 $1,000.00
BEVERLY HILLS, CA 90210
DIRECTOR/ACTOR/PRODUCER -
[Contribution]
PEOPLE FOR MRAZEK

BEATTY, WARREN
10/18/86 $1,000.00
LOS ANGELES, CA 90069
ACTOR -[Contribution]
BELLA ABZUG FOR CONGRESS

BEATTY, WARREN
10/2/86 $1,000.00
LOS ANGELES, CA 90067
ACTOR -[Contribution]
FRIENDS OF MARK GREEN

BEATTY, WARREN MR
4/22/86 $1,000.00
LOS ANGELES, CA 90067
-[Contribution]
DNC SERVICES
CORPORATION/DEMOCRATIC NATIONAL
COMMITTEE

BEATTY, WARREN
3/14/84 $1,000.00
LOS ANGELES, CA 90067
SELF-EMPLOYED -[Contribution]
SIMON FOR SENATE

BEATTY, WARREN
12/10/83 $500.00

LOS ANGELES, CA 90025
-[Contribution]
CRANSTON FOR PRESIDENT COMMITTEE
INC

BEATTY, WARREN
10/19/82 $1,000.00
LOS ANGELES, CA 90067
SELF-EMPLOYED -[Contribution]
BROWN FOR US SENATE

BEATTY, WARREN
3/4/80 $1,000.00
LA, CA 90067
-[Contribution]
KENNEDY FOR PRESIDENT COMMITTEE

BEATTY, WARREN
11/3/80 $1,000.00
LOS ANGELES, CA 90067
PARAMOUNT PICTURES -[Contribution]
HART FOR SENATE CAMPAIGN
COMMITTEE INC

BEATTY, WARREN
11/4/80 $1,000.00
LOS ANGELES, CA 90067
ACTOR/DIRECTOR -[Contribution]
MCGOVERN CAMPAIGN COMMITTEE

BEATTY, WARREN MR
6/29/79 $2,000.00
LOS ANGELES, CA 90067
ACTOR/PROD -[Contribution]
DNC SERVICES
CORPORATION/DEMOCRATIC NATIONAL
COMMITTEE

Figure 35.1   Federal Election Commission contributions

Campaign contributions can also be found in publications, such as the *Political Finance* and *Lobby Reporter* (available online through Lexis and Nexis).

The Congressional Member Honoraria Receipts Report (available online through Lexis and Nexis) contains information on fees paid to members of the U.S. Congress for speeches and personal appearances.

Events

Politicians do not hit the news only because of their actions. Sometimes their simple presence at a public event or private party may be considered newsworthy. This makes it relatively easy to identify their friends, relatives, business associates, and interests. The news databases can provide details of past events, but for upcoming events, there are several additional databases that you might want to try.

Reuters Washington Report (available online through Nexis and Reuters, Ltd.) provides coverage of events in Washington, DC, including press conferences, government hearings, speeches, demonstrations, the President's schedule, Congressional schedules, diplomatic events, and financial items. The calendar of daily activities in the U.S. Congress and the Office of the President can also be found in the BNA Presidential Calendar database (available online through BT North America, Inc., and Westlaw). Congressional News (available online through Congressional Quarterly) provides a daily calendar of events on and off Capitol Hill that influence legislation in the U.S. Congress.

CQ Committee and Floor Schedules (available online through Congressional Quarterly) provides schedules for the U.S. House of Representatives, Senate, joint committees, conference committees, and floor votes for the next day up to three months ahead. For each schedule, this database provides agenda, issue involved, bill number, chairperson, location and time, and names and affiliations of witnesses for each meeting or hearing. StateNet: California includes committee hearing schedules and floor agendas for the state legislature, as does StateNet: Illinois, StateNet: Michigan, StateNet: Ohio, and StateNet: Pennsylvania.

Government Documents

If you would like to find out what bills a Congressional member has worked on or glean some insight into a legislator's interests, some useful government documents can be located online. CIS (available online through LexisNexis) provides citations, with abstracts, to publications produced by the committees and subcommittees of the U.S. Congress.

Other government documents can be found on the Internet at www.fedworld.gov, and an index of documents available through the Government Printing Office can be found through the Government Information Locator Service (GILS) at www.access.gpo.gov/su_docs/gils/index.html.

Chapter 36

We the People

*It's human nature to keep doing something as long as it's
pleasurable and you can succeed at it—which is why the world
population continues to double every 40 years.*

–Peter Lynch

Although this book is focused on locating information about individuals, it should at least be mentioned that many databases available online and on CD-ROM also compile information about groups of us. When information about an individual is not available, group records are sometimes used to extrapolate or make presumptions about individuals within the group.

For example, if you were trying to figure out whether a person was wealthy, and little information was available about the individual, census tract records might be used to determine the average wealth in the subject's neighborhood. It might then be reasonable to assume that the person should fit somewhere within the local range. This is far from a perfect method, but such inferences can be sufficient for certain purposes or as a preliminary screen to determine whether it is worth proceeding further.

Census Records

The United States Bureau of Census collects information on households and businesses throughout the United States, and has done so every ten years since 1790. Data for individual households or persons remains confidential for 72 years under Title 44 of the U.S. Code. The older data is often used by genealogists in order to trace family lineage or gain information about neighbors or others living within a household as of a given point in time. Please refer to Chapter 34: Genealogical Records for more information on the older records.

More recent records are aggregated into groups and made available through many online databases including:

- Annual Demographic Update (available online through Claritas Data Services)

- CENDATA (available online through CompuServe), which contains selected text and numeric data from Census Bureau economic and demographic reports, press releases, and new product announcements

- Claritas Connect (available online through Claritas Data Services)

- DRI U.S. Central (available online through Standard and Poor's DRI)

- Population Demographics (available online through Dialog)

- State Macroeconomic (available online through The WEFA Group)

- SUPERSITE (available online through CompuServe and as part of DRI/McGraw-Hill, which is carried by many online vendors)

Note that the addresses for these and other database vendors mentioned in this chapter can be found in Appendices L and N.

The main menu from the Census database, (available on the Internet at www.census.gov), appears as follows:

Your Gateway Census 2000

Summary File 2 (SF@) is the latest release

      People Estimates • C2SS Area Profiles • Projections • Income • Poverty International • Genealogy • Housing

      Business Economic Census • Government • E-Stats • NAICS • Foreign Trade

      Geography Maps • TIGER • Gazetteer

      Newsroom Releases • Economic Indicators • Minority Links Radio/TV/Photos

      At the Bureau Regional Offices • Doing business with us • About the Bureau

      Special Topics Census Calendar • The 1930 Census • For Teachers • American Community Survey • Statistical Abstract • FedStats

Selecting "People" brings the following choices:

Population and Household Economic Topics

Census 2000
Historical Census Data
American Community Survey
American FactFinder
International Statistics
Genealogy

U.S. 286,966,308
World 6,222,120,369
05:19 EDT May 04, 2002

More Population Clocks
Population and Household Economic Topics

- Estimates

- Projections

- Population Profile

- Journey to Work

- Labor Force

- Language Use

- Age
- Ancestry
- Births
- Children
- Computer Ownership and Use
- Deaths
- Disability
- Education
- Elderly
- Families
- Fertility
- Foreign Born
- Grandparents
- Health Insurance
- Hispanic Origin
- Households and Families
- Income
- Marital Status and Living Arrangements
- Migration
- Occupation
- Overseas U.S. Population
- Poverty
- Program Participation
- Puerto Rico and the Insular Areas
- Race
- Small Area Income and Poverty Estimates
- School Costs
- School Districts
- School Enrollment
- Voting and Registration
- Wealth
- Well-Being
- Working At Home
- Immigration

As you can see, the information is grouped and presented in many ways, but it does not provide enough detail for anyone to know who lives in any given household, their race, age, educational level, employer, income, or any other specific details pertaining to an individual. Viewing information for a particular metropolitan area can be useful, however, in developing an understanding of the general populace of that area or neighborhood.

Some databases emphasize specific sections of the census data. For example, Population by Age, Sex, and Race (available online through GE Information Services [GEIS]) focuses on population and housing information.

The Equal Employment Opportunity information collected by the Census is the focus of EEO Data (available online through Claritas Data Service).

Household Age/Income (available online through The WEFA Group) contains detailed time series of historical data on U.S. household income levels.

Senior Life (available online through Claritas Data Service) contains data from the U.S. Census of Population and Housing, current-year estimates, and five-year forecasts on persons aged 55 or older.

WellCount (available online through NGWIC Ground Water Network) contains counts of the number of U.S. households using private water wells.

Colorado Economic and Demographic Information System (available online through Colorado State Data Center) contains demographic, financial, and employment time series data on Colorado local governments and all fifty states.

Other Demographic and Statistical Databases

Other demographic and statistical databases are available for the United States, such as ECONBASE: Time Series & Forecasts (available online through Dialog), which contains monthly, quarterly, and annual economic time series. Census State Data Centers can be found at www.census.gov/sdc/www.

A good many additional statistical and demographic databases have been created for marketing purposes. These are often compiled from many sources, including telephone directories, census information, surveys, and warrantee cards. Databases such as these can be used to determine the size of the target population before development of an ad campaign or to determine the best location for a new venture, such as a restaurant or grocery store.

Census Projections

Projections of future census information also are available. They are included in some of the databases noted previously, as well as being the focus of New York Forecast Database (available online through The WEFA Group).

Foreign Census Records, Demographics, and Statistics

Census records, demographics, and statistical data are also available for other countries. These databases are examples of those available for the following countries:

Australia

- PC Ausstats (available online through Australian Bureau of Statistics (ABS)

Canada

- Alberta Statistical Information System (available online through Alberta Treasury, Statistics) for the province of Alberta and its census divisions and municipalities

France

- IGAMINFO (available online through SUNIST) for the French regions of Provence, the Cote d'Azur, and the Alps

Mexico

- State population figures are available at www.mexonline.com/estado.htm

Japan

- NRI/E Japan Economic & Business Database (available online through The WEFA Group)

Sweden

- Regionalstatistiska databasen (RSDB) (available online through Sweden Statistiska Centralbyran [SCB])

United Kingdom

- CSO Macro-Economic Data Bank (available online through ADP (U.K.) Ltd., Primark Corporation—Primark Financial Information, Standard and Poor's DRI, The WEFA Group) National Online Manpower Information System (available online through University of Durham) for the U.K.

Many more international statistical agencies, such as the Statistical Office of the European Union, the United Nations Global Statistics System, and the World Data Bank can be found on the Internet. They are indexed by the Glasgow University Library at www.lib.gla.ac.uk/Depts/MOPS/Stats/usefulworld.html

Demographic and Statistical Publications

Demographic and statistical information can also be found in many publications, including newspapers, magazines, books, and journals. Some publications that focus on this type of information are available online as well. They include:

- *The Numbers News* (available online through Nexis)

- *Statistical Abstract of the United States* (available on the Internet at www.census.gov/statab/www)

- *USA Statistics in Brief*, a supplement to Statistical Abstract of the United States (available online at www.census.gov/statab/www/brief.html)

Although census and demographic databases rarely provide access to information on individuals, there are a couple of exceptions to this rule. CAMEO (available online through Bureau van Dijk, SA (BvD)—Electronic Publishing) enables users to confirm an individual's home address, as well as providing a profile of that address based on census information. Det Sentrale Folkeregister (DSF) (available online through the Office of the National Registrar) contains data on all persons in Norway whose domicile is or has been in the country since 1964.

Summary

Although census, demographic, and statistical data may not give us detailed information about an individual, they can tell us something about the environment that a person comes from or lives in. This, in itself, is important when trying to understand a person in the context of his or her surroundings and background.

Where Can I Find More Information?

Books

ADOPTEE/ BIRTHPARENT SEARCH GUIDES

Adoption Reunion Survival Guide: Preparing Yourself for the Search, Reunion, and Beyond
by Julie Jarrell Bailey, Lynn N.Giddens, M.A., Annette Baran,
New Harbinger Pubns;
March 2, 2001
ISBN: 1572242280

Before the Search: An Adoption Searcher's Primer
Michele Heiderer, (Editor)
Ye Olde Genealogie Shoppe,
June 1997
ISBN: 1878311247

Outer Search, Inner Journey: An Orphan and Adoptee's Quest
by Peter Dodds
Aphrodite Publishing

Company; April 1997
ISBN: 1889702242

Search: A Handbook for Adoptees and Birthparents, 3rd edition
by Jayne Askin
Oryx Press; July 10, 1998
ISBN: 1573561150

The Search of a Lifetime
by Kathryn M. Denton,
Teresa M. Cummings
1stBooks Library; October 2000
ISBN: 1587215691

Searching for a Piece of My Soul : How to Find a Missing Family Member or Loved One
by Tammy L. Kling
NTC/Contemporary
Publishing; September 1, 1997
ISBN: 0809230631

BACKGROUND RESEARCH/ INVESTIGATIVE REPORTING BOOKS

Background Investigation for Law Enforcement
by Van Ritch
Carolina Academic Press;
June 1997
ISBN: 0890899010

Be Your Own Detective
by Greg Fallis, Ruth Greenberg
M Evans & Co; February 1999
ISBN: 0871318725

The Big Chill: Investigative Reporting in the Current Media Environment
by Marilyn S. Greenwald (Editor), Joseph Bernt (Editor)
Iowa State University Press;
December 1999
ISBN: 0813828058

Business Intelligence Using Smart Techniques: Environmental Scanning Using Text Mining and Competitor Analysis Using Scenarios and Manual Simulation
by Charles Halliman
Information Uncover; April 4, 2001
ISBN: 0967490626

Check Him Out! The American Woman's Guide to Background Investigations, 2nd Edition
by W. Joseph Ryan
Washington Research Assn; February 15, 2001
ISBN: 0937801178

Check It Out! A Top Investigator Shows You How to Find Out Practically Anything About Anybody in Your Life, 2nd edition
by Edmund J. Pankau
Contemporary Books; December 1998
ISBN: 0809229005

Competitive Intelligence: How to Gather, Analyze, and Use Information to Move Your Business to the Top
by Larry Kahaner
Touchstone Books; February 1998
ISBN: 0684844044

Competitor Intelligence— Strategy, Tools and Techniques for Competitive Advantage
by Andrew Pollard
Financial Times—Prentice

Hall Publishing; February 1999
ISBN: 0273637096

Competitor Intelligence: Turning Analysis into Success (Wiley Series in Practical Strategy)
by D. E. Hussey, Per V. Jenster
John Wiley & Son Ltd.; March 1999
ISBN: 0471984078

Computer-Assisted Investigative Reporting: Development and Methodology (Lea's Communication Series)
by Margaret H. Defleur
Lawrence Erlbaum Assoc; March 1997
ISBN: 0805821635

Digital Evidence and Computer Crime: Forensic Science, Computers, and the Internet
by Eoghan Casey
Academic Pr; March 15, 2000
ISBN: 012162885X

Financial Investigation and Forensic Accounting
by George A. Manning
CRC Press; July 15, 1999
ISBN: 0849304350

Get the Facts on Anyone: Find Out Confidential Information About Any Person or Organization, 3rd edition
by Dennis King
Arco Pub; June 1999
ISBN: 0028628217

The Guide to Background Investigations, 9th Edition
by T.I.S.I.
TISI-Nat'l Employment Screening Service; September 1, 2000
ISBN: 0964238845

High Technology Crime Investigator's Handbook
by Gerald L. Kovacich, William C. Boni
Butterworth-Heinemann; September 15, 1999
ISBN: 075067086X

How to Do Financial Asset Investigations: A Practical Guide for Private Investigators, Collections Personnel, and Asset Recovery Specialists, 2nd edition
by Ronald L. Mendell
Charles C. Thomas Pub Ltd.; April 2000
ISBN: 0398070458

How to Investigate by Computer: 1999
by Ralph Thomas
Thomas Investigative Publications; January 1999
ISBN: 1891247271

Investigating Computer-Related Crime: A Handbook for Corporate Investigators
by Peter Stephenson
CRC Press; September 28, 1999
ISBN: 0849322189

Investigations: 150 Things
by Louis A. Tyska, Lawrence
J. Fennelly
Butterworth-Heinemann; July
1999
ISBN: 0750671823

*Investigative Reporting: A
Study in Technique
(Journalism Media Manual)*
by David Spark
Focal Press; November 1999
ISBN: 0240515439

*Investigator's Guide to Free
Searches on the Internet*
by Ralph Thomas
Thomas Investigative
Publications; August 20,
1998
ISBN: 1891247190

*The Investigator's
Handbook: How to Use
Open Sources and Public
Records to Legally Locate
Information on Anyone*
by Don Ray
National Book Network;
December 15, 2000
ISBN: 1889150177

*The Investigator's Little
Black Book, 2nd edition,
Vol. 2*
by Robert Scott
Crime Time Pub Co; January
1998
ISBN: 0965236927

*Millennium Intelligence:
Understanding and
Conducting Competitive
Intelligence in the Digital
Age*
by Jerry P. Miller (Editor)

Information Today Inc;
March 2000
ISBN: 0910965285

*Online Competitive
Intelligence: Increase Your
Profits Using Cyber-
Intelligence (Online Ease)*
by Helen Burwell, Carl R.
Ernst, Michael Sankey
Facts on Demand Pr; July
1999
ISBN: 1889150088

*The Private Investigator's
Guide*
by John Krause
Picasso Pubns Inc; October
1999
ISBN: 1552790215

*Professional's Guide To
Background Investigations
(Private Investigation)*
by Ralph Thomas
(Photographer), Rod
Richburg (Illustrator), Pat
Pound (Editor)
Thomas Investigative
Publications; April 22, 1999
ISBN: 1891247301

*Super Searchers Do
Business: The Online
Secrets of Top Business
Researchers (Super
Searchers, Vol. 1)*
by Mary Ellen Bates,
edited by Reva Basch
Information Today, Inc.;
August 1999
ISBN: 0910965331

*Super Searchers Go to the
Source: The Interviewing
and Hands-On Information*

*Strategies of Top Primary
Researchers—Online, on the
Phone, and in Person*
by Risa Sacks,
edited by Reva Basch
Information Today, Inc.; 2001
ISBN: 0910965536

*Super Searchers in the
News: The Online Secrets of
Journalists and News
Researchers*
by Paula J. Hane,
edited by Reva Basch
Information Today, Inc.; 2000
ISBN: 0910965455

*The Warroom Guide to
Competitive Intelligence*
by Steven M. Shaker, Mark P.
Gembicki
McGraw-Hill; January 1999
ISBN: 007058057X

GENEALOGICAL RESEARCH GUIDES

*A Genealogist's Guide to
Discovering Your English
Ancestors: How to Find and
Record Your Unique
Heritage*
by Paul Milner, Linda Jonas
Betterway Pubns; August
2000
ISBN: 1558705368

*A Genealogist's Guide to
Discovering Your Female
Ancestors: Special Strategies
for Uncovering Hard-to-
Find Information about Your
Female Lineage*
by Sharon DeBartolo

Carmack
F & W Publications,
Incorporated, March 1998
ISBN: 1558704728

***A Genealogist's Guide to
Discovering Your Germanic
Ancestors: How to Find and
Record Your Unique
Heritage***
by Chris Anderson, Ernest
Thode, S. Chris Anderson
Betterway Pubns; May 2000
ISBN: 1558705201

***A Genealogist's Guide to
Discovering Your Immigrant
& Ethnic Ancestors: How to
Find and Record Your
Unique Heritage***
by Sharon DeBartolo
Carmack
Betterway Pubns; July 2000
ISBN: 1558705244

***A Genealogist's Guide to
Discovering Your Italian
Ancestors: How to Find and
Record Your Unique
Heritage***
by Lynn Nelson
Betterway Pubns; September
1997
ISBN: 1558704264

***Ancestors, Guide to
Discovery: Key Principles
and Processes of Family
History Research***
by Jim Tyrrell
Everton Publishers; June
2000
ISBN: 1890895040

***Cherokee Connections: An
Introduction to Genealogical***

***Connections Pertaining to
Cherokee Ancestors***
Myra Vanderpool Gormley
Genealogical Publishing
Company, Incorporated,
August 1998
ISBN: 0806315792

***Cherokee Proud: A Guide
for Tracing and Honoring
Your Cherokee Ancestors,
2nd edition***
Tony Mack McClure
Chu-Nan-Nee Books,
December 1998
ISBN: 0965572226

***The Complete Beginner's
Guide to Genealogy, the
Internet, and Your
Genealogy Computer
Program***
by Karen Clifford
Genealogical Publishing
Company; January 2001
ISBN: 0806316365

***The Complete Idiot's Guide
to Online Genealogy***
by Rhonda R. McClure,
Shirley Langdon Wilcox
MacMillan Distribution;
November 17, 1999
ISBN: 002863635X

***Digging for Irish Roots:
How to Search for Your
Ancestors***
by Don Cahalan
Ad Infinitum Pr; May 15,
2001
ISBN: 0915474107

***Family Ties in England,
Scotland, Wales & Ireland:
Sources for Genealogical***

Research
by Judith P. Reid
Library of Congress; June
1998
ISBN: 0844409111

***Finding Your German
Ancestors: A Beginner's
Guide***
by Kevan M. Hansen
MyFamily.com, Inc.;
September 1999
ISBN: 0916489833

***Finding Your Roots: How to
Trace Your Ancestors at
Home and Abroad***
by Jeane Eddy Westin, John
J. Stewart (Introduction)
J P Tarcher; January 1999
ISBN: 087477943X

***First Steps in Genealogy: A
Beginner's Guide to
Researching Your Family
History***
by Desmond Walls Allen
Betterway Pubns; August
1998
ISBN: 1558704892

***From Generation to
Generation: How to Trace
Your Jewish Genealogy and
Family History***
by Arthur Kurzweil
HarperCollins Publishers,
Incorporated, March 2001
ISBN: 0765762013

***Genealogy: How to Find
Your Ancestors, Revised
Edition***
by Paul Drake, Margaret

Grove Driskill
ISBN: 0788414763, 2000

Genealogy Online For Dummies®, 2nd Edition
by April Leigh Helm, Matthew L. Helm
Hungry Minds, Inc; May 1999
ISBN: 0764505432

Genealogy Online: Millennium Edition
by Elizabeth Powell Crowe
Computing McGraw-Hill; August 23, 1999
ISBN: 0071351035

Guide to Cuban Genealogical Research
by Peter E. Carr
Clearfield Co; August 18, 2000
ISBN: 0806350288

Guide to Genealogical Research in the National Archives
by United States National Archives and Records Administration
Natl Archives & Record Service; December 2000
ISBN: 1880875217

How to Find Your Family Roots and Write Your Family History, 2nd edition
by William Latham, Cindy Higgins
Santa Monica Pr; March 2000
ISBN: 1891661124

How to Trace Your African-American Roots:

Discovering Your Unique History
by Barbara Thompson Howell
Citadel Pr; January 1999
ISBN: 0806520558

How to Trace Your Jewish Roots: Discovering Your Unique History
by Rabbi Jo David
Citadel Pr; September 2000
ISBN: 0806520426

How to Trace Your Roots: For the Beginning Family Historian
by Mary Haegele
Abacus Associates; March 1, 1999
ISBN: 1896625088

In Search of Your Asian Roots: Genealogical Research on Chinese Surnames
by Sheau-yueh J. Chao
Clearfield Co; January 2000
ISBN: 0806349468

In Search of Your Canadian Roots, 3rd edition
by Angus Baxter
Genealogical Publishing Company, Inc.; January 2000
ISBN: 0806316268

In Search of Your European Roots: A Complete Guide to Tracing Your Ancestors, 3rd edition
by Angus Baxter
Genealogical Publishing Company; February 2001
ISBN: 0806316578

In Search of Your German Roots: The Complete Guide to Tracing Your Ancestors in the Germanic Areas of Europe, 4th edition
by Angus Baxter
Genealogical Publishing Company; January 2001
ISBN: 080631656X

Irish and Scotch-Irish Ancestral Research: A Guide to the Genealogical Records
by Margaret Dickson Falley
Genealogical Publishing Company; January 1, 1998
ISBN: 0806309164

Land and Property Research in the United States
by E. Wade Hone
MyFamily.com, Inc.; March 1998
ISBN: 091648968X

The Librarian's Guide to Genealogical Research (Highsmith Press Handbook Series)
by James Swan
Highsmith Co; October 1998
ISBN: 1579500110

Locating Lost Family Members & Friends: Modern Genealogical Research Techniques for Locating the People of Your Past and Present
by Kathleen W. Hinckley
Betterway Pubns; August 1999
ISBN: 1558705031

Netting Your Ancestors: Genealogical Research on

the Internet
by Cyndi Howells
Genealogical Publishing
Company; 1999
ISBN: 0806315466

*The Sleuth Book for
Genealogists: Strategies for
More Successful Family
History Research*
by Emily Anne Croom
Betterway Pubns; March
2000
ISBN: 1558705325

*The Source: A Guidebook of
American Genealogy*
by Sandra H. Luebking
(Editor), Loretto D. Szucs
MyFamily.com, Inc.; March
1997
ISBN: 0916489671

*Tracing Your Roots:
Locating Your Ancestors at
Home and Abroad*
by Meg Wheeler
Todtri Productions Ltd;
November 1998
ISBN: 188090893X

*The Weekend Genealogist:
Timesaving Techniques for
Effective Research*
by Marcia Yannizze Melnyk
Betterway Pubns; August
2000
ISBN: 1558705465

*There are so many additional
books and guides on genealogy that it was necessary to
exclude books that predate
1997. This does not in any
way reflect on their value or
worthiness for study.*

INTERNET/WEB SEARCHING BOOKS

*The Extreme Searcher's
Guide to Web Search
Engines (2nd Edition)*
by Randolph Hock, Foreword
by Reva Basch; Information
Today, Inc.; 2001
ISBN: 0910965471

*The Invisible Web:
Uncovering Information
Sources Search Engines
Can't See*
by Chris Sherman
and Gary Price
Information Today, Inc.;
August 2001
ISBN: 091096551X

LOCATING PEOPLE

*Celebrity Locator
2001–2002: Where to Locate
the Regular Addresses, E-
Mail Addresses, Web Site
Addresses, and Fan Clubs of
Celebrities*
Axiom Info Resources;
February 2001
ISBN: 0943213398

*Find Anyone (Book &
CD-Rom)*
by Richard R. Johnson, John
H. Wood
Quantum Media; March 1,
1998
ISBN: 1893477002

*How to Find Almost Anyone,
Anywhere*
by Norma Mott Tillman

Rutledge Hill Press; October
1998
ISBN: 1558536574

*How to Locate Anyone in the
Information Age: Secrets of
the Search Company*
by Joanne Kerr, Dana K.
Vian, Rory D. Goshorn
T S C Pubns; January 1998
ISBN: 0966158318

*How to Locate Anyone Who
Is or Has Been in the
Military: Armed Forces
Locator Guide, 8th edition*
by Richard S. Johnson, Debra
Johnson Knox
Military Information
Enterprises; March 1999
ISBN: 1877639508

You Can Find Anybody!
by Joseph Culligan
Jodere Group; November 1,
2000
ISBN: 1588720004

MAILING LIST DIRECTORIES

*Direct Marketing List
Source*
SRDS, 6 issues/year
www.srds.com/

*Direct Marketing Market
Place 2001: The Networking
Source of the Direct
Marketing Industry (Direct
Marketing Market Place,
2001)*
Natl Register Pub Co;

October 2000
ISBN: 0872173437

*Directory of Mailing List
Companies: A Guide to
Mailing List Sources, 14th
edition*
Barry Klein
Todd Publications, January
2001
ISBN: 0915344831

PRIVACY, SECURITY, AND FREEDOM OF INFORMATION BOOKS

*A Citizen's Guide on Using
the Freedom of Information
Act and the Privacy Act of
1974 to Request Government
Records*
Government Printing Office;
March 1999
ISBN: 9990959196

*A Culture of Secrecy: The
Government Versus the
People's Right to Know*
by Athan G. Theoharis
(Editor)
Univ Pr of Kansas; April
1998
ISBN: 070060880X

*Access Denied: Freedom of
Information in the
Information Age*
by Charles N. Davis (Editor),
Sigman L. Splichal (Editor)
Iowa State University Press;
August 2000
ISBN: 0813825679

*Ben Franklin's Web Site:
Privacy and Curiosity from
Plymouth Rock to the
Internet*
by Robert Ellis Smith,
Sangram Majumdar
(Illustrator)
Privacy Journal; June 2000
ISBN: 0930072146

*Compilation of State and
Federal Privacy Laws: 1997,
2nd edition*
by Robert Ellis Smith
Privacy Journal; July 2000
ISBN: 0930072111

*The Complete Guide to E-
Security: Using the Internet
and E-Mail Without Losing
Your Privacy*
by Michael Chesbro
Paladin Pr; November 2000
ISBN: 1581601050

*The Complete Idiot's Guide
to Protecting Yourself Online*
by Preston Grulla
Que; August 1999
ISBN: 0789720353

*Computer and Internet Use
on Campus: A Legal Guide
to Issues of Intellectual
Property, Free Speech, and
Privacy*
by Constance S. Hawke
Jossey-Bass; September 1,
2000
ISBN: 0787955167

*Computerized Monitoring
and Online Privacy*
by Thomas A. Peters
McFarland & Company;
October 1999
ISBN: 0786407069

*The Culture of Secrecy:
Britain, 1832–1998*
by David Vincent
Oxford Univ Press; March
1999
ISBN: 0198203071

*Cyberdanger and Internet
Safety: A Hot Issue*
by Jennifer Lawler
Enslow Publishers, Inc.; June
2000
ISBN: 0766013685

*Cybershock: Surviving
Hackers, Phreakers, Identity
Thieves, Internet Terrorists
and Weapons of Mass
Disruption, 2nd edition*
by Winn Schwartau
Thunder's Mouth Pr; March
30, 2001
ISBN: 156025307X

*Database Nation: The Death
of Privacy in the 21st
Century*
by Simson Garfinkel,
Deborah Russell
O'Reilly & Associates;
January 2001
ISBN: 0596001053

*Delivering Security and
Privacy for E-Business*
by Anup K. Ghosh
John Wiley & Sons; February
15, 2001
ISBN: 0471384216

*The E-Privacy Imperative:
Protect Your Customers'
Internet Privacy and Ensure
Your Company's Survival in
the Electronic Age*

by Mark S. Merkow, James
Breithaupt
AMACOM; May 2001
ISBN: 0814406289

Electronic Democracy:
Using the Internet to
Transform American Politics
(2nd Edition)
by Graeme Browning
Information Today, Inc.;
February 2002
ISBN: 0910965498

The Electronic Privacy
Papers: Documents on the
Battle for Privacy in the Age
of Surveillance
by Bruce Schneier, David
Banisar
John Wiley & Sons; August
25, 1997
ISBN: 0471122971

The End of Privacy
by Charles J. Sykes
St Martins Pr (Trade);
October 1999
ISBN: 0312203500

The End of Privacy: How
Total Surveillance Is
Becoming a Reality
by Reginald Whitaker
New Press; February 2000
ISBN: 1565845692

Freedom of Information and
the Right to Know: The
Origins and Applications of
the Freedom of Information
Act
by Herbert N. Foerstel
Greenwood Publishing
Group; October 1999
ISBN: 0313285462

Freedom of Information:
The Law, the Practice and
the Ideal (Law in Context)
2nd edition
by Patrick Birkinshaw
Northwestern Univ Pr;
August 1997
ISBN: 0406049726

The Hundredth Window:
Protecting Your Privacy and
Security in the Age of the
Internet
by Charles Jennings, Lori
Fena, Esther Dyson
Free Press; June 15, 2000
ISBN: 068483944X

In Pursuit of Privacy: Law,
Ethics and the Rise of
Technology
by Judith Wagner Decew
Cornell Univ Pr; June 1997
ISBN: 0801484111

Information Eclipse: Privacy
& Access in America
by Michael Fraase
Arts & Farces; November
1998
ISBN: 189265900X

Internet Marketing Secrets:
Privacy Marketing and More
by Larry Chiang, Gerri
Detweiler
Triple Option Press; February
2001
ISBN: 0970161409

Internet Privacy
by Harley Hahn
Prentice-Hall, August 1, 2001
ISBN: 0130334480

Internet Privacy for
Dummies

by John Levine, Ray Everett-
Church, Gregg Stebben
Hungry Minds, Inc; July
2001
ISBN: 0764508466

Internet Privacy Protection
Guide
by J. K. Santiago, Patricia
Love (Editor)
Boggy Cove, Inc.; November
1, 1999
ISBN: 0967688000

Invasion of Privacy
by Louis R. Mizell, Jr.
Berkley Pub Group; June
1998
ISBN: 0425160882

Net Crimes and
Misdemeanors:
Outmaneuvering the
Spammers, Swindlers, and
Stalkers Who Are Targeting
You Online
by J. A. Hitchcock; edited
by Loraine Page
Information Today, Inc.; 2002
ISBN: 0910965579

Net Privacy: A Guide to
Developing & Implementing
an Ironclad Ebusiness
Privacy Plan
by Michael Erbschloe, John
R. Vacca
McGraw-Hill Professional
Publishing; March 26, 2001
ISBN: 0071370056

The New Battle over
Workplace Privacy: How Far
Can Management Go? What
Rights Do Employees Have?
Safe Practices to Minimize
Conflict, Confusion, and
Litigation

by William S. Hubbartt
AMACOM; January 1998
ISBN: 0814403573

None of Your Business:
World Data Flows,
Electronic Commerce, & the
European Privacy Directive
by Peter P. Swire, Robert E.
Litan
Brookings Institute;
November 1998
ISBN: 081578239X

Online Consumer Privacy:
What Your Company Needs
to Know Right Now
by Steven Voien (Editor)
Business for Social
Responsibility Education
Fund; January 31, 2001
ISBN: 1931371091

Privacy and Confidentiality
of Health Information (An
AHA Press/Jossey-Bass
Publication)
by Jill Callahan Dennis
Jossey-Bass; September 1,
2000
ISBN: 0787952788

Privacy and Human Rights
1999: An International
Survey of Privacy Laws &
Developments
by David Banisar, Simon
Davies
Electronic Privacy
Information Center; August
13, 1999
ISBN: 189304405X

Privacy for Sale: How Big
Brother and Others Are
Selling Your Private Secrets

for Profit
by Michael Chesbro
Paladin Pr; July 1999
ISBN: 158160033X

Privacy in the Information
Age
by Fred H. Cate
Brookings Institute;
November 1997
ISBN: 0815713150

The Privacy Law
Sourcebook 1999: United
States Law, International
Law, and Recent
Developments
by Marc Rotenberg
Electronic Privacy
Information Center; July 16,
1999
ISBN: 1893044041

Privacy on the Line: The
Politics of Wiretapping and
Encryption
by Whitfield Diffie, Susan
Landau
MIT Press; February 26,
1999
ISBN: 0262541009

The Privacy Plan: How to
Keep What You Own Secret
From High-Tech Snoops,
Lawyers and Con Men
by Robert J. Mintz, Peter S.
Doft; Francis O'Brien &
Sons Publishing Company;
1999
ISBN: 0963997114

Privacy: The Debate in the
United States Since 1945
(Harbrace Books on
America Since 1945)
by Philippa Strum, Gerald W.

Nash, Richard W. Etulain
HBJ College & School Div;
November 1998
ISBN: 0155018809

Privacy-Enhanced Business:
Adapting to the Online
Environment
by Curtis D. Frye
Quorum Books; December
30, 2000
ISBN: 1567203213

Protecting Yourself Online:
The Definitive Resource on
Safety, Freedom, and
Privacy in Cyberspace
by Robert B. Gelman, Esther
Dyson
HarperCollins (paper); March
1998
ISBN: 0062515128

Public Policy and the
Internet: Privacy, Taxes, and
Contract (Hoover Institution
Press Publication, 481.)
by Nicholas Imparato
(Editor)
Hoover Inst Pr; April 2000
ISBN: 0817998926

The Right to Privacy
(Individual Freedom, Civic
Responsibility)
by Brandon Garrett
Rosen Publishing Group;
February 2001
ISBN: 0823932362

The Transparent Society:
Will Technology Force Us to
Choose Between Privacy and
Freedom?
by David Brin
Perseus Pr; June 1, 1999
ISBN: 0738201448

Visions of Privacy: Policy Choices for the Digital Age
by Colin Bennett (Editor), Rebecca Grant (Editor)
Univ of Toronto Pr; July 1999
ISBN: 0802080502

Web of Deception: Misinformation on the Internet
Anne P. Mintz (Editor)
Information Today, Inc.; 2002
ISBN: 0910965609

Web Psychos and Other Horror Stories from the Internet
by Michael A. Banks
Information Today, Inc.; 2003
ISBN: 0910965617

Workplace Privacy: Real Answers and Practical Solutions
by David M. Safon, Worklaw Network
Thompson Publishing Group; July 1, 2000
ISBN: 0967047099

PUBLIC RECORDS RESEARCH GUIDES

Find Public Records Fast, 3rd edition
by Michael L. Sankey (Editor), James R. Flowers (Editor), Carl R. Ernst
Facts on Demand Pr; February 15, 2000
ISBN: 1889150134

The Investigator's Handbook: How to Use Open Sources and Public Records to Legally Locate Information on Anyone
by Don Ray
National Book Network; December 15, 2000
ISBN: 1889150177

The Librarian's Guide to Public Records: The Complete State, County and Courthouse Locator 2000 Edition (Librarians Guide to Public Records 2000), 4th edition
by Michael L. Sankey (Editor), James R. Flowers (Editor), Peter J. Weber
Business Resources Bureau; January 2000
ISBN: 1879792567

Public Records Online, 3rd Rev edition
by Peter J. Weber, Michael L. Sankey (Editor), James R. Flowers (Editor)
Facts on Demand Pr; September 1, 2000
ISBN: 1889150215

Researching Public Records: How to Get Anything on Anybody
by Vincent Parco
Replica Books; October 2001
ISBN: 0735101094

Vital Records Computer Databases
by Linda E. Brinkerhoff
Genealogical Institute; 1998
ISBN: 0940764717

Where to Write for Vital Records: Births, Deaths, Marriages & Divorces
Government Printing Office; May 1999
ISBN: 016036275X

Please note that publication dates given are for the latest edition I was aware of at press time. When ordering any book, be sure you are getting the most current edition.

Please refer to the Naked in Cyberspace *Web site for these and additional titles of interest.*

Periodicals

I'd rather bathe lepers than be interviewed by the press.

—Mother Teresa

ADOPTEE/ BIRTHPARENT SEARCH PUBLICATIONS

Adoptologist
Susan Foglesong
Kansas City Adult Adoptees
Organization
Box 15225
Kansas City, MO 64106

American Journal of Adoption Reform
1139 Bal Harbor Boulevard,
Suite 184
Punta Gorda, FL 33950
(813)637-7477

Birthparents Today
Birthparents Support
Lynn Lape
2905 Orchardgate Court
Cincinnati, OH 45239

Canadopt Newsletter
Canadopt
RR 1
Ilderton, Ont. N0M 2A0

Concerned United Birthparents Newsletter
Concerned United
Birthparents, Inc.
2,000 Walker St.
Des Moines, IA 50317
(515)262-2334

Geborener Deutscher
2300 Ocean Ave.
Brooklyn, NY 11229
http://hometown.aol.com/
wmlgage/gd/gd.htm

International Concerns Committee for Children— Newsletter
International Concerns
Committee for Children
(ICCC)
911 Cypress Drive
Boulder, CO 80303
(303)494-8333

On the Vine
Sweet Pea Press
Box 1852
Appleton, WI 54913

Open Adoption Birthparent
4-Squared Press
721 Hawthorne St.
Royal Oak, MI 48067

The Open Record
Americans for Open Records
(AmFOR)
Box 401
Palm Desert, CA 92261
(619)341-2619

People Searching News
P.O. Box 22611
Fort Lauderdale, FL 33335-
2611
(407)768-2222

PFI Communique
Parent Finders Inc.
P.O. Box 1008
Station F
Toronto, Ont. M4Y 2T7
(416)465-8434

Reunions, the Magazine
P.O. Box 11727
Milwaukee, WI 53211-0727
(414) 263-4567
www.reunionsmag.com

COMPETITIVE AND BUSINESS INTELLIGENCE PUBLICATIONS

Certified Corporate Services
3313 B Bloor St W, Unit 3
Toronto, ON, M8X 1E7
Canada
(416)760-3181

Competitive Intelligence Magazine
Society of Competitive
Intelligence Professionals
1700 Diagonal Rd, Ste 520
Alexandria, VA 22314
(703)739-0696
www.scip.org/news/
cimagazine.asp

Competitive Intelligence Review
John Wiley and Sons, Inc.
605 3rd Ave.
New York, NY 10158
(800)225-5945; (212)850-6000
www.wiley.com/cda/
product/0,,CIR,00.html

Information Solutions
Information Plus, Inc.
14 Lafayette Square, Ste. 2000
Buffalo, NY 14203-1920
(716)852-2220

FUNDRAISING/ PROSPECT RESEARCH PUBLICATIONS

America's Spirit
United Service Organizations

(USO)
USO World Headquarters
Washington Navy Yard
1008 Eberle Place, SE Ste. 301
Washington, DC 20374-5096
(202)610-5700

Animal Aid Communique: A Volunteer Community Service for Emergency Rescue and Humane Education
Animal Aid of Tulsa, Inc.
3307 E. 15th St.
Tulsa, OK 74112
(918)744-1648
www.animalaid.org

APA Psychology Research Funding Bulletin
American Psychological
Association
750 1st St. NE
Washington, DC 20002-4242
(800)374-2721; (202)336-5500
www.apa.org/science/bulletin.
html

Canadian Donors Guide To Fundraising Organizations in Canada
Third Sector Publishing
P.O. Box 744, Sta. A.
Toronto, ON, Canada M5W
1G2
(416)961-6776
www.donorsguide.ca

Canadian FundRaiser
The Hilborn Group Ltd.
Box 86, Station C
Toronto, ON, Canada M6J
3M7
(800)461-1489; (416)696-8146
www.canadianfundraiser.com

Christian Management Report
Christian Management
Association
P.O. Box 4090
San Clemente, CA 92674
(800)727-4262; (949)487-0900
www.christianity.com/cma

The Chronicle of Philanthropy: The Newspaper of the Non-Profit World
The Chronicle of
Philanthrophy
1255 23rd St. NW, Ste. 700
Washington, DC 20037
(202)466-1200
http://philanthropy.com

Connections
Association of Professional
Researchers for Advancement
414 Plaza Drive, Suite 209
Westmont, IL 60559
(630)655-0177
www.aprahome.org/
connections.htm

Currents
Council for Advancement and
Support of Education (CASE)
1307 New York Ave. NW,
Ste. 1000
Washington, DC 20005
(800)554-8536; (202)328-5900
www.case.org

Development Director's Letter: Practical Advice for the Nonprofit Manager
CD Publications
8204 Fenton St.

Silver Spring, MD 20910
(800)666-6380; (301)588-
6380
www.cdpublications.com/
funding/development
director.htm

Dimensions
National Catholic
Development Conference
86 Front St.
Hempstead, NY 11550
(516)481-6000
www.amn.org/ncdc/ncpubs.htm

**Drug Abuse Funding
Monitor**
Capitol City Publishers
1408 N. Fillmore St., Ste. 3
Arlington, VA 22201
(888)854-3080; (703)525-
3080
www.capitolcitypublishers.
com/pubs/drug/index.html

**Foundation & Corporate
Funding Advantage:
Inside Information on
Foundation & Corporate
Giving in a Fast Read
Format**
Progressive Business
Publications
370 Technology Dr.
Malvern, PA 19355
(800)220-5000; (610)695-
8600
www.pbp.com

**Foundation Giving Watch:
The Mon. Report to
Nonprofit Organizations
Seeking Foundation
Support**
The Taft Group
27500 Drake Rd.

Farmington Hills, MI 48331-
3535
(800)347-GALE; (248)699-
4253

FRI Monthly Portfolio
The Taft Group
27500 Drake Rd.
Farmington Hills, MI 48331-
3535
(800)347-GALE; (248)699-
4253

**Friends of Libraries U.S.A.
News Update**
Friends of Libraries U.S.A.
1420 Walnut St., Ste. 450
Philadelphia, PA 19102
(800)9FO-LUSA; (215)790-
1674
www.folusa.com

FRM Weekly
Fund Raising Management
Magazine (FRM)
Hoke Communications, Inc.
224 7th St.
Garden City, NY 11530
(800)229-6700; (516)746-
6700

**Fundraising Ideas:
Over 225 Money Making
Events for Community
Groups, with a Resource
Directory**
McFarland & Co., Inc.,
Publishers
961 Hwy. 88 W
Box 611
Jefferson, NC 28640
(800)253-2187; (336)246-
4460

**Fund-Raising Regulation
Report**
John Wiley and Sons, Inc.
605 3rd Ave.
New York, NY 10158
(800)225-5945; (212)850-
6000

**Healthcare Fund Raising
Newsletter: A Summary of
Healthcare Fund Raising
Activities**
Health Resources Publishing
P.O. Box 456
Allenwood, NJ 08720
(800)516-4343; (732)292-
1100
www.healthresourcesonline.
com/health_grants/2nl.htm

**Jack and Jill of America
Foundation—Intercom**
Jack and Jill of America
Foundation, Inc.
P.O. Box 468
Pickerington, OH 43147-
8976
(614)864-7085
www.jackandjillfoundation.
org/newsletter.asp

**Kiwanis International
Foundation Newsletter**
Kiwanis International
3636 Woodview Trace
Indianapolis, IN 46268-3196
(800)549-2647; (317)875-
8755
http://kif.kiwanis.org

Link to Link
Links
1200 Massachusetts Ave. NW
Washington, DC 20005
(202)842-8686

National Fund Raiser
Barnes Associates Inc.
909 15th St., Ste. 9
Modesto, CA 95354
(800)231-4157; (209)523-8582

Nonprofit World
Society for Nonprofit
Organizations
6314 Odana Rd., Ste. 1
Madison, WI 53719
(800)424-7367; (608)274-9777
http://danenet.danenet.org/snpo/
newpage2.htm

**Planned Giving Today:
The Practical Newsletter
for Gift-Planning
Professionals**
Planned Giving Today
100 2nd Ave. S., Ste. 180
Edmonds, WA 98020-3551
(800)525-5748; (425)744-3837
http://pgtoday.com

Successful Fund Raising
Stevenson Consultants, Inc.
P.O. Box 4528
Sioux City, IA 51104-1105
(712)239-3010
www.stevensoninc.com/
newsletters_sfr.htm

World Federalist Newsletter
World Federalist Association
418 Seventh St. SE
Washington, DC 20003
(800)WFA-0123; (202)546-3950
www.wfa.org/resources/
newsletters

Please note that many additional publications address fundraising from a more narrow perspective, focused on funding of research for a particular disease or cause.

GENEALOGICAL RESEARCH PUBLICATIONS

AAHGS Newsletter—Afro-American Historical and Genealogical Society
Afro-American Historical and
Genealogical Society
Box 73086
Washington, DC 20056-3086
(202)234-5350
www.rootsweb.com/
~mdaahgs/news.html

Acadian Genealogy Exchange
Janet B. Jehn
3265 Wayman Branch Rd.
Covington, KY 41015
(859)356-9825
www.acadiangenexch.com

AFGnewS
American-French
Genealogical Society
Box 2113
Pawtucket, RI 02861-0113
(401)765-6141
www.afgs.org/afgnews.html

Afro-American Historical and Genealogical Society Journal
Afro-American Historical and
Genealogical Society
Box 73086
Washington, DC 20056-3086
(202)234-5350
www.rootsweb.com/~mdaahgs

American-Canadian Genealogist
American-Canadian
Genealogical Society
P.O. Box 6478
Manchester, NH 03108-6478
(603)622-1554
www.acgs.org/acgen/acgen.htm

The American Genealogist
The American Genealogist
P.O. Box 398
Demorest, GA 30535-0398
(706)865-6440
www.americangenealogist.
com/index.html

An Drochaid
Clans & Scottish Societies of
Canada
c/o St. Andrews Church
73 Simcoe St.
Toronto, ON, Canada M5J
1W9
(416)593-0518

APG Quarterly
Association of Professional
Genealogists (APG)
P.O. Box 40393
Denver, CO 80204-0393
www.apgen.org/publications/
index.htm#Quarterly

British Connections
International Society for
British Genealogy and
Family History (ISBGFH)
P.O. Box 3115
Salt Lake City, UT 84110-3115
(801)272-2178
www.genealogysource
catalog.com/ISBGFH.htm

The Constantian
The Constantian Society
840 Old Washington Rd.

McMurray, PA 15317-3228
(724)942-5374

de Halve Maen:
Journal of Dutch American
Colonial History
Holland Society of New York
122 E. 58th St.
New York, NY 10022

The Dinghy
Pentret Press
P.O. Box 2782
Kennebunkport, ME 04046-2782
(207)255-4114

Dorot:
The Journal of the Jewish
Genealogical Society
Jewish Genealogical Society
P.O. Box 6398
New York, NY 10128
(212)330-8257
www.jgsny.org/dorot.htm

Everton's Genealogical
Helper: Magazine
Dedicated to Helping
Genealogists Since 1947
Everton Publishers, Inc.
3223 S. Main
Nibley, UT 84321
www.everton.com/shopper/
index.php (click on the
Genealogy Magazine)

Family Chronicle:
The Magazine for Families
Researching Their Roots
Moorshead Magazines Ltd.
505 Consumers Rd., No. 500
Toronto, ON, Canada M2J
4V8
(416)491-3699
www.familychronicle.com

Family Findings
White Publishing Co.
Box 3343
Jackson, TN 38303-0343

Heritage Magazine
Genealogical Society of
Flemish Americans
18740 13 Mile Rd.
Roseville, MI 48066
(810)776-9579
www.rootsweb.com/~gsfa/
gsfainfo.htm

Flower of the Forest Black
Genealogical Journal
Mullac Publishing
1364 Walker Ave.
Baltimore, MD 21239
(410)323-3883

Genealogical Computing:
A Quarterly Journal
MyFamily.com, Inc.
266 W. Center
Orem, UT 84057
(800)262-3787; (801)426-3500
www.ancestry.com/learn/
main.htm

Genealogical Goldmine
Paradise Genealogical
Society, Inc.
P.O. Box 460
Paradise, CA 95967-0460
(530)877-2330
www.pargenso.org/periodic.
htm

Genealogija
Blazekas Museum of
Lithuanian Culture
6500 S. Pulaski Rd.
Chicago, IL 60629-5136
(773)582-6500

Genealogy Bulletin
Heritage Quest

P.O. Box 329
Bountiful, UT 84011-0329
www.genealogybulletin.com

German Genealogical
Society of America
Newsletter
German Genealogical Society
of America
2125 Wright Ave., Ste. C-9
La Verne, CA 91750-5816
(909)593-0509
http://fecfhs.org/ggsa/
frg-ggsa.html

Germans from Russia
Heritage Society Newsletter
Germans from Russia
Heritage Society
1008 E. Central Ave.
Bismarck, ND 58501
(701)223-6167
www.grhs.com

Heritage Quest Magazine
Heritage Quest
P.O. Box 40
Orting, WA 98360-0040
(253)770-0551
www.heritagequest.com/
genealogy/magazine/index.
html

The Hispanic American
Historical Review
Duke University Press
Florida International
University
206 Chemistry & Physics
Bldg.
University Park
Miami, FL 33199
(305)348-4247
http://dukeupress.edu/
journals/index.shtml

**Immigrant Genealogical
Society Newsletter**
Immigrant Genealogical
Society
P.O. Box 7369
Burbank, CA 91510-7369
(818)848-3122
http://feefhs.org/igs/frg-igs.html

Immigration Digest
Family History World
Genealogical Institute, Inc.
P.O. Box 129
Tremonton, UT 84337-0129
(800)377-6058; (801)250-
6717
www.genealogical-
institute.com

**Irish Families:
An International
Membership Publication**
or **Irish Family Journal**
Irish Genealogical
Foundation
P.O. Box 7575
Kansas City, MO 64116
(816)454-2410
www.irishroots.com

Je Me Souviens
American-French
Genealogical Society
P.O. Box 171
Millville, MA 01529
(508)885-4316

Kinship Kronicle
Rockingham County Chapter
of the New Hampshire
Society of Genealogists
P.O. Box 81
Exeter, NH 03833-0081
(603)436-5824

L'Extuaire Genealogique
Society Genealogique de l'ost
du Quebec
110 Eneche E.
Rimouski, QC, Canada G5L
1X9
(418)724-3242

Main Gazette
Nancy L. Childress Services
3709 W. Gardenia Ave.
Phoenix, AZ 85051-8266

Mennonite Historian
Mennonite Heritage Centre
600 Shaftesbury Blvd.
Winnipeg, MB, Canada R3P
0M4
(204)888-6781
www.mbconf.ca/mbstudies/
historian

NGS Newsmagazine
National Genealogical
Society
4527 17th St. N.
Arlington, VA 22207-2399
(800)473-0060; (703)525-
0050
www.ngsgenealogy.org/
pubsnewsmag.htm

NGS Quarterly
National Genealogical
Society
4527 17th Street North
Arlington, VA 22207-2399
Tel. (703)525-0050
www.ngsgenealogy.org/pub-
squarterly.htm

**North American Manx
Association—Bulletin:
"To Preserve Whate'er is
Left Us of Ancient Heritage"**
North American Manx

Association
24 NW 8th Ave.
Galva, IL 61434
(309)932-8272

Nuestras Raices/Our Roots
Genealogical Society of
Hispanic America
Box 9606
Denver, CO 80209-0606
(720)564-0631
www.gsha.net

The Palatine Immigrant
Palatines to America
611 E. Weber Rd.
Columbus, OH 43211-1097
(614)267-4700
http://genealogy.org/~palam/
about.htm

Pioneer Branches
Northeast Washington
Genealogical Society
c/o Colville Publishing
Library
195 S. Oak
Colville, WA 99114
www.newgs.org/about.htm

**Polish Genealogical
Society—Bulletin**
Polish Genealogical Society
of America, Inc.
984 N. Milwaukee Ave.
Chicago, IL 60622
(773)776-5551
www.pgsa.org

**Presidential Families
Gazette**
Presidential Families of
America
20749 NW 9 CT., 207
Miami, FL 33269-5421
(305)493-0003

Quaker Queries
Ruby Simonson McNeill
6625 N. Sutherlin St.
Spokane, WA 99208-5045
(206)262-3300
www.isle-of-man.com/
interests/genealogy/rama/
index.htm

Research News
Family History World
Genealogical Institute, Inc.
P.O. Box 129
Tremonton, UT 84337-0129
(800)377-6058; (801)250-
6717
www.genealogical-
institute.com

Saguenayensia
Societe Historique du
Saguenay
930 rue Jacques-Cartier Est
CP 456
Chicoutimi, QC, Canada
G7H 5C8
(418)549-2805

The SAR Magazine
National Society Sons of the
American Revolution
P.O. Box 26595
Milwaukee, WI 53226
(414)782-9410
www.sar.org/sarmag/features.
htm

**Schale (Westfalen)
Newsletter**
Illinois College
Jacksonville, IL 62650
(217)245-3460

The Second Boat
Pentref Press
P.O. Box 2782

Kennebunkport, ME 04046-
2782
(207)255-4114

The Septs
Irish Genealogical Society
International
5768 Olson Memorial Hwy.
Golden Valley, MN 55422-
5014
(651)457-4458
www.rootsweb.com/~irish/
septs/index/septs_indcx.htm

**Societe Genealogique
Canadienne-Francaise
Memoires**
Societe Genealogique
Canadienne-Francaise
3440 rue Davidson
Montreal, QC, Canada H1W
2Z5
(514)527-1010
www.sgcf.com

**Swedish American
Genealogist**
Swenson Swedish
Immigration Research Center
P.O. Box 390536
Minneapolis, MN 55439
(612)925-1008
www.augustana.edu/
administration/swenson/sag.
html

**White Eagle:
Journal of the Polish
Nobility Association
Foundation**
Polish Nobility Association
Foundation
Villa Anneslie
529 Dunkirk Rd.
Anneslie, MD 21212-2014
www.geocities.com/athens/
atrium/9615/WhtEagle.htm

*Please note that there are
many additional newsletters
and publications produced by
genealogical and history
associations. There are
dozens that are dedicated to
a particular family or to a
particular county or state,
which are not represented
here. For a more comprehensive list of genealogical periodicals, please refer to:*

**Genealogical Periodical
Annual Index:
Key to the Genealogical
Literature**
Heritage Books, Inc.
1540-E Pointer Ridge Pl.
Bowie, MD 20716
(800)398-7709; (301)390-7709
www.heritagebooks.com

INVESTIGATIVE JOURNALISM & PRIVATE INVESTIGATIVE PUBLICAITONS

**Eagle Investigators' News
An international newsletter
of private investigation and
security**
International Security &
Detective Alliance—ISDA
P.O. Box 6303
Corpus Christi, TX 78466-
6303
(361)888-8060

The IRE Journal
Investigative Reporters and
Editors, Inc. (IRE)
University of Missouri

138 Neff Annex
School of Journalism
Columbia, MO 65211
(573)882-2042
www.ire.org/store/periodi-
cals.html

The Legal Investigator
National Association of Legal
Investigators
6109 Meadowwood
Grand Blanc, MI 48439
(800)266-625
www.nalionline.org/
nalipublications.html

**PI Magazine: America's
private investigation journal (Private Investigator)**
Bob Mackowiak, Ed. & Pub.
755 Bronx Dr.
Toledo, OH 43609
(419)382-0967
www.pimag.com

PIAU Journal
Private Investigators
Association of Utah, Inc.
1733 West 126 South, #223
Riverton, UT 84065
(801)467-9500
www.piau.com/journal.htm

**Private Investigators
Connection:
A Newsletter for
Investigators**
Thomas Publications, Inc.
P.O. Box 33244
Austin, TX 78764
(512)719-3595

**The Professional
Investigator Journal**
Institute of Professional
Investigators

21 Bloomsbury Way
London WC1A 2TH
44 0 1254 680072
www.ipi.org.uk/journal.htm

MAILING LISTS/DIRECT MARKETING PUBLICATIONS

Admarks
Chicago Association of
Direct Marketing
122 S. Michigan Ave., Ste.
1100
Chicago, IL 60603
www.cadm.org/resources

**The Canadian Direct
Marketing Association—
Communicator**
Communicator 1985; CDMA
Update 1985
The Canadian Direct
Marketing Association
1 Concorde Gate, Ste. 607
Don Mills, ON, Canada M3C
3N6
(416)391-2362
www.the-cma.org

**Creative:
The Magazine of Promotion
and Marketing**
Magazines/Creative, Inc.
42 W. 38th St., Rm. 601
New York, NY 10016-6210
(212)840-0160
www.creativemag.com

The DeLay Letter
Whitaker Newsletters, Inc.
313 South Ave.
P.O. Box 340

Fanwood, NJ 07023-0340
(800)359-6049; (908)889-
6336

**Direct Marketing Hints and
Secrets**
Martin Gross
145 E. 27th St. PH C
New York, NY 10016-9067
(212)689-0772

**Direct Response:
The Digest of Direct
Marketing**
Creative Direct Marketing
Group
1815 W. 213th St., Ste. 210
Torrance, CA 90501-2805
(310)212-5727
www.directmarketingcenter.net

Direct
Intertec Publishing
470 Park Ave. S., 7th Fl. N.
New York, NY 10016
(212)683-3540
http://industryclick.com/
magazine.asp?magazineid=
15&siteid=2

DMAW Marketing Advents
Direct Marketing Association
of Washington, DC
7702 Leesburg Pike, Ste. 400
Falls Church, VA 22043-2612
(703)821-3629

**Fred Goss' What's Working
in Direct Marketing**
United Communications
Group
11300 Rockville Pike, Ste.
1100
Rockville, MD 20852-3030
(800)929-4824; (301)287-
2700

Friday Report
Hoke Communications, Inc.
224 7th St.
Garden City, NY 11530
(800)229-6700; (516)746-
6700

Journal of Interactive Marketing
John Wiley & Sons
605 3rd Ave.
New York, NY 10158-0012
(800)225-5945; (212)850-
6000
www.wiley.com

The Marketing Revolution Newsletter
Clement Communications,
Inc.
Concord Industrial Park
10 LaCrue Ave.
P.O. Box 500
Concordville, PA 19331
(800)345-8101; (610)459-
1700
www.clement.com

Non-Store Marketing Report
or **NSM Report**
Maxwell Sroge Publishing,
Inc.
522 Forest Ave.
Evanston, IL 60202
(847)866-1890
www.catalog-news.com/
nsmreport.php3

PCS Direct Marketing Newsletter
PCS Mailing List Company
39 Cross St.
Peabody, MA 01960
(800)532-LIST; (978)532-
7100

**Target Marketing:
The Authoritative
Information Source for
Direct Marketers**
North American Publishing
Co.
401 N. Broad St., 5th Fl.
Philadelphia, PA 19108
(800)627-7689; (215)238-
5263
www.targetonline.com

ONLINE RESEARCH AND DATABASE PUBLICATIONS

**Data Base Alert:
News and Reference Service
for Data Base Users and
Producers**
Knowledge Industry
Publications, Inc.
701 Westchester Ave.
White Plains, NY 10604
(800)800-5474; (914)328-
9157

**EContent:
The Magazine of Electronic
Research & Resources**
Information Today, Inc.
143 Old Marlton Pike
Medford, NJ 08055-8750
(800)300-9868
(609)654-6266
www.econtentmag.com

**Electronic Information
Report:
Empowering industry deci-
sion makers since 1979**
SIMBA Information
11 Riverbend Dr. S
Box 4234

Stamford, CT 06907-0234
(800)307-2529; (203)358-
9900
www.simbanet.com

The Information Freeway Report
Washington Researchers
1655 N. Fort Myer Dr., Ste.
800
Arlington, VA 22209
(703)527-4585

Information Services & Use
I O S Press
Van Diemenstraat 94
Amsterdam, 1013 CN
Netherlands
31-20-688-3355
www.iospress.nl/site/navfr/
navframe2.html

**Information Today:
The Newspaper for Users
and Producers of Electronic
Information Services**
Information Today, Inc.
143 Old Marlton Pike
Medford, NJ 08055-8750
www.infotoday.com/it/itnew.
htm

**Information World Review:
The Information
Community Newspaper**
Information Today, Inc.
143 Old Marlton Pike
Medford, NJ 08055
(800)300-9868;
(609)654-6266
store.yahoo.com/infotoday/
inworrevsub.html

**InternetWeek:
The Newspaper for the
Communications Industry**

C M P Publications, Inc.
600 Community Dr.
Manhasset, NY 11030
(516)562-5000
www.internetwk.com

**Legal Information Alert:
What's New in Legal
Publications, Databases and
Research Techniques**
Alert Publications, Inc.
401 W. Fullerton Pkwy.
Chicago, IL 60614-2810
(773)525-7594
www.alertpub.com

**Link-Up:
The Newsmagazine for
Users of Online Services
and CD-ROM**
Information Today, Inc.
143 Old Marlton Pike
Medford, NJ 08055
(800)300-9868; (609)654-
6266
www.infotoday.com/lu/lunew
.htm

Online Newsletter
Information Intelligence, Inc.
P.O. Box 31098
Phoenix, AZ 85046
(602)996-2283
www.infointelligence.com

Online Product News
Worldwide Videotex
P.O. Box 3273
Boynton Beach, FL 33424-
3273
(407)738-2276
www.wvpubs.com

**Web—Online Services
(Year): Market Analysis
and Forecast**

SIMBA Information
11 Riverbend Dr. S
Box 4234
Stamford, CT 06907-0234
(800)307-2529; (203)358-
9900
www.simbanet.com

PRE-EMPLOYMENT SCREENING AND RECRUITMENT PUBLICATIONS

**Checkpoint:
The Russell Staffing
Resources Workplace
Review**
Russell Staffing Resources
P.O. Box 6279
San Rafael, CA 94903-0279
(800)616-JOBS; (415)781-
1444

**Corporate Security
Newsletter:
Biweekly Intelligence
Tracking Cutting-Edge
Practices, Trends, and New
Technologies for Security
Executives**
Corporate Security
Publishing
1921 Sunderland Pl. NW, Ste.
A
Washington, DC 20036
(202)452-8756
www.infoinc.com/
corpsecurity

Employment Marketplace
Employment Marketplace
12015 Robyn Park Dr.
St. Louis, MO 63131
(314)569-3095
www.eminfo.com

Executive Recruiter News
Kennedy Information
One Kennedy Pl., Rte. 12 S.
Fitzwilliam, NH 03447
(800)531-0007; (603)585-
3101
www.kennedyinfo.com/er/
ern.html

**Labor Relations Reporter
or BNA Labor Relations
Reporter: Series: Labor
Relations Reporter**
The Bureau of National
Affairs, Inc.
1231 25th St., NW
Washington, DC 20037
(202)452-4200
www.bna.com/products/
labor/lelw.htm

The Recruiting Pipeline
The Recruiting Network, Inc.
P.O. Box 68366
Schaumburg, IL 60168-0366
(800)562-6593; (847)524-
8487
www.recruitingpipeline.com

**Recruiting Trends:
The Monthly Newsletter for
the Recruiting Executive**
Kennedy Information
One Kennedy Pl., Rte. 12 S.
Fitzwilliam, NH 03447
(800)531-0007; (603)585-
3101
www.kennedyinfo.com/mt/
rectrends.html

**Smart Workplace Practices:
The Newsletter That Makes
Your HR Work A Lot
Easier**
Independent Small Business
Employers of America
520 S. Pierce, Ste. 224

Mason City, IA 50401
(800)728-3187; (515)424-3187
www.biztrain.com/
membership/smartemployer.htm

Workforce: HR Trends & Tools for Business Results
ACC Communications, Inc.
245 Fischer Ave. A-2
Costa Mesa, CA 92626
(714)751-1883
www.workforceonline.com

Workforce Stability Alert: Strategies and Tactics for Employee Recruitment and Retention
M. Lee Smith, Publishers LLC
P.O. Box 5094
Brentwood, TN 37024-5094
(800)274-6774; (615)373-7517

PRIVACY AND COMPUTER SECURITY PUBLICATIONS

Annual Conference Computer Security Applications
IEEE Computer Society Press
3 Park Ave, 17th Fl.
New York, NY 10017
(714)821-8380
http://computer.org/
proceedings/proceed_a-h.htm

Bank Security Report
Warren, Gorham and Lamont
One Penn Plaza
New York, NY 10119
(212)367-6300

Cipher Newsletter
Technical Committee on Security & Privacy
IEEE Computer Society
1730 Massachusetts Ave. NW
Washington, DC 20036-1992
www.ieee-security.org/cipher.html

Computer & Communications Security Abstracts
MCB—UP Ltd.
Anbar Electronic Intelligence
60-62 Toller Ln.
Bradford, W Yorks, BD8 9BY
United Kingdom
44-1274-777700
http://tamino.anbar.com/
abstracts/ccsa/index.htm

Computer Fraud & Security
Pergamon
The Boulevard, Langford Ln.
East Park
Kidlington, Oxford, OXB 1GB
United Kingdom
65-434-3727
www.elsevier.com/locate/
compfraud

Computer Law and Security Report
Pergamon
The Boulevard, Langford Ln
East Park
Kidlington, Oxford, OXB 1GB
United Kingdom
31-20-485-3757
www.compseconline.com/
compsec/show

Computer Security Alert
Miller Freeman, Inc.
600 Harrison St.
San Francisco, CA 94107
(415)905-2370
https://wow.mfi.com/csi/
order/publications.html

Computer Security Digest
Computer Protection Systems, Inc.
P.O. Box 6121
12275 Appletree Dr.
Plymouth, MI 48170
(313)459-8787

Computer Security Foundations Workshop
IEEE Computer Society Press
3 Park Ave, 17th Fl.
New York, NY 10017
(714)821-8380
http://computer.org/
proceedings/proceed_a-h.htm

Computer Security Journal
Miller Freeman, Inc.
600 Harrison St.
San Francisco, CA 94107
(415)956-3371
https://wow.mfi.com/csi/
order/publications.html

The Computer Security Journal
Computer Security Institute
600 Harrison St.
San Francisco, CA 94107
(415)905-2626
https://wow.mfi.com/csi/
order/publications.html

Computer Security, Auditing and Controls or COM—SAC

Management Advisory
Publications
57 Greylock Rd.
Box 81151
Wellesley, MA 02481
(617)235-2895
www.masp.com/publications/
MAP-2.html

**Computers & Security:
The international journal
devoted to the study of the
technical and managerial
aspects of computer
security**
Pergamon
The Boulevard, Langford Ln.
East Park
Kidlington, Oxford, OXB
1GB
United Kingdom
31-20-485-3757
www.elsevier.com/locate/
compsec

**Computing and
Communications: Law and
Protection Report**
Assets Protection Publishing
P. O. Box 10279
Phoenix, AZ 85064-0279
(602)956-7074

**Cryptologia:
A quarterly journal devoted
to all aspects of cryptology**
U.S. Military Academy;
Department of Mathematics
West Point, NY 10996-9902
(914)938-3200
www.dean.usma.edu/math/
pubs/cryptologia

Datenschutz Nachrichten
Deutsche Vereinigung fur
Datenschutz e.V.
Bonner Talweg 33-35

Bonn, 53113
Germany
49-228-222498
www.aktiv.org/DVD/themen/
dana/dana_start.html

**Datenschutz und
Datensicherung
Recht und Sicherheit der
Informations und
Kommunikationssysteme
or D u D**
Friedrich Vieweg & Sohn
Verlagsgesellschaft mbH
Postfach 58 29
65048 Wiesbaden
Germany
49-611-7878151
www.dud.de

**Datenschutz und
Informationsrecht**
Oesterreichische Gesellschaft
fuer Datenschutz
Sautergasse 20
A-1170 Wien
Austria
43-1-4897893
www.ad.or.at/text/dir.htm

Datenschutz-Berater (DSB)
Verlagsgruppe Handelsblatt
GmbH
Kasernenstr 67
Duesseldorf, 40213
Germany
49-211-887-0
www.vhb.de

**EDPACS:
The E D P audit, control
and security newsletter**
Auerbach Publications
Subsidiary of: C R C Press
(New York)
535 Fifth Ave., Ste. 806

New York, NY 10017
(212)286-1010
www.auerbach-
publications.com/ejournals/
product_info

**E-Commerce Market
Reporter**
E-Commerce Information
Center
1913 Atlantic Ave, Ste F4
Manasquan, NJ 08736
(732)292-1100
www.healthresourcesonline.
com/ecic/22nl.htm

Effector Online Newsletter
Electronic Frontier
Foundation
1550 Bryant St., Ste. 725
San Francisco, CA 94103-
4832
(415)436-9333
www.eff.org/effector

Financial Privacy Report
12254 Nicollet Ave.
Burnsville, MN 55337
(612)895-8757
www.thelibertarian.net/fpr.
html

**FOIA Update (Freedom of
Information Act)**
U.S. Department of Justice
Office of Information and
Privacy
Constitution Ave & Tenth
Sts., NW
Washington, DC 20530-0001
(202)514-5105
www.usdoj.gov/oip/foi-
upd.htm

**Healthcare Data Security
Manual**

American Health Consultants
3525 Piedmont Rd., NE
6 Piedmont Center, Ste. 400
Atlanta, GA 30305
(404)688-2421
www.ahcpub.com/ahc_root_
html/products/newsletters/
hosref.html

**IEEE Symposium on
Security and Privacy**
445 Hoes Ln.
Box 1331
Piscataway, NJ 08854
(800)678-4333
http://computer.org/
proceedings/proceed_r-z.htm

**Information Management
& Computer Security**
MCB University Press Ltd.
60-62 Toller Ln.
Bradford, W Yorks, BD8
9BY
United Kingdom
www.emeraldinsight.com/
imcs.htm

**Information Security
Technical Report**
Pergamon
The Boulevard, Langford Ln.
East Park
Kidlington, Oxford, OXB
1GB
United Kingdom
31-20-485-3757
www.elsevier.com/locate/
infsec

Information Security
International Computer
Security Association
106 Access Rd.
Norwood, MA 02062
(781)255-0200
www.infosecuritymag.com

**Information Systems
Auditor:
Risk Security Control**
International Newsletters
P.O. Box 133
Witney, Oxon, OX8 6ZH
United Kingdom
44-199-3824130
www.intnews/isa.htm

**Information Systems
Control Journal:
A leader in I T governance
and assurance**
Information Systems Audit &
Control Association
3701 Algonquin Rd., Ste.
1010
Rolling Meadows, IL 60008
(847)253-1545
www.isaca.org/jrnlhome.htm

**Information Systems
Security**
535 Fifth Ave., Ste. 806
New York, NY 10017
(212)286-1010
www.auerbach-
publications.com/ejournals/
product_info/product_detail.
asp?id=96

**International Journal of
Information Security**
Springer-Verlag
Heidelberger Platz 3
Berlin, 14197
Germany
49-30-82787-0
http://link.springer.de/link/ser
vice/journals/10207/index.
htm

**Journal of Computer
Security**
IOS Press

Van Diemenstraat 94
Amsterdam, 1013 CN
Netherlands
31-20-688-3355
www.iospress.nl/site/navfr/
navframe2.html

The Lyke Report
Lyke Publications, Inc.
P.O. Box 290
Glenview, IL 60025
(800)725-7714
www.lykepublications.com

Password
Information Systems Security
Association
7044 S 13th St.
Oak Creek, WI 53154
(414)768-8000
www.issa.org

**Privacy and American
Business**
Center for Social & Legal
Research
2 University Plaza, 414
Hackensack, NJ 07601-6209
(201)996-1154
www.pandab.org

**The Privacy and Security
Review**
Thin Man & Associates
4309 Hatch
North Las Vegas, NV 89030
(702)878-7160

**Privacy Commissioner of
Canada Annual Report**
Privacy Commissioner
112 Kent St, 3rd Fl
Ottawa, ON, K1A 1H3
Canada
(800)267-0441; (613)995-
2410

www.privcom.gc.ca/
information/ar/02_04_e.asp

Privacy Journal (Monthly)
P.O Box 28577
Providence, Rhode Island
02908
(401)274-7861
www.townonline.com/
privacyjournal

Privacy Times
Privacy Times, Inc.
P.O. Box 21501
Washington, DC 20009
(202)829-3660
www.privacytimes.com

**Research Trends in
Computer and Data
Security**
Research Information Ltd.
222 Maylands Ave
Hemel Hempstead Rd.
Hemel Hempstead, Herts,
HP3 8LA
United Kingdom
01442-213222

Responsible Computing
National Center for Computer
Crime Data
1222-B 17th Ave.
Santa Cruz, CA 95062
(831)475-4457

**S C Magazine; the interna-
tional journal of computer
security**
West Coast Publishers Inc.
161 Worcester Rd., Ste. 201
Framingham, MA 01701
(508)879-9792
www.scmagazine.com/
scmagazine/scmagazinehome.
html

Securite Informatique
Publi-News
47 rue Aristide Briand
Levallois-Perret, 92300
France
33-1-41499360
www.publi-news.fr

**Security:
The magazine for buyers of
security products, systems
and service**
Business News Publishing
Co.
755 W Big Beaver Rd., Ste.
1000
Troy, MI 48084
(248)362-3700
www.securitymagazine.com

**Security Electronics
Magazine**
Security Electronics
Magazine
Ste. 6, 586-590 Parramatta
Rd.
Petersham, NSW, 2049
Australia
61-2-95600749
www.safecity.com.au/secele.
htm

**Security Watch:
Protecting People, Property
and Assets**
Bureau of Business Practice
7201 McKinney Circle
Frederick, MD 21704
(800)876-9105
www.bbpnews.com/safety/
saf_portal.shtml

**Seguridad en Informatica y
Comunicaciones (SIC)**
Ediciones Coda S.L.
Doctor Esquerdo, 28, So.

1o.D
Madrid, 28028
Spain
34-91-401-0626

**Sicherheit in der
Informations- und
Kommunikationstechnik**
Spektrum Akademischer
Verlag GmbH
Vangerowstr 20
Heidelberg, 69115
Germany
49-6221-9126-0
www.spektrum-verlag.com

**Software Protection:
A journal on the legal, technical and practical aspects
of protecting computer software**
Law & Technology Press
4 Arbolado Ct.
Manhattan Beach, CA 90266-
4937
(310)544-0272
www.totse.com/en/hack/
hack_attack/periodic.html

**Telecom & Network
Security Review**
Pasha Publications Inc.
1600 Wilson Blvd., Ste. 600
Arlington, VA 22209
(703)528-1244

**Virus Bulletin:
The international publication on computer virus prevention, recognition and
removal**
The Pentagon
Abingdon Science Park
Abingdon, Oxon, OX14 3YP
United Kingdom
44-1235-555139
www.virusbtn.com

Zashchita Informatsii-Konfident
Confident Data Security
Association
Pl Proletarskoi Diktatury 2
St Petersburg, 193060
Russian Federation
(812)3251037
http://ssl.eastview.com/cgi-bin/evshop.P20484.htm

PROPERTY MANAGEMENT PUBLICATIONS

Allen Letter
PMN Publishing
P.O. Box 47024
Indianapolis, IN 46247
(317)888-7156
www.mfdhousing.com/gfa/books/index.html (Industry newsletter)

Beijing Fangdichan
or **Beijing Real Estate**
Beijing Fangdichang
Guanliju; (Beijing Real
Estate Administration)
1 Nanwanzi, Nanheyan
Dongcheng-qu
Beijing, 100006
China
5225481

Canadian Property Management
MediaEdge Communications
Inc.
5255 Yonge St., Ste. 1000
North York, ON, M2N 6P4
Canada
(416)512-8186

www.mediaedge.ca/PubSearch.asp

Journal of Property Management
The official publication of the Institute of Real Estate Management
Institute of Real Estate
Management
P.O. Box 109025
430 N Michigan Ave.
Chicago, IL 60610
(312)329-6059; (312)329-6058
www.irem.org/i06-jpm/index.html

Manager's Source Guide:
Serving the Decision Makers of Income Producing Properties
The Adler Group, Inc.
8601 Georgia Ave., 7th Fl.
Silver Spring, MD 20910
(301)588-0681

Mr. Landlord:
The Survival Newsletter for Landlords
Home Rental Publishing
P.O. Box 64442
Virginia Beach, VA 23467
(800)950-2250; (757)424-7997
www.mrlandlord.com/mllshop/subscribe.html

Property Australia
Property Council of Australia
Level 26, Australia Square
(264)278 George St.
Sydney, NSW, 2000
Australia
61-2-9252-3111
www.propertyoz.com.au

Property Management Association Bulletin
Property Management
Association
7900 Wisconsin Ave., Ste.
204
Bethesda, MD 20814-3601
(301)907-9326; (301)587-6543
www.pma-dc.org/publications.html

Property Management Monthly:
Serving decision-makers of income-producing properties
Adler Group, Inc.
8601 Georgia Ave., Ste. 701
Silver Spring, MD 20910-3439
(301)588-0681

Property Management News
K-Rey Publishing Inc.
789 W Pender St., Ste. 920
Vancouver, BC, V6C 1H2
Canada
(604)669-7671

Property Management
M C B University Press Ltd.
60-62 Toller Ln.
Bradford, W Yorks, BD8
9BY
United Kingdom
www.emeraldinsight.com/pm.htm

The Property Professional
National Property
Management Association
1108 Pinehurst Rd.
Dunedin, FL 34698

(813)736-3788
www.npma.org/publications.
htm

Right of Way
International Right of Way
Association
13650 S. Gramercy Pl.
Gardena, CA 90249
(310)538-0233
www.irwaonline.org/row

Organizations

*Please accept my resignation. I don't care to belong to
any club that will have me as a member.*

–Groucho Marx

ADOPTEE/ BIRTHPARENT SEARCH ORGANIZATIONS

AFRICA

Johannesburg Child Welfare Society
P.O. Box 2539
2000 Johannesburg
27 (11)331-0171
www.jhbchildwelfare.org.za

AUSTRALIA

Adopted Persons Support Group, South Australia Inc.
APSG SA Inc
52 Fordingbridge Road
Davoren Park, SA 5113
61 8 8252 527; 61 08 8287 4590
http://users.senet.com.au/~djdelany

Adoption and Family

**Information Service
Department of Human Services**
P.O. Box 39
Rundle Mall
Adelaide SA 5032
9th Floor, Citi Centre,
Building 11 Hindmarsh Square
Adelaide SA 5000
(08)8226 6694
www.adoptions.sa.gov.au

Adoption and Substitute
Care Section P.O. Box 825
Canberra City, ACT 2601
(062)454 11

Adoption Australia—Queensland Origins
Queensland
www.angelfire.com/de/lilyorigins

Adoption Australia Origins Inc.
NSW
www.angelfire.com/or/originsnsw

**Adoption Information Service
Department of Health and Community Services**
448 St. Kilda Rd.
Melbourne, Victoria 3004
(03)9868-7777

Adoption Jigsaw WA, Inc.
P.O. Box 403
Subiaco, WA 6904
(08)9388-1922

Adoption Jigsaw WA, Inc.
P.O. Box 252
Hillarys Perth, WA 6025
09-388-1922

Adoption Jigsaw
Jigsaw Centre
91 Hensman Rd.
Subiaco 6008
09-388-1922

Adoption Jigsaw
P.O. Box 912
New Farm, Queensland 4005
(07)3358-6666

Adoption and Substitute Care Unit
P.O. Box 40596
Casuarina NT 0811
(08)98 2277 077

Adoption Triangle
Cadia House
March Street
Orange, NSW 2800
(02)6363 1744

Adoption Triangle
P.O. Box 96
Jesmond Newcastle
NSW 2299
(049)655 888

Association for Adoptees
14 Rosemary Court
Beenleigh, Queensland 4207
07 3807-6428

Association of Relinquishing Mothers (ARMS)—South Australia
Torrens Building
220 Victoria Square
Adelaide 5000
(08)82216944

Association of Relinquishing Mothers (ARMS)—Western Australia
P.O. Box 60
Tuart Hill, WA 6060
61 (09)367 1211; 447 3970; 390 5603; 444 1214; 335 7961

Australian Relinquishing Mothers Society
P.O. Box 521
Hamilton Hill, WA 6904
08 9336 1337

Australian Relinquishing Mothers
51 North Terrace
Hackney, SA 5069
08-362-2418

Child Migrants Trust
228 Canning Street
North Carlton
Melbourne, Victoria, 3054
(03)9347 7403
www.nottscc.gov.uk/child_migrants/Index.htm

Department Community Welfare
Adoption Section
G.P.O. Box 125-B
Hobart TAS 7002
(002)303 395

Family and Childrens Services
Adoption Branch
189 Royal Street
East Perth WA 6000
(09)426 3444

Family Information Service NSW
Department of Community Services
Adoption Services Branch
P.O. Box 3485
Parramatta NSW 2124
Level 13 Ferguson Centre
100 George Street
Parramatta NSW 2150
(02)689 5961; (02)689 5967; (02)9865 5906

Far West Post Adoption Support Network
http://lisp.com.au/dubbo/adopt.htm

Jigsaw Queensland Inc.
P.O. Box 55
Roma Street Qld 4003
61 (7)3875-1909
http://members.ozemail.com.au/~jigsaw

Jigsaw SA, Inc.
P.O. Box 567
Prospect East SA 5082
48 Watson Ave.
Broadview, SA 5083
(08)8344 7529
www.onkaparingacity.com/services/doc-jigsaw_sa_inc.html

Jigsaw Tasmania
The Secretary
GP.O. Box 989K
Hobart
Tasmania 7001
61 3 6243 6626

Origins (SA)
www.angelfire.com/ok3/originssa

Origins Tasmania
36 Corranga Drive
Chigwell Tasmania 7011
http://216.226.153.57

Post Adoption Resource Centre
P.O. BOX 239
Bondi NSW 2026
(02)9365 3444; 800 024 256
www.bensoc.asn.au/pasc

Vanish (Victorian Adoption Network for Information and Self Help)
199 Cardigan Street
Carlton Victoria 3053
(008)334 043; (03)663 8064; (61 3)9348 2111
http://home.vicnet.net.au/~vanish

War-Babes Down Under
46, Lucknow Street
Mitcham 3132
Victoria
03 9874-8875

AUSTRIA

Osterreichisches Rotes Kreuz (Austrian Red Cross)
Suchdienst
Gusshausstrasse 3
A-1041 Wien
www.roteskreuz.at

BELGIUM

KOBEL–Korea Belgium Association
109 Rue Carton de Wairt,
B-1090 Bruxelles
00 32 3 736 62 40
www.kobel.de

Vereniging voor Kind en Adoptiegezin, VZW
Sulferbergstraat 38
8000 Brugge

CANADA

CANADopt
www.canadopt.ca/index.htm

Alberta

Alberta Adoptee
http://glink2.com/jim/Adoptee2.htm

Birthparents/Relatives Group
2147 - 141st Avenue
Edmonton, AB T5Y 1C4
Box 20089, Beverly Postal
Outlet

Edmonton, AB T5W 5E6
(780)473-1912; (403)478-0197

KNOW NAME Search and Support Group
23 Rosedale Way
Medicine Hat, AB T1B 1X5
(403)526-3143

Parent Finders
P.O. Box 12031
Edmonton, AB T5J 3L2
(780)466-3335

Parent Finders
18 Oslo Close
Red Deer, AB T4N 5A5
(403)434-7712

TRIAD, Calgary Chapter
Box 5114, Stn. A
Calgary, AB T2H 1X1
(403)265-3166
www.triadcanada.ca

British Columbia

Adoptees and Birthparents Seeking Kinfolk
600 Jaschinsky Road
Kelowna, BC V1X 1L8
(250)860-5368

Adoptees and Kinfolk Seeking Relatives (ASK)
2050 Quebec Street
Penticton, BC
(604)493-4319

Adoption Support Group
10220 110th Avenue
Fort St. John, BC V1J 2T9
(250)785-1781

Adoption Support Group
217 11th Avenue

Prince Rupert, BC V8J 2W2
(250)624-4827

Adoptive Families Association of BC
#205, 15463 - 104 Ave.
Surrey, BC V3R 1N9
(604)588-7300
www.bcadoption.com

Birth Mothers Branching Out
(250)592-4126

Canadian Adoptees Reform Association (CARA)
3986 Broadway
Richmond, BC V7E 2Y2
(604)513-9450; (604)241-8255

Cariboo Adoption Support Group
#25-803 Hogsdown Road
Williams Lake, BC V2G 3R2
(250)392-4282

Forget Me Not Family Society
10693 - 135A St.
Surrey, BC V3T 4E3
#7 - 1546 Yew Street
Vancouver, BC V6K 3E4
(604)581-0550

Forget Me Not Family Society
1146 Kent Street
White Rock, BC V4B 4T4
(604)526-6644

Full Circle Birth Parent Support Group
416 Gore Street
Nelson, BC V1L 5B9
(250)352-6122

IMAGINE Search/Support Group
30 Edgewood Rise, NW
Calgary, AL T3A 2T7
(403)245-5005

Parent Finders–Kamloops
Box 84 - Main Postal Station
Kamloops, BC V2C 5K3
(250)372-3906

Parent Finders of Canada (National Office)
and **Canadian Adoption Reunion Register (C.A.R.R.)**
19 English Bluff Road
Delta, BC V4M 2M4
(604)948-1069
www.parentfinders.org

Parent Finders–Prince George
4152 Chestnut Drive
Prince George, BC V2K 2T5
(250)962-2069

Parent Finders–Quesnel
2019 Feldspar Ave.
Quesnel, BC V2J 5S5
(250)747-2323

Parent Finders–Vancouver
19 English Bluff Road
Delta, BC V4M 2M4
(604)948-1069
www.parentfinders.org

Parent Finders–Victoria
686 Hampshire Road
Victoria, BC V8S 4S2
(250)598-9711

Society of Special Needs Adoptive Parents
The United Kingdom

Building
1150 - 409 Granville Street
Vancouver, BC V6C 1T2
(800)663-7627; (604)687-3144
www.snap.bc.ca

TRIAD Canada (TRIAD Society for Truth in Adoption)
P.O. Box 5922, Stn B
Victoria, BC V8R 6S8
(250)474-2280
www.triadcanada.ca

Manitoba

Adoption Connection
P.O. Box 20062 (South)
Brandon, MAN R7A 6Y8

LINKS Post-Legal Adoption Support Group
89 St. Michael Road
Winnipeg, MAN R2M 2K8
(204)257-4742
members.shaw.ca.rkading

New Brunswick

New Brunswick Parent Finders
935 Lansdown Road
Mount Pleasant, NB E7L 4K7
(506)375-6660
www.geocities.com/pfnbca

Newfoundland

Newfoundland Adoption Support Group
P.O. Box 8896
Manuels, Newfoundland
A1X 1C6
(709)834-1895

Parent Finders–Newfoundland
P.O. Box 287
Gander, Newfoundland
A1V 1W6
(709)256-3768; (709)651-2769

Nova Scotia

Parent Finders–Nova Scotia
P.O. Box 791
Lower Sackville, NS B4C 3V3
(902)864-6654

Ontario

Adoptee Issues Support Group
3 - 120 Dundas St.
London, ONT N6A 1G1
(519)858-9247

Adoptees Helping Adoptees
363 McKim St.
Sudbury, ONT P3C 2L4
(705)524-1951; (705)673-2423

Adoption Awareness Support System
129 Loyola Place
Thunder Bay, ONT P7C 5N6
(807)475-7843

Adoption Council of Canada
180 Argyle Avenue, #329
Ottawa, ONT K2P 1B7
(613)235-0344
www.adoption.ca

Adoption Council of Ontario
3216 Younge Street,

Second Floor
Toronto, ONT M4N 2L2
(416)482-0021
www.dreaming.org/~n/aco/
acomain.html

**Adoption Disclosure
Support Group**
#203, 815 Sherbrooke Street
Peterborough, ONT K9J 2R2
(705)740-0483

Adoption Disclosure
Catholic Children's Aid
Society of Toronto
26 Maitland St.
Toronto, ONT M4Y 1C6
(416)395-1527; (416)924-
2100

**Adoption Reform Coalition
of Ontario (ARCO)**
ONT
(613)828-3236; (613)748-
3236
http://members.aol.com/
pfncr/arco.ontario.html

Adoption Roots and Rights
187 Patricia Ave
Dorchester, ONT N0L 1G1
(519)268-3674
www.geocities.com/
adoption_reunion2001

**Adoption Support Kinship
(ASK)**
20 Bloor Street East
P.O. Box 75040
Toronto, ONT M4W 3T3
(416)410-7021

**B and M Search and
Support**
63 Holborn Ave.
Nepean, ONT K2C 3H1
(613)730-1039

**Birth Mothers for Each
Other**
99 Tyndall Ave., #908
Toronto, ONT M4P 1N8
(416)533-9828

**Birth Mothers' Support
Group**
6 Tardree Place
Scarborough, ONT M1R 3X3
(416)757-7604

Birth Parents and Adoptees
North York Support Group
North York, Rishy, ONT
(416)226-3015

**Canadian Adoptee's
Registry Inc.**
94 Bayview Dr.
Barrie, ONT L4N 3P1
(705)728-6512
www.canadianadoptees
registry.org

**Canadian Council of
Birthmothers**
P.O. Box 467, Stn. C
Toronto, ONT M6J 3P5
(416)537-4486
www.nebula.on.ca/canbmothers

CARR Support Group
717, 47 Jakes Avenue
Toronto, ONT M4T 1E2
(416)920-6819

**Coalition for Open Records
(COAR)**
462 Ossington Ave.
Toronto, ONT M6G 3T2
www.geocities.com/
coarontario

**Durham Adoption
Disclosure Support Group**

ONT
(905)433-1551, ext. 2261

**International Reunion
Services**
#203 - 103 John Street, South
Hamilton, ONT L8N 2C2
(905)522-2665

Lost and Found
24 Albert St.
Guelph, ONT N1G 1C6
(519)837-2830

**Orangeville Adoption
Reunion Support Group**
20 Century Drive, #9
Orangeville, ONT L9W 4L5
(519)942-2823

**Parent Finders–Aurora/
Newmarket**
132 Cherrywood Dr.
Newmarket, ONT L3Y 2X7
(905)898-7476

**Parent
Finders–Belleville/Quinte**
P.O. Box 38
42 Wellington Street
Stirling, Ontario K0K 3E0
(613)968-7209; (613)395-
2795

Parent Finders–Brockville
P.O. Box 2002
Brockville, ONT K6V 6N4
(613)925-3383

**Parent Finders–Hamilton/
Burlington**
P.O. Box 91530
Roseland Plaza Postal Outlet
Burlington, ONT L7R 4L6
(905)381-0198; (905)632-
4256

Parent Finders–Kawartha
General Delivery
Cameron, ONT K0M 1G0
(705)359-1172
www.lindsaycomp.on.ca/
parfind.htm

Parent Finders–Kingston
33 Barbara Ave.
Kingston, ONT K7K 2M9
(613)542-0892
http://members.aol.com/
pfncr/index.html

**Parent Finders–Kitchener/
Waterloo**
1873 Townline Road, RR 21
Cambridge, ONT N3C 2V3
(519)658-5590
www.kw.igs.net/
%7Erobmann/pf.html

Parent Finders–London
Westmount Square
Apartments
955 Wonderland Rd., South -
Apt. 812
London, ONT N6K 2X8
(519)472-5017

Parent Finders–Markham
1472 Valley Drive
Stouffville, ONT L1J 7Z3
(905)720-2994; (905)477-
0011

**Parent Finders–National
Capital Region**
P.O. Box 21025, Ottawa
South
Postal Outlet
Ottawa, Ontario K1S 5N1
(613)730-8305
http://members.aol.com/
pfncr/index.html

Parent Finders–Niagara
83, 286 Cushman Road
St. Catherines, ONT L2M
6Z2
(905)938-1092

**Parent Finders–North Bay
Liaison**
122 Labreche Drive
North Bay, ONT P1A 3R5
(705)497-9873

**Parent Finders–Northern
Ontario**
3059 Elm Street
Val Caron, ONT P3N 1E8

**Parent Finders–Sarnia-
Lambton**
Box 58 Evergreen Lane
Camlachie, ONT N0N 1E0
(519)869-6071
www.sarnia.com/groups/
parentfinders

Parent Finders–Toronto
Box 1008, Station F
50 Charles St. E.
Toronto, ONT M4Y 2Y7
(416)465-8434
http://toronto.com/E/V/
TORON/0015/17/33

Parent Finders–Windsor
12 Hill Street, Box 85
Cottam, ONT N0R 1B0
(519)839-4144

**Peterborough Adoption
Disclosure Support Group**
203 - 815 Sherbrooke St.
Peterborough, ONT K9J 2R2
(705)740-0483

**Post Adoption Reunion
Support Group**
24 Lincoln Ave.
Toronto, ONT M6P 1M8
(416)762-4944

**Rejoining the
Circle–Anishnawbe**
Anishnawbe Health Centre
225 Queen St. East
Toronto, ONT M5A 1S4
(416)360-0486

Reuniting in Cornwall
Cornwall, ONT
(613)932-3984; (613)933-
9186
http://members.tripod.com/
reuniting

Searching Lost Families
RR#3
Ayr, ONT N0B 1E0
(519)632-9306
http://home.golden.net/~gail

Searchline of Canada
63 Holborn Avenue
Ottawa, ONT K2C 3H1
(613)825-1640

**Sharing Post Adoption
Issues**
600 Toke St. North
Timmins, ONT P4N 6W1
(705)264-4475

Prince Edward Island

**Parent Finders–Prince
Edward Island**
13 Orlebar St.
Charlottetown, PEI C1A 4R5
(902)892-4069
www.geocities.com/
SiliconValley/Bay/3259/
default.html

Quebec

**Mouvement Retrouvailles
[Canadian Open Records
Movement]**

Bureau 333
150, Grant
Longueuil, QC J4H 3H6
(450)646-1060
www.mouvement-retrou-
vailles.qc.ca

Parent Finders–Montreal
190 Davignon
Dollard-des-Ormeaux, QUE
H9B 1Y5
(514)683-0204
http://home.primus.ca/~pfmtl

Quebec Adoption Quest
P.O. Box 305
Cote St. Luc, QUE H4V 2Y5

Saskatchewan

**Birthmother's Support
Group**
1348 Edward St.
Regina, SK, S4T 4M6
(306)522-2756

TRIAD–Moose Jaw
724 - 3rd Avenue, NW
Moose Jaw, SK S6H 3T2
(306)693-2697

TRIAD–Regina
P.O. Box 33040
Regina, SK S4T 7X2
(306)586-4782

TRIAD–Saskatoon
P.O. Box 1221
Saskatoon, SK S7K 3N2
(306)665-3109

DENMARK

Korea Klubben
Valby Langgade 141 1.tv
D.K-2500 Valby
www.koreaklubben.org

ENGLAND

Adopt-A-Link
60 Downside Rd.
Sutton, Surrey SM2 5HP
081-642-7064

NORCAP
112 Church Road
Wheatley, OX, OX33 1LU
(865)750-554
www.norcap.org.uk

EUROPE

**Campaign for Adoption
Reform in Europe**
St. Stephan's Manse
33 Camperdown Street
Broughty Ferry
Dundee DD5 3AA

FRANCE

**GEN-AB (Genealogies-
Abandonnes)**
B.P. 5010
38821-Grenoble Cedex
33.76.35.63.98

Racines Corennes
Bd de la Grenelles 63
F-75015 Paris

**Service Social d'Aide aux
Emigrants**
Association reconnue d'u-
tilite publique
SIEGE SOCIAL
72, rue Regnault
F-75640 Paris Cedex 13

GERMANY

Deutsches Rotes Kreuz
Generalsekretariat
Suchdienst Munchen

Zentrale Auskunfts- und
Dokumentationsstelle
Infanteriestrabe 7 A
80797 Munchen
www.rotkreuz.de

Hodori (Korea)
Zittauer Str.5
D-33619 Bielefeld

**Internationaler Sozialdienst
Deutscher Zweig e.v.**
Am Stockborn 5-7
60439 Frankfurt
49 69 9580702
www.dsk.de/rds/00766.
htm

IRELAND

A.A.A.
Killmeaque
Naas
Co. Killdare

Adoption Action
c/o 3 Gandon Hall
Lwr Gardiner Street
Dublin 1

Adoption Advice Service
Christ Church Square
Dublin 6
011-353-1-473-2110
www.barnardos.ie/adoption/
index.htm

**Department of Foreign
Affairs**
Adoption Services
Inveagh House
80 St. Stephen's Green
Dublin 2
353 1 4780822; 021-4923121
www.shb.ie/s15/c2b.html

KOREA

Euro-Korean League
Kpobox 1964
Seoul, South Korea, 110-619
82 2 564 2275

**Korean Overseas Adoptees
(KOA)**
K. P.O. Box 1964
Seoul, South Korea 110-619
82.2.720.5251

NETHERLANDS

Adoption Centre
University of Utrecht
Heidelberglaan 1
3584 CS Utrecht

**Stichting International
Social Service**
Laan Copes van Cattenburch
139
NL-2585 GA's-Gravenhage
(31)(70)356 09 67

NEW ZEALAND

Adoption Support Link
GP.O. Box 4164
Auckland

Adoption Support Services
Dept. of Social Services
Private Bag 21
Wellington
04-472-7666

**Hutt Adoption Search and
Support**
P.O. Box 38304
Petone
68-7460

Jigsaw, Inc.
P.O. Box 28-0376
Remuera, Aukland 5
0011 64 9523 3460

Jigsaw, NZ
P.O. Box 38681
Howick, Auckland
(09)533-9191; 09-274-6605

**N.Z. Adoption Education
and Healing Trust**
P.O. Box 11446
Wellington
0064 4 970.3374
www.adoptionreform.org.nz

NORWAY

**Children of the World
(Korea)**
Bogstadveien 27B
0355 Oslo
47 22 69 85 55

SCOTLAND

Birthlink
21 Castle Street
Edinburgh EH2 3DN
0131-225-6441

**Campaign for Adoption
Reform in Europe**
St. Stephan's Manse
33 Camperdown Street
Broughty Ferry
Dundee DD5 3AA

**Family Care and Link
Adoption Registry**
21 Castle Street
Edinburgh EH2 3DN
0131 225-6441

SPAIN

**Servicio Social
Internacional**
Consejo Superior de
Protection de Menores
Condesa de Venadito 34
28027 Madrid

SRI LANKA

Weladama
24 Ebenezer Place
Dehiwala

SWEDEN

AKF (Korea)
Banvallsv.3
S-24293

Weladama
ersens 6
211 42 Malm

SWITZERLAND

Dongari (Korea)
Schindlerstrasse 15
CH8006 Zurich

**Fondation Suisse Du
Service Social International**
10, rue Dr. Alfred-Vincent
CH-1201 Geneva
022-731-67-00

IGADO Schwiez
Postfach 8557
CH-8050 Zuerich
011 41 61 313 85 00

**Schweizerischer
Gemeinnuetziger**

Frauenverein
Zuerichbergstrasse 7
CH-8032 Zuerich
011 41 1 252 57 56

UNITED KINGDOM

Adoption InterLink–UK
www.billsimpson.com

UNITED STATES

Origins USA
www.geocities.com/CapitolH
ill/Parliament/1733/indcx.html

Alabama

Adoption Circle
P.O. Box 240681
Montgomery, AL 36124-0681
(334)288-1671

AL Adoption Alliance
P.O. Box 533
Jackson, AL 36545-0533

Benefiting Birth Parents
2505 32nd Ave. North
Birmingham, AL 35207
(205)324-9676

Orphan Voyage of AL
95 Indian Creek Road, Suite
132
Huntsville, AL 35806
(205)722-0506

Orphan Voyage of AL
1610 Pinehurst Bl.
Sheffield, AL
(205)383-7377

Alaska

ALMA Chapter
P.O. Box 873573
Wasilla, AK 99687

**Concerned United
Birthparents (CUB)**
7105 Shooreson
Anchorage, AK 99504
(907)333-2272

Arizona

**The Adoption Counseling
Home**
11260 N. 92nd St. #1046
Scottsdale, AZ 85260
(602)494-9799
www.geocities.com/
Heartland/Flats/4507

Adoption Counseling Inc.
1038 E. Michigan Ave.
Phoenix AZ 85022
(602)494-9799
www.geocities.com/Heartlan
d/Flats/4507

**Adult Adoptees Support
Group**
7757 E. Marquise Drive
Tucson, AZ 85715
(602)885-6771

ALMA Chapter
P.O. Box 13334
Airpark Station
Scottsdale, AZ 85267-3334

ALMA Southwest Chapter
P.O. Box 4544
Cave Creek, AZ 85327-4544
(602)595-2058

**Concerned United
Birthparents AZ**
2613 N. Saratoga St.
Tempe, AZ 85381
(520)297-4204

**Flagstaff Adoption Search
and Support**
P.O. Box 1031
Flagstaff, AZ 86002

Orphan Voyage
P.O. Box 8245
Scottsdale, AZ
(602)990-1890

Past Present Future
7290 West Shaw Butte Drive
Peoria, AZ 85345
(602)486-3042

**Scottsdale Adoption
Connection**
P.O. Box 2512
Scottsdale, AZ 85251

Search Triad Inc.
P.O. Box 10181
Phoenix, AZ 85064-0181
(480)977-1320; (480)834-
7417
http://home.att.net/~kchgchu/
home.html

**TRACE (Transatlantic
Children's
Endeavors)(U.K.)**
P.O. Box 1541
Sierra Vista, AZ 85636
(602)458-5509

**Tracers, Ltd. (Ireland,
Germany)**
Box 18511
Tucson AZ 85731-8511
(602)885-5958

Tracers, Ltd.
9141 E. 38th Street
Tucson, AZ 85731-1851
(520)885-5958

TRIAD
7155 E. Freestone Drive
Tucson, AZ 85730
P.O. Box 12806
Tucson, AZ 85732
(602)790-6320; (520)881-
8250; (520)331-9259;
(520)297-4204

Arkansas

Adoption Triad
1912 Sanford Dr. #2
Little Rock, AR 72207-6428

AR Adoption Triad
602 Prospect Avenue
Hot Springs, AR 71901

**Arkansas Adoption
Connection**
5220 Park Avenue
Fort Smith, AR 72903
www.arkansasadoption.com/
index.html

Arkansas Research
P.O. Box 303
Conway, AR 72032
www.arkansasresearch.com

California

**Adoptee/Birthparent
Connection**
8820 Kennedy Lane
San Miguel, CA 93451
(805)467-2707

**Adoptees Identity Discovery
(AID)**
P.O. Box 2159
Sunnyvale, CA 94087-2159
(408)737-2222

Adoptees Research Assn.
P.O. Box 304
Montrose, CA 91020-0304

Adoptees Search Workshop
P.O. Box 039
Harbor City, CA 90710

**Adoptees', Birthparents'
Association**
P.O. Box 33
Camarillo, CA 93011
(805)583-4306, (805)482-
8667

**Adoption Council of
Orange County**
P.O. Box 10857
Costa Mesa, CA 92627

Adoption Reality
2180 Clover St.
Simi Valley, CA 93065

**Adoption Support Group of
Santa Monica**
1452 26th St., #103
Santa Monica, CA 90404
(310)829-1438

Adoption With Truth
66-C Panoramic Way
Berkeley, CA 94704
(415)704-9349

**Adult Adoptees and
Birthparents Support
Group**
260 Maple Ct, Suite 124
Ventura, CA 93003
(805)644-1930

ALMA Chapter
P.O. Box 1233
Simi Valley, CA 93062

ALMA Chapter
P.O. Box 191514
Sacramento, CA 95819-7514

ALMA Chapter
P.O. Box 2341
Alameda, CA 94501-2341
(510)523-4774

ALMA Chapter
P.O. Box 271
Vina, CA 96092

ALMA Chapter
P.O. Box 9425
Canoga Park, CA 91309-
0425

**Amerasian Network
(Cambodia, Japan, Korea,
Laos, Okinawa , Phillipine
Islands, Thailand, Vietnam)**
10725 Ellis Ave.
Suite 1
Fountain Valley, CA 92708

**ANSWERS–Post Adoption
Reunion Education
Network**
Box 337
Diablo, CA 94528
(925)831-0730

**Association for Korean
Adoptees (AKA)**
P.O. Box 87291
San Diego, CA 92138-7291

Baby Girl Jane Does
319 Virginia Ave.
San Franciso, CA 94110

**Bay Area Birthmothers
Association**
1546 Great Hway., #44
San Francisco, CA 94122
(415)564-3691

The Birth Connection
P.O. Box 277434
Sacramento, CA 95827-7434

**Birthparent Connection
and Adoption Connection
of San Diego**
P.O. Box 230643
Encinitas, CA 92023
(619)753-8288

C.A.R.S.
P.O. Box 6058
Huntington Beach, CA 92615

**California Adoption Triad
Search**
P.O. Box 26598
San Diego, CA 92196
(619)689-0598

**Caring Adoptees' Search
Exchange**
74-300 Candlewood St., #1
Palm Desert, CA 92260
(619)340-0344

**Central Coast Adoption
Support Group**
1718 Long Branch
Grover City, CA 93433

Coming Out of the Dark
841 W. Branna Is Road #25
Isleton, CA 95641

**Concerned United
Birthparents (CUB)**
14820 Figueras Road
La Mirada CA 90638
(714)521-4204
www.cubirthparents.org/
member.htm

**Concerned United
Birthparents (CUB)**

1787 Michon Drive
San Jose, CA 95124

**Concerned United
Birthparents (CUB)**
P.O. Box 230457
Encinitas, CA 92023
(800)822-2777
www.cubirthparents.org

**Concerned United
Birthparents (CUB)**
26821 Preciados Drive
Mission Viejo, CA 92691

**Concerned United
Birthparents (CUB)**
423 Hill St.
San Francisco CA 94114

**Concerned United
Birthparents (CUB)**
P.O. Box 816
El Toro, CA 92630

**Concerned United
Birthparents (CUB)**
Carlsbad, CA
(619)930-9322

**Concerned United
Birthparents (CUB)**
Terra Bella, CA
(209)535-4084

**Concerned United
Birthparents (CUB), Los
Angeles Branch**
686 South Arroya Parkway
#106
Pasadena, CA 91105
www.cubirthparents.org/
lacub.htm

**Concerned United
Birthparents (CUB), San**

Diego Branch
30021 Los Nogales Rd.
Temecula, CA 92591
(619)685-7673; (619)571-
0291
www.cubirthparents.org/
sdcub.htm

Dolphin Search
339 Magdalena Drive
Oceanside, CA 91257

**Family Search Services
(Italy)**
Box 587
Camarillo, CA 93011-0587

Full Circle
13661 Fairmont Way
Tustin, CA 92780
(714)544-4752
www.fullcircleca.org

Full Circle
PMB #159
270 S Bristol, Suite 101
Costa Mesa, CA 92626
(949)574-0141

**Grover City, Central Coast
Adoption Group**
Grover City, CA
(805)481-4086

**Hand in Hand Adoption
Support**
391 Teasdale St.
Thousand Oaks, CA 91360

**Independent Search
Consultants**
P.O. Box 10857
Costa Mesa, CA 92627
www.iscsearch.org

Isleton, Coming Out of the Dark
(916)777-5028

L.A.County Adoption Search Association (LACASA)
P.O. Box 1461
Roseville, CA 95661
(916)784-2711

Los Angeles, Italian Searches
Los Angeles, CA
(213)558-4775

MayDay Project for Birthmothers
P.O. Box 8445
Berkeley, CA 94707-8445

Mendo Lake Adoption Triad
620 Walnut Avenue
Ukiah, CA 95482
(707)468-0648

Mendo Lake Adoption Triad
P.O. Box 487
Hopland, CA 95449

**Moreno Valley
3 Hearts Adoption Gp.**
Moreno Valley, CA
(909)924-1401

Next Life
34111 Wildwood Canyon Rd., Sp#3
Yucaipa, CA 92399
(909)795-4972

Open Adoption Group and Info Line
P.O. Box 3506

Santa Cruz, CA 95063-3506
(831)429-2252

Parenting Resources
250 El Camino Real #111
Tustin, CA 92680

Post Adoption Center for Education and Research (PACER)(HQ)
P.O. Box 743
Corte Madera, CA 94976-0743
(925)935-6622
www.pacer-adoption.org

Post Adoption Center for Education and Research (PACER)
1053 Filbert Street
San Francisco, CA 94133

Post Adoption Center for Education and Research (PACER)
Berkeley, CA
(510)287-8981

**Post Adoption Center for Education and Research (PACER)
Contra Costa/Tri-Valley**
Contra Costa, CA
(925)828-4644

Post Adoption Center for Education and Research (PACER)
East Bay Adoptees
Oakland, CA
(415)868-2355

Post Adoption Center for Education and Research (PACER)
P.O. Box 309
Orinda, CA 94563-0309

Post Adoption Center for Education and Research East Bay Birthmothers/Marin Triad
Larkspur, CA
(415)381-1503

Post Adoption Center for Education and Research
Menlo Park, CA
(650)482-9813

Post Adoption Center for Education and Research
Oakland, CA
(510)643-4637

Post Adoption Center for Education and Research Sacramento Triad
Sacramento, CA
(916)965-4583

Post Adoption Center for Education and Research San Francisco Adoptees
San Francisco, CA
(415)868-2355; (415)647-2417; (415)285-0322

Post Adoption Center for Education and Research Sonoma County Birthmothers
(707)527-7803

Post Adoption Center for Education and Research Sonoma County Triad
Sebastopol, CA
(415)898-8938

Post Adoption Center for Education and Research South Bay/Peninsula Triad
(650)325-9510

Post Adoption Center for
Education and Research
Yuba City Triad
Yuba City, CA
(530)458-4125

**Professional Adoption
Search Team**
P.O. Box 24095
San Jose, CA 95154-4095
(408)978-5430

PURE, Inc.
P.O. Box 638
Westminster, CA 92663

Reconnections
1191 Eastside Rd.
El Cajon, CA 92020
(619)449-1713

Reconnections of California
41669 Zinfandel Ave.
Temecula, CA 92591
(909)695-1152
http://thorn.adnc.com/
~oncall/recon.html

**ReConnections of Tulare-
Kings Counties**
3728 S. Chatham
Visalia CA 93277
(209)627-3308

**Redwood Area Adoption
Triad Support**
818 Redwood Dr.
Garberville, CA 95542
(707)247-3452

Research
P.O. Box 2837
Petaluma, CA 94953-2837

ROOTS
P.O. Box 40564
Bakersfield, CA 93304-0564

S.C.A.N.
P.O. Box 230643
Encinitas, CA 92023

**San Fernando Valley Triad
Search/Support**
P.O. Box 16656
North Hollywood, CA 91615
(818)347-9690

Search Company
1020 Second Street, Suite A
Encinitas, CA 92024
(760)944-6752

**Search Finders of
California**
P.O. Box 24595
San Jose, CA 95154
(408)356-6711

Search Group of Poway
13626 Catawba Dr.
Poway, CA 92064
(760)736-9073

Second Abandonment
2323 Eastern Canal
Venice, CA

Severed Strings
P.O. Box 2203
Fullerton, CA 92633

Snoop Sisters
P.O. Box 129
Soulsbyville, CA 95372-0129

Triad Research
300 Golden West
Shafter, CA 93263

Triad Support Group
P.O. Box 172
Torrance, CA 90507
(310)541-8499

Triad Ties
P.O. Box 1178
Colusa, CA 95932
(530)458-4125

**Triple Hearts Adoption
Triangle**
P.O. Box 51082
Riverside, CA 92517-2082
(909)854-3240
http://biz.com/triplehearts

**Vista, Adopt Reunion
Support**
Vista, CA
(760)726-1924

Colorado

**Adoptees and Birthparents
Together**
5213 Miners Creek Ct.
Ft. Collins, CO 80525

Adoptees in Search
P.O. Box 24556
Denver, CO 80224-0556
(303)232-6302
http://members.aol.com/
aisdenver/adoption.htm

Adoptees in Search
P.O. Box 323
Contract Sta. 27
Lakewood, CO 80215

Adoptees Support Group
420 N. Nevada
Colorado Springs, CO 80224
(719)471-8522

AIS in Boulder
4631 Carter Trail
Boulder, CO 80301
(303)530-7241

Birthparents' Group
Box 16512
Colorado Springs, CO 80935

**Concerned United
Birthparents (CUB)**
10511 West 104th Avenue
Broomfield, CO 80020

**Concerned United
Birthparents (CUB)**
2538 Keller Farm Dr.
Boulder, CO 80304
(303)447-8112

**Concerned United
Birthparents (CUB)**
2895 Springdale Lane
Boulder, CO 80303
(303)825-3430

**Concerned United
Birthparents (CUB),
Denver Branch**
P.O. Box 2137
Wheat Ridge, CO 80034-2137
(303)825-3430
www.cubirthparents.org/
denvercub.htm

Lambs in Search
3578D Parkmoor Village
Drive
Colorado Springs, CO 80917

**Orphan Voyage (National
HQ)**
2141 Road 2300
Cedaredge, CO 81413

Re-Unite
P.O. Box 7945
Aspen, CO 81612
(303)927-2400

**Search and Support of
Denver**
805 S. Ogden
Denver, CO 80209
(303)778-8612

Connecticut

**Adoption
Answers–Support-Kinship**
8 Homestead Dr. S.
Glastonbury, CT 06073
(203)633-3130

Adoption Healing
2-F2 Hadik Parkway
So. Norwalk, CT 06854
(203)846-3281; (203)866-
6475; (203)866-8988

**Adoption Search
Connection**
1203 Hill Street
Suffield, CT 06078

Birthparent Support Group
9 Whitney Road
Columbia, CT 06237
(203)228-0076

**Concerned United
Birthparents (CUB)**
P.O. Box 558
Bethel, CT 06801
(203)633-3130

**Concerned United
Birthparents
(CUB)/A.A.S.K.**
8 Homestead Drive
S. Glastonbury, CT 06073

**National Adoption Reunion
Registry**

P.O. Box 2494
Danbury, CT 06813-2494

Ties That Bind
P.O. Box 3119
Milford, CT 06460
(203)874-2023

Delaware

Adoption Forum of DE
New Castle, DE 19720
(302)633-4743
www.delawarehelpline.org
(Enter program name)

Finders Keepers, (HQ)
P.O. Box 748
Bear, DE 19701-0748
(302)834-8888
http://finderskeepers.faith
web.com/index.htm

District of Columbia

**American Adoption
Congress (AAC)**
1000 Connecticut Avenue,
N.W., Suite 9
Washington, D.C. 20036
P.O. Box 42730
Washington, D.C. 20015
(800)274-6736; (202)483-
3399
www.americanadoption
congress.org

Florida

Active Voices in Adoption
P.O. Box 24-9052
Coral Gables, FL 33124

**Adoptee Birth Family
Connection
(Dale, Broward, and Palm
Beach Counties)**
P.O. Box 22363
Fort Lauderdale, FL 33335
(305)370-7100
www.birthfamily.com

**Adoptees Search and
Referral Source**
P.O. Box 3412
Holiday, FL 34690-3412
(813)942-1462

**Adoption and Family
Counseling**
P.O. Box 6581
Ft. Myers, FL 33911

**Adoption and Family
Reunion Center (AFRC)**
162 SW 48th St.
Cape Coral, FL 33914
(800)477-7335; (941)549-
2093

**Adoption Connection of
Manasota**
Manasota, FL
(941)747-0447

**Adoption Connection of
Panama City**
6459 Oak Shore Drive
Panama City, FL 32404
(904)871-6916

**Adoption Connection of
South Florida
(serving Adoptees of SW
Broward County)**
3100 Hunter Road
Ft. Lauderdale, FL 33331

Adoption Helpletter
P.O. Box 5929

Lake Worth, FL
(407)738-0921

**Adoption Search and
Support Group of
Tallahassee**
P.O. Box 3504
Tallahassee, FL 32315
(904)893-0004
www.tfn.net/doc/adoption.
search.group

**Adoption Support and
Knowledge of FL
Serving NE/NW Broward
Co.**
11646 NW 19 Drive
Coral Springs, FL 33071

**Adoption Triad of the
Treasure Coast**
6666 SE Windsong Ln., #401
Stuart, FL 34997
(561)287-4366

**Adoption Triangle
Ministries**
Musser Foundation
P.O. Box 1860
Cape Coral, FL 33910
1105 Cape Coral Parkway
Cape Coral, FL 33904
(800)477-7335; (813)542-
1342

**Adoption Triangle
(Serving SE/W Palm Beach
County)**
1301 NW 2nd Ave.
Delray Beach, FL 33444

ALMA Chapter
Bonnie Rogers
P. O. Box 4358
Ft Lauderdale, FL 33338
(954)462-0958

**Birthmother's Support
Group of Tallahassee**
1522 Doolittle Avenue
Tallahassee, FL 32310
(904)574-2787

**BMOMs (Birth Mothers of
Minors)**
Miami, FL 33156
(305)971-0785

**Christian Adoptees Support
Exchange**
2354 Willard Street
Ft. Myers, FL 33901

Circle of Hope
(Sondi Hill)
3530 Pine Tree Court, #A-2
Greenacres, FL 33463
(561)967-7079

**Concerned United
Birthparents (CUB)**
P.O. Box 1117
St. Augustine, FL 32085-
1117

**Daniel Memorial Adoption
Information Center**
134 East Street Church Street
Jacksonville, FL 32202

Enigma Research
P.O. Box 5929
Lake Worth, FL 33466-5929

Forever Families
(904)377-6455

**Christian Adoptees Support
Exchange (CASE)**
2354 Willard Street
Ft. Myers, FL 33901

**Mid-Florida Adoption
Reunions**

P.O. Box 3475
Belleview, FL 32620-3475
(352)307-9600

Mother and Child Reunion
2219 SW Mt. Vernon St.
Port St Lucie, FL 34953
(407)878-9101

National Organization for Birthfather Adoption Reform
1139 Bal Harbor Blvd.
Punta Gorda, FL 33950
(813)575-0948; (941)637-7477

Organized Adoption Search Information Services (OASIS)(National HQ)
P.O. Box 53-0761
Miami Shores, FL 33153
(305)947-8788; (305)948-8933

Orphan Voyage Chapter at Tampa
13906 Pepperrell Drive
Tampa, FL 33624
(813)961-1393

Orphan Voyage of Florida
Paton House
1122 Marco Place
Jacksonville, FL 32207-4043
(904)292-9200

Orphan Voyage-at-St. Augustine
P.O. Box 5495
St. Augustine, FL 32085
(904)810-5596

Searches International
1600 West 64th Street
Hialeah, FL 33012-6106

St. Johns Co. S/S Group
2629 Gorda Bella Ave.
St. Augustine FL 32086
(904)797-8830

Tallahassee Adoption
(904)893-7193

Tampa Bay Adoption Connection
(813)268-7438

Tree Search Research
P.O. Box 117
Sharpes, FL 32959-0117

Triad Adoption Search/Support
3408 Neptune Drive
Orlando, FL 32804
(407)843-2760

Triad of Central Florida
2359 Summerfield Rd.
Winter Park, FL 32792
(407)644-7665

Triad of Hope
5815 24th Street
Vero Beach, FL 32966
(561)567-8340

Triad Search and Support Group
3408 Neptune Drive
Orlando, FL 32804
(407)843-2760

Triad/Orlando
2359 Summerfield Rd.
Winter Park, FL 32792
(407)644-7665

Voices in Adoption
P.O. Box 24-9052
Coral Gables, FL 33124
(305)667-0387

Georgia

Adoptee and Birthparent Connection
4565 Pond Lane
Marietta, GA 30062
(404)642-9063

Adoptee and Birthparent Connection
P.O. Box 851
Roswell, GA 30077

Adoptee Birthparent Connection
1836 Walthall Dr., NW
Atlanta, GA 30318
(404)705-5257

Adoptee's Search Network
3317 Spring Creek Dr.
Conyers, GA 30208

Adoption Angels and Extensions
ALARM Network Rep.
4565 Pond Lane
Marietta, GA 30062

Adoption Beginnings
2550-320 Sandy Plains Rd. #275
Marietta, GA 30066

Adoption Beginnings
P.O. Box 440121
Kennesaw, GA 30144
(770)971-5263

Adoption Connection of Georgia
1469 Raider Dr.
Dalton, GA 30720

Adoption Information Services (AIS)

558 Dovie Place
Lawrenceville, GA 30045
(770)339-7236

**Atlanta
Birthparent/Adoptee**
Hammond Park Community
Center
6005 Glen Ridge Drive
Atlanta, GA 30328
(770)422-6486

**Bridges in Adoption
Connection**
6810 Wright Road
Atlanta, GA 30328

**Concerned United
Birthparents (CUB)**
3374 Aztec Rd. #35 C
Doraville, GA 30340

Families First
1105 W. Peachtree St. NE
P.O. Box 7948, Stn. C
Atlanta, GA 30357
(404)853-2800

HOME BASE
4245 Match Point Dr.
Augusta, GA 30909

Hawaii

Access Hawaii and CUB
Box 1120
Hilo, HI 96721

Adoption Circle of Hawaii
P.O. Box 61723
Honolulu, HI 96839-1723
(808)591-3834

Adoption Support Group
P.O. Box 8377
Honolulu, HI 96815

CARE
55 Niuki Circle
Honolulu, HI 96815

**Committee/Adoption
Reform/Educ.**
55 Niuiki Circle
Honolulu, HI 96821
(808)373-9747

**Concerned United
Birthparents (CUB)**
P.O. Box 37838
Honolulu, III
(808)239-5819

**Concerned United
Birthparents (CUB)**
15-2682 He's St.
Pahoa, HI 96778

Idaho

Adoption Support Group
P.O. Box 2316
Ketchum, ID 83340
(208)726 8543

Adoption Support Group
P.O. Box 1435
Ketchum, ID 83340

Search Finders of Idaho
P.O. Box 7941
Boise, ID 83707
(208)375-9803

Search Finders
1512 Shenandoah
Boise, ID 83712-6659
(208)384-1054

SearchLight
P.O. Box 5341
Coeur d'Alene, ID 83814
(208)667-8751

Triad Endeavors
P.O. Box 249
Pinehurst, ID 83850
(208)682-4280

Illinois

AAC
1201 South Firth Street
Springfield, Il 62704
(217)789-0796

AAC/CUB
835 Ridge Ave., #208
Evanston, IL 60202
(708)328-1686

**Adoptees/Birth/Adoptive
Parents Together**
729 Zaininger Ave.
Naperville, IL 60563
(630)778-0636

**The Adoption Connection,
Illinois**
452 Central
Highland Park, IL 60035

Adoption Network, Chicago
1489 Ashbury Lane West
Roselle, IL 60172
(630)539-9162

**Adoption Search and
Support Group**
638 S. Randolph
Macomb, IL 61455
(309)837-9174

Adoption Triangle
Children's Home and Aid
Society of Illinois
1819 South Neil, Suite D
Champaign, Il 61820
(217)359-8815

Adoption Triangle
Dept. of Children and Family
Services
200 S. Wyman, Suite 200
Rockford, IL 61101-1232
(815)987-7117

Adoption Triangle
P.O. Box 384
Park Forest, IL 60466
(219)365-0574; (708)481-
8916

Adoption Triangle
512 Oneida Street
Joliet, IL 60435
(815)722-4999

Adoption Triangle
Rockford
318 N. Church St.
Rockford, Il 61101

Belleville, Lost Connection
(618)235-9409

Children Remembered
P.O. Box 234
Northbrook 60065-0234
(847)291-3572

Concerned United
Birthparents (CUB)
734 Noyes St. #M3
Evanston, IL 60201
(847)439-7644, (708)869-
3921

Concerned United
Birthparents (CUB)
Macomb, IL
(309)836-3809

Family Counseling
Center/Catholic Social

Services
Birth Mother Support Group
10 Henson Place, Suite C
Champaign, IL 61820
(217)352-6565

The Family Tree
P.O. Box 233
Libertyville, Il 60048

Healing Hearts, Inc.
P.O. Box 136
Stanford, IL 61774
(309)379-5401

Healing Hearts, Inc.
P.O. Box 606
Normal, IL 61761
(309)820-0230; (309)452-
9849

Heritage Finders
1337 Park Dr.
Montgomery, IL 60538
(630)851-0677

Hidden Birthright
100 Cumberland
Rochester, Il 62563-9238

IL Council for Adoption
Reform
244 Latrobe Avenue
Northfield, IL 60093
(708)441-7581

The Lost Connection
2661 North Illinois Street,
Suite 147
Belleville, IL 62221
(618)235-9409

Midwest Adoption Center
3166 Des Plaines River Road

Des Plaines, IL 60018
(708)298-9096

Missing Pieces
P.O. Box 7541
Springfield, IL 62791-7541
(217)787-8450

People Searching for People
P.O. Box 5442
Rock Island, IL 61204-5442

Search Connection, Ltd
P.O. Box 2425
Bridgeview, IL 60455
(708)430-9133

Search Research
P.O. Box 48
Chicago Ridge, Il 60415

Truth Seekers
P.O. Box 366
Prospect Heights, IL 60070-
0366
(708)342-0056

Truth Seekers in Adoption
P.O. Box 366
Mount Prospect, IL 60056
(708)342-8742

Indiana

A.B.S.E.N.T. (Adoptee,
Birthparent, Siblings
Enlightenment Network of
Thornton)
711 W Plum Street
Thorntown, IN 46071-1249
(317)436-7257

Adoptees' Identity Doorway
P.O. Box 361
South Bend, IN 46624
(219)272-3520

Adoption Circle
401 Beechwood Drive
Beech Grove, IN 46107-1137
(317)592-1998

Adoption Support and Info.
Alliance of Muncie
P.O. Box 1125
Muncie, IN 47308

Adoption Triangle
7361 Wilson Place
Merrillville, IN 46410-4445
(219)736-5515

The Adoption Triangle
3012 East Amy Lane
Bloomington, IN 47408

Anonymous By Adoption
P.O. Box 12132
Ft. Wayne, IN 46862-2312

Common Bond
110 N Sheridan St
Kendallville, IN 46755-1869
(219)343-0777

Coping With Adoption
61 Country Farm Road
Peru, IN 46970
(317)472-7425

Double Heritage
1533 N 500 W
Marion, IN 46952
(765)384-5885

**Full Circle Adoption
Support Group**
2205 E 74th St.
Indianapolis, IN 46240-3109
P.O. Box 2904
Indianapolis, IN 46206
(317)255-7135; (317)592-
1998

Indiana Adoption Coalition
P.O. Box 1292
Kokomo, IN 46903
(317)453-4427; (765)472-
7425

**Lafayette Adoption
Search/Support
Organization**
1100 N 9th St., Ste. 102
Lafayette, IN 47904
(317)567-4139

**Lafayette Adoption
Search/Support
Organization**
5936 Lookout Drive
West Lafayette, IN 47906

**Past and Present
Association**
3548 Revere Court
Lake Station, IN 46405

Reflections
1211 Blueberry Ct.
Evansville, IN 47710-5801
(812)428-7987

Reflections
7401 Washington Avenue
Evansville, IN 47715-4513

**Search Committee of
Madison County**
P.O. Box 523
Anderson, IN 46015

Search for Tomorrow
P.O. Box 441
New Haven, IN 46774
(219)749-4392

Searching for Answers
R#4, Box 29A
Loogootee, IN 47553

**Support of Search
Indiana Adoption Coalition**
P.O. Box 1292
Kokomo, IN 46901
(317)453-4427

Iowa

The Adoptive Experience
1105 Fremont
Des Moines, IA 50316

The Adoption Experience
Rte. 5, Box 22
Osceola, IA 50213

**Concerned United
Birthparents (CUB)**
130 33rd Avenue SW
Cedar Rapids, IA 52404

**Concerned United
Birthparents (CUB)**
Boone, IA
(515)432-9356

**Concerned United
Birthparents (CUB)**
Iowa City, IA
(319)339-4357

**Concerned United
Birthparents (CUB)**
500 Kimberly Lane
Des Moines, IA 50317

**Concerned United
Birthparents, National HQ
(CUB)**
2000 Walker Street
Des Moines, IA 50317
(800)822-2777; (515)263-
9558; (515)282-7549

Family Search Services
P.O. Box 30106
Des Moines, IA 50310-
0106
(515)255-0356

ORIGINS, Inc
4300 Ashby Avenue
Des Moines, IA 50310-
3540
(515)277-7700

Kansas

**Adoption Concerns
Triangle**
411 SW Greenwood
Topeka, KS 66606-1231
(785)235-6122

**Adoption Concerns
Triangle**
1427 N. Harrison
Topeka, KS 66608

**Adoption Concerns
Triangle**
1242 NE 39th St.
Topeka, KS 66617

**Getting to Know You
Search and Support
Group**
1770 S Roosevelt
Wichita, KS 67218
(316)682-2244

**Great Bend, Triadoption
Group**
Great Bend, KS
(316)792-1393

Reunions Ltd.
2611 East 25th
Topeka, KS 66605

Wichita Adult Adoptees
4551 S. Osage St.
Wichita, KS 67217-4743
(316)522-8772

Kentucky

Adoptee Awareness
P.O. Box 23242
Anchorage, KY 40223
(502)245-2811

Binding Together
P.O. Box 197328
Louisvile, KY 40259
(502)961-0512

Birthmothers Sharing
P.O. Box 73184
Bellevue, KY 41073-0184
(502)491-0172, (502)271-
5926

**Concerned United
Birthparents (CUB)**
9803 Encino Court
Louisville, KY 40223-1148
(502)423-1438

Louisiana

**Adoptees' Birthrights
Committee**
25 Osborne Ave.
Kenner, LA 70065
(504)443-1012

**Adoptees' Birthrights
Committee**
P.O. Box 9442
Metarie, LA 70005
(504)835-4284

**Adoption Connection of
LA**
7301 W Judge Perez
Suite 311

Arabi, LA 70032
(504)454-7728

**Adoption Connection of
LA**
P.O. Box 6921
Metairie, LA 70009

**Adoption Connection of
LA**
P.O. Box 7213
Metairie, LA 70010

**Adoption Search
Organization**
8154 Longwood Dr.
Denham Springs, LA
70726

**Adoption Triad Network,
Inc.**
P.O. Box 3932
Lafayette, LA 70502
(318)984-3682

Lost and Found
18343 Weatherwood Drive
Baton Rouge, LA 70817-
3924

Maine

**Adoption Search
Consultants of ME**
P.O. Box 2793
So. Portland, ME 04116
(207)842-6622

**Adoption Support Group
of Penobscot Bay**
Taylor's Point
Tenant's Harbor, ME
04860
(207)372-6322

**Concerned United
Birthparents (CUB)**

RFD #2
Hilton Lane
North Berwick, ME 03906

**Concerned United
Birthparents (CUB)**
Route #1, Box 1017
West Paris, ME 04289

SearchRight Inc.
P.O. Box 506
Yarmouth, ME 04096
(207)846-9555

Maryland

**Adoptee Birth Family
Connection**
Mt. Zion United Methodist
Church
Route 70
Myersville, MD
(301)271-3037

**Adoptee-Birthparent
Support Network (ABSN of
the DC Metro Area)**
P.O. Box 6485
Columbia MD 21045-6485
(202)686-4611

Adoptees In Search (AIS)
P.O. Box 41016
Bethesda, MD 20824
(301)656-8555; (301)656-
8553

**Adoption Connection
Exchange**
1301 Park Avenue
Baltimore, MD 21217

**Adoption Contact Search
and Reunion**
311 W Saratoga St.
Baltimore, MD 21201
(410)767-7730

**Adoption Triad Support
Group**
Bibelots Book Store
2080 York Road
Timonium, MD
(410)308-1888

**Concerned United
Birthparents (CUB)**
14914 Nighthalk Lane
Bowie, MD 20716-1033

**Concerned United
Birthparents (CUB)**
327 Dogwood Road
Millersville, MD 21108
(410)544-0083

**Concerned United
Birthparents (CUB)**
P.O. Box 151
Mount Airy, MD 21777

**Concerned United
Birthparents (CUB)**
P.O. Box 15258
Chevy Chase, MD 20825
(202)966-1640; (301)298-
1011
www.geocities.com/
Heartland/Village/6789

**Concerned United
Birthparents (CUB)**
St. Mark's Church
Ellicott City, MD
(410)554-2218

ENCORE
R.D. #8, Box 419
York, PA
(800)772-0203; (410)466-
0222

Lost or Found
7290 Shirley Dr.

Easton, MD 21601
(410)820-5138

Searchlight Inc.
P.O. Box 441
Glen Dale, MD 20769
(410)262-8894

SEEK
P.O. Box 26
Hydes, MD 21082-0026
(410)592-7156

**Western Maryland
Adoption Srch/Support**
1427 Church St.
Cumberland, MD 21502
(301)724-4705

Massachusetts

Adoption Connection (AC)
11 Peabody Square, #6
Peabody, MA 01960
(978)532-1261
www.adoptionconnection.
qpg.com

Adoption Healing
44 Wareham Lake Shore
Drive
E. Wareham, MA 02538
(508)295-9755

**Adoption Triad Seeking
Support**
10 W Hollow Lane
Webster, MA 01570
(508)949-1919

C.A.R.E.S.
20 Blanchard St.
Harvard, MA 01451
(508)772-2699

**Cape Cod Adoption
Connection**
P.O. Box 336
Brewster, MA 02631
(508)896-7332

**Center for Family
Connections**
P.O. Box 383246
Cambridge, MA 02238
(800)KINNECT

**Concerned United
Birthparents (CUB) Open
Doors**
395 A Washington St.
Braintree, MA
(781)302-4602

**Concerned United
Birthparents (CUB)**
Boyslton, MA
(508)869-6774

**Concerned United
Birthparents (CUB),
Boston Chapter**
P.O. Box 380396
Cambridge, MA 02238-3246
(508)443-3770
http://cub-boston.freeyellow.
com

**Healing Adoption—
Completing the Circle**
P.O. Box 684
Bridgewater, MA 02324-
0684
(508)697-8772

Raynham Adoption Group
P.O. Box 684
Bridgewater, MA 02324
(508)697-8772

**TRY-Resource/Referral
Center**
P.O. Box 989

Northampton, MA 01061-
0989
(413)584-6599

Vinyard Haven
Open Circle, MA
(508)693-6727

Michigan

**Adoptee-Birth Parent
Group**
Catholic Social Services
117 N. Division
Ann Arbor, MI 48104

**Adoptees Search for
Knowledge (ASK)**
P.O. Box 762
East Lansing, MI 48826-0762
(517)321-7291

**Adoption Circle Support
Group**
4925 Packard
Ann Arbor, MI 48108-1521
(313)971-9781

Adoption Connections
P.O. Box 293
Cloverdale, MI 49035-0293
(616)623-8060

**Adoption Identity
Movement**
22646 Michigan
Dearborn, MI 48124-2116
(313)730-0055

**Adoption Identity
Movement**
37231 Tall Oak Drive
Clinton Twp., MI 48036-
1644
(810)263-5530

**Adoption Identity
Movement**
P.O. Box 337
Kakaska, MI 49646
(616)258-9710

**Adoption Identity
Movement of Michigan**
P.O. Box 5414
Traverse City, MI 49696-
5414
(231)922-1986

**Adoption Identity
Movement**
P.O. Box 72
Ortonville, MI 48462

**Adoption Identity
Movement**
P.O. Box 812
Hazel Park, MI 48030-0812
(810)548-6291; (248)548-
6291

**Adoption Identity
Movement**
P.O. Box 9783
1434 South Lawn Drive, SW
Grand Rapids, MI 49509
(616)531-1380

**Adoption Identity
Movement**
P.O. Box 930086
Wixom, MI 48393-0086
(248)669-1237

Adoption Insight
P.O. Box 171
Portage, MI 49081
(616)327-1999

**Adoption Support of St.
Claire County**
2008 Katherine St.
Port Huron, MI 48060

Birth Bond
1015 E. Columbia St.
Mason, MI 48854

**Birthparent and Adult
Adoptee Support Group**
21700 Northwestern #1490
Southfield, MI 48075-4901
(248)423-2770

**Bonding By Blood,
Unlimited**
4710 Cottrell Road
Rural Route No. 5
Vassar, MI 48768

**Bonding By Blood,
Unlimited**
5845 Waterman Road
Vassar, MI 48768-9790
(517)823-8248

**Concerned United
Birthparents (CUB)**
1270 Grosvenor Hwy
Palmyra, MI 49268-9732
(517)486-3444

**Concerned United
Birthparents (CUB)**
Saginaw, MI
(517)792-5876

**Informed Adoption
Network**
P.O. Box 6084
Ann Arbor, MI 48106-6084
(313)482-1697

**Kalamazoo Birthparent
Support Group**
P.O. Box 2183
Portage, MI 49081-2183
(616)324-9987

**Mid-Michigan Adoption
Identity**
13636 Podunk Road
Cedar Springs, MI 49319

Missing in Adoption (MIA)
4198 East Cedar Lake Drive
Greenbush, MI 48738-9703

**Port Huron Adoption
Support Group**
(313)982-9774

**Post Adoption Support
Services**
1221 Minnesota Ave.
Gladstone, MI 49837
(906)428-4861

**Post Adoption Support
Services**
Route #1, Box 360
Bellaire Road
Baraga, MI 48809

Retraced Roots
P.O. Box 892
Ludington, MI 49431
(616)843-8409

Retraced Roots
765 Peterson Rd.
Muskegon, MI 49445

Roots and Reunions
210 Barbeau St.
Sault Sainte Marie, MI
49783-2402
(906)635-5922

**Tri-County Genealogical
Society**
21715 Brittany
Eastpointe, MI 48021-2503
(810)774-7953

Truth in the Adoption Triad
2642 Kansas Street
Saginaw, MI
(517)777-6666

Truth in the Adoption Triad
1815 Sunrise Drive
Caro, MI 48723
(517)672-2054

Minnesota

**Concerned United
Birthparents (CUB),
Twin Cities Area Branch**
6429 Mendelssohn Lane
Edina, MN 55343-8424
(612)938-5866; (612)930-9058
www.cubirthparents.org/
slpcub.htm

Korean Adoption Registry
14735 Highway 65 NE
Ham Lake, MN 55304
(612)434-6638

**Leaf/Minnesota Reunion
Registry and Support**
23247 Lofton Court North
Scandia, MN 55073

**Liberal Education for
Adoptive Families (LEAF)**
1295 Omaha Ave. N.
Stillwater, MN 55082
(651)436-2215

**Liberal Education for
Adoptive Families (LEAF)**
23247 Lofton Court No.
Scandia, MN 55073-9752
(612)436-2218

MAK (Korea)
P.O. Box 25852

St. Paul, MN 55125
(612)305-2892

Orphan Voyage
Bloomington, MN
(612)943-9037

Someone's Child Network
Bloomington, MN
(612)544-9976

Mississippi

**Adoption Information
Network**
P.O. Box 4154
Meridian, MS 39304
5917 5th Street
Meridian, MS 39307-6126
(601)482-7556

**Mississippi Adoption
Network**
30 North Hill Parkway, Apt.
B4
Jackson, MS 39206-5591

Missouri

Adoptee Searches Inc.
P.O. Box 803
Chesterfield, MO 63006-
0803
(800)434-0020

**Adoption Search of
Missouri**
P.O. Box 1153
St. Anne, MO 63074

**Adoption Search of
Missouri**
9434 Bristol Ave.
St. Louis, MO 63117

**Baldwin Post Adopt
Support**

Ballwin, MO 63022
(314)281-8921

Birthmom Support
P.O. Box 505
Springfield, MO 65801-0505
(417)889-4207

Birthparent Connection
(serving St. Louis and
Central Illinois)
121 Weiss Avenue
St. Louis, MO 63125
(314)544-2520; (314)776-
7011

**Carson Baxter Support
Group**
5061 Pernod Ave.
St. Louis, MO 63139
(314)351-4492

**Concerned United
Birthparents (CUB)**
7000 Jackson
Kansas City, MO 63142

Connecting Adoptees
P.O. Box 30252
Kansas City, MO 64112
(816)333-5656

**Kansas City Adult Adoptees
Org.**
P.O. Box 11828
Kansas City, MO 64138
(816)229-4075

**Kansas City Adult Adoptees
Org.**
P.O. Box 15225
Kansas City, MO 64106
(913)262-0836; (816)356-
5213

**Missouri Adoption Reform
Coalition**

708-B Demarest Dr.
Columbia, MO 65202-3048
(573)635-4575

**PAST (Post Adoption
Support Team)**
Deaconess West Hospital
503 Des Peres Road
St. Louis, MO

Search for Life
Route #2, Box 93
Birth Tree, MO 65438

The Searcher's Forum
830 Marshall Avenue
Webster Groves, MO 63119-
2003

**Support Open Adoption
Records Search/Support
Group**
4589 Hopewell Road
Wentzville, MO 63385
(314)828-5726

Montana

Missoula Adoption Reunion
4104 Barbara Lane
Missoula, MT 59803
(406)251-4158

**Montana Post Adoption
Center**
P.O. Box 634
Helena, MT 59624
(406)449-3266

Nebraska

Adoption Triad Midwest
P.O. Box 489
Fullerton, NE 68638
(308)536-2633

Adoption Triad Midwest
P.O. Box 45273
Omaha, NE 68132
P.O. Box 37273
Omaha, NE 68137
3711 N 108th Street
Omaha, NE 68164
(402)493-8047

**Concerned United
Birthparents (CUB)**
9621 Parker Street
Omaha, NE 68114
(402)397 6394

**Concerned United
Birthparents (CUB)**
4075 W. Airport Rd.
Grand Island, NE 68803
(308)384-3571

Operation Identity (OI)
13101 Blackstone Rd NE
Albuquerque, NM 87111
(505)293-3144

Nevada

**Adoptees Search
Connection**
9713 Quail Springs St.
Las Vegas, NV 89117

**Truth of Adoption Searches
and Support (TASS)**
1810 N. Decatur Blvd., #204
Las Vegas, NV 89109
(702)631-7101

New Hampshire

Adoption Bonding Circle
67 Ann Avenue
Charlestown, NH 03603
(603)826-4806

Adoption Bonding Circle
RR #2, Box #125
Claremont, NH 03743

Circle of Hope
P.O. Box 127
Somersworth, NH 03878
(603)692-6320

**Living in Search of Answers
(LISA)**
P.O. Box 215
Gilsum, NH 03448 0215
(603)357-5218

Pieces of Yesterday
P.O. Box 1703
Manchester, NH 03105

New Jersey

**Adopt Reunion Coalition
Jersey Shore**
3047 Governor's Crossing
Wall, NJ 07719
(908)681-6348

**Adoption Reunion
Coalition of New Jersey**
15 Fir Place
Hazlett, NJ 07730
(908)739-9365

Adoption Support Group
500-48 Auten Road
Somerville, NJ 08876

**Adoption Support Group of
Central NJ**
P.O. Box 362
Belle Meade, NJ 08502
(908)725-1457; (609)279-
0211

**Adoption Support Group of
South Jersey**

32 Trotters Lane
Smithville, NJ 08201-3804
(609)748-8126

**Adoption Support Network
Inc.**
505 W. Hamilton Ave, #207
Linwood, NJ 08221
(609)653-4242

**Adoptive Parents for Open
Records**
Morristown, NJ
(973)267-8698

**ALMA Society–Adoptees'
Liberty Movement
Association (ALMA)**
P.O. Box 85
Denville, NJ 07834
(973)586-1358

**Connected Hearts Adoption
Triad**
c/o Presbyterian Church
170 Watchung Ave.
North Plainfield, NJ 07060
(732)227-0607

Finders Keepers II
32 Trotters La.
Smithville, NJ 08205

Lookup U.K.
P.O. Box 8015
Paramus, NJ 07653-8015
www.lookupuk.com/main.
html

**New Jersey
Coalition/Openness in
Adoption–South Jersey
Chapter**
206 Laurel Place
Laurel Springs, NJ 08021
(609)784-7432

New Jersey Coalition/Openness in Adoption
29 Hill Street
Morristown, NJ 07960
(201)292-2440

Origins
P.O. Box 556
Whippany, NJ 07981-0556
(973)428-9683

Sharing Hope: Adoption Reunion Experience
55 Highland Drive
Barnegat, NJ 08005
(609)698-7121

West Central Search/Support of New Jersey
P.O. Box 3604
Trenton, NJ 08629

New Mexico

Concerned United Birthparents (CUB)
548 Brighton
Los Alamos, NM 87544
(505)672-3976

Concerned United Birthparents (CUB)
358 Joya Loop
Los Alamos, NM 87544

Geborener Deutscher (Switzerland)
805 Alvarado N.E.
Albuquerque, NM 87108
(505)268-1310

Leonie Boehmer
805 Alvarado, NE
Albuquerque, NM 87108
(505)268-1310

Operation Identity
13101 Blackstone Road, NE
Albuquerque, NM 87111
(505)293-3144

Operation Identity (Germany, Austria, Switzerland)
805 Alvardo, N.E.
Albuquerque, NM 87108
(505)268-1310

Operation Identity
1818 Somervell St, NE
Albuquerque, NM 87112
(505)275-9952

New York

aka World (Korean adoptees in New York)
P.O. Box 6037
FDR Station
New York, NY 10150
(212)386-9201
www.alsoknownasinc.org/splash.html

A.N.G.E.L.S.
14 Baylor Circle
Rochester, NY 14624
(716)234-1864

Adoptee Liberty Movement Association (ALMA)
P.O. Box 727
Radio City Station
New York, NY 10101-0727
(212)581-1568

Adoptees In Reunion
11 Janet Lane
Glen Cove, NY 11542
(516)759-9054

Adoptees Information Service
19 Marion Avenue
Mount Vernon, NY 10552

Adoption Circle Capitol District
P.O. Box 9025
Schenectady, NY 12309

Adoption Circle Long Island
421 Jackson Street
Oceanside, NY 11572

Adoption Circle Putnam
North Brewster Road
Brewster, NY 10509-9804

Adoption Circle Westchester
P.O. Box 311
Shenorock, NY 10587

Adoption Crossroads (HQ)
444 E. 76th St.
New York, NY 10021
(212)988-0110; (914)268-0283
www.adoptioncrossroads.org

Adoption Crossroads
74 Lakewood Drive
Congers, NY 10920
(914)268-0283; (845)268-0283
www.adoptioncrossroads.org

Adoption Crossroads
Schenectady, NY
(518)370-2558

Adoption Get-together in Northern Westchester
Lincolndale/Somers, NY
(914)248-5060

Adoption in Recovery
Rte 1, Box 224 A
Petersburg, NY 12138
(518)658-2972

Adoption Kinship
P.O. Box 182
Vestal, NY 13851
(607)772-6793

**Adoption Parent Group of
Orange County Inc.**
P.O. Box 156
Chester, NY 10918-0156
(914)651-7075

Adoption Support Group
57 Little Neck Road
Centerport, NY 11721-1614

**Always Support for
Adopted People**
12 Sunset Ave. So.
Farmingdale, NY 11735
(516)694-4289; (516)798-7160

**Always Support for
Adopted People**
134 Jerusalem Avenue
Massapequa, NY 11758

ANSWERS
P.O. Box 67
Woodstock, NY 12498
(914)657-6213

B.I.R.T.H.
7 Cheryl Place
Massapequa, NY 11758

B.K.I.D.S.
P.O. Box 43
Erin, NY 14838
(607)739-2957

**Birthparent Support
Network (HQ)**
P.O. Box 120
N. White Plains, NY 10603
(914)682-2250

**Birthparent Support
Network (BSN)**
Queensbury, NY
(518)798-2133

**Birthparent Support
Network (BSN)**
37 Sylvia Lane
Plainview, NY 11803

**Birthparent Support
Network (BSN)**
P.O. Box 34
Old Bethpage, NY 11804
(516)931-5925

**Birthparents, Adoptees,
Adoptive Parents United in
Support (BUS)
(serving Western NY)**
P.O. Box 299
Victor, NY 14425
(716)924-0410

**Candid Adoption Talk
(CAT)**
175-A Fawn Hill Road
Tuxedo, NY 10987
(914)351-3306

**Candid Adoption Talk
(CAT)**
20 Fitzgerald Court
Monroe, NY 10950-4423
(914)783-1027

**Champlain Valley Adoptive
Families**
6 Grace Avenue
Plattsburgh, NY 12901

**Concerned United
Birthparents (CUB)**
Cazenovia, NY
(315)655-9137

**Concerned United
Birthparents**
Petersburg, NY
(518)658-2972

**Council for Equal Rights in
Adoption**
401 East 74th Street
Suite 17D
New York, NY 10021
(212)988-0110

**Hudson Valley Adoption
Search and Reunion
Support Group**
P.O. Box 67
Woodstock, NY 12498
(914)657-6213

**International Social Service
American Branch**
390 Park Avenue South
New York, NY 10016
(212)532-6350

Kin Quest, Inc.
89 Massachusetts Ave.
Massapequa, NY 11758
(516)541-7383

**Manhattan Birthparents'
Group**
P.O. Box 20137
Cherokee Station
New York, NY 01028-0051
(212)289-6782

Missing Connection
P.O. Box 712
Brownville, NY 13615
(315)782-6245

Missing Pieces
P.O. Box 8041
Massena, NY 13662
(315)764-5970

Post Adoption Center for Education and Support (PACES)
P.O. Box 1223
Amherst, NY 14226-7223
(716)837-0787

Post Adoption Center of Western New York
104 Cazenovia
Buffalo, NY
(716)824-3967

Reunions: The Next Step
305 E. 40th St., #12V
New York, NY 10016
(212)867-1918

The Right to Know
P.O. Box 52
Old Westbury, NY 11568

Triad United Support
P.O. Box 299
Victor, NY 14564

Triangle of Truth
P.O. Box 2039
Liverpool, NY 13089
(315)622-0620

W.A.I.F., Inc.
201 East 28th Street
New York, NY 10016-8538

North Carolina

Adoptees Search of Enlightenment
365 W. Illinois Avenue
Southern Pines, NC 28387
(910)695-0603

Adoption Connections
P.O. Box 4153
Chapel Hills, NC 27515
(919)967-5010

Adoption Information Exchange (AIE)
46 Fairfax Avenue
Asheville, NC 28806

Adoption Information Exchange (AIE)
P.O. Box 1917
Matthews, NC 28106
(704)846-8025; (704)537-5919

Adoption Information Exchange (AIE)
P.O. Box 471921
Charlotte, NC 28247
(704)537-5919

Adoption Issues and Education
P.O. Box 768
Vanceboro, NC 28586
(919)975-1510

Adoption Issues and Education
P.O. Box 8314
Greenville, NC 27835

Adoption Reunion Connection
P.O. Box 1447
Dunn, NC 28335
(910)892-1072

Adoption Search Consultants
P.O. Box 1917
Matthews, NC 28106
(704)846-8025

Birth Mothers Easing the Hurt
Rte. 4, Box 252-I
Dobson, NC 27017

Birth Mothers Easing the Hurt
P.O. Box 266
Dobson, NC 27017
(910)386-4274

Birth Mothers Easing the Hurt
P.O. Box 7003
Lexington, NC 27295

Carolina Adoption Triangle
116 West Queen Street
Hillsborough NC 27278
(919)732-2751

Children's Home Society of NY
P.O. Box 114608
Greensboro, NC 27415-4608
(336)834-8222

L. Giddens Adoption Information Exchange
8539 Monroe Road
Charlotte, NC 28212

Missing Links
8714 Lowwoods Circle
Charlotte, NC 28214
(704)391-2693

North Carolina Adoption Connections
Ashville, NC
(704)254-8248

North Carolina Adoption Connections
P.O. Box 4153
Chapel Hill, NC 27515
(919)967-5010

North Carolina Adoption Connections
Raleigh, NC
(919)876-8564

North Carolina Adoption Connections
Youngsville, NC
(919)556-8355

Sunflower Birthmoms Group
1404 Granada Drive
Fayetteville, NC 28314
(901)487-1434
www.bmom.net

Ohio

Adoptees' Foreign Searches
P.O. Box 360074
Strongsville, OH 44136
(216)238-1004

The Adoption Connection
P.O. Box 2482
Youngstown, OH 44512
(216)792-3546

Adoption Network
205 W 30th St
Room 14
Lorain, OH 44055
(440)244-1060

Adoption Network
302 Overlook Park Dr.
Cleveland, OH 44110
(216)261-1511

Adoption Network Cleveland
291 E. 222nd St., Room 229
Cleveland, OH 44123-1751
(216)261-1511
www.AdoptionNetwork.org

Adoption Triad Support Center
5900 S.O.M. Center Rd, #273
Cleveland, OH 44094
(216)943-2118

Adoption Triangle Unity
4144 Packard Road
Toledo, OH 43613-1938
(419)244-7072

Birthmother's Support Group
324 E. Siebenthaler Ave.
Dayton, OH 45405
(937)277-4881

Birthparents Support
3423 Bluerock Rd
Cincinatti, OH 45239
(513)741-0929

Birthright
6779 Manchester Road
Clinton, OH 44216

Chosen Children
311 Springbrook
Dayton, OH 45405
(937)274-8017

Concerned United Birthparents (CUB)
13 Meadowbrook Dr
Perrysburg, OH 43551
(419)874-4471

Concerned United Birthparents (CUB) Perrysburg Branch
2544 Bonnie Lane
Maumee, OH 43537

Concerned United Birthparents (CUB) Toledo Branch
6704 Inglewood

Holland, OH 43610
(419)865-9604

Families Blessed by Adoption
74 Clinton Road
Chillicothe, OH 45601

Full Circle
11690 Symes Valley Drive
Loveland, OH 45140

Mt. Gilead Reunite Inc
Mt. Gilead, OH
(419)946-9443

Ohio Adoptee Searches
P.O. Box 856
Waynesville, OH 45068-0856
(513)897-2409

Pieces of Yesterday
856 Pine Needles Dr
Dayton, OH 45458-3329
(937)436-0593

Re-Connections
3782 Skyline Drive
Beavercreek, OH 45432

Reunite, Inc. (OH and WV)
P.O. Box 694
Reynoldsburg, OH 43068

Sunshine Reunions
1175 Virginia Avenue
Akron, OH 44306
(216)773-4691

Oklahoma

Adoptees As Adults
8220 NW 114th Street
Oklahoma City, OK 73132

Adoptees As Adults
7908 Hemingford Court #A
Oklahoma City, OK 73120

**Adoption Connection
(specializing in Arkansas
and Oklahoma)**
Rt. 1, Box 613
Roland, OK 74954
(918)427-0453

**Adoption Triad of
Oklahoma**
RR3 Box 210
Owasso, OK 74055-9369
(918)646-6179

Oklahoma Adoption Triad
P.O. Box 471008
Tulsa, OK 74147

Oklahoma Adoption Triad
P.O. Box 2503
Broken Arrow, OK 74013

Shared Heartbeats
P.O. Box 12125
Oklahoma City, OK 73157
(405)943-4500

Shepherd's Heart
1158 Stevens Court N
Newella, OK 74857
(405)391-2397

Tulsa Adoption Tree
Tulsa, OK
(918)445-1493

Oregon

**Adoptee Birthfamily
Connection**
P.O. Box 50122
Eugene, OR 97405
(541)345-6710

A.N.S.R.S., Inc.
9203 SW Cree Circle
Tualatin, OR 97062-9046
(503)692-5794

The Circle
P.O. Box 415
Ashland, OR 97520-0415
(541)482-5554

Family Ties
4537 Souza Street
Eugene, OR 97402
(503)461-0752

Family Ties
3185 Lincoln
Eugene, OR 97405

**Oregon Adoptive Rights
Association (O.A.R.A.)**
715 N. 10
Springfield, OR 97477

**Oregon Adoptive Rights
Assoc. (OARA)**
P.O. Box 882
Portland, OR 97207
(503)235-3669

Portland DADS
Portland, OR
(503)222-1111

**Southern Oregon Adoptive
Rights**
1076 Queens Branch Road
Rogue River, OR 97537

**Southern Oregon Adoptive
Rights**
1605 SW K Street
Grants Pass, OR 97526-2638

Pennsylvania

Adoption Connection
Harrisburg, PA
(717)652-4310

Adoption Connection
Lansdale, PA
(215)361-9679

Adoption Connection
St Mary's, PA
(814)781-7312

Adoption Forum (HQ)
P.O. Box 12502
Philadelphia, PA 19151
(215)238-1116

**Adoption Forum, Berks
County**
(610)777-9742; (610)367-
4371

**Adoption Forum, Bucks
County**
20 Runnemede V2
New Hope, PA 18938
(215)892-2695

**Adoption Forum, Chester
County**
(610)384-0863

**Adoption Forum, Delaware
County**
(610)328-1874

**Adoption Forum, Delaware
State**
(302)324-2903

**Adoption Forum, Lehigh
County**
(610)797-0447

**Adoption Forum,
Montgomery County**
(610)705-0311

Adoption Healing
(412)481-3187

Adoption Healing
Family Services of Western
46th and Hatfield Streets
Pittsburgh, PA 15201
(412)687-0100

Adoption Healing
3329 Perryville Ave
Apt. A
Pittsburgh, PA 15205
(412)322-5607

**Adoption Lifeline of
Altoona**
412 28th Avenue
Altoona, PA 16601

**Adoptees Liberty
Movement Association
(ALMA)**
P.O. Box 53735
Philadelphia, PA 19105
(215)561-2525

ENCORE
PRD #8, Box 419
York, PA 17403
(800)772-0203, access code
04; (717)428-2829

HOPE
P.O. Box 272
Downingtown, PA 19335
(610)873-4756

Lost Loved Ones
621 W. Crawford Street
Ebensburg, PA 15931
(814)472-7525

**Open Line Adoption
Connection**
Oil City, PA 16301
(814)677-7850

ORIGINS
Box 1032 Hemlock Farms
Hawley, PA 18428
(717)775-9729

**Parents/Adoptees Support
Together (PAST)**
8130 Hawthorne Dr
Erie, PA 16509
(814)899-1493

**The Pennsylvania Coalition
for Openness in Adoption
(PACFOA)**
20 Runnemede V2
New Hope, PA 18938
(215)862-2695

**Pittsburgh Adoption
Connection**
37 Edgecliff Road
Carnegie, PA 15106
(412)279-2511

**Pittsburgh Adoption
Lifeline**
Altoona, PA
(724)443-3370

**Pittsburgh Adoption
Lifeline**
P.O. Box 52
Gibsonia, PA 15044

Potsdam Family Finders
30 Grant St.
Potsdam, NY 13676

Searching
P.O. Box 7446
Harrisburg, PA 17113-0446
(717)939-0138

Puerto Rico

Dept. of Social Services
P.O. Box 11398

Santurce
Puerto Rico 00910
(809)723-0303

Rhode Island

Lost and Found
457 Carter Avenue
Pawtucket 02861
(401)726-3033

**Parents and Adoptees
Liberty Movement (PALM)**
Riverside
(401)437-1811

**Parents and Adoptees
Liberty Movement (PALM)**
861 Mitchell's Lane
Middletown, RI 02840

Yesterday's Children
77 Homer Street
Providence, RI 02903

South Carolina

A.A.L.M. Triad
1725 Atascadero Drive
Columbia, SC 29206

**Adoptees and Birthparents
in Search**
263 Lemonade Road
Pacolet, SC 29372

**Adoptees and Birthparents
in Search**
8137 Ramsgate Road
North Charleston, SC 29406

**Adoptees and Birthparents
in Search**
P.O. Box 13
Lexington, SC 29071-0013
(803)356-0059

Adoptees and Birthparents in Search
P.O. Box 5551
West Columbia, SC 29171
(803)791-1133

Adoption and Family Reunion Center
Box 103
Pacolet, SC 29373

Adoption Family Connection
P.O. Box 239
Moore, SC 29369
(803)574-0681

Adoption Reunion Connection
263 Lemonade Road
Pacolet, SC 29372
(803)474-3479

Adoption Reunion Search/Support
P.O. Box 239
Moore, SC 29369

Adoption Search For Life
303 Brighton Road
Anderson, SC 29621
(803)224-8020

Birthmothers Support Group
10839 Dorchester Rd
Summerville, SC 29485
(843)821-5043

Bits and Pieces
P.O. Box 380
Norris, SC 29667

Bits and Pieces
P.O. Box 85
Liberty, SC 29657
(864)879-9010

Ever Check Where?
Roebuck, SC
(864)576-7593

Home Base
Box 7966
N. Augusta, SC 29841

South Dakota

ALMA Chapter
1325 South Bahnson
Sioux Falls, SD 57103

Concerned United Birthparents (CUB)
41004 259th Street
Mitchell, SD 57301
(605)996-6691

Tennessee

Adoption Support and Education
921 Belvoir Hills Dr.
East Ridge, TN 37412
(615)622-5341

Concerned United Birthparents (CUB)
Morristown, TN
(615)586-8427

Concerned United Birthparents (CUB)
Nashville
(615)354-9754

F.A.I.T.H.
P.O. Box 294
Kingsport, TN 37662
(615)378-4679

Family Finders
122 Bass Drive
Mt. Juliet, TN 37122

Free Adoptees in Their Heritage
P.O. Box 294
Kingsport, TN 37662

Group for Openness in Adoption
518 Gen'l G. Patton Rd
Nashville, TN 37221
(615)646-8116

Openness in Adoption
518 General George Patton Road
Nashville, TN 37221

Right to Know
5182 Oak Meadow Avenue
Memphis, TN 38134
(901)373-7049; (901)386-2197

Right to Know
P.O. Box 34334
Bartlett, TN 38134

ROOTS
P.O. Box 9662
Knoxville, TN 37940
304 Arbuts Lane
Knoxville, TN 37919
(615)691-7412

U.F.O.
P.O. Box 290333
Nashville, TN 37229-0333

Texas

Adoptees/Birth Parents In Search
4208 Roxbury
El Paso, TX 79922
(915)581-0478

Adoptees Liberty Movement Association of

Austin (ALMA)
P.O. Box 14089
Austin, TX 78761

Adoption Counseling and Search
206 Lochaven
San Antonio, TX 78213
(210)341-2070

Adoption Healing
LLUMC (Rm 2)
5324 W N W Hwy
Dallas, TX
(972)513-0606

Adoption Knowledge Affiliates
P.O. Box 402033
Austin, TX 78704
(512)442-8252

Adoption Reform Group
706 Gresham
Smithville, TX 78957

Adoption Search and Support
Box 371
Pasadena, TX 77501

Adoption Triad Forum
P.O. Box 832161
Richardson, TX 75081

Austin-Post Adoption Services
510 W 26th Street
Austin, TX 78705
(512)472-9251

Birth Parents/Adoptees Support Group (U.K.)
4038 Clayhead Rd.
Richmond, TX 77469

DePelchin–Search/Support Group
100 Sandman
Houston, TX 77007
(713)802-7724

DFW Support Groups
5025 N Central Expressway, # 3026
Dallas, TX 75205-3447
(972)414-3639

Homeward Bound
P.O. Box 11032
Ft. Worth, TX 76110
(817)732-1319

Love, Roots and Wings
10432 Achilles
El Paso, TX 79924

Marywood Search Support Group
510 W. 26th St.
Austin, TX 78705
(512)472-9251

Methodist Family Services
6487 Whitby Road
San Antonio, TX 78240
(210)696-2410 ext. 122

Orphan Voyage
1305 Augustine Court
College Station, TX 77840
(409)764-7157

Orphan Voyage
5811 Southminister
Houston, TX 77035
(713)723-1762

Overseas Brats
P.O. Box 29805
San Antonio, TX 78229
(210)349-1394

Post Adoption Center
8600 Wurzbach Rd, #1110
San Antonio, TX 78240-4334
(210)614-0299

Right to Know
P.O. Box 1409
Grand Prairie, TX 75050

Searchline of Texas
1516 Old Orchard
Irving, TX 75061
(214)445-7005

Texas Coalition for Adoption Reform and Education
P.O. Box 832161
Richardson, TX 75083-2161

Triad Support Group
4208 Roxbury
El Paso, TX 79922

Triangle Search
5730 Crest Grove
Corpus Cristi, TX 78415

Utah

Adoption Connection of Utah
1349 Mariposa Avenue
Salt Lake City, UT 84106
(801)278-4858

Search Finders of Utah/L.A.M.B.
672 East 2025 South
Bountiful, UT 84010
(801)298-8520

Vermont

Adoption Alliance of Vermont
104 Falls Road
Shelburne, VT 05482

Adoption Alliance of Vermont
107 Twin Oaks
South Burlington, VT 05403

Adoption Alliance of Vermont
17 Hopkins Street
Rutland, VT 05701

Adoption Alliance of Vermont
613 Hill's Pt. Rd.
Charlotte, VT 05445
(802)425-2478

Adoption Alliance of Vermont
91 Court Street
Middlebury, VT 05753
(802)388-7569

Adoption Connections
P.O. Box 401
Putney, VT 05346

Adoption Search/Support Network (ASSN)
RR1 Box 83
East Calais, VT 05650
(802)456-8850

B and C Research Assistance
P.O. Box 1451
St. Albans, VT 05478
(802)527-7507; (802)524-9825

Beacon of Vermont
P.O. Box 152
Bakersfield, VT 05441-0152

BEACON
P.O. Box 83
Bridgeport, VT 05734-0083

Birthmothers Against Adoption
P.O. Box 424
Concord, VT 05824
(802)695-8107

Concerned United Birthparents (CUB)
403 White Birch Lane
Williston, VT 05495-7704
(802)860-3975

Friends in Adoption
P.O. Box 1228
Middletown Springs, VT 05757

Virgin Islands

DCYF Post Adoption Unit
Spenceley Bldg. 3rd floor
Charlotte Amalie
St. Thomas, VI 00802
(809)774-4393

Virginia

Adopted Bikers Assn.
P.O. Box 36317
Richmond, VA 23236-6317
(804)323-4129

Adoptee-Birthparent Support Network (ABSN)
P.O. Box 8273
McLean, VA 22106-8273
(202)628-4111

Adoptee-Birthparent Support Network (ABSN)
P.O. Box 8273
McLean, VA 22106
(202)628-4111; (202)686-4611

Adoptees and Natural Parents Organization

(ANPO)
949 Lacon Drive
Newport News, VA 23608
(757)874-9091

Adoptees Support
8630 Granby Street
Norfolk, VA 23503

Adult Adoptees in Search
P.O. Box 203
Ferrum, VA 24088-0203

Parents and Adoptees in Search
3932 Durette Drive
Richmond, VA 23237

Parents and Adoptees Together
7608 Hillside Avenue
Richmond, VA 23229

Washington

Adoptee Support Circle
123 Draper Valley Rd.
Port Angeles, WA 98362
(360)452-2212

Adoption Resource Center Children's Home Society of Washington, Northwest Branch
3300 NE 65th St.
Seattle, WA 98115
(206)524-6020

Adoption Search and Counseling Consultants
6201 15th Ave. NW #P210
Seattle, WA 98107
(206)284-8538; (206)782-4491

Association of Confidential Intermediaries
123 Draper Valley Rd.
Port Angeles, WA 98362
(360)452-2212

Bastard Nation
21904 Marine View Drive S.
PMB 138
Des Moines, WA 98198
(415)704-3166
www.bastards.org

Concerned United Birthparents (CUB)
10014 NE 35th Street
Vancouver, WA 98662

Grays Harbor Adoption Triangle
63 Bear Gulch Rd
Aberdeen, WA 98520
(360)533-6953

My Family Ties
P.O. Box 9306
Tacoma, WA 98409
(206)588-9407

Open Arms
6816-135 Ct., NE
Redmond, WA 98052

Oregon Adoption Rights Assoc.
P.O. Box 2692
Battle Ground, WA 98604
(360)263-3937

Search and Reconciliation
14320 SE 170
Renton, WA 98058

Seattle Birthparent Support Group
1024 NE 180th St
Seattle, WA 98155
(206)362-7840

Touched by Adoption
205 Brock St. #7
Walla Walla, WA 99362

Tri-Cities Adoption Search/Support Group
2130 Hoxie Avenue
Richmond, WA 99352
(509)546-0363

Washington Adoptees Rights Movement (WARM)
1119 Peacock Lane
Burlington, WA 98233

Washington Adoptees Rights Movement (WARM)
20 Hall Avenue
Yakima, WA 98902

Washington Adoptees Rights Movement (WARM)
408 SW 175th Place
Seattle, WA 98166-3758

Washington Adoptees Rights Movement (WARM)
5950 6th Ave. South # 107
Seattle, WA 98108
(206)767-9510

Washington Adoptees Rights Movement (WARM)
9901 SE Shoreland Drive
Bellevue, WA 98004

Washington Adoptees Rights Movement (WARM)
P.O. Box 2667
Olympia, WA 98507

Washington Adoptees Rights Movement (WARM)
Route #1, Box 101
303 E Paradise Rd
Spangle, WA 99031
(509)448-3740

Washington Adoption Reunion Movement
5950 Sixth Avenue South
Suite 107
Seattle, WA 98108-3317
(206)767-9510

West Virginia

Legacies
826 Honaker Lane
Charleston, WV 25312
(304)984-0305

Lineages
P.O. Box 1264
Huntington, WV 25714

Mending Hearts
2509 24th Street
Parkersburg, WV 26101
(304)428-8119

Society's Triangle
411 Cabell Court
Huntington, WV 25714

Wisconsin

Adoption Information and Direction
P.O. Box 516
4308 Heffron St
Stevens Point, WI 54481
(715)345-1290

Adoption Information and Direction
P.O. Box 875
Green Bay, WI 54305-0875

Adoption Information and Direction
P.O. Box 2043
Oshkosh, WI 54903

Adoption Resource Network
P.O. Box 8221
Eau Claire, WI 54702-8221
(715)835-6695

Adoption Root Retraced
N5080 17th Avenue
Mauston, WI 53948

Adoption Roots Traced
N6795 Highway A, Lot #44
Lake Mills, WI 53551
(414)648-2917

Adoption Search and Support
P.O. Box 174
Coon Valley, WI 54623-0174
(608)452-3146

Adoption Triad Outreach
P.O. Box 370691
Milwaukee, WI 53237
(414)483-3533
www.adoptiontriad.org

Common Bonds
280 D North Campbell Road
Oshkosh, WI 54901

Fox Valley Friends in Adoption
1032 Forestedge Dr.
KauKauna, WI 54130
(414)766-3213

ICARE–Wisconsin Adoption Reunion Registry
N 5080 17th Ave
Mauston, WI 53948
(608)847-5563

Milestone Search and Support
3214 Berkshire Road

Janesville, WI 53546
(608)754-4005

Mix and Match/Contact Point
P.O. Box 1141
Manitowoc, WI 54221-1141
(414)683-2225

Open Ends of Adoption
1219 Hobart Drive
Green Bay, WI 54304-1458

Orphan Voyage
Madison, WI
(608)845-3463

Wyoming

Adults Affected by Adoption
1408 Hugur
Cheyenne, WY 82001

Please refer also to Appendix K for Adoption Registries and the groups that maintain them.

ASSET SEARCH ORGANIZATIONS

The Asset Search Industry Association (ASIA)
2000 L Street NW, Suite 200
Washington, DC 20036
(202)416-1616

CONSUMER CREDIT ASSOCIATIONS

Consumer Data Industry Association
1090 Vermont Ave., N.W.

Suite 200
Washington, DC 20005-4905
(202)371-0910
www.cdia.online.org

FUNDRAISING/ PROSPECT RESEARCH ORGANIZATIONS

INTERNATIONAL

Association of Fundraising Professionals (AFP)
1101 King St., Suite 700
Alexandria, VA 22314
(800)666-FUND; (703)684-0410
www.nsfre.org

UNITED STATES
Alabama

Alabama Planned Giving Council
2000 Southbridge Parkway, Ste. 590
Birmingham, AL 35209
(205)802-7575

Alaska

Alaska Planned Giving Council
550 W. Seventh Ave., Ste. 1980
Anchorage, AK 99501-3594
(907)258-6565

Arizona

Friends of the Journal of Arizona History
2525 E. Broadway Blvd. 200
Tucson, AZ 85716-5350

Planned Giving Roundtable of Arizona
Arizona Community Foundation
2122 E. Highland Ave., Ste. 400
Phoenix, AZ 85016
(602)381-1400
www.premiumadministration.com/Planned%20Giving%20first%20Try.htm

Planned Giving Roundtable of Southern Arizona
United Way of Greater Tucson
P.O. Box 13290
Tucson, AZ 85732
(520)722-6000

Arkansas

United Way of Southeast Arkansas (UWSA)
P.O. Box 8702
Pine Bluff, AR 71611-8702
(870)534-2153
www.unitedway.org/local.cfm?ID=04230&zip=00000

California

Central Coast Planned Giving Council
KCBX Public Radio
4100 Vachell Ln.
San Luis Obispo, CA 93401
(805)781-3020

The Grantsmanship Center (TGCI)
P.O. Box 17220
Los Angeles, CA 90017
(213)482-9860
www.tgci.com/index.html

Inland Empire Planned Giving Roundtable
Major and Planned Giving
University of California, Riverside
257 Highlander Hall
Riverside, CA 92521
(909)787-6449
http://infrasite.goingv.com/ie

Nevada Planned Giving Roundtable
Riordan and McKinzie
300 S. Grand, 29th Fl.
Los Angeles, CA 90071
(213)229-8504

Northern California Planned Giving Council
Morgan, Miller and Blair
1676 N. California Blvd., Ste. 200
Walnut Creek, CA 94596-4137
(925)937-3600
www.greatorgs.com/ncpage

Planned Giving Council of Santa Cruz and Monterey Counties
Hospice Caring Project of Santa Cruz Co.
6851 Soquel Ave.
Aptos, CA 95003
(831)688-5819

Planned Giving Council of Ventura County
Smith and Smith Associates
4200 Clear Valley Dr.
Encino, CA 91436-3316
(818)784-5542

Planned Giving Forum of Sacramento
Wells Fargo Bank
Sacramento, CA 95814
(916)440-4449

Planned Giving Roundtable of Orange County
Tax and Financial Group
4001 MacArthur Blvd.
Newport Beach, CA 92660
(949)223-8529
www.pgrtoc.org

Planned Giving Roundtable of San Diego
Young Men's Christian Association of San Diego County
4715 View Ridge Ave., Ste. 100
San Diego, CA 92123
(619)292-4034

Planned Giving Roundtable of Santa Barbara
Rehabilitation Foundation
427 Camino Del Remedio
Santa Barbara, CA 93101-1310
(805)683-3788

Planned Giving Roundtable of Southern California
P.O. Box 1695
Oak View, CA 93022
(805)649-4565
www.pgrtsc.org

San Joaquin Valley Planned Gifts Council
Price, Paige and Stewart
677 Scott Ave.
Clovis, CA 93612
(559)299-9540

Silicon Valley Planned Giving Council
WealthPlan
1550 S. Bascom Ave., Ste. 150
Campbell, CA 95008
(408)369-7555

Colorado

Colorado Planned Giving Roundtable
The Colorado Episcopal Foundation
1234 Bannock St.
Denver, CO 80204
(303)534-6778
www.cpgr.org

Connecticut

Planned Giving Group of Connecticut
Planned Giving
Arthritis Foundation
25 Beverly Rd.
Wethersfield, CT 06109
(860)563-3828

District of Columbia

Planned Giving Study Group of Greater Washington, D.C.
Theological College
400 Michigan Ave., Northeast
Washington, DC 20017
(202)756-4905

Florida

Lutheran Planned Giving Council
246 Woodingham Trail
Venice, FL 34292
(941)408-9096
www.lpgc.org

Miami-Dade County Planned Giving Council
Crockett and Chasen, P.A.
420 Lincoln Rd., No. 338
Miami Beach, FL 33139
(305)674-9222
www.plannedgivingmiami.org

Naples Council on Planned Giving
Wollman, Strauss and Associates, P.A.
5129 Castello Dr., Ste. 1
Naples, FL 34103
(941)435-1533

Northwest Florida Planned Giving Council
Lakeview Foundation
1221 W. Lakeview Ave.
Pensacola, FL 32501
(850)469-3782

Planned Giving Council of Broward County
Northern Trust Bank
1100 E. Las Olas Blvd.
Ft. Lauderdale, FL 33301-2387
(954)527-3939

Planned Giving Council of Central Florida
Sun Trust Bank, Central FL
P.O. Box 3838
Mailcode 1073
Orlando, FL 32802-3838
(407)237-4246

Planned Giving Council of Indian River
United Way of In.R.C.
P.O. Box 1960
Vero Beach, FL 32961-1960
(561)567-8900

Planned Giving Council of Lee County
SW Florida Community Foundation, Inc.
12734 Kenwood Ln., Ste. 72
Ft. Myers, FL 33907
(941)274-5900

Planned Giving Council of Miami-Dade County
www.plannedgivingmiami.org

Planned Giving Council of Northeast Florida
Association Services
P.O. Box 550780
Jacksonville, FL 32255-0780
(904)821-0994

Planned Giving Council of Palm Beach County
Chase Manhattan Private Bank, NA
205 Royal Palm Way
Palm Beach, FL 33480
(561)838-8712

Southwest Florida Planned Giving Council
Bershon and Associates
1800 Second St., No. 892
Sarasota, FL 34236
(941)952-1440

Tampa Bay Area Planned Giving Council
5318 Balsam St.
New Port Richey, FL 34652
(727)849-1122
www.pgtampabay.org

Treasure Coast Planned Giving Council
4597 SE Windsor Ct.
Stuart, FL 34997
(561)223-9731

Georgia

Association of Fund-Raising Distributors and Suppliers (AFRDS)

P.O. Box 420187
5775 Peachtree-Dunwoody
Rd., Ste. 500-G
Atlanta, GA 30342
(404)252-3663
www.afrds.org

**Georgia Planned Giving
Council**
The Salvation Army
1424 NE Expressway
Atlanta, GA 30329
(404)728-1318

Hawaii

**Hawaii Planned Giving
Council**
University of Hawaii
Foundation
2444 Dole St., Bachman 101
Honolulu, III 96822
(808)956-9714

Idaho

**Southwest Idaho Planned
Giving Council**
St. Luke's Health Foundation
190 E. Bannock,
Boise, ID 83712
(208)381-2123

Illinois

**Central Illinois Planned
Giving Council**
Illinois State University
401 Hovey Hall
Campus Box 3060
Normal, IL 61790-3060
(309)438-7178
www.cipgc.org

**Chicago Council on
Planned Giving**
231 S. LaSalle
Chicago, IL 60697-0246
(312)828-8028

**Suburban Chicago Planned
Giving Council**
Benedictine University
5700 College Rd.
Lisle, IL 60532
(630)829-6079

Indiana

**American Association of
Fund-Raising Counsel
(AAFRC)**
10293 N. Meridian St., Ste.
175
Indianapolis, IN 46290-1130
(800)46-AAFRC; (212)481-
6705

**Kentucky Planned Giving
Council**
St. Meinrad Archabbey
Development Office
St. Meinrad, IN 47577-1025
(812)357-6501

**National Committee on
Planned Giving (NCPG)**
233 McCrea St., Ste. 400
Indianapolis, IN 46225
(317)269-6274

**Northwest Indiana Planned
Giving Group**
Legacy Foundation, Inc.
1000 E. 80th Place
Twin Towers S-503
Merrillville, IN 46410
(219)736-1880

**Planned Giving Council of
Northeast Indiana**
Parkview Hospital
Foundation
2200 Randalia
Ft. Wayne, IN 46805
(219)480-5021

Iowa

**Mid-Iowa Planned Giving
Council**
Syverson, Strege, Sandager
and Co.
4200 Corporate Dr., Ste. 100
West Des Moines, IA 50266
(515)225-6000

**Northwest Iowa Planned
Giving Council**
110 W. 4th St.
P.O. Box 1252
Spencer, IA 51301
(712)262-9177

**Quad City Planned Giving
Council**
Genesis Foundation
1227 E. Rusholme St.
Davenport, IA 52803
(319)421-6865

**Tri-State Gift Planning
Council**
Mercy Health Center
250 Mercy Dr.
Dubuque, IA 52001
(319)589-8107

Kansas

**Central Kansas Planned
Giving Roundtable**
Newton Healthcare
Foundation
600 Medical Center Dr.
P.O. Box 548
Newton, KS 67114-0548
(316)283-5200

Kentucky

**Central Kentucky Planned
Giving Council**
Northwestern Mutual/Robert

W. Baird, Inc.
3166 Custer Rd.
Lexington, KY 40517
(606)272-8685

**Mayfield-Graves County
United Way**
P.O. Box 47
Mayfield, KY 42066
(502)247-7454

Louisiana

**Greater New Orleans
Council of National Council
of Planned Giving**
Jewish Endowment
Foundation
234 Loyola Bldg., Ste. 806
New Orleans, LA 70112
(504)524-4559

Maine

**Maine Planned Giving
Council**
Private Banking and Investing
Key Bank
P.O. Box 4000
Bangor, ME 04402-4000
(207)945-0713
www.mpgc.org

Maryland

**Allegheny Planned Giving
Alliance**
129-9 W. Patrick St.
Frederick, MD 21701
(301)698-4886

**Chesapeake Planned Giving
Council**
PSA Financial Center
1447 York Rd.
Lutherville, MD 21093-6032
(410)821-7766

**National Capital Gift
Planned Council**
12424 Pretoria Dr.
Silver Spring, MD 20904
(301)572-2099
www.ncgpc.org

Planned Giving Council
PSA Financial Center
1447 York Rd.
Lutherville, MD 21093-6032
(410)821-7766

**Potomac Council on
Planned Giving**
Albright, Crumbacker, Moul
and Itell
44 N. Potomac St.
Hagerstown, MD 21740
(301)739-5300

Massachusetts

**National Association of
State Charity Officials
(NASCO)**
Office of Attorney General
1 Ashburton Pl.
Boston, MA 02108
(617)727-2200
www.nasconet.org

**Planned Giving Council of
Cape Cod**
The Community of Jesus,
Inc.
P.O. Box 1094
Orleans, MA 02653
(508)255-1094

**Planned Giving Group of
New England**
200 Reservoir St., Ste. 309A
Needham, MA 02494
(781)444-6861
www.pggne.org

**Southeastern Massachusetts
Planned Giving Council**
426 Plain St.
Marshfield, MA 02050
(781)837-9921

Michigan

**Heartland Council on
Planned Giving**
Hillsdale College
33 E. College
Hillsdale, MI 49242
(517)437-7341

**Mid-Michigan Planned
Giving Council**
Laine Appold Co., P.C.
720 Livingston
Bay City, MI 48708
(517)893-3588

**Northern Michigan Council
of National Committee on
Planned Giving**
Bagley Incorporated
18654 Center Rd.
Traverse City, MI 49686-
9769
(616)223-7992

**Planned Giving Roundtable
of Southeast Michigan**
19251 Mack Ave., Ste., No.
380
Grosse Pointe Woods, MI
48236
(313)343-9009

**Western Michigan Planned
Giving Group**
The Grand Rapids
Foundation
161 Ottawa NW, Ste. 209-C
Grand Rapids, MI 49503
(616)454-1751
www.wmpgg.org

Minnesota

Minnesota Planned Giving Council
Piper Jaffray, Inc.
2200 Piper Jaffray Plaza
444 Cedar St.
St. Paul, MN 55101
(612)298-1655
www.mnpgc.org

Missouri

Mid-America Planned Giving Council
Commerce Bank
118 W. 47th St.
Kansas City, MO 64112
(816)234-2568

St. Louis Planned Giving Council
Mercantile Trust Co. N.A.
8820 Ladue Rd.
St. Louis, MO 63124-2096
(314)889-0734
www.slpgc.org

Nebraska

Planned Giving Council of Nebraska
P.O. Box 6402
Omaha, NE 68106
(402)558-1701

New Hampshire

Upper Valley Planned Giving Council
16 Rip Rd.
Hanover, NH 03755
(603)643-2609

New Jersey

Gift Planning Council at New Jersey

P.O. Box 42
Princeton, NJ 08542-0042
www.giftplanning-nj.org
index.htm

Princeton Area Planned Giving Council
Rutgers University Foundation,
Winants Hall
7 College Ave.
New Brunswick, NJ 08901
(732)932-8808

United Fund of Westfield
301 N. Ave., W
Westfield, NJ 07090
(908)233-2113
http://westfieldnj.com/
unitedfund

New Mexico

New Mexico Planned Giving Council
Swaim, Schrandt and Davidson, PC
4830 Juan Tabo NE, Ste. F
Albuquerque, NM 87111
(505)237-0064

New York

Gift Planning Group of Northeastern New York
1206 Godfrey Ln.
Niskayuna, NY 12309
(518)346-1400

Long Island Planned Giving Council
Philanthropy Planning Center
100 Quentin Roosevelt Blvd.
Garden City, NY 11530-4854
(516)794-4089

National Society of Fund Raising Executives, Genesee Valley Chapter
183 E Main St., Ste. 1200
Rochester, NY 14604
(716)797-0876

Planned Giving Council of Upstate New York
Roberts Wesleyan College
2301 Westside Dr.
Rochester, NY 14624
(716)594-6200

Western New York Planned Giving Consortium
Foundation of Jewish Philanthropies
787 Delaware Ave.
Buffalo, NY 14209
(716)882-1166

North Carolina

North Carolina Planned Giving Council
WFU Baptist Medical Center
3775 Vest Mill Rd., Ste. C
Winston-Salem, NC 27157-1021
(336)716-6031
www.ncpgc.org

Ohio

Central Ohio Planned Giving Council
The Ohio State University,
401 Fawcett Center
2400 Olentangy River Rd.
Columbus, OH 43210-1061
(614)688-5699

Greater Cincinnati Planned Giving Council
Talbot Wolf Ahearn

102 Hetherington Ln.
Cincinnati, OH 45246
(513)772-6887

**Greater Dayton Planned
Giving Council**
Dayton Foundation
2100 Kettering Tower
Dayton, OH 45423
(937)222-0410

**North Central Ohio
Planned Giving Council
(NCOPGC)**
Ashland University
401 College Ave.
Ashland, OH 44805
(419)289-5072

**Northern Ohio Planned
Giving Council**
Huntington National Bank
Corporate Financial Center
5900 Landerbrook Dr., Ste.
150
Mayfield Heights, OH 44124
(216)515-0261

**Springfield Council on
Planned Giving**
Wallace and Turner, Inc.
616 N. Limestone St.
P.O. Box 209
Springfield, OH 45501
(937)324-8492

**Toledo Area Planned Giving
Council**
St. Vincent Mercy Medical
Center Foundation,
2213 Cherry St.
Toledo, OH 43608
(419)251-8959

Oklahoma

**Oklahoma Planned Giving
Council**

Mee, Mee and Hoge, LLP
1900 City Place
204 N. Robinson Ave.
Oklahoma City, OK 73102
(405)232-5900

Oregon

**Northwest Planned Giving
Roundtable**
Charitable Estate and Gift
Advisor
Providence Health System in
Oregon
9205 SW Barnes Rd.
Portland, OR 97225-6622
(503)216-2226
www.nwpgrt.org

Pennsylvania

**Delaware Valley Planned
Giving Council**
The Curtis Institute of Music
1726 Locust St.
Philadelphia, PA 19103
(215)893-5279

First Foundation
1417 N. Delphos St.
Kokomo, IN 46901-2566

**Pittsburgh Planned Giving
Council (PPGC)**
Waynesburg College
51 W.College St.
Waynesburg, PA 15370
(724)852-3369

**Susquehanna Valley
Planned Giving Council**
Blue Ball National Bank
P.O. Box 445
Hershey, PA 17033-0445
(717)354-4541

Rhode Island

**Planned Giving Council of
Rhode Island**
Jewish Federation of Rhode
Island
130 Sessions St.
Providence, RI 02906-3497
(401)421-4111

South Carolina

**South Carolina Planned
Giving Council**
Wheat First Butcher Singer
1901 Main St., Ste. 620
MC1101
NationsBank Plaza
Columbia, SC 29201
(800)332-6637

South Dakota

**South Dakota Planned
Giving Council**
South Dakota Community
Foundation
207 E. Capitol
Box 296
Pierre, SD 57501
(605)224-1025

Tennessee

**Greater Chattanooga Area
Planned Giving Council**
Shumaker and Thompson,
P.C.
First Tennessee Bank Bldg.
701 Market St., Ste. 500
Chattanooga, TN 37402
(423)265-2214

**Greater Memphis Planned
Giving Council**
Legacy Wealth Management
1755 Kirby Parkway,

Ste. 330
Memphis, TN 38120
(901)758-9006

**Middle Tennessee Planned
Giving Council**
Vanderbilt University, 105
Kirkland Hall
Nashville, TN 37240
(615)343-3113

Texas

**Central Texas Chapter of
National Committee of
Planned Giving**
Clark, Thomas and Winters
P.O. Box 1148
Austin, TX 78767-1148
(512)472-8800

**Lone Star Chapter of
National Committee of
Planned Giving**
First Financial Services
Bank of Commerce Tower
Ft. Worth, TX 76102
(817)332-4500

**North Texas Chapter of
National Committee of
Planned Giving**
The Nautilus Group
15305 Dallas Parkway, No.
1050 LB15
Dallas, TX 75248
(972)720-6616

**Planned Giving Council of
Houston**
Chase Bank of Texas
P.O. Box 2558
Houston, TX 77252-8037
(713)216-0451

**San Antonio Regional
Council of National**

**Committee of Planned
Giving**
Texas Military Institute
20955 Tejas Trail West
San Antonio, TX 78257
(210)698-7171

Utah

**Utah Planned Giving
Roundtable**
First Security Bank
P.O. Box 30007
Salt Lake City, UT 84130
(801)246-5451

Vermont

**Upper Valley Planned
Giving Council**
P.O. Box 88
Quechee, VT 05059
(802)296-3642
www.uvpgc.org

Virginia

**Association for Healthcare
Philanthropy (AHP)**
313 Park Ave., Ste. 400
Falls Church, VA 22046
(703)532-6243
www.go-ahp.org

**Blue Ridge Planned Giving
Study Group**
Ferrum College
P.O. Box 1000
Ferrum, VA 24088
(540)365-4330

**Virginia Association of
Fund Raising Executives**
951 E. Byrd St.
Richmond, VA 23219-4040
www.vafre.org

**Virginia Planned Giving
Study Group**
Hunton and Williams
951 E. Byrd St.
Richmond, VA 23219-4074
(804)788-8641

Washington

**Inland Northwest Planned
Giving Council**
Gonzaga Preparatory School
1224 E. Euclid
Spokane, WA 99207
(509)489-6302

**Planned Giving Council of
Eastern Washington**
The Salvation Army
1102 Carriage Sq. Dr.
Grandview, WA 98930
(800)659-7747

**Washington Planned Giving
Council**
Seattle University
Broadway and Madison
Adm. 120
Seattle, WA 98122
(206)296-6103

Wisconsin

**Planned Giving Council of
Eastern Wisconsin**
Milwaukee Foundation
1020 N. Broadway
Milwaukee, WI 53202
(414)272-5805

**Wisconsin Planned Giving
Council**
Hurley, Burish and Milliken,
S.C.
301 N. Broom St.
Madison, WI 53713-2067
(608)257-0945

GENEALOGICAL RESEARCH ASSOCIATIONS

ARGENTINA

Asociación de Genealogía Judía de Argentina
Juana Azurduy 2223, P. 8,
(1429)Buenos Aires
www.agja.org.ar/index.htm

AUSTRALIA

Australiasian Association of Genealogists and Record Agents
P.O. Box 268
Oakleigh, Victoria 3166
www.aagra.asn.au

Australasian Federation of Family History Organizations (AFFHO)
6/48 May St.
Bayswater, WA 6053
61 8 92714311
www.affho.org

Australian Jewish Genealogical Society, Adelaide
c/o Beit Shalom Synagogue
P.O. Box 47
Stepney, SA 5069

Australian Jewish Genealogical Society, Brisbane
3/23 Lucinda St, Taringa,
Brisbane, Queensland 4068

Australian Jewish Genealogical Society, Canberra
C/O ACT Jewish Community

Inc.
P.O. Box 3105
Manuka
Australian Capital Territory,
2603

Australian Jewish Genealogical Society, Victoria
P.O. Box 189
Genhuntly, Melbourne
Victoria 3163
61-3-9571-8251
www.ajgs.exist.com.au

Australian Jewish Genealogical Society, Perth
P.O. Box 225
Claremont, WA 6912

Australian Jewish Genealogical Society, Sydney
P.O. Box 154
Northbridge
Sydney, NSW 1560
61-2-9958-6317
www.zeta.org.au/~feraltek/ge
nealogy/ajgs

Society of Australian Genealogists
Richmond Villa
120 Kent St.
Sydney, NSW 2000
Australia
61 2 92473953
www.sag.org.au

AUSTRIA

Genealogical and Heraldry Society
Heraldisch-Genealogische
Gesellschaft
Gesellschaft ADLER

Universitaetsstrasse 6/9b
P.O. Box 220
A-1096 Vienna

BELGIUM

Jewish Genealogical Society of Belgium
74 Avenue Stalingrad
B-1000 Bruxelles, Belgique
32-2-512.19.63

CANADA

Abbotsford Genealogical Society
P.O. Box 672
Abbotsford, BC V2S 6R7
members.shaw.ca/Abby-
Genealogy/welcome.html

Alberta Genealogical Society
Prince of Wales Armouries
Heritage Centre
#116, 10440 - 108 Ave
Edmonton AB T5H 3Z9
(780)424-4429
www.compusmart.ab.ca/
abgensoc

Association de Recherches Généalogiques et Historiques d'Auvergne (ARGHA)
Maison des Associations
Rue des Saulées
63400 Chamalieres
http://web.nat.fr/argha/
default.asp

Association for Canadian Jewish Studies
Department of
Religion/Concordia
University

1455 de Maisonneuve West
Montreal, QC H3G 1M8
http://fcis.oise.utoronto.ca/
~acjs

**Bruce County Genealogical
Society**
P.O. Box 1083
Port Elgin, ON, N0H 2C0
www.compunik.com/bcgs

**Canadian Association for
Irish Studies**
St. Michael's College
81 St. Mary Street
Toronto ONT M5S 1J4
www.erin.utoronto.ca/cais

**Canadian Federation of
Genealogical and Family
History Societies**
227 Parkville Bay
Winnipeg, MB, R2M 2J6
www.geocities.com/Athens/
Troy/2274

**Centre de recherches
généalogiques du Québec**
11440, 54ième Avenue,
Montréal, QC H1E 2J1
(514)881-9633
www.cam.org/~cdrgduq

**Fédération québécoise des
sociétés de généalogie**
Case postale 9454
Sainte-Foy, QC G1V 4B8
www.federationgenealogie.
qc.ca

**French-Canadian
Genealogical Society
(FCGS)**
or **Société généalogique
canadienne-française
(SGCF)**
3440, rue Davidson

Montréal QC H1W 2Z5
(514)527-1010
www.sgcf.com/anglais/
welcome.htm

**Genealogical Association of
Nova Scotia**
P.O.Box 641
Station "Central"
Halifax, NS B3J 2T3
(902)454-0322
www.chebucto.ns.ca/
Recreation/GANS/index.html

**Genealogical Institute of
the Maritimes**
or **Institut généalogique des
provinces Maritimes**
P.O. Box 3142
Halifax South Postal Station
Halifax, NS B3J 3H5
http://nsgna.ednet.ns.ca/gim

**Genealogical Society of NB
Saint John Chapter**
Box 2423
Main Stn Post Office
Saint John, NB E2L 3V9
www.sjfn.nb.ca/community_
hall/G/GENEXXXX.html

**Germans from Russia
Heritage Society–The
Alberta Chapter**
247 Huntridge Way NE,
Calgary, AB Canada, T2K
4C4
www.grhs.com/chapters/
alberta.html

**Icelandic Memorial Society
of Nova Scotia**
RR #4, Middle
Musquodoboit, NS B0N 1X0
www.nova-scotia-
icelanders.ednet.ns.ca

**Jewish Genealogical
Institute of British
Columbia**
#206 - 950 West 41st Ave.
Vancouver, BC V5Z 2N7,
(604)321-9870
www.geocities.com/
Heartland/Hills/4441

**Jewish Genealogical Society
of Canada (Toronto)**
P.O. Box 446, Station "A"
Willowdale, ONT M2N 5T1
www.jgstoronto.ca

**Jewish Genealogical Society
of Montreal**
5599 Edgemore Ave
Montreal, QC H4W 1V4
(514)484-0100
www.gtrdata.com/jgs-
montreal

**Jewish Genealogical Society
of Southern Alberta**
1607 90th Avenue SW,
Calgary, AB T2V 4V7
www.jewishgen.org/jgssa

**Jewish Genealogy Society
of Ottawa**
c/o Greenberg Families
Library
Soloway JCC
1780 Kerr Ave
Ottawa, ONT K2A 1R9
(613)995-9227(W)or
(613)731-0876 (H)
www.jgstoronto.ca/Ottawa.
html

**La Société généalogique de
l'est du Québec**
110, Évêché est, Local L-
120, Rimouski, QC G5L 1X9
(418)724-3242

Jewish Heritage Centre of Western Canada, Genealogical Institute
C116 - 123 Doncaster St.
Winnipeg, MB, R3N 2B2,
(204)477-7460,
www.jhcwc.org/geninst.htm

Le Club de généalogie de Longueuil
763, rue Després
Longueuil
(450)670-1869
www.club-genealogie-longueuil.qc.ca

Newfoundland and Labrador Genealogical Society
Colonial Building, Military Road
St. John's, NF A1C 2C9
(709)754-9525
www3.nf.sympatico.ca/nlgs

Nova Scotia Genealogy Network Association
P.O. Box 248
Shelburne NS B0T 1W0
http://nsgna.ednet.ns.ca

Ontario Genealogical Society–Elgin County Branch
Box 20060
St. Thomas, ONT N5P 4H4
http://home.ican.net/~bedmonds/ElginOGS

Ontario Genealogical Society–Essex County Branch
P.O. Box 2, Station "A"
Windsor, ONT N9A 4H0
www.rootsweb.com/~onsxogs/ogs1.htm

Ontario Genealogical Society–Hamilton Branch
Box 904, LCD 1
Hamilton, ONT L8N 3P6
www.hwcn.org/link/HBOGS

Pictou County Genealogy and Heritage Society
P.O. Box 1210
Pictou, NS B0K 1H0
www.rootsweb.com/~nspcghs

Prince Edward Island Genealogical Society Inc.
P.O. Box 2744
Charlottetown, PEI C1A 8C4
www.islandregister.com/peigs.html

Shelburne County Genealogical Society
168 Water Street, P.O. Box 248
Shelburne, NS B0T 1W0
(902)875-4299
http://nsgna.ednet.ns.ca/shelburne/index.php

Société de généalogie de Québec
Salle 4266
Pavillon Louis-Jacques-Casault
Cité Universaire
Case Postale 9066
Sainte-Foy, QC G1V 4A8
(418)651-9127
www.genealogie.org/club/sgq

South Shore Genealogical Society
68 Bluenose Drive
P.O. Box 901
Lunenburg, NS B0J 2C0
(902)634-4794
www.rootsweb.com/~nslssgs

Ukranian Genealogical and Historical Society of Canada (UGHSC)
R. R. #2
Cochrane, Alberta T0L 0W0
www.feefhs.org/ca/frgughsc.html

FRANCE

Association Française de Généalogie
www.afg-2000.org

Association Généalogique de l'Oise
Ancien Hôtel-Dieu Saint-Nicolas-du-Pont
3, rue Jeanne d'Arc
60200 Compiegne
B.P. n°10626 - 60206
Compiegne Cedex
03 44 86 14 30
http://ag-oise.genealogie.to

Association Généalogique de Relevés et de Recherches
Secrétariat de l'A.G.R.R.
Mairie de Champdivers
39500 Champdivers

Associations généalogiques des Provinces du Nord
SGHPN
45 Avenue Denis Cordonnier - F
59139 Wattignies
www.genenord.tm.fr

Association Généalogique du Pays de Bray
Espace Social et Communal d'Animation Léo Lagrange
E.S.C.A.L.L.
Boulevard Albert Charvet
76270 Neufchâtel-en-Bray
http://site.voila.fr/agpb7660

Association Parisienne de Généalogie Normande
49 rue St-Georges
75009 Paris
www.chez.com/apgn

Cercle de Genealogie Juive
14, rue Saint-Lazare
75009 Paris
33 1 40 23 04 90
www.genealoj.org

GenAmi, Association de Généalogie Juive Internationale
76 rue de Passy
F-75016 Paris
33 1 45 24 35 40
http://asso.genami.free.fr

Genealogie Algerie Maroc Tunisie
Maison Maréchal A. Juin–29,
avenue de Tübingen
13090 Aix-en-Provence
04 42 95 19 49
www.aix-assu.org/gamt/gamt.html

International Confederation of Genealogy and Heraldry (ICGH)
or
Confederation Internationale de Genealogie et d'Heraldique (CIGH)
49 rue des Granges
F-25000 Besancon

GERMANY

Deutschet Arbeitsgemeinschaft Genealogischer Verbande (DAGV)

Vereine
An der Baumschule 7
D-50374 Erftstadt-Lechenich
49 2235 73104

Hamburger Gesellschaft für jüdische Genealogie e.V.
Staatsarchiv, Kattunbleiche
19, D-22011, Hamburg
0049-40-428 313138

IRELAND

Association of Professional Genealogists in Ireland
c/o The Honorary Secretary
30 Harlech Crescent
Clonskeagh
Dublin 14
http://indigo.ie/~apgi

ISRAEL

Galilee Genealogical Society
Hoshaya, M. P. O.
Hamovil 17915
972 (0)6 646-8180

Israel Genealogical Society (IGS)
P.O. Box 4270
91041 Jerusalem
972 2 424147
www.isragen.org.il

Israel Genealogical Society (IGS)–Jerusalem Branch
Mevakshei Derech Building
22 Shai Agnon Boulevard
Jerusalem
www.isragen.org.il

Israel Genealogical Society (IGS)–Negev Branch
Kehilat Magen Avraham
Synagogue

Rehov Ad-Ad 11
Omer
www.isragen.org.il

Israel Genealogical Society (IGS)–Netanya Branch
AACI : 28 Shmuel Hanatziv
Netanya
www.isragen.org.il

Israel Genealogical Society (IGS)–Tel-Aviv Branch
Rothshild Boulevard 16
Tel-Aviv 66881
972-3-5177760
www.isragen.org.il/btn/bible-museum.htm

Jewish Family Research Association (JFRA)
P.O. Box 10099
61100 Tel Aviv
972-3-699-2813

MEXICO

Biblioteca Nacional de Mexico
Instituto de Investigaciones Bibliograficas
Universidad Nacional
Autonoma de Mexico
Centro Cultural, Ciudad
Universitaria
Delegacion Coyoacan
Apdo. 29-124
04510

Colonia Juarez Branch Genealogical Library
Colonia Juarez
Chihuahua

MONACO

Association Généalogique and Héraldique des Alpes-

Maritimes et de Monaco (AGHAMM)
Archives Départementales
des Alpes-Maritimes
Centre Administratif
Départemental
Route de Grenoble
06036 Nice Cedex
www.multimania.com/numa/
aghamm.html

NETHERLANDS

**Afdeling
Computergenealogie Van
De Nederlandse
Genealogische
Vereniging–Gens Data**
Postbus 19114
3501 DC Utrecht

**Dutch Society for Jewish
Genealogy (DSJG)**
Nederlandse Kring voor
Joodse Genealogie (NKJG)
Abbringstraat 1
NL-1447 PA Purmerend,
Netherlands
31 299 644498

**Nederlandse Kring voor
Joodse Genealogie**
or **Netherlands Society for
Jewish Genealogy**
Abbingstraat #1, 1447 P.A.
Purmerend
31 299-644498
www.nljewgen.org

PORTUGAL

**Associacao Portuguesa de
Genealogia**
Rua Marques da Fronteira,
127, 2.º
P-1000 LISBOA

**Instituto Portugues de
Heraldica**
Convento do Carmo
Largo do Carmo
P-1200 LISBOA

SOUTH AFRICA

**Jewish Genealogy Society of
Johannesburg**
Box 1388
Parklands 2121
27 (11)887-7764

SPAIN

**Asociacion de Diplomados
en Genealogia**
Heraldica y Nobiliaria
Alcala, 20-2a Oficina 7-B
Edificio Teatro "Alcazar"
28014 Madrid

**Instituto International De
Genealogia y Heraldica**
Asociacion de Hidalgos
Calle Atocha 94,
Madrid

SWEDEN

**Jewish Genealogical Society
of Sweden**
c/o Gerber
Box 7427
103 91, Stockholm
46-8-679 29 17
http://ijk-s.se/genealogi

SWITZERLAND

**Schweizerische Vereinigung
fur Judische Genealogie**
Scheuchzerstrasse 154
8006 Zurich
41 1 361 71 54
www.eye.ch/swissgen/ver/
jeinfo-d.htm

UNITED KINGDOM
ENGLAND

**Anglo-German Family
History Society**
14 River Reach
Teddington, Middx TW11
9QL
44 20 89772731

**Association of Genealogists
and Researchers in
Archives (AGRA)**
29 Badgers Close
Horsham, W. Sussex RH12
5RU
www.agra.org.uk

**Federation of Family
History Societies (FFHS)**
Birmingham and Midland
Institute
Benson Rm.
Margaret St.
Birmingham, W. Midlands
B3 3BS
44 7041 492032
www.ffhs.org.uk

**Institute of Heraldic and
Genealogical Studies**
79-82 Northgate
Canterbury CT1 1BA
44 1227 768664
www.ihgs.ac.uk

**Irish Genealogical Research
Society (IGRS)**
c/o The Irish Club
83 Eaton Sq.
London SW1W 9AJ
44 171 2354164

**Jewish Genealogical Society
of Great Britain**
P.O. Box 13288

London N3 3WD
44-1923-825-197
www.jgsgb.org.uk

Society of Genealogists
14 Charterhouse Bldgs.
Goswell Rd.
London EC1M 7BA
44 171 2518799
www.sog.org.uk

SCOTLAND

Aberdeen and NE Scotland Family History Society
164 King St.
Aberdeen AB24 5BD
44 (0)1224 646323
www.anesfhs.f9.co.uk

Alloway and Southern Ayrshire Family History Society
c/o Alloway Public Library
Doonholm Road
Alloway AYR KA7 4QQ
www.maybole.org/history/res
ources/asafhs.htm

Association of Scottish Genealogists and Record Agents (ASGRA)
51/3 Mortonhall Road
Edinburgh EH9 2HN
www.asgra.co.uk

Scottish Genealogy Society (SGS)
Library and Family History
Centre
15 Victoria Terrace
Edinburgh EH1 2JL
44 131 2203677
www.sol.co.uk/s/scotgensoc

Northern Ireland

Ulster Historical Foundation (UHF)
12 College Sq.
E Belfast BT1 6DD
44 1232 332288
www.irishroots.net/
AntmDown.htm

WALES

Association of Family History Societies of Wales
Peacehaven
Badgers Meadow
Pwllmeyric
Chepstow, Mon, NP16 6UE
or
5, Beaufort Avenue
Redhill, Hereford HR2 7PZ
www.rootsweb.com/~wlsafhs

UNITED STATES
Alabama

Afro-American Historical and Genealogical Society–Freedom Trail
220 Oak Dr.
Lowndesboro, AL 36752

Afro-American Historical and Genealogical Society–North Alabama
P.O. Box 11754
Huntsville, AL 35814

Alabama Genealogical Society, Inc.
Samford University Library
P.O. Box 2296
Birmingham, AL 35229-0001
www.familyhistory.com/
societyhall/viewmember.asp?
societyid=6

Autauga Genealogical Society
P.O. Box 680668
Prattville, AL 36068-0668
www.rootsweb.com/~alags

Baldwin County Genealogical Society
P.O. Box 108
Foley, AL 36536-0108

Birmingham Genealogical Society
P.O. Box 2432
Birmingham, AL 35201
www.birminghamgenealogy.
org

Dekalb County Genealogical Society, Inc.
P.O. Box 681087
Fort Payne, AL 35968-1612

Genealogy Society of Washington County
P.O. Box 399
Chatom, AL 36518
http://members.aol.com/JOR-
DANJM2/WCGS.html

Mobile Genealogical Society
P.O. Box 6224
Mobile, AL 36660-6224
(334)432-MGS-4
www.siteone.com/clubs/mgs/
index.html

Montgomery Genealogical Society, Inc.
P.O. Box 230194
Montgomery, AL 36123-0194
www.rootsweb.com/~almgs

Natchez Trace Genealogical Society (NTGS)
P.O. Box 420
Florence, AL 35631-0420

North Central Alabama Genealogical Society
P.O. Box 13
Cullman, AL 35056-0013
http://home.HiWAAY.net/~lthurman/society.htm

Northeast Alabama Genealogical Society, Inc.
P.O. Box 8268
Gadsden, AL 35902
www.geocities.com/Heartland/Ranch/5952

Pea River Historical and Genealogical Society (PRHGS)
P.O. Box 310628
Enterprise, AL 36331-0628
(334)393-2901
www.rootsweb.com/~alprhgs

Tennessee Valley Genealogical Society
P.O. Box 1568
Huntsville, AL 35807
http://hiwaay.net/~white/TVGS/tvgs.html

Many historical societies in Alabama can also be found at www.archives.state.al.us/referenc/hsglist.html.

Arizona

Afro-American Historical and Genealogical Society–Tucson Chapter
http://AZTucson.com/nonprofit/aahgs-tucson

Apache Genealogy Society
Sierra Vista Public Library
Maria Bishop Room

P. O. Box 1084
Sierra Vista, AZ 85636-1084

Arizona Genealogical Advisory Board (AzGAB)
P.O. Box 5641
Mesa, AZ 85211-5641
www.azgab.org

Arizona Genealogical Computer Interest Group
P.O. Box 51498
Phoenix, AZ 85076-1498
www.agcig.org

Arizona State Genealogical Society
P.O. Box 42075
Tucson, AZ 85733-2075
(520)513-ASGS
www.rootsweb.com/~asgs

Black Family History Society
P.O. Box 1515
Gilbert, AZ 85299-1515

Cherokee Family Ties
516 N. 38th St.
Mesa, AZ 85205

Cochise Genealogical Society
P.O. Box 68
Pirtleville, AZ 85626
www.mycochise.com

Czech and Slovak Genealogical Society of Arizona
7311 N. 69th Drive
Glendale, AZ 85303
www.rootsweb.com/~azcsgsa

Family History Society of Arizona

P.O. Box 63094
Phoenix, AZ 85082-3094

Genealogical Society of Yuma, Arizona
P.O. Box 2905
Yuma, AZ 85366-2905
www.gsya.org

Genealogical Workshop of Mesa
P.O. Box 6052
Mesa, AZ 85216
http://members.cox.net/gwom

Greater Phoenix Jewish Genealogical Society
P.O. Box 4063
Scottsdale, AZ 85261-4063

Green Valley Genealogical Society
P.O. Box 1009
Green Valley, AZ 85622-1009

Hispanic Family History Society
3607 S. Kenneth Pl.
Tempe, AZ 85282

Jewish Historical Society of Arizona
720 W. Edgewood Ave.
Mesa, AZ 85210-3513

Jewish Historical Society of Southern Arizona, Genealogy Group
4181 E Pontatoc Canyon Dr
Tucson, AZ 85718-5227
(520)299-4486

Lake Havasu Genealogical Society
P.O. Box 953

Lake Havasu City, AZ 86405-0953
www.rootsweb.com/~azlhgs

**Mohave County
Genealogical Society**
400 W Beale St
Kingman, AZ 86401-5797
www.citlink.net/~mocohist/
museum/geneal.htm

Monte Vista Genies
Monte Vista Village Resort
Pueblo Rm
8865 E. Baseline Rd
Mesa, AZ 85208-5309

**Northern Arizona
Genealogical Society**
P.O. Box 695
Prescott, AZ 86302-0695
www.rootsweb.com/~aznags

**Northern Gila County
Genealogical Society**
107 E Lone Pine Dr.
Payson, AZ 85541-5558
P.O. Box 952
Payson, AZ 85547-0952
(928)474-2139

**Ohio Genealogical
Society–Arizona Chapter**
P.O. Box 677
Gilbert, AZ 85299-0677

**Phoenix Genealogical
Society**
4607 W Rovey Ave
Glendale, AZ 85301-5323
P.O. Box 38703
Phoenix, AZ 85069-8703
www.geocities.com/
Heartland/Valley/5752

Polish Genealogical Interest

Group of Arizona
2015 E. Redmon Dr.
Tempe, AZ 85283
www.azneighbors.com/212

Sedona Genealolgy Club
P.O. Box 4258
Sedona, AZ 86340.
http://fp.sedona.net/
genealogy/index.htm

**Sierra Vista Genealogical
Society**
P.O. Box 1084
Sierra Vista, AZ 85636-1084
www.rootsweb.com/~azsvgs

**Sun Cities Genealogical
Society**
P.O. Box 1448
Sun City, AZ 85372

**Tri-State Genealogical
Society**
P.O. Box 9689
Fort Mohave, AZ 86427

**West Valley Genealogical
Society/ Sun City
Genealogical Society, Inc.**
P.O. Box 1448
Sun City, AZ 85372-1448
(623)933-4945
www.rootsweb.com/~azwvgs/
index.htm

*Additional genealogical and
historical societies in Arizona
can be found at www.azgab.
org/pages/societies.htm.*

Arkansas

**Afro-American Historical
and Genealogical
Society–Arkansas Chapter**

P.O. Box 4294
Little Rock, AR 72214
www.rootsweb.com/
~mdaahgs/arkansas

**Ancestors Unknown
Genealogy Society**
P.O. Box 164
Conway, AR 72033
www.ancestorsunknown.org

**Arkansas Genealogical
Society**
P.O. Box 908
Hot Springs, AR 71902-0908
www.rootsweb.com/~args

**Arkansas Roots–Southeast
Arkansas Genealogical
Society**
Regional Archives
119 West College
Monticello, AR

**Baxter County, Arkansas,
Historical and Genealogical
Society**
P.O. Box 1611
Mountain Home, AR 72654
www.baxtercountyonline.
com/bchgs

**Bradley County
Genealogical Society**
P.O. Box 837
Warren, AR 71671-0837
(870)226-5959; (870)226-7675
www.rootsweb.com/~
arbradle/bradcogensoc.shtml

**Clay County Genealogical
and Historical Society**
361 W. Main St.
Piggott, AR 72454
(501)598-3666

Greene County Historical and Genealogical Society
120 N. 12th St.
Paragould, AR 72450
www.couchgenweb.com/
arkansas/greene/gchgs.htm

Madison County Genealogical and Historical Society
P.O. Box 427
Huntsville, AR 72740
(501)738-6408

Melting Pot Genealogical Society (MPGS)
P.O. Box 936
Hot Springs, AR 71902
(501)624-0229; (501)262-4975

Northwest Arkansas Genealogical Society
P.O. Box 796
Rogers, AR 72757-0796
(501)273-3890

Orphan Train Heritage Society of America (OTHSA)
614 E. Emma Ave., No. 115
Springdale, AR 72764-4634
(501)756-2780

Tri-County Genealogical Society
P.O. Box 580
Marvell, AR 72366
(501)829-2772
www.couchgenweb.com/
arkansas/tricou/society.htm

Union County Genealogical Society
c/o Barton Library
501 W. 8th Street

El Dorado, AR 71730
(870)862-3198; (870)863-5447

Additional genealogical societies in Arkansas can be found at www. genealogyforum.rootsweb. com/gfaol/resource/AR/GS.htm.

California

African American Genealogical Society of Northern California
P.O. Box 27485
Oakland, CA 94602-0985
www.aagsnc.org

Antelope Valley Genealogical Society
P.O. Box 1049
Lancaster, CA 93584-1049
www.qnet.com/~toiyabe/avgs

Armas de España
3 Rancho Jurupa Place
Phillips Ranch, CA 91766
(714)623-1440

Association of Jewish Genealogical Society
Orange County Chapter
2370 1-D Via Mariposa W.
Laguna Hills, CA 92653
(949)855-4692

The Augustan Society, Inc. (AS)
P.O. Box 75
Daggett, CA 92327-0075
(760)254-9223
www.augustansociety.org

The Augustan Society, Inc.
P.O. Box P

Torrance, CA 90508-0210
(310)320-7766

Conejo Valley Genealogical Society
P. O. Box 1228
Thousand Oaks, CA 91358-0228
http://pages.prodigy.net/
jimcolvin/cvgspage/
P3ReqInfo.html#Questions

The Computer Genealogy Society of San Diego
P.O. Box 370357
San Diego CA 92137-0357
(619)670-0960
www.cgssd.org

Croatian Genealogical Society (CGS)
2527 San Carlos Ave.
San Carlos, CA 94070
(800)935-2429; (650)592-1190

The Cuban Index
P.O. Box 15839
San Luis Obispo, CA 93406
(909)473-0713; (909)864-7869

East Bay Genealogical Society (EBGS)
P.O. Box 20417
Oakland, CA 94620-0417
(510)482-2479; (510)451-9599
www.katpher.com/EBGS/
EBGS.html

Genealogical Society of Hispanic America
P.O. Box 2472
Santa Fe Springs, CA 90670-0472

**Genealogical Society of
Morongo Basin**
P.O. Box 234
Yucca Valley, CA 92286-
0234
(760)365-9201; (760)365-
2224
www.yuccavalley.com/
genealogy

**Genealogical Society of
North Orange County
California (GSNOCC)**
P.O. Box 706
Yorba Linda, CA 92885-0706

**Genealogical Society of
Santa Cruz County**
P.O. Box 72
Santa Cruz, CA 95063
(831)420-5794

**Genealogical Society of
Siskiyou County**
P.O. Box 225
Yreka, CA 96097
(530)842-6018

**German Genealogical
Society of America (GGSA)**
2125 Wright Ave, C-9
La Verne, CA 91750-0517
(909)593-0509; (909)593-
6786
www.feefhs.org/ggsa/frg-
ggsa.html

**German Research
Association (GRA), Inc.**
P.O. Box 711600
San Diego, CA 92171-1600
http://feefhs.org/gra/frg-
gra.html

**Hi-Desert Genealogical
Society**
P.O. Box 1271

Victorville, CA 92393
http://vvo.com/comm/hdgs.htm

Hispanic Family History
4522 Indian Hills
Riverside, CA 92501
(714)788-2188

**Hispanic Family History
Research**
4275 Edgewood
Riverside, CA 92506

**Immigrant Genealogical
Society (IGS)**
1310B Magnolia Blvd.
P.O. Box 7369
Burbank, CA 91510-7369
(818)848-3122
http://feefhs.org/igs/frg-
igs.html

**Jewish Genealogical Society
of Los Angeles (JGSLA)**
P.O. Box 55443
Sherman Oaks, CA 91413-
0443
(818)771-5554
www.jgsla.org

**Jewish Genealogical Society
of Orange County**
2370-1D Via Mariposa
Laguna Woods, CA 92653
(714)278-2896
www.jewishgen.org/jgsoc

**Jewish Genealogical Society
of Palm Springs**
40111 Portulaca Court
Palm Desert, CA 92260-2332
(760)340-6554

**Jewish Genealogical Society
of Sacramento**
2351 Wyda Way

Sacramento, CA 95825-1160
(916)486-0906 x361
www.jewishgen.org/jgs-
sacramento

**Los Angeles Westside
Genealogical Society**
P.O. Box 10447
Marina del Rey, CA 90295-
6447
www.genealogy-
la.com/lawgs.shtml

**Merced County
Genealogical Society**
P.O. Box 3061
Merced, CA 95340
(209)722-2169
www.rootsweb.com/~camcgs

**Orange County California
Genealogical Society**
P.O. Box 1587
Orange, CA 92856-1587
http://occgs.com

**Placer County Genealogical
Society**
P.O. Box 7385
Auburn, CA 95604-7385
(530)887-2646
www.webcom.com/gunruh/
pcgs.html

Portuguese Ancestry
1155 Santa Ana
Seaside, CA 93955
(408)899-2112
www.dholmes.com/ancestry.
html

**Questing Heirs
Genealogical Society, Inc.**
P.O. Box 15102
Long Beach, CA 90815-0102
www.cagenweb.com/questing

San Diego African-American Genealogy Research Group
P.O. Box 740240
San Diego, CA 92174-0240
(619)566-7566

San Diego Geneological Society
1050 Pioneer Way, Ste. E
El Cajon, CA 92020
(619)588-0065
www.rootsweb.com/~casdgs

San Diego Jewish Genealogical Society
P.O. Box 927089
San Diego, CA 92192-7089
(858)459-2074
www.homestead.com/sdjgs

San Fernando Valley Genealogical Society
P.O. Box 3486
Winnetka, CA 91396-3486
www.rootsweb.com/~casfvgs

San Francisco Bay Area Jewish Genealogical Society (SFBAJGS)
P.O. Box 471616
San Francisco, CA 94147-1616
(415)666-0188; (650)964-9657
www.jewishgen.org/sfbajgs

Santa Barbara County Genealogical Society
P.O. Box 1303
Goleta, CA 93116-1303
(805)884-9909
www.cagenweb.com/santabarbara/sbcgs

Santa Clara County Historical and Genealogical Society
3345 Lochinvar Ave
Santa Clara, CA 95051-5387
(408)615-2986
www.katpher.com/SCCHGS

Shasta County Genealogical Society
P.O. Box 994652
Redding, CA 96099-4652
(530)241-4540; (530)246-2858

Society of Hispanic Historical and Ancestral Research (SHHAR)
P.O. Box 5294
Fullerton, CA 92635
(714)773-1510

Society of Hispanic Historical and Ancestral Research (SHHAR)
P.O. Box 490
Midway City, CA 92655-0490

Solano County Genealogical Society
P.O. Box 2494
Fairfield, CA 94533
(707)446-6869

Sonoma County Genealogical Society
P.O. Box 2273
Santa Rosa, CA 95405-0273
(707)539-2858

South Bay Cities Genealogical Society
P.O. Box 11069
Torrance, CA 90510-1069
www.rootsweb.com/~casbcgs

South Orange County California Genealogical Society
P.O. Box 4513
Mission Viejo, CA 92690-4513
www.rootsweb.com/~casoccgs

Southern California Genealogical Society and Family Research Library
417 Irving Drive
Burbank, CA 91504
(818)843-7247
www.scgsgenealogy.com

Tuolumne County Genealogical Society, The Golden Roots of Mother Lode
P.O. Box 3956
Sonora, CA 95370
(209)532-1317

Vandenberg Genealogical Society
P.O. Box 81
Lompoc, CA 93438-0081
(805)737-1170; (805)733-2965

Additional genealogical and historical societies in California can be found at www.cagenweb.com/re/losangeles/langesoc.htm.

Colorado

Association of Professional Genealogists
P.O. Box 40393
Denver, CO 80204-0393
(303)422-9371
www.apgen.org

Boulder Genealogical Society
P.O. Box 3246
Boulder, CO 80307-3246
www.rootsweb.com/~bgs

Colorado Council of Genealogical Societies
P.O. Box 24379
Denver, CO 80224-0379
(303)642-7262
www.rootsweb.com/~coccgs

Colorado Genealogical Society (CGS)
P.O. Box 9218
Denver, CO 80209-0218
(303)571-1535

Columbine Genealogical and Historical Society
P.O. Box 2074
Littleton, CO 80161-2074
(303)795-1150
www.rootsweb.com/~cocghs/index.htm

The Foothills Genealogical Society
P.O. Box 150382
Lakewood, CO 80215-0382
www.rootsweb.com/~cofgs/index.htm

Genealogical Society of Hispanic American
P.O. Box 9606
Denver, CO 80209-0606
(719)561-0585; (310)390-0748

Jewish Genealogical Society of Colorado
6965 East Girard Ave.
Denver, CO 80224-2901
(303)756-6028
www.jewishgen.org/jgs-colorado

Mesa County Genealogical Society
P.O. Box 1506
Grand Junction, CO 81502
www.gj.net/mcgs

Pikes Peak Computer Genealogists
3958 Stanton Street
Pikes Peak, CO 80907-4537

Prowers County Genealogical Society
P.O. Box 928
Lamar, CO 81052-0928
(719)336-4507; (719)336-5408

Weld County Genealogical Society
P.O. Box 278
Greeley, CO 80632
www.rootsweb.com/~cowcgs

Additional genealogical societies can be found at www.rootsweb.com/~coccgs.

Connecticut

Afro-American Historical and Genealogical Society–Hartford
P.O. Box 320063
Hartford, CT 06132-0063

International Genealogy and Heraldry Fellowship of Rotarians (IFRG)
10 Fox Tail Ln.
Brookfield, CT 06804
(203)775-2854

Jewish Genealogical Society of Connecticut
P.O. Box 524

Middletown, CT 06457-0524
(203)268-2923
www.geocities.com/jgsct

Polish Genealogical Society of Connecticut
8 Lyle Rd.
New Britain, CT 06053-2104
(860)223-5596

Delaware

Delaware Genealogical Society
505 N. Market St.
Wilmington, DE 19801-3091
(302)655-7161; (302)292-0701
http://delgensoc.org

District of Columbia

Afro-American Historical and Genealogical Society, Inc. (AAHGS)
P.O. Box 73086
Washington, DC 20056
(202)234-5350; (202)829-8970
www.rootsweb.com/~mdaahgs

Jewish Genealogy Society of Greater Washington, DC
P.O. Box 31122
Bethesda, MD 20824-1122
(202)546-5239
www.jewishgen.org/jgsgw

National Society, Daughters of the American Colonists (DAC)
2205 Massachusetts Ave. NW
Washington, DC 20008
(202)667-3076

National Society, Daughters of the American Revolution (DAR)
1776 D St. NW
Washington, DC 20006-5392
(202)628-1776

Florida

Afro-American Historical and Genealogical Society–Central Florida Chapter
P.O. Box 1347
Orlando, FL 32802-1347
www.rootsweb.com/~flcfaahg

Charlotte County Genealogical Society
P.O. Box 2682
Port Charlotte, FL 33949-2682
(941)637-6208

Citrus County Genealogical Society
P.O. Box 2211
Inverness, FL 34451-2211
(352)382-2129

Dominican Institute of Genealogy (DIG)
EPS A306
P.O. Box 52-4121
Miami, FL 33184
(809)686-8849; (809)687-3992; (809)563-5277

Genealogical Society of Okaloosa County
P.O. Drawer 1175
Ft. Walton Beach, FL 32549
(850)243-4589; (850)689-1535

Historic Ocala/Marion County Genealogical Society
P.O. Box 1206
Ocala, FL 34478-1206

Jacksonville Jewish Genealogical Society
2710 Strasbourg Ct.
Ponte Vedra, FL 32082-2947
(904)285-4626

Jewish Genealogical Society of Broward County
P.O. Box 17251
Ft. Lauderdale, FL 33318-7251
(954)472-5455

Jewish Genealogical Society of Greater Miami, Inc.
5850 SW 13th St.
Miami, FL 33144-5704
(305)266-3350

Jewish Genealogical Society of Greater Orlando
P.O. Box 941332
Maitland, FL 32794-1332
(407)644-3566
http://members.aol.com/JGSGO

Jewish Genealogical Society of Palm Beach County, Inc.
P.O. Box 7796
Delray Beach, FL 33482-7796
(561)483-1060

Jewish Genealogical Society of Tallahassee
820 Live Oak Plantation Rd.
Tallahassee, FL 32312-2413
(850)385-3323

Jewish Genealogical Society of Tampa Bay
4270 Rudder Way
New Port Richey, FL 34652-4466
(727)539-4521 (days);
(727)842-5789 (evenings)

Lee County Genealogical Society
P.O. Box 150153
Cape Coral, FL 33915

Palm Beach County Genealogical Society
P.O. Box 1746
West Palm Beach, FL 33402
(561)832-3279

Pan-American Indian Association (Pan-Am)
8335 Sevigny Dr.
North Ft. Myers, FL 33917-1705
(941)731-7029; (941)543-7727

Southern Genealogist's Exchange Society (SGES)
P.O. Box 2801
Jacksonville, FL 32203
(904)387-9142

Suwannee Valley Genealogical Society
P.O. Box 967
Live Oak, FL 32064-0967
(904)362-0528

Georgia

Afro-American Historical and Genealogical Society - Atlanta
P.O. Box 162516
Atlanta, GA 30321-2516

**Bartow County
Genealogical Society**
P.O. Box 993
Cartersville, GA 30120-0993
(770)606-0706; (770)382-6676

**Cobb County Genealogical
Society (CCGS)**
P.O. Box 1413
Marietta, GA 30061-1413
(770)434-0507

**First Families of Georgia
1733-1797 (FFG)**
15 Watson Dr.
Newnan, GA 30263

**International Association of
Jewish Genealogical
Societies (IAJGS)**
4430 Mt. Paran Pkwy. NW
Atlanta, GA 30327-3747
(404)261-8662

**Jewish Genealogical Society
of Georgia, Inc.**
P.O. Box 681022
Marietta, GA 30068-0018
(404)352-8700
www.jewishgen.org/jgsg

**Northwest Georgia
Historical and Genealogical
Society (NGHGS)**
P.O. Box 5063
Rome, GA 30162-5063
(706)234-2110

**Savannah Area
Genealogical Association
(SAGA)**
P.O. Box 15385
Savannah, GA 31416
(912)354-2708

**Southwest Georgia
Genealogical Society**

(SGGS)
P.O. Box 4672
Albany, GA 31706
(912)435-9659

Hawaii

**Jewish Genealogical Society
of Hawaii**
237 Kuumele Pl
Kailua, HI 96734-2958
(808)262-0030

Idaho

**Kootenai County
Genealogical Society**
c/o Hayden Lake Library
8385 N. Government Way
Hayden Lake, ID 83835
(208)772-5612

Illinois

**Afro-American Historical
and Genealogical
Society–Little Egypt**
207 Lendview Dr.
Carbondale, IL 62901

**Afro-American Historical
and Genealogical Society
Chicago Chapter (AAHGS
PLR)**
P.O. Box 438652
Chicago, IL 60643
(773)821-6473; (773)487-1739

**Champaign-Urbana Jewish
Genealogy Society**
808 La Sell Dr.
Champaign, IL 61820-6820
(217)359-3102

**Daughters of Union
Veterans of the Civil War
1861-1865 (DUV)**
503 S. Walnut St.
Springfield, IL 62704-1932
(217)544-0616; (316)263-8026

**Effingham County
Genealogical and Historical
Society**
P.O. Box 1166
Effingham, IL 62401-1166
(217)342-2210

**Fulton County Historical
and Genealogical Society
(FCHGS)**
45 N. Park Dr.
Canton, IL 61520
(309)647-0771

**Hardin County Historical
and Genealogical Society**
P.O. Box 72
Elizabethtown, IL 62931
(618)287-2361; (618)289-4319

**Illiana Jewish Genealogical
Society (IJGS)**
P.O. Box 384
Flossmoor, IL 60422-0384
(708)957-9457; (708)748-5503
www.lincolnnet.net/ijgs

**Jewish Genealogical Society
of Illinois**
P.O. Box 515
Northbrook, IL 60065-0515
(312)666-0100
www.jewishgen.org/jgsi

**Knox County Genealogical
Society**

P.O. Box 13
Galesburg, IL 61402-0013
(309)483-6504

**Lawrence County
Genealogical Society**
Rt. 1, Box 44
Bridgeport, IL 62417
(618)945-8021

**McHenry County Illinois
Genealogical Society
(MCIGS)**
P.O. Box 184
Crystal Lake, IL 60039-0184
(815)653-9459

Indiana

**Adams County Indiana
Genealogical Society**
P.O. Box 33
Geneva, IN 46740
http://users.rootsweb.com/
~inadams/acigs.htm

**Allen County Genealogical
Society of Indiana**
P.O. Box 12003
Fort Wayne, IN 46862
www.ipfw.edu/ipfwhist/
historgs/acgsi.htm

**Jewish Genealogy Society of
Indiana**
P.O. Box 68280, Indianapolis,
IN 46268-0280
(317)388-0632

**Northwest Territory
Genealogical Society
(NTGS)**
Lewis Historical Library-
LRC 22
Vincennes University
Vincennes, IN 47591
(812)888-4330

**Owen County Historical &
Genealogical Society**
P.O. Box 569
Spencer, IN 47460
www.owen.in.us/owenhist/
owen.htm

Iowa

**American/Schleswig-
Holstein Heritage Society
(ASHHS)**
P.O. Box 313
Davenport, IA 52805-0313
(319)284-4184; (319)843-
2531

**Audubon County
Genealogical Society**
505 Brayton Street
Audubon, IA 50025-1301

**Dubuque County-Key City
Genealogical Society**
P.O. Box 13
Dubuque, IA 52004-0013

**Greene County
Genealogical Society**
P.O. Box 133
Jefferson, IA 50129
(515)386-8111; (515)386-
4784

**Howard-Winneshiek
Genealogy Society**
P.O. Box 362
Cresco, IA 52136
(319)547-4278

**Iowa Genealaogical Society,
Washington County
Chapter**
P.O. Box 446
Washington, IA 52353
(319)653-2726; (319)653-
6979

Iowa Genealogical Society
P.O. Box 7735
Des Moines, IA 50322-7735
(515)276-0287

**Iowa Genealogical Society,
Carroll County Chapter**
P.O. Box 21
Carroll, IA 51401
(712)792-4710; (712)792-
5880

**Iowa Genealogical Society,
Cherokee County Chapter**
P.O. Box 247
Cleghorn, IA 51014
(712)436-2624

**Iowa Genealogical Society,
Des Moines County
Chapter**
P.O. Box 493
Burlington, IA 52601

**Iowa Genealogical Society,
Humboldt County Chapter**
30 6th St. N.
Humboldt, IA 50548
(515)332-2155; (515)332-
1022

**Iowa Genealogical Society,
Keo Mah County Chapter**
Keo-Mah Library
Adjoining Penn Central Mall,
South Side
Oskaloosa, IA 52577-0616
(515)673-6507

**Iowa Genealogical Society,
Lucas County Chapter**
c/o Free Public Library
Family History Rm.
803 Braden
Chariton, IA 50049-1742
(515)774-5514; (515)535-
2704

**Iowa Genealogical Society,
Taylor County Chapter**
Box 8
Gravity, IA 50848
(712)537-2475

**Iowa Genealogical Society,
Wayne County Chapter**
c/o Le Compte Library
110 S. Franklin
Corydon, IA 50060-1518
(515)872-1621

**Iowa Genealogical Society,
Webster County Chapter**
P.O. Box 1584
Ft. Dodge, IA 50501

**Iowa Genealogy Society,
Van Buren County Chapter**
P.O. Box 158
Keosauqua, IA 52565
(319)293-3766

**Jefferson County
Genealogical Society**
2791 240th St
Fairfield, IA 52556-8518
(515)472-4667

**Lee County Genealogical
Society (of Iowa)**
P.O. Box 303
Keokuk, IA 52632-0303
(319)524-4121

**Mills County Genealogical
Society (MCGS)**
Glenwood Public Library
109 N. Vine
Glenwood, IA 51534
(712)527-5252

**Monroe County
Genealogical Society
(MCGS)**

Albia Public Library
203 Benton Ave. E
Albia, IA 52531
(515)932-5477; (515)932-
2469

**Palo Alto County
Genealogical Society**
Geneology Room
Smith Wellness/Library
Center
707 N. Superior,
Emmetsburg, IA 50536
(712)842-4009

**Pottawattamie County
Genealogical Society**
Box 394
Council Bluffs, IA 51502
(712)325 3121; (712)322-
1171

**Sac County Genealogical
Society**
P.O. Box 54
Sac City, IA 50583
(712)662 4094

**Scott County Iowa
Genealogical Society**
P.O. Box 3132
Davenport, IA 52808-3132

Kansas

**Cherokee County Kansas
Genealogical-Historical
Society**
100 S. Tennessee
P.O. Box 33
Columbus, KS 66725
(316)429-2992

**Cowley County
Genealogical Society**
1518 E. 12th St.

Winfield, KS 67156
(316)221-4591; (316)221-
4584

**Finney County
Genealogical Society**
P.O. Box 592
Garden City, KS 67846

**Flint Hills Genealogical
Society (FHGS)**
P.O. Box 555
Emporia, KS 66801

**Harper County
Genealogical Society**
1002 Oak
Harper, KS 67058
(316)896-2959

**Kansas Council of
Genealogical Societies**
P.O. Box 3858
Topeka, KS 66604-6858
(316)431-2125; (316)692-
3620

**Kansas Genealogical
Society**
Village Square Mall - 2601
Central
P.O. Box 103
Dodge City, KS 67801
(316)225-1951

**Montgomery County
Genealogical Society
(MCGS)**
Box 444
Coffeyville, KS 67337
(316)251-0716

**Osborne County
Genealogical and Historical
Society**
929 N. 2nd St

Osborne, KS 67473-1629
(785)346-2418

**Phillips County
Genealogical Society**
P.O. Box 114
Phillipsburg, KS 67661
(785)543-5325; (785)543-
2352

**Rawlins County
Genealogical Society**
102 S. 6th St.
P.O. Box 203
Atwood, KS 67730
(913)626-3805

**Reno County Genealogical
Society**
P.O. Box 5
Hutchinson, KS 67504-0005
(316)663-2804

**Revolutionary Mexican
Historical Society**
Sunset Ridge Road
Ozawkie, KS 66070
(913)945-3800

**Riley County Genealogical
Society**
2005 Claflin Road
Manhattan, KS 66502
(785)565-6495

Kentucky

**Adair County Genealogical
Society**
P.O. Box 613
Columbia, KY 42728
www.rootsweb.com/~kyacgs/
index.html

**Bullitt County Genealogical
Society**

P.O. Box 960
Shepherdsville, KY 40165
(502)538-6428

**Fayette County
Genealogical Society**
P.O. Box 8113
Lexington, KY 40533-8113
(606)278-9966

**Fulton County Genealogical
Society (FCGS)**
P.O. Box 1031
Fulton, KY 42041

**Hart County Historical
Society (HCHS)**
P.O. Box 606
Munfordville, KY 42765-
0606
(502)524-0101

**Hopkins County
Genealogical Society**
P.O. Box 51
Madisonville, KY 42431
(270)825-2680

**Kentucky Genealogical
Society (KGS)**
P.O. Box 153
Frankfort, KY 40602
(502)223-7541; (502)564-
8300

**Mason County Genealogical
Society (MCGS)**
P.O. Box 266
Maysville, KY 41056
(606)759-7257; (606)759-
5078

**National Society, Sons of
the American Revolution
(NSSAR)**
1000 S. 4th St.

Louisville, KY 40203
(502)589-1776

**Southern Kentucky
Genealogical Society
(SKGS)**
P.O. Box 1782
Bowling Green, KY 42102-
1782
(502)843-9452

**Webster County Historical
and Genealogical Society
(WCHGS)**
P.O. Box 215
Dixon, KY 42409
(502)639-5170; (502)639-
5042

Louisiana

**Ark-La-Tex Genealogical
Association (ALTGA)**
P.O. Box 4462
Shreveport, LA 71134-0462
(318)746-4598

**Comite des Archives de la
Louisiane (CAL)**
P.O. Box 44370
Baton Rouge, LA 70804
(225)387-4264; (225)355-
9906

**East Ascension
Genealogical and Historical
Society**
P.O. Box 1006
Gonzales, LA 70707-1006
(504)644-1869

**Evangeline Genealogical
and Historical Society
(EGHS)**
P.O. Box 664
Ville Platte, LA 70586
(318)457-0324

Genealogical Research
Society of New Orleans
(GRSNO)
P.O. Box 51791
New Orleans, LA 70151
(504)581-3153

Jefferson Genealogical
Society
P.O. Box 961
Metairie, LA 70004-0961
(504)466-4711

Jewish Genealogical Society
of New Orleans
P.O. Box 7811
Metairie, LA 70010
(504)888-3817
www.jewishgen.org/jgsno

Natchitoches Genealogical
and Historical Association
P.O. Box 1349
Natchitoches, LA 71458-
1349
(318)357-2235

Southwest Louisiana
Genealogical Society
(SWLGS)
P.O. Box 5652
Lake Charles, LA 70606-
5652
(318)477-3087

St. Bernard Genealogical
Society
P.O. Box 271
Chalmette, LA 70044
(504)279-1610

Maine

York County Genealogical
Society (YCGS)
P.O. Box 431

Eliot, ME 03903
(207)439-4243

Maryland

Afro-American Historical
and Genealogical Society—
Baltimore
P.O. Box 9366
Baltimore, MD 21229-3125

Afro-American Historical
and Genealogical Society—
Central Maryland
P.O. Box 2774
Columbia, MD 21045

The Afro-American
Historical and Genealogical
Society, Inc.—Prince
George's County, Maryland
Chapter
P.O. Box 44772
Ft. Washington, MD 20744-
9998
www.rootsweb.com/
~mdaahgs/pgcm

Afro-American Historical
and Genealogical Society
P.O. Box 1848
Germantown, MD 20875-
1848

Anne Arundel Genealogical
Society
P.O.Box 221
Pasadena, MD 21123
www.geocities.com/Yosemite
/Trails/4256/gensoc.htm

Baltimore County
Genealogical Society
P.O. Box 10085
Towson, MD 21285-0085
(410)750-9315; (410)665-
8769

Calvert County Genealogy
Society
P.O. Box 9
Sunderland, MD 20689
(410)535-0839

Frederick County
Genealogical Society
P.O. Box 234
Monrovia, MD 21770
(301)831-5781; (301)834-
9907

Genealogical Club of the
Montgomery County
Historical Society
Beall-Dawson House
103 W. Montgomery Ave.
Rockville, MD 20850
(301)340-2974; (301)762-
1492

Genealogical Society of
Cecil County
Box 11
Charlestown, MD 21914
(410)658-6062; (410)287-
8793

Howard County
Genealogical Society
P.O. Box 274
Columbia, MD 21045
(301)776-1393

Jewish Genealogy Society
of Greater Washington
(JGSGW)
P.O. Box 31122
Bethesda, MD 20824-1122
(301)362-2634

Jewish Genealogical Society
of Maryland
c/o Jewish Community
Center

3506 Gwynbrook Ave.
Owings Mills, MD 21117-
1498
(443)255-8228

**Lower Delmarva
Genealogical Society
(LDGS)**
P.O. Box 3602
Salisbury, MD 20802-3602
http://bay.intercom.net/ldgs/in
dex.html

**National Society
Descendants of Early
Quakers (NSDEQ)**
3202 Superior Ln.
Bowie, MD 20715-1919

**National Society Women
Descendants of the Ancient
and Honorable Artillery
Company (DAH)**
P.O. Box 453
Abingdon, MD 21009-0453
(410)515-1824

**Order of Americans of
Armorial Ancestry (OAAA)**
408 Sassafras Ct.
Bel Air, MD 21015-6022
(410)515-1824

**Prince Georges County
Genealogical Society**
P.O. Box 819
Bowie, MD 20718-0819
(301)773-9507

**St. Marys Genealogical
Society**
P.O. Box 1109
Leonardtown, MD 20650
(301)373-5764; (301)373-
8458

Massachusetts

**Acadian Cultural Society
(ACS)**
P.O. Box 2304
Fitchburg, MA 01420-8804

**Afro-American Historical
and Genealogical Society—
New England**
P.O. Box 93
Chelmsford, MA 01824

**American-Portuguese
Genealogical Society**
P.O. Box 644
Tanton, MA 02780

**Essex Society of
Genealogists (ESOG)**
P.O. Box 313
Lynnfield, MA 01940
(978)664-9279

**General Society of
Mayflower Descendants
(GSMD)**
P.O. Box 3297
Plymouth, MA 02361
(508)746-3188

**Jewish Genealogical Society
of Greater Boston**
P.O. Box 610366
Newton Highlands, MA
02461-0366
(617)796-8522
www.jgsgb.org

**Massachusetts Genealogical
Council**
P.O. Box 5393
Cochituate, MA 01778
(781)784-5664

**Plymouth County
Genealogists**
P.O. Box 7025
Brockton, MA 02301-7025
(508)588-2253

**Society for Spanish and
Portuguese History**
Boston College
Chestnut Hill, MA 021567

**Western Massachusetts
Genealogical Society
(WMGS)**
P.O. Box 80206
Forest Park Sta.
Springfield, MA 01108

Michigan

**Genealogical Society of
Flemish Americans (GSFA)**
18740 13 Mile Rd.
Roseville, MI 48066
(810)776-9579

**Jewish Genealogical Society
of Michigan**
30141 High Valley Rd.
Farmington Hills, MI 48331-
2169
(248)661-0668, (248)661-
8515
www.jgsmi.org

Minnesota

**The Anoka County
Genealogical Society**
P.O. Box 48126
Coon Rapids, MN 55448-
0126
http://freepages.genealogy.
rootsweb.com/
~relativememory

Czechoslovak Genealogical
Society International
(CGSI)
P.O. Box 16225
St. Paul, MN 55116
(651)739-7543; (612)941-
8746

Mississippi

Alcorn County
Genealogical Society
P.O. Box 1808
Corinth, MS 38835-1808
www.avsia.com/acgs

Order of the First Families
of Mississippi 1699–1817
P.O. Box 821
Natchez, MS 39121-0821
(601)442-0018

Tippah County Historical
and Genealogical Society
308 N. Commerce St.
Ripley, MS 38663
(601)837-7773

Missouri

Afro-American Historical
and Genealogical Society—
Landon Cheek
P.O. Box 23804
St. Louis, MO 63121-0804

Afro-American Historical
and Genealogical Society—
Magic
P.O. Box 300972
Kansas City, MO 64139-0972

American Family Records
Association (AFRA)
P.O. Box 15505
Kansas City, MO 64106

Audrain County Area
Genealogical Society
c/o Mexico-Audrain County
Library
305 W. Jackson St.
Mexico, MO 65265

Barry County Genealogical
and Historical Society
P.O. Box 291
Cassville, MO 65625

Daniel Boone and Frontier
Families Research
Association
1770 Little Bay Rd.
Hermann, MO 65041
(573)943-6423

Douglas County Historical
and Genealogical Society
(DCHGS)
P.O. Box 986
Ava, MO 65608
(417)683-5799

Harrison County
Genealogical Society
2307 Central St.
Bethany, MO 64424
(660)425-2459

Irish Genealogical
Foundation (IGF)
P.O. Box 7575
Kansas City, MO 64116
(816)454-2410

Jewish Genealogical Society
of St. Louis
Affiliated with United
Hebrew Congregation
13039 Musket Court
St. Louis, MO. 63146-4371
(314)434-2566
www.jewishgen.org/jgs-
StLouis

Laclede County
Genealogical Society
P.O. Box 350
Lebanon, MO 65536
(417)532-4069

Livingston County
Genealogical Society
c/o Livingston County
Library
450 Locust St.
Chillicothe, MO 64601
(816)646-0547

Oregon County
Genealogical Society
P.O. Box 324
Alton, MO 65606

Platte County Genealogical
Society
P.O. Box 103
Platte City, MO 64079
(816)858-3599

Ray County Genealogical
Association
901 W. Royle St.
Richmond, MO 64085
(816)776-2305; (816)776-
2872

Reynolds County
Genealogy and Historical
Society
P.O. Box 281
Ellington, MO 63638-0281
(573)663-3233; (573)663-
2675

St. Charles County
Genealogical Society
P.O. Box 715
St. Charles, MO 63302
(314)724-6668; (314)947-
1762

Texas County Genealogical and Historical Society
P.O. Box 12
Houston, MO 65483
(417)967-2946; (417)967-3484

Montana

Dawson County Tree Branches
A Genealogical Society
203 Mulberry Dr.
P.O. Box 1275
Glendive, MT 59330
(406)365-2026; (406)365-4014

Lewis and Clark County Genealogical Society
P.O. Box 5313
Helena, MT 59604
(406)442-2380; (406)443-6479

Nebraska

Adams County Genealogical Society
P.O. Box 424
Hastings, NE 68902-0424
(402)463-5838
http://incolor.inetnebr.com/achs/acgs.html

Cheyenne County Genealogical Society
P.O. Box 802
Sidney, NE 69162
(308)254-2325; (308)254-4732

Hooker County Genealogical Society
P.O. Box 280
Mullen, NE 69152

(308)546-2458; (308)546-2756

Nebraska State Genealogical Society
P.O. Box 5608
Lincoln, NE 68505

Saline County Genealogical Society
P.O. Box 24
Crete, NE 68333

Seward County Genealogical Society
P.O. Box 72
Seward, NE 68434-0072
(402)532-7635; (402)643-4830

Thayer County Genealogical Society
P.O. Box 387
Belvidere, NE 68315-0387
(402)768-7313; (402)768-6845

Washington County Genealogical Society
210 S. 17th
Blair, NE 68008
(402)426-3617; (402)478-4819

Nevada

Clark County Nevada Genealogical Society
P.O. Box 1929
Las Vegas, NV 89125-1929
(702)225-5838

Jewish Genealogical Society of Southern Nevada
P.O. Box 29342
Las Vegas, NV 89126

(702)871-9773; (702)363-8230

Pursuing Our Italian Names Together (POINT)
Box 14966, Dept. EA
Las Vegas, NV 89114-4966
(702)257-6628

New Hampshire

American-Canadian Genealogical Society (ACGS)
P.O. Box 6478
Manchester, NH 03108-6478
(603)622-1554
www.acgs.org

Genealogical and Historical Association of New Hampshire
P.O. Box 6478
Manchester, NH 03108
(603)622-1554

Jewish Genealogical Society of New Hampshire
P.O. Box 1019
Manchester, NH 03105-1019
(603)623-1212
www5.netmart.com/jgsnh

Piscataqua Pioneers (PP)
RR 2 Box 668
Center Barnstead, NH 03225-9103
(603)269-4371

Rockingham Society of Genealogists
P.O. Box 81
Exeter, NH 03833-0081
(603)436-5824

Strafford County Genealogical Society
P.O. Box 322
Dover, NH 03821-0322
(603)664-9090; (603)664-9080

New Jersey

Afro-American Historical and Genealogical Society–New Jersey
785 Sterling Dr. E.
South Orange, NJ 07079

Descendants of Colonial Tavern Keepers: Flagon and Trencher
850-A Thornhill Ct.
Lakewood, NJ 08701-6661
(732)920-3279

Genealogical Society of Bergen County
P.O. Box 432
Midland Park, NJ 07432

Jewish Genealogical Society of Bergen County, New Jersey (JGSBCNJ)
135 Chestnut Ridge Rd.
Montvale, NJ 07645
(201)384-8851
www.erosenbaum.netfirms.com/jgsbc

Jewish Genealogical Society of North Jersey
c/o YM-YWHA of North Jersey
1 Pike Rd.
Wayne, NJ 07470-2494
(973)595-0100 x236
http://community.nj.com/cc/jgsnorthjersey

Jewish Genealogical Society of Philadelphia
109 Society Hill
Cherry Hill, NJ 08003
(856)424-6860

Morris Area (NJ) Jewish Genealogical Society
21 Rolling Hill Dr.
Morristown, NJ 07960
(973)993-1744 (day);
(973)829-0242 (evening)

New Mexico

Alamogordo Genealogy Society
P.O. Box 734
Alamogordo, NM 88310-0734
http://hometown.aol.com/iwitchell/myhomepage/heritage.html

DeColores, Inc.
2633 Granite N.W.
Albuquerque, NM 87104

New York

Afro-American Historical and Genealogical Society–JSS Greater New York
P.O. Box 022340
Brooklyn, NY 11201-0049
(212)330-7882

Amenia Historical Society (AHS)
Rt. 22, P.O. Box 22
Amenia, NY 12501
(914)373-9376; (914)373-8069

Brookfield Township Historical Society (BTHS)

Box 143
Brookfield, NY 13314
(315)899-5893; (315)899-3348

Buffalo Irish Genealogical Society
245 Abbott Rd.
Buffalo, NY 14220
(716)662-1164

Capital District Genealogical Society (CDGS)
P.O. Box 2175
Empire State Plaza Sta..
Albany, NY 12220-0175
(518)482-9374; (518)438-7507

Center of Puerto Rican Studies
Hunter College East
695 Park Avenue
New York, NY 10021
(212)772-5686

Central New York Genealogical Society
P.O. Box 104
Colvin Sta.
Syracuse, NY 13205

Genealogical Association of English-Speaking Researchers in Europe (GAESRE)
HQ USAREUR
CMR 420, Box 142
APO New York, NY 09063

General Society, Sons of the Revolution (SR)
Fraunces Tavern Museum
54 Pearl St.
New York, NY 10004
(212)425-1776

Heritage and Genealogical Society of Montgomery County
Railroad St.
P.O. Box 1500
Fonda, NY 12068-1500
(518)853-8186; (518)853-8187

Hispanic Institute
612 W. 116th Street
New York, NY 10027

Hispanic Society of America
Audubon Terrace
613 W. 155th Street
New York, NY 10032
(212)926-2234

Italian Genealogy Group (IGG)
P.O. Box 626
Bethpage, NY 11714

Jewish Genealogical Society (JGS)
P.O. Box 6398
New York, NY 10128
(212)330-8257

Jewish Genealogical Society of Rochester, NY
265 Viennawood Drive
Rochester, NY 14618-4465
(716)271-2118

Jewish Genealogical Society, Inc.
15 W. 16th Street
New York, NY 1011
(212)294-8326
www.jgsny.org

Jewish Genealogy Society of Buffalo
3700 Main St.
Amherst, NY 14226-3233
(716)833-0743

Jewish Genealogy Society of Long Island
37 Westcliff Drive
Dix Hills, NY 11746-5627
(631)549-9532
www.jewishgen.org/jgsli

JGS of the Capital District
P.O. Box 5002
Albany, NY 12205-0002
(518)462-4815

La Casa De La Herencia Puertorriqueña
or
The Puerto Rican Heritage House
1 East 104th Street, 5th floor
New York, NY 10029
(212)722-2600

Livingston County Genealogical Society
P.O. Box 303
Nunda, NY 14517-0303

Madison County Historical Society (MCHS)
435 Main St.
P.O. Box 415
Oneida, NY 13421
(315)363-4136

Nassau County Historical Society (NCHS)
P.O. Box 207
Garden City, NY 11530
(516)747-1141

Niagara County Genealogical Society
215 Niagara St.
Lockport, NY 14094-2605
(716)439-7600

Northern New York American-Canadian

Genealogical Society (NNY-ACGS)
P.O. Box 1256
Plattsburgh, NY 12901-0120
(518)834-5401; (518)561-5728

Russian Nobility Association in America (RNAA)
971 1st Ave.
New York, NY 10022
(212)755-7528

Society of Daughters of Holland Dames (SDHD)
620 Park Ave.
New York, NY 10021
(212)249-4949; (212)410-3554

Western New York Genealogical Society (WNYGS)
P.O. Box 338
Hamburg, NY 14075

North Carolina

Afro-American Historical and Genealogical Society—NorthCarolina/ Piedmont-Triad
P.O. Box 36254
Greensboro, NC 27416

Afro-American Historical and Genealogical Society–Raleigh
4401 Lewinsburg No. A
Raleigh, NC 27604

Alleghany Historical-Genealogical Society (AHGS)
P.O. Box 817

Sparta, NC 28675
http://horace.ls.net/~ahgs

**American Society for
Ethnohistory**
Duke University Press
6697 College Station
Durham, NC 27708

**Descendants of the Signers
of the Declaration of
Independence (DSDI)**
202 Campden Way
Greenville, NC 27858

**Durham-Orange
Genealogical Society**
P.O. Box 4703
Chapel Hill, NC 27515-4703

**Forsyth County
Genealogical Society**
P.O. Box 5715
Winston-Salem, NC 27113
(919)724-0714

**North Carolina
Genealogical Society
(NCGS)**
P.O. Box 1492
Raleigh, NC 27602

**Onslow County
Genealogical Society**
P.O. Box 1739
Jacksonville, NC 28541-1739
(910)347-5287

**Randolph County
Genealogical Society**
P.O. Box 4394
Asheboro, NC 27204
(910)318-6815

**Society of Richmond
County Descendants
(SRCD)**

P.O. Box 848
Rockingham, NC 28380
(910)997-6641

Ohio

**Adams County
Genealogical Society**
P.O. Box 231
West Union, OH. 45693
www.rootsweb.com/~ohacgs

**African American
Genealogy Group of the
Miami Valley (AAGGMV)**
P.O. Box 485
Yellow Spring, OH 45387-
1224
(937)767-1949
www.coax.net/people/lwf/aag
gmv.htm

**The Alliance Genealogical
Society**
P.O. Box 3630
Alliance, OH 44601
www.rootsweb.com/~ohags

**Ashland County Ohio
Genealogy Society**
Box 681
Ashland OH 44805
www.rootsweb.com/
~ohacogs/indextwo.html

**Ashtabula County
Genealogical Society, Inc.
(OGS #83)**
860 Sherman Street
Geneva, OH 44041-9101
www.ashtabulagen.org

**Athens County Chapter of
the Ohio Genealogical**

Society
Athens County Historical
Society and Museum
65 N. Court Street
Athens, OH 45701-2506
(740)592-2280
http://frognet.net/~achsm

**Auglaize Co. Genealogical
Society**
P.O. Box 2021
Wapakoneta, OH 45895-0521
www.rootsweb.com/~
ohaugogs/index.html

**Columbus Jewish Historical
Society**
1175 College Ave.
Columbus OH 43209-2890
(614)238-6977
www.gcis.net/cjhs

**Jewish Genealogical Society
of Dayton**
P.O. Box 60338
Dayton OH 45406-0338
(937)277-3995

**Jewish Genealogical Society
of Greater Cincinnati**
3101 Clifton Ave.
Cincinnati, OH 45220-2488
(513)631-0233

**Jewish Genealogy Society
of Cleveland**
996 Eastlawn Drive
Highland Heights, OH
44143-3126
(440)449-2326

**Muskingum County
Genealogical Society
(MCGS)**

P.O. Box 2427
Zanesville, OH 43702-2427
(614)453-0391

**Ohio Genealogical Society
(OGS)**
713 S. Main St.
Mansfield, OH 44907-1644
(419)756-7294

**Ohio Genealogical Society,
Greene County Chapter**
P.O. Box 706
Xenia, OH 45385
(937)429-4012

**Palatines to America (Pal-
Am)**
611 E Weber Rd.
Columbus, OH 43211-1097
(614)267-4700

**Palatines to America (Pal-
Am)**
Capital University
Columbus, OH 43209-2394
(614)236-8281; (614)236-
8371

**Transylvania Saxon
Genealogy and Heritage
Society, Inc. (TSGHS)**
P.O. Box 3319
Youngstown, OH 44513-3319
http://feefhs.org/ah/hu/tsghs/
frgtsghs.html

**Wayne County
Genealogical Society**
Box 856
Wooster, OH 44691-0856
(330)264-2911

Oklahoma

**Adair County Historical &
Genealogical Association**

www.rootsweb.com/~okadair/
achga.html

**Logan County Genealogical
Society**
406 E. Oklahoma
P.O. Box 1419
Guthrie, OK 73044-1419
(405)282-8492; (405)586-
2551

**Major County Genealogical
Society**
P.O. Box 74
Fairview, OK 73737
(580)227-4500

**Pittsburg County
Genealogical and Historical
Society**
113 E. Carl Albert Pkwy.
McAlester, OK 74501-5039
(918)426-0388

**Society of Descendants of
Colonial Hispanics**
Brooks Enterprises
1718 West Robinson St., 1A
Normon, OK 73069-7311

Oregon

**Crook County Genealogical
Society**
246 N. Main St.
Prineville, OR 97754
(503)447-3715

**The Eugene Oregon Jewish
Genealogy Study Group**
2352 Van Ness
Eugene, OR 97403-1862
(541)345-8129
www.users.qwest.net/
~cfleishman/eugenegen.html

**Jewish Genealogical Society
of Oregon**
6651 S.W. Capitol Highway
Portland, OR 97219-1992
(503)244-0111
www.rootsweb.com/~orjgs

**Oregon Mennonite
Historical and Genealogical
Society (OMHGS)**
5326 Briar Knob Loop NE
Scotts Mills, OR 97375-9615
(503)873-6406

Pennsylvania

**African American
Genealogical Group**
P.O. Box 17
Philadelphia, PA
(215)572-6063
www.aagg.org

**Afro-American Historical
and Genealogical Society—
Western Pennsylvania**
P.O. Box 5707
Pittsburgh, PA 15208

**Blair County Genealogical
Society**
431 Scotch Valley Rd.
Hollidaysburg, PA 16648
(814)696-3492

**Bucks County Genealogical
Society (BCGS)**
P.O. Box 1092
Doylestown, PA 18901
(215)230-9410

**Centre County
Genealogical Society**
P.O. Box 1135
State College, PA 16804
(814)466-2246

Crawford County Genealogical Society
848 N. Main St.
Meadville, PA 16335
(814)724-6080

Genealogical Research Society of Northeastern Pennsylvania
210 Grant St.
P.O. Box 1
Olyphant, PA 18447-0001
(570)383-7661

Genealogical Society of Southwestern Pennsylvania
P.O. Box 894
Washington, PA 15301-0894
(724)222-7022

Jewish Genealogical Society of Greater Philadelphia (JGSGP)
109 Society Hill
Cherry Hill, NJ 08003-2402
(856)424-6860
www.jewishgen.org/jgsp

Jewish Genealogical Society of Pittsburgh
2127-31 5th Ave.
Pittsburgh, PA 15219-5505
(412)471-0772

Lancaster Mennonite Historical Society (LMHS)
2215 Millstream Rd.
Lancaster, PA 17602-1499
(717)393-9745; (717)393-9746

Mercer County Genealogical Society
P.O. Box 812
Sharon, PA 16146
(412)346-5117; (412)981-4360

Northampton County Historical and Genealogical Society (NCHGS)
107 S. 4th St.
Easton, PA 18042
(610)253-1222

Venango County Genealogical Club
2 Central Ave
Oil City, PA 16301-2734

Puerto Rico

Arzobispado de San Juan
Apartado 1967
San Juan, PR 00902-1967
(809)727-7373

Instituto de Cultura Puertorriqueña
Av. Ponce de Leo 500
P.O. Box 4184
San Juan, PR 00905

Sociedad Puertorriqueña De Genealogia
Calle GEA - 9
Urb. Apolo
Guaynabo, PR 00657

Sociedad Puertoriqueña De Genealogia
103 Avenida Universidad
Suite No. 239
Rio Piedras, PR 00925

Rhode Island

American-French Genealogical Society (AFGS)
Box 2113
Pawtucket, RI 02861
(401)765-6141
www.afgs.org

South Carolina

Afro-American Historical and Genealogical Society–Columbia
P.O. Box 8836
Columbia, SC 29202

Aiken-Barnwell Genealogical Society
P.O. Box 415
Aiken, SC 29802-0415
(803)649-9273
www.ifx.net/~lhutto/page2.html

South Carolina Genealogical Society, Old Edgefield District Chapter
104 Courthouse Sq.
P.O. Box 546
Edgefield, SC 29824
(803)637-4010

Sumter County Genealogical Society
219 W. Liberty St.
P.O. Box 2543
Sumter, SC 29150
(803)773-9144

South Dakota

Aberdeen Area Genealogical Society
P.O. Box 493
Aberdeen, SD 57402-0493
www.rootsweb.com/~sdbrown/genrsrc.html#AAGS

Hyde County Historical and Genealogical Society (HCHGS)
P.O. Box 392
113 Iowa South
Highmore, SD 57345-0392
(605)852-3103

Tennessee

Afro-American Historical and Genealogical Society - Nashville
3047 Woodlawn Dr.
Nashville, TN 37215

Carroll County Historical Society (CCHS)
640 N. Main St.
McKenzie, TN 38201
(901)352-3510

Obion County Historical Society
P.O. Box 241
Union City, TN 38281
(901)885-2322

Roane County Genealogical Society
P.O. Box 297
Kingston, TN 37763
(423)376-9905; (423)376-6018

Weakley County Genealogical Society (WCGS)
P.O. Box 894
Martin, TN 38237

Texas

Afro-American Historical and Genealogical Society–Houston
P.O. Box 750877
Houston, TX 77275-0877

Anderson County Genealogical Society
P.O. Box 2045
Palestine, TX 75802-2045
users.tvec.net/bonniew/acgs/acgs2.htm

Angelina County Genealogical Society of Texas
P.O. Box 150631
Lufkin, TX 75915-0631
www.rootsweb.com/~txacgs

Arlington Genealogical Society
c/o Arlington Public Library, Genealogy Collection
101 E. Abram St.
Arlington, TX 76010
(817)459-6900
www.users.ticnet.com/stevem/ags.htm

Athens Genealogical Organization
510 Seneca Drive
Athens, TX 75751
(903)675-2878
http://bunhun.freeyellow.com/page2.html

The Austin Genealogical Society
P.O. Box 1507
Austin, TX 78767-1507
www.AustinTxGenSoc.org

Canary Islands Descendants of San Antonio
305 West Kings Highway
San Antonio, TX 78212

Cass County Genealogical Society
P.O. Box 880
Atlanta, TX 75551
(903)796-2107

Cherokee County Genealogical Society
P.O. Box 1332
Jacksonville, TX 75766
(409)824-2485; (903)586-8750

Comal County Genealogy Society
P.O. Box 310160
New Braunfels, TX 78131-0160
(210)625-8766; (512)259-1355

Dallas Jewish Historical Society, Genealogy Division
7900 Northaven Road
Dallas, TX 75230-3392
(214)369-8373
www.dvjc.org/history/genealogy.shtml

Denton County Genealogical Society
P.O. Box 424707
TWU Station
Denton, TX 76204
(940)382-0464

East Bell County Genealogical Society (EBCGS)
2613 Forest Tr.
Temple, TX 76502;
(254)773-4711

Ft. Bend County Genealogical Society
P.O. Box 274
Richmond, TX 77469

Genealogical Society of Kendall County
P.O. Box 623
Boerne, TX 78006-0623

Greater Houston Jewish Genealogical Society
7115 Belle Park Dr.
Houston, TX 77072-2417
(281)495-9211

Hispanic Genealogical Society of Houston
P.O. Box 231271
Houston, Texas 77223-1271

Houston County Historical Commission
Houston County Courthouse, 1st Fl.
Crockett, TX 75835
(409)544-3255; (409)544-3269

Hutchinson County Genealogical Society
625 Weatherly St.
Borger, TX 79007
(806)274-3530

Kerrville Genealogical Society
505 Water St.
Kerrville, TX 78028
(830)257-8422

Lamar County Genealogical Society
P.J.C. Box 187-2400
Clarksville
Paris, TX 75460
(903)782-0448

Los Bexareños Genealogical Society
4867 Castle Sword
San Antonio, TX 78218
P.O. Box 1935
San Antonio, TX 78297
(210)822-1526

Mid-Cities Genealogical Society (MCGS)
P.O. Box 407
Bedford, TX 76095-0407
(817)868-0920

Montgomery County Genealogical Society (MCGS)
P.O. Box 867
Conroe, TX 77305-0867
(409)756-8625

San Antonio Jewish Genealogical Society
12500 NW Military Dr.
San Antonio, TX 78231-1871
(210)302-6860

South Plains Genealogical Society (SPGS)
P.O. Box 6607
Lubbock, TX 79493-6607
(806)747-1319; (806)793-7191

Spanish American Genealogical Association (SAGA)
9601 Cosner
Corpus Christi, TX 78415
(512)854-9145

Stephens County Genealogical Society
P.O. Box 350
Breckenridge, TX 76424
(254)559-8471; (254)559-2723

Texas State Genealogical Society
3219 Meadow Oaks Dr.
Temple, TX 76502-1752
(254)778-2073

Walker County Genealogical Society
P.O. Box 1295
Huntsville, TX 77342
(409)294-9431; (409)295-5551

Ward County Genealogical Society
400 E. 4th St.
Monahans, TX 79756
(915)943-6312

Wood County Genealogical Society
P.O. Box 832
Quitman, TX 75783
(903)763-4191

Utah

Armenian Genealogical Society (AMGS)
P.O. Box 1383
Provo, UT 84603-1383
http://feefhs.org/am/frg-amgs.html

The Cuban Genealogical Society
2552 Tamara Drive
P.O. Box 2650
Salt Lake City, UT 84110-2650
(801)968-7312

Dutch Family Heritage Society (DFHS)
2463 Ledgewood Dr.
West Jordan, UT 84084
(801)967-8400

Federation of East European Family History Societies (FEEFHS)
P.O. Box 510898
Salt Lake City, UT 84151-0898
(801)288-1501; (801)284-5917

Genealogical Institute (GI)
P.O. Box 129
Tremonton, UT 84337
(800)377-6058

Genealogical Society of Utah
or **Genealogical Society of the Church of Jesus Christ of Latter-day Saints**
or **Family and Church History Department of the Church of Jesus Christ of Latter-Day Saints**
50 E. North Temple
Salt Lake City, UT 84150
(801)240-2331
www.familysearch.org

Institute of Genealogy and History for Latin America (IGHL)
316 West 500 North
St. George, UT 84770
(801)628-4944

Progenitor Genealogical Society (PGS)
P.O. Box 345
Paradise, UT 84328
(435)245-9386

Vermont

Vermont French Canadian Genealogical Society
P.O. Box 65128
Burlington, VT 05406-5128
http://members.aol.com/ vtfcgs/genealogy

Welsh-American Genealogical Society
60 Norton Ave.
Poultney, VT 05764-1029

Virginia

Afro-American Historical and Genealogical Society - Hampton Roads

P.O. Box 2448
Newport News, VA 23609-2448

Afro-American Historical and Genealogical Society - Richmond
5858 Westover Dr. No. A
Richmond, VA 23225

Afro-American Historical and Genealogical Society - Tidewater
P.O. Box 10522
Virginia Beach, VA 23450

Genealogical Society of Page County, Virginia
P.O. Box 734
Luray, VA 22835
(540)743-6867; (540)778-2111

Jewish Genealogical Society of Tidewater
7300 Newport Ave.
Norfolk, VA 23505
(757)351-2190

Mt. Vernon Genealogical Society
1500 Shenandoah Rd.
Alexandria, VA 22308-0000
(703)765-4573; (703)765-4645

Presidential Families of America (PFA)
1435 Willow Lake Dr.
Charlottesville, VA 22902

Virginia Genealogical Society
5001 W. Broad St., No. 115
Richmond, VA 23230-3023
(804)285-8954

Washington

Jewish Genealogical Society of Washington State
3633-86th St SE
Mercer Island, WA 98040-3612
(206)232-2666
http://members.tripod.com/ ~JGSWS

Okanogan County Genealogical Society
263 Old Riverside Hwy.
Omak, WA 98841
(509)826-1686; (509)422-3944

Pacific County Genealogical Society
P.O. Box 843
Ocean Park, WA 98640
(360)665-2737; (360)665-4495

Whitman County Genealogical Society
P.O. Box 393
Pullman, WA 99163-0393
(509)332-2386

West Virginia

Kanawha Valley Genealogical Society (KVGS)
P.O. Box 8555
South Charleston, WV 25303
(304)776-1037

Mingo County Genealogical Society
P.O. Box 2581
Williamson, WV 25661
(304)237-4646

Morgan County Historical and Genealogical Society
P.O. Box 52
Berkeley Springs, WV 25411
(304)258-2569

Nicholas County Historical and Genealogical Society
P.O. Box 443
Summersville, WV 26651
(304)872-2478; (304)872-1096

West Virginia Genealogical Society and Library
P.O. Box 249
Elkview, WV 25071
(304)965-1179

Wetzel County Genealogical Society
P.O. Box 464
New Martinsville, WV 26155

Wisconsin

Ashland and Bayfield Counties Wisconsin Genealogical Society
Rte. 1, Box 139
Mason, WI 54856
(715)765-4597

Bay Area Genealogical Society (BAGS)
P.O. Box 283
Green Bay, WI 54305-0283
(414)494-9286

Chippewa County Genealogical Society
1427 Hilltop Blvd.
Chippewa Falls, WI 54729
(715)723-3715

French Canadian/Acadian Genealogists of Wisconsin

P.O. Box 414
Hales Corners, WI 53130-0414
(414)284-5636
www.fcgw.org

Grant County Genealogical Society
P.O. Box 281
Dickeyville, WI 53808-0281
(608)568-3124

Sauk County Historical Society (SCHS)
P.O. Box 651
Baraboo, WI 53913
(608)356-1001

Sheboygan County Genealogical Society (SCGS)
518 Water St,
Sheboygan Falls, WI 53085-1455
(414)467-4667

Stevens Point Area Genealogical Society
c/o Portage County Library
1001 Main St.
Stevens Point, WI 54481
(715)341-1555; (715)346-1548

Walworth County Genealogical Society (WCGS)
P.O. Box 159
Delavan, WI 53115-0159
(608)752-8816; (414)728-3719

Waukesha County Genealogical Society
P.O. Box 1541
Waukesha, WI 53187-1541

Wisconsin Jewish Genealogical Society
9280 N. Fairway Drive
Milwaukee, WI 53217-1317
(414)351-2190

Wisconsin Slovak Historical Society (WSHS)
P.O. Box 164
Cudahy, WI 53110-0164
(414)697-4038

Wyoming

Fremont County Genealogical Society
1330 W. Park Ave.
Riverton, WY 82501
(307)856-5310

Additional genealogical and historical societies in the U.S. can be found at www. daddezio.com/society/hill.

VENEZUELA

Family History Center Church of Latter Day Saints
2da Avenida de Campo Alegre, No.14
Urb. Campo Alegre, Chacao
Apartado 62569, Caracas

OCEI
Avenida Boyaca
Edf. Fundacion La Salle, P.B. 3
Caracas

Venezuelan Institute of Genealogy (VIG)
or
Instituto Venezolano de

Genealogia (IVG)
10a Transversal
No. 2 Altamira
Caracas 1061-A
58 2 2635217

INVESTIGATIVE JOURNALISM AND PRIVATE INVESTIGATIVE ORGANIZATIONS

CANADA

Canadian Association of Journalists (CAJ)
St. Patrick's Bldg.
1125 Colonel By Dr.
Carleton University
Ottawa, ON K1S 5B6
Canada
(613)526-8061
www.eagle.ca/caj

UNITED KINGDOM

Association of British Investigators (ABI)
10 Bonner Hill Rd.
ABI House
Kingston upon Thames
Surrey KT1 3EP,
England
44 181 5463368
www.assoc-britishinvestigators.org.uk

Institute of Professional Investigators
21 Bloomsbury Way
London WC1A 2TH
44(0)20 7242 6696
www.ipi.org.uk

World Association of Detectives, Inc. (WAD)
P.O. Box 333
Brough HU15 1XL
England
44 1482 665577
www.wad.net

UNITED STATES

Association of Christian Investigators
2553 Jackson Keller, Suite 200
San Antonio, TX 78230
(210)342-0509
www.a-c-i.org

Association of Professional Investigators and Security Providers
P.O. Box 4244
Metuchen, NJ 08840
(732)494-1266; (570)223-2971

Center for Investigative Reporting (CIR)
500 Howard St., Ste. 206, 2nd Fl.
San Francisco, CA 94105-3008
(415)543-1200
www.muckraker.org

Council of International Investigators (CII)
2150 North 107th St., No. 205
Seattle, WA 98133-9009
(888)759-8884; (206)361-8869
www.cii2.org

Find the Children
3030 Nebraska Ave., No. 207
Santa Monica, CA 90404-4111

(888)477-6721; (310)998-8444
www.findthechildren.com

Fund for Investigative Journalism (FIJ)
P.O. Box 40339
Washington, DC 20016
(202)362-0260
www.fij.org

Global Investigators Network
P.O. Box 2434
La Grange, IL 60525
(708)579-1776
www.ginetwork.com

International Security and Detective Alliance (ISDA)
P.O. Box 6303
Corpus Christi, TX 78466-6303
(361)888-8060

Investigative Reporters and Editors (IRE), Inc.
School of Journalism
138 Neff Annex
Columbia, MO 65211
(573)882-2042
www.ire.org

ION (Investigators Online Network)
P.O. Box 40970
Mesa, AZ 85274-0970
(800)338-3463; (480)730-8088
www.ioninc.com

National Association of Investigative Specialists (NAIS)
P.O. Box 33244
Austin, TX 78764
(512)719-3595
www.pimall.com/nais/home.html

National Association of
Traffic Accident
Reconstructionists and
Investigators
(NATARI)
717 Cypress Ct.
North Wales, PA 19454-1167
(215)672-4784
www.natari.org

National Council of
Investigation and Security
Services
1730 M Street, N.W.
Suite 200
Washington, DC 20036
www.nciss.com

Society of Professional
Investigators
INVESTICORP, INC.
705 Bedford Ave.
Suite C
Bellmore, NY 11710
www.spionline.org

World Association of
Detectives (WAD), Inc.
P.O. Box 441000-301
Aurora, CO 80044
(800)962-0516
www.wad.net

Arizona

Arizona Association of
Licensed Private
Investigators, Inc.
P.O. Box 2129
Phoenix, AZ 85001
www.aalpi.com

California

Certified Investigative
Professionals, Inc.

140 Encinitas Blvd., No. 440
Encinitas, CA 92024
www.cipi.org

Colorado

Professional Private
Investigators Association of
Colorado
P.O. Box 9801
Denver, CO 80209
(303)430-4802
www.ppiac.org

Connecticut

Connecticut Association of
Licensed Private
Investigators (CALPI)
136 Stratton Brook Rd
Simsbury, CT. 06070-2309
(860)651-4200
http://users.ntplx.net/~calpi

Florida

Florida Association of
Licensed Investigators
P.O. Box 12483
Tallahassee, FL 32317
(888)845-3254
www.fali.com

Northwest Florida
Association of Private
Investigators
www.watson-co.com/nwfapi

South Florida Investigators
Association
P.O. Box 891
Fort Lauderdale, FL 33302
http://sofloridainvestigators.
org

Illinois

Associated Detectives of
Illinois, Inc.
4350 Di Paolo Center
Suite #D
Glenview, IL 60025
(847)824-8400
www.the-adi.com

Indiana

Indiana Association of
Professional Investigators,
Inc.
(317)248-9295; (317)823-
2244
www.IN.gov/iapi

Indiana Society of
Professional Investigators
984 Logan Street, Ste. 1
Noblesville, IN 46060
www.indianainvestigators.com

Iowa

Iowa Association of Private
Investigators
P.O. Box 4924
Des Moines, IA 50306
(515)848-3401
www.iowa-investigators.com

Kansas

Kansas Association of
Private Investigators
P.O. Box 2111
Overland Park, KS 66201-
1111
(913)294-4300
www.kapi.org

Louisiana

Louisians Private
Investigators Association,

Inc.
P.O. Box 3311
Baton Rouge, LA 70821-
3311
www.lpia.net

Maine

**Maine Licensed Private
Investigators Association**
P.O. Box 1645
Portland, ME 04104-1645;
(207)772-3999 Ext. 3
http://mlpia.org

Massachusetts

**Center for Campus
Organizing (CCO)**
165 Friend St. M/S, No. 1
Boston, MA 02114-2025
(617)725-2886

**Licensed Privated
Detectives Association of
Massachusetts**
140 Wood Rd Suite 200
Braintree, MA 02184
http://lpdam.org

Michigan

**Michigan Council of
Private Investigators**
P.O. Box 790
Garden City, MI 48136
(800)266.MCPI
www.mcpihome.com

Minnesota

**Minnesota Association of
Private Investigators**
411 Lexington Parkway,
Suite G
St. Paul, MN 55104
www.mapi.org

Mississippi

**Mississippi Professional
Investigators Association**
P.O. Box 1012
Tupelo, MS 38802-1012
www.mpia.com

Nevada

**Nevada Investigators
Association**
P.O. Box 94735
Las Vegas, NV 89193
(702)669-4847

New Hampshire

**New Hampshire League of
Investigators, Inc.**
P.O. Box 108
Concord, NH 03302
(603)753-6734
www.mv.com/ipusers/magee

New Jersey

**New Jersey Licensed
Private Investigators
Association**
Eastern Associates
P.O. Box 10781
Fairfield, NJ 07004
www.njlpia.com
www.njlpia.net
www.njlpia.org

New York

**Associated Licensed
Detectives of New York
State**
35 West 35th Street
New York, NY 10001
(212)947-3700
www.aldonys.org

North Carolina

**North Carolina Association
of Private Investigators
(NCAPI)**
P.O. Box 61238
Raleigh, NC 27661-1238
www.ncapi.org

Ohio

**Ohio Association of
Security and Investigation
Services (OASIS)**
41 South High Street
Columbus, OH 43215
(614)227-4595
www.JHandA.com/oasis

Oklahoma

**Oklahoma Private
Investigators Association**
P.O. Box 4120
Tulsa, OK 74159-0120
(800)299-2241; (405)235-
0214
www.opia.com

Oregon

**Oregon Association of
Licensed Investigators, Inc.**
P.O. Box 2705
Portland, OR 97208
(503)224-3531
www.oali.org

Pennsylvania

**Pennsylvania Association of
Licensed Investigators
(PALI)**
P.O. Box 60036
Harrisburg, PA 17106-0036
(800)443-0824
www.pali.org

Rhode Island

**Licensed Private Detectives
Association of Rhode Island**
255 Main Street
Pawtucket, RI 02860
(401)727-2290
http://lpdari.org

South Carolina

**South Carolina Association
of Legal Investigators**
P.O. Box 5012
Anderson, SC 29623-5012
(864)231-8446
www.scalinv.com

Texas

**North Texas Private
Investigators Association**
P.O. Box 59997
Dallas, TX 75229
www.ntpia.org

**South Texas Private
Investigators**
P.O. Box 58172
Webster, TX 77598
(281)351-0530

**Texas Association of
Licensed Investigators, Inc.**
P.O. Box 702641
Dallas, TX 75370-2641
(877)444-TALI; (972)492-8801
www.tali.org

Utah

**Private Investigators
Association of Utah (PIAU)**
1733 West 126 South, #223
Riverton, UT 84065
(801)467-9500
www.piau.com

Virginia

**Coalition of Virginia
Private Investigator and
Security Associations**
P.O. Box 7600
Alexandria, VA 22307
(703)360-4848

**Private Investigator
Business Owners
Association of Virginia**
P.O. Box 7600
Alexandria, VA 22307-0600
(703)360-4848

**Private Investigators
Association of Virginia
(PIAVA)**
10617 Jones St., Ste. 201-B
Fairfax, VA 22030-5116
(703)273-1200
www.pimall.com/piav

Washington

**Pacific Northwest
Association of Investigators,
Inc. (PNAI)**
P.O. Box 61592
Vancouver, WA 98666-1592
www.pnai.com

**Washington Association of
Legal Investigators**
10002 Aurora Avenue
Suite 1133
Seattle, WA 98133-7225
(206)625-9254
www.WALI.org

Wisconsin

**Professional Association of
Wisconsin Licensed
Investigators (PAWLI)**
P.O. Box 20817
Milwaukee WI 53220
www.pawli.com

ORGANIZATIONS INVOLVED IN PRIVACY RIGHTS, COMPUTER PRIVACY, OR FREEDOM OF INFORMATION

**American Booksellers
Foundation for Free
Expression (BFFE)**
139 Fulton St., Ste. 302
New York, NY 10038
(212)587-4025
www.abffe.org

**American Society for
Industrial Security (ASIS
International)**
1625 Prince St.
Alexandria, VA 22314-2818
(703)519-6200
www.asisonline.org

**American Society of Access
Professionals (ASAP)**
1444 I Street, Ste. 700
Washington, DC 20005-6542
(202)712-9054
www.AccessPro.org

**American Society of
Newspaper Editors (ASNE)**
11690B Sunrise Valley Dr.
Reston, VA 20191-1409
(703)453-1122
www.asne.org

**Arab Permanent
Committee for Information
(APCI)**
c/o LEA
Information Administration
Midan Attahrir, Tahrir Sq.
P.O. Box 11642
Cairo, Egypt
20 2 5750511; 20 2 5752966

Associated Press Broadcast Services (APB)
1825 K Street NW, Ste. 710
Washington, DC 20006-1202
(800)821-4747(202)736-1100
www.apbroadcast.com

Associated Press Managing Editors (APME)
50 Rockefeller Plz.
New York, NY 10020
(212)621-1500
www.apme.com/index.shtml

Association for Federal Information Resources Management (AFFIRM)
c/o Intermertics
1595 Spring Hill Rd., Ste. 600
Vienna, VA 22182-2228
(703)827-2606
www.affirm.org

Australian Civil Liberties Union (ACLU)
Box 1137
Carlton, VIC 3053
Australia
61 3 93478671
www.go.to./aclu

Canadian Society for Industrial Security Inc. (CSIS)
Societe Canadienne de la Surete Industrielle (SCSI)
2700 Lancaster Rd., Unit 102
Ottawa, ON, Canada K1B 4T7
(800)461-7748; (613)738-1920
www.csis-scsi.org

Catholic Press Association (CPA) of the United States and Canada
3555 Veterans Memorial

Hwy., Unit 0
Ronkonkoma, NY 11779
(516)471-4730
http://catholicpress.org

The Children's Legal Centre (CLC)
University Of Essex
Wivenhoe Park
Colchester
Essex CO4 3SQ, England
44 1206 873820; 44 1206 872466
www2.essex.ac.uk/clc

Committee to Protect Journalists (CPJ)
330 7th Ave., 12th Fl.
New York, NY 10001
(212)465-1004; (212)465-9344
www.cpj.org

Computer Security Institute (CSI)
600 Harrison St.
San Francisco, CA 94107
(415)947-6320
www.gocsi.com

Freedom of Information Center (FOI)
University of Missouri
127 Neff Annex
Columbia, MO 65211
(573)882-4856
http://web.missouri.edu/~foiwww

Freedom of Information Clearinghouse (FOIC)
P.O. Box 19367
Washington, DC 20036
(202)588-7790
www.citizen.org/litigation/free_info

IEEE Computer Society (CS)
1730 Massachusetts Ave. NW
Washington, DC 20036-1992
(202)371-0101
http://computer.org

Information Systems Security Association (ISSA)
7044 S. 13th St.
Oak Creek, WI 53154
(800)370-4772; (414)768-8000
www.issa.org

Institute of Internal Auditors (IIA)
249 Maitland Ave.
Altamonte Springs, FL 32701-4201
(407)830-7600
www.theiia.org

International Association for Computer Systems Security (IACSS)
6 Swathmore Ln.
Dix Hills, NY 11746
(631)499-1616
www.iacss.com

International Federation of Free Journalists (IFFJ)
4 Overton Rd.
London N14 4SY, England
44 181 3602991

Internet Society
11150 Sunset Hills Rd., Ste. 100
Reston, VA 20190-5321
(703)326-9880
www.isoc.org

Investigative Reporters and Editors
138 Neff Annex

University of Missouri
School of Journalism
Columbia, MO 65211
(573)882-2042
www.ire.org

**Joint Stock Company
International Media Center
STB**
1 Shevtsova St.
03773 Kyiv, Ukraine
380 44 4462060; 380 44
4462060

**Journalism Education
Association**
Kansas State University
103 Kedzie Hall
Manhattan, KS 66506-1505
(785)532-5532; (785)532-
7822
www.jea.org

LibertyTree Network (LTN)
100 Swan Way
Oakland, CA 94621-1428
(800)927-8733; (510)568-
6047
www.liberty-tree.org

**Media Access Project
(MAP)**
950 18th St. NW
Washington, DC 20006-2202
(202)232-4300
www.mediaaccess.org

The Media Institute
1000 Potomac St., N.W. Suite
301
Washington, DC 20007
(202)298-7512
www.mediainst.org

**Media Institute of Southern
Africa (MISA)**

Private Bag 13386
Windhoek, Namibia
264 (61)232975
www.misanet.org

**National Association of
Attorneys General**
750 First St., N.E. Suite 1100
Washington, DC 20002
(202)326-6000
www.naag.org

**National Association to
Protect Individual Rights**
P.O. Box 7371
Fairfax Station, VA 22039-
7371
(703)425-5347

**National Center for
Computer Crime Data
(NCCCD)**
1222 17th Ave., Ste. B
Santa Cruz, CA 95062
(408)475-4457

**National Center for
Freedom of Information
Studies**
Loyola University of Chicago
820 N. Michigan Ave.
Chicago, IL 60611
(312)915-8662

**National Employment
Lawyers Association
(NELA)**
600 Harrison St., Ste. 535
San Francisco, CA 94107
(415)227-4655
www.nela.org/home_ns.htm

**National Freedom of
Information Coalition**
400 S. Record St., Sixth
Floor

Dallas, TX 75202
(214)977-6658
www.nfoic.org

**National Institute for
Computer-Assisted
Reporting**
University of Missouri
School of Journalism
138 Neff Annex
Columbia, MO 65211
(573)882-0684
www.nicar.org

**National Press
Photographers Association
(NPPA)**
3200 Croasdaile Dr., Ste. 306
Durham, NC 27705
(919)383-7246
www.nppa.org/default.cfm

**Office of Information and
Privacy**
U.S. Department of Justice
Flag Building Suite 570
Washington, DC 20530
(202)514-4251
www.usdoj.gov/oip/oip.html

**Ohio Center for Privacy
and the First Amendment**
Kent State University
School of Journalism and
Mass Communications
130 Taylor Hall
Kent, OH 44242
(330)672-2572
www.jmc.kent.edu/cfp/cfp.htm

Privacy International
Morgan Towers
Bromley BR1 3QE, England
44 181 4020737; 44- 7960-
523-679
www.privacyinternational.org

Privacy International
Washington Office
1718 Connecticut Ave, NW,
Suite 200
Washington, DC 20009
(202)483-1217
www.privacyinternational.org

Public Citizen
1600 20th St., N.W.
Washington, DC 20009
(202)588-1000
www.citizen.org

Quill and Scroll Society
University of Iowa
School of Journalism and
Mass Communications
Iowa City, IA 52242
(319)335-5795
www.uiowa.edu/~quill-sc

**Radio-Television News
Directors Association**
1000 Connecticut Ave., N.W.
Suite 615
Washington, DC 20036
(202)659-6510
www.rtnda.org

**Reporters Committee for
Freedom of the Press
(RCFP)**
1815 N. Fort Myer Dr., Ste.
900
Arlington, VA 22209
(703)807-2100
www.rcfp.org

Security on Campus Inc.
215 W. Church Rd., Suite
200
King of Prussia, PA 19406-
3207
(610)768-9330
www.campussafety.org

**Society of Professional
Journalists/Sigma Delta Chi
Foundation (SDX)**
3909 N. Meridian St.
Indianapolis, IN 46208-4011
(317)927-8000
http://spj.org

**Special Interest Group on
Management Information
Systems (SIGMIS)**
c/o Membership/Marketing
Department
1515 Broadway, 17th Fl.
New York, NY 10036
(212)869-7440
www.acm.org/sigmis

**Student Press Law Center
(SPLC)**
1815 N. Fort Myer Dr., Ste.
900
Arlington, VA 22209-1817
(703)807-1904
www.splc.org

**TruSecure (formerly
National Computer
Security Association
(NCSA))**
1200 Walnut Bottom Rd.
Carlisle, PA 17013
(717)258-1816
(800)488-4595

PROCESS SERVER ASSOCIATIONS

**California Association of
Photocopiers and Process
Servers**
530 Bercut Dr., Ste. G
Sacramento, CA 95814-0101
(916)444-8963
www.capps.org

**National Association of
Professional Process
Servers (NAPPS)**
P.O. Box 4547
Portland, OR 97208-4547
(800)477-8211; (503)222-
4180
www.napps.com

PROFESSIONAL RESEARCH ASSOCIATIONS THAT ARE KNOWLEDGEABLE ABOUT ONLINE SEARCHING

**American Intellectual
Property Law Association**
2001 Jefferson Davis
Highway, Suite 203
Arlington, VA 22202
(703)415-0780
www.aipla.org

**American Library
Association**
50 East Huron Street
Chicago, IL 50511-2795
(312)944-6780
www.ala.org

**American Society for
Information Science and
Technology (ASIS)**
8720 Georgia Avenue, Suite
501
Silver Spring, MD 20910-
3602
(301)495-0900
www.asis.org

**Association of Independent
Information Professionals
(AIIP)**

7044 S. 13th St.
Oak Creek, WI 53154
(414)766-0421
www.aiip.org

**Chartered Institute of
Patent Agents**
Staple Inn Buildings
High Holborn
London WC1V 7PZ, England
44 171 4059450
www.cipa.org.uk

**Copyright Society of the
USA (CSUSA)**
1133 Avenue of the Americas
New York, NY 10036
(212)354-6401
http://law.dukc.cdu/
copyright/index.htm

**European Communities
Trade Mark Association**
Bisschoppenhoflaan 286
Box 5
B-2100 Deurne-Antwerpen,
Belgium
32/3-326 47 23
www.ecta.org

**European Information
Researchers Network
(EIRENE)**
c/o Instant Library Limited
Charnwood Wing, GR&TC
Ashby Road
Loughborough
Leicestershire LE11 3GS
United Kingdom
44 01509 268 292
www.eirene.com

**Intellectual Property
Society of Australia and
New Zealand Inc.**
GPO Box 2491V
Melbourne VIC 3001

Australia
(61 3)9722 2877
www.ipsanz.com.au

**International Intellectual
Property Alliance**
1747 Pennsylvania Avenue
NW, 12th Floor
Washington, DC 30006
(202)833-4198
www.iipa.com

**International Intellectual
Property Association**
1255 223rd St. NW, Suite
850
Washington, DC 20037
(202)785-1814

**International Trademark
Association (INTA)**
1133 Avenue of the Americas
New York, NY 10036
(212)768-9887
www.inta.org

**International Trademark
Center**
Chateau Hof van Lyere
Hofeinde 2
B-2240 Zandhoven, Belgium
32 3 4845511

**Japan Intellectual Property
Association**
www.jipa.or.jp

**Japan Patent Information
Organization**
www.japio.or.jp

**Los Angeles Copyright
Society**
7049 Century Park, E. 34th
Floor
Century City, CA 90067-
3208

(310)205-8373
www.copr.org

**Medical Library
Association
Mental Health Librarians
Section (MLA-MHLS)**
c/o Medical Libraries
Association
65 E. Wacker Pl., Ste. 1900
Chicago, IL 60601-7298
(312)419-9094
www.mlanet.org

**National Council of
Intellectual Property Law
Associations (NCIPLA)**
1255 23rd St. NW, Ste. 200
Washington, DC 20037
(202)466-2396
www.ncipla.org

**Pacific Intellectual Property
Association**
P.O. Box 3477
Grand Central Station
New York, NY 10163

**Patent and Trade Mark
Group (PATMG)**
39-41 North Road
London, N7 9DP
United Kingdom
www.patmag.ork.uk

**Patent and Trademark
Office Society (PTOS)**
P.O. Box 2089
Arlington, VA 22202
www.ptos.org

**Patent Office Professional
Association (POPA)**
P.O. Box 2745
Arlington, VA 22202
(703)305-3000; (703)308-
0818
www.popa.org

Special Libraries Association (SLA)
1700 18th St. NW
Washington, DC 20009-2514
(202)234-4700
www.sla.org

Trade Marks, Patents and Designs Federation (TMPDF)
25 Southhampton Bldg.
London WC2A 1AW,
England
44 171 2423923

Trademark Society (TMS)
NTEU Local 245
2900 Crystal Dr.
P.O. Box 2631
East Station
Arlington, VA 22202
(703)308-9101; (703)308-9112

VPP
Uhlandstrasse 1
D-47239 Duisburg, Germany
49 2151 940236
www.vpp-patent.de

PROPERTY MANAGEMENT ORGANIZATIONS

Clinton County Property Managers Association
P.O. Box 397
Mulberry, IN 46058-0397
(765)296-3466; (765)659-9485

Hong Kong Association of Property Management Companies

P.O. Box 47160
Morrison Hill Post Office
Wanchai, Hong Kong
852 29608181
www.hkapmc.org.hk

Institute of Real Estate Management (IREM)
430 N. Michigan Ave.
Chicago, IL 60611-4090
(800)837-0706; (312)329-6000
www.irem.org

National Property Management Association (NPMA), Inc.
1102 Pinehurst Rd.
Oaktree Center
Dunedin, FL 34698
(727)736-3788
www.npma.org

National Property Management Association, Antelope Valley Chapter
www.edwards.af.mil/npma

National Property Management Association, Austin Chapter
SW Texas State University
601 University Dr.
San Marcos, TX 78666
(512)245-2294

National Property Management Association, Bay Area Chapter
Stanford University
122 Encina Commons
Sta., M/C 6025
Stanford, CA 94305-6025
www.npma-bayareachapter.org

National Property Management Association, Capitol City
2095 Rexford Rd.
Montgomery, AL 36116

National Property Management Association, Circle City Chapter
1640 Stable Circle
Indianapolis, IN 46239
(317)230-5099

National Property Management Association, Cochise Chapter
2813 E. Broadway Blvd.
Tucson, AZ 85716

National Property Management Association, Columbia Basin Chapter
P.O. Box 871
Richland, WA 99352

National Property Management Association, CSRA Chapter
1201 Huntcliff Trace
Aiken, SC 29801

National Property Management Association, Delaware Valley Chapter
874 Concord Pl.
Lansdale, PA 19446

National Property Management Association, Duke City Chapter
2729 Valencia, NE
Albuquerque, NM 87110

National Property Management Association, Federal Center Chapter
7818 Whistling Pines Ct.
Ellicott City, MD 21043

National Property
Management Association,
Gateway Chapter
1002 N. Brampton Dr.
St. Charles, MO 63304

National Property
Management Association,
Gold Canyon Chapter
2124 N. Lazona Dr.
Mesa, AZ 85203

National Property
Management Association,
Great Salt Lake Chapter
229 W. 800 S.
Bountiful, UT 84010

National Property
Management Association,
Great Smoky Mountain
Chapter
2344 Connors Creek Circle
Knoxville, TN 37932
www.ornl.gov/npma

National Property
Management Association,
Gulf Coast Chapter
260 Carmel Dr.
Mandeville, LA 70448

National Property
Management Association,
Harbor Lights Chapter
6059 Tamar Dr.
Columbia, MD 21045

National Property
Management Association,
Hoosiers Chapter
Aerospace Communications
7310 Innovation,
P.O. Box 3700
Ft. Wayne, IN 46801

National Property
Management Association,
Johnson Space Center
754 Seamaster Dr.
Houston, TX 77062

National Property
Management Association,
Kings Bay Chapter
Budget and Finance Division
Bldg. No. 28,
U.S. Department of Treasury
Brunswick, GA 31524

National Property
Management Association,
Lady Liberty Chapter
430 Jeffrey Ave.
East Meadow, NY 11554

National Property
Management Association,
Land of Enchantment
Chapter
RR 1 Box 120 E.
Santa Fe, NM 87501

National Property
Management Association,
Las Vegas Chapter
1013 Shadow Mountain Pl.
Las Vegas, NV 89108

National Property
Management Association,
Long Island Chapter
430 Jeffrey Ave.
East Meadow, NY 11554

National Property
Management Association,
Los Angeles Chapter
23852 Pacific Coast Hwy.
PMB No. 244
Malibu, CA 90265
http://home.earthlink.net/~
npmala

National Property
Management Association,
Macu Chapter
George Mason University
4400 University Dr./MSN,
1A1
Fairfax, VA 22030-4444

National Property
Management Association,
Magic City Chapter
513 Fox Hunt Circle
Longwood, FL 32750-3349
(407)306-2794

National Property
Management Association,
Mission Chapter
10260 Campus Point Dr.
MS-F2
San Diego, CA 92121

National Property
Management Association,
Mokan Chapter
P.O. Box 2228
Lees Summit, MO 64063
www.or.blm.gov/npma/
crnpma/Mokan.htm

National Property
Management Association,
Monte Diablo Chapter
University of California
1 Cyclotron Rd., 69 102
Berkeley, CA 94720

National Property
Management Association,
Natural State Chapter
Little Rock, AR
www.aristotle.net/~
ciannacone/index.html

National Property
Management Association,

New York Upstaters Chapter
174 Ledgewood Rd.
Rochester, NY 14615

National Property Management Association, North Atlantic Chapter
60 Concord St.
Gyro Lab
Wilmington, MA 01887
http://members.aol.com/
npmanac/index.htm

National Property Management Association, North Star Chapter
8800 Winnetka Ave., S.
Bloomington, MN 55431
(612)921-6647

National Property Management Association, North Texas Chapter
4717 Miami Dr.
Garland, TX 75043
(972)205-7486

National Property Management Association, Northwest Chapter
14715 SE 138th Pl.
Renton, WA 98059
www.geocities.com/npmanw/
index.htm

National Property Management Association, Nova Chapter
6544 Cypress Point Rd.
Alexandria, VA 22312

National Property Management Association, Nutmeg Chapter
60 Devine Rd.
Suffield, CT 06078

www.geocities.com/
nutmegchapter

National Property Management Association, Ohio Valley Chapter
718 W. Aberdeen Dr.
Trenton, OH 45067

National Property Management Association, River City Chapter
AEROJET
P.O. Box 13222 20019 5570
Sacramento, CA 95813-6000

National Property Management Association, Rocket City Chapter
Huntsville, AL
www.npmahsv.org

National Property Management Association, Saddleback Chapter
11851 Scandia St.
Garden Grove, CA 92845
www.geocities.com/Athens/
Aegean/5146

National Property Management Association, Saguaro Chapter
4215 E. Morrow Dr.
Phoenix, AZ 85050

National Property Management Association, San Fernando Valley Chapter
7821 A Orion Ave.
P.O. Box 7713
Van Nuys, CA 91409
http://members.aol.com/
dhalstead/sfvnpma

National Property Management Association, Santa Barbara Island Chapter
248 Camino Toluca Ave.
Camarillo, CA 93010

National Property Management Association, Shamrock Chapter
86 S. Cobb Dr.
Department 15-15 zone
Marietta, GA 30063

National Property Management Association, Shuttle Chapter
3805 Sentry Dr.
Cocoa, FL 32926

National Property Management Association, Sooner Chapter
AMQ-160
P.O. Box 25082
Oklahoma City, OK 73125
(405)954-5102
www.or.blm.gov/npma/
States/sooner.htm

National Property Management Association, Southeast Chapter
2135 Shadyhill Terr.
Winter Park, FL 32792

National Property Management Association, Suncoast Chapter
2511 Lantana Ln.
Palmetto, FL 34221

National Property Management Association, Sunflower Chapter
2019 Rosewood Ct.
Derby, KS 67037

National Property
Management Association,
Western Federal Chapter
7183 W. Crystal Rd.
Glendale, AZ 85308
www.or.blm.gov/npma

National Property
Management Association,
Western Federal Chapter
8801 W. Belleview Ave.
Littleton, CO 80123
www.or.blm.gov/npma/index.
htm

National Property
Management Association,
Western Spaceport Chapter
616 Colbert Dr.
Lompoc, CA 93436

National Property
Management Association,
Yankee Chapter
State of Connecticut
Comptrollers
55 Elm St.
Hartford, CT 06106
www.npma.org/chconn.htm

Property Management
Association, Inc. (PMA)
7900 Wisconsin Ave, Ste. 204
Bethesda, MD 20814
(301)657-9200
www.pma-dc.org

PUBLIC RECORDS RESEARCH ORGANIZATIONS

National Public Records
Research Association
(NPRRA)

3200 Croasdaile Dr., No. 603
Durham, NC 27705
(919)384-0434; (919)383-0044
www.nprra.org

SKIP-TRACER AND COLLECTION AGENCY ASSOCIATIONS

American Collectors
Association, International
(ACA)
ACA Center
4040 W. 70th St.
Minneapolis, MN 55435-4199
(612)926-6547
www.collector.com

American Recovery
Association (ARA)
One Seine Ct., Ste. 505
P.O. Box 6788
New Orleans, LA 70114
(504)366-7377
www.repo.org

Associated Collection
Agencies of Colorado and
Wyoming
2170 S. Parker Rd., No. 263
Denver, CO 80231
(303)750-9764

Associated Collection
Agencies
10200 W. 44th Ave.
Wheat Ridge, CO 80033
(303)422-7905

California Receivers
Forum–Bay Area Chapter

P.O. Box 1838
San Leandro, CA 94577-0718
www.receivers.org

California Receivers
Forum–LA/Orange County
Chapter
954 La Mirada St
Laguna Beach, CA 92651
(949)497-3673 x200
www.receivers.org

California Receivers
Forum–Sacramento Valley
Chapter
928 Second St.
Sacramento, CA 95814-2201
www.receivers.org

California Receivers
Forum–San Diego Chapter
954 La Mirada St
Laguna Beach, CA 92651
(949)497-3673 x200
www.receivers.org

International Association of
Commercial Collectors
(IACC)
4040 W. 70th St.
Minneapolis, MN 55435
(952)925-0760
www.commercialcollector.
com/index.htm

Michigan Association of
Collection Agencies
P.O. Box 1760
Warren, MI 48090
(810)558-1000

National Association of
Investigative Specialists
(NAIS)
P.O. Box 33244
Austin, TX 78764

(512)719-3595
www.pimall.com/nais/nais.j.
html

**National Consumer Credit
Consultants (NCCC)**
780 W. Army Trail Rd., Ste.
208
Carol Stream, IL 60188
(800)736-1036

**National Finance Adjusters
(NFA)**
1370 W. North Ave.
Baltimore, MD 21217
(410)728-2400
www.nfa.org

**Pennsylvania Collectors
Association**
717 N. 2nd St., Ste 300
Harrisburg, PA 17102
(717)238-1222

Time Finance Adjusters
728 Fentress Blvd.
Daytona Beach, FL 32114
(800)874-0510; (386)274-
4210
www.tfaguide.com

TENANT SCREENING ASSOCIATIONS

**National Association of
Screening Agencies (NASA)**
Penthouse
2020 Pennsylvania Ave. NW
Washington, D.C. 20006
877-900-NASA
www.n-a-s-a.com

Databases That Include Biographies

Once the implicit aim of biography
was to uplift ... now it is to unveil.

–Mark Feeney

African-American History and Culture
Facts on File, Inc.
11 Penn Plaza, 15th Fl.
New York, NY 10001-2006
(800)322-8755; (212)290-8090
Online: Facts on File, Inc.

The African American Biographical Database (AABD)
ProQuest Inc.
300 N. Zeeb Rd.
P.O. Box 1346
Ann Arbor, MI 48106-1346
(800)521-0600; (734)761-4700
Online: Bell and Howell Information and Learning

AGORA-DOCUMEN-TAIRE (ADOC)
Agence France-Presse (AFP)
13, place de la Bourse
B.P. 20
F-75002 Paris, France
33 1 40414646
Online: DataStar,

Europeenne de Donnees,
Infomart Dialog Ltd. (IDL),
LexisNexis, Bell and Howell
Information and Learning

Almanac of American Politics
National Journal Group Inc.
1501 M St. NW, Ste. 300
Washington, DC 20005
(800)207-8001; (202)739-8400
Online: LexisNexis, State Net
Internet: National Journal Group Inc. at http://nationaljournal.com, State Net at www.statenet.com

American Indian History and Culture
Facts on File, Inc.
11 Penn Plaza, 15th Fl.
New York, NY 10001-2006
(800)322-8755; (212)290-8090
Online: Facts on File, Inc.

American Men and Women of Science or AMWS Online
Gale Group
27500 Drake Rd.
Farmington Hills, MI 48331
(800)877-4253
Online: Suspended until Spring 2003

AP Alert/Political or Associated Press Political Service
The Associated Press (AP)
50 Rockefeller Plaza
New York, NY 10020
(212)621-1500
Online: Bell and Howell Information and Learning, LexisNexis

Artists in Canada
National Gallery of Canada Research Library and Archives
P.O. Box 427, Sta. A
Ottawa, ON, Canada K1N 9N4
(613)990-0585

Online: Canadian Heritage Information Network (CHIN)

Associated Press-Candidate Biographies
The Associated Press (AP)
50 Rockefeller Plaza
New York, NY 10020
(212)621-1500
Online: LexisNexis

Australian Architecture Database (ARCH)
Stanton Library
234 Miller St.
North Sydney, NSW 2060, Australia
61 2 99368400
Internet: Informit Online at www.informit.com.au

AUSTROM
or **Australian Social Science Law and Education Databases**
RMIT Publishing
P.O. Box 12058
A'Beckett St.
Melbourne, VIC 8006, Australia
61 3 99258100
Internet: Informit Online at www.informit.com.au

BASELINE
BASELINE, INC.
838 Broadway, 4th Fl.
New York, NY 10003
(800)242-7546; (212)254-8235
Online: BASELINE, INC.

BASELINE Celebrity Bios
BASELINE, INC.
838 Broadway, 4th Fl.
New York, NY 10003
(800)242-7546; (212)254-8235
Online: LexisNexis, also as part of BASELINE

BIODOC
R.H. Neirijnck
Zomerstraat 4
B-8310 Brugge, Belgium
3250 352471
3250 352471
Online: Europeenne de Donnees

Biography Master Index (BMI)
Gale Group
27500 Drake Rd.
Farmington Hills, MI 48331-3535
(800)877-4253; (248)699-4253
Online: Dialog
Internet: DialogWeb at www.dialogweb.com and InfoTrac (Gale Group) at http://infotrac.galenet.com

Biography Resource Center (BioRC)
Gale Group
27500 Drake Rd.
Farmington Hills, MI 48331-3535
(800)877-4253; (248)699-4253
Internet: InfoTrac (Gale Group) at http://infotrac.galenet.com

Bowker Biographical Directory
R.R. Bowker
121 Chanlon Rd.
New Providence, NJ 07974
(888)269-5372; (908)464-6800

Online: Dialog, LexisNexis
Internet: DialogWeb at www.dialogweb.com

The Complete Marquis Who's Who ONLINE (MWW)
Reed Elsevier Inc.
Marquis Who's Who
121 Chanlon Rd.
New Providence, NJ 07974
(800)521-8110
(800)323-3288
Online: Dialog, SilverPlatter Information Inc.

Contemporary Authors
Gale Group
27500 Drake Rd.
Farmington Hills, MI 48331-3535
(800)877-4253; (248)699-4253
Internet: InfoTrac (Gale Group) at http://infotrac.galenet.com

CQ Member Profiles
Congressional Quarterly Inc. (CQ)
1414 22nd St. NW
Washington, DC 20037
(800)432-2250; (202)887-6279
Online: Congressional Quarterly Inc. (CQ) and as part of CQ.com OnCongress and Washington Alert

DBE
K.G. Saur Verlag GmbH and Co.
Ortlestrasse 8
D-81373 Munich, Germany

49 89 769020
Online: GENIOS

**Dictionary of German
National Biography (DBE)
or Deutsche Biographische
Enzyklopadie**
K.G. Saur Verlag
Ortlerstrasse 8
D-81373 Munich, Germany
49 89 769020
Online: GENIOS

**Dictionary of Literary
Biography (DLB)**
Gale Group
27500 Drake Rd.
Farmington Hills, MI 48331-
3535
(800)877-4253; (248)699-
4253
Internet: InfoTrac (Gale
Group) at
http://infotrac.galenet.com

**DISCovering Authors
Modules**
Gale Group
27500 Drake Rd.
Farmington Hills, MI 48331-
3535
(800)877-4253; (248)699-
4253
Online: Student Resource
Center
Internet: InfoTrac (Gale
Group) at
http://infotrac.galenet.com

DISCovering Biography
Gale Group
27500 Drake Rd.
Farmington Hills, MI 48331-
3535
(800)877-4253; (248)699-
4253

Internet: InfoTrac (Gale
Group) at
http://infotrac.galenet.com

DISCovering Collection
Gale Group
27500 Drake Rd.
Farmington Hills, MI 48331-
3535
(800)877-4253; (248)699-
4253
Internet: InfoTrac (Gale
Group) at
http://infotrac.galenet.com

**EBSCOlearn Social
Studies–Biography**
EBSCO Publishing
10 Estes St.
Ipswitch, MA 01938
(800)653-2726; (800)758-
5995; (978)356-6500
Online: EBSCO Publishing

Gale Biographies
Gale Group
27500 Drake Rd.
Farmington Hills, MI 48331-
3535
(800)877-4253; (248)699-
4253
Online: Nexis

**George Eastman House
Interactive Catalog**
George Eastman House
International Museum of
Photography
George Eastman House
900 East Ave.
Rochester, NY 14607
(716)271-3361
Internet: George Eastman
House International Museum
of Photography at
www.geh.org

KnowUK
ProQuest Inc.
300 N. Zeeb Rd.
P.O. Box 1346
Ann Arbor, MI 48106-1346
(800)521-0600; (734)761-
4700
Online: Bell and Howell
Information and Learning

**Korean Biographical
Dictionary**
Moojin Mirae Research
Institute
RM/705, Namsan Park Hotel
72-8
Heiyun-Dong 2-ka, chung-ku
Seoul, Republic of Korea
82 2 7523212
Online: Moojin Mirae
Research Institute

**Korean Integrated
Newspaper Database
System (KINDS)**
Korean Press Institute
12th Fl., Korea Press Center
Bldg.
25 1-Ga, Taepyong-Ro,
Chung-Gu
Seoul 100-746, Republic of
Korea
82 2 3981654
Online: Chollian, HiTEL,
Nownuri, and Unitel Co. Ltd.

Korean People
The Munhwa Ilbo
68, Chung-Jung Ro Iga,
Chungku
Seoul 100-151, Republic of
Korea
822 37015864
Online: Chollian and HiTEL

KUKA
Kustannusosakeyhtio Otava
P.O. Box 134
FIN-00121 Helsinki, Finland
919961
Online: TT-Tietopalvelut Oy

Literature Resource Center (LRC)
Gale Group
27500 Drake Rd.
Farmington Hills, MI 48331-3535
(800)877-4253; (248)699-4253
Internet: InfoTrac (Gale Group) at
http://infotrac.galenet.com

Major Authors Online
Gale Group
27500 Drake Rd.
Farmington Hills, MI 48331-3535
(800)877-4253; (248)699-4253
Internet: InfoTrac (Gale Group) at
http://infotrac.galenet.com

MAPERS
Munzinger-Archiv GmbH
Albersfelder Str. 34
D-88273 Ravensburg, Germany
49 0751 769 37 0
Online: GENIOS
Internet: Munzinger-Archiv GmbH at
www.munzinger.com

MAPOP
Munzinger-Archiv GmbH
Albersfelder Str. 34
D-88273 Ravensburg, Germany

49 0751 769 37 0
Online: GENIOS
Internet: Munzinger-Archiv GmbH at
www.munzinger.com

Marquis Who's Who (MWW)
Refer to The Complete Marquis Who's Who Online

Marquis Who's Who in American Regional Publications
Reed Elsevier, Inc.
Marquis Who's Who
121 Chanlon Rd.
New Providence, NJ 07974
(800)323-3288; (908)771-6800
Online: Dialog, Nexis
Internet: DialogWeb at
www.dialogweb.com

Marquis Who's Who Topical Library
Reed Elsevier, Inc.
Marquis Who's Who
121 Chanlon Rd.
New Providence, NJ 07974
(800)323-3288; (908)771-6800
Online: Dialog, LexisNexis
Internet: DialogWeb at
www.dialogweb.com

MASPORT
Munzinger-Archiv GmbH
Albersfelder Str. 34
D-88273 Ravensburg, Germany
49 0751 769 37 0
Online: GENIOS
Internet: Munzinger-Archiv GmbH at
www.munzinger.com

The New York Times Biographical File
The New York Times Company
New York Times On-Line Services
520 Speedwell Ave.
Morris Plains, NJ 07950
(973)829-0036
Online: LexisNexis

People Library
LexisNexis
9443 Springboro Pike
P.O. Box 933
Dayton, OH 45401-0933
(800)227-9597; (937)865-6800
Online: LexisNexis

Scribner Writers Series
Charles Scribner's Sons
1633 Broadway, 23rd Fl.
New York, NY 10019
(800)877-4253; (800)223-1244
Internet: InfoTrac (Gale Group) at
http://infotrac.galenet.com

Standard and Poor's Register–Biographical
Standard and Poor's
55 Water St.
New York, NY 10041-0003
(800)221-5277; (212)438-7280
Online: CompuServe Interactive Services, Dialog, LexisNexis
Internet: CompuServe Information Service—Knowledge Index at
www.compuserve.com, and DialogWeb at www. dialogweb.com

**The Top 100 People
(Biographies)**
Indigo Publications
142, rue Montmartre
F-75002 Paris, France
33 1 44882610
Internet: Indigo Publications at
www.africaintelligence.com/d
ossiers/p_gp.asp

**Union List of Artist Names
(ULAN)**
J. Paul Getty Trust
1200 Getty Center Dr., Ste.
300
Los Angeles, CA 90047-1680
(310)440-6348
Online: J. Paul Getty Trust

**The Washington Post
Biographical Stories**
The Washington Post News
Research Center
1150 15th St. NW, 5th Fl.
Washington, DC 20071
(202)334-6762
Online: LexisNexis and as
part of The Washington Post
(available online through Bell
and Howell Information and
Learning, Dialog, European
Information Network
Services, Factiva, FT Profile,
Newsbank, Inc., Nexis, and
West Group–Westlaw)
Internet: Washington Post at
www.washingtonpost.com

Who's Who
Cyber JoongAng
Glastower 7th Floor, 946-1
Daechi-dong Kangnam-ku
Seoul 135-708, Republic of
Korea
82 2 21859200
Online: Cyber JoongAng
Who's Who in American

Art
International Labour Office
(ILO)
Bureau of Statistics
4, route de Morillons
CH-1211 Geneva,
Switzerland
41 227 997149
Online: LexisNexis

**Who's Who in American
Politics**
International Labour Office
(ILO)
Bureau of Statistics
4, route de Morillons
CH-1211 Geneva,
Switzerland
41 227 997149
Online: LexisNexis

**Who's Who in European
Business and Industry**
WHO'S WHO Edition
GmbH
Starnberger Weg 62
D-82205 Gilching, Germany
49 8105 390653
Online: GENIOS

**Who's Who in Germany
(WIW)**
or **Who's Who in Germany**
Verlag Schmidt-Roemhild
Kronprinzenstrasse 13
D-45128 Essen, Germany
49 201 81300
Online: GENIOS

**Who's Who in Russia and
the Commonwealth of
Independent States**
or **Who's Who Directory**
Russian Information and
Communications Agency
(RUSSICA)

Spartakovskaya St. 13
107066 Moscow, Russia
095 9325610
Online: MagnaTex
International Inc.–COMMU-
NICATE!, Nexis,
SovInfoLink, and as part of
Lexis Country Information
Service

Who's Who in Technology
Gale Group
27500 Drake Rd.
Farmington Hills, MI 48331-
3535
(800)877-4253; (248)699-
4253
Online: Questel Orbit and as
part of Gale Biographies

**Wilson Biographies Plus
Illustrated**
H.W. Wilson Company
950 University Ave.
Bronx, NY 10452
(800)367-6770; (718)588-
8400
Internet: WilsonWeb at
www.hwwilson.com/
Databases/biobank.htm

**Wilson Biography Index
Plus**
H.W. Wilson Company
950 University Ave.
Bronx, NY 10452
(800)367-6770; (718)588-
8400
Online: OCLC Epic, OCLC
FirstSearch Catalog, Ovid
Technologies, Inc.,
SilverPlatter Information, Inc.
Internet: WilsonWeb at
www.hwwilson.com/
Databases/biobank.htm

World Biographical Dictionary of Artists
K.B. Saur Verlag GmbH and Co.
Ortlerstrasse 8
D-81373 Munich, Germany
49 89 769020
Online: GENIOS Wirtschaftsdatenbanken

World Biographical Index
K.B. Saur Verlag GmbH and Co.
Ortlestrasse 8
D-81373 Munich, Germany
49 89 769020
Online: K.G. Saur Verlag GmbH and Co.

The World's Best Poetry
Roth Publishing, Inc.
175 Great Neck Rd.
Great Neck, NY 11021
(800)899-7684; (516)466-3676
Internet: Lit Finder, Inc. at www.litfinder.com

Please note that general encyclopedias have been omitted from this section, as they have been listed in Appendix F. Some specialized encylopedias are listed here. Professional directories, some of which contain biographical information, are listed in Appendix D.

Book Directory Databases

Outside of a dog, a book is man's best friend.
Inside of a dog, it's too dark to read.

—Groucho Marx

Academia
or Academia Online
Baker & Taylor, Inc.
Electronic Business and
Information Services
2709 Water Ridge Pkwy.
Charlotte, NC 28217
(800)775-1800; (704)357-3500
Online: Baker & Taylor, Inc.
Electronic Business and
Information Services

Archival Resources
Research Libraries Group,
Inc. (RLG)
1200 Villa St.
Mountain View, CA 94041-1100
(800)537-7546; (650)691-2333
Internet: Research Libraries
Group, Inc. (RLG)–Eureka,
and at
www.rlg.org/eureka.html

Australia and New Zealand
Books in Print (ANZBiP)

RMIT Publishing
P.O. Box 12058
A'Beckett St.
Melbourne, VIC 8006,
Australia
61 3 99258100
Online: SilverPlatter
Information Inc.

Automated Library
Information System (ALIS)
Danmarks Tekniske
Videncenter (DTV)
Anker Engelunds Vej 1
DK-2800 Lyngby, Denmark
45 45257200
Online: Danmarks Tekniske
Videncenter (DTV)

BIBLIODATA
Die Deutsche Bibliothek
Adickesallee 1
D-60322 Frankfurt am Main,
Germany
49 69 15250
Online: STN International
and GENIOS

Bibliografia Espanola
(BIBL)
Ministerio de Educacion y
Cultura
Abdon Terradas, 7
E-28015 Madrid, Spain
34 91 5439366
Online: Ministerio de
Educacion y Cultura
(ESPANA), Secretaria
General Tecnica, Puntos de
Informacion Cultural (PIC)

BNBMARC
British Library
National Bibliographic
Service
BLAISE
Boston Spa
Wetherby, W. Yorkshire LS23
7BQ, England
44 1937 546585
Online: BLAISE

Book Review Index (BRI)
Gale Group
27500 Drake Rd.

Farmington Hills, MI 48331-3535
(800)877-4253; (248)699-4253
Online: Dialog

BookFind-Online (BFOL)
Book Data, Ltd.
Globe House
1 Chertsey Rd.
Twickenham TW1 1LR,
England
44 20 88438600
Online: ddp/ADN
Allgemeiner Deutscher
Nachrichtendienst GmbH

Books in Print®
R.R. Bowker
630 Central Ave.
New Providence, NJ 07974
(888)269-5372
Online: Ameritech Library
Services—Vista, CARL
Corporation, Dialog, EBSCO
Publishing, K.G. Saur Verlag
GmbH & Co., LexisNexis,
OCLC EPIC, OCLC
FirstSearch Catalog, Ovid
Online, Ovid Technologies,
Inc., SilverPlatter Information
Inc.
Internet: InfoTrac Web at
http://infotrac.galegroup.com
and R.R. Bowker at
www.bowker.com/bip

**Books In Print® With Book
Reviews**
R.R. Bowker
630 Central Ave.
New Providence, NJ 07974
(888)269-5372
Online: R.R. Bowker

Books Out-of-Print™
R.R. Bowker
630 Central Ave.
New Providence, NJ 07974
(888)269-5372
Online: K.G. Saur Verlag
GmhB & Co.

**British Library Catalogue:
Document Supply Centre
(Monographs)**
or **British Library Books at
Boston Spa**
British Library
Document Supply Centre
Boston Spa
Wetherby, W. Yorkshire LS23
7BQ, England
(800)932-3575; 44 1937
546060
Online: BLAISE, also part of
The British Library Public
Catalogue

Burk-Sok
Bibliotekstjanst AB/Library
Service Ltd. (BTJ)
P.O. Box 200
S-221 82 Lund, Sweden
46 46 180000
Online: Bibliotekstjanst
AB/Library Service Ltd.
(BTJ)

CANUC:H
National Library of Canada
Acquisitions and
Bibliographic Services
Branch
Union Catalogue Division
395 Wellington St.
Ottawa, ON, Canada K1A
0N4
(613)997-7990
Online: Ovid Technologies,
Inc. and part of AMICUS

Canadian Online Library
System

CANUC:S
National Library of Canada
Acquisitions and
Bibliographic Services
Branch
Union Catalogue Division
395 Wellington St.
Ottawa, ON, Canada K1A
0N4
(613)997-7990
Online: As part of AMICUS
Canadian Online Library
System

**Children's Literature
Comprehensive Database
(CLCD)**
Children's Literature
7513 Shadywood Rd.
Bethesda, MD 20817-2065
(800)469-2070
Online: bigchalk.com and
Children's Literature
Internet: bigchalk
www.bigchalk.com/cgi-bin/WebObjects/WOPortal.
woa/wa/BCCorpDA/display?
type=Corporates&page=
products/clcd.html

CHOIX
Services Documentaires
Multimedia, Inc. (SDM)
75, de Port-Royal Est, bureau
300
Montreal, QC, Canada H3L
3T1
(514)382-0895
Online: Services
Documentaires Multimedia,
Inc. (SDM)

Collective Catalog of Belgium
or Dutch Collective Catalogus van Belgie; French Catalogue Collectif de Belgique
National Conference of University Chief Librarians
NFWO
Egmontstraat 5
B-1050 Brussels, Belgium
32 2 5129110
Online: Ministere Belge des Affaires Economiques, Centre de Traitement de l'Information BELINDIS (CCBE)

Computer Book Bytes
Baker & Taylor, Inc.
Information and Entertainment Services
2709 Water Ridge Pkwy.
Charlotte, NC 28217
(800)775-1800; (704)357-3500
Online: Baker & Taylor, Inc. Information and Entertainment Services

Electre
Electre
35, rue Gregoire de Tours
F-75006 Paris, France
33 1 44412800
Online: Electre

English Short-Title Catalogue 1473-1800 (ESTC)
University of California at Riverside
Center for Bibliographical Studies and Research (CBSR)
Tomas Rivera Library
CBSR 016

Riverside, CA 92521
(909)787-2388
Online: BLAISE
Internet: Research Libraries Group, Inc. (RLG), Eureka at www.rlg.org/eureka.html and Research Libraries Information Network (RLIN) at www.rlg.org/rlin.html

General Catalog
John Wiley & Sons, Inc.
605 Third Ave.
New York, NY 10158-0012
(800)879 4539; (212)850-6000
Online: Inforonics, Inc.

Hand Press Book Database
Consortium of European Research Libraries (CERL)
25 Southampton Buildings, Rooms 45-47
London WC2A 1AW, England
44 20 78310927
Internet: Research Libraries Group, Inc. (RLG)—Eureka at www.rlg.org/eureka.html

International Bibliography of Book Reviews of Scholarly Literature on the Humanities and Social Sciences (IBR)
Zeller Dietrich
Bibliographischer Verlag
Hirschberger Str. 17 b
D-49086 Osnabruck, Germany
49 541 404590
Online: GBV
Verbundzentrale (GBV/VZ)

Japanese Books
Japan National Diet Library
Information System Division

10-1, 1-Chome
Nagato-cho, Chiyoda-ku
Tokyo 100-8924, Japan
81 3 35812331
Online: Japan National Diet Library Information System Division

KSIAZKI Data Base
Politechnika Wroclawska
Biblioteka Glowna i Osrodek Informacji Naukowo-Technicznej
Wybrzeze S. Wyspianskiego 27
50-370 Wroclaw, Poland
48 71 3282707
Online: Politechnika Wroclawska Biblioteka Glowna i Osrodek Informacji Naukowo-Technicznej

LC MARC: Books All
or **Machine-Readable Cataloging - Books All; Books Master File; Library of Congress Computerized Catalog (LCCC)**
U.S. Library of Congress Cataloging Distribution Service
101 Independence Ave., S.E.
Washington, DC 20541-4912
(800)255-3666; (202)707-6100
Online: BLAISE, Dialog, University of Tsukuba—Science Information Processing Center, WilsonWeb
Internet: DialogWeb at www.dialogweb.com

Library Information System (LIBRIS)
Sveriges Kungl. Biblioteket

P.O. Box 5039
S-102 41 Stockholm, Sweden
46 8 7833900
Internet: Sveriges Kungl.
Biblioteket at
www.libris.kb.se

Libros en Venta
Ministerio De Educacion y
Cultura
Subdireccion general Del
Libro
Agencia Espanol ISBN
Santiago Rusinol 8
28040 Madrid, Spain
5368 83032
Online: Ministerio de
Educacion y Cultura
(ESPANA) Secretaria
General Tecnica Puntos de
Informacion Cultural (PIC)

**Management Books and
Resources**
Anbar Electronic Intelligence
60/62 Toller Lane
Bradford, W. Yorkshire BD8
9BY, England
44 1274 785277
Online: Anbar Electronic
Intelligence

**Nasjonalbibliografiske Data
1962–**
or **Norwegian National
Bibliographic File 1962–;
NBDATA**
The National Library of
Norway (Nasjonalbiblioteket)
Drammensveien 42
Postboks 2674 Solli
N-0103 Oslo, Norway
47 81500188
Online: The National Library
of Norway
(Nasjonalbiblioteket)

**National Diet Library
Catalog of Foreign Books**
or **Foreign Book**
Japan National Diet Library
Information System Division
10-1, 1-Chome
Nagato-cho, Chiyoda-ku
Tokyo 100-8924, Japan
81 3 35812331
Online: Japan National Diet
Library Information System
Division

New Titles On-Line (NTO)
Blackwell Book Service
6024 SW Jean Rd., Bldg. G
Lake Oswego, OR 97035
(800)547-6426; (503)684-
1140
Online: Blackwell Book
Service

Norsk bokfortegnelse
or **Norbok**
University of Oslo Library
Bibliographic Services
Department
Drammensveien 42
Postboks 2674 Solli
N-0103 Oslo, Norway
47 81500188
Online: University of Oslo
Library Bibliographic
Services Department, and as
part of Nasjonalbibliografiske
data 1962–

**OCLC Online Union
Catalog (OLUC)**
or **WORLDCAT**
OCLC Online Computer
Library Center, Inc.
6565 Frantz Rd.
Dublin, OH 43017-3395
(800)848-5878; (614)764-
6000

Online: OCLC EPIC, OCLC
FirstSearch Catalog, OCLC
Online Computer Library
Center, Inc., STN
International
Internet: OCLC FirsSearch
Catalog at
http://firstsearch.oclc.org and
STN International at
telnet://stnk.fiz-karlsruhe.de

**OzLife: Australian
Biography and Book
Review Index**
The National Library of
Australia
Parkes Pl.
Canberra, ACT 2600,
Australia
61 2 62621111
Online: The National Library
of Australia

**Poole's Plus: The Digital
Index of the Nineteenth
Century**
Paratext, Inc.
111-M Carpenter Dr.
Sterling, VA 20164
(703)318-0285
Online: Paratext, Inc.

**Register of Preservation
Microforms**
British Library
Register of Preservation
Microforms
96 Euston Rd.
London NW1 2DB, England
44 0207 4127629
Online: BLAISE

Sambok
or **Norsk samkatalog for
boker**
University of Oslo Library

Bibliographic Services
Department
Drammensveien 42
Postboks 2674 Solli
N-0103 Oslo, Norway
47 81500188
Online: University of Oslo
Library Bibliographic
Services Department

**SCIPIO: Art and Rare
Book Sales Catalogs**
Research Libraries Group,
Inc. (RLG)
1200 Villa St.
Mountain View, CA 94041-
1100
(800)537-7546; (650)691-
2333
Internet: Research Libraries
Group, Inc. (RLG) Eureka
www.rlg.org/eureka.html and
CitaDel Service at
www.rlg.org/cit-sci.html

**Svensk bibliografi
1700–1829, Luckan**
Sveriges Kungl. Biblioteket
P.O. Box 5039
S-102 41 Stockholm, Sweden
46 8 7833900
Online: Sveriges Kungl.
Biblioteket

TENTTU–Books
Helsinki University of
Technology—Library
Teknillisen Korkeakoulun
Kirjasto
P.O. Box 1000
Otakaari 1
FIN-02150 Espoo, Finland
358 9 4511
Online: Teknillinen
Korkeakoulu Atkeskus

The Title Source II
Baker and Taylor, Inc.
Electronic Business and
Information Services
2709 Water Ridge Pkwy.
Charlotte, NC 28217
(800)775-1800; (704)357-
3500
Online: Baker and Taylor,
Inc. Electronic Business and
Information Services

**Whitaker's Books in Print
(WBIP)**
or **British Books in Print
(BBIP)**
J. Whitaker and Sons, Ltd.
12 Dyott St.
London WC1A 1DF, England
44171 4206000
Online: BLAISE, Dialog

**The Whole Story: 3000
Years of Sequels and
Sequences**
RMIT Publishing
P.O. Box 12058
A'Beckett St.
Melbourne, VIC 8006,
Australia
61 3 99258100
Online: SilverPlatter
Information Inc.

Wilson Book Review Digest
H.W. Wilson Company
950 University Ave.
Bronx, NY 10452
(800)367-6770; (718)588-
8400
Online: Bell & Howell
Information and Learning,
CompuServe Information
Service, Dialog, OCLC
EPIC, OCLC FirstSearch
Catalog, SilverPlatter

Information, Inc., WilsonWeb

**Wilson Cumulative Book
Index (CBI)**
H.W. Wilson Company
950 University Ave.
Bronx, NY 10452
(800)367-6770; (718)588-
8400
Online: Bell & Howell
Information and Learning,
Dialog, OCLC EPIC, OCLC
FirstSearch Catalog, Ovid
Technologies, Inc., ProQuest
Inc., SilverPlatter Information
Inc., WilsonWeb

Business Credit and Company Financial Databases

Borrow causes sorrow.

—Yiddish proverb

Account Data
Account Data A/S
Howitzvej 60, 6
DK-2000 Frederiksberg,
Denmark
38861149
Online: Account Data A/S

AMADEUS: Analyse MAjor Databases from EUropean Sources
Bureau van Dijk, SA (BvD)
Electronic Publishing
Ave. Louise 250
Box 14
B-1050 Brussels, Belgium
32 2 6390606
Internet: Bureau van Dijk,
SA (BvD)- Electronic
Publishing at
http://amadeus1.bvdep.com/
cgi/template.dll?product=2

Asian Company Profiles
FBR Data Base Inc.
P.O. Box 12-118

Taipei, Taiwan
886 2 28754355
Online: DataStar, Dialog,
Factiva, FBR Data Base Inc.,
Financial Times Electronic
Publishing (FTEP),
LexisNexis, Profound
Inc.–The Dialog Corporation,
Reuters Group PLC
Internet: DataStarWeb at
www.dialog.com/info/
products/datastar-index.shtml
and DialogWeb at
www.dialogweb.com

BANKSCOPE
Bureau van Dijk, SA (BvD)
Electronic Publishing
Ave. Louise 250
Box 14
B-1050 Brussels, Belgium
32 2 6390606
Internet: Bureau van Dijk,
SA (BvD)- Electronic
Publishing at
http://bankscope.bvdep.com/
cgi/template.dll?product=4

Best's Statement File–Life/Health
A.M. Best Company, Inc.
Ambest Rd.
Oldwick, NJ 08858
(908)439-2200
Online: A.M. Best Company,
Inc.

Best's Statement File–Property/Casualty
A.M. Best Company, Inc.
Ambest Rd.
Oldwick, NJ 08858
(908)439-2200
Online: A.M. Best Company,
Inc.

BIS
or **Banking Information Source**
Dowon International
New Seoul Bldg., Rm. 405
Yeooksam-dong No. 405,
Kangnam-gu
Seoul, Republic of Korea

822 5013106
Online: Dialog, Dowon
International, LexisNexis
Internet: DialogWeb at
www.dialogweb.com

BISNES Plus
INFOTRADE N.V.
Stationsstraat 30 b2
B-1702 Groot-Bijgaarden,
Belgium
32 2 4818283
Online: DataStar, INFO-
TRADE N.V.
Internet: DataStarWeb at
www.dialog.com/info/
products/datastar-index.shtml

**Business Who's Who of
Australia (BWWA)**
Dun and Bradstreet
Marketing Pty. Ltd.
19 Havilah St.
Chatswood, NSW 2067,
Australia
61 2 99352700
Online: Dun and Bradstreet
Marketing Pty. Ltd.
Internet:
http://bww.dnb.com.au/
default.asp

**Canadian Federal
Corporations and Directors**
Infomart Dialog Ltd. (IDL)
333 King St. E
Toronto, ON, Canada M5A
4R7
(800)668-9215; (416)350-
6001
Online: Infomart Online

**CanCorp Plus Canadian
Financial Database**
Micromedia Ltd.
20 Victoria St.

Toronto, ON, Canada M5C
2N8
(800)387-2689; (416)362-
5211
Online: DataStar, Dialog,
Infomart Dialog Ltd. (IDL),
Infomart Online, LexisNexis
and as part of: Compact D
Internet: DataStarWeb at
www.dialog.com/info/
products/datastar-index.shtml
and DialogWeb at
www.dialogweb.com

Cards Database
AFX News Ltd.
Fitzroy House
13-17 Epworth St.
London EC2A 4DL, England
44171 2532532
Online: DataStar, Dialog, FT
Profile, LexisNexis
Internet: DataStarWeb at
www.dialog.com/info/
products/datastar-index.shtml
and DialogWeb at
www.dialogweb.com

CIFARBASE
or **CIFAR Balance Sheets
and Data of International
Enterprises**
Center for International
Financial Analysis and
Research, Inc. (CIFAR)
P.O. Box 3228
Princeton, NJ 08543-3228
(609)520-9333
Online: Center for
International Financial
Analysis and Research, Inc.
(CIFAR)

**COMLINE Japanese
Corporate Directory**

COMLINE Business Data,
Inc.
1-12-5 Hamamatsucho,
Minto-ku
Tokyo 105, Japan
03 5401 4567
Online: DataStar
Internet: DataStarWeb at
www.dialog.com/info/
products/datastar-index.shtml

**Commercial Register
Switzerland**
or **Handelsregister Schweiz**
Orell Fuessli Verlag AG
Dietzingerstrasse 3
CH-8036 Zurich, Switzerland
41 14667247
Online: GENIOS

Compact D
Primark Corporation
Primark Financial
Information Division
Disclosure Inc.
5161 River Rd.
Bethesda, MD 20816
(800)754-9690; (800)846-
0365; (301)951-1753
Internet: Primark
Corporation–Primark
Financial Information
Division–Disclosure Inc. at
www.primark.com/
GuidetoSEC.pdf

**Company & Management,
Financial Market
Information**
Korea Management
Consulting & Credit Rating
Corp. (KMCC)
An-won Bldg., 14-15,
Youido-dong
Seoul 150-010, Republic of
Korea

8223685500
Online: Korea Management
Consulting & Credit Rating
Corp. (KMCC), Nownuri

**Company Data
Direct/International**
Mergent FIS, Inc.
60 Madison Ave., 6th Fl.
New York, NY 10010
(800)342-5647; (212)413-
7670
Internet: Mergent FIS, Inc.at
www.fisonline.com

Company Data Direct/U.S.
Mergent FIS, Inc.
60 Madison Ave., 6th Fl.
New York, NY 10010
(800)342-5647; (212)413-
7670
Internet: Mergent FIS, Inc.at
www.fisonline.com

Company Dossier
LexisNexis
9443 Springboro Pike
P.O. Box 933
Dayton, OH 45401-0933
(800)227-9597; (937)865-
6800
Online: LexisNexis

Company Intelligence
Gale Group
27500 Drake Rd.
Farmington Hills, MI 48331-
3535
(800)877-4253; (248)699-
4253
Online: DataStar, Dialog,
LexisNexis
Internet: DataStarWeb at
www.dialog.com/info/
products/datastar-index.shtml
and DialogWeb at www.
dialogweb.com

Company Library
LexisNexis
9443 Springboro Pike
P.O. Box 933
Dayton, OH 45401-0933
(800)227-9597; (937)865-
6800
Online: LexisNexis

Company ProFile
Gale Group
27500 Drake Rd.
Farmington Hills, MI 48331-
3535
(800)877-4253; (248)699-
4253
Online: Ameritech Library
Services–Vista, CARL
Corporation
Internet: InfoTrac (Gale
Group) at
http://infotrac.galenet.com

Companyline
Profound Inc.–The Dialog
Corporation
11000 Regency Pkwy, Ste
10
Cary, NC 27511
(919)462-8600
Online: Profound Inc.–The
Dialog Corporation

Comparative Profiler
Integra Information, Inc.
245 Main St. 101
Chester, NJ 07930-2569
(800)780-2660; (908)879-
0400
Internet: Integra Information,
Inc. at www.integrainfo.com

COMPMARK
Standard & Poor's
55 Water St.
New York, NY 10041-0003

(800)221-5277; (212)438-
7280
Online: Standard & Poor's

**Consumer Credit
Information**
National Information &
Credit Evaluation Inc.
(NICE)
Ah-tac Bldg 1337-20
Seocho-2dong Scocho-ku
Seoul, Republic of Korea
82 2 34755600
Online: Chollian, HiTEL,
Unitel Co. Ltd., and as part
of Nice-Tips

Corporate Canada Online
Globe Information Services
444 Front St. W.
Toronto, ON, Canada M5V
2S9
(800)268-9128; (416)585-
5250
Online: Info Globe Online

COSMOS 1
Teikoku Databank America,
Inc.
747 Third Ave., 25th Fl.
New York, NY 10017
(212)421-9805
Online: DIALOG, G-Search
Ltd., LexisNexis, Profound
Inc.–The Dialog Corporation,
Thomson Financial Securities
Data (TFSD)
Internet: DialogWeb at
www.dialogweb.com

**Creditreform-Datenbank-
Dienst (CREFO)**
or **Creditreform–Company
Profiles**
Verband der Vereine

Creditreform e.V.
Hellersbergstr. 12
Postfach 101552
D-41460 Neuss, Germany
49 2131 109300
Online: DataStar, GBI,
GENIOS, LexisNexis, ORT,
Verband der Vereine
Creditreform e.V.
Internet: DataStarWeb at
www.dialog.com/info/
products/datastar-index.shtml

CRETOP
Korea Credit Guarantee Fund
254-5, Kongduk-dong, Mapo-
Gu
Seoul 121-744, Republic of
Korea
8227104764
Online: Korea Credit
Guarantee Fund, Unitel

**D&B Dun's Financial
Records Plus (DFR Plus)**
Dun & Bradstreet, Inc.
One Diamond Hill Rd.
Murray Hill, NJ 07974-1218
(800)234-3867; (908)665-
5000
Online: CompuServe
Interactive Services, Dialog,
Factiva Information America
(IA) Internet: DialogWeb at
www.dialogweb.com

**D&B Dun's Market
Identifiers (DMI)**
Dun & Bradstreet, Inc.
One Diamond Hill Rd.
Murray Hill, NJ 07974-1218
(800)234-3867; (908)665-
5000
Online: AT&T EasyLink
Services, DataStar,

CompuServe Interactive
Services, GEnie, Factiva,
Information America (IA),
West Group—Westlaw,
Youvelle Renaissance Group
Internet: DataStarWeb at
www.dialog.com/info/
products/datastar-index.shtml

**D&B European Dun's
Market Identifiers (EDMI)**
Dun & Bradstreet, Inc.
One Diamond Hill Rd.
Murray Hill, NJ 07974-1218
(800)234-3867; (908)665-
5000
Online: AT&T EasyLink
Services, CompuServe
Interactive Services, Dialog,
European Information
Network Services (EINS),
NIFTY-SERVE, West
Group–WESTLAW
Internet: DialogWeb at
www.dialogweb.com

**D&B European Financial
Records**
Dun & Bradstreet, Ltd.
Holmers Farm Waye
High Wycombe, Bucks. HP12
4UL, England
44 1494 422000
Online: DataStar, Dialog, FT
Profile
Internet: DataStarWeb at
www.dialog.com/info/
products/datastar-index.shtml
and DialogWeb at
www.dialogweb.com

**D&B Global Corporate
Linkages**
Dun & Bradstreet, Inc.
One Diamond Hill Rd.
Murray Hill, NJ 07974-1218

(800)234-3867; (908)665-
5000
Online: Dialog
Internet: DialogWeb at
www.dialogweb.com

**D&B Norge–SVAR
DIREKTE**
Dun & Bradstreet Norge AS
Okernveien 145
Postboks 34 Okern
N-0508 Oslo, Norway
47 22915334
Online: Dun & Bradstreet
Norge AS

**D&B's Business
Information Report (BIR)**
Dun & Bradstreet, Inc.
One Diamond Hill Rd.
Murray Hill, NJ 07974-1218
(800)234-3867; (908)665-
5000
Online: West Group–Westlaw

**Danish Companies: Full
Financial Data**
Kobmandsstandens
Oplysningsbureau A/S
Gammel Mont 4
DK-1117 Copenhagen K,
Denmark
45 33111200
Online: DataStar
Internet: DataStarWeb at
www.dialog.com/info/
products/datastar-index.shtml

**Disclosure Corporate
Snapshots**
Primark Corporation
Primark Financial
Information Division
Disclosure Inc.
5161 River Rd.

Bethesda, MD 20816
(800)754-9690; (800)846-
0365; (301)951-1753
Online: OCLC FirstSearch
Catalog

Disclosure SEC Database
Primark Corporation
Primark Financial
Information Division
Disclosure Inc.
5161 River Rd.
Bethesda, MD 20816
(800)754-9690; (800)846-
0365; (301)951-1753
Online: ADP Financial
Information Services
(ADP/FIS), CompuServe
Interactive Services,
DataStar, Factiva,
LexisNexis, Quotron
Systems, Inc., and as part of
Compact D, Global Access
and M.A.I.D. (Market
Analysis and Information
Database)
Internet: DataStarWeb at
www.dialog.com/info/
products/datastar-index.shtml

**Dun & Bradstreet Nordic
Financial Records (DNFR)**
Dun & Bradstreet, Ltd.
Holmers Farm Waye
High Wycombe, Bucks.
HP12 4UL, England
44 1494 422000
Online: DataStar
Internet: DataStarWeb at
www.dialog.com/info/
products/datastar-index.shtml

**Dun & Bradstreet Soliditet
Business & Credit
Information**
Dun & Bradstreet Sverige

AB
Sundbybergsvagen 1
P.O. Box 1506
S-171 29 Solna, Sweden
46 851901000
Internet: Dun & Bradstreet
Sverige AB at
www.dbsverige.se/default.htm

Duns Business Records Plus
Information America (IA)
Marquis One Tower
245 Peachtree Center Ave.,
Ste. 1400
Atlanta, GA 30303
(800)235-4008; (404)479-
6500
Online: Information America
(IA)

DunsPrint Canada
Dun & Bradstreet Canada
5770 Hurontario St.
Mississauga, ON, Canada
L5R 3G5
(800)463-6362; (905)568-
6000
Online: Dun & Bradstreet
Canada

EDGAR Plus
Primark Corporation
Primark Financial
Information Division
Disclosure Inc.
5161 River Rd.
Bethesda, MD 20816
(800)754-9690; (800)846-
0365; (301)951-1753
Online: LexisNexis, Primark
Corporation–Primark
Financial Information
Division–Disclosure Inc. and
Internet: Global Access at
www.primark.com/
GuidetoSEC.pdf

Electric Utility Financials
Haver Analytics
60 E. 42nd St., Ste. 3310
New York, NY 10165
(212)986-9300
Online: GE Information
Services

**ESEI (Erhvervs- og
Selskabsstyrelsen Eksterne
Informationssystem)**
Erhvervs- og
Selskabsstyrelsen (EOGS)
Danish Commerce and
Companies Agency (DCCA)
Kampmannsgade 1
DK-1780 Copenhagen V,
Denmark
45 33307700
Internet: Erhvervs- og
Selskabsstyrelsen (EOGS)-
Danish Commerce and
Companies Agency
(DCCA) at www.
publi-com.dk index2.htm

**ESPICOM Pharmaceutical
& Medical Company
Profiles**
ESPICOM Business
Intelligence
Lincoln House
City Fields Business Park
City Fields Way
Chichester, W. Sussex PO20
6FS, England
44 1243 533322
Online: Dialog
Internet: DialogWeb at
www.dialogweb.com

EURIDILE
France Institut National de la
Propriete Industrielle (INPI)
26 bis, rue de Saint
Petersbourg

F-75800 Paris, France
33 1 5304 5414
Online: ORT

European Business Browser
OneSource Information
Services
300 Baker Ave., Ste. 303
Concord, MA 01742-2131
(800)554-5501; (978)318-
4300
Internet: OneSource
Information Services at
www.onesource.com/index.htm

**Europe's 15,000 Largest
Companies**
ELC Publishing Ltd.
109 Uxbridge Rd.
Ealing
London W5 5TL, England
181 5662288
Online: Chamber World
Network–Asia Intelligence
Wire

FIB Database
or **Firmen-Info-Bank**
AZ Bertelsmann Direct
GmbH
Carl-Bertelsmann-St 161s
D-33311 Gutersloh, Germany
052 41 805438
Online: GBI, GENIOS
Internet: AZ Bertelsmann
Direct GmbH at www.az.
bertelsmann.de/static/index.
html

**Financial Analysis Made
Easy (FAME)**
Jordans Ltd.
21 St. Thomas St.
Bristol BS1 6JS, England
44 117 9230600

Online: DataStar, FT Profile,
Jordans Ltd. and as part of
Waterlow Signature
Internet: Bureau van Dijk, SA
(BvD) Electronic Publishing
at http://fame3.bvdep.com/
cgi/template.dll?product=1
and DataStarWeb at
www.dialog.com/info/
products/datastar-index.shtml

**FIRMENINFORMATIO-
NEN–Numeric (FINN)**
or **FINF-Numeric;
Company Information
(COIN); Creditreform-
Bilanzdatenbank**
Verband der Vereine
Creditreform e.V.
Hellersbergstr. 12
Postfach 101552
D-41460 Neuss, Germany
49 2131 109300
Online: DataStar, GBI,
GENIOS
Internet: DataStarWeb at
www.dialog.com/info/
products/datastar-index.shtml

FIS Company Archives
Mergent FIS, Inc.
60 Madison Ave., 6th Fl.
New York, NY 10010
(800)342-5647; (212)413-
7670
Online: As part of Company
Data Direct/U.S.
Internet: Mergent FIS, Inc.at
www.fisonline.com

Foretagsfakta
KreditFakta AB
S-11390 Stockholm, Sweden
46 8 7365600
Fax: 46 8 7365160
Online: KreditFakta AB

FP Corporate Survey
The Financial Post Datagroup
333 King St. E.
Toronto, ON, Canada M5A
4N2
(800)661-7678; (416)350-
6500
Online: Infomart Dialog Ltd.
(IDL), Infomart Online

**German Macro and
Financial Data**
Haver Analytics
60 E. 42nd St., Ste. 3310
New York, NY 10165
(212)986-9300
Internet: Haver Analytics at
www.haver.com

Global Access
Primark Corporation
Primark Financial
Information Division
Disclosure Inc.
5161 River Rd.
Bethesda, MD 20816
(800)754-9690; (800)846-
0365; (301)951-1753
Internet: Primark
Corporation–Primark
Financial Information
Division–Disclosure Inc. at
www.primark.com

Global Business Browser
OneSource Information
Services
300 Baker Ave., Ste. 303
Concord, MA 01742-2131
(800)554-5501; (978)318-
4300
Internet: OneSource
Information Services at
www.onesource.com/index.htm

Global Scan
Equifax PLC

Godmersham Park
Godmersham
Canterbury, Kent CT4 7DT,
England
44 1227 81300
Online: BT Telecom Gold,
FT Profile

**High-growth Small and
Medium Enterprise
Directory**
Small and Medium Industry
Promotion Corporation
(SMIPC)
24-3, Yoido-dong,
Youngdcungpo-Gu
Seoul 150-718, Republic of
Korea
82 2 7696593
Online: Small and Medium
Industry Promotion
Corporation (SMIPC)

Hoover's Online
Hoover's, Inc.
1033 La Posada Dr., Ste. 100
Austin, TX 78752-3812
(800)486-8666; (888)310-
6087; (512)374-4500
Online: Hoover's, Inc.
Internet: Limited information
available through Hoover's at
www.hoovers.com

Hoppenstedt Austria
Verlag Hoppenstedt GmbH
Havelstrasse 9
Postfach 100139
D-64201 Darmstadt,
Germany
49 6151 3800
Online: Austria Presse
Agentur (APA), DataStar,
GBI
Internet: DataStarWeb at
www.dialog.com/info/

products/datastar-index.shtml
and GBI at http://engl.gbi.de

Hoppenstedt Benelux
ABC voor Handel en
Industrie C.V.
Koningin Wilhelminalaan 16
NL-2012 JK Haarlem,
Netherlands
31 235 327033
Online: ABC voor Handel en
Industrie C.V., DataStar,
Questel Orbit
Internet: DataStarWeb at
www.dialog.com/info/
products/datastar-index.shtml
and Questel at telnet://
questel.questel.fr

**Hoppenstedt
Bilanzdatenbank Banken
(HOBB)**
or **Hoppenstedt Balance
Sheets Banking
Establishments**
Verlag Hoppenstedt GmbH
Havelstrasse 9
Postfach 100139
D-64201 Darmstadt,
Germany
49 6151 3800
Online: GENIOS,
LexisNexis, and as part of
Datastream–Investext

**Hoppenstedt
Bilanzdatenbank
Industrieunternehmen
(HOBI)**
or **Hoppenstedt Balance
Sheets of Industrial
Enterprises**
Verlag Hoppenstedt GmbH
Havelstrasse 9
Postfach 100139
D-64201 Darmstadt,

Germany
49 6151 3800
Online: GENIOS

**Hoppenstedt
Bilanzdatenbank
Versicherungen (HOBV)**
or **Hoppenstedt Balance
Sheets of Insurance
Companies**
Verlag Hoppenstedt GmbH
Havelstrasse 9
Postfach 100139
D-64201 Darmstadt,
Germany
49 6151 3800
Online: GENIOS, Primark
Corporation–Primark
Financial Information
Division–Datastream
Internet: Primark
Corporation–Primark
Financial Information
Division–Datastream
International Ltd. at
www.datastream.com

Hoppenstedt Germany
or **Hoppenstedt German
Companies**
Verlag Hoppenstedt GmbH
Havelstrasse 9
Postfach 100139
D-64201 Darmstadt,
Germany
49 6151 3800
Internet: Verlag Hoppenstedt
GmbH at www.company
database.de/endex.html

**ICC British Company
Annual Reports**
ICC Information Ltd.
Field House
72 Oldfield Rd.
Hampton

Middlesex TW12 2HQ,
England
44 20 84818800
Online: DataStar, Dialog
Internet: DataStarWeb at
www.dialog.com/info/
products/datastar-index.shtml
and DialogWeb at
www.dialogweb.com

ICC British Company Financial Reports

ICC Information Ltd.
Field House
72 Oldfield Rd.
Hampton
Middlesex TW12 2HQ,
England
44 20 84818800
Online: DataStar, DIALOG,
GBI, Primark
Corporation–Primark
Financial Information
Division–Datastream
Internet: DataStarWeb at
www.dialog.com/info/
products/datastar-index.shtml
and DialogWeb at
www.dialogweb.com

INFOCHECK

Equifax PLC
Godmersham Park
Godmersham
Canterbury, Kent CT4 7DT,
England
44 1227 81300
Online: DataStar, Equifax
PLC, The Infocheck Group,
Ltd.
Internet: DataStarWeb at
www.dialog.com/info/
products/datastar-index.shtml

Intelliscope

Intelligence Data, Inc.

22 Thomson Pl.
Boston, MA 02210
(800)654-0393; (617)856-
1890
Internet: Intelligence Data,
Inc. at intelliscope.
intelligencedata.com/index.
jsp

International Dun's Market Identifiers (IDMI)

Dun & Bradstreet, Inc.
One Diamond Hill Rd.
Murray Hill, NJ 07974-1218
(800)234-3867; (908)665-
5000
Online: AT&T EasyLink
Services, Bell & Howell
Information and Learning,
CompuServe Interactive
Services, Dialog, Factiva,
Information America (IA),
NIFTY-SERVE, West
Group–Westlaw
Internet: DialogWeb at
www.dialogweb.com

Investext

Thomson Financial Securities
Data (TFSD)
Two Gateway Center
Newark, NJ 07102
(888)989-8373; (973)622-
3100
Online: Bell & Howell
Information and Learning,
CompuServe Interactive
Services, Data Downlink
Corporation, DataStar,
Dialog, European
Information Netrowk
Services (EINS), Factiva, FIZ
Technik, FT Profile, I/PLUS
Direct, STN International,
Thomson Financial Securities
Data (TFSD), and as part of

Lexis Financial Information
Service, Research Bank Web
Internet: DataStarWeb at
www.dialog.com/info/
products/datastar-index.shtml
and DialogWeb at
www.dialogweb.com

ISIS: InSurance Information and Statistics

Bureau van Dijk, SA (BvD)
Electronic Publishing
Ave. Louise 250
Box 14
B-1050 Brussels, Belgium
32 2 6390606
Internet: Bureau van Dijk, SA
(BvD)- Electronic Publishing
at www.bvdep.com/Product
Page.asp?product=ISIS

Italian Company Financial Profiles

Databank S.p.A.
Via dei Piatti 11
I-20123 Milan, Italy
39 2 809556
Online: DataStar
Internet: DataStarWeb at
www.dialog.com/info/
products/datastar-index.shtml

Jane's World Defence Industry

Jane's Information Group
Sentinel House
163 Brighton Rd.
Coulsdon, Surrey CR5 2YH,
England
44 20 87003703
Internet: Jane's Information
Group at
http://catalogue.janes.com/
wrld_def_ind.shtml

JEWEL
Jordans Ltd.
21 St. Thomas St.
Bristol BS1 6JS, England
44 117 9230600
Online: Jordans Ltd.

Jobson's Online
or **Dun & Bradstreet**
Jobson's Online
Dun and Bradstreet
Marketing Pty. Ltd.
19 Havilah St.
Chatswood, NSW 2067,
Australia
61 2 99352700
Online: Dun and Bradstreet
Marketing Pty. Ltd.

JordanWatch: British
Companies
Jordans Ltd.
21 St. Thomas St.
Bristol BS1 6JS, England
44 117 9230600
Online: DataStar
Internet: DataStarWeb at
www.dialog.com/info/
products/datastar-index.shtml

Key British Enterprises
Financial Performance
Dun & Bradstreet, Ltd.
Holmers Farm Waye
High Wycombe, Bucks.
HP12 4UL, England
44 1494 422000
Online: DataStar
Internet: DataStarWeb at
www.dialog.com/info/
products/datastar-index.shtml

Kompass U.K. Register
Kompass International
Neuenschwander SA
Saint Laurent

F-73800 Cruet, France
33 479 652508
Online: as part of Kompass
Worldwide Database

Korean Company Directory
Korean Trade Market
Information Co., Ltd.
Pung-an Bldg., Rm. 501
385-108, Hapchong-Dong,
Mapo-ku
Seoul, Republic of Korea
822 3227611
Online: Korean Trade Market
Information Co., Ltd.

Korean Company
Information
National Information &
Credit Evaluation Inc.
(NICE)
Ah-tae Bldg 1337-20
Seocho-2dong Seocho-ku
Seoul, Republic of Korea
82 2 34755600
Online: Chollian, HiTEL,
Nownuri, Unitel Co. Ltd.,
and as part of Nice-Tips

Kreditschutzverband:
Austrian Companies
(KSVA)
Kreditschutzverband von
1870
Zelinkagasse 10
A-1010 Vienna, Austria
43 1 53484400
Online: Austria Presse
Agentur (APA), DataStar,
GBI, Kreditschutzverband
von 1870
Internet: DataStarWeb at
www.dialog.com/info/
products/datastar-index.shtml

Luottotietokanta
or **Credit Information**
Database
Suomen Asiakastieto Oy
P.O. Box 16
FIN-00581 Helsinki, Finland
358 9 14886523
Online: Suomen Asiakastieto
Oy

Luxemburgs ABC for Trade
and Industry
or **Luxembourgs ABC voor**
Handel en Industrie
ABC voor Handel en
Industrie C.V.
Koningin Wilhelminalaan 16
NL-2012 JK Haarlem,
Netherlands
31 235 327033
Online: ABC voor Handel en
Industrie C.V., GBI, DataStar,
LexisNexis and as part of
Hoppenstedt Benelux
Internet: DataStarWeb at
www.dialog.com/info/
products/datastar-index.shtml

Market & Business
Development
Market & Business
Development Ltd. (MBD)
Barnett House
53 Fountain St.
Manchester M2 2AN,
England
44 161 2478600
Online: DataStar, FT PRO-
FILE, Mintel International
Group, Ltd., Reuters Group
PLC, Thomson Financial
Securities Data (TFSD)
Internet: DataStarWeb at
www.dialog.com/info/
products/datastar-index.shtml

Market Guide
Market Guide, Inc.
2001 Marcus Ave., Ste. S.
200, 2nd Fl.
Lake Success, NY 11042
(516)327-2400
Online: ADP Financial
Information Services
(ADP/FIS), Argus Research
Corporation, Bridge
Information Systems,
Inc.–Knight-Ridder Financial
Information Group, CDA
Investment Technologies –
CDA/Wiesenberger, Dialog,
Interactive Data Corporation,
Market Guide, Inc., Quotron
Systems, Inc., Shark
Information Systems, Telerate
Systems Inc., Telescan, Inc.,
Thomson Financial Securities
Data (TFSD), Track Data
Corporation, Vickers Stock
Research Corporation, and as
part of Dial/Data, and
Investext
Internet: DialogWeb at
www.dialogweb.com

Media General Plus
Media General Financial
Services, Inc. (MGFS)
301 E. Franklin St.
P.O. Box 85333
Richmond, VA 23293
(800)775-8118; (800)775-
8118; (804)775-8000
Online: Dialog
Internet: DialogWeb at
www.dialogweb.com

**New Straits Times
Company Database**
New Straits Times Press
(Malaysia) Berhad

Balai Berita
31 Jalan Riong
59100 Kuala Lumpur,
Malaysia
603 2823131
Online: Chamber World
Network–Asia Intelligence
Wire

NICE-TIPS
National Information &
Credit Evaluation Inc.
(NICE)
Ah-tae Bldg 1337-20 Seocho-
2dong Seocho-ku
Seoul, Republic of Korea
82 2 34755600
Online: National Information
& Credit Evaluation Inc.
(NICE)

**Pharmaceutical Company
Profiles**
IMS HEALTH Incorporated
IMS HEALTH Global
Services
7 Harewood Ave.
London NW1 6JB, England
44 20 73935757
Online: DataStar, Dialog,
STN International and as part
of Companies on the Web
Internet: DataStarWeb at
www.dialog.com/info/
products/datastar-index.shtml
and DialogWeb at
www.dialogweb.com

**PIMS Competitive Strategy
Data Base**
Strategic Planning Institute
1030 Massachusetts Ave.
Cambridge, MA 02138
(617)491-9200
Online: Strategic Planning
Institute

Pratt's Stats
Business Valuation Resources
7412 SW Beaverton Hillsdale
Hwy., Ste. 106
Portland, OR
(888)BUS-VALU; (503)291-
7963
Internet: NVST Business
Valuation Resources at
http://NVST.com/val

**Professional Investor
Report (PIR)**
Factiva
P.O. Box 300
Princeton, NJ 08543-0300
(800)832-1234; (609)520-
4000
Online: Factiva, Track Data
Corporation

Publi-com
Erhvervs- og
Selskabsstyrelsen (EOGS)
Danish Commerce and
Companies Agency (DCCA)
Kampmannsgade 1
DK-1780 Copenhagen V,
Denmark
45 33307700
Online: Erhvervs- og
Selskabsstyrelsen (EOGS)-
Danish Commerce and
Companies Agency (DCCA)

QUICK I
Dun & Bradstreet Finland Oy
PL 42, Vattuniemenkatu 21A
FIN-00211 Espoo, Finland
358 9 25344400
Online: Dun & Bradstreet
Finland Oy

Research Bank Web
Thomson Financial Securities
Data (TFSD)

Two Gateway Center
Newark, NJ 07102
(888)989-8373; (973)622-3100
Online: Thomson Financial
Securities Data (TFSD)

The S&W Database
or French Company
Balance Sheets
Chambre de Commerce et
d'Industrie de Paris (CCIP)
Direction de l'Information
Economique (DIE)
2, rue de Viarmes
F-75001 Paris, France
33 1 55653643
Online: DataStar
Internet: DataStarWeb at
www.dialog.com/info/
products/datastar-index.shtml

SCRL Bilans Plus
AXETUDES–Coface SCRL
5, Alfred de Vigny
F-75008 Paris, France
33 1 42122345
Online: Questel Orbit
Internet: Questel at
telnet://questel.questel.fr

SCRL French Companies
Financial Profiles
AXETUDES–Coface SCRL
5, Alfred de Vigny
F-75008 Paris, France
33 1 42122345
Online: DataStar
Internet: DataStarWeb at
www.dialog.com/info/
products/datastar-index.shtml

SEC Online
Primark Corporation
Primark Financial
Information Division

Disclosure Inc.
5161 River Rd.
Bethesda, MD 20816
(800)754-9690; (800)846-0365; (301)951-1753
Online: Bloomberg Financial
Markets, Bridge Inforamtin
Systems, Inc.–Knight-Ridder
Financial Information Group,
Dialog, Factiva, I/PLUS
Direct, Information America
(IA), LexisNexis, Primark
Corporation–Primark
Financial Information
Division–Disclosure Inc.,
Telescan, Inc., Thomson
Financial Securities Data
(TFSD), Track Data
Corporation,
West Group–Westlaw
Internet: DialogWeb at
www.dialogweb.com

Skyminder.com
CRIBIS-CRIF Business
Information Services
Island Center, Ste. 1040
2701 North Rocky Point Dr.
Tampa, FL 33607
(813)636-0981
Online: CRIBIS-CRIF
Business Information
Services

Standard & Poor's
Corporate Descriptions
plus NEWS
Standard & Poor's
55 Water St.
New York, NY 10041-0003
(800)221-5277; (212)438-7280
Online: Dialog, FactSet Data
Systems, Inc., LexisNexis
Internet: DialogWeb at
www.dialogweb.com

Standard & Poor's
MarketScope
Standard & Poor's
MarketScope Services
55 Water St.
42nd Floor
New York, NY 10041-0003
(800)233-2310
Online: Beta Systems,
Bloomberg Financial
Markets, Bridge, Bunker
Ramo, CompuServe
Interactive Services, Factiva,
Shark Information Systems,
Standard & Poor's, Telerate
Systems Inc., Telescan, Inc.,
Track Data Corporation
Internet: Standard & Poor's
at www.advisorinsight.com

Supplier Evaluation
Dun & Bradstreet, Inc.
One Diamond Hill Rd.
Murray Hill, NJ 07974-1218
(800)234-3867; (908)665-5000
Online: Dialog
Internet: DialogWeb at
www.dialogweb.com

Teikoku Japanese
Companies
Teikoku Databank America,
Inc.
747 Third Ave., 25th Fl.
New York, NY 10017
(212)421-9805
Online: DataStar, Dialog, G-Search Ltd., LexisNexis,
Nikkei Telecom
Internet: DataStarWeb at
www.dialog.com/info/
products/datastar-index.shtml
and DialogWeb at
www.dialogweb.com

Thomson Bank Directory
Thomson Financial
Corporate Communications
22 Thomson Pl., 11F2
Boston, MA 02210
(877)983-4636; (617)856-
4636
Online: SilverPlatter
Information Inc.

Thomson Savings Directory
Thomson Financial
Corporate Communications
22 Thomson Pl., 11F2
Boston, MA 02210
(877)983-4636; (617)856-
4636
Online: LexisNexis

ThomsonDirect.com
Thomson Financial Securities
Data (TFSD)
Two Gateway Center
Newark, NJ 07102
(888)989-8373; (973)622-
3100
Online: Thomson Financial
Securities Data (TFSD)

Transdata WebReports
TransData Corporation, Ltd.
P.O. Box 1883
North Sydney, NSW 2059,
Australia
61 2 99225544
1800-622447; 888-522-6038
Internet: TransData
Corporation, Ltd. at
www.webreports.net/subs/we
breports.cfm

**TRW Business Credit
Profiles**
Experian
505 City Pkwy. W., 3rd Fl.
Orange, CA 92868

(888)397-3742; (800)972-
0322; (714)385-7712
Online: CompuServe
Interactive Services, Dialog
Internet: DialogWeb at
www.dialogweb.com

TSR-VAN
Tokyo Shoko Research, Ltd.
(TSR)
Shinichi Bldg., 9-6, 1-Chome
Shinbashi
Minato-ku
Tokyo 105-0004, Japan
81 3 35742211
Online: Tokyo Shoko
Research, Ltd. (TSR)

U.S. Business Browser
OneSource Information
Services
300 Baker Ave., Ste. 303
Concord, MA 01742-2131
(800)554-5501; (978)318-
4300
Internet: OneSource
Information Services at
www.onesource.com/index.htm

**U.S. Energy Company
Financials**
Haver Analytics
60 E. 42nd St., Ste. 3310
New York, NY 10165
(212)986-9300
Online: GE Information
Services

**UCs
Kreditupplysningsregister**
or **Business Info Covering
Sweden**
Upplysningscentralen UC AB
S-11496 Stockholm, Sweden
86709000

Online: Upplysningscentralen
UC AB

**U.K. and European Risk
Management Reports**
Dun & Bradstreet, Ltd.
Holmers Farm Waye
High Wycombe, Bucks. HP12
4UL, England
44 1494 422000
Online: Dun & Bradstreet,
Ltd.

U.K. Business Browser
OneSource Information
Services
300 Baker Ave., Ste. 303
Concord, MA 01742-2131
(800)554-5501; (978)318-
4300
Internet: OneSource
Information Services at
www.onesource.com/index.htm

Value Line DataFile
Value Line
Institutional Services
220 E. 42nd St.
New York, NY 10017
(800)531-1425; (212)907-
1550
Online: The DAIS Group,
Inc., FactSet Data Systems,
Inc., FAME Information
Services, Inc., Global
Information Technologies,
Salomon Smith Barney
Holdings, Inc., Shaw Data
Services, Inc., Vestek
Systems Inc.

**Ward's Business Directory
of U.S. Private and Public
Companies**
Gale Group
27500 Drake Rd.

Farmington Hills, MI 48331-
3535
(800)877-4253; (248)699-
4253
Online as part of Company
Intelligence, Gale Business
Resources, and InSite2

Worldscope
or Disclosure Worldscope
Database
Primark Corporation
Primark Financial
Information Division
Disclosure Inc.
5161 River Rd.
Bethesda, MD 20816
(800)754-9690; (800)846-
0365; (301)951-1753
Online: Bell & Howell
Information and Learning,
Bridge Information Systems,
Inc.–Knight-Ridder Financial
Information Group, Primark
Corporation–Primark
Financial Information
Division–Datastream,
Factiva, FactSet Data
Systems, Inc., FAME
Information Services, Inc.,
LexisNexis, OCLC
FirstSearch Catalog,
Profound Inc.–The Dialog
Corporation, Sandpoint
Company–Sandpoint Hoover,
Vestek Systems Inc., and as
part of Compact D and
Global Access

Worldscope Emerging
Markets Database
Primark Corporation
Primark Financial
Information Division
Disclosure Inc.
5161 River Rd.

Bethesda, MD 20816
(800)754-9690; (800)846-
0365; (301)951-1753
Online: CompuServe
Interactive Services, Dialog,
LexisNexis
Internet: DialogWeb at
www.dialogweb.com

Yritys-Suomi Online
Helsinki Media Blue Book
Hoylaamotie 1 D
PL 100
FIN-00040 Helsinki, Finland
358 9 1201
Online: Helsinki Media Blue
Book

Professional and Staff Directory Databases

Professional: (n)1. A person following a profession,
especially a learned profession. 2. One who earns a living
in a given or implied occupation: "hired a professional to
decorate the house." 3. A skilled practitioner; an expert.

The American Heritage Dictionary
of the English Language: Fourth Edition, 2000

Albi Avvocati e Procuratori
Corte Suprema di Cassazione
d'Italia
Centro Elettronico di
Comumentazione (CED)
Via Damiano Chiesa 24
I-100136 Rome, Italy
396 33081
Online: Corte Suprema di
Cassazione d'Italia–Centro
Elettronico di
Documentazione (CED)

Aspen Law & Business
Directory of Corporate
Counsel
Aspen Law & Business
1165 Avenue of the Americas
37
New York, NY 10036-2601
(800)638-8437; (212)894-
8484
Online: West Group–Westlaw

ASTERI
Maatalouden tutkimuskeskus
(MTT)
Agricultural Research Centre
of Finland (MTT)
FIN-31600 Jokioinen,
Finland
358 341881
Online: Maatalouden
tutimuskeskus (MTT)–
Agricultural Research Centre
of Finland (MTT)

BASELINE Celebrity
Contacts
BASELINE, INC.
838 Broadway, 4th Fl.
New York, NY 10003
(800)242-7546; (212)254-
8235
Online: LexisNexis, and as
part of BASELINE

BASELINE Company
Profiles
BASELINE, INC.
838 Broadway, 4th Fl.
New York, NY 10003
(800)242-7546; (212)254-
8235
Online: LexisNexis, and as
part of BASELINE

BEST Great Britain
Community of Science, Inc.
1629 Thames St., Ste. 200
Baltimore, MD 21231
(410)563-5382
Online: Community of
Science, Inc.

California Lobbyists/PACs
Directory
California Journal, Inc.
2101 K St.
Sacramento, CA 95816

(916)444-2840
Online: Information for
Public Affairs, Inc.
(IPA)–StateNet

**California State
Government Directory**
California Journal, Inc.
2101 K St.
Sacramento, CA 95816
(916)444-2840
Online: Information for
Public Affairs, Inc. (IPA)–
StateNet

**Canadian Federal
Corporations and Directors**
Infomart Dialog
333 King St. E
Toronto, ON Canada M5A
4R7
(800)668-9215; (416)350-
6001
Online: Infomart Online
(DCFC)

The Capital Source
National Journal Group Inc.
1501 M St. NW, Ste. 300
Washington, DC 20005 USA
(800)207-8001; (202)739-
8400
Online: LexisNexis, National
Journal Group Inc.

**Congressional Member
Profile Report**
LexisNexis
9443 Springboro Pike
P.O. Box 933
Dayton, OH 45401-0933
(800)227-4908; (937)865-
6800
Online: LexisNexis

**Congressional Staff
Directory**

Congressional Quarterly, Inc.
CQ Press
1414 22nd St., NW
Washington, DC 20037
(800)638-1710; (202)822-
1475
Online:Congressional
Quarterly, Inc. (CQ)
Internet: Congressional
Quarterly, Inc.–CQ Press at
http://csd.cq.com

**D&B Dun's Electronic
Business Directory (EYP)
Dun & Bradstreet**
3 Sylvan Way
Parsippany, NJ 07054
(800)223-1026; (973)605-
6000
Online: AT&T EasyLink
Services, CompuServe
Information Service, Dialog,
West Group–Westlaw, and as
part of Dun's Market
Identifiers
Internet: DialogWeb at
www.dialogweb.com

D&B UK Executive Report
Dun & Bradstreet Ltd.
5th Fl., Westminster House
Portland St.
Manchester, Greater
Manchester M1 3HU,
England
44 161 4555119
Online: Dun & Bradstreet
Ltd.

**Deutsche
Unternehmensberater**
Bundesverband Deutscher
Unternehmensberater BDU
e.V
Friedrich Wilhelm-Str. 2
D-53113 Bonn, Germany

228 91610
Online: GENIOS
Wirtschaftsdatenbanken

**Directory of Directors
Electronic Edition**
or **Financial Post Directory
of Directors**
The Financial Post Datagroup
333 King St. E.
Toronto, ON, Canada M5A
4N2
(800)661-7678; (416)350-
6500
Online: Infomart Dialog Ltd.
(IDL), Infomart Online

Executive Affiliation
Information America (IA)
Marquis One Tower, Ste.
1400
245 Peachtree Center Ave.
Atlanta, GA 30303
(800)235-4008; (404)479-
6500
Online: Information America

ExpertNet
ExpertNet, Ltd.
2514 Royal Ridge Dr.
Crete, IL 60417
(800)888-8318; (708)672-
3078
Online: West Group–Westlaw

**Federal Political and
Government Directory**
Info-One International Pty.
Ltd.
Level 3, 2 Elizabeth Plaza
North Sydney, NSW 2060,
Australia
612 99595075
Online: Info-One
Internatioanl Pty. Ltd.

Hoppenstedt Austria
Verlag Hoppenstedt GmbH
Havelstrasse 9
Postfach 100139
D64201 Darmstadt, Germany
06151 3800
Online: Austria Presse
Agentur (APA), DataStar,
BGI
Internet: DataStarWeb at
www.dialog.com/info/
products/datastar-index.shtml
and GBI at http://engl.gbi.de

**ICC British Directors
Database**
ICC Information Ltd.
Field House
72 Oldfield Rd.
Hampton
Middlesex TW12 2HQ,
England
44 20 84818800
Online: DataStar
Internet: DataStarWeb at
www.dialog.com/info/
products/datastar index shtml

**Jane's International ABC
Aerospace Directory**
Jane's Information Group
Sentinel House
163 Brighton Rd.
Coulsdon, Surrey CR5 2YH,
England
44 20 87003703
Internet: Jane's Information
Group at www.janes.com

Kvinder pa linien
or **Women on Line**
KVINFO–The Danish Centre
for Information on Women
and Gender
Christians Brygge 3

DK-1219 Copenhagen K,
Denmark
45 33135088
Online: KVINFO–The
Danish Centre for
Information on Women and
Gender
Internet: Skyrr og Elias at
www.polinfodk/kvinfo

The Leadership Library
Leadership Directories, Inc.
104 5th Ave.
New York, NY 10011 USA
(212)627-4140
Internet: Leadership
Directories, Inc. at
www.leadershipdirectories.com

**Lexis State Corporation
Information Library
(INCORP)**
LexisNexis
9443 Sprinboro Pike
P.O. Box 933
Dayton, OH 45401-0933
(800)227-4908; (937)865-
6800
Online: LexisNexis

Literature Library
YEIN Information Co., Ltd.
401 Post Office, 234-4, Kui-
Dong
Kwang, Jin-gu
Seoul 133-201, Republic of
Korea
8224466064
Online: Infoshop

**Lloyd's Ship Owners,
Managers, and Parent
Companies File**
Lloyd's Maritime
Information Services Ltd.
69-77 Paul St.

London, EC2A 4LQ,
England
44 171 5531000
Online: Lloyd's Maritime
Inforamtion Services Ltd.
(LMIS) and as part of
Seadata

**Martindale-Hubbell Law
Directory Online**
Martindale Hubbell
Reed Reference Publishing
Group
121 Chanlon Rd.
New Providence, NJ 07974
(800)526 4902; (908)464-
6800
Online: LexisNexis
Internet: Martindale-Hubbell
Lawyer Locator at
www2.martindale.com

NNDC Address List
Brookhaven National
Laboratory
National Nuclear Data Center
(NNDC)
Bldg. 197D
P.O. Box 5000
Upton, NY 11973-5000
(516)344-2901
Online: Brookhaven National
Laboratory–National Nuclear
Data Center (NNDC)

PARAD Online
Bonnier Business Publishing
Group
AffarsData
P.O. Box 3188
S-103 63 Stockholm, Sweden
08 7365919
Online: Bonnier Business
Publishing Group–AffarsData

PDQ (Physician Data Query)
U.S. National Cancer Institute
Bethesda, MD 20892
(301)496-6644
Online: DIMDI (Deutsches Institut fuer Medizinische Dokumentation und Information)

Riksdagsinformation, LEDREG
Sveriges riksdag
S-100 12 Stockholm, Sweden
46 8 7864000
Online: Rixlex

Scott's Directories
Infomart Dialog
333 King St. E
Toronto, ON, Canada M5A 4R7
(800)668-9215; (416)350-6001
Online: Infomart Online (DSCT)

Simmons Top Management Insights
Simmons Market Research Bureau, Inc. (SMRB)
309 W. 49th St.
New York, NY 10019 USA
(212)373-8900
Online: Simmons Market Research Bureau, Inc. (SMRB)

Singapore Architects and Designers Directory
Times Trade Directories Pte. Ltd.
Times Centre
1 New Industrial Rd.
Singapore 536196, Singapore

65284 8844
Online: Chamber World Network–Asia Intelligence Wire, as as part of Chamber World Network (CWN)

StateNet
2101 K Street
Sacramento, CA 95816
(916)444-0840
Online: State Net
Internet: State Net at www.statenet.com

Technical Advisory Service for Attorneys (TASA)
Technical Advisory Service, Inc.
1166 DeKalb Pike
Blue Bell, PA 19422-1853
(800)523-2319; (800)329-8272; (610)275-8272
Online: West Group–Westlaw

Texas Faculty Profiles
Texas Innovation Network System (TINS)
3500 W. Balcones Center Dr.
Austin, TX 78759
(800)645-8324
Online: Texas Innovation Network System (TINS)

West's Legal Directory
West Group
620 Opperman Dr.
Eagan, MN 55123
(800)328-9352; (651)687-7000
Online: West Group–Westlaw

Refer to Chapter 15: Biographies, Chapter 18: Staff, Professional and Other Directories, and Appendix A: Databases That Include Biographies, for other examples of databases that can be used as professional directories. Note that Business Credit and Company Financial Records also often contain listings of key executives, so refer to Chapter 24 and Appendix C for these.

Please note that there are many Web sites of licensing and regulatory agencies containing directories of those licensed in various professions. These may also be used as professional directories. Refer to Chapter 7: Pre-Employment Screening for examples of these.

Other Directory Databases Containing Employee Information

Work is the refuge of people who have nothing better to do.

–Oscar Wilde

ABC Belge pour le Commerce et l'Industrie
ABC pour le Commerce et l'Industrie C.V.
Doomveld 1B28
B-1731 Asse, Belgium
02 4630213
Internet: ABC pour le Commerce et l'Industrie C.V. at www.abc-d.be

ABC Europe Production Europex
Europe Export Edition GmbH
P.O. Box 100262
D-64202 Darmstadt 1, Germany
06151 38920
Online: FIZ Technik, STN International

ABC Germany
or **ABC der Deutschen Wirschaft; German**

Buyers' and Sellers' Guide; Info Bonds
ABC der Deutschen Wirtschaft
Verlagsgesellschaft mbH
ABC Publishing Group
P.O. Box 100262
D-64202 Darmstadt, Germany
6151 38920
Internet: FIZ Technik at www.fiz-technik.de

ABC Luxembourgeois pour le Commerce et l'Industrie
ABC pour le Commerce et l'Industrie C.V.
Doomveld 1B28
B-1731 Asse, Belgium
02 4630213
Internet: ABC pour le Commerce et l'Industrie C.V. at www.abc-d.be

ABC voor Handel en Industrie
or **ABC for Trade and Industry**
ABC voor Handel en Industrie C.V.
P.O. Box 190
NL-2000 AD Haarlem, Netherlands
31 235319031
Online: ABC voor Handel en Industrie C.V., DataStar, GBI, LexisNexis, and as part of Hoppenstedt Benelux
Internet: DataStarWeb at www.dialog.com/info/products/datastar-index.shtml, LexisNexis at www.lexisnexis.com

ABCDienstverleners
or **Dutch Directory of Business Services; ABC Services**
ABC voor Handel en

Industrie C.V.
P.O. Box 190
NL-2000 AD Haarlem,
Netherlands
31 235319031
Online: ABC voor Handel en
Industrie C.V., DataStar, GBI,
LEXISNEXIS and as part of
Hoppenstedt Benelux
Internet: DataStarWeb at
www.dialog.com/info/
products/datastar-index.shtml,
LexisNexis at www.lexis
nexis.com

**American Library
Directory (ALD)**
R.R. Bowker
121 Chanlon R.d
New Providence, NJ 07974
(888)BOWKER2; (908)464-
6800
Online:Dialog, LexisNexis
Internet: DialogWeb at
www.dialogweb.com,
LexisNexis at www.
lexisnexis.com

**Australian Rural Research
in Progress (ARRIP)**
Australia Commonwealth
Scientific and Industrial
Research Organisation
(CSIRO)
CSIRO Information
Technology Services
700 Blackburn Rd.
Private Bag 89
Clayton, VIC 3002, Australia
03 9518 5900
Online: RMIT
Publishing–Informit
Electronic Publishing &
Training

**Belgisch ABC voor Handel
en Industrie**
ABC voor Handel en
Industrie C.V.
P.O. Box 190
NL-2000 AD Haarlem,
Netherlands
31 235319031
Online: ABC voor Handel en
Industrie C.V., GBI, and as
part of Hoppenstedt Benelux

**BioScan: The Worldwide
Biotech Industry Reporting
Service**
American Health Consultants
3525 Piedmont Rd.
Bldg. 6, Ste. 400
Atlanta, GA 30305
(800)688-2421; (404)262-
7436
Online: Knowledge Express
Data Systems–Knowledge
Express

**BizEkon News–Soviet
Business Directory**
or **BizEkon Companies in
the C.I.S.**
Russian Information and
Communications Agency
(RUSSICA)
Spartakovskaya St. 13
107066 Moscow, Russia
095 9325610
Online: GBI, LexisNexis,
MagnaTex International
Inc.–COMMUNICATE!,
SovInfoLink, and as part of
Soviet News

Dun & Bradstreet Germany
Dun & Bradstreet Ltd.
5th Fl., Westminster House
Portland St.
Manchester, Greater

Manchester M1 3HU,
England
44 161 4555119
Online: DataStar,
Questel–Orbit, and as part of
DBZZ
Internet: DataStarWeb at
www.dialog.com/info/
products/datastar-index.shtml

**Dun & Bradstreet (Israel)
Ltd.**
Dun & Bradstreet (Israel)
Ltd.
City Palace
27 Hamered St.
68125 Tel Aviv, Israel
9723 5103355
Online: DataStar, FIZ
Technik
Internet: DataStarWeb at
www.dialog.com/info/
products/datastar-index.shtml,
Dun & Bradstreet (Irsrael)
Ltd. at www.dnb.com/
country/il.asp

Dun & Bradstreet Italy
Via dei Valtorta
48-20127 Milano
Italy
02 28455 1
www.dnb.it/index.html

**Dun & Bradstreet United
Kingdom**
50-100 Holmers Farm Way
High Wycombe
Buckinghamshire
HP12 4UL
England
44 (0) 1494 422000
44 (0) 870 243 2344

ESSOR
Union Francaise des

Annuaires Porfessionnels
(UFAP)/ESSOR
130 av des Bouleaux
BP 36
F-78192 Trappes Cedex,
France
0130138200
Online: Questel–Orbit
Internet: Questel–Orbit at tel-
net://questel.questel.fr

EUDISED
or **European
Documentation and
Information System for
Education**
Council of Europe
European Documentation and
Information System for
Education (EUDISED)
F-67075 Strasbourg Cedex,
France
33 0 388 41 25 81
Online: European
Information Network
Services (EINS)

EURISTOTE
Commission of the European
Communities (CEC)
Directorate-Genearl
Batiment Jean Monnet
Plateau du Kirchberg
L-2920 Luxembourg,
Luxembourg
430134226
Online: Commission of the
European Communities
(CEC)– European
Commission Host
Organization (ECHO)

Finnish Export Companies
Finnish Foreign Trade
Association
Arkadiankatu 4-6 B

P.O. Box 908
SF-00101 Helsinki, Finland
204 6951
Online: GBI

Foundation Directory
The Foundation Center
79 Fifth Ave.
New York, NY 10003-3050
(212)620-4230
Online: Dialog
Internet: DialogWeb at
www.dialogweb.com

Health Devices Sourcebook
ECRI
5200 Butler Pike
Plymouth Meeting, PA 19462
(610)825-6000
Online: Dialog, dimdi
(Deutsches Institut fuer
Medizinische Dokumentation
and Information
Internet: DialogWeb at
www.dialogweb.com

Holland Exports
ABC voor Handel en
Industrie C.V.
P.O. Box 190
NL-2000 AD Haarlem,
Netherlands
31 235319031
Online: ABC voor Handel en
Industrie C.V. (ABCX)
Internet: ABC voor Handel
en Industrie C.V. at
www.abc-d.nl

**Japanese Government and
Public Research in Progress**
Japan Science and
Technology Corporation,
Information Center for
Science and Technology
(JICST)

5-3, Yonbancho
Chiyoda-ku
Tokyo 102, Japan
81 3 52148413
Online: STN International

**Kompass Central/Eastern
Europe**
Kompass International
Neuenschwander SA
Saint Laurent
F-73800 Cruet, France
33 479 652508
Online: Dialog
Internet: DialogWeb at
www.dialogweb.com

KOMPASS-FRANCE
Kompass France S.A.
66, quai du Marechal Joffre
F-92415 Courbevoie Cedex,
France
33 1 41165100
Online: Kompass France S.A.

KOMPASS Israel
Kompass Israel Ltd.
P.O. Box 50384
29 Hamered St.
64253 Tel-Aviv, Israel
03 6470033
Online: Dialog
Internet: DialogWeb at
www.dialogweb.com

**Kompass Middle
East/Africa/Mediterranean**
Kompass International
Neuenschwander SA
Saint Laurent
F-73800 Cruet, France
33 479 652508
Online: Dialog
Internet: DialogWeb at
www.dialogweb.com

KOMPASS Online
Bonnier Information Services
Saltmatargatan 8, Box 3223
S-10364 Stockholm, Sweden
08 229120
Online: Bonnier Business
Publishing Group–AffarsData

Kompass U.K.
Reed Information Services
Windsor Court
East Grinstead House
East Grinstead, W. Sussez
RH19 1XA, England
0342 326972
Online: Dialog
Internet: DialogWeb at
www.dialogweb.com

Kompass USA
Kompass International
Neuenschwander SA
Saint Laurent
F-73800 Cruet, France
33 479 652508
Online: Dialog
Internet: DialogWeb at
www.dialogweb.com

Kompass Western Europe
Kompass International
Neuenschwander SA
Saint Laurent
F-73800 Cruet, France
33 479 652508
Online: Dialog, Kompass
International
Neuenschwander SA
Internet: DialogWeb at
www.dialogweb.com

Lexis State Corporation Information Library (INCORP)
LexisNexis
9443 Springboro Pike

P.O. Box 933
Dayton, OH 45401-0933
(800)227-4908; (937)865-6800
Online: LexisNexis
Internet: LexisNexis at
www.lexisnexis.com

Nordres
Teknillisen Korkeakoulun
Kirjasto
Helsinki University of
Technology Library
P.O. Box 7000
FIN-02015 Espoo, Finland
0 4514120
Online:Teknillinen
Korkeakoulu Atkeskus

Ofertas de Tecnologia
Instituto de la Pequena y
Mediana Empresa Industrial
(IMPI)
Paseo de la Castellana 141
E-28046 Madrid, Spain
341 5829312
Online: Instituto de la
Pequena y Mediana Empresa
Industrial (IMPI)

Research Centers and Services Directories (RCSD)
Gale Group
27500 Drake Rd.
Farmington Hills, MI 48331-3535
(800)877-4253; (248)699-4253
Online: Dialog
Internet: DialogWeb at
www.dialogweb.com,
InfoTrac (Gale Group) at
http://infotrac.galenet.com

SANI
or **Italian National Register of Companies**
CERVED International S.A.
rue de l'Industrie 22
B-1040 Bruxelles, Belgium
322 5141300
Online: CERVED
International S.A.

SIEPPO/Kirjastot
University of Helsinki
Science Library
P.O. Box 26
FIN-00014 Helsinki,
Fincland
3580 70844114
Online: University of
Helsinki–Computing Center

Sveriges Handelskanlendera
Bonnier Information Services
Saltmatargatan 8, Box 3223
S-10364 Stockholm, Sweden
08 229120
Online: Telenor Foretagsinfo

TEKTRAN (Technology Transfer Automated Retrieval System)
U.S. Department of
Agriculture
Agricultural Research Service
(ARS)
Room 403, Bldg. 006,
BARC-West
10300 Baltimore Ave.
Beltsville, MD 20705-2350
(301)504-5345
Online: Knowledge Express
Data Systems, Knowledge
Express

Thomas Register Online
Thomas Publishing Company

Thomas Online
Five Penn Plaza
New York, NY 10001
(212)290-7200
Online: CompuServe
Information Service, Dialog
Internet: DialogWeb at
www.dialogweb.com,
Inforonics, Inc. at
www.inforonics.com/cli/cli_c
lients.html#thomas

*Please note that many other
databases contain the names
of executives, researchers, or
other personnel. Financial
and Business Credit
Databases often contain the
names of executives and
directors. These can be found
in Appendix C. Professional
Directory Databases are
found in Appendix D, and
personnel names can also be
found within them.*

General Encyclopedia Databases

When I am king, they shall not have bread and shelter only,
but also teachings out of books, for a full belly is little worth
where the mind is starved.

–Mark Twain, *The Prince and the Pauper*

Academic American Encyclopedia
The Grolier Multimedia Encyclopedia is based on the text of the Academic American Encyclopedia. Please refer to that listing.
Online: Prodigy

The Canadian Encyclopedia
Stewart House Publishing Inc.
290 Queen Street North Suite 210
Etobicoke ON M9C 5K4
(866)574-6873x213;
(416)695-7981
Internet: www.the canadianencyclopedia.com

Compton's Interactive Encyclopedia
The Learning Company
Compton's NewMedia
314 Erin Dr.
Knoxville, TN 37919-6201

(423)558-8270
Online: America Online; The Learning Company

Computer Desktop Encyclopedia
Computer Language Company
5521 State Park Rd.
Point Pleasant, PA 18950
(215)297-8082
Online: Computer Language Company

The Concise Columbia Encyclopedia
Columbia University Press
562 W. 113th St.
New York, NY 10025
(800)944-8648; (212)666-1000
Online: Microsoft Corporation and Internet: www.bartleby.com/65

Electric Library
Infonautics Corporation

900 W. Valley Rd., Ste. 1000
Wayne, PA 19087-1830
(800)860-9227; (610)971-8840
Online: Infonautics Corporation and Internet: www.encyclopedia.com

Encarta Online
Microsoft Corporation
One Microsoft Way
Redmond, WA 98052-6394
(425)882-8080
Internet: http://encarta.msn.com/reference

Encyclopaedia Britannica Online
Encyclopaedia Britannica Customer Service Department
310 S. Michigan Avenue
Chicago, IL 60604
(800)522-8656; (312)294-2104
Internet: www.eb.com

Encyclopaedia of the Orient
LexicOrient
Urtegata 32b
0187 OSLO
NORWAY
NO 976 538 242
Internet: http://i-cias.com/e.o/index.htm

Encyclopedia Americana Online
Grolier Interactive Inc.
90 Sherman Tpke.
Danbury, CT 06816
(800)243-7256; (203)797-3271
Internet: As part of Grolier
http://auth.grolier.com/cgi-bin/authV2

Encyclopedia Smithsonian
Smithsonian Information
SI Building, Room 153
Washington, DC 20560-0010
(202)357-2700
Internet:
www.si.edu/resource/faq

Everyman's Encyclopaedia
J.M. Dent & Sons Ltd.
91 Champham High St.
London SW4A 7TA, England
171 6229933
Online: Dialog and as part of
CompuServe Knowledge
Index

Funk & Wagnalls New Encyclopedia
Primedia
One International Blvd., Ste.
630
Mahwah, NJ 07495-0017
(201)529-6900
Online: EBSCOhost and
Internet:

http://search.epnet.com/login.asp?profile=fw

Grolier Multimedia Encyclopedia
Grolier Interactive Inc.
90 Sherman Tpke.
Danbury, CT 06816
(800)243-7256; (203)797-3271
Internet: As part of Grolier:
http://auth.grolier.com/cgi-bin/authV2

Lands and Peoples
Grolier Interactive Inc.
90 Sherman Tpke.
Danbury, CT 06816
(800)243-7256; (203)797-3271
Internet: As part of Grolier:
http://auth.grolier.com/cgi-bin/authV2

The New Book of Knowledge
Grolier Interactive Inc.
90 Sherman Tpke.
Danbury, CT 06816
(800)243-7256; (203)797-3271
Internet: As part of Grolier:
http://auth.grolier.com/cgi-bin/authV2

Nueva enciclopedia Cumbre en linea
Grolier Interactive Inc.
90 Sherman Tpke.
Danbury, CT 06816
(800)243-7256; (203)797-3271
Internet: As part of Grolier:
http://auth.grolier.com/cgi-bin/authV2

Nupedia
Nupedia.com
3585 Hancock Street
Suite A
San Diego, CA 92110
(619)296-1732
Internet: www.nupedia.com

Otava's Electronic Encyclopedia or
Otavan yleistietosanakirja
Kustannusosakeyhtio Otava
P.O. Box 134
FIN-00121 Helsinki, Finland
919961
Online: TT-Tietopalvelut Oy

World Book Multimedia Encyclopedia or
World Book Online
World Book, Inc.
525 W. Monroe St., 20th Fl.
Chicago, IL 60661
(800)967-5325; (312)876-2200
Internet: www.
worldbookonline.com/
wbol/wbAuth

News Databases

*You can never get all the facts from just one newspaper,
and unless you have all the facts, you cannot make proper
judgments about what is going on.*

–Harry S. Truman

Academic ASAP
Gale Group
27500 Drake Rd.
Farmington Hills, MI 48331-3535
(800)877-4253; (248)699-4253
Internet: InfoTrac (Gale Group) at http://infotrac.galenet.com

Academic Index
Gale Group
27500 Drake Rd.
Farmington Hills, MI 48331-3535
(800)877-4253; (248)699-4253
Online: CARL Corporation, DataStar, Dialog
Internet: CompuServe Information Service–Knowledge Index, DataStarWeb at www.dialog.com/info/products/datastar-index.shtml, DialogWeb at www.

dialogweb.com InfoTrac (Gale Group)at http://infotrac.galenet.com

Academic Search FullTEXT Family (Premier, Elite, Select)
EBSCO Publishing
10 Estes St.
Ipswitch, MA 01938
(800)653-2726; (800)758-5995; (978)356-6500
Online: EBSCOHost

Actualite Quebec
or **CD Actualite Quebec**
CEDROM-SNI Inc.
825, Avenue Querbes, Ste. 200
Outremont, QC, Canada H2V 3X1
(800)565-5665; (514)278-6060
Internet: CEDROM-SNI Inc. at www.cedrom-sni.qc.ca/index.asp

Aerzte-Zeitung Datenbank
Aerzte-Zeitung
Verlagsgesellschaft mbH
Am Forsthaus Gravenbruch 5
D-63263 Neu-Isenburg,
Germany
49 61023060
Online: DataStar, GENIOS
Internet: DataStarWeb at www.dialog.com/info/products/datastar-index.shtml

ANSA
or **Italian General News Service; Agenzia Nazionale Stampa Associata**
Agenzia ANSA
94, via delle Dataria
I-00187 Rome, Italy
39 6 67741
Internet: DataStarWeb at www.dialog.com/info/products/datastar-index.shtml

Arizona Republic/Phoenix Gazette/Arizona Business

Gazette
Phoenix Newspapers,
Inc.–Library, LI-18
P.O. Box 100
Phoenix, AZ 85001
(602)444-8114
Online: Dialog, Factiva
Internet: CompuServe
Interactive
Services–Knowledge Index,
DataStarWeb at www.
dialog.com/info/products/
datastar-index.shtml and
DialogWeb at www.
dialogweb.com and at
Phoenix Newspapers,
Inc.–Library, LI-18 at
www.azcentral.com

ArticleSearch
Bibliotekstjanst AB/Library
Service Ltd. (BTJ)
P.O. Box 200
S-221 00 Lund, Sweden
046 180000
Online: Bibliotekstjanst
AB/Library Service Ltd.
(BTJ)

**Asia Intelligence Wire
(AIW)**
Financial Times Electronic
Publishing (FTEP)
Fitzroy House
13-17 Epworth St.
London EC2A 4DL, England
(800)007-777; 44 171
8257777
Online: Dialog, FT
Discovery, FT Profile, and as
part of FT Newswatch
Internet: DialogWeb at
www.dialogweb.com

Asian Economic News
Kyodo News International, Inc.

50 Rockefeller Plaza, Rm.
803
New York, NY 10020
(800)536-3510; (212)397-
3723
Online: As part of Newsletter
Database

**Asia-Pacific Business
Journals**
The Dialog Corporation
DataStar
The Communications Bldg.
48 Leicester Sq.
London WC2H 7DB,
England
(800)334-2564; 080-0
690000; 44 171 9306900
Online: Dialog
Internet: DataStarWeb at
www.dialog.com/info/
products/datastar-index.shtml
and DialogWeb at
www.dialogweb.com

Asia-Pacific News
The Dialog Corporation
Dialog
11000 Regency Pkwy., Ste.
10
Cary, NC 27511
(800)334-2564; 080-0
690000; (919)462-8600
Online: Dialog
Internet: DialogWeb at
www.dialogweb.com

ASIA-PACIFIC
Aristarchus Knowledge
Industries Inc.
P.O. Box 45610
Seattle, WA 98105
Online: Dialog
Internet: DialogWeb at
www.dialogweb.com

**Associated Press
Newswires–Plus**
The Associated Press (AP)
50 Rockefeller Plaza
New York, NY 10020
(212)621-1500
Online: West Group–Westlaw
Internet: West
Group–Westlaw at
web2.westlaw.com

Associated Press Newswires
The Associated Press (AP)
50 Rockefeller Plaza
New York, NY 10020
(212)621-1500
Online: West Group–Westlaw
Internet: West
Group–Westlaw at
web2.westlaw.com

Baltic Business Information
COBALT Finland Oy
P.O. Box 10
FIN-00931 Helsinki, Finland
93401355
Online: COBALT Finland Oy

BBC International Reports
British Broadcasting
Corporation (BBC)
BBC Worldwide Monitoring
Caversham Pk.
Reading RG4 8TZ, England
44 118 9469289
Online: Factiva, FT Profile,
LexisNexis, NewsBank, Inc.,
Profound Inc.–The Dialog
Corporation, Reuters Group
PLC
Internet: BBC at www.
monitor.bbc.co.uk and
LexisNexis at www.
lexisnexis.com

BizEkon News–Soviet Economic Press Report
Russian Information and Communications Agency (RUSSICA)
Spartakovskaya St. 13
107066 Moscow, Russia
095 9325610
Online: LexisNexis, MagnaTex International Inc.–COMMUNICATE!, SovInfoLink, and as part of Soviet News, West Group–Westlaw
Internet: LexisNexis at www.lexisnexis.com and West Group–Westlaw at web2.westlaw.com

BridgeNews
Bridge Information Systems, Inc.
Knight Ridder Financial Information Group
3 World Financial Center
New York, NY 10281
(800)927-2734; (212)372-7100
Internet: Bridge Information Systems, Inc.–Knight Ridder Financial Information Group at www.bridge.com

British Universities Newsreel Project (BUNP)
British Universities Film & Video Council (BUFVC)
77 Wells St.
London W1P 3RE, England
44 20 73931500
Online: British Universities Film & Video Council (BUFVC)

Burrelle's Broadcast Database

Burrelle's Information Services
75 E. Northfield Rd.
Livingston, NJ 07039-9873
(800)876-3342; (973)992-6600
Online: Bell & Howell Information and Learning, Burrelle's Information Services

Burrelle's TV Transcripts
Burrelle's Information Services
75 E. Northfield Rd.
Livingston, NJ 07039-9873
(800)-876-3342; (973)992-6600
Online: Bell & Howell Information and Learning

Business & Industry (B&I)
Gale Group
27500 Drake Rd.
Farmington Hills, MI 48331-3535
(800)877-4253; (248)699-4253
Online: CHEST (Combined Higher Education Software Team), Data Downlink Corporation, DataStar, Dialog, FT Profile, Gale Group, GENIOS, LexisNexis, OCLC FirstSearch Catalog, Primark Corporation–Primark Financial Information Division–Disclosure Inc., and as part of Business Reference Suite
Internet: ChemWeb, Inc. at www.chemweb.com, DataStarWeb at www.dialog.com/info/products/datastar-index.shtml, DialogWeb at www.dialogweb.com,

LexisNexis at www.lexis-nexis.com

Business Dateline
ProQuest Inc.
300 N. Zeeb Rd.
P.O. Box 1346
Ann Arbor, MI 48106-1346
(800)521-0600; (734)761-4700
Online: CompuServe Interactive Services, Dialog, Factiva, LEXIS NEXIS, OCLC EPIC
Internet: DialogWeb at www.dialogweb.com and LexisNexis at www.lexisnexis.com

Business Source Elite
EBSCO Publishing
10 Estes St.
Ipswitch, MA 01938
(800)653-2726; (800)758-5995; (978)356-6500
Online: EBSCOHost

Business Source Premiere
EBSCO Publishing
10 Estes St.
Ipswitch, MA 01938
(800)653-2726; (800)758-5995; (978)356-6500
Online: EBSCOHost

Canadian Magazine Article Summaries FullTEXT or **Canadian MAS FullTEXT**
EBSCO Publishing
10 Estes St.
Ipswitch, MA 01938
(800)653-2726; (800)758-5995; (978)356-6500
Online: EBSCOHost

Canadian MAS FullTEXT Select
EBSCO Publishing
10 Estes St.
Ipswitch, MA 01938
(800)653-2726; (800)758-5995; (978)356-6500
Online: EBSCOHost

Canadian Newspapers
Southam, Inc.
1450 Don Mills Rd.
Don Mills, ON, Canada M3B 2X7
(416)445-6641
Online: Dialog
Internet: DialogWeb at www.dialogweb.com

CBCA Fulltext Business
Micromedia Ltd.
20 Victoria St.
Toronto, ON, Canada M5C 2N8
(800)387-2689; (416)362-5211
Online: Axiom, Dialog, Infomart Dialog, Infomart Online, Voyageur
Internet: DialogWeb at www.dialogweb.com

CBCA Fulltext Reference
Micromedia Ltd.
20 Victoria St.
Toronto, ON, Canada M5C 2N8
(800)387-2689; (416)362-5211
Online: Axiom, Voyageur

CNN News Transcripts
Cable News Network (CNN)
1 CNN Center
Atlanta, GA 30303-2705
(404)827-1500

Online: Bell & Howell Information and Learning, LexisNexis
Internet: Cable News Network (CNN) at http://cnn.com/TRAN-SCRIPTS and LexisNexis at www.lexisnexis.com

Command News
The Canadian Press (CP)
36 King St. E.
Toronto, ON, Canada M5C 2L9
(800)434-7578; (416)364-0321
Online: The Canadian Press (CP)

COMTEX Top Headlines
COMTEX News Network, Inc.
4900 Seminary Rd., Ste. 800
Alexandria, VA 22311-1811
(800)266-8399; (703)820-2000
Online: COMTEX News Network, Inc., GEnie–Youvelle Renaissance Group

CPI.Q
Gale Group
27500 Drake Rd.
Farmington Hills, MI 48331-3535
(800)877-4253; (248)699-4253
Internet: InfoTrac (Gale Group) at http://infotrac.galenet.com

Current Digest of the Post-Soviet Press
Current Digest of the Post-Soviet Press

3857 N. High St.
Columbus, OH 43214
(614)292-4234
Online:LexisNexis
Internet: LexisNexis at www.lexisnexis.com

Daily Digest of the Russian Press
Russian Information and Communications Agency (RUSSICA)
Spartakovskaya St. 13
107066 Moscow, Russia
095 9325610
Online: LexisNexis, MagnaTex International Inc.–COMMUNICATE!, SovInfoLink, West Group–Westlaw and as part of Soviet News
Internet: LexisNexis at www.lexisnexis.com, West Group–Westlaw at web2.westlaw.com

Dialog Headlines
The Dialog Corporation
Dialog
11000 Regency Pkwy., Ste. 10
Cary, NC 27511
(800)334-2564; 080-0 690000; (919)462-8600
Online: Dialog
Internet: DialogWeb at www.dialogweb.com

DIALOGSelect
The Dialog Corporation
Dialog
The Communications Bldg.
48 Leicester Sq.
London, WC2h 7DB, England
(800)334-2564; 44 171

9306900
Online: Dialog
Internet: DialogWeb at
www.dialogweb.com

Dow Jones Interactive
Dow Jones & Company, Inc.
P.O. Box 300
Princeton, NJ 08543-0300
(800)832-1234; (609)520-
4000
Online: Factiva

Dow Jones International News
Dow Jones & Company, Inc.
P.O. Box 300
Princeton, NJ 08543-0300
(800)832-1234; (609)520-
4000
Online: Factiva

Dow Jones News/Retrieval
Dow Jones & Company, Inc.
P.O. Box 300
Princeton, NJ 08543-0300
(800)832-1234; (609)520-
4000
Online: Factiva

Dow Jones Text Library
Dow Jones & Company, Inc.
P.O. Box 300
Princeton, NJ 08543-0300
(800)832-1234; (609)520-
4000
Online: Factiva

Early Edition–U.S.
The Dialog Corporation
Dialog
11000 Regency Pkwy., Ste.
10
Cary, NC 27511
(800)334-2564; 080-0
690000; (919)462-8600

Online: Dialog
Internet: DialogWeb at
www.dialogweb.com

EIU on the Internet
The Economist Group
The Economist Intelligence
Unit, Ltd. (EIU)
15 Regent St.
London SW1Y 4LR, England
44 20 78301007
Internet: The Economist
Group–The Economist
Intelligence Unit, Ltd. (EIU)
at www.eiu.com

EIU Online
The Economist Group
The Economist Intelligence
Unit, Ltd. (EIU)
15 Regent St.
London SW1Y 4LR, England
44 20 78301007
Online: Bloomberg Financial
Markets, DataStar, Dialog,
FT Profile, Institute for
Scientific Information (ISI),
LexisNexis, Primark
Corporation–Primark
Financial Information
Division–Datastream,
Profound Inc.–The Dialog
Corporation, and as part of
MarkIntel
Internet: DataStarWeb at
www.dialog.com/info/prod-
ucts/datastar-index.shtml and
DialogWeb at www.
dialogweb.com, The
Economist Group–The
Economist Intelligence Unit,
Ltd. (EIU) at www.eiu.com
and LexisNexis at www.
lexisnexis.com/lncc

EIU TradeWire
The Economist Group
The Economist Intelligence
Unit, Ltd. (EIU)
15 Regent St.
London SW1Y 4LR, England
44 20 78301007
Internet: The Economist
Group–The Economist
Intelligence Unit, Ltd. (EIU)
at www.eiu.com

Ethnic NewsWatch
SoftLine Information, Inc.
20 Summer St.
Stamford, CT 06901
(800)524-7922; (203)975-
8292
Online: EBSCOHost, Factiva,
LexisNexis, Profound
Inc.–The Dialog Corporation,
SoftLine Information, Inc.
Internet: LexisNexis at
www.lexis-nexis.com

Euromoney Publications PLC
Nestor House
Playhouse Yard
London EC4V 5EX, England
171 7798888
Online: DataStar
Internet: DataStarWeb at
www.dialog.com/info/
products/datastar-index.shtml

Europe Intelligence Wire
Financial Times Electronic
Publishing (FTEP)
Fitzroy House
13-17 Epworth St.
London EC2A 4DL, England
(800)007-777
44 171 8257777
Online: Financial Times
Electronic Publishing (FTEP)

Feature Information
JoongAng Ilbo New Media
Inc.
7th fl., Sunhwa-dong 7,
Chung-ku
Seoul 100-759, Republic of
Korea
82 2 7519533
Online: Chanelli, Chollian,
HiTEL , Infoshop, JOINS,
JoongAng Ilbo New Media
Inc.

Federal News Service
Federal News Service
620 National Press Bldg.
Washington, DC 20045
(800)211-4020; (202)347-
1400
Online: Dialog, Federal News
Service
Internet: DialogWeb at
www.dialogweb.com

**Financial Times Business
Reports: Eastern Europe**
Financial Times Electronic
Publishing (FTEP)
Fitzroy House
13-17 Epworth St.
London EC2A 4DL, England
(800)007-777
44 171 8257777
Online: DataStar, LexisNexis
Internet: DataStarWeb at
www.dialog.com/info/
products/datastar-index.shtml
and LexisNexis at www.lexis-
nexis.com/lncc

The Frontrunner
Bulletin New Network, Inc.
(BNN)
8150 Leesburg Pike Ste. 501
Vienna, VA 22182-2714
Online: LexisNexis, West

Group–Westlaw
Internet: Congressional
Quarterly Inc. (CQ) at
www.cq.com, LexisNexis at
www.lexisnexis.com and
West Group–Westlaw at
web2.westlaw.com

**General BusinessFile ASAP
International**
Gale Group
27500 Drake Rd.
Farmington Hills, MI 48331-
3535
(800)877-4253; (248)699-
4253
Internet: InfoTrac (Gale
Group) at
http://infotrac.galenet.com

General BusinessFile ASAP
Gale Group
27500 Drake Rd.
Farmington Hills, MI 48331-
3535
(800)877-4253; (248)699-
4253
Internet: InfoTrac (Gale
Group) at
http://infotrac.galenet.com

**General Periodicals ASAP
Abridged**
Gale Group
27500 Drake Rd.
Farmington Hills, MI 48331-
3535
(800)877-4253; (248)699-
4253
Internet: InfoTrac (Gale
Group) at
http://infotrac.galenet.com

**General Periodicals Index
(GPI)**
Gale Group

27500 Drake Rd.
Farmington Hills, MI 48331-
3535
(800)877-4253; (248)699-
4253
Internet: InfoTrac (Gale
Group) at
http://infotrac.galenet.com

**General Reference Center
Gold**
Gale Group
27500 Drake Rd.
Farmington Hills, MI 48331-
3535
(800)877-4253; (248)699-
4253
Internet: InfoTrac (Gale
Group) at
http://infotrac.galenet.com

**General Reference Center
Select**
Gale Group
27500 Drake Rd.
Farmington Hills, MI 48331-
3535
(800)877-4253; (248)699-
4253
Internet: InfoTrac (Gale
Group) at
http://infotrac.galenet.com

General Reference Center
Gale Group
27500 Drake Rd.
Farmington Hills, MI 48331-
3535
(800)877-4253; (248)699-
4253
Internet: InfoTrac (Gale
Group) at
http://infotrac.galenet.com

G-Search Database
G-Search Ltd.

Loop-X Bldg., 9th Floor
3-9-15, Kaigan, Minato-ku
Tokyo 108-0022, Japan
81 3 55424381
Online: G-Search Ltd.
Internet: G-Search Ltd. at
www.g-search.or.jp

INFO-LATINOAMERICA
National Information
Services Corporation (NISC)
Wyman Towers
3100 St. Paul St.
Baltimore, MD 21218
(410)243-0797
Internet: National
Information Services
Corporation (NISC)–
BiblioLine at www.nisc.com

**Information on Serial
Feature Articles**
JoongAng Ilbo New Media
Inc.
7th fl., Sunhwa-dong 7,
Chung-ku
Seoul 100-759, Republic of
Korea
82 2 7519533
Online: HiTEL
Internet: JoongAng Ilbo New
Media Inc. at
http://ad.joins.com/english/
indcx.asp

**InfoTrac Custom
Newspapers**
Gale Group
27500 Drake Rd.
Farmington Hills, MI 48331-
3535
(800)877-4253; (248)699-
4253
Internet: InfoTrac (Gale
Group) at
http://infotrac.galenet.com

InfoTrac OneFile
Gale Group
27500 Drake Rd.
Farmington Hills, MI 48331-
3535
(800)877-4253; (248)699-
4253
Internet: InfoTrac (Gale
Group) at
http://infotrac.galenet.com

ITINET
Innovative Telematics, Inc.
11115 SW 134th Ct.
Miami, FL 33186-4312
Online: Innovative
Telematics, Inc.

JoongAng Ilbo
JoongAng Ilbo New Media
Inc.
7, Soonhwa-dong, Chung-ku/
Seoul 100-759, Republic of
Korea
82 3 7515114
Online: HiTEL
Internet: JoongAng Ilbo New
Media Inc. at
english.joins.com

**Knight-Ridder/Tribune
Business News (KRTBN)**
Knight Ridder
50 W. San Fernando St.
San Jose, CA 95113
(408)938-7700
Dialog
Infomart Dialog Ltd. (IDL)
Infomart Online
Internet: DialogWeb at
www.dialogweb.com and
Infomart Online at
telnet://otta04.infomart.ca

Kookje Shinmun
Kookje Shinmun Co., Ltd.

76-2, Geoje-dong, Yonje-ku
Pusan 611-070, Republic of
Korea
82 51 5005261
Online: Chollian
Internet: Kookje Shinmun
Co., Ltd. at
www.kookje.co.kr

**Korean Integrated
Newspaper Database
System (KINDS)**
Korean Press Institute
12th Fl., Korea Press Center
Bldg.
25 1-Ga, Taepyong-Ro,
Chung-Gu
Seoul 100-746, Republic of
Korea
82 2 3981654
Online: Chollian, HiTEL,
Infoshop, Nownuri, Unitel
Co. Ltd.

**LexisNexis Academic
Universe**
LexisNexis
9443 Springboro Pike
P.O. Box 933
Dayton, OH 45401-0933
(800)227-9597; (937)865-
6800
Online: LexisNexis
Internet: LexisNexis at
https://web.lexisnexis.com/
universe

Magazine Index
Gale Group
27500 Drake Rd.
Farmington Hills, MI 48331-
3535
(800)877-4253; (248)699-
4253
Online: CARL Corporation,
DataStar, DIALOG

Internet: CompuServe Interactive Services–Knowledge Index, DataStarWeb at www.dialog.com/info/products/datastar-index.shtml and DialogWeb at www.dialogweb.com and InfoTrac (Gale Group) at http://infotrac.galenet.com

MAS FullTEXT Ultra or Magazine Article Summaries FullTEXT Ultra
EBSCO Publishing
10 Estes St.
Ipswitch, MA 01938
(800)653-2726; (800)758-5995; (978)356-6500
EBSCO Publishing

MAS FullTEXT or Magazine Article Summaries FullTEXT
EBSCO Publishing
10 Estes St.
Ipswitch, MA 01938
(800)653-2726; (800)758-5995; (978)356-6500
Online: Ameritech Library Services–Vista, CARL Corporation

MasterFILE FullTEXT
EBSCO Publishing
10 Estes St.
Ipswitch, MA 01938
(800)653-2726; (800)758-5995; (978)356-6500
Online: OCLC EPIC

The McGraw-Hill Companies Publications Online
McGraw-Hill Companies, Inc.

1221 Avenue of the Americas
New York, NY 10020
(800)262-4729
Online: Bell & Howell Information and Learning, Dialog, Factiva, LexisNexis
Internet: DialogWeb at www.dialogweb.com and LexisNexis at www.lexisnexis.com

Mideast/Africa Library
LexisNexis
9443 Springboro Pike
P.O. Box 933
Dayton, OH 45401-0933
(800)227-9597; (937)865-6800
Online: LexisNexis
Internet: LexisNexis at www.lexisnexis.com

Miller Freeman Industry and Product News
Miller Freeman, Inc.
600 Harrison St.
San Francisco, CA 94107
(800)444-4881; (415)905-2200
Online: DataStar
Internet: DataStarWeb at www.dialog.com/info/products/datastar-index.shtml

Multimedia Database
G-Search Ltd.
Loop-X Bldg., 9th Floor
3-9-15, Kaigan, Minato-ku
Tokyo 108-0022, Japan
81 3 55424381
Internet: G-Search Ltd. at www.g-search.or.jp

New Zealand Newspapers
West Group–Westlaw
610 Opperman Dr.

Eagan, MN 55123-1396
(800)937-8527; (651)687-7000
Online: West Group–Westlaw
Internet: West Group–Westlaw at web2.westlaw.com

Newsearch
Gale Group
27500 Drake Rd.
Farmington Hills, MI 48331-3535
(800)877-4253; (248)699-4253
Online: Dialog
Internet: CompuServe Interactive Services–Knowledge Index and DialogWeb at www.dialogweb.com

NewsEdge Insight
NewsEdge Corporation
80 Blanchard Rd.
Burlington, MA 01803
(800)252-9980; (781)229-3000
Internet: NewsEdge Corporation at www.newsedge.com

NewsEdge Live
NewsEdge Corporation
80 Blanchard Rd.
Burlington, MA 01803
(800)252-9980; (781)229-3000
Internet: NewsEdge Corporation at www.newsedge.com

Newsfile
British Broadcasting Corporation (BBC)
BBC Worldwide Monitoring

Caversham Pk.
Reading RG4 8TZ, England
44 118 9469289
Internet: BBC at www.
monitor.bbc.co.uk

Newsletter Database
Gale Group
27500 Drake Rd.
Farmington Hills, MI 48331-3535
(800)877-4253; (248)699-4253
Online: Bell & Howell
Information and Learning,
DataStar, Dialog, European
Information Network
Services (EINS), Factiva, FT
Profile, I/PLUS Direct
(NLS), STN International,
Thomson Financial Securities
Data (TFSD)
Internet: DataStarWeb at
www.dialog.com/info/
products/datastar-index.shtml
and DialogWeb at
www.dialogweb.com and
InfoTrac (Gale Group) at
http://infotrac.galenet.com

NewsLibrary
MediaStream, Inc.
One Commerce Sq.
2005 Market St., Ste. 1020
Philadelphia, PA 19103
(800)888-6195; (215)239-4100
Internet: MediaStream, Inc.
at
www.newslibrary.com/nlsite/i
ndex.html

Newsline
Profound Inc.–The Dialog
Corporation

11000 Regency Pkwy., Ste.
10
Cary, NC 27511
(919)462-8600
Online: Profound Inc.–The
Dialog Corporation

**Newspaper & Periodical
Abstracts**
Bell & Howell Information
and Learning
300 N. Zeeb Rd.
Ann Arbor, MI 48106-1346
(800)521-0600; (734)761-4700
Online: CARL Corporation,
Dialog, OCLC EPIC, OCLC
FirstSearch Catalog
Internet: DialogWeb at
www.dialogweb.com

Newspaper Abstracts Daily
Bell & Howell Information
and Learning
300 N. Zeeb Rd.
Ann Arbor, MI 48106-1346
(800)521-0600; (734)761-1346
Online: Dialog
Internet: DialogWeb at
www.dialogweb.com

Newspaper Abstracts
Bell & Howell Information
and Learning
300 N. Zeeb Rd.
Ann Arbor, MI 48106-1346
(800)521-0600; (734)761-1346
Online: Dialog, OCLC
FirstSearch Catalog, Ovid
Technologies, Inc.
Internet: DialogWeb at
www.dialogweb.com

Newspaper Source
EBSCO Publishing
10 Estes St.
Ipswitch, MA 01938
(800)653-2726; (800)758-5995; (978)356-6500
Online: EBSCOHost

NewsWatch
NewsWare, Inc.
56 Pine St.
New York, NY 10005
(212)509-9700
Online: NewsWare, Inc.

Newswire ASAP
Gale Group
27500 Drake Rd.
Farmington Hills, MI 48331-3535
(800)877-4253; (248)699-4253
Online: Dialog
Internet: DialogWeb at
www.dialogweb.com

Newzindex
Fact Finders On-Line
Ltd.P.O. Box 37-689
Parnell
Auckland, New Zealand
Online:Centre d'Etudes
Prospectives et
d'Informations
Internationales (CEPII),
Fairfax Holdings–AUSINET

Nordiska Nyhetsbyraer
Tidningarnas Telegrambyra
AB (TT)
Kungsholmstorg 5
SE-105 12 Stockholm,
Sweden
46 8 6922600
Online: Suomen
Tietotoimisto Oy

**Periodical Abstracts
PlusText**
ProQuest Inc.
300 N. Zeeb Rd.
P.O. Box 1346
Ann Arbor, MI 48106-1346
(800)521-0600; (734)761-
4700
Online: Dialog, ProQuest Inc.
Internet: DialogWeb at
www.dialogweb.com

Polinfo
Polinfo
Radhuspladsen 37
DK-1785 Copenhagen V,
Denmark
45 33471450
Online:
Hjaelpemiddelinstituttet,
Politikens
Informationsvirksomhed
(Polinfo), UNI-C

Presscom
Presscom Australia
121 King William St.
Adelaide, SA 5000, Australia
61 88206 2559
Internet: Nexus Information
Service at
www.nexus.edu.au/nexus4

PressLink Online
MediaStream, Inc.
One Commerce Sq.
2005 Market St., Ste. 1020
Philadelphia, PA 19103
(800)888-6195; (215)239-
4100
Internet: NewsCom-
PressLink at
www.newscom.com

Primary Search
EBSCO Publishing
10 Estes St.
Ipswitch, MA 01938
(800)653-2726; (800)758-
5995; (978)356-6500
Online: EBSCOHost

PROMT
or **Predicasts Overview of
Markets and Technology**
Gale Group
27500 Drake Rd.
Farmington Hills, MI 48331-
3535
(800)877-4253; (248)699-
4253
Online: Bell & Howell
Information and Learning,
DataStar, Dialog, FT Profile,
GENIOS, I/PLUS Direct,
Questel Orbit, STN
International, Thomson
Financial Securities Data
(TFSD)
Internet: DataStarWeb at
www.dialog.com/info/
products/datastar-index.shtml
and DialogWeb at
www.dialogweb.com and
InfoTrac (Gale Group) at
http://infotrac.galenet.com

ProQuest Asian Business
ProQuest Inc.
300 N. Zeeb Rd.
P.O. Box 1346
Ann Arbor, MI 48106-1346
(800)521-0600; (734)761-
4700
Online: Bell & Howell
Information and Learning

ProQuest Direct
ProQuest Inc.
300 N. Zeeb Rd.

P.O. Box 1346
Ann Arbor, MI 48106-1346
(800)521-0600; (734)761-
4700
Online: Bell & Howell
Information and Learning

**ProQuest European
Business**
ProQuest Inc.
300 N. Zeeb Rd.
P.O. Box 1346
Ann Arbor, MI 48106-1346
(800)521-0600; (734)761-
4700
Online: Bell & Howell
Information and Learning

**ProQuest Full-Text
Newspapers**
ProQuest Inc.
300 N. Zeeb Rd.
P.O. Box 1346
Ann Arbor, MI 48106-1346
(800)521-0600; (734)761-
4700
Online: Bell & Howell
Information and Learning

ProQuest Newsstand
ProQuest Inc.
300 N. Zeeb Rd.
P.O. Box 1346
Ann Arbor, MI 48106-1346
(800)521-0600; (734)761-
4700
Online: Bell & Howell
Information and Learning
Dialog
Internet: DialogWeb at
www.dialogweb.com

Regional News Library
LexisNexis
9443 Springboro Pike
P.O. Box 933

Dayton, OH 45401-0933
(800)227-9597; (937)865-
6800
Online: LexisNexis
Internet: LexisNexis at
www.lexisnexis.com

Resource/One Select Full Text
ProQuest Inc.
300 N. Zeeb Rd.
P.O. Box 1346
Ann Arbor, MI 48106-1346
(800)521-0600; (734)761-
4700
Online: Bell & Howell
Information and Learning

Resource/One
ProQuest Inc.
300 N. Zeeb Rd.
P.O. Box 1346
Ann Arbor, MI 48106-1346
(800)521-0600; (734)761-
4700
Online: Bell & Howell
Information and Learning

Retail News
Verdict Research Limited
Newlands House
40 Berners St.
London W1P 4DX, England
44 20 72556400
Online: Verdict Research
Limited

Reuters Business Briefing (RBB)
or **Reuters Business Briefing Search for Web; RBB Search Web**
Factiva
105 Madison Ave., 10th Fl.
New York, NY 10016
(800)369-8474
Online: Factiva

Reuters North America News Service
Reuters Group PLC
85 Fleet St.
London EC4P 4AJ, England
44 171 2501122
Online: Reuters Group PLC

Reuters North American Business News Service
Reuters Group PLC
85 Fleet St.
London EC4P 4AJ, England
44 171 2501122
Online: Reuters Group PLC

Reuters South Africa Online Report
Reuters Group PLC
85 Fleet St.
London EC4P 4AJ, England
44 171 2501122
Online: Reuters Group PLC

Reuters U.S. Company News
Reuters Group PLC
85 Fleet St.
London EC4P 4AJ, England
44 171 2501122
Online: Reuters Group PLC

Reuters U.S. Market News
Reuters Group PLC
85 Fleet St.
London EC4P 4AJ, England
44 171 2501122
Online: Reuters Group PLC

Reuters U.S. Oddly Enough Online Report
Reuters Group PLC
85 Fleet St.
London EC4P 4AJ, England
44 171 2501122
Online: Reuters Group PLC

Reuters U.S. Online Report PLUS
Reuters Group PLC
85 Fleet St.
London EC4P 4AJ, England
44 171 2501122
Online: Reuters Group PLC

Reuters U.S. Technology Report
Reuters Group PLC
85 Fleet St.
London EC4P 4AJ, England
44 171 2501122
Online: Reuters Group PLC

Rubber and Plastics News
Crain Communications, Inc.
740 N. Rush St.
Chicago, IL 60611-2590
(312)649-5200
Online: Factiva, LexisNexis,
Profound Inc.–The Dialog
Corporation, Reuters Group
PLC, and as part of
Newsletter Database
Internet: LexisNexis at
www.lexisnexis.com

South American Business Information (SABI)
COMTEX News Network,
Inc.
4900 Seminary Rd., Ste. 800
Alexandria, VA 22311-1811
(800)266-8399; (703)820-
2000
Online: COMTEX News
Network, Inc., Dialog
Internet: DialogWeb at
www.dialogweb.com

South Asia News Wires
AAP Information Services
Asia Pulse
Level 7, The AAP Centre

Locked Bag 21, Grosvenor
Pl.
Sydney, NSW 2000, Australia
61 2 93228634
Online: Asia Pulse

Standard & Poor's Daily News
Standard & Poor's
55 Water St.
New York, NY 10041-0003
(800)221-5277; (212)438-7280
Online: Dialog, LexisNexis
Internet: CompuServe
Interactive
Services–Knowledge Index,
DialogWeb at www.
dialogweb.com and
LexisNexis at www.
lexisnexis.com

The Summary of World Broadcasts (SWB)
British Broadcasting
Corporation (BBC)
BBC Worldwide Monitoring
Caversham Pk.
Reading RG4 8TZ, England
44 118 9469289
Online: DataStar, FT Profile
Internet: BBC at www.
monitor.bbc.co.uk,
DataStarWeb at
www.dialog.com/info/
products/datastar-index.shtml

SuperTOM+
Gale Group
27500 Drake Rd.
Farmington Hills, MI 48331-3535
(800)877-4253; (248)699-4253
Internet: InfoTrac (Gale

Group) at
http://infotrac.galenet.com

Tire Business
Crain Communications, Inc.
740 N. Rush St.
Chicago, IL 60611-2590
(312)649-5200
Internet: Crain
Communications, Inc. at
www.tirebusiness.com/
subscriber/headlines.phtml

Today's News
Infomart Dialog Ltd. (IDL)
333 King St. E
Toronto, ON, Canada M5A
4R7
(800)668-9215; (416)350-6001
Online: Infomart Online

Top News Library
LexisNexis
9443 Springboro Pike
P.O. Box 933
Dayton, OH 45401-0933
(800)227-9597; (937)865-6800
Online: LexisNexis
Internet: LexisNexis at
www.lexisnexis.com

TOPICsearch
EBSCO Publishing
10 Estes St.
Ipswitch, MA 01938
(800)653-2726; (800)758-5995; (978)356-6500
Online: EBSCOHost

Transcripts: News Events and Congressional Hearings
Congressional Quarterly Inc.
(CQ)
1414 22nd St. NW

Washington, DC 20037
(800)432-2250; (202)887-6279
Online: Congressional
Quarterly Inc. (CQ)
Internet: Congressional
Quarterly Inc. (CQ) at
www.cq.com

Transport Europe
Europe Information Service,
s.a.
Ave. Adolphe Lacomble 66
B-1030 Brussels, Belgium
32 2 7377709
Online: Chamber World
Network–Asia Intelligence
Wire, Context Ltd., GENIOS,
Infonautics, Inc., INFO-
TRADE N.V., LexisNexis,
Reuters Group PLC,
Thomson Financial Securities
Data (TFSD), and as part of
Newsletter Database
Internet: EIS at isnet.eis.be/
content/Default.asp,
LexisNexis at www.
lexisnexis.com

TV & Radio Transcripts Daily
Federal Document Clearing
House, Inc.
201 Pennsylvania Ave., SE
Suite 119
Washington, DC 20003
(301)883-2492
Online: Dialog, Factiva,
Infonautics, Inc., LexisNexis,
Reuters Group PLC
Internet: DialogWeb at
www.dialogweb.com,
LexisNexis at www.
lexisnexis.com

U.S. Business Browser
OneSource Information

Services
300 Baker Ave., Ste. 303
Concord, MA 01742-2131
(800)554-5501; (978)318-
4300
Internet: OneSource
Information Services at
www.onesource.com/index.htm

U.S. Business Reporter
The Dialog Corporation
Dialog
11000 Regency Pkwy., Ste.
10
Cary, NC 27511
(800)334-2564; 080-0
690000; (919)462-8600
Online: Dialog
Internet: DialogWeb at
www.dialogweb.com

U.S. Press
Congressional Quarterly Inc.
(CQ)
1414 22nd St. NW
Washington, DC 20037
(800)432-2250; (202)887-
6279
Internet: Congressional
Quarterly Inc. (CQ) at
www.cq.com

U.K. Business Browser
OneSource Information
Services
300 Baker Ave., Ste. 303
Concord, MA 01742-2131
(800)554-5501; (978)318-
4300
Internet: OneSource
Information Services at
www.onesource.com/index.htm

Uutisarkisto
Startel, Inc.
P.O. Box 35

FIN-00089 Sanomat, Finland
358 9 1221
Online: Startel, Inc.

Vocational Search
EBSCO Publishing
10 Estes St.
Ipswitch, MA 01938
(800)653-2726; (800)758-
5995; (978)356-6500
Online: EBSCOHost

**Wilson Reader's Guide Full
Text Mega Edition**
H.W. Wilson Company
950 University Ave.
Bronx, NY 10452
(800)367-6770; (718)588-
8400
Online: Dialog, SilverPlatter
Information Inc., WilsonWeb
Internet: DialogWeb at
www.dialogweb.com

**Wilson Reader's Guide Full
Text Mini Edition**
H.W. Wilson Company
950 University Ave.
Bronx, NY 10452
(800)367-6770; (718)588-
8400
Online: SilverPlatter
Information Inc., WilsonWeb

Wireline
Profound Inc.–The Dialog
Corporation
11000 Regency Pkwy., Ste.
10
Cary, NC 27511
(919)462-8600
Online: Profound Inc.–The
Dialog Corporation

World Library
LexisNexis
9443 Springboro Pike

P.O. Box 933
Dayton, OH 45401-0933
(800)227-9597; (937)865-
6800
Online: LexisNexis
Internet: LexisNexis at
www.lexisnexis.com

World Reporter
The Dialog Corporation
Dialog
11000 Regency Pkwy., Ste.
10
Cary, NC 27511
(800)334-2564; 080-0
690000; (919)462-8600
Online: DataStar, Dialog,
Factiva, FT Discovery, FT
Profile, Profound Inc.–The
Dialog Corporation
Internet: DataStar Web at
www.dialog.com/info/
products/datastar-index.shtml
and DialogWeb at
www.dialogweb.com

*Please note that there are
many additional news databases available online, each
covering a single publication,
or possibly two. These are
also often available through
their own Web sites.*

Databases That Include Photographs

"What is the use of a book," thought Alice,
"without pictures or conversations?"
—Lewis Carroll, *Through the Looking Glass*

AccuNet/AP Photo Archive
AccuWeather, Inc.
385 Science Park Rd.
State College, PA 16803
(800)566-6606; (814)235-8600
Online: AccuWeather, Inc.

The African American Biographical Database (AABD)
ProQuest Inc.
300 N. Zeeb Rd.
P.O. Box 1346
Ann Arbor, MI 48106-1346
(800)521-0600; (734)761-4700
Online: ProQuest Inc.

African-American History and Culture
Facts on File, Inc.
11 Penn Plaza, 15th Fl.
New York, NY 10001-2006
(800)322-8755; (212)290-8090
Online: Facts on File, Inc.

AFT Sports Database for Sydney Olympics
Or AFP at the Olympics
Agence France-Presse (AFP)
13, place de la Bourse
B.P. 20
F-75002 Paris, France
33 1 40414646
Online: Agence France-Presse (AFP)

Air & Space Magazine
Smithsonian Institution
Air and Space Magazine
901 D St. SW
Washington, DC 20024
(202)287-3733
Online: Air and Space Magazine, Smithsonian Institution

American Civil War Research Database
Historical Data Systems, Inc.
P.O. Box 196
Kingston, MA 02364
Online: Historical Data Systems, Inc.

American Drama
ProQuest Inc.
300 N. Zeeb Rd.
P.O. Box 1346
Ann Arbor, MI 48106-1346
(734)761-4700
Online: ProQuest Inc.

American Historical Images
Facts on File, Inc.
11 Penn Plaza, 15th Fl.
New York, NY 10001-2006
(800)322-8755; (212)290-8090
Online: Facts on File, Inc.

American Indian History & Culture
Facts on File, Inc.
11 Penn Plaza, 15th Fl.
New York, NY 10001-2006
(800)322-8755; (212)290-8090
Online: Facts on File, Inc.

American Journey: The Civil War
Gale Group
27500 Drake Rd.
Farmington Hills, MI 48331-3535
(800)877-4253; (248)699-4253
Online: Gale Group, PSM Online

American Journey: The Cold War
Gale Group
27500 Drake Rd.
Farmington Hills, MI 48331-3535
(800)877-4253; (248)699-4253
Online: Gale Group, PSM Online

American Journey: The Constitution and Supreme Court
Gale Group
27500 Drake Rd.
Farmington Hills, MI 48331-3535
(800)877-4253; (248)699-4253
Online: Gale Group, PSM Online

American Journey: Westward Expansion
Gale Group
27500 Drake Rd.
Farmington Hills, MI 48331-3535
(800)877-4253; (248)699-4253
Online: Gale Group, PSM Online

American Journey: Women in America

Gale Group
27500 Drake Rd.
Farmington Hills, MI 48331-3535
(800)877-4253; (248)699-4253
Online: Gale Group, PSM Online

American Memory
U.S. Library of Congress
101 Independence Ave.
Washington, DC 20540
(202)707-5000
Online: U.S. Library of Congress

The AMICO Library
Art Museum Image Consortium (AMICO)
2008 Murray Ave., Ste. D
Pittsburgh, PA 15217
(412)422-8533
Internet: Research Libraries Group, Inc. (RLG)—Eureka at www.rlg.org/amico/index.html

Art Today
ArtToday.com, Inc.
3240 N. Dodge Blvd., Ste. F
Tucson, AZ 85716-1469
(800)881-8503; (520)881-8101
Online: ArtToday.com, Inc.

Bettmann Archive Forum
CompuServe Interactive Services
5000 Arlington Centre Blvd.
P.O. Box 20212
Columbus, OH 43220-2913
(800)848-8990; (614)457-8600
Online: CompuServe Interactive Services

Business Periodicals Global
ProQuest Inc.
300 N. Zeeb Rd.
P.O. Box 1346
Ann Arbor, MI 48106-1346
(800)521-0600; (734)761-4700
Online: ProQuest Inc.

Business Periodicals Research
ProQuest Inc.
300 N. Zeeb Rd.
P.O. Box 1346
Ann Arbor, MI 48106-1346
(800)521-0600; (734)761-4700
Online: ProQuest Inc.

Business Periodicals Select
ProQuest Inc.
300 N. Zeeb Rd.
P.O. Box 1346
Ann Arbor, MI 48106-1346
(800)521-0600; (734)761-4700
Online: ProQuest Inc.

California Museum of Photography Database (CMP)
University of California, Riverside
California Museum of Photography
3824 Main St.
Riverside, CA 92501
(909)787-4787
Online: California Museum of Photography, University of California, Riverside

Collins COBUILD on CD-ROM
COBUILD
HarperCollins Publishers

Westmere
50 Edgbaston Park Rd.
Birmingham B15 2RX,
England
44 121 4143926
Online: Reuters Group PLC

CP Pictures Archive
The Canadian Press (CP)
36 King St. E.
Toronto, ON, Canada M5C
2L9
(800)434-7578; (416)364-
0321
Online: The Canadian Press
(CP)

Daily Life Through History
Greenwood Publishing
Group, Inc.
Greenwood Electronic Media
88 Post Rd. W.
P.O. Box 5007
Westport, CT 06881-5007
(203)226-3571
Online: Greenwood
Electronic Media

**Deike Unterhaltung &
Gedenktage**
VerlagHorst Deike KG
P.O. Box 100452
D-78404 Konstanz, Germany
49 7531 81550
Online: GENIOS

The Detroit News
Detroit News
615 W. Lafayette Blvd.
Detroit, MI 48226
(800)678-6400; (313)222-
2300
Online: Detroit News,
LexisNexis, ProQuest Inc.

**DISCovering Multicultural
America**
Gale Group
27500 Drake Rd.
Farmington Hills, MI 48331-
3535
(800)877-4253; (248)699-
4253
Internet: InfoTrac (Gale
Group) at
http://infotrac.galenet.com

Euro 2000 Sports Database
Or Euro 2000 from AFP
Agence France-Presse (AFP)
13, place de la Bourse
B.P. 20
F-75002 Paris, France
33 1 40414646
Online: Agence France-
Presse (AFP)

FACTS.com
Facts on File, Inc.
11 Penn Plaza, 15th Fl.
New York, NY 10001-2006
(800)322-8755; (212)290-
8090
Online: Facts on File, Inc.

Galleri NOR
or **Nasjonalbibliotekets
Nasjonale fotodatabase**
Nasjonalbibliotekavdelinga i
Rana (NBR)
Langneset 29
P.O. Box 278
N-8601 Mo, Norway
47 75125460
Online:
Nasjonalbibliotekavdelinga i
Rana (NBR)

**History Resource Center:
U.S.**
Gale Group

27500 Drake Rd.
Farmington Hills, MI 48331-
3535
(800)877-4253; (248)699-
4253
Internet: InfoTrac (Gale
Group) at
http://infotrac.galenet.com

Homework Helper
Infonautics, Inc.
900 W. Valley Rd., Ste. 1000
Wayne, PA 19087
(800)860-9227; (610)971-
8840
Online: Prodigy

ImageForum
Agence France-Presse (AFP)
13, place de la Bourse
B.P. 20
F-75002 Paris, France
33 1 40414646
Online: Agence France-
Presse (AFP)

Major Authors Online
Gale Group
27500 Drake Rd.
Farmington Hills, MI 48331-
3535
(800)877-4253; (248)699-
4253
Online: Gale Group

Den Nationale Billedbase
Det Kongelige Bibliotek
(KB)
Soren Kirkegaards Plds 1
DK-1016 Copenhagen K,
Denmark
45 33474747
Internet: Det Kongelige
Bibliotek (KB) at www.kb.dk

North Korea Database
Cyber JoongAng

Glastower 7th Floor, 946-1
Daechi-dong Kangnam-ku
Seoul 135-708, Republic of
Korea
82 2 21859200
Online: Cyber JoongAng

Our Star
ABC Net Co. Ltd.
6F, Sam-dae-yang Bd.
Okeum-dong, Songpa-ku
Seoul 138-130, Republic of
Korea
8224004000
Online: Chollian, HiTEL,
Infoshop, Nownuri, Unitel
Co. Ltd.

Palmer's Full Image Online
ProQuest Inc.
300 N. Zeeb Rd.
P.O. Box 1346
Ann Arbor, MI 48106-1346
(800)521-0600; (734)761-
4700
Online: Bell & Howell
Information and Learning

People Online
People Magazine
Time & Life Bldg.
Rockefeller Center
New York, NY 10020
(212)522-1212
Online: CompuServe
Interactive Services

PressLink Online
MediaStream, Inc.
One Commerce Sq.
2005 Market St., Ste. 1020
Philadelphia, PA 19103
(800)888-6195; (215)239-
4100
Online: MediaStream, Inc.

**Reuters South Africa
Online Report**
Reuters Group PLC
85 Fleet St.
London EC4P 4AJ, England
44 171 2501122
Online: Reuters Group PLC

**Reuters U.S. Online Report
PLUS**
Reuters Group PLC
85 Fleet St.
London EC4P 4AJ, England
44 171 2501122
Reuters Group PLC

**Scribner Writers
Series–Comprehensive
Edition**
Charles Scribner's Sons
1633 Broadway, 23rd Fl.
New York, NY 10019
(800)877-4253; (800)223-
1244
Internet: InfoTrac (Gale
Group) at
http://infotrac.galenet.com

**Scribner Writers
Series–Selected Authors
Edition**
Charles Scribner's Sons
1633 Broadway, 23rd Fl.
New York, NY 10019
(800)877-4253; (800)223-
1244
Internet: InfoTrac (Gale
Group) at
http://infotrac.galenet.com

Seymour
Picture Network
International, Ltd.
2000 14th St. N.
Arlington, VA 22201
(800)764-7427; (703)807-

2740
Online: Picture Network
International, Ltd.

SIRS Discoverer
SIRS Mandarin, Inc.
P.O. Box 272348
Boca Raton, FL 33427-2348
(800)232-7477; (561)994-
0079
Online: SIRS Mandarin, Inc.

SIRS Renaissance
SIRS Mandarin, Inc.
P.O. Box 272348
Boca Raton, FL 33427-2348
(800)232-7477; (561)994-
0079
Online: SIRS Mandarin, Inc.

Sun Herald
Sun Herald
61 92823052
Internet–West
Group–Westlaw at
web2.westlaw.com

Texas Almanac
The Dallas Morning News
508 Young St.
P.O. Box 655237
Dallas, TX 75265
(800)431-0010; (214)977-
8222
Internet: Infotrac at
http://infotrac.galenet.com

**UPI Newspictures Online
Photo Gallery**
United Press International
(UPI)
1510 H St. NW
Washington, DC 20005
(202)898-8000
Online: UPI

Who's Who
Cyber JoongAng

Glastower 7th Floor, 946-1
Daechi-dong Kangnam-ku
Seoul 135-708, Republic of
Korea
82 2 21859200
Online: Cyber JoongAng

**Wilson Biographies Plus
Illustrated**
H.W. Wilson Company
950 University Ave.
Bronx, NY 10452
(800)367-6770; (718)588-
8400
Internet: WilsonWeb at
www.hwwilson.com/Databas
es/biosplusi.htm

**Wilson Current Biography
Illustrated**
H.W. Wilson Company
950 University Ave.
Bronx, NY 10452
(800)367-6770; (718)588-
8400
Internet: WilsonWeb at
www.hwwilson.com/
Databases/cbillus.htm

**Wilson Junior Authors &
Illustrators**
H.W. Wilson Company
950 University Ave.
Bronx, NY 10452
(800)367-6770; (718)588-
8400
Internet: WilsonWeb at
www.hwwilson.com/
Databases/jrauthors.htm

Yeong Nam Il Bo News
The Yeongnam Ilbo
Yeongnam Ilbo
111, Shinchon-Dong, Dong-
Ku
Taegu, Republic of Korea

8253 7575324
Online: Chollian, HiTEL,
Nownuri, Unitel Co. Ltd.,
The Yeongnam Ilbo

Databases Containing Quotations and/or Speeches

The object of oratory alone is not truth, but persuasion.

—Lord Macaulay

3500 Good Quotes for Speakers
Sylvia Lieberman
2325 Ocean Ave.
Brooklyn, NY 11229
(718)339-8642
Online: LexisNexis
Internet: LexisNexis at
www.lexisnexis.com

Academic Abstracts FullTEXT Ultra
EBSCO Publishing
10 Estes St.
Ipswitch, MA 01938
(800)653-2726; (800)758-5995; (978)356-6500
Online: EBSCO Publishing

The African American Biographical Database (AABD)
ProQuest Inc.
300 N. Zeeb Rd.
P.O. Box 1346

Ann Arbor, MI 48106-1346
(800)521-0600; (734)761-4700
Online: Bell & Howell
Information and Learning

African-American History and Culture
Facts on File, Inc.
11 Penn Plaza, 15th Fl.
New York, NY 10001-2006
(800)322-8755; (212)290-8090
Online: Facts on File, Inc.
Internet: Facts on File, Inc. at
www.factsonfile.com

American Banker News Service
American Banker–Bond
Buyer
One State St. Plaza, 27th Fl.
New York, NY 10004
(800)221-1809; (212)803-8333

Online: Dialog
Internet: DialogWeb at
www.dialogweb.com

American Journey: Civil Rights in America
Gale Group
27500 Drake Rd.
Farmington Hills, MI 48331-3535
(800)877-4253; (248)699-4253
Internet: Gale Group–PSM
Online at
www.galegroup.com/psm

American Journey: The African-American Experience
Gale Group
27500 Drake Rd.
Farmington Hills, MI 48331-3535
(800)877-4253; (248)699-4253

Internet: Gale Group–PSM
Online at
www.galegroup.com/psm

**American Journey: The
Hispanic-American
Experience**
Gale Group
27500 Drake Rd.
Farmington Hills, MI 48331-
3535
(800)877-4253; (248)699-
4253
Internet: Gale Group–PSM
Online at
www.galegroup.com/psm

**American Journey:
Westward Expansion**
Gale Group
27500 Drake Rd.
Farmington Hills, MI 48331-
3535
(800)877-4253; (248)699-
4253
Internet: Gale Group–PSM
Online at
www.galegroup.com/psm

**American Journey: Women
in America**
Gale Group
27500 Drake Rd.
Farmington Hills, MI 48331-
3535
(800)877-4253; (248)699-
4253
Internet: Gale Group–PSM
Online at
www.galegroup.com/psm

American Memory
U.S. Library of Congress
101 Independence Ave.
Washington, DC 20540
(202)707-5000

Internet: U.S. Library of
Congress at
http://memory.loc.gov/amme
m/amhome.html

**Associated Press-Campaign
News**
The Associated Press (AP)
50 Rockefeller Plaza
New York, NY 10020
(212)621-1500
Online: LexisNexis
Internet: LexisNexis at
www.lexisnexis.com

The Budget Database
Globe Information Services
444 Front St. W.
Toronto, ON, Canada M5V
2S9
(800)268-9128; (416)585-
5250
Online: Info Globe Online

**Business & Management
Practices (BaMP)**
Gale Group
27500 Drake Rd.
Farmington Hills, MI 48331-
3535
(800)877-4253; (248)699-
4253
Online: Data Downlink
Corporation, Dialog,
GENIOS, LexisNexis,
NERAC, Inc., OCLC Online
Computer Library Center,
Inc., Primark
Corporation–Primark
Financial Information
Division–Disclosure Inc.,
SilverPlatter Information Inc.
Internet: DialogWeb at
www.dialogweb.com, Gale
Group at
www.galegroup.com,
LexisNexis at www.
lexisnexis.com and as part of

Gale Group's Business
Reference Suite

Canada Budget Database
QL Systems Limited
QUICKLAW
St. Andrew's Tower, Ste. 901
275 Sparks St.
Ottawa, ON, Canada K1R
7X9
(800)387-0899; (613)238-
3499
Online: QL Systems
Limited–QUICKLAW

Canada NewsWire (CNW)
Canada NewsWire, Ltd.
10 Bay St., Ste. 914
Toronto, ON, Canada M5J
2R8
(416)863-9350
Online: Bell & Howell
Information and Learning,
Dialog, Factiva, Info Globe
Online, Infomart Dialog Ltd.
(IDL), Infomart Online,
LexisNexis, QL Systems
Limited—QUICKLAW
Internet: DialogWeb at
www.dialogweb.com

**Canadian Business &
Current Affairs (CBCA)**
or **CBCA Fulltext Business**
Micromedia Ltd.
20 Victoria St.
Toronto, ON, Canada M5C
2N8
(800)387-2689; (416)362-
5211
 Online: SilverPlatter
Information Inc.
Internet: Micromedia Ltd. at
http://circ.micromedia.on.ca

Canadian Speeches/ISSUES of the Day
Canadian Speeches
P.O. Box 250
Woodville, ON, Canada K0M 2T0
(705)439-2580
Online: Infomart Dialog Ltd. (IDL), Infomart Online

Capital Gains Tax
Australian Tax Practice (ATP)
100 Harris St.
Pyrmont, NSW 2009, Australia
61 2 85877600
Online: Australian Tax Practice (ATP)

Congressional Record
U.S. Government Printing Office (GPO)
Office of Electronic Information Dissemination Services (SDE)
732 N. Capitol St.
Washington, DC 20402
(888)293-6498; (202)512-1530
Online: LexisNexis, West Group–Westlaw
GPO Access and as part of LEGI-SLATE
Internet: LexisNexis at www.lexisnexis.com, U.S. Government Printing Office (CPO)–Office of Electronic Dissemination Services (SDE) at www.access.gpo.gov/su_docs /aces/aces150.html

Consumer InSite
Intelligence Data, Inc.
22 Thomson Pl.

Boston, MA 02210
(800)654-0393; (617)856-1890
Internet: Intelligence Data, Inc. at www.iac-insite.com/about.htm

CQ Weekly Report
or **Congressional Quarterly Weekly Report**
Former Database Name: CQ Weekly Report
Congressional Quarterly Inc. (CQ)
1414 22nd St. NW
Washington, DC 20037
(800)432-2250; (202)887-6279
Online: Bell & Howell Information and Learning, Congressional Quarterly Inc. (CQ)

Dansk Nationallitteraert Arkiv (DNA)
or **Danish National Archive of Literature**
Det Kongelige Bibliotek (KB)
Soren Kirkegaards Plds 1
DK-1016 Copenhagen K, Denmark
45 33474747
Online: Forlaget MAGNUS A/S–Skattekartoteket
Internet: Det Kongelige Bibliotek (KB) at www.kb.dk/index-en.htm

Douglass: Archives of American Public Address
Northwestern University
633 Clark St.
Evanston, IL 60208
(847)491-3741
Online: Northwestern University

The Executive Speaker
The Executive Speaker (TES)
P.O. Box 292437
Dayton, OH 45429
(937)294-8493
Online: LexisNexis
Internet: LexisNexis at www.lexisnexis.com

Federal News Service
Federal News Service
620 National Press Bldg.
Washington, DC 20045
(800)211-4020; (202)347-1400
Online: Dialog, Federal News Service
Internet: DialogWeb at www.dialogweb.com

The Forex Watch
Technical Data
22 Thompson Pl.
Boston, MA 02210
(617)345-2526
Online: Telerate Systems Inc.

Information and Technology Transfer Database (ITTD)
International Research and Evaluation (IRE)
21098 IRE Control Center
Eagan, MN 55121
(888)888-9245; (612)888-9635
Online: International Research and Evaluation (IRE)

International Economic Calendar
Technical Data
22 Thompson Pl.
Boston, MA 02210
(617)345-2526
Online: Telerate Systems Inc.

Journalisten-Pool-Datenbank
or **Up-to-Date Economic News for Journalists**
DIMIS compress
Wirtschaftsinformationen
Pressehaus II Heussalle 2-10
D-53113 Bonn, Germany
49 228 241958
Internet: GENIOS at
www.genios.de

Landmark Documents in American History
Facts on File, Inc.
11 Penn Plaza, 15th Fl.
New York, NY 10001-2006
(800)322-8755; (212)290-8090
Online: Facts on File, Inc.
Internet: Facts on File, Inc. at
www.factsonfile.com

LOGOS
La Documentation Francaise
Banque d'Information
Politique et d'Actualite
(BIPA)
124, rue Henri Barbusse
F-93308 Aubervilliers Cedex,
France
01 40157277
Online: Questel Orbit

Luthers Werke (Weimar Edition)
ProQuest Inc.
300 N. Zeeb Rd.
P.O. Box 1346
Ann Arbor, MI 48106-1346
(800)521-0600; (734)761-4700
Online: Bell & Howell
Information and Learning

Lyrics
Bibliotekstjanst AB/Library

Service Ltd. (BTJ)
P.O. Box 200
S-221 82 Lund, Sweden
46 46 180000
Online: Bibliotekstjanst
AB/Library Service Ltd.
(BTJ)

MarketNews
Market News International
100 William St.
New York, NY 10038-4512
(800)284-1401; (212)509-4444
Online: Market News
International, Telerate
Systems Inc.

MAS FullTEXT Ultra
or **Magazine Article Summaries FullTEXT Ultra**
EBSCO Publishing
10 Estes St.
Ipswitch, MA 01938
(800)653-2726; (800)758-5995; (978)356-6500
Online: EBSCO Publishing

MAS Online Plus
or **Magazine Article Summaries Online Plus**
EBSCO Publishing
10 Estes St.
Ipswitch, MA 01938
(800)653-2726; (800)758-5995; (978)356-6500
Online: EBSCO Publishing

MasterFILE Elite
EBSCO Publishing
10 Estes St.
Ipswitch, MA 01938
(800)653-2726; (800)758-5995; (978)356-6500
Online: EBSCO Publishing

MasterFILE Premier
EBSCO Publishing
10 Estes St.
Ipswitch, MA 01938
(800)653-2726; (800)758-5995; (978)356-6500
Online: EBSCO Publishing

MasterFILE Select
EBSCO Publishing
10 Estes St.
Ipswitch, MA 01938
(800)653-2726; (800)758-5995; (978)356-6500
OCLC EPIC
Online: EBSCOHost

Middle Search Plus
EBSCO Publishing
10 Estes St.
Ipswitch, MA 01938
(800)653-2726; (800)758-5995; (978)356-6500
Online: EBSCOHost

Multicultural Australia and Immigration Studies (MAIS)
Former Database Name:
Multicultural Australia
Information System
Australia Department of
Immigration and
Multicultural Affairs
P.O. Box 25
Belconnen, ACT 2616,
Australia
02 62642455
Internet: Informit Online at
www.informit.com.au

NBC Professional
Federal Document Clearing
House, Inc.
201 Pennsylvania Ave., SE
Suite 119

Washington, DC 20003
(301)883-2492
Online: LexisNexis
Internet: LexisNexis at
www.lexisnexis.com

The New York Times (NYT)
The New York Times
Company
New York Times On-Line
Services
520 Speedwell Ave.
Morris Plains, NJ 07950
(973)829-0036
Online: DataStar, Dialog,
Factiva, LexisNexis, OCLC
EPIC, OCLC FirstSearch
Catalog
Internet: DataStarWeb at
www.dialog.com/info/
products/datastar-index.shtml,
DialogWeb at www.
dialogweb.com, LexisNexis
at www.lexisnexis.com

**The Official Index to The
Times, 1906–1980**
ProQuest Inc
300 N. Zeeb Rd.
P.O. Box 1346
Ann Arbor, MI 48106-1346
(800)521-0600; (734)761-
4700
Online: Bell & Howell
Information and Learning

Primary Search
EBSCO Publishing
10 Estes St.
Ipswitch, MA 01938
(800)653-2726; (800)758-
5995; (978)356-6500
Online: EBSCOHost

**Project Vote Smart
Database**

Center for National
Independence in Politics
Project Vote Smart
129 NW 4th St., Ste. 204
Corvallis, OR 97330
(541)754-2746
Internet: Center for National
Independence in
Politics–Project Vote Smart at
www.vote-smart.org/
index.phtml

RAPID
European Commission
Spokesman's Service
200, rue de la Loi
B-1049 Brussels, Belgium
322 2956332
Online: European
Commission–Office for
Official Publications

REUTERS Markets 3000
Reuters Group PLC
85 Fleet St.
London EC4P 4AJ, England
44 171 2501122
Internet: Reuters Group
PLC–Reuters Web at
www.reuters.com

**Riksdagsinformation,
Riksdagens arbet**
or **Agenda of Parliament**
Sveriges riksdag
S-100 12 Stockholm, Sweden
46 8 7864000
Online: Rixlex

Riksdagstrycket, ANF
Sveriges riksdag
S-100 12 Stockholm, Sweden
46 8 7864000
Online: Rixlex

SIRS Government Reporter
SIRS Mandarin, Inc.

P.O. Box 272348
Boca Raton, FL 33427-2348
(800)232-7477; (561)994-
0079
Online: SIRS Mandarin, Inc.

**The Summary of World
Broadcasts (SWB)**
British Broadcasting
Corporation (BBC)
BBC Worldwide Monitoring
Caversham Pk.
Reading RG4 8TZ, England
44 118 9469289
Online: DataStar, FT PRO-
FILE
Internet: BBC at www.
monitor.bbc.co.uk,
DataStarWeb at www.
dialog.com/info/products/
datastar-index.shtml

**United Kingdom Law
Journal Library**
LexisNexis
9443 Springboro Pike
P.O. Box 933
Dayton, OH 45401-0933
(800)227-9597; (937)865-
6800
Online: LexisNexis
Internet: LexisNexis at
www.lexisnexis.com

*Please note that transcripts,
which are excellent sources
of quotations and speeches,
are found in Appendix G:
News Databases.*

Telephone Directories

*The telephone is a good way to talk to people
without having to offer them a drink.*

–Fran Lebowitz

Acxiom Directories–Biz
Acxiom Corporation
P.O. Box 2000
Conway, AR 72032-2000
(800)922-9466; (501)342-
1000
Internet: OCLC FirstSearch
Electronic Collections Online
at www.ref.oclc.org

Acxiom Directories–Home
Acxiom Corporation
P.O. Box 2000
Conway, AR 72032-2000
(800)922-9466; (501)342-
1000
Internet: OCLC FirstSearch
Electronic Collections Online
at www.ref.oclc.org

**American Business
Directory**
or **Business
America–ONLINE**
infoUSA, Inc.
5711 S. 86th Circle
P.O. Box 27347
Omaha, NE 68127-0347

(800)321-0869; (888)274-
5325; (402)593-4500
Dialog

**Big Yellow: Yellow Pages on
the Web**
Bell Atlantic Corporation
1095 Ave. of the Americas
New York, NY 10036
(800)621-9900; (212)395-
2121
Online: Bell Atlantic
Corporation

BizFile
infoUSA, Inc.
5711 S. 86th Circle
P.O. Box 27347
Omaha, NE 68127-0347
(800)321-0869; (888)274-
5325; (402)593-4500
Online: CompuServe
Interactive Services

BusinessCanada
infoUSA, Inc.
5711 S. 86th Circle
P.O. Box 27347

Omaha, NE 68127-0347
(800)321-0869; (888)274-
5325; (402)593-4500
Online: infoUSA, Inc.,
LexisNexis
Internet: LexisNexis at www.
lexisnexis.com

**Den Elektroniske
Katalogen**
Telenor Media AS
Box 21 Ullem
N-0311 Oslo, Norway
22736000
Online: Telenor Media AS

**Den Elektroniske
Telefonbog**
Teledanmark, Jydsk Telefon
Sletvej 30
DK-8310 Arhus-Tranbjerg J,
Denmark
89453135
Online: Teledanmark, Jydsk
Telefon

DirectoryNET InfoNOW
DirectoryNET, Inc.

4555 Mansell Rd., Ste. 230
Alpharetta, GA 30022
(800)733-1212; (770)521-0100
Online: DirectoryNET, Inc.

FaxGuident
Telia InfoMedia Interactive
AB
P.O. Box 818
S-161 24 Bromma, Sweden
86341700
Online: Telia InfoMedia
Interactive AB

Infotel
Helsingin Puhelin Oy (HPY)
P.O. Box 148
FIN-00131 Helsinki, Finland
358 96061
Online: Helsingin Puhelin Oy
(HPY)

MetroNet
Metromail Corporation
360 E. 22nd St., Ste. 4
Lombard, IL 60148-4989
(800)793-2536; (630)620-3012
Online: Metromail
Corporation

MetroNet EDA Access
Metromail Corporation
360 E. 22nd St., Ste. 4
Lombard, IL 60148-4989
(800)793-2536; (630)620-3012
Online: Metromail
Corporation

NummerGuiden
Telia InfoMedia Interactive
AB
P.O. Box 811
S-161 24 Bromma, Sweden

46 8 7043500
Online: Telia InfoMedia
Interactive AB

NYNEX Interactive Yellow Pages
Bell Atlantic Corporation
1095 Ave. of the Americas
New York, NY 10036
(800)621-9900; (212)395-2121
Online: Bell Atlantic
Corporation

OMHP
Finland Oikeusministerio
Tietohallintotoimisto
Bureau of Data Management
P.O. Box 157
SF-13101 Haemeenlinna,
Finland
358 171531
Online: TT-Tietopalvelut Oy

Les Pages Pro
France Telecom
6, place d'Alleray
F-75505 Paris, France
Online: France Telecom

People Finder
Information America (IA)
Marquis One Tower
245 Peachtree Center Ave.,
Ste. 1400
Atlanta, GA 30303
(800)235-4008; (404)479-6500
Online: Information America
(IA)

Pro CD Biz
Pro CD, Inc.
5711 South 86 Circle
Omaha, NE 68127
(800)331-6681;

(800)99-CD-ROM
Online: OCLC EPIC

Pro CD Home
Pro CD, Inc.
5711 South 86 Circle
Omaha, NE 68127
(800)331-6681; (800)99-CD-ROM
Online: OCLC EPIC

Pro CD Phone
Pro CD, Inc.
5711 South 86 Circle
Omaha, NE 68127
(800)331-6681; (800)99-CD-ROM
Online: EBSCOHost

Research Centers and Services Directories (RCSD)
Gale Group
27500 Drake Rd.
Farmington Hills, MI 48331-3535
(800)877-4253; (248)699-4253
Online: Dialog
Internet: InfoTrac (Gale
Group) at
http://infotrac.galenet.com,
DialogWeb at www.
dialogweb.com

Sahkoinen puhelinluettelo
Suomen Numeropalvelu Oy
Ruoholahdenkatu 8
FIN-00121 Helsinki, Finland
96937741
Online: Suomen
Numeropalvelu Oy

STELA
Moscow City Telephone
Network

Referral-Information Center
Novy Arbat Ave. 2
121019 Moscow, Russia
095 2038618
Online: Moscow City
Telephone Network–Referral
Information Center

U.S. Businesses
infoUSA, Inc.
5711 S. 86th Circle
P.O. Box 27347
Omaha, NE 68127-0347
(800)321-0869; (888)274-
5325; (402)593-4500
Online: Dialog, infoUSA,
Inc. Internet: DialogWeb at
www.dialogweb.com

Windex
Cyber JoongAng
Glastower 7th Floor, 946-1
Daechi-dong Kangnam-ku
Seoul 135-708, Republic of
Korea
82 2 21859200
Online: Cyber JoongAng

*Please note that the
business telephone directories
that include sales figures or
other financial information
have been included in
Appendix C.*

Adoption and Reunion Registries

It's never too late to have a happy childhood.

–Tom Robbins

INTERNATIONAL

Please note that the registries found were assumed to be international if registrants from various countries were found within them, more than one country was allowed on their registration form, and there was no statement otherwise limiting them.

Adoptee/Birth Parent Free Search Registry
www.adopting.org/supporta.html

Adoptees and Birth Family Registry
Adoptee Birthfamily
Connections
Angry Grandmas Registry
www.birthfamily.com/registry

Adoption Reunion Registries
www.geocities.com/
kerrylynn_52/Adoption
Registries.html

AdoptionRegistry.com
Adoption.com
www.AdoptionRegistry.com

Adoptions Records Database
Adoption Search
by Peace Monastery
www.skylace.net/adoption

Adoption Search & Find Registry
www.geocities.com/
Heartland/ridge/2755

Adoption Searches and Reunion Registry
www.geocities.com/
Wellesley/Garden/1525

Adoption Triad Outreach International Adoption Reunion Registry
www.adoptiontriad.org/
registry.htm

The ALMA Society Registry
Adoptees' Liberty Movement
Association
P.O. Box 85
Denville, NJ 07834

Arvin Publications Free Adoption Registry
www.arvinpublications.com

The Birthmother Tree
http://members.tripod.com/~
binky3

BirthQuest Online International Searchable Database
www.birthquest.org

Black Market Adoptee's Registry (U.S. and Canada)
www.geocities.com/
Heartland/Garden/2313/
index.htm

Closing the Gap Registry (U.S. and Canada)
http://members.tripod.com/
Diana_Crystal/
ClosingTheGap.html

Eyes Wide Open Registry
www.geocities.com/
Wellesley/3686

FindMe
www.findme.org/index.cfm?
fuseaction=Main

**Free International Adoption
Registry**
Adoption Triad Outreach
www.adoptiontriad.org/
registry/board/yabb.pl

**G Spot United States
Adoption Registry**
www.aci.net/schaefer/page60.
html

Gina's Adoption Registry
www.geocities.com/
Heartland/Flats/6403/
searchregistry.html

**International Soundex
Reunion Registry (I.S.R.R.)**
(This is the most important
adoption/reunion registry
now available.)
P.O. Box 2312
Carson City, NV 89702-2312
(702) 882-7755
www.isrr.net

**Kayhhs' Radical Opinions
Registries**
www.geocities.com/
Heartland/8529

**Kindred Pursuits, The
CANADopt Registry
(Canada and U.S.)**
http://nebula.on.ca/canadopt

**Lisa's Adoption Search
Pages**

http://millennium.
fortunecity.com/bankhead/
378

Lost and Missing Relatives
CyberPages International Inc.
www.cyberpages.com/
LOSTPRSN.HTM

**Lost n Found Adoption
Registry**
www.niwot.net/adopt

**Lynches Adoption Reunion
Registry**
www.geocities.com/
heartland/acres/9942/
registry.html

Metro Reunion Registry
www.geocities.com/
Heartland/Flats/3666

PBN Adoption Post
www.pbnreunion.com/
adoptionpostings.htm

Relatively Seeking
The Seeker Magazine
www.the-seeker.com/
relative.htm

Relinquished Registry
Catholic Charities
http://freeweb.wpdcorp.com/
relinquished

ReunionRegistry
www.reunionregistry.com/
default.asp

**Searching for Siblings
Registry**
http://sibsearch.8m.com

**The Seekers of the Lost
International Free Adoption**

**and Missing Persons
Registry**
www.seeklost.com

World Wide Registry
http://adoptionsearching.com/
birth.html

**www.Reunion.com
Adoption Registry**
ReuNet–The Reunion
Network
www.highschoolalumni.com

AUSTRALIA
Australia Adoption Registry
www.geocities.com/
HotSprings/4427/AUS.html

**Origins Tasmania's
Registry
for Australian Black
Market Adoptees**
www.users.bigpond.com/
Tonilivesey/registry.htm

CANADA
**British Columbia's
Adoption Reunion Registry**
202–1600 West 6th Avenue
Vancouver, British Columbia
V6J 1R3
(604) 736-7917
www.adoptionreunion.net

**The Ideal Maternity
Home–Home of the
Butterbox Babies**
www3.ns.sympatico.ca/
bhartlen

Canada Adoption Registry
www.geocities.com/
HotSprings/4427/Canada.html

Canadian Adoptees Registry Inc.
www.canadianadoptees
registry.org

Family Ties Adoption Search Canada Database
www.geocities.com/family
tiescanada/index.html

GERMANY
Germany Adoption Registry
www.geocities.com/
HotSprings/4427/Germany.
html

GREECE
S.E.A.S.Y.P. Greek Reunion Registry
www.seasyp.gr

IRELAND
Ireland Adoption Registry
www.geocities.com/
HotSprings/4427/Ireland.html

Irish Adoption Contact Register
Adopted Peoples Association
www.adoptionireland.com/
register/index.htm

For Northern Ireland, please refer to "United Kingdom."

KOREA
topseeknow.com
http://topseeknow.com/
index2.htm

NEW ZEALAND
New Zealand Adoption Registry
www.geocities.com/
HotSprings/4427/NZL.html

PHILIPPINES
Philippines Adoption Registry
www.geocities.com/
HotSprings/4427/PHL.html

SOUTH AFRICA
Adoption Reunions South Africa
http://members.tripod.com/
adoption_reunions/index.htm

SOUTH KOREA
South Korea Adoption Registry
www.geocities.com/
HotSprings/4427/SKorea.html

UNITED KINGDOM
Please note that adoptees in the U.K. are entitled to access their original birth certificates and may have access to certain other records.

England
Adopted Children Register
Office of Population Census and Surveys, (OCPS)
The General Register Office
Smedley Hydro
Trafalgar Road
Birkdale
Southport, U.K. PR8 2HH
44 (0)1 514 714 313

England Adoption Registry
www.geocities.com/
HotSprings/4427/England.html

Northern Ireland
General Register Office
Oxford House
49-55 Chichester Street
Belfast

BT1 4HL
44 (0)1 232 252 000

Scotland
Family Care (and Scottish Birth-Link Register)
21 Castle Street
Edinburgh
EH2 3DN

General Register Office (Scotland)
New Register House
Edinburgh
EH1 3YT

Wales
Adopted Children Register
Office of Population Census and Surveys, (OCPS)
The General Register Office
Smedley Hydro
Trafalgar Road
Birkdale
Southport
Southport, U.K. PR8 2HH
44 (0)1 514 714 313

UNITED STATES
Please note that the registries found were assumed to be U.S. national if various U.S. addresses were found within them, there was no statement otherwise limiting or extending them, and only U.S. states were allowed within their online registration form.

Adoptees and Birthparents for Open Records Nationwide (A.B.O.R.N.)
Rt. 4, Box 361
Adrian, MO 64720
(877)748-7979, ext. 856
http://members.tripod.com/
ABORN.Webring/Aborn

AdoptionRegistry.Net
www.adoptionregistry.net

**Family Ties Adoption
Search Database**
www.geocities.com/
heartland/ranch/1049/
index100.html

**Helping
Angels–Missing/Lost
Family/Friends**
http://members.tripod.com/~
KarenTA/missing.htm

**Search Registry Page for
All Whose Life Has Been
Affected by an Adoption
Facilitiated by Catholic
Charities**
www.geocities.com/
Heartland/Pointe/5576

**Twins & Triplets Search
Registry**
http://hometown.aol.com/
CEEART/index10.html

**United States Adoption
Registry**
www.geocities.com/
HotSprings/4427/
UnitedStates.html

Alabama
*Please note that Alabama is
an open records state, allowing adult adoptees unre-
stricted access to original
adoption information.*

**Alabama Adoptees
Searching**
www.geocities.com/
HotSprings/4427/ALA.html

**Alabama Birthlink Online
Reunion Registry**

www.alabama-
adoption.org/birthlink/
registry/registry.html

Office of Adoption
Alabama Department of
Human Resources
Family Services Division
50 N. Ripley Street
Montgomery, AL 36130
(334) 242-9500
www.dhr.state.al.us/fsd/
adopt.asp

Alaska
*Please note that Alaska is an
open records state, allowing
adult adoptees unrestricted
access to original adoption
information.*

Alaska Adoptees Searching
www.geocities.com/
HotSprings/4427/AKA.html

Bureau of Vital Statistics
Alaska Department of Health
and Social Services
P.O. Box 110675
Juneau, AK 99811-0675
(907) 465-3392
www.hss.state.ak.us/dph/bvs
/birth/default.htm

Arizona
**Arizona Adoptees
Searching**
www.geocities.com/
HotSprings/4427/AZA.html

**Arizona Adoption Reunion
Registry**
www.angelfire.com/az2/
azreunionregistry
www.geocities.com/Heartland
/Meadows/7173/registry.html

Arkansas
**Arkansas Adoptees
Searching**
www.geocities.com/
HotSprings/4427/ARA.html

**Arkansas Mutual Consent
Voluntary Adoption
Registry**
Arkansas Department of
Human Services
Division of Children and
Family Services
P.O. Box 1437, Slot 808
Little Rock, AR 72203-1437
(501)682-8462
www.state.ar.us/dhs/
adoption/mcvar.htm

Arkansas Reunion Registry
www.geocities.com/Heartland
/Bluffs/3592/AR.html

**Crystal Ladies Adoption
Registry (for Arkansas,
Missouri,
Oklahoma, and Texas)**
www.crystallady.com/
adopreg.htm

California
**California Adoptees
Searching**
www.geocities.com/
HotSprings/4427/CAA.html

**California Adoption Search
& Reunion**
www.angelfire.com/ca4/CASR

**California Mutual Consent
Registry**
www.100megsfree3.com/
levgen/cmcr.html

Consent Program
California Department of
Social Services
Adoptions Branch
744 P Street, M/S 19-67
Sacramento, CA 95814
(916) 322- 3778
www.childsworld.org/
adoption/fa_359.htm

Colorado
**Adoptees in Search (Denver,
CO)**
http://user.aol.com/
aisdenver/adoption.htm

**Colorado Adoptees
Searching**
www.geocities.com/
HotSprings/4427/COA.html

**Colorado Mutual Consent
Registry**
www.nmia.com/~rema2/
coreg.html

**Colorado Voluntary
Adoption Registry**
Health Statistics and Vital
Records
Colorado Department of
Public Health and
Environment
4300 Cherry Creek Drive
South (HSVR-VR-A1)
Denver, CO 80246-1530
(303) 692-2188
www.cdphe.state.co.us/hs/
aboutadoptionregistry.html

Connecticut
**Connecticut Adoptees
Searching**
www.geocities.com/
HotSprings/4427/CTA.html

**Department of Children
and Families**
Office of Foster and Adoption
Services
505 Hudson St.
Hartford, CT 06106
(860)550-6450; (860)550-
6453; (860)550-6578
www.state.ct.us/dcf/
AdoptPics/adoption%
20search.htm

Delaware
**Delaware Adoptees
Searching**
www.geocities.com/
HotSprings/4427/DEA.html

**Delaware Adoption
Reunion Registry**
www.geocities.com/Heartland
/Acres/4392

District of Columbia
**District of Columbia
Adoptees Searching**
www.geocities.com/
HotSprings/4427/DCA.html

Florida
Children of Hope (FL)
http://home.att.net/
~MDNicholas/children.html

**The Cole Baby Registry
(Miami, FL)**
www.geocities.com/Heartland
/Fields/9298/Colebaby.html

**Common Bond Free Search
Registry (FL)**
www.angelfire.com/fl/
commonbond/
membersearches.html

Finding in Florida
http://users.yourvillage.com/
pattyann/flmain.htm

Florida Adoptees Searching
www.geocities.com/
HotSprings/4427/FLA.html

**Florida Adoption Reunion
Registry (FARR)**
Department of HRS-CYF
1317 Winewood Blvd., Bldg
8, Room 100
Tallahassee, FL 32399-0700
(904) 488-8000
http://users.yourvillage.com/
pattyann/FARR.htm

**Florida Online Family
Finders (F.O.F.F.)**
www.geocities.com/Heartland
/Woods/2677

Georgia
**Georgia Adoptees
Searching**
www.geocities.com/
HotSprings/4427/GAA.html

**Georgia Adoption Reunion
Registry**
Families First/Office of
Adoptions
2 Peachtree Street, N.W.
Suite 323
Atlanta, GA 30303-3142
(888)328-0055; (404)657-
3555
www.adoptions.dhr.state.ga.
us/reunion.htm
www.adoptions.dhr.state.ga.
us/pstadopt2.htm#reunion

**N. Georgia Reunion
Registry**
www.geocities.com/Heartland
/Bluffs/3592/GA.html

Silent Legacy–Hicks Clinic Birth Registry (McCaysville, GA)
www.hicksclinic.com

Hawaii
Hawaii Adoptees Searching
www.geocities.com/
HotSprings/4427/HIA.html

Island of Hawaii–Adoption Records
Family Court, Third Circuit
345 Kekuanaoa St., Room 40
Hilo, HI 96720

Island of Kauai–Adoption Records
Family Court, Fifth Circuit
3059 Umi St.
Lihue, Kauai, HI 96766

Islands of Maui, Molokai, Lanai–Adoption Records
Family Court, Second Circuit
2145 Main St., Suite 226
Wailuku, Maui, HI 96793

Island of Oahu–Adoption Records
Family Court, First Circuit
P.O. Box 3498
Honolulu, HI 96811-3498
(808)539-4424

Idaho
Grain of Life Registry (ID)
www.geocities.com
/wildfyres_registry/id.html

Idaho Adoptees Searching
www.geocities.com/
HotSprings/4427/IDA.html

Idaho Voluntary Adoption Registry

Idaho Department of Health and Welfare
Bureau of Vital Records and Health Statistics
450 W. State St. First Floor
P.O. Box 83720
Boise, Idaho 83720-0036
(208)334-5990
www2.state.id.us/dhw/vital_stats/adopt/var.htm

Illinois
Illinois Adoptees Searching
www.geocities.com/
HotSprings/4427/ILA.html

Illinois Adoption Registry
Illinois Department of Public Health
535 West Jefferson Street
Springfield, IL 62761
(877)323-5299; (217)557-5159
www.idph.state.il.us/vital/iladoptreg.htm

Indiana
Indiana Adoptees Searching
www.geocities.com/
HotSprings/4427/INA.html

Indiana Adoption History Registry
Indiana State Registrar
Indiana State Department of Health
P.O. Box 7125
Indianapolis, IN 46206-7125
www.state.in.us/isdh/bdcertifs/history.htm

Indiana Searching
www.geocities.com/
heartland/country/9577

Iowa
Iowa Adoptees Searching
www.geocities.com/
HotSprings/4427/IAA.html

Iowa Reunion Registry
www.wildfyre-registries.com/IA/ia.html

IOWASEARCH
www.fortunecity.com/
millennium/cedar/512/
search.html

Kansas
Please note that Kansas is an open records state, allowing adult adoptees unrestricted access to original adoption information.

Kansas Adoptees Searching
www.geocities.com/
HotSprings/4427/KSA.html

Kansas Department of Health and Environment (KDHE)
Vital Statistics
Adoption Clerk
900 SW Jackson
Topeka, KS 66612-2221
(785)296-1400
www.kdhe.state.ks.us/vital

Kentucky
Kentucky Adoptees Searching
www.geocities.com/
HotSprings/4427/KYA.html

Kentucky Adoption Reunion Registry
66.70.142.206/aboutus.htm

Kentucky's Adoption Search Services
Kentucky Department for Social Services
275 East Main Street
Grankfort, KY 40621
(502)564-2147
http://aborn.org/state/Not
Answered/Kentucky.html

Ole Kentucky Home Registry
www.geocities.com/Heartland/Bluffs/3592/KY.html

Louisiana
Louisiana Adoptees Searching
www.geocities.com/HotSprings/4427/LAA.html

Louisiana Adoption Database
www.angelfire.com/la2/adoption/page16.htm

Louisiana Adoption Registry
Louisiana Voluntary Registry
Department of Social Services
Office of Community Services
1967 North St.
Post Office Box 3318
Baton Route, Louisiana 70821
(800)259-2456; (504)342-9922
www.dss.state.la.us/offocs/html/registry.html

Sellers Baptist Children's Home & Adoption Center (New Orleans, LA)
http://members.aol.com/CEdwa49620/sbch.html

Maine
Adoption Reunion Registry
Office of Vital Records
Deputy State Registrar
221 State Street
11 State House Station
Augusta, ME 04333-0011
(207) 287-3181

www.state.me.us/dhs/bohodr/ovrpage.htm

Maine Adoptees Searching
www.geocities.com/HotSprings/4427/MEA.html

The Maine Registry
www.angelfire.com/me2/themaineregistry/index.html

Tammy's Adoption Search Page & Registry for Maine, New Hampshire, Rhode Island & Vermont
www.angelfire.com/nh/redmomma/index.html

Maryland
Maryland Adoptees Searching
www.geocities.com/HotSprings/4427/MDA.html

Mutual Consent Voluntary Adoption Registry
Maryland Department of Human Resources
Social Services Administration
311 W. Saratoga Street
Baltimore, Maryland 21201-3521
(800)39-ADOPT; (410) 767-7423; (410) 767-7372
www.dhr.state.md.us/voladpr.htm

Massachusetts
Adoption Search Coordinator
Department of Social Services
24 Farnsworth St.
Boston, MA 02210
(800)548-4802 ext. 558;
(617)748-2240

Massachusetts Adoptees Searching
www.geocities.com/HotSprings/4427/MAA.html

The Massachusetts Registry
http://hometown.aol.com/Espaura/MAadopt.html

Michigan
Michigan Adoptees Searching
www.geocitics.com/HotSprings/4427/MIA.html

Michigan Central Adoption Registry
Michigan Family Independence Agency
P.O. Box 30037
300 South Capitol Ave.
Lansing, MI 48909
(517)373 3513
www.michiganadoption.com/MichiganSearch/release_of_info.html#central

Michigan Listings
www.geocities.com/heartland/7233

The Michigan Mutual Consent Registry
www.michiganadoption.com/S&S/mi_registry.htm

MoonMist's Michigan Registry
MoonMist's Adoptees & Birth Parents of Michigan
http://members.tripod.com/~MoonMist69/form.html

Minnesota
Minnesota Adoptees Searching

www.geocities.com/
HotSprings/4427/MNA.html

Minnesota Department of Health (MDH)
P.O. Box 64975
St. Paul, MN, 55164-0975
(612)676-5129
www.health.state.mn.us/divs/
chs/data/bd_1.htm

Minnesota Fathers' Adoption Registry
Minnesota Department of
Health
717 Delaware Street
Southeast
P.O. Box 9441
Minneapolis, MN 55440-
9441
(888)345-1726; (612)676-
5466
www.health.state.mn.us/divs/
chs/registry/resourc.htm

Minnesota Registry
www.wildfyre-registries.
com/MN/mn.html

Mississippi
Centralized Adoption Records File
Bureau of Vital Records
Mississippi State Department
of Health
71 Stadium Drive
P.O. Box 1700
Jackson, MS 39215-1700
www.msdh.state.ms.us/phs/
rules5.htm

Mississippi Adoptees Searching
www.geocities.com/
HotSprings/4427/MSA.html

Mississippi Reunion Registry
www.geocities.com/Heartland
/Bluffs/3592/MS.html

Missouri
Adoption Information Registry
Division of Family Services
P.O. Box 88
Jefferson City, MO 65103-
0088
(573)751-6529
www.dss.state.mo.us/dfs/
adoir.htm

Crystal Ladies Adoption Registry (for Arkansas, Missouri, Oklahoma, and Texas)
www.crystallady.com/
adopreg.htm

Missouri Adoptees Searching
www.geocities.com/
HotSprings/4427/MOA.html

Montana
Montana Adoptees Searching
www.geocities.com/
HotSprings/4427/MTA.html

Montana Reunion Registry
www.wildfyre-registries.
com/MT/mt.html

Nebraska
Biological Father Registry
Nebraska Health and Human
Services System
Vital Statistics
P.O. Box 95065
Lincoln, NE 68509-5065
(402)471-9097

www.hhs.state.ne.us/adp/
biofather.htm

Nebraska Adoptees Searching
www.geocities.com/
HotSprings/4427/NEA.html

Nebraska Reunion Registry
www.wildfyre-registries.
com/NE/ne.html

Nevada
Nevada Adoptees Searching
www.geocities.com/
HotSprings/4427/NVA.html

Nevada State Adoption Registry
711 East Fifth Street
Carson City, NV 89701
(775)684-4400
http://dcfs.state.nv.us/page51.
html

New Hampshire
New Hampshire Adoptees Searching
www.geocities.com/
HotSprings/4427/NHA.html

Tammy's Adoption Search Page & Registry for Maine, New Hampshire, Rhode Island & Vermont
www.angelfire.com/nh/
redmomma/index.html

New Jersey
DYFS Adoption Registry
New Jersey Department of
Human Services
Division of Youth and Family
Services
Adoption Registry
Coordinator

P.O. Box 717
Trenton, NJ 08625-0717
(609) 984-6800; (609) 292-8816
www.state.nj.us/
humanservices/adoption/
registryframe.html

New Jersey Adoptees Searching
www.geocities.com/
HotSprings/4427/NJA.html

New Mexico
Children, Youth and Families Dept.
P.O. Drawer 5160
Santa Fe, NM 87502
(800)610-7610

New Mexico Adoptees Searching
www.geocities.com/
HotSprings/4427/NMA.html

New Mexico Adoption Registry
http://nmar.freeservers.com

New York
Adoption and Medical Information Registry
New York State Department of Health
P.O. Box 2602
Albany, NY 12237-2602
(518)474-9600
www.health.state.ny.us/
nysdoh/consumer/vr.htm

New York Adoptees Searching
www.geocities.com/
HotSprings/4427/NYA.html

New York Adoption Database

www.geocities.com/
SouthBeach/Lights/9645/
dbase.htm

Our Lady of Victory Infant Home (aka Father Baker's) (Lackawanna, NY)
www.angelfire.com/ny/
olvadoption/index.html

The Springer Connection (Springer Private Hospital, Union, NY)
www.homestead.com/
springerconnection/index.html

North Carolina
North Carolina Adoptees Searching
www.geocities.com/
HotSprings/4427/NCA.html

North Dakota
The Dakotas Registry
www.wildfyre-registries.
com/CAK/dak.html

North Dakota Adoptees Searching
www.geocities.com/
HotSprings/4427/NDA.html

Ohio
Ohio Adoptees Searching
www.geocities.com/
HotSprings/4427/OHA.html

Ohio Adoption Registry
Ohio Department of Health
Vital Statistics
35 East Chestnut Street
P.O. 15098
Columbus, OH 43215-0098
(614) 728-6489
www.odh.state.oh.us/Birth/
adopt.htm

Ohio Adoption Resource Exchange
30 East Broad St.
Columbus, OH 43266-0423

Ohio Reunion Registry
http://ohioadoptee.com/enter.
html

Oklahoma
Crystal Ladies Adoption Registry (for Arkansas, Missouri, Oklahoma, and Texas)
www.crystallady.com/
adopreg.htm

Oklahoma Adoptees Searching
www.geocities.com/
HotSprings/4427/OKA.html

Oklahoma DHS Adoption Reunion Registry
Mutual Consent Voluntary Registry
Department of Human Resources
Children & Family Services
Adoption Section
P.O. Box 25352
Oklahoma City, OK 73125
(877)OKSWIFT; (405)521-2475
www.okdhs.org/adopt/
reunion.htm

Oklahoma_Registry
http://groups.yahoo.com/
group/Oklahoma_Registry

Oregon
Please note that Oregon is an open records state, allowing adult adoptees unrestricted access to original adoption information.

Oregon Adoptees Searching
www.geocities.com/
HotSprings/4427/ORA.html

**Voluntary Adoption
Registry**
State Office for Services to
Children and Families
Adoption Registry
2nd Floor South
500 Summer Street NE, E71
Salem, OR 97301-1068
(503)945-6643; (503)945-
5670
www.scf.hr.state.or.us/ar/
index.htm

Pennsylvania
**Adoption Medical History
Registry**
Hillcrest, Second Floor
P.O. Box 2675
Harrisburg, PA 17105-2675
(800)227-0225
www.adoptpakids.org/
paemedicalhist.asp

**Pennsylvania Adoptees
Searching**
www.geocities.com/
HotSprings/4427/PAA.html

Rhode Island
**Rhode Island Adoptees
Searching**
www.geocities.com/
HotSprings/4427/RIA.html

**Rhode Island Family Court
Adoption Registry**
www.geocities.com/Heartland
/Forest/4191/index.html

**Tammy's Adoption Search
Page & Registry for Maine,
New Hampshire, Rhode
Island & Vermont**

www.angelfire.com/nh/
redmomma/index.html

South Carolina
**South Carolina Adoptees
Searching**
www.geocities.com/
HotSprings/4427/SCA.html

South Dakota
The Dakotas Registry
www.wildfyre-registries.
com/DAK/dak.html

**South Dakota Adoptees
Searching**
www.geocities.com/HotSprin
gs/4427/SDA.html

Voluntary Registry
Dept. of Social Services
Child Protective Services
700 Governors Drive
Richard F. Kneip Bldg.
Pierre, SD 57501
(605)773-3227

Tennessee
**Adoption Advanced Notice
Registry**
Tennessee Department of
Human Services
Department of Children's
Services
Post-Adoption Services
436 Sixth Avenue North
Nashville, TN 37243-1290
(615)532-5637
www.state.tn.us/youth/
adoption/advancednotice.htm

**Tennessee Adoptees
Searching**
www.geocities.com/
HotSprings/4427/TNA.html

**Tennessee Adoption
Registry**
www.geocities.com/Heartland
/Flats/9073/regentry.html

**Tennessee Mama's
Adoption Registry**
www.geocities.com/Heartland
/Bluffs/7446

Tennessee Reunion Registry
www.geocities.com/Heartland
/Bluffs/3592/reunion.html

Texas
Central Adoption Registry
Texas Department of Health
Bureau of Vital Statistics
P.O. Box 140123
Austin, TX 78714-0123
(512)458-7388
www.tdh.state.tx.us/bvs/car/
car.htm

**Crystal Ladies Adoption
Registry (for Arkansas,
Missouri, Oklahoma and
Texas)**
www.crystallady.com/
adopreg.htm

**Edna Gladney Reunion
Registry (Edna Gladney
Agency)**
www.geocities.com/
voasearch/gladney.html

**Homestead Reunion
Registry (Homestead
Maternity Home &
Adoption Agency)**
www.geocities.com/
voasearch/homestead.html

**Hope Cottage Reunion
Registry**

www.geocities.com/
voasearch/hopecottage.html

Lena Pope Reunion Registry (Lena Pope Maternity Home)
www.geocities.com/
voasearch/lenapope.html

Rest Cottage Registry (Rest Cottage Maternity Home & Adoption Agency)
www.geocities.com/
voasearch/restcottage.html

Texas Adoptees Searching
www.geocities.com/
HotSprings/4427/TXA.html

Texas Adoption Search Registry
www.txcare.org/searchreg/
index.shtml

Texas Reunion Registry
http://millenium.fortunecity.
com/wacky/713/index.htm

Volunteers of American Registry
www.wildfyre-registries/
VOA/voa.html

Utah
Adoption Reunion Registry
Department of Health
Vital Statistics
288 N. 1460 W.
Salt Lake City, UT 84114-2855
(801) 538-6363
www.archives.state.ut.us/
referenc/adopt.htm

Utah Adoptees Searching
www.geocities.com/
HotSprings/4427/UTA.html

Vermont
Tammy's Adoption Search Page & Registry for Maine, New Hampshire, Rhode Island, & Vermont
www.angelfire.com/nh/
redmomma/index.html

Vermont Adoptees Searching
www.geocities.com/
HotSprings/4427/VTA.html

Vermont Adoption Registry–Finding Your Roots
Social and Rehabilitation Services
103 South Main Street
Waterbury, VT 05671
(802) 241-2122
www.state.vt.us/srs/
adoption/registry.html

Virginia
Child Protective Services Central Registry
Virginia Department of Social Services
730 East Broad Street
Second Floor
Richmond, VA 23219-1849
(804)692-1290
www.dss.state.va.us/form/pdf
/032-02-151_4.pdf

Virginia Adoptees Searching
www.geocities.com/
HotSprings/4427/VAA.html

Virginia Adoption Registry
www.geocities.com/Heartland
/Plains/6436

Washington
Washington Adoptees Searching
www.geocities.com/
HotSprings/4427/WAA.html

West Virginia
Mutual Consent Registry
West Virginia Department of Health and Human Resources
Bureau for Children and Families
Office of Social Services
Services to Children and Families
Capitol Complex
Building 6, Room B 850
Charleston, WV 25305
(304)558-2933
www.wvdhhr.org/oss/staff.htm

West Virginia Adoptees Searching
www.geocities.com/
HotSprings/4427/WVA.html

Wisconsin
Adoption Records Search Program
P.O. Box 8916
Madison, WI 53708-8916
(608)266-7163
www.dhfs.state.wi.us/
Children/adoption/adsearch.htm

ICARE Wisconsin Adoptee–Birth Family Registry
www.icareregistry.com

Wisconsin Adoptees Searching
www.geocities.com/
HotSprings/4427/WIA.html

Wyoming
Putative Father Registry

Department of Family
Services
Adoption Services
Hathaway Building, 3rd Floor
2300 Capitol Avenue
Cheyenne, WY 82002
http://dfsweb.state.wy.us/
CHILDSVC/UPDATES/
ADOPTION/putativefather.
jpg

**Wyoming Adoptees
Searching**
www.geocities.com/
HotSprings/4427/WYA.html

**Wyoming Confidential
Intermediaries Program**
Adoption Consultant
Department of Family
Services
Hathaway Building, Room
366
2300 Capitol Avenue
Cheyenne, WY 82002-0710
(307)777-3570
http://dfsweb.state.wy.us/
CHILDSVC/UPDATES/
ADOPTION/adultadoption.htm
http://dfsweb.state.wy.us/
CHILDSVC/UPDATES/
ADOPTION/access.htm

Wyoming Registry
www.wildfyre-registries.
com/WY/wy.html

**VIET NAM
Adopted Vietnamese
International (AVI)**
www.darlo.tv/indigo/
Vietnam1.html

**Vietnamese Adoptee
Network, Inc.**
www.van-online.org

Consumer Online Systems

With so much information now online,
it is exceptionally easy to simply dive in and drown.

–Alfred Glossbrenner

America Online, Inc.
8619 Westwood Center Dr.
Vienna, VA 22182-2285
(800)824-6364; (703)448-8700
www.aol.com

CompuServe Information Services
5000 Arlington Centre Blvd.
Columbus, OH 43220
(800)848-8990; (614)457-8600
www.compuserve.com

Delphi Internet Services Corporation
620 Avenue of the Americas
New York, NY 10011
(800)695-4005; (212)462-5000
www.delphi.com

GE Information Services (GEIS)
401 N. Washington St.
Rockville, MD 20850
(301)340-4000
www.geis.com

The Internet
Owned by no one, Internet service is provided by thousands of Internet Service Providers (ISPs). For a list of ISPs, see The List at www.thelist.com

Prodigy Services Company
446 Hamilton Ave.
White Plains, NY 10601
(800)776-0845; (914)993-8000
myhome.prodigy.net

Public Records Producers and Vendors

*That miscellaneous collection of a few wise
and many foolish individuals, called the public.*

–John Stuart

*Although there are many
other companies that offer
online public records, tenant
and employee screening, and
related services, the following list is an attempt to identify only those companies
that are producers of proprietary databases of this type.*

Accufax
P.O. Box 3563
Tulsa, OK 74153
(800)256-8898; (918)627-
2226
www.accufax-us.com

Accu-Source, Inc.
8585 N. Stemmons Freeway
Suite M-26
Dallas, TX 75247
(817)589-7408
www.accu-source.com

Acxiom Corporation
1 Information Way
P.O. Box 8180
Little Rock, AR 72203-0180

(501)342-1000
www.acxiom.com

**Agency Records/Rapid
Information Services**
Box 310175
Newington, CT 06131-0175
(800)777-6655; (860)667-
1617
http://AgencyRecords.com

**American Insurance
Services Group**
a unit of Insurance Services
Office, Inc.
545 Washington Boulevard
Jersey City, NJ 07310-1686
(201)469-3140
www.iso.com/AISG/index.
html

**Ameridex Information
Systems**
P.O. Box 51314
Irvine, CA 92619-1314
http://Kadima.com

AmeriFind
or **DCS Information**

Systems
or **Dallas Computer
Services Inc.**
500 N. Central Expressway,
Suite 280
Plano, TX 75074
(800)394-3274; (972)422-
3600
www.dnis.com

Aristotle Industries
50 E Street, S.E.
Washington, DC 20003
(202)554-3563
www.aristotle.com/default.asp

**Atlantic Magellan
Corporation**
301 Merchant's Drive
Norcross, GA 30093
(770)414-5442
http://66.43.146.166/
magellan/default.htm

**AutoTrackXP
ChoicePoint Inc.**
4530 Conference Way South
Boca Raton, FL 33431
(800)279-7710
www.dbt.com

Avert, Inc.
301 Remington Street
Fort Collins, CO 80524
(888)606-7869
www.avert.com

Background Information Services, Inc.
1800 30th Street, Ste. 213,
Boulder, CO 80301
(800)433-6010; (303)442-3960
www.bisi.com

Carfax, Inc.
a subsidiary of the R.L. Polk
Company
www.carfax.com

ChoicePoint Online
1000 Alderman Dr.
Alpharetta, GA 30005
(800)333-3365
www.choicepointonline.com

Commercial Information Systems, Inc.
P.O. Box 69174
Portland, OR 97201-0174
(800)454-6575
www.cis-usa.com

Confi-chek
1816 19Th Street
Sacramento, CA 95814
(800)821-7404
www.confi-chek.com

CT Corporation System
a Division of CCH Legal
Information Systems
1633 Broadway, 30th Fl.
New York, NY 10019
(800)624-0909
www.cch-lis.com

DAC Services
a division of TISI
4500 South 129th E. Ave.
Suite 200
Tulsa, OK 74134-5885
(800)331-9175
www.dacservices.com

DAMAR Real Estate
3610 Central Avenue
Riverside, CA 92506
(800)873-2627

DBT Online Inc.
or **Database Technologies, Inc.**
a ChoicePoint company
4530 Conference Way South
Boca Raton, FL 33431
(561)982-5363
www.dbtonline.com

DataQuick Information Systems, Inc.
9620 Towne Centre Drive
San Diego, CA 92121
(888)604-DATA; (858)597-3100
www.dataquick.com

Dun & Bradstreet, Inc.
One Diamond Hill Rd.
Murray Hill, NJ 07974-1218
(800)234-3867; (908)665-5000
www.dnb.com

Environmental Data Resources Inc.
3530 Post Road
Southport, CT 06490
(800)352-0050
www.edrnet.com

Experian
North American Headquarters

505 City Parkway West
Orange, CA 92868
(714)385-7000
www.experian.com

Explore Information Services
4920 Moundview Drive
Red Wing, MN 55066
(800)531-9125; (651)385-2284
www.exploredata.com

Fidelifacts Metropolitan Inc.
42 Broadway
Suite 1548
New York, NY 10004
(212)425-1520
www.fidelifacts.com

Finance and Commerce Daily
a Dolan Media Company
730 2nd Ave S # 100
Minneapolis, MN
(612)333-4244

General Information Services (GIS)
a Division of Policy
Management Systems
Corporation
P.O. Box 353
Chapin, SC 29036
(888)GEN INFO
www.geninfo.com

Hogan Information Services
14000 Quail Springs Parkway
Suite 4000
Oklahoma City, OK 73134
(405)302-6954
www.hoganinfo.com

Hollingsworth Information Services, Inc.

10761 Perkins Road
Suite A
Baton Rouge LA 70810
(504)769-2156
http://rouge.net

The Info*Center Inc.
940 North St. Extension
Feeding Hills, MA 01030-
1336
(800)462-3033; (413)786-
7987
www.infocredit.com

Information America (IA)
a ChoicePoint company
(Refer to DBT Online)
www.dbtonline.com

Informus Corporation
2001 Airport Road, Suite 201
Jackson, MS 39208
(800)364-8380
www.informus.com

**Insurance Information
Exchange**
3001 Earl Rudder Fwy S.
College Station, TX 77845
(800)683-8553
www.iix.com

Intelligence Network Inc.
1224 Rogers St.
Clearwater, FL 34616-5903
(813)449-0072

LexisNexis
9443 Springboro Pike
P.O. Box 933
Dayton, OH 45401-0933
(800)227-9597; (937)865-
6800
www.lexisnexis.com

**Lloyd's Maritime
Information Services**

1200 Summer Street
Stamford, CT 06905
(800)423-8672; (203)359-
8383
www.lmis.com

**Merlin Information
Services**
215 South Complex Drive
Kalispell, MT 59901
(800)367-6646
www.merlindata.com

MIB Group, Inc.
P.O. Box 105
Essex Station
Boston, MA 02112
(617)426-3660
www.mib.com

**Motznik Computer Services
Inc.**
8301 Briarwood, Suite 100
Anchorage, AK 99518
(907)344-6254
www.motznik.com

**National Credit
Information (NCI)Network**
a division of W.D.I.A.
Corporation
P.O. Box 53247
Cincinnati, OH 45253
(513)522-3832
www.wdia.com

New Mexico Technet Inc.
5921 Jefferson NE
Albuquerque, NM 87109
(505)345-6555
www.technet.nm.org

Nexis
Refer to LexisNexis

**Ohio Professional
Electronic Network (OPEN)**
1650 Lake Shore Dr., Suite

350
P.O. Box 549
Columbus OH 43204-4895
(800)366-0106; (614)481-
6999
www.openonline.com

PACER Service Center
Administrative Office of the
U.S. Courts
P.O. Box 780549
San Antonio, TX 78278
(800)676-6856; (210)301-
6440
http://pacer.psc.uscourts.gov

Plat System Services Inc.
12450 Wayzata Blvd.
Suite 108
Minnetonka, MN 55305
(952)544-0012
www.platsystems.com

Pollock & Co.
27 Garfield Street
Newington, CT 06111
(860)667-1617

Property Data Center Inc.
7100 E Belleview Ave # 110
Englewood, CO 80111
(303)850-9586
www.pdclane.com/default.asp

Public Data Corporation
38 E. 29th St., 8th Fl.
New York, NY 10016-7911
(212)519-3063
www.pdcny.com

**Rental Research Services
or Employment Research
Services**
11300 Minnetonka Mills Rd.
Minnetonka, MN 55305-5151
(800)328-0333; (952)935-
5700
www.rentalresearch.com

Rhino Referral Systems
157 Glynwood Ave
Lafayette, LA
(337)234-1450

The Screening Network
from IRSC
a ChoicePoint company
(800)640-4772
www.screeningnetwork.com

Search Network Ltd.
2 Corporate Place, Suite 210
1501 42nd Street
West Des Moines, IA 50266
(800)383-5050; (515)223-
1153
www.searchnetworkltd.com

Statens Vegvesen (SVV)
Grenseveien 97
P.O. Box 8037 Dep
N-62885000 Oslo, Norway
47 22074300
http://hotell.nextel.no/stvv/
infoside.html

**Superior Information
Services, LLC**
P.O. Box 8787
Trenton, NJ 08650
(800)848-0489
www.superiorinfo.com

**Trans-Union DATEQ
Network Inc.**
5555 Triangle Parkway
Norcross, GA 30092
(770)613-2860

**TransUnion Employment
Screening Services, Inc.**
6111 Oak Tree Blvd.
Cleveland, Ohio 44131
(800)853-3228
www.tuess.com

Vegdirektoratet
P.O. Box 8142 Dep
N-0033 Oslo, Norway
47 22073500

Verifacts, Inc.
7326 27th Street West
Suite C
University Place, WA 98466
(800)568-5665; (253)565-
9109
www.verifacts.com

West Group–WESTLAW
610 Opperman Dr.
Eagan, MN 55123-1396
(800)937-8527; (651)687-
7000
web2.westlaw.com

Other Database Vendors

As long as one keeps searching, the answers come.

—Joan Bucz

There are hundreds of online database vendors. The following list represents only a small sampling of these vendors. It is my intention to include the major vendors who offer a broad base of databases, as well as the vendors whose databases I have found to be most helpful researching information on individuals (in addition to those listed in Appendices L and M).

ABC voor Handel en Industrie C.V
P.O. Box 190
NL-2000 AD Haarlem,
Netherlands
31 235319031
www.abc-d.nl/abc-guides/en/pend/index.html

AccuWeather, Inc.
385 Science Park Rd.
State College, PA 16803
(800)566-6606;

(814)235-8600
www1.accuweather.com

ADP Network Services, Inc.
175 Jackson Plaza
Ann Arbor, MI 48106
(800)829-2206; (313)769-6800

ADP (UK) Ltd.
ADP House
2 Pine Trees
Chertsey Ln.
Staines
Middlesex, Greater London
TW18 3Ds, England
44 1784 429000

Alberta Treasury, Statistics
Rm. 259 Terrace Bldg.
9515 107th St.
Edmonton, AB, Canada T5K 2C3
(403)427-3099

American Chemical Society (ACS)
1155 16th St., NW

Washington, DC 20036
(800)333-9511; (202)293-9704
http://pubs.acs.org

American Society of Civil Engineers (ASCE)
1801 Alexander Bell Dr.
Reston, VA 20191-4400
(800)548-2723; (703)295-6300
www.pubs.asce.org

ARK Information Services
11 NewFetter Ln., 10th Floor
London EC44 1JN, England
171 8153975

Association IBISCUS
1 bis, rue du Havre
F-75008, Paris, France
01 42942434

Australian Bureau of Statistics (ABS)
Cameron Offices
P.O. Box 10
Belconnen, ACT 2616,

Australia
62020 ABOST AA

BASELINE, INC.
838 Broadway, 4th F.
New York, NY 10003
(800)242-7546; (212)254-
8235
www.pkbaseline.com

BELINDIS
or **Ministere Belge des
Affaires
Economiques–Centre de
Traitement de
l'Information**
North Gate III, Blvd. E.
Jacqmain 154
B-1000 Brussels, Belgium
322 2064283

**Bell & Howell Information
and Learning**
300 N. Zeeb Rd.
P.O. Box 1346
Ann Arbor, MI 48106-1346
(800)521-0600; (734)761-
4700
www.bellhowell.
infolearning.com

BT North America, Inc.
40 E. 52nd St., 14th Fl.
New York, NY 10022
(800)872-7654; (212)418-
7800

**The Bureau of National
Affairs, Inc.**
1231 25th St., NW
Washington, DC 20037
(800)452-7773; (202)452-
4200

**Bureau van Dijk, SA
(BvD)–Electronic
Publishing**

Ave. Louise 250
Box 14
B-1050 Brussels, Belgium
32 2 6390606
www.bvdep.com

**Burrelle's Information
Services**
75 E. Northfield Rd.
Livingston, NJ 07039-9873
(800)876-3342; (973)992-
6600
www.burrelles.com

Callassure
3637 4th St., N., Ste. 330
St. Petersburg, FL 33704

**Cambridge Scientific
Abstracts (CSA)**
7200 Wisconsin Ave., Ste.
601
Bethesda, MD 20814-4823
(800)843-7751; (301)961-
6700
www.csa.com

**Canadian Heritage
Information Network
(CHIN)**
15 Eddy St., 4th Fl.
Hull, PQ Canada K1A 0M5
(800)520-2446; (819)994-
1200
www.chin.gc.ca

The Canadian Press
36 King St. E
Toronto, ON Canada M5C
2L9
(800)434-7578; (416)364-
0321
www.cp.org

CARL Corporation
3801 E. Florida Ave.
Suite 300

Denver, CO 80210
(303)758-3030

Cartermill Ltd
Technology Centre
St. Andrews
Fife KY16 9EA, Scotland
1334 477660

CDA/Investnet
1455 Research Blvd.
Rockville, MD 20850
(800)933-4446; (954)384-
1500
www.cda.com

**Center for International
Financial Analysis and
Research, Inc.**
P.O. Box 3228
Princeton, NJ 08543-3228
(609)520-9333

**CERVED International,
S.A**
rue de l'Industrie 22
B-1040 Bruxelles, Belgium
322 5141300

**Chamber World
Network–Asia Intelligence
Wire**
14 Wall St., Ste. 1220
New York, NY 10005-2101
(212)645-2464

ChemWeb, Inc.
34-42 Cleveland St
London W1P 6LB, England
www.chemweb.com

Chollian
65-228, Hangangro 3ga
Youngsan-Gu
Seoul, Republic of Korea
822 2207002
www.chollian.net

Claritas Data Services
53 Brown Rd.
Ithaca, NY 14850
(800)234-5997; (607)257-0567
www.claritas.com

Colorado State Data Center
1313 Sherman St., Rm. 521
Denver, CO 80203
(303)866-4819

Congressional Quarterly
1414 22nd St. NW
Washington, DC 20037
(800)638-1610; (202)887-
8500
www.cq.com

COSMOSNET
or **Teikoku Databank,
Litd.–COSMOSNET**
5-20 Minami Aoyama 2-
Chrome
Minato-ku
Tokyo 107-860, Japan
813 34044311

DataStar
The Communications
Building
48 Leicester sq.
London WC2H 7DB England
(800)334-2564; 44 171
9306900
www.dialog.com/info/
products/datastar-index.shtml

**DBC Sports–Computer
Sports World**
675 Grier Dr.
Las Vegas, NV 89119
(800)321-5562

Det Kongelige Bibliotek
P.O. Box 2149
DK-1016
Copenhagen K, Denmark

45 33474747
www.kb.dk

Dialog
The Communications
Building
48 Leicester sq.
London WC2H 7DB England
(800)334-2564; 44 171
9306900
www.dialogweb.com

**DIMDI (Deutsches Institut
fuer Medizinische
Dokumentation und
Information)**
Weisshausstr. 27
Postfach 420580
D-50899 Cologne, Germany
0221 47241
www.dimdi.de

**Dow Jones & Company,
Inc.**
P.O. Box 300
Princeton, NJ 08543-0300
(800)832-1234; (609)520-
4000
www.dowjones.com/corp/
index.html

DRI-WEFA
24 Hartwell Ave.
Lexington, MA 02173-3154
(800)933-3374; (781)863-
5100
www.dri-wefa.com

Dun & Bradstreet Australia
19 Havilah St.
Chatswood, NSW 2065,
Australia

Dun & Bradstreet Canada
5770 Hurontario St.
P.O. Box 6200, Station A
Mississauga, ON, Canada

L5R 3G5
(800)234-3867; (905)568-
6000
www.dnb.ca

**Dun & Bradstreet Business
Credit Services**
One Diamond Hill Rd.
P.O. Box 27
Murray Hill, NJ 07974-0027
(800)362-3425; (908)665-
5000
www.dnb.com

**Dun & Bradstreet France
S.A.**
17, ave. de Choisy
Le Palatino
F-75643 Paris Cedex 13,
France
www.dbfrance.com

Dun & Bradstreet Ltd.
5th Floor, Westminster House
Portland St.
Manchester, Greater
Manchester M1 3HU,
England
44 161 4555119

EBSCOhost and **EBSCO
Publishing**
10 Estes St.
Ipswich, MA 01938
(800)653-2726; (508)356-
6500
www.epnet.com

**European Information
Network Services**
c/o The British Library
Science Reference
Information Service
25 Southampton Bldgs.
London WC2A 1AW,
England
44 171 4127946
www.eins.org

Europeenne de Donnees (ASPO)
164 Ter, rue d'Aguesseau
F-93100 Boulogne-
Billancourt, France
331 41868686

Factiva
105 Madison Avenue
10th Floor
New York, NY 10016
Americas: (800)369-7466;
(609)627-2000
Europe: 44.207.208.0000
Australia and Asia:
61.2.8272.4600
www.factiva.com

FactSet Data Systems, Inc.
One Greenwich Plaza
Greenwich, CT 06830
(203)863-1500

Federal News Service
620 National Press Bldg.
Washington, DC 20045
(800)969-3677; (202)347-
1400
www.fnsg.com

**FIZ Technik
(Fachinformationszentrum
Technik e.V.)**
Ostbahnhofstr. 13-15
D-60314 Frankfurt am Main,
Germany
49 69 4308225
www.fiz-technik.de

FT PROFILE
Fitroy House
13-17 Epworth St.
London EC2A, 4DL England
44 171 8257777

Gale Group
27500 Drake Rd.

Farmington Hills, Mi 48331-
3535
(800)347-4253; (248)699-
4253
http://infotrac.galegroup.com

**GE Information Services
(GEIS)**
401 N. Washington St.
Rockville, MD 20850
(301)340-4000
www.geis.com

**GENIOS
Wirschaftsdatenbanken**
Gartnerweb 4-8
D-60322 Frankfurt
am Main 1, Germany
www.genios.de

**Gesellschaft fur
Betriebswirtschaftliche
Information mbH (GBI)**
Freischuetzstr. 96
Postfach 810360
D-81927 Munich, Germany
4989 99287923
www.gbi.de
http://engl.gbi.de

**Global Access/Primark
Corporation**
Monmouth House
58-64 City Rd.
London EC1Y 2AL, England
44 171 2503000
www.primark.com

Global Meeting Line, Inc.
1345 Oak Ridge Turnpike,
P.M.B. 357
Oak Ridge, TN 37830
(865)482-6451

**H.W. Wilson
Company–WilsonWeb**
950 University Ave.
Bronx, NY 10452

(800)367-6770; (718)588-
8400
www.hwwilson.com

Haver Analytics
60 E. 42nd St., Ste 3310
New York, NY 10165
(212)986-9300
www.haver.com

HITEL
Sera B/D, 50-1
Nonhyn-Dong, Gangnan-Gu
Seoul, Republic of Korea
www.hitel.net

The Infocheck Group, Ltd.
Godmersham Park
Godmersham
Canterbury, Kent CT4 7DT,
England
44 1227 81300

Infomart Dialog
333 King St. E
Toronto, ON Canada M5A
4R7
(800)668-9215; (416)350-
6001
www.infomart.com

Infomart Online
1450 Don Mills Rd.
Don Mills, ON Canada M3B
2X7
(800)668-9215; (416)442-
2223

Infonautics Corporation
900 W. Valley Rd.
Ste. 1000
Wayne, PA 19087-1830
(800)860-9227; (610)971-
8840

Information for Public Affairs, Inc. (IPA)–StateNet
2101 K St.
Sacramento, CA 95816-4920
(916)444-0840
www.statenet.com

INFOTRADE N.V.
Stationstraat, 30 b2
B-1702 Groot-Bijgaarden,
Belgium
32 2 4818283
www.infotrade.be

Intelex Corp.
P.O. Box 859
Charlottesville, VA 22902-0859
(804)970-2286

Interactive Data Corporation
22 Crosby Dr.
Bedford, MA 01730-1402
(617)306-6999

International Research and Evaluation (IRE)
21098 IRE Center
Eagan, MN 55121
(888)888-9245; (612)888-9635

Israel National Center of Scientific and Technological Information (COSTI)
Atidim Scientific Park
Devorah-Haneviah St.
61430 Tel-Aviv, Israel
3 492040

Jane's Information Group
1340 Braddock Pl. Ste 300
Alexandria, Va 22314-1657
(800)824-0768;

(703)683-3700
www.janes.com

Jordans Ltd.
21 St. Thomas St.
Bristol BS1 6JS, England
1179 230600

K.G. Saur Verlag GmbII & Co
Ortlerstrasse 8
D-81373 Munich, Germany
49 89 769020
www.saur.de

Kompass France S.A.
66, quai du Marechal Joffre
F-92415 Courbevoie Cedex,
France
33 1 41165100

Lda Mope
Rua de Santa Marta
43 E/F 4th Floor
1100 Lisbon, Portugal
3522996

Legi-Slate
10 G St., NE, Ste. 500
Washington, DC 20002
(800)733-1131; (202)898-2300

Legi-Tech
2101 K St.
Sacramento, CA 95816-4920

MagnaTex International., COMMUNICATE!
1173 Rockrimmon Rd.
Stamford, CT 06903
(800)777-9246
(203)322-2569

MILITRAN, Inc.
P.O. Box 490

Southeastern, PA 19399-0490
(800)426-9954; (610)687-3900

Ministerio de Educacion, Deporte Cultura y (ESPANA)
Avda. Juan de Herrera 2
28040 Madrid, Spain
5 495991
www.mcu.es/homemcu.html

National Adoption Center (NAC)
1500 Walnut St., Ste 701
Philadelphia, PA 19102
(215)735-9988
www.adopt.org

National Information Services Corporation
Wyman Towers, Ste. 6
3100 St. Paul St.
Baltimore, MD 21218
(410)243-0797

National Library of Canada
Information Technology
Services
395 Wellington St.
Ottawa, ON
Canada K1A 0N4
(613)997-7000

NewsBank, Inc.
5050 Tamiami Trail North,
Ste. 110
Naples, FL 34103
(800)762-8182; (941)263-6004
www.newsbank.com

NewsEdge Corporation
80 Blanchard Rd.
Burlington, MA 01803
(800)252-9980;

(781)313-5900
www.newsedge.com

NIFTY-SERVE
26-1, Minami-oi 6-chome
Shinagawa-ku
Tokyo 140, Japan
813 54715800

OCLC
- EPIC
- Firstsearch Catalog
- Firstsearch Electronic
Collections Online
6565 Frantz Rd.
Dublin, OH 43017-3395
(800)848-5878; (614)764-
6000
www.oclc.org/home

Organization of American
States, General Secretariat
1889 F St., NW
Washington, DC 20006-4413
(202)458-3725
www.oas.org

Ovid Technologies, Inc.
333 Seventh Ave.
New York, NY 10001
(800)950-2035; (212)563-
3006
www.ovid.com

Profound Inc.–The Dialog
Corporation
The Communications
Building
48 Leicester sq.
London WC2H 7DB England
(800)334-2564; 44 171
9306900
www.profound.co.uk

QL Systems Limited
St. Andrew's Tower, Ste. 901
275 Sparks St.
Ottawa, ON Canada

K1R 7X9
(800)387-0899;
(613)238-3499

Questel Orbit
4, rue des Colonnes
F-75082, Paris, France
33 1 55045200
www.questel.orbit.com
Research Bank Web
or **Thomson Financial**
Services, Inc.
22 Thomson Pl
Boston, MA 02210
(888)989-8373; (617)856-
2704
www.investext.com

Reuters Information
Services, Inc.
1700 Broadway
New York, NY 10019
(212)603-3300
www.reuters.com

RIXLEX
Riksdagen
S-100 12 Stockholm, Sweden
87865333

SilverPlatter Information,
Inc.
100 River Ridge Dr.
Norwood, MA 02062-5043
(800)343-0064; (781)769-
2599
www.silverplatter.com

Simmons Market Research
Bureau, Inc. (SMRB)
420 Lexington Ave.
New York, NY 10170
www.smrb.com

SovInfoLink
or **Russian Information and**
Communications Agency

(RUSSICA)
Spartakovskaya St. 13
107066 Moscow, Russia
095 9325610

The Sports Network
95 James Way
Stes. 107 and 109
Southampton, PA 18966
(215)942-7890
www.sportsnetwork.com

Standard & Poor's
Compustat
7400 S. Alton Court
Englewood, CO 80112
(800)525-8640; (303)771-
6510
www.compustat.com

Star Temporaries
8133 Leesburg Pike, Ste. 305
Vienna, VA 22182-2706

STN International
The Scientific & Technical
Information Network
VIZ Karlsruhe
P.O. Box 2465
D-76012 Karlsruhe, Germany
07247 808555
www.fiz-
karlsruhe.de/stn.html

SUNIST
B.P. 7229
34184 Montpellier Cedex,
France

Sveriges Kungl
P.O. Box 5039
S-102 41
Stockholm, Sweden
46 8 7833900

Sweden Statistiska
Centralbyran(SCB)

Statistical Databases Division
S-115 81 Stockholm, Sweden

Telerate Systems Inc.
a Bridge Company
Harborside Financial Center
600 Plaza Two
Jersey City, NJ 07311
(201)860-4000
www.telerate.com/home.html

**Texas Innovation Network
System (TINS)**
3500 W. Balcones Center Dr.
Austin, TX 78759
(800)645-8324

**Thomson Financial
Investment Banking and
Capital Markets Group**
Two Gateway Center
Norwalk, NJ 07102
(888)989-8383; (973)622-
3100
www.tfibcm.com

TT-Tietopalvelut Oy
P.O. Box 406
FIN-02003 Espoo, Finland

**U.S. Federal Election
Commission**
999 E. St., NW
Washington, DC 20463
(800)424-9530; (202)694-
1250
www.fec.gov

Umea Universitet
SE-901 87
Umea, Sweden
46 90 786 68 75

Unitel
942-1, Daechei-Dong,
Gangnam-Ku
Seoul, Republic of Korea
8225284600

University of Durham
Chief Clerk's Office
Old Shire Hall
Durham DH1 3HP, England
191 3742925
www.dur.ac.uk

University of Oslo Library
Bibliographic Services Dept.
Drammensveien 42
N-0242 Oslo, Norway
4722 859126
www.ub.uio.no

Vestek Systems, Inc.
388 Market St., Suite 700
San Francisco, CA 94111
(415)498-6340

The WEFA Group
1110 Vermont Ave., NW
Washington, DC 20005
(202)775-0610
www.fdic.gov

Companies and Associations That Can Help to Remove Your Name from Mailing and Telephone Lists

In good times, people want to advertise;
in bad times, they have to.

–Bruce Barton

Acxiom Corporation
Attn: Opt-outs / Consumer
Advocacy
P.O. Box 2000
Conway AR 72033-2000
(501)342-2722

Abacus Direct
P.O. Box 1478
Broomfield, CO 80038-1478
(800)518-4453; (303)410-5294

Alabama's Do Not Call List
Public Service Commission
P. O. Box 304260
Montgomery, AL 36130-4260
(877)727-8200
www.psc.state.al.us

Alaska's Do Not Call List (Anchorage)
(907)564-1133

Alaska's Do Not Call List (South Central)
(907)761-2635

Alaska's Do Not Call List (Other)
(907)835-2231; (907)265-5600

American Business Information, Inc.
Attn: Product Quality
P.O. Box 27347
Omaha NE 68127

American Family Publishers
P.O. Box 62000

Tampa FL 33662
(800)237-2400

Arizona's Telemarketing Abuse Information
Arizona Secretary of State's Office
1700 W. Washington Street
Phoenix, AZ 85007
(800)458-5842; (602)542-6187
www.sosaz.com/business_services/ts/TeleSolicit_brochure.htm

Arkansas' Do Not Call List
Office of the Attorney General
323 Center Street, Suite 200
Little Rock, Arkansas 72201
(877)866-8225; (501)682-1334
www.donotcall.org

Canada's Do Not Mail Service
Canadian Marketing Association
1 Concorde Gate
Suite 607
Don Mills, Ontario M3C 3N6
Canada
(416)391-2362
www.cornerstonewebmedia.
com/cma/submit.asp

Consumer.net
www.consumer.net
and http://privacy.net

Database America
Compilation Department
470 Chestnut Ridge Rd.
Woodcliff Lake, NJ 07677-7604
(800)223-7777

DMA's E-mail Preference Service
www.the-dma.org/consumers/
optoutform_emps.shtml

DMA's Mail Preference Service
Preference Service Manager
Direct Marketing Association
1120 Avenue of the Americas
New York, NY 10036-6700
www.the-dma.org/cgi/
offmailinglistdave

DMA's Telephone Preference Service
Preference Service Manager
Direct Marketing Association
1120 Avenue of the Americas
New York, NY 10036-6700
www.the-dma.org/cgi/
offtelephonedave

Donnelly Marketing, Inc.
416 S. Bell Avenue
Ames, IA 50010
(515)956-8000

Dunn & Bradstreet
Customer Service
899 Eaton Avenue
Bethlehem, PA 18025

EcoFuture
www.ecofuture.org/jnkmail.
html

Equifax
P.O. Box 105873
Atlanta GA 30348
(800)567-8688
www.equifax.com/contact_us
/personal_credit_rpt.html

Experian
Consumer Opt Out
701 Experian Parkway
Allen, TX 75013
(800)353-0809
www.experian.com/
customer/mail.html#

Federal Trade Commission
www.ftc.gov/privacy/
protect.htm

Florida's Do Not Call List
Division of Consumer
Services
(800)HELP-FLA
www.800helpfla.com

Georgia's No-Call List
(877)426-6225
www.ganocall.com

Germany's Do Not Mail List

DDV Robinson-Liste
Postfach 1401
71243 Ditzingen
07156/ 95 10 10
http://privacy.net/OptOut/
mpsde.asp

Haines & Co.
Criss-Cross Directory
Attn: Director of Data
Processing
8050 Freedom Ave., NW
North Canton, OH 44720
(800)562-8262

Idaho's Attorney General's No Call List
700 W. Jefferson Street
P.O. Box 83720
Boise, ID 83720-0010
(208)334-2424
www2.state.id.us/ag

Junk Mail Busters
Suite 4 Embarcadero Center
San Francisco, CA 94111

Junkbusters
www.junkbusters.com/ht/en/
self.html

Kentucky's No More Calls Please
Attorney General's Office
1024 Capital Center Drive
Frankfort, KY 40601
(502)696-5398
www.law.state.ky.us/cp/
nocall.htm

Metromail Corp.
Consumer Services
901 West Bond
Lincoln, NE 68521
(800)228-4571, Ext. 4633

Missouri's No Call List
(573)751-3321
www.ago.state.mo.us

New York's Do Not Call List
Office of the Attorney General
(800)771-7755
www.oag.state.ny.us/
consumer/tips/
telemarketing.html

Oregon No Call List
(877)700-6622
www.ornocall.com

R. L. Polk & Company
Attention: Opt-Out Coordinator
26955 Northwestern Highway,
Southfield MI 48034-8455
(800)873-7655

Privacy Rights Clearinghouse
1717 Kettner Ave. Suite 105
San Diego, CA 92101
(619)298-3396
www.privacyrights.org

Private Citizen, Inc.
P.O. Box 233
Naperville, IL 60566
(630)393-2370
www.private-citizen.com

Stop Junk Mail Association
3020 Bridgeway #150
Sausalito, CA 94965
(800)827-5549

Tennessee Solicitor Do Not Call Program
(615)741-2904 ext.162
www2.state.tn.us/tra/nocall.htm

Trans Union Marketing List Opt-Out
TransUnion LLC's Name Removal Option
P.O. Box 97328
Jackson, MS 39288-7328
(888)567-8688
www.transunion.com/
personal/OptOut.asp

U.K. Do Not Mail List
The Mail Preference Service
Freepost 22
London W1E 7EZ
http://privacy.net/OptOut/mps
uk.asp

Have I Missed Anything?

A computer lets you make more mistakes faster than any invention in human history—with the possible exceptions of handguns and tequila.

–Mitch Ratliffe

Updates to the material in *Naked in Cyberspace* can be found at www.technosearch.com/naked. If there are sources that I've missed, errors made, or anything that you think should be covered that you did not find in *Naked in Cyberspace*, please send your comments and updates to calane@technosearch.com.

Thank you.

About the Author

After earning her bachelor's degree in psychology, Carole A. Lane spent more than a decade designing databases and systems in the medical and consumer credit fields. Throughout her career, she has been involved with personal records, which took on greater emphasis when she opened her research firm, TechnoSearch, Inc., in 1993.

Carole has served on the advisory board of the Special Libraries Association and on the board of directors of the Association of Independent Information Professionals, and she is a member of Mensa.

Carole has taught classes on locating personal records online and information brokering, and has testified before the Federal Trade Commission and the California Joint Legislative Task Force on Personal Information and Privacy. She has written articles on various subjects including locating people, privacy online, market research, and Customer Relationship Management (CRM). Carole is also a frequently requested speaker at conferences throughout the United States (and occasionally beyond). She has appeared on numerous television shows (including *Good Morning America*, *World News Tonight*, *The Montel Williams Show*), radio programs (such as "Sunday Rounds on National Press Radio"), and in print publications (for example, *Time*, *Money*, *Washington Post*).

Carole makes her home in Vista, California along with her husband, Barry Wang; son, Skylar; and daughter, Alexandra.

Index

F

J

M

O

P

Q

R

S

T

U

V

Z

More CyberAge Books from Information Today, Inc.

Web of Deception
Misinformation on the Internet

Edited by Anne P. Mintz • Foreword by Steve Forbes

Intentionally misleading or erroneous information on the Web can wreak havoc on your health, privacy, investments, business decisions, online purchases, legal affairs, and more. Until now, the breadth and significance of this growing problem have yet to be fully explored. In *Web of Deception*, Anne P. Mintz brings together 10 information industry gurus to illuminate the issues and help you recognize and deal with the flood of deception and misinformation in a range of critical subject areas.

2002/278 pp/softbound/ISBN 0-910965-60-9 $24.95

Net Crimes & Misdemeanors
Outmaneuvering the Spammers, Swindlers, and Stalkers Who Are Targeting You Online

By J.A. Hitchcock • Edited by Loraine Page

Cyber crime expert J.A. Hitchcock helps individuals and business users of the Web protect themselves, their children, and their employees against online cheats and predators. Hitchcock details a broad range of abusive practices, shares victims' stories, and offers advice on how to handle junk e-mail, "flaming," privacy invasion, financial scams, cyberstalking, and indentity theft. She provides tips and techniques that can be put to immediate use and points to the laws, organizations, and Web resources that can aid victims and help them fight back. Supported by a Web site.

2002/384 pp/softbound/ISBN 0-910965-57-9 $24.95

Electronic Democracy, 2nd Edition
Using the Internet to Transform American Politics

By Graeme Browning • Foreword by Adam Clayton Powell III

In this new edition of *Electronic Democracy*, award-winning journalist and author Graeme Browning details the colorful history of politics and the Net, decribes key Web-based sources of political information, offers practical techniques for influencing legislation online, and provides a fascinating, realistic vision of the future.

2002/200 pp/softbound/ISBN 0-910965-49-8 $19.95

Smart Services
Competitive Information Strategies, Solutions, and Success Stories for Service Businesses

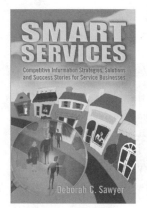

By Deborah C. Sawyer

Here is the first book to focus specifically on the competitive information needs of service-oriented firms. Author, entrepreneur, and business consultant Deborah C. Sawyer illuminates the many forms of competition in service businesses, identifies the most effective information resources for competitive intelligence (CI), and provides a practical framework for identifying and studying competitors in order to gain a competitive advantage. *Smart Services* is a roadmap for every service company owner, manager, or executive who expects to compete effectively in the Information Age.

2002/256 pp/softbound/ISBN 0-910965-56-0 $29.95

Millennium Intelligence
Understanding and Conducting Competitive Intelligence in the Digital Age

By Jerry P. Miller and the Business Intelligence Braintrust

With contributions from the world's leading business intelligence practitioners, here is a tremendously informative and practical look at the CI process, how it is changing, and how it can be managed effectively in the Digital Age. Loaded with case studies, tips, and techniques, chapters include: What is Intelligence?; The Skills Needed to Execute Intelligence Effectively; Information Sources Used for Intelligence; The Legal and Ethical Aspects of Intelligence; Small Business Intelligence; Corporate Security and Intelligence; … and much more!

2000/276 pp/softbound/ISBN 0-910965-28-5 $29.95

Internet Business Intelligence
How to Build a Big Company System on a Small Company Budget

By David Vine

According to author David Vine, business success in the competitive, global marketplace of the 21st century will depend on a firm's ability to use information effectively—and the most successful firms will be those that harness the Internet to create and maintain a powerful information edge. In *Internet Business Intelligence*, Vine explains how any company can build a complete, low-cost, Internet-based business intelligence system that really works. Here is a savvy, no-nonsense approach to using the Internet to solve everyday business problems and stay one step ahead of the competition.

2000/448 pp/softbound/ISBN 0-910965-35-8 $29.95

Building and Running a Successful Research Business
A Guide for the Independent Information Professional

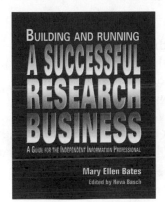

By Mary Ellen Bates • Edited by Reva Basch

This is *the* handbook every aspiring independent information professional needs to launch, manage, and build a research business. Mary Ellen Bates covers everything from "is this right for you?" to closing the sale, managing clients, promoting your business on the Web, and tapping into powerful information sources beyond the Web. Bates, a popular author and speaker and a long-time successful independent info pro, reveals all the tips, tricks, and techniques for setting up, running, and growing your own information business.

2002/360 pp/softbound/ISBN 0-910965-62-5 $29.95

Super Searchers Make It on Their Own
Top Independent Information Professionals Share Their
Secrets for Starting and Running a Research Business

By Suzanne Sabroski • Edited by Reva Basch

If you want to start and run a successful Information Age business, read this book. Here, for the first time anywhere, 11 of the world's top research entrepreneurs share their strategies for starting a business, developing a niche, finding clients, doing the research, networking with peers, and staying up-to-date with Web resources and technologies. You'll learn how these super searchers use the Internet to find, organize, analyze, and package information for their clients. Most importantly, you'll discover their secrets for building a profitable research business.

2002/336 pp/softbound/ISBN 0-910965-59-5 $24.95

Internet Prophets
Enlightened E-Business Strategies for Every Budget

By Mary Diffley

In *Internet Prophets*, Diffley speaks directly to the skeptics, serving up straightforward e-commerce advice that will help even the most technophobic executive do more business on the Web. This readable, easy-to-use handbook is the first to detail the costs of proven e-commerce strategies, matching successful techniques with budgetary considerations for companies of all types and sizes. *Internet Prophets* gets down to the nitty-gritty that every businessperson wants to know: "What's it going to cost?"

2001/366 pp/softbound/ISBN 0-910965-55-2 $29.95

net.people
The Personalities and Passions Behind the Web Sites

By Eric C. Steinert and Thomas E. Bleier

In *net.people*, get up close and personal with the creators of 36 of the world's most intriguing online ventures. For the first time, these entrepreneurs and visionaries share their personal stories and hard-won secrets of Webmastering. You'll learn how each of them launched a home page, increased site traffic, geared up for e-commerce, found financing, dealt with failure and success, built new relationships—and discovered that a Web site had changed their life forever.

2000/317 pp/softbound/ISBN 0-910965-37-4 $19.95

The Librarian's Internet Survival Guide
Strategies for the High-Tech Reference Desk

By Irene E. McDermott • Edited by Barbara Quint

In this authoritative and tremendously useful guide, Irene McDermott helps her fellow reference librarians succeed in the bold new world of the Web. *The Survival Guide* provides easy access to the information librarians need when the pressure is on: Trouble-shooting tips and advice, Web resources for answering reference questions, and strategies for managing information and keeping current. In addition to helping librarians make the most of Web tools and resources, McDermott covers a full range of important issues including Internet training, privacy, child safety, helping patrons with special needs, building library Web pages, and much more.

2002/296 pp/softbound/ISBN 1-57387-129-X $29.50

The Modem Reference
The Complete Guide to PC Communications, 4th Edition

By Michael A. Banks

Now in its fourth edition, this popular handbook explains the concepts behind computer data, data encoding, and transmission, providing practical advice for PC users who want to get the most from their online operations. In his uniquely readable style, techno-guru Mike Banks takes readers on a tour of PC data communications technology, explaining how modems, fax machines, computer networks, and the Internet work. He shows how data is communicated between computers all around the world, demystifying terminology, hardware, and software. A must-read for students, professional online users, and all computer users who want to maximize their PC fax and data communications capabilities.

2000/306 pp/softbound/ISBN 0-910965-36-6 $29.95

The Invisible Web
Uncovering Information Sources Search Engines Can't See

By Chris Sherman and Gary Price

Most of the authoritative information accessible over the Internet is invisible to search engines. This "Invisible Web" is largely comprised of content-rich databases from universities, libraries, associations, businesses, and government agencies. Award-winning authors Chris Sherman and Gary Price introduce you to top sites and sources and offer tips, techniques, and analysis that will let you pull needles out of haystacks every time. Supported by a dedicated Web site.

2001/450 pp/softbound/ISBN 0-910965-51-X $29.95

The Extreme Searcher's Guide to Web Search Engines
A Handbook for the Serious Searcher, 2nd Edition

By Randolph Hock • Foreword by Reva Basch

"Ran Hock is the Mario Andretti of Web searching."

—Chris Sherman/*The Invisible Web*

In this completely revised and expanded version of his award-winning book, the "extreme searcher," Randolph (Ran) Hock, digs even deeper, covering all the most popular Web search tools, plus a half-dozen of the newest and most exciting search engines to come down the pike. This is a practical, user-friendly guide supported by a regularly updated Web site.

2001/250 pp/softbound/ISBN 0-910965-47-1 $24.95

International Business Information on the Web
Searcher Magazine's Guide to Sites and Strategies for Global Business Research

By Sheri R. Lanza • Edited by Barbara Quint

"A valuable tool for any business researcher who needs to locate global information."   —*Information Today*

Here is the first ready-reference for effective worldwide business research, written by experienced international business researcher Sheri R. Lanza and edited by *Searcher* magazine's Barbara Quint. This book helps readers identify overseas buyers, find foreign suppliers, investigate potential partners and competitors, uncover international market research and industry analysis, and much more.

2001/380 pp/softbound/ISBN 0-910965-46-3 $29.95

Super Searchers Go to the Source
The Interviewing and Hands-On Information Strategies of Top Primary Researchers—Online, on the Phone, and in Person

By Risa Sacks • Edited by Reva Basch

For the most focused, current, in-depth information on any subject, nothing beats going directly to the source—to the experts. This is "Primary Research," and it's the focus of the seventh title in the Super Searchers series. From the boardrooms of America's top corporations, to the halls of academia, to the pressroom of the *New York Times*, Risa Sacks interviews 12 of the best primary researchers in the business. These research pros reveal their strategies for integrating online and "off-line" resources, identifying experts, and getting past gatekeepers to obtain information that exists only in someone's head. Supported by the Super Searchers Web page.

2001/420 pp/softbound/ISBN 0-910965-53-6 $24.95

Super Searcher, Author, Scribe
Successful Writers Share Their Internet Research Secrets

By Loraine Page • Edited by Reva Basch

The impact of the Internet on the writing profession is unprecedented, even revolutionary. Wired writers of the 21st century use the Internet to do research, to collaborate, to reach out to readers, and even to publish and sell their work. Here, *Link-Up* editor Loraine Page draws out gems of wisdom from 15 leading journalists, book authors, writing instructors, and professional researchers in the literary field. These super-searching scribes share their online tips, techniques, sources, and success stories and offer advice that any working writer can put to immediate use. Supported by the Super Searchers Web page.

2002/226 pp/softbound/ISBN 0-910965-58-7 $24.95

Super Searchers Cover the World
The Online Secrets of International Business Researchers

By Mary Ellen Bates • Edited by Reva Basch

Here, twenty skilled researchers from government organizations, multi-national companies, universities, libraries, and research firms around the world share the secrets of successful international business research. Interviewed by super searcher Mary Ellen Bates, experts from the U.S., U.K., Japan, China, Italy, Argentina, Mexico, and the Netherlands reveal the tips, techniques, sites, and strategies they use every day. You'll learn how they reach beyond borders, overcome language barriers, cope with cultural biases, evaluate unfamiliar sources, and much more. Supported by the Super Searchers Web Page.

2001/290 pp/softbound/ISBN 0-910965-54-4 $24.95

Super Searchers on Mergers & Acquisitions
The Online Research Secrets of Top Corporate Researchers and M&A Pros

By Jan Davis Tudor • Edited by Reva Basch

"If you have even the slightest interest in researching M&A information, read this book."   *—ONLINE*

The sixth title in the "Super Searchers" series is a unique resource for business owners, brokers, appraisers, entrepreneurs, and investors who use the Internet and online services to research Mergers & Acquisitions (M&A) opportunities. Leading business valuation researcher Jan Davis Tudor interviews 13 top M&A researchers, who share their secrets for finding, evaluating, and delivering critical deal-making data on companies and industries. Supported by the Super Searchers Web page.

2001/208 pp/softbound/ISBN 0-910965-48-X $24.95

Super Searchers on Health & Medicine
The Online Secrets of Top Health & Medical Researchers

By Susan M. Detwiler • Edited by Reva Basch

With human lives depending on them, skilled medical researchers rank among the best online searchers in the world. In *Super Searchers on Health & Medicine*, medical librarians, clinical researchers, health information specialists, and physicians explain how they combine traditional sources with the best of the Net to deliver just what the doctor ordered. If you use the Internet and online databases to answer important health and medical questions, these Super Searchers will help guide you around the perils and pitfalls to the best sites, sources, and techniques. Supported by the Super Searchers Web page.

2000/208 pp/softbound/ISBN 0-910965-44-7 $24.95

Super Searchers in the News
The Online Secrets of Journalists and News Researchers

By Paula J. Hane • Edited by Reva Basch

Professional news researchers are a breed apart. The behind-the-scenes heroes of network newsrooms and daily newspapers, they work under intense deadline pressure to meet the insatiable, ever-changing research needs of reporters, editors, and journalists. Here, for the first time, 10 news researchers reveal their strategies for using the Internet and online services to get the scoop, check the facts, and nail the story. If you want to become a more effective online searcher and do fast, accurate research on a wide range of moving-target topics, don't miss Super Searchers in the News. Supported by the Super Searchers Web page.

2000/256 pp/softbound/ISBN 0-910965-45-5 $24.95

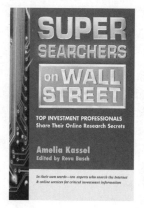